THE OFFICIAL®
PRICE GUIDE TO
GLASSWARE

THE OFFICIAL®
PRICE GUIDE TO
GLASSWARE

MARK PICKVET

FIRST EDITION

House of Collectibles • New York

Important Notice. All of the information, including valuations, in this book has been compiled from the most reliable sources, and every effort has been made to eliminate errors and questionable data. Nevertheless, the possibility of error, in a work of such immense scope, always exists. The publisher will not be held responsible for losses that may occur in the purchase, sale, or other transaction of items because of information contained herein. Readers who feel they have discovered errors are invited to *write* and inform us, so they may be corrected in subsequent editions. Those seeking further information on the topics covered in this book are advised to refer to the complete line of *Official Price Guides* published by the House of Collectibles.

 This is a registered trademark of Random House, Inc.

Published by: House of Collectibles
201 East 50th Street
New York, NY 10022

Distributed by Ballantine Books, a division of Random House, Inc., New York, and simultaneously in Canada by Random House of Canada Limited, Toronto.

Manufactured in the United States of America

ISSN: 0743-8699

ISBN: 0-876-37953-6

Text design by Holly Johnson

Cover design by Kristine Mills
Cover photo by George Kerrigan

First Edition: April 1995

10 9 8 7 6 5 4 3

CONTENTS

Acknowledgments   vii

Introduction: *A brief overview of glass collecting*   3

Market Review and Pricing Techniques   5

Chapter 1—Foreign Glass and Glassmaking: *The world history and evolution of glassmaking. Foreign glass price guide for the 19th and 20th centuries*   9

Chapter 2—Pressed Glass: *The Early and Middle American periods of glass, including the origin and history of glassmaking in America. Pressed glass price guide for the 19th and early 20th centuries*   65

Chapter 3—Cut Glass: *The Brilliant Period of American glass, America's finest crystal; price guide for 1880–1915*   127

Chapter 4—American Art Glass: *From Tiffany to Steuben. Art glass price guide for the late 19th and early 20th centuries*   157

Chapter 5—Carnival Glass: *America's fad. Carnival glass price guide for the early 1900s to the 1920s*   221

Chapter 6—Depression Glass: *America's Great Depression. Depression glass price guide for the 1920s and 1930s*   288

Chapter 7—Modern and Miscellaneous American Glass: *Price guide for American glassware from the 1940s, along with older miscellaneous items*   367

Appendices   439

Appendix 1—Periodicals and Clubs   441

Appendix 2—Museums   444

Appendix 3—Glossary   446

Appendix 4—Manufacturers' Marks   478

Bibliography   488

ACKNOWLEDGMENTS

Naturally, a project of this magnitude is never completed alone. There are many, many people who helped along the way, and I sincerely hope that I do not forget anyone: Robin Rainwater, Louis Pickvet, Jr., Leota Pickvet, Louis Pickvet III, Fairy Pickvet, Juli Pickvet, Andrea Pickvet, Michael Pickvet, Bill Willard, Kathy Willard, Tom Smith, Sandra Smith, David Smith, Ella Kitson, Robert Darnold, Sue Darnold, Rachel Moore, Ward Lindsay, Robert Davidson, Rick Patterson, Joe Renner, David Renner, Linda Renner, Paul Traviglia, Jennifer Hood, Robert Lutton, William Smola, Dr. Fred Svoboda, Dr. Arthur Harshman, Dr. David Churchman, Dr. Howard Holter, Dr. Mark Luca, and members of the SGCA.

Librarians and personnel from the following libraries: Carnegie Institute, Chrysler Museum Library, Corning Museum of Glass Library, Detroit Public Library, Fenton Art Glass Company Library, Flint Public Library, Harvard Widener Library, Historical Society of Pennsylvania, Library of Congress, Milwaukee Public Library, New York Public Library Annex, Toledo–Lucas County Library, Toledo Museum of Art Library, and the Libraries of the University of Michigan.

Museum and company personnel: Christine Mack from the Allen Memorial Art Museum; Andora Morginson from the Art Institute of Chicago; Barbara Anderson from the Bergstrom-Mahler Museum; William Blenko, Jr., Richard Blenko, and Virginia Womack from the Blenko Glass Company; M. E. Walter from the Block China Corporation; Bernard C. Boyd, Susan Boyd, and Luke Boyd from the Boyd Art Glass Company; Sarah Nichols from the Carnegie Museum of Art; Donna Sawyer, Rosemary Dumais, Gary Baker, and Peter Dubeau from the Chrysler Museum; Jane Shadel Spillman, Jill Thomas-Clark, and Virginia Wright from the Corning Museum of Glass; Darlene Antonellis-LaCroix from the Currier Gallery of Art; Frank Fenton from the Fenton Art Glass Company; Cathleen Latendresse from the Henry Ford Museum; Jack Wilkie from The Franklin Mint; Lisa Gibson from the Gibson Glass Company; Jim Hill from the Greentown Glass Museum; Carrie Brankovich from the Lotton Art Glass Company; Katherine McCracken from the National Heisey Glass Museum; Philip F. Hopfe from the New England Crystal Company; Donna Baron of Old Sturbridge Village; Peter Moore from the Pilgrim Glass Corporation; Kirk Nelson from the Sandwich Glass Museum; Paula Belanger of the Showcase Antique Center; Sheila Machlis Alexander from the Smithsonian Institute; Sandra Knudsen from the Toledo Museum of Art; the Havenmeyer collection at the University of Michigan Museum of Art; and William Hosley and Linda Roth from Wadsworth Athenaeum.

Finally, for the glass artisans of the past and present, from the blowers and cutters down to the polishers and packers, thanks for giving us so much.

THE OFFICIAL®
PRICE GUIDE TO

GLASSWARE

INTRODUCTION

Take a deep, close look at the crystal ball. It is no ordinary ball, for this is a witch's ball, an object of myth, legend, and extreme fascination and desirability. One such legend has it that old blind witches used them to see with. The visual sensations in the immediate viewing range were often replaced by happenings in distant lands and events far into the future.

What do you see? A vision? The future? A past or upcoming event? A dream perhaps? Look again. It is merely a high grade of crystal free of any visible flaws. It has been worked with precision into a heavy, solid sphere with clarity rivaling that of the clearest natural spring waters. It is simply glass, an object of beauty and worth to the owner and collector.

Such is the way many collections begin. Something within the object itself captures the eye, an emotion, or a need. Once it is acquired, many a collector is born. Soon another just like it is found, and then another, and yet another!

Glass collecting is a broad category, covering everything from Tiffany lamps valued at over $100,000 to souvenir tumblers worth $1. In between are glass items pressed into mechanical machines both old and new, art glass products from around the world, brilliantly cut crystal wares, fancy engraved designs, Carnival and other iridescent forms, colored glassware of the Depression era, modern patterns, wildlife, novelty items, miniatures, and on and on.

The book has been divided into seven major categories along with several helpful appendices. The appendices include a good deal of reference information on the current market, periodicals, clubs, museums, manufacturers' marks, a glossary that includes information on specific glass companies (past and present), and pricing information. It cannot be emphasized enough that the prices listed here should serve as a general guide only and are not intended to set prices. Please see Market Review and Pricing Techniques for more information.

Each chapter begins with a brief history, but the pricing organization varies somewhat from chapter to chapter. Pressed pattern and Depression glass are listed alphabetically by pattern name. Cut glass is alphabetized by company name since so many manufacturers produced the same patterns and basic cuttings. Carnival glass contains a list by pattern name but also includes miscellaneous pieces made by certain manufacturers. Modern, Art, and Foreign listings include both manufacturers and pattern names; patterns are used when there is sufficient variety of pieces to list separately. The modern section also contains some miscellaneous older listings that do not fit within the other categories (fruit or canning jars for example).

In conclusion, there is one small favor that I ask of you. If you discover any mistakes, errors, discrepancies, or inconsistencies or have some new or interesting information available that you would like to share, I would be happy to hear from you. Please write to Mark Pickvet, P.O. Box 90404, Flint, MI 48509.

Please include a self-addressed, stamped envelope for a response and adequate return postage for any photographs you might send (that is, if you prefer that they be returned). I am away at times but do my best to answer any correspondence that I receive.

I wish you the best in your collecting endeavors.

—*Mark Pickvet*

MARKET REVIEW AND PRICING TECHNIQUES

THE MARKET

Over the past two decades, glass collectors have proliferated to an astounding degree. Proof of this can be found in the number of new books and new magazines devoted to glassware published, small art glass companies founded, and clubs organized, and the growing general interest. There are now frequent shows, auctions, and national advertising devoted solely to glass collecting.

For the most part, the hub of the glass world in the United States is still in the East and Midwest. Historically, factories sprang up in Massachusetts, Pennsylvania, New York, West Virginia, Ohio, and Indiana. With the exception of Bartlett-Collins in Oklahoma, all glass manufacturing in America through the Depression years occurred east of the Mississippi River. As a result, prices and availability are adversely affected for those living in the western half of the country.

As the years go by, supply is becoming a problem that directly influences pricing. Pressed, cut, art, and Carnival glass are generally available only through auctions, choice shows, and exclusive dealers. Depression and even some modern glass are slowly following the trends of their predecessors; however, both are still available through general shows and common dealers.

PRICING

With the huge variety of glass shows, numerous auctions, and national advertising, prices are becoming more standardized for glass collectibles. The values listed in this book should serve as a general guide only. They are not intended to set prices; rather, they are determined from hundreds of these shows, dealers, auctions, mail order listings, experts in the field, and private collectors. Neither the author nor the publisher assumes responsibility for any losses that might possibly be incurred as a result of using this guide. The purpose of this book is to provide the most up-to-date and realistic prices for rare as well as common collectible glassware.

Prices listed in this book are based on glass in excellent or mint condition. Glass that is chipped, heavily scratched, cracked, or poorly finished or that has other major problems has very little value. Age, condition, demand, availability, and other factors are directly relevant to pricing. Take special note that dealers pay only about one-half to two-thirds of the quoted prices. The categories themselves involve several different aspects regarding condition and are outlined as follows.

Pressed Glass

Pressed patterns are the oldest styles of glass priced in this guide. They are, for the most part, 19th-century hand-pressed items that vary a good deal in consistency. Further complicating matters is the general lack of patents and therefore numerous companies and individuals making the same designs in different molds. The end result is objets with wide variations in shape, pattern, type, and general formula. Ribbing may be thicker or thinner, vines may be single or double, gridding or checkering maybe be narrow or wide, and even clear glass tends to a pale purple tinge with age. Manganese in the basic formula is responsible for amethyst coloring; a little too much coupled with prolonged exposure to the sun is responsible for this tinting.

Beware of tinging as well as serious flaws within old pattern glass. Some clear Depression patterns and reproductions are at times confused with older and more valuable pressed designs. Thinner examples can be quite fragile, but for the most part, the formulas used in pressed glass have held together well. One last item of note is to look out for irregular, out-of-balance, slightly stretched pieces or those that appear off-center, including the pattern.

Art Glass

There is simply no other category of glass that requires as much attention as art glass. Pieces that run into the thousands and even the hundreds of thousands of dollars deserve the following ten-point plan:

1. **Mint Condition.** The tiniest chip or crack; any missing portion; any part that is repaired or reground; discoloration; staining; internal bubbles that have burst; variations in cutting, engraving, or enameling; or any problems, no matter how minor, should at the very least reduce the prices listed in this guide. The only exception would be for a few minor scratches on the underside of the base on which the object rests.

2. **The Source or Dealer.** A knowledgeable and reputable dealer is essential when purchasing. A dealer should stand by the work, which might turn out to be a reproduction or even a fake. A signed certificate of authenticity should pose no difficulty from a dealer, auction house, or similar organization.

3. **Appraisal.** Get a second opinion if there is the least bit of doubt. Museum personnel, licensed appraisers, or others with knowledge in the field should be called upon.

4. **Education.** There is no substitute for experience in the art glass field. Reading and studying books, visiting museums and art galleries, speaking with dealers and visiting their shops, and attending auctions even as if only a nonbidding participant can all enhance one's knowledge in this category.

5. **Marks and Signatures.** Learn to recognize the *exact* marks and signatures of the various makers, particularly for the items or producers you are most interested in. The simplest of forgeries is that of a well-known maker's mark applied to what was previously an unmarked object of lesser quality and value.

6. **Low Prices.** Glass objects of rarity and significant value are rarely sold for small fractions of their actual worth. Carder, Steuben, Tiffany, Gallé, and the like are simply not found at flea markets and rummage sales. The majority of art glass was purchased in the past almost exclusively by the upper echelons of society.

7. **High Prices.** On the flip side of No. 6, do not get caught up in bidding wars at auctions in the heat of the moment. At times, collectors searching for a matching or highly desirable piece may pay very exorbitant prices; of course, if you are the one who has found the piece of your dreams, it is, after all, your money! Visiting a few

galleries, signing up on "Want Lists" from specific dealers, and a bit of traveling may get you the piece you are looking for without excessive bidding.

8. **Age.** Older glass will usually have some telltale sign of wear. A slight bit of fading that does not detract from the item's overall appearance may be evident. Tiny or random scratches on the base are common for art glass, simply because the object has stood in one place for so long. A piece that appears brand-new just might be!

9. **Color.** No matter how close they come, the colors of reproduction glassware always seem to differ slightly or to a larger degree from the originals. Much of this is due to the original formulas and ingredients utilized in the glassmaking process. Sand, lead, and other additives are nearly impossible to duplicate through the decades, especially when they are obtained from different sources or regions. The raw materials and sand banks of a hundred years ago no longer exist in some parts of the country. The slightest variation in color, shade, or hue from known examples can clue one to the existence of a reproduction.

10. **Be Choosy.** If the other nine requirements have been satisfied, there is still a question that arises concerning the individual design. Ill-formed, twisted, or unnatural shapes are sometimes referred to as "grotesque" and may look quite odd or lack value as compared to graceful, free-flowing objects of beauty. Aside from the practical side, a true object of art should capture your imagination and stir an emotion (unless you are buying for investment or reselling).

Cut Glass

Like art glass, cut glass was also an exclusive product for the wealthy. Due to the extremely heavy lead content as well as the extensive hand-cutting, hand-engraving, and hand-polishing involved, reproductions of the original cut patterns have not been made using these methods. Because of the thick heavy cuts, some lead cut glass has a thickness that exceeds one-half inch! One of the biggest mistakes people make is the assumption that thick glass is strong and durable. Cut glass is fragile because cutting weakens the glass structurally, especially deeper and asymmetrical cutting.

Quality and condition are the two most prevalent factors when inspecting cut glass. Light refraction, a natural crystal gleam, is far superior to a cheaper acid finish. Uniform weight, balance, and thickness; true symmetrical cuts that are sharp and precise; a lack of cloudiness; and a resonating bell-like sound when tapped with a fingernail are all determining factors of quality. Nicks, tiny chips, discoloration, a dull finish, and scratches all reduce the value of fine cut glass. Any major flaws such as heavy scratching or chipping render the object virtually worthless.

Carnival Glass

Originally, this glass was produced as a cheap substitute for art glass; however, prices for some Carnival glass have easily reached the art glass level. Less expensive common items should be given the same general visual and hand inspection as with all glassware. For rare and incredibly valuable items, such as red Carnival, follow the ten-point procedure outlined under art glass.

Since Carnival glass is characterized by an iridescent metal flashing, that is the one area of inspection that differentiates it from most other glassware. The iridization should flow smoothly and consistently over the entire object. Gaps, discolorations, dull areas from excessive wear, or any incomplete flashing reduces the price. The base color in most pieces should be observed only on the underside; if it can be viewed in significant areas or portions on the outside, it may be a sign that the iridization has worn off or was incomplete.

Reproductions pose problems in Carnival glass. Some iridized Depression glass and later iridized examples resemble the original Carnival designs. Naturally, those that cause the most severe problems are new pieces made in the original molds. Fortunately, there are some companies (e.g., Imperial) that marked the new wares ("IG") to distinguish them from the old.

Depression Glass

In no other category is the chip as much of a factor as in Depression glass. As a rule, most Depression glass was mass produced cheaply in machines in great quantities for the general public. Because of constant everyday use and thinner designs that were no longer hand-cut, chipping is a severe problem with Depression glass. Foots, rims, lids, handles, joints, and so on should all be carefully inspected for chips. Run your finger around these places with your eyes closed to discover chips by touch.

Minor flaws—such as an occasional tiny air bubble, slight inconsistent coloring from piece to piece, tiny trails of excess glass, and so on—do not detract from the value of Depression glass. A typical Depression mold might last for thousands of machine pressings, and it was impossible to match perfectly batch after batch of color. As a result, it is possible to accumulate a matching-patterned set of over fifty pieces that vary slightly in color. Major flaws—such as excess scratching, large trails of glass, rough mold lines, chips, missing pattern designs, and so on—all render Depression glass virtually worthless.

Reproductions pose a few difficulties; however, there appear to be major differences in the new versions. The most prevalent difference is color. New reproduction colors appear washed out, dull, and not as attractive as the originals. Other differences involve dimensions and new colors that were not produced in the older original versions.

Modern Glass

There is little to report on glass produced within the past fifty years or so. In short, it should be in nothing less than new condition. Occasionally, enameling on cheaper advertising or character glass may fade or scratch easily, but if abundant, less-than-perfect items should be passed over unless they are highly desired and quite scarce. Even brand-new items should be inspected for any damage or flaws that may have occurred in the manufacture, transport, or shipping or simply from being moved around constantly on display shelves.

CHAPTER 1

FOREIGN GLASS AND GLASSMAKING

A question that may never be answered fully is what brought about the development or discovery of glass. Some believe that its invention was completely by accident. Legend has it that a desert nomad in ancient Egypt lit a wood fire in a sand pit, and the ashes fused with the sand into a glassy substance. Further experimentation was carried on from there until a workable material was created. No matter how, archaeological records or surviving glass objects date from the time of the Egyptians roughly 3,500 years ago.

The prime ingredients of glass are silica, a form of sand, and ashes from plants and trees. Ash is an alkali that aids the sand in melting at a lower temperature. Stabilizing substances like carbonate of soda or lime are crushed into fine powders and added to the batch. They not only assist in the fusion process but also protect against excessive moisture. Metals and other ingredients or additives were altered through the centuries, but the basic formula has for the most part remained intact.

The Egyptian technique of core-forming did not change for centuries, until the rise of the Roman Empire. The first step in core-forming is the construction of a base or core, ordinarily a mixture of clay and dung. Hot glass was then spun around the core. The core-formed glass was quite dark or opaque and was often decorated with brightly colored glass threads that were woven around it.

The average citizens of ancient Egypt usually were not in possession of such ornaments as the new glassware. It was reserved for the wealthy, such as high priests, nobles, the pharaoh's assistants, and even the pharaoh himself. Core-formed objects were usually made into containers for ointments, oils, and perfumes. These artistic items were present on thrones, buried with mummies in their cases, and even placed in the tombs of pharaohs.

Core-forming was the exclusive method of early glassmaking, but advances and new ideas followed as the centuries passed. The Mesopotamians cast glass into moldlike containers. Simple clay molds may have lasted for only one good cast, but molds did have their beginning here. Another innovation of the Mesopotamians was the addition of an extra step in the finishing process. After casting, the surface of the glass was polished by revolving wheels fed with abrasives. These basic techniques of mold casting and polishing were adopted later by European and American glassmakers.

The second significant step in the history of glassmaking, other than its actual discovery, was the art of glassblowing. Around 50 B.C., or just over 2,000 years ago, the Romans developed the process of blowing short puffs of air through a hollow metal tube into a gather or molten blob of glass. Glassmakers would heat up a batch of glass to the melting point, inflate a bubble quickly at the end of the rod, and then work it quickly, while it was still warm, into many shapes and sizes. Glassblowing was the first significant alternative to the ancient methods of casting and core-forming.

With the advent of blowing, glass was no longer a luxury product created exclusively for the wealthy. The Romans produced a great variety of glass, and fortunately a good deal of it survived or was re-created from archaeological digs. The most popular or common items blown were drinking vessels. Drinking cups were primarily used for drinking fermented beverages. Gladiator beakers and souvenir beakers depicting gruesome gladiator scenes, battles, heroes, chariots, and so forth were designed for drinking wine. Glass was also blown into molds, and bottles were often decorated with the same scenery. Other popular shapes blown from glass included figureheads, gods and goddesses, and particularly grapes or grape clusters to celebrate wine and the vine it was derived from. The same grape patterns can be found in 19th-century, Carnival, and Depression wares.

The Romans experimented with many styles of decorating that were also adapted later. The Greeks had borrowed cutting techniques from the Mesopotamians but learned to cut shallow grooves and hollows more precisely, similar to that applied to gemstones. The Romans advanced further with cutting, engraving, and polishing with the use of stone and wooden wheels. A glass object was held against a wheel and fed with an abrasive paste. Shallow, deep, and fancy cuts were made, based for the most part on the cutter's skill.

Enameling developed long before glassware. The painting of cave walls, rocks, clay, pottery, and so forth have been a part of every culture since the dawn of civilization. The Romans enameled their glassware much as we do today, only without the complex machinery. With the Romans, colored glass was pulverized into a powder, mixed with oils like a paint, and then applied to a glass article. The piece was then reheated to permanently fuse the enamel. For the most part, Romans manipulated cold glass and cold painting.

Up until the 5th century, the Romans ruled the Western world, and the advances by the West were found somewhere within their vast empire. In the East, China delved into glassmaking in the form of beads, jewelry, and jadelike carved glass figurines, at about the same time as the Romans. Much of it was exported or traded away since glass was not highly regarded. The Chinese spent more time and effort creating the finest porcelain in the world for the coming centuries. Not until the 18th and 19th centuries would glass become somewhat popular in China. Cut-glass snuff bottles for inhaling opium and porcelain replicas of vases were made of glass. In the Middle East (the Islamic world) and later in Europe advances in the history of glassmaking can be traced.

Islamic glass dates as far back as the 8th century. The Romans had experimented with some cameo or relief cutting, but the Islamic cutters took it a step further. Relief cutting is a difficult, time-consuming, and expensive process. It involves outlining a design on a glass surface and then carefully cutting away part of the background in order to leave the original design raised in relief. Relief-cut glass was once again reserved for the upper echelon of society. Plants, geometric patterns, fish, quotations from the Koran, and a wide variety of other designs were highlighted by highly skilled artists in relief on vases, perfume sprinklers, beakers, bottles, and many other articles.

Common items for ordinary people might include bowls, bottles, and drinking glasses, primarily for wine consumption. Enameling was also done on lamps that housed oil for fuel and floating wicks. The period of Islamic glass ended very early in the 15th century, when, in 1401, the Mongol conqueror Tamerlane destroyed Damascus and captured the glass artisans. He brought them and their skills to Samarkand.

In the Middle ages, glassmaking nearly became extinct in Europe. A few primitive vessels such as bowls and drinking vessels were created but hardly anything of note for decades. In the 12th century the rise in power of the Catholic church was responsible for a new chapter in glassmaking history.

Gothic architecture and the creation of the stained glass window brought glassmaking out of the Dark Ages. Stained materials from oils, plants, and vegetable matter were added to the basic ingredients of glass. Glass colored with experimental metals was cast into flat cakes, cut into small pieces, and then formed into mosaics. Brilliantly colored glass was included in some of the finest European architecture. Huge cathedral windows, sparkling in shades of all the basic colors, adorned the greatest and most elaborate churches ever, such as Notre Dame and Westminster Abbey.

In the new millennium, the first glassmakers guild was formed, and Venice became the hub of the glassmaking world; by the early 13th century Venice was the trade center of the Western world. Venetian glassmakers formed a guild to guard their trade secrets as commercial production of glass flourished once again.

The glass industry in Venice was ordered by proclamation to move all operations to the nearby island of Murano because the hazards associated with the great furnace fires could easily destroy the entire city if an accident occurred in one of the glass houses. The glass trade was such an integral part of the commerce of Venice that Venetian glassmakers were forbidden by law to leave Murano. The penalty for escape was death, though many did manage to do so.

It was not all that unfortunate for the glass craftsmen living and working on Murano. Their skills and reputation were highly regarded, and their daughters were allowed to marry noblemen. For the most part the city of Venice had a Western world monopoly on the art of glassmaking. Their craftsmen held the secrets for furnace construction, glass formulas (including the ideal proportion of ingredients), and the use of tools and toolmaking. Knowledge was passed down to their sons or to those rarely admitted to the guild. The secrets were well guarded until 1612, when Antonio Neri made them available in his book titled *L'Arte Vetraria*, which translates into *The Art of Glass*. Neri was a master glass craftsman and understood the complete process involved in its production. It is easy to see that Neri enjoyed his trade, for he is famous for writing: "Glass is more gentle, graceful, and noble than any metal and its use is more delightful, polite, and sightly than any other material at this day known to the world."*

The biggest impact the Venetians were to have on the evolution of glassmaking was the development of cristallo in the 16th century. Next to the discovery of glass itself by the Egyptians and the invention of glassblowing by the Romans, the creation of a nearly colorless glass formula was a very significant innovation. The glass was adapted to the world's finest mirrors, far superior to those made of bronze, steel, or polished silver. Venetians produced glass beads for jewelry and rosaries that rivaled gemstones. Glass jewelry was also used for barter in the African slave trade.

Venetian glass was produced in colors that would resurface in art glass in the 19th century and Depression glass in America in the early 20th. Emerald green, dark blue, amethyst, reddish-brown and, later in the 17th century, a milky-white glass—all flowed steadily from the factories on Murano. The monopoly and production of fine Venetian glass dominated the world market through most of the 17th century.

*Neri, Antonio, Venice, Italy: *L'Arte Vetraria*, pamphlet on glassmaking, early 17th century.

Glass was a significant factor in science and technological advances. Clear optical lenses for microscopes, telescopes, improved eyeglasses, test tubes, beakers, flasks, tubing, and a host of other laboratory apparatus were vital for scientific experimentation. The Venetian cristallo did not interfere with chemicals, and one could easily observe chemical reactions and the results through the clear glass. As with most glass to this point in time, the finest Venetian styles were created for the wealthy. People of importance in the West graced their tables with glass wine goblets, fancy bowls, and vessels created in Venice. The Venetian glass cutters were the first to use diamond point engraving. Up to the 17th century, India was the sole source of diamonds, and the majority of trade between East and West passed through Venice. With diamonds readily available, the glass artisans of Venice adapted them to their cutting wheels.

The one serious complaint about Venetian glass was its inherent frail nature. There was no question that the glass was exquisite and the best in the world to that point, but it was thin, fragile, and not easily transported since it broke easily in shipment. The quest for a more durable and stronger formula would be pursued by the English.

Shortly after the time of the Venetians, a few other glass houses sprang up around northern Europe. Europe was still in the midst of the feudal system, and a few glass houses existed near the manors of noblemen. Wood ashes or potash was readily available and aided in the melting of the sand mixture. Heavy concentrations of iron in the soil produced glass of a pale or murky green color. These so-called "Forest Glasshouses" made windows and drinking vessels of poor quality; however, both were very practical items.

Huge drinking vessels were particularly popular in Germany, where beer could be drunk in large quantities. Some held several quarts, and amazingly enough, some drinkers tried to drain them in a single gulp. Some lost their bets, and others succeeded; but the practice was frowned upon by some; Martin Luther referred to these vessels as "Fool's Glasses."

In the late 16th and 17th centuries, Germans and Bohemians began cutting and decorating their glass. Their drinking glasses contained patriotic designs, coats of arms, biblical figures and references, mythological figures, and scenes of daily life. They experimented with the formulas of making glass and actually developed a form of crystal that was easier to cut than the thin Venetian cristallo. In Bohemia and Brandenburg specifically, this new glass could be cut on rapidly rotating stone and copper wheels. The Germans were responsible for the perfection of wheel engraving and engraved many of the same designs as were enameled. As the center of the West's trade shifted away from Venice, so did the advances in glassmaking. The English adopted the Venetian style and then began their own unique technological advances beyond those of the experts at Murano.

This early world history certainly has its relevance in the past two centuries of glassmaking. Sand and ash are still the two primary ingredients for its production. Many of the colors used in art and Depression glass were invented or perfected long ago. Enameling, wheel cutting, cameo engraving, and other decorating techniques can be traced far into the distant past. However, there was still room for significant improvement and experimentation. Both would occur in Europe and America.

England did little in the way of original glassmaking until the 17th century. In the 13th century, English artisans did manage to produce some window glass and a few crude drinking glasses. In 1571, Giacomo Verzelini and nine other Italian glassmakers escaped to London from Antwerp. Three years later Verzelini received a patent from Queen Elizabeth to create glass in the Venetian style, whose secrets he was familiar with. For the next 100 years, England was well on its way to becoming the world leader in the production of practical glassware.

In 1615, English glassmakers were forced to switch from wood to coal as fuel for their furnaces. Wood was outlawed because of a severe shortage; what was available was reserved for ship building. Coal posed special problems, for it was dirtier and the fumes produced could easily ruin molten glass during the blowing process.

The first significant item that England produced for export was the "Black Bottle" in the mid-17th century. It was actually a very dark green due primarily to iron and other elements present in the sand utilized in the glass formulas. It was nearly black, which actually served to protect the contents from light. The bottle was made of thick glass that was very durable; unlike the fragile, thin Venetian glassware, the black bottle rarely broke in shipping. Throughout the mid-17th and 18th centuries, England was the largest supplier of bottles in the Western world.

A more important goal of English glassmakers was to find a cross between the delicate clear Venetian glass with the strong thick black bottle. They preferred the elegance and clarity of cristallo coupled with the durability of the black bottle. The solution arrived in 1676 with George Ravenscroft. Ravenscroft was an English glassmaker who had lived and studied for several years in Venice. He would forever etch his name in the history of glass development by perfecting a formula for heavy lead glass that is still regarded as an excellent formula today.

The new batch held great advantages and was a significant factor in ending the Venetian dominance. When heated, it remained in a workable condition for a longer period of time, which in turn allowed the glass artisan to indulge in fancier and more time-consuming endeavors. It was superior in clarity, weight, strength, and light-capturing ability. The workability of the first true lead crystal was responsible for a host of new stem formations, particularly in goblets. Airtwists, teardrops, knops or knobs, balusters, and others all refracted light as never before. With Ravenscroft's discovery, the English truly succeeded in their goal.

The English further experimented with refraction in their cutting techniques. Prior to the early 18th century, England borrowed cutting techniques from the Germans and Bohemians. The new style began with covering the surface of a glass object with an orderly geometric pattern of facets. This technique, combined with the new crystal formula, maximized refraction, which in turn produced a brilliant sparkling effect. This new beautifully patterned cut glass was applied to chandeliers, candlesticks, centerpieces, and drinking glasses. Previously, rooms in typical English homes were dark; candles were heavily taxed and, therefore, expensive. Glass served to lighten things up, and it replaced candles until it too became too popular and was also subject to taxation.

The new lead glass could be formed into thicker articles and was much easier to cut than the Venetian glass. Sturdier everyday items like firing and dram glasses followed in the late 18th century. Firing glasses obtained their name from being slammed upon the table since the resulting noise of several simultaneously sounded like a group musket firing. Firing glasses were built with extremely thick bases and withstood the abuse inflicted upon them in taverns. The base might be as much as an inch thick.

Durable glass products from England were exported in large quantities. Some was shipped to the Far East in the 17th century but much more in the 18th. The English East India Company exported significant amounts of glass to India, second only to what they shipped to America.

In 1780, Parliament lifted a 35-year ban on the exportation of Irish glass. Irish glass was tax-free, and many of England's skilled glassworkers moved to Ireland. English and Irish glass was virtually identical in style and impossible to distinguish one from the other except for marks. Glassworkers in Ireland turned out huge quantities for American markets across the Atlantic. Glassmaking cities such as Dublin, Belfast, Cork, and probably the most famous city for fine glass, Waterford, survived well into the 19th century. Some companies have been reorganized, such as Waterford, and continue to operate today.

America's founding fathers and people who had access to glassware on America's East Coast used British- and Irish-made glass well into the 1820s, until the invention of the mechanical pressing machine. Glassware imported by America included water tumblers, decanters, firing glasses, wine glasses and other stemware, rummers, drams, fluted glasses, finger basins, bottles, punch jugs, liquors or cordials, salts, mustards, butter keelers, globes, and anything else the English and Irish factories turned out.

When American companies geared up in the 19th century, England and Ireland lost a significant share of their largest market; they still exported a good deal of glass to America. More glass found its way into domestic life, and more decorations were applied to it. Landscapes, architecture, city views, nature, and portraiture were all engraved, stained, or enameled on English glassware. Beakers often contained entire maps of famous battles as well as scenes of daily life.

In 1845, Parliament finally removed the excise tax on English glass. By the 1850s, England still had the reputation of producing some of the finest glassware in the world. In 1851, the World's Fair in London, dubbed "The Great Exposition of the Works of Industry of All Nations," contained a huge display of glass. The Crystal Palace Exposition featured a giant building containing 400 tons of sheet glass, or about 300,000 hand-blown panes. The displays and products at this exhibit could not but help stimulate the glass industry.

The Crystal Palace Exposition. Courtesy of the Corning Museum of Glass.

Complete matching table sets of glassware that would later be produced in great quantity in America during the Great Depression had their roots in England. Table service items included stemmed drinking glasses in many different shapes and sizes, water beakers, beer tankards, decanters, bowls, sugar bowls and creamers, salt shakers, butter dishes, honey jars, flower vases, candlestick holders, bonbon dishes, carafes and pitchers, and so on.

A variety of glass items other than tableware was made in England too: jugs, water basins, powder boxes, jewelry dishes and boxes, toothbrush holders, soap dishes, and other glass objects. The hand pressing method invented in America was available in England very soon after its initial development. Paperweights were popular in England in the mid-19th century. England and other European countries were the first to spark a revival of cameo cut glass, which had not been present for centuries, since the time of the Islamic glass cutters. John Northwood was credited with the revival of relief cutting in cameo colors. A blue or plum color cased in white with classic Greek and Roman themes was raised in relief on vases, flasks, plaques, and many other items.

England began and then followed the art glass trends in the later 19th century. Thomas Webb and his sons were one of the largest producers of Cameo, Burmese, Peachblow, and a variety of other designs. Several English firms also adopted the cheaper Carnival glassmaking techniques from America in the 20th century. With the help of the English, Australian glass houses were built, and they also produced Carnival glass. The later 19th century was a significant period for the entire European community as others joined in.

The biggest impact the French would have in the world of glassmaking was the leadership role in the Art Nouveau movement. Eugene Rousseau and Emile Gallé were the initial French designer-artists and first displayed their fancy glass at the Paris Exposition Universelle. From the time Admiral Perry opened trade with Japan to the West, Rousseau was deeply influenced by Oriental Art. This renewed interest in Orientalism in the form of rugs, porcelain, prints, paintings, and so on was also popular in America throughout the Art Nouveau period. Rousseau and Gallé did not limit themselves to Far Eastern influence but rather combined it with traditional German and Italian Renaissance shapes. Gallé more than Rousseau was the inspiration for this period. The new art form not only appeared in glass but in architecture, paintings, posters, book illustrations, furniture, wallpaper, fabric, embroidery, jewelry, and numerous other mediums. Unlike many of the cut glass manufacturers, Gallé signed his works, which sparked others to continue this tradition.

Art glass was richly ornamental, with little in the way of rules. It was full of originality, displaying crackle effects, metal particles, asymmetrical designs, long sinuous lines, weaving tendrils, flowing rhythms, and wild color effects. Colors and opaqueness were experimented with, and impractical items made of glass had no constructive use except for display and value as a work of art. Whimsies abounded, and such things as insects, animals, fruits, paperweights, and other recurring themes in nature were all re-created in glass. Rather than typical pretty floral designs, thistle pines, pinecones, and simple grains of wheat were represented on this glass. There were no set limits or traditions to follow.

Gallé went on to direct the highly acclaimed Nancy School of Art in Nancy, France. The institute dedicated itself to originality, innovation, and artistic achievement in glass. In the 1880s and 1890s, the city of Nancy became the hub of the art glass movement in Europe. Enameled, gilded, and engraved glass, as well as bizarre color effects, were all part of Gallé's designs; however, he is most noted for his superb cameo relief creations in glass. Nancy attracted many other noted figures, such as Jean Daum, second only to Gallé in reputation. When Gallé died in 1904, the quality of work in his factory suffered, and many believe that this event was the beginning of the decline of an era.

One other noteworthy French designer and artisan was René Lalique. Lalique began his career as a maker of art glass jewelry in the 1890s. He was commissioned by Coty Parfums to produce fancy decorative perfume bottles for Coty's various fragrances. From this point, the true artist was born, and Lalique's famous creations branched into glass sculpture. Figurals, nudes, vases, and even car hood ornaments were formed into frosted crystal works of art. He experimented a little with colors but worked primarily with crystal. Many of his creations contain several separate views such as a bowl formed by three kneeling nude figures.

Other European countries were part of the Art Nouveau movement. Austrian makers included Johannn Lutz, E. Bakalowits, and Moser and Sons; Val St. Lambert was a famous glass city in Belgium; the islands near Venice continued to produce millefiore designs dating back to the 13th century; and even famous American artists like Tiffany and Carder visited Europe to gain firsthand knowledge and ideas of glassmaking trends.

The rest of this chapter is devoted to pricing trends in foreign glassware primarily from the past two centuries. Please see Market Review and Pricing Techniques for an explanation of the guides contained within this work.

ALEXANDRITE THOMAS WEBB AND SONS, ENGLAND, 1890s–EARLY 1900s

Object	Price
Bowl, Finger, 5", Fluted, Matching Underplate	$700.00
Bowl, Finger with Matching Underplate, Honeycomb Pattern	2000.00
Creamer, 3" Tall, Pitcher Style, Thumbprint Pattern	2000.00
Goblet, 8½" Tall, Wafer Base, Textured Leaves on Stem	2000.00
Match Holder with Square Top, 3" Square, 2½" Tall, Diamond Quilted Pattern	750.00
Pitcher, 5½" Tall, Petal Top, Applied Handle	1750.00
Plate, 5½", Crimped, Thumbprint Pattern	850.00
Plate, 6", Rippled	900.00
Tazza, 1½" × 4½", Amber Pedestal Feet, Diamond Quilted Pattern	750.00
Toothpick Holder, 2½" Tall, Dark or Light Color Shading	900.00
Toothpick Holder, 3" Tall, Globe-Shaped Body, Square Top	700.00
Toothpick Holder, 3" Tall, Ruffled	625.00
Tumbler, 3" Tall, Honeycomb Pattern	825.00
Vase, 4" Tall, Jack-in-the-Pulpit Style, Honeycomb Pattern	1050.00
Vase, 6" Tall, Ruffled, Honeycomb Pattern	750.00
Wine Glass, 4½" Tall, Honeycomb Pattern	1000.00
Wine Glass, 4½" Tall, Thumbprint Pattern	1250.00

This English art glass consists of gradual shading from pale yellow or amber to a pinkish rose color and finally to blue. See additional material under Thomas Webb & Sons near the end of the chapter.

AUSTRALIAN CARNIVAL GLASS   1918–1930s

Object	Price
Bowl, 5", Kookaburra (Bird) Pattern, Marigold or Purple	*$50.00*
Bowl, 5", Thunderbird Pattern, Marigold or Purple	*50.00*
Bowl, 5½", Australian Swan Pattern, Marigold (Purple $100.00)	*50.00*
Bowl, 9", Kangaroo Pattern, Marigold (Purple $110.00)	*85.00*
Bowl, 9", 12-Sided, Kingfisher Pattern, Marigold (Purple $200.00)	*150.00*
Bowl, 9", Thunderbird Pattern, Marigold or Purple	*90.00*
Bowl, 9½", Australian Swan Pattern, Marigold (Purple $125.00)	*60.00*
Bowl, 10", Kiwi Pattern, Marigold (Amethyst $200.00)	*150.00*
Bowl, 10", Kookaburra (Bird) Pattern, Marigold or Purple	*100.00*
Bowl, Berry, Heavy Banded Diamond Pattern, Marigold or Purple	*85.00*
Bowl, Berry, Magpie Pattern, Marigold	*55.00*
Bowl, Octagonal, Emu Pattern, Marigold, Purple, or Amber	*100.00*
Bowl, Pin-Up Square on Stem Pattern, Marigold or Purple	*100.00*
Cake Plate, Butterfly Bower Pattern, Marigold or Purple	*150.00*
Cake Plate, Ostrich Pattern, Marigold, Amethyst, or Purple	*250.00*
Compote, Butterflies and Bells Pattern, Marigold or Purple	*150.00*
Compote, Butterflies and Waratah Pattern, Marigold (Amethyst $300.00)	*150.00*
Compote, Butterfly Bower Pattern, Marigold or Purple	*125.00*
Compote, Ostrich Pattern, Marigold or Purple	*175.00*
Compote, Rose Panels Pattern, Marigold	*150.00*
Compote, S-Band Pattern, Marigold or Amethyst	*75.00*
Compote, Wild Fern Pattern, Marigold (Purple $200.00)	*150.00*
Epergne, Sungold Pattern, White	*200.00*
Mug, Souvenir, Paneled Flute Design, Inscribed "Greetings From Mr. Gambier," Marigold (White $125.00)	*100.00*
Pitcher, Water, Banded Diamond Pattern, Marigold, Amethyst, or Purple	*1500.00*
Pitcher, Water, Beaded Spears Pattern, Marigold, Amethyst, or Purple	*300.00*
Plate, 5¼", Golden Cupid Pattern, Crystal with Gold	*75.00*
Plate, 9", Golden Cupid Pattern, Crystal with Gold	*100.00*
Tumbler, Banded Diamond Pattern, Marigold, Amethyst, or Purple	*450.00*
Tumbler, Beaded Spears Pattern, Marigold, Amethyst, or Purple	*100.00*
Tumbler, Vertical Grape Pattern, Light Marigold	*30.00*
Vase, Shallow Bowl with Flower Holder in Center, 3-Tiered Threaded Design, Ice Green	*65.00*

The most famous Australian factory to produce Carnival glass was the Crystal Glass Works Ltd. in the city of Sydney. The majority of glass was produced in marigold, purple, and amethyst.

AUSTRIAN GLASS   19TH CENTURY–PRESENT

Object	Price
Bowl, 4¾", Iridescent Purple with Pink and White Threading	*$200.00*
Brandy Glass, 5¾" Tall, Crystal	*8.00*
Compote, 3¾" Tall, Lime Green with Black Foot, Enameled Black Lattice Design	*250.00*
Goblet, 8" Tall, Iridescent Light Green	*225.00*
Goblet, 8½" Tall, Crystal, Curved Stem, Kirkland Design	*10.00*

Lamp, 13" Tall, Metal Base, 10" Iridescent Amber Shade with Pink Threading ... *$1500.00*

Paperweight, Round, 1 1/2" Diameter, Multicolor Center with Edelweiss and Gentian Floral Design ... *55.00*

Royal Pumpkin Coach (Cinderella's), 3" Tall, Drawn by 2 Mice, Mirrored Base, Gold Crown, Chain, Wheel Hubs, and Visor ... *75.00*

Shot Glass, Square, 2 1/2" Tall, 2 oz. Crystal with Etched Floral Pattern around Glass ... *20.00*

Shot Glass, 2 3/4" Tall, Crystal with Gold Rim and Multicolored Enameled Flags and Coat of Arms ... *10.00*

Vase 3 1/4" Tall, Ruffled, Iridescent Blue with Gold Vines and Jeweled Butterflies ... *500.00*

Vase, 4 1/8" Tall, Iridescent Gold with Amber Spots ... *325.00*

Vase, 6 1/2" Tall, Light Orange with Deep Amethyst Rim and Handle ... *400.00*

Vase, 7" Tall, Silver Rim, Iridescent Green with Applied Serpent Design ... *375.00*

Vase, 8" Tall, Conch Seashell-Shaped, Iridescent Gold with Green Seashell Foot ... *400.00*

Vase, 9 3/4" Tall, Scalloped, Iridescent Yellow with Orange Design on Base ... *500.00*

Vase, 10 3/8" Tall, Ruffled, Iridescent Purple with Silver Overlay ... *850.00*

Vase, 12" Tall, Iridescent Yellow with Gilding ... *550.00*

Older Austrian glass from several factories can be difficult to distinguish from other European makers due to the country's historical association with Germany, Bohemia, and the Austrio-Hungarian Empire. Often (as at auctions), Austrian glass products are combined with other miscellaneous European glassware, which might include French, English, German, and that of other countries.

BACCARAT GLASS COMPANY FRANCE, 1765–19TH CENTURY, 1953–PRESENT

Object *Price*

Angel with Trumpet Figure, 6" Tall, Crystal ... *$165.00*

Bottle, Scent, 4" Tall, White and Gold (Cyclamen) ... *525.00*

Bottle, Scent, 4 1/4" Tall, Rose Tiente Swirl Design ... *85.00*

Bottle, Scent, 4 1/2" Tall, Front Label (Mitsonko) ... *100.00*

Bottle, Scent, 6 3/4" Tall, Rose Tiente Swirl Design ... *110.00*

Bottle, Scent, 7 1/2" Tall, Rose Tiente Swirl Design ... *135.00*

Bowl, 5 1/2", 2" Tall, Amberina Swirl Design ... *85.00*

Bowl, Rose, 5", Rose Tiente Swirl Design ... *75.00*

Box with Cover, Rectangular (3" × 2"), Rose Tiente Swirl Design ... *100.00*

Candlestick, 7" Tall, Footed, Swirled Amberina Shading ... *75.00*

Carafe, Tumble-Up, Rose Tiente Swirl Design ... *100.00*

Cologne Bottle with Stopper, 5" Tall, Swirled Amberina Shading ... *125.00*

Compote, 4" Tall, Amberina ... *175.00*

Cordial, Amber with Gold Geese Decoration ... *25.00*

Cougar Head, 5 1/2" Tall, 5" Wide, Crystal ... *375.00*

Dachshund, 3 1/4" Tall, 6" Long, Crystal ... *175.00*

Decanter with Stopper, 9 1/2" Tall, Amber, Gold Geese Decoration ... *150.00*

Decanter with Stopper, 13" Tall, Etched Floral Design ... *225.00*

Decanter with Stopper, 14" Tall, Cut and Etched (for JG Monnet & Co.) ... *225.00*

Duck, 1 5/8" Tall, 2 5/8" Long, Crystal, Amethyst, Amber, or Emerald Green ... *90.00*

Epergne, Bronze Mounts, Onyx Footed Plinth, Amberina Shading ... *325.00*

Epergne, 15" Tall, Marbled Base, Swirled Amberina Shading ... *325.00*

Frog, 1 3/4" Tall, 1 7/8" Long, Amber or Moss Green ... *85.00*

Goblet, 5" Tall, Engraved Grape and Vine Design, Signed *$175.00*
Heart Shape, 3" Long, Amethyst, Blue, or Green *100.00*
Horse Head, 4¹/₂" Tall, 5³/₄" Long, Crystal *190.00*
Inkwell with Silverplated Lid, 2³/₄" Tall, Square, Floral Design *85.00*
Ladybug, 1¹/₄" Tall, 2¹/₄" Long, Crystal, Amber, Light Green, or Yellow *90.00*
Lamp, 4" Tall, Rose Tiente Swirl Design, Fairy Figure, Circular Base *275.00*
Lamp, Peg, 8" Tall, Ruffled Shades, Rose Tiente Swirl Design *500.00*
Lamp, Hurricane, 22" Tall, Bobeche with 4¹/₂" Prisms, Amberina *600.00*
Loch Ness Monster, 4 Pieces, 3³/₄" Tall, 9" Long, Crystal *300.00*
Mother with Child Figurine, 9¹/₄" Tall, Crystal *250.00*
Mug, Swirled Amberina Shading, Thumbprint Pattern *100.00*
Paperweight, 2⁵/₈", 10 Twisted Ribbons Radiating from a Millefiore Center *525.00*
Paperweight, 3¹/₈", Double Clematis Design *1750.00*
Paperweight, Sulphide, Faceted, Crystal Alexander the Great Design *300.00*
Paperweight, Sulphide, Faceted, Crystal Julius Caesar Design *300.00*
Paperweight, Sulphide, Faceted, Crystal Charlemagne Design *400.00*
Paperweight, Sulphide, Faceted, Crystal Winston Churchill Design *625.00*
Paperweight, Sulphide, Faceted, Crystal Admiral DeGrasse Design *350.00*
Paperweight, Sulphide, Faceted, Crystal Dwight D. Eisenhower Design *450.00*
Paperweight, Sulphide, 2¹/₂", Ben Franklin Design (Antique) *1250.00*
Paperweight, Sulphide, Faceted, Crystal John F. Kennedy Design *475.00*
Paperweight, Sulphide, Faceted, Red and White Overlaid John F. Kennedy Design .*1500.00*
Paperweight, Sulphide, Faceted, Crystal Martin Luther King Design *300.00*
Paperweight, Sulphide, 3" Faceted, Robert E. Lee Design, 1955 . . . .*325.00*
Paperweight, Sulphide, 3", Faceted, Crystal Abraham Lincoln Design *425.00*
Paperweight, Sulphide, 4", Faceted, Crystal Mount Rushmore Design *425.00*
Paperweight, Sulphide, Faceted, Crystal Napoleon Design *300.00*
Paperweight, Sulphide, Faceted, Crystal Thomas Paine Design *375.00*
Paperweight, Sulphide, Faceted, Crystal Peter the Great Design *300.00*
Paperweight, Sulphide, Faceted, Pope John XXIII Design *125.00*

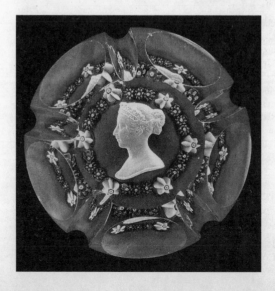

Baccarat glass. Courtesy of the Corning Museum of Glass.

Paperweight, Sulphide, 2³/₄", Pope Pius XII Design, Signed "David," 1959 . . . . . . *$125.00*
Paperweight, Sulphide, 3¹/₄", Faceted Outer Canes, Faceted Queen Elizabeth Design, 1977
. . . . *.300.00*
Paperweight, Sulphide, 3¹/₄", Queen Victoria Design (Antique) . . . . *.500.00*
Paperweight, Sulphide, Faceted, Crystal Harry Truman Design, Gold Base . . . . *.475.00*
Paperweight, Sulphide, Faceted, Crystal George Washington Design . . . . *.500.00*
Paperweight, Sulphide, Faceted, Crystal Woodrow Wilson Design . . . . *.425.00*
Paperweight, Packed Canes Design, Dated 1956 . . . . *.275.00*
Paperweight, Scattered Canes, Muslin Background, Dated 1846 . . . . *1750.00*
Plate, Rose Tiente Swirl Design . . . . *.50.00*
Shaving Brush Holder, Rose Tiente Swirl Design . . . . *.100.00*
Shot Glass, 2¹/₄" Tall, Flared, Millefiori Paperweight Base . . . . *.250.00*
Soap Dish, 4¹/₂" Across, 2" Tall, Vaseline . . . . *.50.00*
Tumbler, 3³/₄" Tall, Rose Tiente Swirl and Gold Floral Design . . . . *.250.00*
Tumbler, 4" Tall, Rose Tiente Swirl Design . . . . *.75.00*
Vase, 7" Tall, Cylindrical, Crystal, Cut Ovals . . . . *.85.00*
Vase, 7" Tall, Ovoid Design, Hexagonal Top, Crystal . . . . *.200.00*
Vase, 8" Tall, French Cameo, Signed . . . . *.400.00*
Vase, 8" Tall, Coiled Snake Design, Signed . . . . *.350.00*
Vase, 10" Tall, Opalescent, Scenic View with Birds Design . . . . *.400.00*
Vase, 12" Tall, Jack-in-the-Pulpit Design, Amethyst . . . . *.275.00*

The original Baccarat company was most famous for high-quality millefiori and
other paperweights in the mid-19th century; however, they did produce a variety of
other art glass objects. Since 1953, they have resumed paperweight production and
are also noted for high-quality clear lead crystal products.

BOHEMIAN GLASS   GERMANY, 17TH CENTURY–PRESENT

Object	*Price*
Beaker, 5³/₈" Tall, Ruby Red, Deer and Trees Decoration	*$100.00*
Bowl, 6", Engraved Castle, Deer, and Foliage Designs	*.100.00*
Bowl, Cranberry Overlay, Various Enameled Designs	*.125.00*
Candlestick, 9" Tall, Ruby and Crystal Cut, Bird or Deer Decoration	*.75.00*
Chalice, 6" Tall, Fluted, Footed, Crystal to Ruby Coloring, Stag Design	*.125.00*
Compote, 9", White to Green, Multicolored Floral Design	*.175.00*
Decanter with Stopper, 9" Tall, Opaque Shading of Pink to White, Cut Floral Design	*325.00*
Decanter with Stopper, Ruby Red, Building and Floral Design	*.125.00*
Decanter with Stopper, 12" Tall, Narrow, Etched and Cut Patterns	*.175.00*
Goblet, 5¹/₂" Tall, Ruby Red Scroll Design	*.125.00*
Goblet, 7" Tall, Ruby Red, Battle Monument Baltimore Decoration	*.500.00*

Jar, 13" Tall, Applied Prunts, Footed, Enameled Design of Man with Drinking Cup, Verse on
Reverse Side . . . . *.300.00*
Mantel Lustre, 12" Tall, Tulip Form Top, Hanging Crystal Prisms, Green with White Over-
lay, Enameled Floral Design . . . . *.400.00*
Mantel Lustre, 13" Tall, Tulip Form Top, Hanging Crystal Prisms, Green with White Over-
lay, Enameled Floral Design . . . . *.450.00*
Mantel Lustre, 14" Tall, Ruby Red with Gilding and Enameled Floral Design . . . . . . *.425.00*
Medallion, Oval (2" × 1¹/₂"), Crystal, Nude Figure of Woman with Loincloth, Basket on
Head . . . . *.350.00*

Mug, Beer, 5¹/₂" Tall, Cranberry to Clear Etched $75.00
Plate, 12", Crystal, Engraved Building Design in 4 Views 550.00
Pokal, 16" Tall, Ruby Red, Niagara Falls and Building Decoration 2100.00
Pokal with Cover, 8" Tall, Ruby Red and Crystal, Floral and Building Scenery 1250.00
Pokal with Faceted Finial, 24" Tall, Green with Multicolored Shield and Grape Decoration
....3500.00
Stein, 5" Tall, Ruby Red, Niagara Falls Decoration 325.00
Stein, 5¹/₈" Tall, Ruby Red, Floral Paneled Design 350.00
Stein, 5¹/₂" Tall, Ruby Red, Hunting Dog and Forest Decoration 350.00
Stein, 6¹/₄" Tall, Ruby Red, Castle, Scroll, and Vine Decoration 350.00
Tumbler, 3³/₄" Tall, Ruby Red, Windmill Decoration 75.00
Tumbler, 4" Tall, Crystal, Engraved Chalet with Heavy Grass, Lake, and Bridge Scene 175.00
Urn with Cover, 22" Tall, Ruby Red, Stag and Woodland Scene 625.00
Vase, 5" Tall, Crystal, Engraved Cameo Face of Woman 125.00
Vase, 7¹/₂" Tall, Multicolored Swirl Design 100.00
Vase, 8¹/₄" Tall, Cased with White, Enameled Floral Design 125.00
Vase, 8¹/₄" Tall, Scalloped, Cobalt Blue Overlay 150.00
Vase, 9" Tall, Emerald Green with White and Gold Enameled Floral Design 225.00
Vase, 10" Tall, Cut Windows, Blue, Yellow, and Ruby Red Coloring 225.00
Vase, 10 ¹/₂" Tall, Cobalt Blue Encased in Crystal 100.00
Vase, 11" Tall, Crystal, Many Engraved Miniature Crescent Moons Design 125.00
Wine Glass, 6" Tall, Crystal, Engraved Pinwheel Design 50.00
Wine Glass, Knob Stem, Dark Ruby Red, Monkey Design 75.00

The original Bohemian glass was characterized by heavy stone engraving overlaid with colored glass. A later design included the cutting of two layers of colored glass. The object was then gilded or enameled. In terms of area, Bohemia is now part of western Czechoslovakia. Individual items can be difficult to date because the glass has been continuously produced for over 300 years.

Mantel Lustres are decorative candle holders or vases for use above fireplaces.

BRISTOL GLASS EUROPE (ENGLAND, FRANCE, GERMANY, AND ITALY), 18TH–19TH CENTURIES

Object   *Price*
Basket, 10¹/₂" Tall, Ruffled, Pink Opaline, Bird Design $200.00
Biscuit Jar with Silverplated Cover, 7¹/₂" Tall, Tan Birds and Foliage with Silverplated Handle and Rim 225.00
Bowl, 7", Lily Shape, Amethyst Color 55.00
Cologne Bottle with Gold Ball Stopper, 4" Tall, Green with Gold Dot and Star Design 100.00
Cologne Bottle with Ball Stopper, 5³/₄" Tall, Turquoise with Gold Band and Enameled Floral Design 85.00
Cologne Bottle with Stopper, 10" Tall, Pink with Gold Band and Foliage Design ...150.00
Ewer, 10" Tall, Clambroth with Blue Edging 75.00
Pitcher, Water, 8¹/₂" Tall, Applied Crystal Handle, Light Green with Enameled Floral and Birds Design 90.00
Salt Dip, Rectangular, White with Multicolred Enameled Floral Deisgn 50.00
Sweetmeat Jar, 5" Tall, Silverplated Rim, Cream with Multicolored Enameled Floral Design
....135.00
Urn With Cover, 15" Tall, Enameled Floral Design 150.00

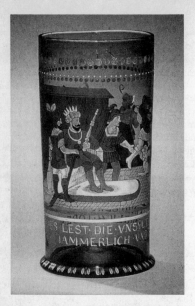

Bristol glass. Photo by Robin Rainwater.

Vase, 3³/₄" Tall, Turquoise with Gold Bands and Multicolored Enameled Florals with White Dots *$75.00*

Vase, 5¹/₄" Tall, Turquoise with Gold Bands and Floral Design *125.00*

Vase, 6¹/₂" Tall, Brown with Gold Floral Design *85.00*

Vase, 7¹/₄" Tall, Opaque Gray with Multicolored Enameled Boy or Girl *90.00*

Vase, 8¹/₂" Tall, Cylindrically Shaped, Blue with Multicolored Enameled Floral, Butterfly, and Building Design *95.00*

Vase, 10" Tall, Handled, Enameled Green Design *150.00*

Vase, 10" Tall, Enameled Gold and Pink Floral Design *125.00*

Vase, 11¹/₂" Tall, Pink with Multicolored Enameled Angel in Chariot Design *175.00*

Vase, 11³/₄" Tall, Opal, Enameled Floral Design *115.00*

Vase, 13¹/₂" Tall, Amethyst Tint, Enameled Floral Design *135.00*

Vase, 14¹/₂" Tall, Cone-Shaped, Blue with White Floral Design *225.00*

Vase, 14¹/₂" Tall, Dark Gray with Red and White Floral Design *175.00*

Bristol glass is usually characterized by an opaque or semiopaque base color, which is further decorated by use of enamels. It originated in Bristol, England, and spread to other parts of Europe. A little of it was produced in America by The New England Glass Company and a few others.

CANADIAN GLASS   MID-1820S–PRESENT

Object	Price
Bowl, 8", Footed, Athenian Pattern, Dominion Glass Co.	*$75.00*
Bowl, 8", Pressed Maple Leaf Pattern	*50.00*
Bowl, 8", Rayed Heart Pattern, Dominion Glass Co.	*90.00*
Butter Dish with Cover, Athenian Pattern, Dominion Glass Co.	*90.00*

Butter Dish with Cover, Rayed Heart Pattern, Dominion Glass Co. *$125.00*

Canning Jar, Amber, Embossed "Canadian Queen," 1 Quart (rare) *325.00*

Canning Jar with Zinc Cover, Embossed "Best," 1 Quart *3.00*

Canning Jar with Glass Lid, Clear with Embossed "Improved Gem," 1 Pint *6.00*

Canning Jar with Glass Lid, Clear with Embossed "Improved Gem," 1 Quart *8.00*

Canning Jar with Glass Lid, Clear with Embossed "Perfect Seal," 1 Pint *6.00*

Canning Jar with Glass Lid, Clear with Embossed "Perfect Seal," 1 Quart *8.00*

Celery Dish, 9" Oblong, Rayed Heart Pattern, Dominion Glass Co. *100.00*

Compote, 7" Diameter, Pressed Maple Leaf Pattern *55.00*

Cookie Jar with Silverplated Lid and Top Handle, Silverplated Beaver Finial on Handle, 10½" Tall, Enameled Grape Decoration *325.00*

Creamer, Athenian Pattern, Dominion Glass Co. *55.00*

Creamer, 4" Tall, Pitcher Style, 2-Handled, Cut Maple Leaf Pattern *175.00*

Creamer, Rayed Heart Pattern, Dominion Glass Co. *75.00*

Goblet, 5½" Tall, Pressed Honeycomb Pattern with Faceted Design within Combs, Copper Wheel Engraved, Diamond Glass Co., 1890s *150.00*

Goblet, 6" Tall, Pressed Raspberry Pattern, 1890s *75.00*

Hat, 2¾" Tall, Canadian Pillar Pattern, Lamont Glass Co., 1890s *65.00*

Lamp, 14" Tall, Bronze Base, Cobalt Blue with Enameled Palm Trees Design, Jefferson Glass Co. *1250.00*

Lamp, Kerosene, 16" Tall, Emerald Green Base and Globe, #102 Style, Dominion Glass Co., 1880s *275.00*

Lamp, 18" Tall, Opal with Enameled Water Scene with Two Sailing Ships, Jefferson Glass Co. *675.00*

Canadian glass. Reproduced from an early 20th-century trade catalog.

Canadian glass. Reproduced from an early 20th-century trade catalog.

Nappy, 4", Athenian Pattern, Dominion Glass Co. *$35.00*

Paperweight, 2¹/₂" Tall, 10³/₈" Circumference, Opal 5-Petal Lily on Multicolor Chips Background, Cobalt Blue Writing: "Souvenir de Wallaceburg, Ont," 1910s *300.00*

Paperweight, 3¹/₈" Tall, 10¹/₈" Circumference, Cased 5-Petal Lily on Bubble Stem, Opal Glass Petals with Emerald Green and Multicolored Chips Background, 1890s *325.00*

Pitcher, Milk, 6¹/₂" Tall, Cut Buzzstar Pattern *275.00*

Pitcher, Water, 11¹/₂" Tall, Footed, Pressed Maple Leaf Pattern *225.00*

Pitcher, 11¹/₂" Tall, 64 oz., Cut Colonial Pattern *375.00*

Pitcher, Water, 10³/₈" Tall, Footed, Hand-Blown Crystal, Excelsior Glass Co., 1880s .*175.00*

Salt and Pepper Shakers, 3" Tall, Milk Glass, Pressed Butterfly and Tassel Pattern . .*85.00*

Salver, 9" Diameter, 5¹/₂" Tall, Athenian Pattern, Dominion Glass Co. *85.00*

Spooner, Rayed Heart Pattern, Dominion Glass Co. *65.00*

Sugar, 3¹/₂" Tall, 2-Handled, Cut Maple Leaf Pattern *125.00*

Sugar with Cover, Athenian Pattern, Dominion Glass Co. *75.00*

Sugar with Cover, Rayed Heart Pattern, Dominion Glass Co. *100.00*

Toothpick Holder, 2¹/₄" Tall, Pressed Canadian Beaded Oval and Fan Pattern *60.00*

Tumbler, 5" Tall, Diamond Crosscut Pattern *75.00*

Tumbler, 5¹/₂" Tall, Cut Buzzstar Pattern *85.00*

Vase, 8" Tall, Slender Form, Ruffled, 4 Long Fluted Design *45.00*

Vase, 11" Tall, Footed, Ruffled, Long Flutes with Pressed Floral Band at Top, Jefferson Glass Co. *85.00*

Canadian glass is often ignored in the collector field (except for Canadian collectors); however, a good deal of glass was made in Canada dating as far back as the mid-1820s. The Mallorytown Glass Works in Ontario was the first to produce glass, and others followed pressed, art, and cut glass trends of Europe and America. Much of the glass made in Canada in the 19th century was very practical (i.e., bottles, tumblers, tableware, windows, fruit or canning jars, etc.). Dominion (several pressed patterns such as "Rayed Heart" and "Athenian") and Diamond were two successful companies that followed Mallorytown. Dominion eventually became Jefferson, a major producer of Art Nouveau lamps.

CLICHY FRANCE, 1840S–1880S, 1950S–PRESENT

Object   *Price*

Paperweight, 2¹/₄", Con Mill, 4 Rows in Blue and White Basket *$1500.00*

Paperweight, 2¹/₄", 30 Pink and White Swirled Threads *1250.00*

Paperweight, 2¹/₂", Cin Mill, Turquoise with Cane Gar and Florets *725.00*

Paperweight, 2¹/₂" Multicolored Densely Packed Millifiore Design, Signed *3500.00*

Paperweight, 2⁵/₈", Checkered Barber Pole Design with 18 Canes, Twists, and Filigree Rods *2750.00*

Paperweight, 2⁵/₈", Two-Tone Green and White Spiral Design *350.00*

Paperweight, 2³/₄", Multicolored Mill Canes with Pink and Green Rose *850.00*

Paperweight, 2³/₄", Pattern Mill, Faceted, Canes with Rose and 5 Rings *850.00*

Paperweight, 3", Con Mill, Star Cane Cluster with 3 Rings and Rose *1250.00*

Paperweight, 3", Con Mill, 8-Point Star Cane in Basket *1825.00*

Paperweight, 3", Pinwheel, 44 Amethyst Rods, White Tubes and Turquoise Floret .*1500.00*

Paperweight, 3", Scattered Mill, Pink Rose in Center *850.00*

Paperweight, 3¹/₈", Large Dark Pink Camomile Design *650.00*

Paperweight, 3¹/₈", Crystal with Dark Emerald Green 4-Leaf Clover *2250.00*

Paperweight, 3½", Multicolored Florettes Separated by Varied Threaded White Strips . .*$800.00*
Paperweight, 3¾", Con Mill, Cane Gar, 7-Rose Design (1 in Center) *750.00*
Paperweight, Sulphide, 2¾", White Cameo of Comte de Chambord on Deep Cobalt Blue
Ground *550.00*
Paperweight, Sulphide, 3⅜", Translucent Ground, Alfred de Musset Design *600.00*

The French classic period of paperweight manufacturing ran from about 1845 to
1860. The factories in the town of Clichy, like Baccarat and St. Louis, produced
many weights, then closed during the later Art Nouveau period. A revival of paperweight production occurred in the 1950s in all of these famous French glassmaking
towns.

CRYSTAL MINIATURES VARIOUS COMPANIES,
1970S–PRESENT

Object	*Price*
Airplane, F-14 Tomcat, 1" Tall, 2⅝" Long	. . . .*$115.00*
Airplane, F/A-18 Hornet, 1" Tall, 1¾" Long	. . . .*100.00*
Airplane, Stealth Fighter, 2" Long	. . . .*40.00*
Airplane, 2⅛" Long, 2¼" Wingspan	. . . .*125.00*
Anchor, Ship's, 1½" Tall, Gold Chain	. . . .*50.00*
Angel Fish, 1¾" Long, Frosted Fins	. . . .*50.00*
Apple, 1¼" Tall, Rainbow Colors	. . . .*55.00*
Balloon, Hot Air, 1½" Tall, Red Basket	. . . .*75.00*
Basket of Violets, 1¼" Tall	. . . .*70.00*
Bear, 1⅛" Tall, Holding Pink Balloon, Black Eyes and Nose	. . . .*35.00*
Bear, 1¼" Tall, Grandma or Grandpa with Spectacles	. . . .*60.00*
Bear, 1⅜" Tall, Scuba Diving Bear with Treasure Fish and Swimming Fish	. . . .*95.00*
Bear, 1½" Tall, with Captain's Hat and Stern Wheel	. . . .*60.00*
Bear, 1½" Tall, Red Heart and "I Love You" Disk	. . . .*40.00*
Bear, 1⅝" Tall, with Gold Club, Green Cap, Amethyst Ball, and Red Feet	. . . .*85.00*
Bear, 1¾" Tall, with Party Hat, Cake, and Horn	. . . .*50.00*
Bear, 1¾" Tall, with Baseball Bat	. . . .*75.00*
Bear, 1¾" Tall, with Tennis Racket	. . . .*75.00*
Bear, 2⅛" Tall, with Golf Club and Ball	. . . .*120.00*
Bears, 2⅜" Tall, 2 at Candlelight Dinner on Circular Base, Moonlit Window in Background	
. . . .*150.00*	
Bee Bumble, ½" Tall, ⅝" Long	. . . .*25.00*
Butterfly, 1" Long, Octagonal Base with Pink Flower	. . . .*45.00*
Candle, Christmas, 1½ Tall, Holly Berries on Base	. . . .*30.00*
Cannon, 2" Tall, 2⅝" Long, 3" Round Mirror Base, 3 Black Cannonballs	. . . .*175.00*
Car, 1⅝" Long, Red Tailights	. . . .*60.00*
Carousel, 2¼" Tall, 1⅛" Diameter, 2 Horses	. . . .*100.00*
Carousel Horse, 2½" Tall, 1½" Square Base	. . . .*65.00*
Carousel Horse with Bear Holding Balloon, 2⅜" Tall	. . . .*100.00*
Castle, 3" Tall, Slender, Amber Base, 2" Wide	. . . . :. . . .*70.00*
Castle on Green Base, 1" Tall	. . . .*35.00*
Castle with Changing Color Base, 2¼" Tall, Rainbow Stairway on Base	. . . .*150.00*
Castle with Changing Color Base, 2½" Tall, Rainbow Stairway on Base	. . . .*225.00*
Castle with Changing Color Base, 4³⁄₁₆" Tall, Camelot	. . . .*550.00*

Cat, ⁵/₈" Tall, Siamese Kitten, Black Ears and Feet $25.00

Cat, ³/₄" Tall, 1³/₄" Long, Crouched 35.00

Cat, 1" Tall, Kitten with Red Ball 65.00

Cat, 1³/₈" Tall, Siamese Mother, Black Ears and Feet 50.00

Cat Sitting in Rocking Chair, 3" Tall 90.00

Cat Staring at Fish in Fish Bowl, 1³/₄" Tall 100.00

Cats, 1¹/₂" Tall, Mother with Kitten 75.00

Cats, 1¹/₂" Tall, 1" Across, 2 Kittens Together 45.00

Cats in a Basket, 1" Tall, 2¹/₂" Long, 2 Sleeping 60.00

Chick, 1" Tall, Chubby, Silver Feet and Beak 35.00

Chickens, 1" Tall, Circular Base, 2 Chicks and Red Hearts 50.00

Christmas Tree, 2" Tall, with Tiny Kitten and Present 60.00

Christmas Tree, 3³/₈" Tall, with Tiny Kitten and Present 90.00

Christmas Tree with Presents, 6" Tall, 6" Diameter, Colorful Accents, Limited Edition (1000) 900.00

Church, 2³/₄" Tall, ³/₄" Square Base, Rainbow Colors 160.00

Cocker Spaniel, ¹/₂" Tall, Puppy 15.00

Cocker Spaniel, ³/₄" Tall 20.00

Cottage, Honeymoon, 1³/₄" Tall, Multicolored Accents 125.00

Crab, 1¹/₈" Tall, 1¹/₂" Long, Claws Up 50.00

Crab, Hermit, 1¹/₂" Long 50.00

Dog, ⁷/₈" Tall, Puppy, Black Eyes and Nose 30.00

Dog with Doghouse, 1" Tall 65.00

Dolphins, 2¹/₄" Tall, 2 (1 with Ball), Rainbow Base 45.00

Dragonfly, 1⁵/₈" Long, Thin Silver Thread Bones 65.00

Dragster, 4" Long, Red Exhaust Vents 100.00

Duck, ³/₄" Long, Black Eyes and Yellow Beak 30.00

Fire Engine, 1¹/₂" Long 75.00

Fish, Puffer, ³/₄" Tall, 1⁵/₈" Long 50.00

Frog, ¹/₂" Tall 15.00

Gingerbread House on Square Mirrored Base, 2¹/₂" Tall, Multicolored 175.00

Hippopotamus, 1¹/₄" Long, Black Eyes, Red Mouth 30.00

Horse, Rocking, 2" Tall, 2¹/₄" Long 70.00

House Victorian, 3" Tall, Multicolored Accents 250.00

Hummingbird, ⁵/₈" Tall, 1" Long 50.00

Ice Cream Sundae, 1" Tall, Multicolored Accents 40.00

Jack-in-the-Box, 1³/₈" Tall, Multicolored Accents 50.00

Knight, 3" Tall, with Shield and Sword 65.00

Koala Bears on Mirrored Base, 1¹/₂" Tall, 2 Bears Sharing a Heart 75.00

Lighthouse, 2¹/₂" Tall, Gold Circular Base 55.00

Lighthouse with Changing Color Base, 2¹/₂" Tall, Rainbow Stairway on Base 125.00

Meadowlark, 1³/₈" Tall 45.00

Moose, ⁷/₈" Tall 30.00

Moose, 1" Tall, 1¹/₂" Long 50.00

Mouse, ¹/₂" Long 10.00

Mouse, 1³/₄" Tall, Grampa or Grandma on Rocking Chairs 75.00

Otter, ¹/₂" Tall, 1¹/₄" Long 55.00

Owl, 1" Tall 20.00

Panda Bear, ³/₄" Tall, Black Ears, Arms, and Legs 25.00

Penguin, 1¹/₂" Tall 45.00

Pig, ⁷/₈" Tall, Black Eyes and Pink Nose 30.00

Pigs in Race Car, 1¼" Tall, 2½" Long, 2 Pigs *$85.00*
Pineapple, 1¼" Tall .... *.50.00*
Rabbit, ½" Tall, ¾" Long, Lop-Eared .... *.20.00*
Rabbit with Pool Table, Cue Stick and Balls, 1⅛" Tall .... *.85.00*
Rabbit, 1½" Tall, Skiing .... *.60.00*
Rabbit in Basket, 2" Tall, Red Bow and Base .... *.45.00*
Rabbits, 1" Tall, 2" Across, 2 Bunnies Sharing a Heart .... *.55.00*
Rabbits on Beach under Palm Tree, 1⅞" Tall .... *.125.00*
Raccoon, 1" Tall, Black Eyes, Nose, and Tail .... *.40.00*
Sail Boat, 1⅛" Tall, 1" Square Base .... *.30.00*
Scorpion, 2¾" Long, Tail Up .... *.75.00*
Seal, Baby, ½" Tall, ¾" Long, Silver Whiskers .... *.15.00*
Sheep, 1¼" Tall, Black Legs and Face .... *.40.00*
Shell with Faux Pearl, 1" Tall, 1" Long .... *.35.00*
Ship, Cruise, 2¼" Long, 1" Tall .... *.110.00*
Slot Machine, 1¾" Tall, Gold and Red Accents .... *.110.00*
Slot Machine, 2¼" Tall, Gold and Red Accents, Black Ball on Handle .... *.150.00*
Snail, ¾" Tall .... *.12.00*
Snail, 1" Tall .... *.15.00*
Snowman on Skis, 1⅛" Tall, Red Scarf .... *.45.00*
Space Shuttle on Green Globe Base, 3" Tall .... *.350.00*
Squirrel, 1½" Tall, Black Eyes, Holding Acorn .... *.40.00*
Starship Enterprise, Star Trek, Red and Yellow Accents .... *.115.00*
Stork, 3" Tall, with Baby in Beak .... *.75.00*
Swan, ¾" Tall, 1" Long .... *.40.00*
Taj Mahal, 4½" Tall, 4" Square, Limited Edition (2000) .... *.750.00*
Tank, M-1A, 1⅜" Tall, 2¼" Long .... *.90.00*
Telephone, ¾" Tall, Red or Black Buttons .... *.45.00*
Train Engine, 1¼" Tall, 2" Long .... *.110.00*
Turkey, 1⅝" Long .... *.70.00*
Turtle, 1⅛" Long .... *.15.00*
Tweety Bird Sculpture, 2⅜" Tall (Looney Tunes) .... *.125.00*
Vase, 2" Tall, 6 Red Roses with Green Stems .... *.65.00*
Yosemite Sam on Wooden Base, 3½" Tall (Looney Tunes) .... *.125.00*

These tiny pieces have only been around for the past 20 years or so and are already highly collectible. They are made throughout Europe (i.e., Austria, Germany, Sweden, France, Ireland, etc.) and are found mostly in jewelry and fine gift stores. A few are made in the United States as well. Most are faceted; animals are the most popular medium, though new unique and larger items are appearing constantly! Colors are primarily used for accents, though some pieces contain more surface area of color than crystal.

CZECHOSLOVAKIAN GLASS 1918–1992

Object   *Price*
Basket, 5½" Tall, Crystal Thorn Handle, Red with Streaking *$150.00*
Basket, 8" Tall, Black with Ruffled Yellow Top, Black Handle .... *.125.00*
Biscuit Jar with Cover, 6½" Tall, 4¾" Diameter, Crystal, Diamond Pattern, Ceska ... *.75.00*
Bowl, 5½", Footed, Came Cut Dark Green on Light Orange .... *.425.00*

Bowl, 8¹/₂", 4³/₄" Tall, Crystal, Striped Pattern, Ceska *$50.00*

Bowl, 12", Flared, Red .... *.65.00*

Box with Cover, 4" Across, Ruby Red with Cut Floral Design .... *.75.00*

Candlestick, 10¹/₂" Tall, Orange with Multicolored Base .... *.50.00*

Decanter with Stopper, Green with Gold Trim .... *.55.00*

Decanter with Stopper, Cone-Shaped, Ruby Red Handle, Opalescent Crackle Design225.00

Ice Bowl with Insert, 7" Diameter, 5¹/₂" Tall, Crystal, Vertical Ribbed Design, Ceska *.90.00*

Lamp, 9" Tall, Crystal Bubble Sphere on Pedestal with Art Deco Dancer .... *.475.00*

Perfume Bottle with Crystal Figural Stopper, 5¹/₂" Tall, Amber .... *.225.00*

Perfume Bottle with Nude Figural Stopper, 6¹/₂" Tall, Amethyst .... *.400.00*

Perfume Bottle with Stopper, 6¹/₄" Tall, Crystal with Blue Art Deco Design .... *.225.00*

Perfume Bottle with Stopper, 7" Tall, Crystal, Daffodils Design .... *.125.00*

Perfume Bottle with Stopper, 7¹/₂" Tall, Crystal, Cut Hobstar Design .... *.75.00*

Pitcher, Water, 10" Tall, Topaz with Green Streaking and Blue Threading .... *.150.00*

Pitcher, Water, 11¹/₂" Tall, Black Handle, Orange with Colorful Jungle Bird Design *.150.00*

Vanity Set, 4-Piece (Small Water Bottle with Stopper, Oval Dish, and Tray), Crystal, Beaded Medallion Pattern .... *.75.00*

Vase, 4" Tall, Hexagonal, Footed, Multicolored Spatter Design .... *.50.00*

Vase, 4¹/₂" Tall, Cobalt Blue Spatter Design .... *.55.00*

Vase, 5¹/₂" Tall, Ruffled, White with Rose Interior .... *.75.00*

Vase, 6" Tall, Ruffled, Cased Blue with White Interior .... *.175.00*

Vase, 6¹/₄" Tall, Orange with Silver-Deposit Floral Design .... *.45.00*

Vase, 6¹/₂" Tall, 4 Blown Applied Crystal Feet, Orange Curved Figure 6 Design ...... *.75.00*

Vase, 7" Tall, Frosted with Horses Raised in Relief .... *.100.00*

Vase, 7¹/₈" Tall, Jack-in-the-Pulpit Style, Orange with Black Spots .... *.75.00*

Vase, 7¹/₂" Tall, Crystal Crackle with Embossed Floral Design .... *.35.00*

Vase, 8" Tall, Ruffled, Tangerine Blue Design .... *.110.00*

Vase, 8" Tall, Ruffled, Yellow with Black Snake Design .... *.200.00*

Vase, 8¹/₂" Tall, Ruffled, Blue with Pink Interior .... *.100.00*

Vase, 8¹/₂" Tall, Black-Lined Rim, Orange with Enameled Black Medallions .... *.75.00*

Vase, 9" Tall, Tri-Corner Top, Gloss Black Over Orange Design .... *.85.00*

Vase, 9¹/₂" Tall, Fan Style, Amber with Blue Threading .... *.110.00*

Vase, 11" Tall, Square, Emerald Green with Floral Design in Relief .... *.250.00*

Vase, 13" Tall, Canary Yellow with Black Handles .... *.100.00*

Vase, 15¹/₂" Tall, 3⁷/₈" Diameter, Tapers in at Top, Crystal with 12 Interlocking Circles *325.00*

Whiskey Tumbler, 2¹/₂" Tall, Green with Gold Trim (Matches Decanter Above) ..... *.10.00*

Czechoslovakia was officially recognized as a separate country in 1918. Before breaking up in 1992, a good deal of glass was made by several firms. Much of it is simply marked "Czechoslovakia" or "Made in Czechoslovakia," but older items contain a wide variety of manufacturer's marks. It was made in many styles from colored art (especially orange) to engraved crystal.

DAUM, NANCY GLASS   DAUM GLASS, FRANCE,
1880S–1910S

Object   *Price*

Beaker, 4¹/₂" Tall, Footed, Green with Gold Flowers *$150.00*

Bowl, 3³/₄", Translucent Blue, Green, and Yellow, Butterfly Design .... *.2500.00*

Bowl, 6", Yellow, Orange, and Blue Enameled Mulberry and Floral Cameo Design *.1100.00*

Bowl, 10", Pedestal Base, Cameo *$1250.00*

Bowl, 12", Amber, Etched Triangles in Panels *900.00*

Box, Square with Hinged Domed Cover, 6" Diameter, Cameo River Scene *3500.00*

Box with Hinged Cover, 3" Diameter, Leaves and Berries with Grasshopper on Cover, Signed "A. Walter" *5000.00*

Box with Hinged Cover, 6" Tall, Green and Blue with Pyramid on Cover, Signed "A. Walter" *3000.00*

Decanter with Red Stopper, 11" Tall, Crystal with Gray Streaking *350.00*

Egg, Glass with Glass Base, Gilded Pedestal Foot, 5" Tall, Opalescent, Acid Etched with Cameo Engraved Ducks *1750.00*

Lamp, 7" Tall, Marble Base, Green and Brown Forest Lake Scene *2250.00*

Lamp, 7½" Diameter Shade, Amber Base, Red Floral Cameo Design *10,000.00*

Paperweight, 10", Sea Nymph Rising from Surface, Signed "Cheret" *6000.00*

Pitcher, Water, Tortoiseshell Cameo Design, Signed *450.00*

Salt Dip, 2" Square, 1" Tall, Yellow Floral Cameo Design, Enameled Design *1750.00*

Sherbet, 4¼" Tall, Apricot with Gold Mica *125.00*

Tray, 7" Long, Salamander with Ivy Leaves and Yellow Blossoms, Signed "A. Walter" *4500.00*

Tray, 7½" Long. Triangular, Gray with Mallard Duck Faces, Signed "A. Walter" ...*2750.00*

Tumbler, 4¾" Tall, Green Leaves and Purple Violets Design *1500.00*

Tumbler, Wooded Winter Snow Scene, Signed *375.00*

Vase, 4" Tall, Amber, Sailing Ship Design *1000.00*

Vase, 4¾" Tall, Pale Green with Large Air Bubbles *275.00*

Vase, 5" Tall, Pedestal Foot, Cameo Ducks Design *2500.00*

Vase, 5" Tall, Violet Pedestal Foot, Yellow and Turquoise Color *1000.00*

Vase, 5¼" Tall, Red Millifiore Design *850.00*

Vase, 6½" Tall, Frosted with Pine Forest and Lake Scene *450.00*

Vase, 6¾" Tall, 3-Layered Cameo *550.00*

Vase, 7" Tall, 5" Diameter, Cameo Red and Yellow on Aqua, Floral Design, Signed "A. Walter" *2000.00*

Daum glass. Photo by Mark Pickvet.

Vase, 8" Tall, 8" Diameter, Flared, Vertical Ribs, Gray *$1000.00*
Vase, 9" Tall, Light Blue to Cobalt Blue Shading, Gold Mica *2600.00*
Vase, 10" Tall, Slender, Blue, Orange, and Yellow Cameo Berry Cluster Design . . .*1750.00*
Vase, 10¼" Tall, Enameled Joan of Arc Design *2250.00*
Vase, 13" Tall, Ovoid Shape, Yellow with Etched Leaves *2250.00*
Vase, 13½" Tall, Cone-Shaped, Footed, Yellow with Enameled Flower Blossoms . .*6500.00*
Vase, 14" Tall, Gold Gilded on Amethyst, Cameo Iris and Dragonfly Design *2100.00*
Vase, 16" Tall, Green and Gold Gilt on Yellow, Cameo *1750.00*
Vase, 18" Tall, Red and Yellow Spatter with Gold Mica *1250.00*
Vase, 20" Tall, Applied Black Berries on Dark Gray Ground *750.00*
Wine Goblet, Engraved and Enameled Lily Design, Signed *350.00*
Woman Figurine, 7" Tall, Seated with Head in Hands, Yellow, Signed "A. Walter" *2000.00*

Daum, next to Gallé, was one of the most important factories producing French art glass, including cameo designs. Other techniques utilized were intaglio, inlaid, enameled, acid cutting, and copper wheel engraving. Almaric Walter was one famous artisan who worked at the Verreries Artistiques des Freres Daum factory.

ENGLISH CAMEO GLASS 1850S–1890S

Object *Price*
Bowl, Rose, 3½", White on Rose Mother-of-Pearl, Wild Rose Design, Diamond Quilted Pattern *$1750.00*
Bowl, 4" Tall, 6" Diameter, Ruffled, Pink on White Satin with Apple Blossoms, Signed "Stevens & Williams" *850.00*
Bowl, 5", 2" Tall, White on Cranberry, Floral Design, Signed "Webb" *850.00*
Bowl, 6" Tall, White on Blue, Dragon Design (Webb) *2500.00*
Bowl, 7", Aqua on Blue, Seaweed and Shell Design *2500.00*
Cup, Loving, 7½" Tall, 3 Applied Handles, Light Gold on Dark Gold (Webb) *350.00*
Epergne, 10½" Tall, White on Red, Mirrored Base, Floral Design *4500.00*
Perfume Bottle with Cut Stopper, 4" Tall, White on Saffron, Floral Design, Signed "Webb" *1500.00*
Perfume Bottle with Faberge Stopper, 3¾" Tall, White on Blue, Floral Design . . .*7000.00*
Platter, 14" Round, 4-Color (White, Red, Light Blue, and Tan Florals) on Green Cameo (Webb) *8000.00*
Saucer, 6", White Circular Floral Design on Rust (Stevens & Williams) *750.00*
Sweetmeat Jar with Silver Cover, 6" Tall, White on Light Blue, Fancy Leaf Design *2000.00*
Vase, 5" Tall, White on Blue Mother-of-Pearl, 5" Diameter, Apple Blossom Design, Diamond Quilted Pattern *2000.00*
Vase, 5" Tall, White on Blue, Floral Design, Signed "Stevens & Williams" *1500.00*
Vase, 5" Tall, White on Red, Honeysuckle Design, Signed "Webb" *1500.00*
Vase, 5" Tall, White on Yellow, Violets and Leaves Design *1750.00*
Vase, 6" Tall, White on Blue, Floral Design *2000.00*
Vase, 6" Tall, White on Citron, Signed "Webb" *2000.00*
Vase, 6 Tall, White on Amethyst, Beetle and Nasturtiums Design, Signed "Stevens & Williams" *3500.00*
Vase, 6½" Tall, White on Amber to Rose Shading, Ovoid Geranium Design, Signed "Webb" *1250.00*
Vase, 7" Tall, Blue with White Figure, Signed "Woodall" *7500.00*
Vase, 7" Tall, Rose on White, Scroll Design, Signed "Webb" *1500.00*
Vase, 7" Tall, White on Tan, Signed "Stevens & Williams" *1500.00*

English cameo glass. Photo by Mark Pickvet.

Vase, 7½" Tall, Tan with White Figure, Signed "Woodall & Webb" *$8500.00*
Vase, 8" Tall, White Woman with Harp (Siren) on Brown, Signed "Geo. Woodall" .*7500.00*
Vase, 8" Tall, White on Yellow, Tall Grass Design, Signed "Woodall" *3500.00*
Vase, 8" Tall, White on Blue, Rose Design, Signed (Stevens & Williams) *2000.00*
Vase, 8" Tall, White on Red Mother-of-Pearl (Webb) *5000.00*
Vase, 8¼" Tall, Classic 2-Handled Style, White Child on Black (Joseph Northwood) *7500.00*
Vase, 9" Tall, White on Blue, Floral Design on Body and Neck *3250.00*
Vase, 9" Tall, White on Peachblow, Floral Design, Signed "Webb" *5000.00*
Vase, 9" Tall, White on Red, Signed "Stevens & Williams" *1500.00*
Vase, 9¾" Tall, White on Reddish-Orange, Bird, Dragonfly, and Iris Design, Signed "Webb"
. . . .*3250.00*
Vase, 10" Tall, White on Red, Signed "Webb" *3500.00*

Assorted English cameo glass. Photo by Robin Rainwater. Courtesy of the Corning Museum of Glass.

Vase, 11½" Tall, White on Red, Signed "Webb" *$3600.00*
Vase, 11¾" Tall, Opalescent White on Blue (Webb) *3750.00*
Vase, 11¾" Tall, Classic 2-Handled Style, White Floral and Stork Design on Dark Blue
. . . .*4000.00*
Vase, 12" Tall, Gourd-Shaped, White on Yellow, Horsemen Design *4000.00*
Vase, 12" Tall, Banded Neck, White on Peach, Floral Design, Signed "Stevens & Williams"
. . . .*3250.00*
Vase, 12" Tall, White on Red, Floral and Plums Design, Signed "Stevens & Williams" .*3250.00*
Vase, 12½" Tall, Mother-of-Pearl (Ivorylike), Signed "Webb" *3750.00*
Vase, 13" Tall, Tan with White Figures, Signed "Woodall & Webb" *10,000.00*
Vase, 23½" Tall, White on Red, Foxgloves Design (Webb) *7500.00*

Cameo glass is made in two or more layers; the first (inner) is usually a dark color, and the casing (outer) is white. Classic, floral, natural, and other scenes were carved in as many as five layers. The technique was applied by other nations such as France. The primary English makers were Thomas Webb & Sons and Stevens & Williams.

ENGLISH CARNIVAL GLASS   1910–EARLY 1930S

Object   *Price*
Banana Dish, Moonprint Pattern, Marigold (Sowerby) *$150.00*
Basket, Thin Handle, Alternating Diamonds with Floral Design, Marigold (Davisons of Gateshead) *65.00*
Boat, Row (Used for Holding Pens/Pencils), Daisy Block Pattern, Marigold or Amethyst (Sowerby) (Aqua Opalescent $400.00) *275.00*
Bonbon Dish, Illinois Daisy Pattern, Marigold (Davisons of Gateshead) *55.00*
Bowl, 4", Intaglio Daisy Pattern, Marigold (Sowerby) *30.00*
Bowl, 7", Footed, Diving Dolphins Pattern, Marigold (Sowerby) (Blue, Green, or Amethyst $250.00) *150.00*
Bowl, 7¾", Intaglio Daisy Pattern, Marigold (Sowerby) *55.00*
Bowl, 8", Moonprint Pattern, Marigold (Sowerby) *60.00*
Bowl, 10", Grape and Cherry Pattern, Marigold (Sowerby) (Blue $200.00) *85.00*
Bowl, Oval or Round, Finecut Rings Pattern, Marigold (Guggenheim) *45.00*
Bowl, Hobstar and Cut Triangles Design, Marigold (Green or Amethyst $90.00) *75.00*
Bowl, Illinois Daisy Pattern, Marigold (Davisons of Gateshead) *75.00*
Bowl, Oval or Round, Footed, Lea Pattern, Marigold or Amethyst (Sowerby) *60.00*
Bowl, Pineapple Pattern, Marigold (Sowerby) (Blue or Purple $75.00) *55.00*
Bowl, Prism and Cane Pattern, Marigold (Sowerby) (Purple $100.00) *65.00*
Bowl, Rose, Classic Arts Pattern, Marigold (Davisons of Gateshead) *150.00*
Bowl, Rose, Hobstar and Cut Triangles Design, Marigold (Green or Amethyst $90.00) *75.00*
Bowl, Rose, Intaglio Daisy Pattern, Marigold (Sowerby) *65.00*
Bowl, Rose, Vining Leaf Variant Design, Marigold *300.00*
Bowl with Cover, Diamond Pinwheel Pattern, Marigold (Davisons of Gateshead) *45.00*
Butter Dish, 10" Diameter, Cathedral Pattern (Davisons of Gateshead) (Amethyst or Blue $60.00) *45.00*
Butter Dish, Hobstar Reversed Pattern, Marigold, Blue, or Amethyst (Davisons of Gateshead) *65.00*
Butter Dish, Moonprint Pattern, Marigold (Sowerby) *125.00*
Butter Dish, Split Diamond Pattern, Marigold (Davisons of Gateshead) *85.00*

Butter Dish, Triands Pattern, Marigold *$65.00*

Butter Dish with Cover, Beaded Swirl Pattern, Marigold (Davisons of Gateshead) . . .*75.00*

Butter Dish with Cover, Finecut Rings Pattern (Guggenheim) *90.00*

Butter Dish with Cover, Rose Garden Pattern, Marigold (Blue, Green, Amethyst, or Purple $300.00) *150.00*

Cake Stand, Finecut Rings Pattern, Marigold (Guggenheim) *75.00*

Carafe, Daisy and Cane Pattern, Marigold (Sowerby) *100.00*

Casserole Dish with Cover, Fruit and Berries Pattern (Blue $350.00) *300.00*

Celery Dish, Finecut Rings Pattern, Marigold (Guggenheim) *55.00*

Celery Vase, Heavy Prisms Pattern, Marigold (Davisons of Gateshead) (Blue or Purple $110.00) *90.00*

Celery Vase, Triands Pattern, Marigold *65.00*

Chalice, 7" Tall, Cathedral Pattern, Marigold (Davisons of Gateshead) (Amethyst or Blue $100.00) *85.00*

Coaster, Rayed-Star Design, Marigold *40.00*

Compote, Beaded Swirl Pattern, Marigold (Davisons of Gateshead) *40.00*

Compote, Cathedral Pattern, Marigold (Davisons of Gateshead) (Amethyst or Blue $60.00) *50.00*

Compote, Daisy and Cane Pattern, Marigold (Sowerby) *35.00*

Compote, Diamond Pinwheel Pattern, Marigold (Davisons of Gateshead) *50.00*

Compote, Hobstar and Cut Triangles Design, Marigold (Green or Amethyst $90.00) . .*75.00*

Compote, Pineapple Pattern, Blue or Purple (Sowerby) *75.00*

Compote, Stippled Diamond Swag Design, Marigold, Blue, or Green *80.00*

Cookie Jar, Illinois Daisy Pattern, Marigold (Davisons of Gateshead) *90.00*

Cordial, Zipper Stitch Pattern, Marigold *45.00*

Creamer, Apple Panels Pattern, Marigold (Sowerby) (Blue $45.00) *35.00*

Creamer, Cathedral Pattern, Marigold (Davisons of Gateshead) *50.00*

Creamer, Diamond Ovals Pattern, Marigold (Sowerby) *35.00*

Creamer, Diamond Top Pattern, Marigold *40.00*

Creamer, Finecut Rings Pattern, Marigold (Guggenheim) *60.00*

Creamer, Footed, Lea Pattern, Marigold or Amethyst (Sowerby) *55.00*

Creamer, Moonprint Pattern, Marigold (Sowerby) *55.00*

Creamer, Pineapple Pattern, Marigold (Sowerby) (Blue or Purple $75.00) *55.00*

Creamer, Rose Garden Pattern, Marigold (Blue, Green, Amethyst, or Purple $100.00) *55.00*

Creamer, Split Diamond Pattern, Marigold (Davisons of Gateshead) *50.00*

Creamer, Triands Pattern, Marigold *55.00*

Decanter with Stopper, Zipper Stitch Pattern, Marigold *375.00*

Epergne, Cathedral Pattern, Marigold (Davisons of Gateshead) *500.00*

Flower Holder, Cathedral Pattern, Marigold (Davisons of Gateshead) *90.00*

Frog, Flower with Base, Hobstar Reversed Pattern, Marigold (Davisons of Gateshead) *65.00*

Hen Dish with Cover, Marigold (Sowerby) *75.00*

Hen Dish with Cover, Miniature, Marigold (Sowerby) *200.00*

Jam Jar, Finecut Rings Pattern, Marigold (Guggenheim) *60.00*

Jam Jar with Cover, Moonprint Pattern, Marigold (Sowerby) *75.00*

Paperweight, Sphinx Design, Amber *650.00*

Pitcher, Milk, Fans Pattern, Marigold (Davisons of Gateshead) *100.00*

Pitcher, Milk, Moonprint Pattern, Marigold (Sowerby) *125.00*

Pitcher, Milk, Rose Garden Pattern, Marigold (Blue, Green, Amethyst, or Purple $750.00) *450.00*

Pitcher, Water, Banded Grape and Leaf Pattern, Marigold *500.00*

Pitcher, Water, Beaded Swirl Pattern, Marigold (Davisons of Gateshead) *100.00*

Plate, Hobstar and Cut Triangles Design, Marigold (Green or Amethyst $90.00) $75.00

Powder Box with Cover, Paneled, Sculptured Lady Handle on Lid, Marigold (Davisons of Gateshead) *125.00*

Powder Jar, Classic Arts Pattern, Marigold (Davisons of Gateshead) *150.00*

Spittoon, Daisy and Cane Pattern, Blue (Sowerby) *225.00*

Spooner, Hobstar Reversed Pattern, Marigold (Davisons of Gateshead) *65.00*

Spooner, Rose Garden Pattern, Marigold (Blue, Green, Amethyst, or Purple $90.00) ..*50.00*

Spooner, Triands Pattern, Marigold *55.00*

Sugar, Apple Panels Pattern, Marigold (Sowerby) (Blue $45.00) *35.00*

Sugar, Diamond Ovals Pattern, Marigold (Sowerby) *35.00*

Sugar, Diamond Top Pattern, Marigold *40.00*

Sugar, Moonprint Pattern, Marigold (Sowerby) *55.00*

Sugar, Rose Garden Pattern, Marigold (Blue, Green, Amethyst, or Purple) *55.00*

Sugar, Split Diamond Pattern, Marigold (Davisons of Gateshead) *50.00*

Sugar, Sunken Daisy Pattern, Marigold (Blue $55.00) *40.00*

Sugar, Triands Pattern, Marigold *55.00*

Sugar Dish with Cover, Finecut Rings Pattern, Marigold (Guggenheim) *75.00*

Sugar Dish with Cover, Beaded Swirl Pattern (Davisons of Gateshead) *65.00*

Sugar Dish with Cover, Signet Pattern, Marigold *80.00*

Swan Dish with Cover, Marigold (Sowerby) (Amethyst or Purple $225.00) *175.00*

Toothpick Holder, Banded Diamond and Fans Pattern, Marigold *85.00*

Tray, Serving, Zipper Stitch Pattern, Marigold *150.00*

Tumbler, Banded Grape and Leaf Pattern, Marigold *125.00*

Vase, 6¹/₂" Tall, Pinwheel Pattern, Marigold (Green, Purple, or Amethyst $100.00; Blue $150.00) *75.00*

Vase, 7" Tall, Classic Arts Pattern, Marigold (Davisons of Gateshead) *175.00*

Vase, 10" Tall, Classic Arts Pattern, Marigold, (Davisons of Gateshead) *225.00*

Vase, 13¹/₂" Tall, Fine Prisms and Diamonds Pattern, Marigold, Blue, Green, or Purple *90.00*

Vase, Finecut Rings Pattern, Marigold (Guggenheim) *75.00*

Vase, Footed Prisms Pattern, Marigold (Sowerby) (Blue or Green $100.00) *50.00*

Vase, Moonprint Pattern, Marigold (Sowerby) *65.00*

Vase, Pebble and Fan Pattern, Vaseline (Cobalt Blue or Amber $500.00) *125.00*

Vase, Rose Garden Pattern, Blue, Green, Amethyst, or Purple *250.00*

Vase, Sea Gull Design, Marigold *850.00*

Vase, Spiralex Pattern, Marigold, Blue, Green, or Amethyst *75.00*

Vase, Square, Diamond Pattern, Blue *150.00*

Vase, Sunflower and Diamond Pattern, Marigold (Blue $100.00) *75.00*

Vase, Tropicana Pattern, Marigold *1250.00*

Vase, Vining Leaf Variant Design, Marigold *300.00*

Carnival glass first arrived in England from America, and as it caught on, several factories began making it. The three most noted producers were Davisons of Gateshead, Guggenheim Ltd. of London, and the Sowerby Company of Gateshead-on-Tyne.

FRENCH CAMEO GLASS
1850S–EARLY 20TH CENTURY

Object   *Price*

Ashtray, 6" Across, Pate de Verre Design (A. Walter) *$750.00*

Basket, 7" Tall, Black, Red, and Yellow Floral Design (Daum) *$650.00*

Bowl, 2¹/₂", Crystal on Orange, Berries and Leaves Design, Signed (Gallé) *950.00*

Bowl, Rose, 3" Tall, Black on Gold and Pink Satin, Lake and Forest Scene (De Vez) *1100.00*

Bowl, 13¹/₂", Bun Feet, Wine on Rust, Flower Cluster Design (La Verre Francais) . .*2100.00*

Chandelier, 13" Tall, Burgundy to Brown on Yellow, Trumpet Flower Design on Conical Shade (La Verre Francais) *3000.00*

Compote, 4", Brown and Rust on Yellow, Clear Interior, Village Scene with River and Mountains (De Vez) *1250.00*

Ewer, 9" Tall, Thistle Design (Roux Chalon) *550.00*

Goblet, 8" Tall, Blue Floral Design (Gallé) *1000.00*

Lamp, 15" Tall, Dark Red Shade and Base, Egyptian Scene (Degue) *3500.00*

Lamp, 19" Tall, Green and Pink Floral Design *1250.00*

Lamp, 21" Tall, Blue, Amber, and Green on Translucent White, Signed "LeMaitre" *2250.00*

Perfume Bottle with Stopper, 6¹/₂" Tall, Orange and Brown Floral and Bird Design on Amber (D'Argental) *1250.00*

Pitcher, 6" Tall, Shaded Orange and White (Schneider) *425.00*

Powder Jar with Cover, 6" Tall, Red Carved Flowers on Green Ground, Signed (Gallé) *2000.00*

Tumbler, 4" Tall, Signed (Gallé) *450.00*

Vase, 3" Tall, Amethyst and Crystal, Orchid Design (Verrerie D'Art) *900.00*

Vase, 3¹/₂" Tall, Purple on White, Rose and Thorn Design (Weis) *700.00*

Vase, 4" Tall, Rust on Amber, Lakeside Scene, Signed "De Vez" *525.00*

Vase, 4¹/₄" Tall, Multicolor Enameled Landscape Scene (Legras) *850.00*

Vase, 5" Tall, Green on Light Yellow, Maple Leaves and Pod Design (Legras) *375.00*

Vase, 5¹/₂" Tall, Purple Sweet Peas on Frosted Ground, Signed (Galle) *750.00*

Vase, 6" Tall, Amethyst on Frosted Ground, Floral and Foliage Design (D'Argental) .*450.00*

Vase, 6" Tall, Green on Chartreuse, Morning Glory Design (Arsall) *1250.00*

Vase, 6" Tall, Violet and Crystal Foliage Design (Vessiere) *650.00*

Vase, 7" Tall, Blue, Enameled Floral Design (St. Louis) *900.00*

Vase, 8" Tall, Burgundy on Amber, Winding River and Trees Design (De Vez) *1250.00*

Vase, 8" Tall, Matte Crystal and Enamel Design (Baccarat) *650.00*

Vase, 8" Tall, Red to Black, Blue Foot (Richard) *375.00*

Vase, 9" Tall, Pate de Verre Design (Argy-Rousseau) *1500.00*

Vase, 9¹/₂" Tall, Footed, Urn-Shaped, Purple on Pink and Orange, Swag Design (La Verre Francais) *1000.00*

Vase, 10" Tall, Slender Bottle Form, Red and Green on Light Green to Red Shading (D'Argental) *1500.00*

Vase, 10" Tall, 3-Color, Olive Green to Blue to Rose Floral Design, Signed (Gallé) .*2250.00*

Vase, 10" Tall, Purple on Yellow, Lilies and Iris Design (Arsall) *1750.00*

Vase, 11" Tall, Brown and Red Floral Design *850.00*

Vase, 11" Tall, Purple on Multicolored Ground, Floral Design (Degue) *1000.00*

Vase, 11" Tall, Shaded Red and Yellow Mums (DeVez) *750.00*

Vase, 11¹/₂" Tall, Light Pink with Purple and Green Irises (Arsall) *2000.00*

Vase, 11¹/₂" Tall, Red and Amethyst Floral Design (Monthoye) *550.00*

Vase, 12" Tall, Brown and Red, Ship Design (D'Argental) *750.00*

Vase, 13" Tall, Elongated Feet, Dark Brown on Green and Rust, Trees and Fence Design (D'Argental) *1500.00*

Vase, 14" Tall, Green, Enameled Floral Design *650.00*

Vase, 15" Tall, Footed, Gray, Orange, and Red, Cherry Branch Design (Ledoux) . . .*1000.00*

Vase, 15" Tall, Fruit and Vine Design (Gallé) *850.00*

Vase, 15" Tall, Purple Columbine Blossoms on Frosted Gray, Signed (Gallé) *4750.00*

French cameo glass. Photo by Mark Pickvet. Courtesy of the Corning Museum of Glass.

Vase, 16" Tall, Bulbous, Pink on Gray, Grapevine Design (Legras) *$1750.00*
Vase, 17" Tall, Light Orange with Brown and Green Mottling, Grape and Leaf Design .*2000.00*
Vase, 17" Tall, Burgundy on Amber Grapevines Design (D'Argental) *2250.00*
Vase, 18" Tall, Footed, Multicolored on Yellow and Rust, Art Deco Floral Design (La Verre Francais) *1750.00*
Vase, 19" Tall, Footed, Brown on Yellow, Geese Design (La Verre Francais) *2500.00*
Vase, 22" Tall, Cylindrically Shaped, Orange on Light Green Floral Top (La Verre Francais) *3250.00*
Whiskey Tumbler, 2" Tall, Floral Pattern *325.00*
Wine Glass, 8½" Tall, Bell-Shaped, Cranberry to Clear, Double Teardrop Design (D'Argental) *425.00*
Wine Glass, Teardrop Stem, Amethyst to Clear, Cut Hobstar and Fern Pattern (D'Argental) *525.00*

Cameo glass is made in two or more layers; the first (inner) is usually a dark color, and the casing (outer) is white. Classic, floral, natural, and other scenes were carved in as many as five layers. The technique was applied by other nations, such as England (see English Cameo Glass). Gallé, Daum, and a host of others were noted for some of the finest cameo glass ever produced.

Beware of "French" cameo glass produced by Romania since the 1960s, much of it signed with the older signatures. Also, for other examples see "Daum, Nancy Glass."

GALLÉ, EMILE,   FRANCE, 1874–EARLY 1900S

Object   *Price*
Biscuit Jar with Cover, 8" Tall, Footed, Purple on Light Gray Cameo, Flower Blossom Design, Signed *$2000.00*
Bowl, 4½", Dark Green with Enameled Tropical Flowers, Signed *1750.00*
Bowl, Oblong Boat-Shaped (7" × 5"), Brown Design on Peach to Green Cameo, Tree and Stream Scene, Signed *1500.00*

Bowl, 8", Ruffled, Amber with Enameled Flowers and Dragonflies, Signed "Emile Gallé Fecit" *$675.00*

Bowl, 8¹/₂", Pedestal Base, Signed *550.00*

Champagne Glass, 5¹/₄" Tall, Etched and Enameled, Signed *325.00*

Chandelier, 9" Diameter, Cameo Orange on Light Blue, Dragonfly and Tulip Design, Signed *7500.00*

Compote, 4", Enameled Pink Flowers Interior, Carved Leaf Design Exterior *1000.00*

Compote, 6¹/₂", Enameled Pink Pods Interior, Frosted Exterior with Maple Leaves . . *1100.00*

Cup, Footed, Light Amber, Enameled Thistle Design, Signed *600.00*

Decanter with Handle and Stopper, 8" Tall, Amber with Enameled Pink Thistle Design, Signed *1500.00*

Decanter with Stopper, 8¹/₄" Tall, Enameled Lady in Dress, Signed "Gallé" *1750.00*

Ewer, 8" Tall, Amber with Gilding and Multicolored Floral Design, Signed *2250.00*

Lamp, Candle, 7" Tall, Pedestal Stand, Multicolored Cameo Floral Design, Signed . *2250.00*

Lamp, 17" Tall, Pink Dome Shade, Trumpet Base, Cameo Grape and Vine Design, Signed *12,500.00*

Lamp, 19¹/₄" Tall, Pelican Design on Bronze Base, Sprayed Flower Blossoms on Shade, Signed *110.00*

Medallion, Napoleon Profile, 3¹/₂" Diameter, Signed *275.00*

Perfume Bottle with Frosted Stopper, 4¹/₂" Tall, Cameo Green on Green Fern Design, Signed *2250.00*

Perfume Bottle with Stopper, 4³/₄" Tall, Enameled Scene of Man in Boat on Lake, Signed *2000.00*

Pitcher, 3" Tall, Green Serpent Handle, Enameled Red and Brown Floral Design, Signed *1750.00*

Pitcher, 3" Tall, Frosted Handle, Enameled Bleeding Hearts Design, Signed *1250.00*

Ring Tree, 11³/₄" Tall, Crystal Tree with Enameled Insects on Base *1000.00*

Saucer, Light Amber, Enameled Thistle Design, Signed *325.00*

Left: Gallé glass. Photo by Mark Pickvet. Right: Gallé glass. Photo by Mark Pickvet. Courtesy of the Corning Museum of Glass.

Shot Glass, 2¹/₂" Tall, Pink and Green on Frosted Cameo, Maple Seed Design, Signed .*$750.00*

Tumbler, 4¹/₂" Tall, Enameled Arabesques, Signed *250.00*

Vase, 2" Tall, Miniature, Pinecone Decoration, Signed *225.00*

Vase, 3³/₄" Tall, Miniature, Blue and Green Floral Design, Signed *750.00*

Vase, 4¹/₂" Tall, Dark Red with Enameled Green and Gold Lizard, Signed "Gallé" . . .*575.00*

Vase, 5" Tall, Cabbage-Shaped, Signed *350.00*

Vase, 5" Tall, Scalloped, Pinched Sides, Oriental Algae and Starfish Design, Signed *8000.00*

Vase, 6¹/₂" Tall, Cameo Violet on Frosted to Yellow Shading, Signed *1250.00*

Vase, 7" Tall, Slender, Brown on Yellow Cameo, Hyacinth Design, Signed *750.00*

Vase, 9¹/₂" Tall, Various Applied Ceramic Decorations, Signed *500.00*

Vase, 10" Tall, Light Tan with Enameled Floral Design, Signed *1750.00*

Vase, 11¹/₂" Tall, Hexagonal Shape, Brown and Tan Cameo Foliage, Signed *3500.00*

Vase, 13¹/₄" Tall, Flask-Shaped, Poppy Blossoms Design, Signed *7500.00*

Vase, 19" Tall, Inverted Cylinder, Tan on Ice Blue Cameo, Lily Design, Signed . . .*2000.00*

Vase, 20¹/₄" Tall, Jack-in-the-Pulpit Style, Foliage and Flower Blossoms Design, Signed
. . . .*8500.00*

Vase, 21" Tall, Slender Form, Snails on Base, Cameo Lake Scene with Birds, Trees, and
Boats *10,000.00*

Vase, 24³/₄" Tall, Butterflies and Iris Blossoms Design, Signed *9000.00*

Whiskey Tumbler, 2³/₄" Tall, White, Blue, and Green Cameo on Crystal and Pink Background, 4-Petal Flower Design, Signed *750.00*

The leader of the Art Nouveau movement in Europe, Gallé was a designer and innovator and was noted most for the revival of cameo engraving in multiple layers. He also was careful in signing all of his creations, which inspired others to do so (see French Cameo Glass for additional listings).

GERMAN GLASS 20TH CENTURY

Object	*Price*

Apple, 3¹/₂" Tall, 3" Diameter, Long Stem *$25.00*

Bowl, Salad, 10", 5¹/₂" Tall, Silver-Plated Base Crystal, Diamond and Oval Pattern *30.00*

Brandy Snifter, 6¹/₂" Tall, Crystal *5.00*

Egg, 3¹/₄" Tall, 12 oz. Weight, Crystal with Frosted Blue Finish, All-Over Floral Design *35.00*

Hummel Figurines, 2" Tall, Frosted Crystal (for Mother, Little Sweeper, March Winds, Sister, Soloist, or Village Boy), Goebel *50.00*

Hummel Figurines, 3" Tall, Frosted Crystal (Apple Tree Girl, the Botanist, Meditation, Merry Wanderer, the Postman, Visiting an Invalid), Goebel *65.00*

Mug, Barrel-Shaped, Crystal with Etched Grape and Leaf Pattern, Green Handle *8.00*

Pear, 4" Tall, 2¹/₂" Wide, Long Stem *25.00*

Photo Frame, 11¹/₄" × 9¹/₂" Rectangle, Crystal with Diamond and Shell Border *45.00*

Pilsener Glass, 9¹/₂" Tall, 14 oz., Crystal *5.00*

Stein, 8¹/₂" Tall, Pewter Lid and Finial on Handle, Deep Blue with Engraved Fisherman in Water and Ducks, Limited Edition (250) *275.00*

Stein, 9¹/₂" Tall, Pewter Lid and Finial on Handle, Ruby Red with Engraved Stag and Woodlands *200.00*

Stein, 10⁵/₈" Tall, Pewter Lid and Finial on Handle, Crystal with Etched Apple Tree and Garden Design *135.00*

Thimble, Crystal with Handpainted Amish Symbol *25.00*

Thimble, Cyrstal with Handpainted Heart and Leaves *25.00*

Thimble, Crystal, Cut Diamond Pattern *20.00*

Thimble, Crystal with Cut Diamond Pattern and Gold Base *$22.00*
Thimble, Crystal with Engraved Owl Design *20.00*
Thimble, Crystal with Etched Edelweiss Flower *16.00*
Thimble, Crystal with Rainbow Colored Glass Decorations *20.00*
Thimble, Lavender, Light Blue, Ruby Red, or Yellow with Etched Floral and Grape Design
. . . .*18.00*
Thimble, Ruby-Flashed Crystal with Etched Hummingbird *25.00*
Thimble, Stein-Shaped with Gold-Plated Lid and Handle, Green with Etched Star Design
. . . .*18.00*
Thimble Blown within a Miniature Antique Milk Bottle, 2" Tall, Crystal *12.00*
Vase, 6½" Tall, Heart-Shaped Top, Grooved Sides, Crystal, Gorham *35.00*
Vase, 8½", Fan-Shaped, Crystal, Star and Lovebird Cuts *35.00*
Wine Glass, 6 oz., Green Base and Stem, Crystal Bowl with Gold Rim and Gold Leaf and
Grape Design *10.00*

German glass has been made for centuries, but the listings above include modern
examples only. Older items can be found under Bohemian Glass. Of course, many
of the modern examples include thimbles, crystal Hummels, fancy steins, and a variety of other collectibles.

IRISH GLASS   18TH CENTURY–PRESENT

Object   *Price*
Apple, 3¼" Tall, Crystal with 40 Shades of Green Kerry Glass $40.00
Biscuit Jar with Cover, 8" Tall, Crystal with Diamond Cuts, Galway *90.00*
Bowl, 4¾", Crystal with Diamond Cuts, Tipperary *40.00*
Candle Holder, 6" Long, Aladdin's Lamp Style, Crystal with Diamond and Straight Cuts,
Tipperary *40.00*
Candy Dish, 4⅛" Tall, Footed, Crystal-Cut Diamond and Fan Design, Tipperary *25.00*
Chandelier, 24" Tall, 21" Wide, Crystal with Cut Diamonds, 5-Light, Brass Fittings *1650.00*
Clock, Miniature Grandfather, 4½" Tall, Crystal Diamond Cuts, Galway *70.00*
Cornucopia Nut Dish, Footed, Crystal with Diamond and Oval Cuts, Galway *75.00*
Creamer, 4" Tall, Pitcher Style, 10 oz., Crystal with Cross Cuts, Tipperary *40.00*
Football, 3¾" Long, Crystal with Cut Threads, Tipperary *100.00*
Globe, 4¾" Tall, Crystal with Etched Continents, Diamond-Cut Crystal Base, Cavan Crystal
. . . .*140.00*
Mug, Coffee, 5½" Tall, 8 oz., Low Handle, Crystal with Etched Harp, Shamrocks and "Irish
Coffee" *20.00*
Paperweight, 3½" Tall, Oval-Globe Shape, Ocean Blue Swirled Design, Kerry Glass .*30.00*
Paperweight, 4" Tall, Slender Oval Egglike Shape, Crystal with 40 Shades of Green and a
Stone from Blarney *50.00*
Paperweight, 4½" Tall, Oval-Globe Shape, Crystal with 40 Shades of Green Swirls, Kerry
Glass *30.00*
Pig Figurine, 3½" Long, 2" Tall, Crystal with 40 Shades of Green Swirls *40.00*
Pine Cone, 3¾" Tall, Crystal, Rough-Edged Faceted Diamond Cuts *100.00*
Pitcher, Water, 7¾" Tall, 20 oz., Crystal with Fan Cuts, Tipperary *75.00*
Plate, 8¼", Diamond Cuts with Etched Claddagh Coat of Arms, Galway *85.00*
Sherbet, 4¾" Tall, Crystal with Etched Shamrocks *35.00*
Slipper, Crystal, 3" Tall, 6⅛" Long, Tipperary *45.00*
Tumbler, 4¾" Tall, 5 oz., Footed, Crystal with Fan Cuts, Tipperary *30.00*
Tumbler, 3" Tall, 9 oz., Cashel Pattern, Tipperary *25.00*

Tumbler, 12 oz., Old Fashioned Style, Crystal with Etched Shamrocks *$8.00*
Vase, 3" Tall, Crystal with Diamond and Oval Cuts, Tipperary *25.00*
Vase, 5" Tall, Crystal with Diamond and Fan Cuts, Tipperary *40.00*
Vase, 7" Tall, Castle Shape, Crystal-Cut Diamond and Fan, Tipperary *75.00*
Vase, 8" Tall, Crystal with Cut Diamonds and Leaves, Galway *70.00*
Wine Goblet, 8 oz., Crystal with Etched Harps *10.00*

Glass has been made in Ireland for centuries, and much of it was and still is imported to the United States. The most famous name is Waterford (separate listings), but the cities of Cork and Dublin also house large factories and have produced significant quantities of glass in the past. A few of the newest rivals of Waterford's cut crystal are Tipperary, Galway, and Kerry glass.

LALIQUE GLASS   RENÉ LALIQUE, FRANCE, LATE 19TH CENTURY–PRESENT

Object   *Price*
Ashtray, 4½" Long, 8 Girls' Faces around the Edge *$125.00*
Ashtray, 5½" Long, Fish with Bubbles Design, Signed "R. Lalique" *250.00*
Ashtray, Mouse in Center, Yellow, Signed "R. Lalique, France" *425.00*
Beaker, 4" Tall, 6 Panels of Classical Standing Figures *150.00*
Birds, Flying, 12" Tall, Framed, Signed "R. Lalique" *2500.00*
Birds, Love, Menu Holder, Framed, Signed "R. Lalique" *250.00*
Bowl, 8", Opalescent, Mermaids Design *1500.00*
Bowl, 8", Berry Foot, Gray, Mistletoe Design, Signed "R. Lalique" *325.00*
Bowl, 8", Opalescent Blue, Nudes Design in Relief *750.00*
Bowl, 9½", Opal, Fish and Waves Design, Signed "R. Lalique, France" *950.00*
Bowl, 9½", Footed, Dog and Foliage Design, Signed "R, Lalique, France" *950.00*

Lalique glass. Photo by Mark Pickvet.

Lalique glass. Photo by Mark Pickvet.

Bowl, 9¹/₂", Opal, Dahlias Design, Signed "R. Lalique, France" *$900.00*

Bowl, 10", Amber Finish, Black Flower Design, Signed "R. Lalique, France" *1000.00*

Bowl, 10", Opal, Peacock Feather Design, Signed "R. Lalique, France" *950.00*

Bowl, 12", Fish and Bubbles Design *550.00*

Bowl, Rose, 5³/₄", Frosted, Ball-Shaped Flower Blooms and Stems *275.00*

Box, 4", Diameter, Black Rooster and Wheat Design, Signed "Lalique" (without Original Box $4000.00) *6000.00*

Buffalo Figurine, 4¹/₂" Tall, Frosted *250.00*

Candlestick, 6" Tall, Embossed Geomeric Designs, Signed *250.00*

Cat, Sitting, 8¹/₄" Tall, Satin Frosted Finish *225.00*

Chandelier, Bowl Form with 4 Chains, 14" Diameter, Framed Design, Signed "R. Lalique" *3000.00*

Clock, Pendulet, 4¹/₂" Square, Opal, Nudes, Signed "R. Lalique" *2500.00*

Falcon Mascot, 6" Tall, Framed, Signed "R. Lalique" *1000.00*

Fish, Angel, 2" Tall, 2¹/₈" Long, Various Frosted Colors, Signed "Lalique France" ...*100.00*

Fish, 5" Tall, Polished Crystal *75.00*

Girl, Nude with Goat, 4" Tall, Signed "Lalique" *325.00*

Hood Ornament, 6¹/₄" Long, Frosted Dragonfly Design *5000.00*

Hood Ornament, Fish Design, 3⁷/₈" Tall, Frosted, Signed "R. Lalique, France" *3500.00*

Hood Ornament, 5" Tall, 5 Rearing Horses Design *4500.00*

Inkwell, 6" Diameter, Spiraled Serpents, Signed "R. Lalique" *3500.00*

Jardiniere, 5¹/₄" Diameter, 2 Antelope-Designed Handles *2500.00*

Lizard Figurine, 6¹/₂" Tall, Green *250.00*

Mascot, Kneeling Nudes Bending Backward, 5" Tall, Signed "R. Lalique, France" .*4000.00*

Owl Figurine, 3" Tall *125.00*

Paperweight, Owl, 3¹/₂", Frosted *150.00*

Paperweight, Eagle Head, 4¹/₂", Amber *1250.00*

Perfume Bottle with Ball Stopper, 8" Tall, Disk Form, Nina Ricci Brand *250.00*

Perfume Bottle with Stopper, 3¹/₂" Tall, Framed Crystal, Deux Fleurs Brand, Signed "R. Lalique, France" *425.00*

Perfume Bottle with Stopper, 4¹/₂" Tall, 4 Paneled Turtles with Heads Back *6250.00*

Perfume Bottle with Stopper, 6" Tall, Transparent Brown Finish, Coty Amber Antique Brand, Signed "R. Lalique" *1250.00*

Perfume Bottle with Stopper, 6" Tall, Footed, Framed Design, Roses Brand, Signed "R. Lalique" *725.00*

Perfume Bottle with Stopper, 7" Tall, Black Enamel, Forvil Le Parfum Brand, Signed "R. Lalique, France" $825.00
Plate, 8", Engraved Hunting Dog, Signed "Lalique" *500.00*
Plate, Collector, 1965 ....*1000.00*
Plate, Collector, 1966, Dream Rose, 8½" *350.00*
Plate, Collector, 1967 ....*225.00*
Plate, Collector, 1968 through 1976 ....*125.00*
Plate, 9", Opalescent Seashell Design *1000.00*
Powder Box with Cover, 3⅝" Diameter, Dancing Nudes and Garland Design *375.00*
Rooster Mascot, 8" Tall, Framed, Signed "R. Lalique, France" *675.00*
Seal, 5¼" Tall, Frosted on Jagged Clear Crystal Base *950.00*
Sparrow, 4¼" Long, Satin Frosted Finish *125.00*
Tray, 15½" Oval, Clear and Frosted Carnation Blossoms Design *1000.00*
Vase, 4¾" Tall, 4" Wide, Dampierre Design *375.00*
Vase, 5" Tall, Footed, Frosted Swirled Body with 2 Applied Doves *225.00*
Vase, 5" Tall, Bulbous, Fish Design *850.00*
Vase, 5¼" Tall, Male Nudes in Base "Holding Up" Vessel *2750.00*
Vase, 6" Tall, Black on Opal Coloring, Band of Rabbits Design, Signed "R. Lalique"*1500.00*
Vase, 6¾" Tall, Globe-Shaped, Swimming Fish with Lengthy Fins and Tails *350.00*
Vase, 7" Tall, Frosted, Nesting Birds Design *375.00*
Vase, 7" Tall, Globe Shape, Frosted, Antelope Design, Signed *375.00*
Vase, 7" Tall, Globe Shape, Blue, Fern Leaf Design, Signed "R. Lalique" *1250.00*
Vase, 7¼" Tall, 6 Nudes Holding Urns Design *2250.00*
Vase, 8" Tall, Gray, Ibex and Floral Design, Signed "R. Lalique, France" *1750.00*
Vase, 8" Tall, 2 Doves Design, Signed "Lalique" *375.00*
Vase, 8½" Tall, Blue Opal, Snail Shell Design, Signed "R. Lalique, France" *2250.00*
Vase, 9¼" Tall, Globe-Shaped, Allover Molded Fish Design *1750.00*
Vase, 9½" Tall, Opal, 4 Pairs of Lovebirds, Signed "R. Lalique, France" *3250.00*
Vase, 9½" Tall, Globe-Shaped, Dark Gray, Large Fish Design, Signed "R. Lalique" .*20,000.00*
Vase, 9½" Tall, 6 Alternating Panels of Female Nudes *4000.00*

Lalique glass. Photo by Robin Rainwater.

Vase, 10" Tall, Ovoid Shape, Framed Archers Design *$4000.00*
Vase, 10" Tall, Bulbous, Amber, Coiled Serpent Design, Signed "R. Lalique" *18,000.00*
Vase, 10" Tall, Smoke-Colored Eagles and Feathers Design *3500.00*
Vase, 11" Tall, Tapered Neck, Frosted, Mythological Creatures' Design *1500.00*
Vase, 13¼" Tall, Black, Alligator and Pineapple Branch Design, Signed "R. Lalique" *12,500.00*
Wine Glass, 6" Tall, Crystal and Frosted, Dancing Nudes on Stem *175.00*
Yorkshire Terrier, 2½" Tall, Frosted *300.00*

René Lalique worked in the 1890s as a jeweler making paste glass jewelry. M. F. Coty contracted Lalique to design perfume bottles, and Lalique's glass creations made him France's premier designer of the 20th century.

Lalique's figure glass is usually made of quality lead crystal and may be frosted or enameled; a few rare items were produced in black. The figures are often formed into useful objects and may be molded or blown in several identical views. Figures also may be cameo engraved, heavily etched, and contain smooth satiny acidized or pearlized finishes.

Dating is a big problem with Lalique glass. Older molds have been reused, but some signed marks are helpful. Up to his death in 1945, most were marked "R. Lalique." The "R" was dropped a little later. Other pieces may contain "R. Lalique, France" as a signature.

LISMORE   WATERFORD CRYSTAL LTD., 1951–PRESENT

Object	*Price*
Bell, 3" Tall, Ring Handle	*$50.00*
Biscuit Jar with Cover, 7" Tall	*150.00*
Bowl, 4", 2¼" Tall	*40.00*
Bowl, 5"	*70.00*
Bowl, 9½"	*140.00*
Brandy Snifter	*50.00*
Carafe,Wine, 22 oz.	*150.00*
Champagne Glass	*40.00*
Claret Glass	*40.00*
Cordial Glass	*30.00*
Creamer, Pitcher Style, 3" Tall	*50.00*
Decanter, Ship's, with Faceted Stopper, 9½" Tall	*250.00*
Decanter, Whiskey, 10" Tall	*265.00*
Decanter, Wine	*225.00*
Honey Jar with Cover, 4⅛" Tall	*85.00*
Perfume Bottle with Brass Top and Atomizer, 4½" Tall	*80.00*
Pitcher, Milk, 24 oz.	*140.00*
Salt and Pepper Shakers, 6" Tall, Round Feet, Silver-Plated Tops	*125.00*
Sauce Boat, Small Cup-Pitcher Style, 8 oz.	*60.00*
Sherbet	*50.00*
Shot Glass, 1.6 oz., 2½" Tall	*30.00*
Sugar Bowl, 1¾" Tall	*35.00*
Sugar Shaker with Silver-Plated Top, 8" Tall	*70.00*
Tumbler, 5 oz.	*30.00*
Tumbler, 9 oz., Old-Fashioned Style	*35.00*
Tumbler, 10 oz.	*40.00*

Tumbler, 10 oz., Iced Tea, Footed *$50.00*
Tumbler, 12 oz., Old-Fashioned Style *40.00*
Vase, Bud, 4" Tall *45.00*
Vase, 8¹/₂" Tall, Round Base *100.00*
Vase, 9" Tall, Wedge and Olive Cuts *175.00*
Wine Glass, 10 oz. *60.00*
Wine Glass, Red or White *40.00*
Wine Glass, Oversized *95.00*

"Lismore" is one of the new Waterford's most popular cut patterns. For older as well as other newer items, see the Waterford listings near the end of this chapter.

LOETZ GLASS   AUSTRIA, 1840S–EARLY 1900S

Object	*Price*
Basket, Bride's, Red with Enameled Designs, Silver Holder	*$750.00*
Basket, 10" Tall, Amber with Iridescent Blue Threading, Prunt Handle	*.850.00*
Bowl, 2¹/₂", Miniature, Green Papillon with Silver Deposit	*350.00*
Bowl, 6¹/₂", Ruffled, 3 Applied Purple Handles	*125.00*
Bowl, 9", Ruffled, Iridescent Purple	*400.00*
Bowl, 9¹/₂", Scalloped, Iridescent Gold Leaf Design	*500.00*
Bowl, 12", Iridescent Gold, Applied Glass Decoration	*550.00*
Bowl, Rose, 4", Iridescent Shades of Red	*100.00*
Bowl, Rose, 4¹/₂", Staghorn Base, Green with Purple Threading	*400.00*
Candlestick, 10" Tall, Red and Green Fern Design	*300.00*
Chalice, 5¹/₂" Tall, Iridescent Blue-Green, Tear Drop Design	*2500.00*
Cookie Jar with Silver-Plated Cover, Pink Florette Design	*375.00*
Epergne, 4 Green Trumpet-Style Lilies and Small Baskets Design	*600.00*
Ewer, 6" Tall, Iridescent Green with Applied Handles	*525.00*
Jar with Cover, 8" Diameter, Cameo Floral Design, Signed "Leotz"	*750.00*
Lamp, Candle, 12" Tall, Gold Spotted Shade and Base, Red and Green Leaves Design	*750.00*
Lamp, Table, 20" Tall, Bronze Serpent Base, Iridescent Threaded Green Globe Shade	*5000.00*
Pitcher, 5¹/₂" Tall, Square Top, Ribbed Handle, Iridescent White Crackle Design	*550.00*
Pitcher, Syrup, with Silverplated Lid, 8" Tall, Iridescent Cobalt Blue	*1000.00*
Toothpick Holder, Silver Overlay Design	*200.00*
Vase, 4¹/₂" Tall, Iridescent Silver to Blue, Signed "Loetz"	*550.00*
Vase, 5" Tall, Iridescent Gold, Signed "Loetz"	*325.00*
Vase, 6" Tall, Pinched Sides, Iridescent Blue	*575.00*
Vase, 6" Tall, Iridescent Blue to Gold, Lily Pad Design, Signed "Loetz"	*525.00*
Vase, 6" Tall, Iridescent Gold, Signed "Loetz"	*350.00*
Vase, 6" Tall, Iridescent Green	*150.00*
Vase, 6" Tall, Iridescent Purple to Silver, Signed "Loetz"	*375.00*
Vase, 6¹/₂" Tall, Iridescent Yellow to Gold, Blue and Platinum Wave Design	*1750.00*
Vase, 6¹/₂" Tall, Green with Blue Serpent around Neck	*450.00*
Vase, 7" Tall, Bottle Form, Applied Iridescent Grape Design	*175.00*
Vase, 7" Tall, 13" Diameter, 3-Lobed Rim, Iridescent Green to Silver to Blue, Swirls and Spots Design	*1500.00*
Vase, 8", Pinched Sides, Iridescent Blue Swirl Design	*600.00*
Vase, 8" Tall, Ruffled, Opalescent Green Swirl Design	*175.00*
Vase, 8" Tall, Pedestal Base, Iridescent Bronze	*225.00*

Vase, 9" Tall, Pinched Sides, Iridescent Blue to Gold with Pink Highlights *$650.00*
Vase, 9" Tall, Bronze Holder, Ruffled, Iridescent Gold Wavy Design *1500.00*
Vase, 9¼" Tall, Bronzed Leaf and Floral Design on Green Cameo *1750.00*
Vase, 9¾" Tall, Pinched, Ribbed, Iridescent Gold *750.00*
Vase, 10" Tall, Iridescent Gold with Silver Overlay *1000.00*
Vase, 11" Tall, Iridescent Bronze with Purple Threading *1000.00*
Vase, 12" Tall, Ruffled, Blue with Pink Interior *275.00*
Vase, 12" Tall, Iridescent Gold, Floral Decoration *600.00*
Vase, 12" Tall, Iridescent Dark Blue to Light Blue *750.00*
Vase, 12" Tall, Ruffled, Iridescent Crystal with Pink Interior *275.00*
Vase, 12½" Tall, Iridescent Blue to Green *650.00*
Vase, 13" Tall, Amber with Gold and Rose Decoration *300.00*
Vase, 13¼" Tall, Bronzed Leaves on Yellow *2000.00*
Vase, 14" Tall, Green on Gray Cameo, Butterfly and Floral Design *1500.00*
Vase, 19" Tall, Iridescent Blue and Silver Peacock Design *1250.00*

The original Loetz Glassworks was founded in 1840 in Western Austria (Klostermule). They earned a reputation early on as a maker of high-quality glassware. During the Art Nouveau period, they produced iridescent glass similar to that of Carder at Steuben and Tiffany. A few other Loetz originals include threaded glass and cameo designs. Identification can be difficult since much of Loetz's work was not signed, and at times cheaper imitation iridescent glass has been attributed to Loetz.

MID-EASTERN GLASS 1980S–PRESENT

Object   *Price*
Bowl, 3", Silver Decoration at Top, Cinnamon Red, Dark Green, or Ultramarine, Israel *$50.00*
Bowl, 5", Silver Decoration at Top, Cinnamon Red, Dark Green, or Ultramarine, Israel *95.00*
Creamer, 4½" Tall, Silver Handle and Decoration at Top, Cinnamon Red, Dark Green, or Ultramarine, Israel *70.00*
Perfume Bottle with Gold Stopper, 5" Tall, Hand Blown, Amethyst with Gold Accents, Egypt *30.00*
Perfume Bottle with Gold Stopper, 5½" Tall, Hand Blown, Amber with Gold Accents *30.00*
Perfume Bottle with Gold Stopper, 5½" Tall, Hand Blown, Rose Red with Gold Accents, Egypt *35.00*
Perfume Bottle with Gold Stopper, 6½" Tall, Hand Blown, Aquamarine with Gold Accents, Egypt *35.00*
Salt Cellar, 2" Tall, Silver Overlay Decoration, Cinnamon Red, Dark Green, or Ultramarine, Israel *55.00*
Sugar, 5" Tall, Silver Lid and Decoration at Top, Cinnamon Red, Dark Green, or Ultramarine, Israel *70.00*
Vase, 6" Tall, Silver Stem and Trailings, Cinnamon Red, Dark Green, or Ultramarine, Israel *70.00*
Vase, 6½" Tall, Silver Stem and Trailings, Cinnamon Red, Dark Green, or Ultramarine, Israel *75.00*
Vase, 8" Tall, Silver Stem and Trailings, Cinnamon Red, Dark Green, or Ultramarine, Israel *90.00*
Vase, 9½" Tall, Silver Stem and Trailings, Cinnamon Red, Dark Green, or Ultramarine, Israel *125.00*
Vase, 12" Tall, Silver Stem and Trailings, Cinnamon Red, Dark Green, or Ultramarine, Israel *275.00*

Though glass was first invented in Egypt thousands of years ago, the ancient glass of the region (such as Islamic) is housed in museums, and rarely are such items offered for sale. Modern examples from 20 years ago or less are suddenly springing up on the collector market. The Israeli pieces listed are made by David Barak in his studio in Herzlia, Israel.

MILLEFIORE GLASS   VENICE, ITALY, 14TH CENTURY–PRESENT

Object	Price
Bowl, Finger, 2", 2 Applied Crystal Handles, Pink, Green, and White Canes	*$60.00*
Bowl, Finger, 3", Blue Ground	*100.00*
Bowl, 4", 2 Applied Crystal Handles, Blue and White Canes	*85.00*
Bowl, 6", Brass Holder	*225.00*
Creamer, 4" Tall, Scattered Design on White Ground	*225.00*
Cruet with Stopper, 5" Tall, Allover Millefiore, Including Handle and Stopper	*400.00*
Cup, 2¼" Tall	*75.00*
Epergne, 16" Tall, Bowl with 3 Ruffled Trumpet-Style Vases	*300.00*
Goblet, 7½" Tall, Crystal Stem and Base, Multicolored Canes	*200.00*
Lamp, 7" Tall, Dome Shade, Millefiore Base	*325.00*
Lamp, 10" Tall, Shade and Base in Lavender Cane Form	*425.00*
Lamp, 19" Tall, 9"-Diameter Dome Shade, Millefiore Shade and Base	*750.00*
Paperweight, 3", Allover Crowned Design	*100.00*
Saucer (Matches Cup)	*50.00*
Sugar with Cover, 4" Tall, Blue	*250.00*
Toothpick Holder, 2¾" Tall, Blue Ground	*85.00*
Tumbler, 4" Tall, Blue and Green Millefiore Design	*175.00*
Vase, 4" Tall, Miniature, Blue Ground	*150.00*
Vase, 6¼" Tall, Cobalt Blue with Multicolored Canes	*225.00*
Vase, 8" Tall, Ruffled, Applied Crystal Handle, Multicolored Canes	*200.00*
Vase, 8" Tall, 2-Handled, Millefiore Design in Curving Rows	*375.00*
Vase, 8" Tall, Blue Ground	*750.00*
Vase, Dragonfly with Netting Design, Signed	*850.00*

Millefiore glass. Courtesy of the Corning Museum of Glass.

Vase, Ruffled, Violet Ground *$200.00*

Millefiore is an ancient glass technique in which tiny multicolored glass disks are imbedded into the surface of an object to produce a mosaic effect. The term means "thousand flowers," for each little disk is made to resemble flowers. The disks were made by slicing fused glass canes or cylindrical rods. These cross sections were in turn arranged in a desired pattern, refired, and shaped into the desired item. The pieces listed above are Venetian designs from the later 19th and early 20th centuries. Very few American pieces were made in this style (Carder's "Tessera" is one example).

MOSER GLASS   CZECHOSLOVAKIA, 1850S–PRESENT

Object	*Price*
Basket, 6" Tall, 6½" Diameter, Malachite, Woman and Cherubs Design, Marked "Moser/Carlsbad"	*$175.00*
Bowl, 5", Cut Panels, Signed "Moser-Alexandrite"	*250.00*
Box with Hinged Cover, 3" Tall, 4" Diameter, Malachite, Nude Woman on Cover, Marked "Moser/Carlsbad"	*175.00*
Box with Hinged Cover, 5", Ball Feet, Cameo Gold Amazon Warriors on Cobalt Blue	*525.00*
Box with Hinged Cover, 5¾", Cranberry, Gold Vines	*175.00*
Candlestick, 4" Tall, Amethyst, Signed	*100.00*
Candlestick, 14" Tall, Cranberry Overlay with Gilded Scrolls	*725.00*
Chalice, 6¾" Tall, Amethyst to Crystal, Gold Leaves Design	*675.00*
Compote, Blue and Crystal Floral Decoration, Gold Rim	*150.00*
Cruet with Stopper, 5" Tall	*275.00*
Decanter with Stopper, 12½" Tall, Cranberry, Gold Grapes	*625.00*
Decanter with Stopper, 16" Tall, Applied Prunts and Glass Jewels	*500.00*
Ewer, 9" Tall, Cornucopia-Shaped, Pedestal Base, Aquamarine with Gold Foliage and Flowers	*1000.00*
Ewer, 11½" Tall, Multicolored Beads, Enameled Floral Design	*750.00*
Ewer, 12" Tall, Multicolored Leaves on Amber Base, Blue Handle	*850.00*
Perfume Bottle with Cut Stopper, 3" Tall, Amethyst Prism-Cut Design	*275.00*
Perfume Bottle with Stopper, 4½" Tall, Cobalt Blue with Gold Figures	*175.00*
Perfume Bottle with Stopper, 10" Tall, Crystal with Heavy Gold Decoration	*525.00*
Pitcher, Water, 8¼" Tall, Footed, Amber with Blue Trim	*450.00*
Pitcher, Water, 10" Tall, 4 Gilded Feet, Green with Multicolored (Including Gold) Floral and Scroll Design	*600.00*
Tumbler, 4¼ Tall, Cranberry with Gold Floral Design	*100.00*
Urn, 14" Tall, White to Cranberry Cut, Enameled Floral Design with Gold	*800.00*
Vase, 3" Tall, Cobalt Blue, Gold Bands, Enameled Oriental Woman Design	*175.00*
Vase, 3½" Tall, Miniature, Amethyst	*125.00*
Vase, 5" Tall, Gold Foliage with Enameled Acorns and Oak Leaves	*250.00*
Vase, 5" Tall, Malachite, Nude Woman and Floral Design, Marked "Moser/Carlsbad"	*150.00*
Vase, 6½" Tall, Amethyst, Gold Rim, Engraved Tulips Design	*375.00*
Vase, 7" Tall, Amber and Blue, Enameled Floral Design	*750.00*
Vase, 8" Tall, 6" Diameter, 4-Footed, Blue Floral Design with Gold Scrolling	*1000.00*
Vase, 8¾" Tall, Smoke Crackle, Enameled Orchid Design	*800.00*
Vase, 9½" Tall, Malachite, Nude Woman and Grapes Design, Marked "Moser/Carlsbad"	*225.00*

Vase, 9½" Tall, Ruffled, Pink Flowers with Gilding *$225.00*
Vase, 10", Handled, Overall Enamel Design, Signed *650.00*
Vase, 10" Tall, Amethyst, Gold Trim, Birds and Lily Pads Design *500.00*
Vase, 10" Tall, 3" Diameter, Cameo Poppy Design *2500.00*
Vase, 10" Tall, Bulbous, Cobalt Blue, Signed *175.00*
Vase, 11" Tall, Cobalt Blue, Gold Rim, Engraved Elephants and Palm Trees *2000.00*
Vase, 11½" Tall, Crystal with Intaglio Engraved Purple Flowers *775.00*
Vase, 15" Tall, Flared, Crystal to Green with Engraved Floral Design *850.00*
Vase, 20" Tall, Trumpet Form, Gold Feet and Border, Light Purple with Enameled Nude Design *1000.00*
Vase, 22" Tall, Handled, Emerald Green with Gold Leaves, Dutchman in Reverse Design *1500.00*
Whiskey Tumbler, 3" Tall, Cranberry with Gold Grapes *100.00*

The original Moser Glass Works was founded by Leo Moser in Karlsbad (presently Karlovy-Vary), Czechoslovakia. Moser began his career by doing commission portrait engraving on glass for wealthy patrons of health spas. In his own factory, he further developed artistic forms, including orchid-colored glass named Alexandrite (separate from Webb's); carved animal forms, especially birds in flight; carved floral designs; gold leaf and other enameling, etc.

Items marked "Malachite" are characterized by swirled layers of dark green shades (just like the mineral it is named after).

NAILSEA GLASS ENGLAND, LATE 18TH CENTURY–PRESENT

Object *Price*
Bottle, Bellows, 11" long, Crystal with Pine and White Loopings *$110.00*
Bowl, Finger, 4", Crystal with Blue and White Streaking *100.00*
Bowl, Finger, 4½", 4-Fold Rim, Chartreuse with White Loopings *85.00*
Bowl, 4¼" Tall, 2¼" Tall, Citron with White Looping *125.00*
Candlestick, 10" Tall, Bulb Stem, Cone-Shaped Base, Crystal with White Loopings *175.00*
Cologne Bottle, 5⅜" Tall, Milk White with Blue and Cranberry Loopings, Crystal Stopper with Blue, Pink, and White Loopings *500.00*
Flask, 6½" Tall, Milk White with Dark Blue Loopings *125.00*
Flask, 7¼" Tall, Crystal with Cranberry and White Loopings *125.00*
Flask, 7⅜" Tall, Cobalt Blue with White Loopings *150.00*
Lamp, 7" Tall, Blue Shade with White Loopings *625.00*
Mug, 5½" Tall, Crystal with Blue and White Loopings *325.00*
Pitcher, Water, 9½" Tall, Applied Crystal Handle and Feet, Cranberry with White Loopings *1000.00*
Powder Horn Novelty, 12" Long, Light and Dark Blue Shading with White Loopings *175.00*
Rolling Pin, 19" Long, Crystal with Pink Loopings *125.00*
Salt Dip, 3²/₄" Diameter, Footed, Crystal with White Loopings *175.00*
Witch Ball, 4½" Diameter, Crystal with Thin White Loopings *200.00*

This glass obtained its name from the small town of Nailsea, England. The first factory produced novelty items, and a particular style developed. It was characterized by colored or crystal glass decorated with contrasting loops, swirls, or spirals. The style spread to other parts of England and even a little to America.

PEACHBLOW   THOMAS WEBB & SONS, ENGLAND,
1890S–EARLY 1900S

Object   *Price*

Biscuit Jar with Cover, 6" Tall, Pine Needles and Butterfly Design with Gold Decoration
....*$1000.00*
Bowl, 2½", 3¾" Tall, Gold Buterfly and Pine Needles Design *300.00*
Bowl, Rose, 2¾", 3" Tall, 8-Crimped *250.00*
Cologne Bottle with Stopper, 5" Tall *600.00*
Vase, 3¾" Tall, 2¾" Diameter, Gold Prunus Design *375.00*
Vase, 4½" Tall, Gold Flowers with Silver Centers Design.....................*500.00*
Vase, 5" Tall, Footed, Applied Crystal Flowers and Leaves *500.00*
Vase, 5¾" Tall, 3" Diameter, Gold Floral and Insect Design *300.00*
Vase, 5¾" Tall, Coralene Seaweed Design...................................*350.00*
Vase, 6" Tall, Ruffled, Blue Interior, Enameled Floral Design *275.00*
Vase, 6½" Tall, 3½" Diameter, Gold Prunus and Bee Design *475.00*
Vase, 7" Tall, 4" Diameter, Gold Prunus Design *350.00*
Vase, 7" Tall, Gold Floral, Leaves, and Dragonfly Design......................*750.00*
Vase, 7¼" Tall, Gold Prunus Design *275.00*
Vase, 7½" Tall, Gold Bands, Floral, and Butterfly Design......................*825.00*
Vase, 7½" Tall, Gold and Purple Floral Design *225.00*
Vase, 8" Tall, Pinched Sides, Acid-Cut *750.00*
Vase, 8" Tall, Slender, Lined *625.00*
Vase, 8¼" Tall, Horizontal Ribbing, White Interior *200.00*
Vase, 8½" Tall, Gold Branches with Blossoms and Leaves Design..............*475.00*
Vase, 9⅞" Tall, Bottle-Shaped, Gold Floral and Leaves Design ....._____.*475.00*
Vase, 10" Tall, 6" Diameter, Gold Prunus Design *750.00*
Vase, 11¾" Tall, 5¾" Diameter, Clear Feet and Floral Design *800.00*
Vase, 15" Tall, 7" Diameter, Rose Shaded to Pink, Gold Floral and Birds Design ...*1250.00*

Peachblow was originally made in America and usually shades from a rose pink at
the top to white or grayish-white at the bottom. See the end of the chapter for more
on Thomas Webb & Sons.

PEKING GLASS   CHINA, 1680–EARLY 20TH CENTURY

Object   *Price*

Bowl, 7", Blue on White Cameo, Floral Design *$225.00*
Bowl, 7", Multicolored Flowers, Leaves, and Butterfly Design on White Cameo *350.00*
Bowl with Cover, 7½", Red on White Cameo, Bird on Floral Branches Design *400.00*
Candlestick, 6" Tall, Dragon Foot, Green Cased Center with Oak Leaf Top *125.00*
Cup, 3½" Tall, Flared, Blue on White Cameo, Dragon and Cloud Design *250.00*
Snuff Bottle, 2¼" Tall, White with Green Floral Design *100.00*
Urn with Cover, Teakwood Stand, Blue and White Floral Stand *225.00*
Vase, 6" Tall, Red on White Cameo, Butterflies and Peony Design *175.00*
Vase, 8" Tall, Cameo Yellow Floral Design on White *225.00*
Vase, 8½" Tall, Bulbous, Red on White Cameo, Floral Design *250.00*
Vase, 9" Tall, Red on White Cameo, Birds and Pine Tree Design *275.00*
Vase, 9" Tall, Green on White Cameo, Raven and Pine Tree Design *275.00*

Peking glass. Photo by Robin Rainwater.

Vase, 9¼" Tall, Red on White Cameo, Monkey in Pine Tree Design *$300.00*
Vase, 9¼" Tall, Yellow on White Cameo, Butterfly and Peony Design *300.00*
Vase, 10" Tall, Blue on White Cameo, Bird in Floral Tree Design *325.00*
Vase, 10" Tall, Yellow on White Cameo, Monkey in Pine Tree Design *350.00*
Vase, 10" Tall, Gourd Shape, Red on White Cameo, Peony Design *325.00*
Vase, 10¼" Tall, Hexagonal, Red on White Cameo, Floral Panel Design *375.00*
Vase, 12" Tall, Bulbous, White with Dark Red Floral Design *275.00*
Vase, 12" Tall, Red on White Cameo, Butterflies and Peonies Design *550.00*
Vase, 12½" Tall, Red on White Cameo, Floral Design *600.00*

Glassware in China was made to resemble the more desirable porcelain. Glass was considered inferior and only an imitation by the Chinese; however, they experimented with opaque glassware, including cameo designs. The name "Peking" is also attributed to glassware made in other cities in China (such as Po-shan); the final finish was applied in Peking factories.

PELOTON GLASS BOHEMIA (WESTERN CZECHOSLOVAKIA), 1880–EARLY 20TH CENTURY

Object   *Price*
Biscuit Jar with Cover, 6" Tall, Multicolored Threading on Opal White *$500.00*
Biscuit Jar with Silverplated Cover and Handle, 7" Tall *625.00*
Bowl, Rose, 2½", 6-Crimped, Multicolored Threading on Opal White *200.00*
Bowl, Rose, 2½", 6-Crimped, Cyrstal Feet, Multicolored Threading on Lavender *225.00*
Bowl, Rose, 2½", 6-Crimped, Wishbone Feet, Multicolored Strings on Cased Pink ...*225.00*
Cruet with Crystal Stopper, 7" Tall, Pastel Filaments on Light Blue Ground *300.00*
Pitcher, Water, 7½" Tall, Clear and White Threading, Enameled Leaves and Floral Design
....*400.00*
Pitcher, Water, 8" Tall, Crystal Overshot Style *350.00*
Plate, 7", Single Colors on a Translucent Ground *325.00*
Vase, 3" Tall, Miniature, Applied Legs, Violet *300.00*
Vase, 3⅛" Tall, Crystal with White Threading *200.00*

Vase, 3 3/4" Tall, 6-Petal Feet, 4-Corner Top, Multicolored Threaded Design	$325.00
Vase, 4" Tall, Folded Tri-Corner Top, Multicolored Threading on Opal White	375.00
Vase, 4" Tall, Bulbous, Ribbed, Pastel Strings on Pink Shading	575.00
Vase, 5" Tall, Tri-Corner Top, Blue and White Threading	325.00
Vase, 5 3/8" Tall, Ruffled, Yellow and White Threading	350.00
Vase, 6" Tall, Crimped, Multicolored Threading on Crystal to Lavender Shading	425.00
Vase, 6 3/4" Tall, Yellow with White Interior and Threading	350.00
Vase, 7" Tall, 5 Wishbone Feet, Ribbed, Multicolored Threading on Opal White	475.00
Vase, 8" Tall, Tiny Multicolored Flaking on Opal White	450.00
Vase, 9" Tall, Multicolored Threading on Opal White	475.00
Vase, 13" Tall, Multicolored Threading on Opal White	625.00

This design was first patented by Wilhelm Kralick in 1880 and is characterized by short random lengths and shapes of colored streaks (or threads) on an opaque, colored base. The base is most often opal white. The streaking was added by rolling the threads directly into the base when the article was removed from the oven. Pieces were also further decorated by enameling.

PERTHSHIRE PAPERWEIGHTS LTD. CRIEFF, SCOTLAND, 1970–PRESENT

Object	*Price*
Bowl, 4 1/2", Blue Rim, White Vertical Latticino Bands, Millefiore Base	$125.00
Inkwell, 7 1/2" Tall, Millefiore Base and Stopper	450.00
Paperweight, 2 7/8", Mill Heart on Red Ground	200.00
Paperweight, 2 7/8", Opal Blue Ground, Multicolored	750.00
Paperweight, 3", Pattern Mill, Central Cane with Ribbon Twist and Other Canes	125.00
Paperweight, Panda, 3", Translucent Blue, Limited Edition (300)	750.00
Paperweight, 3 1/8", 86-Petal Dahlia in Canes	675.00
Paperweight, 3 1/2", Sea Horse and 2 Fish, Pink Seaweed, Crab, and Shell	350.00
Perfume Bottle with Glass Swirl Threaded Stopper, Millefiore Base	175.00
Shot Glass, 2 7/8" Tall, 5-Petal Yellow Lampwork Flower on Translucent Blue Ground	80.00
Tumbler, Millefiore Base	100.00

Perthshire has been in business only since 1970, and already many of their limited editions are valued at over $500. Perthshire is one of many companies (most are French) who have sparked a great revival in paperweight making and collecting.

SABINO ART GLASS FRANCE, 1920S–1930S, 1960S–1970S

Object	*Price*
Bird, Perched	$65.00
Bird, Wings Down	75.00
Birds Figure, 2 Babies Perched on Branch	25.00
Birds Figure, 2 Birds, 3 1/2" Tall, 4 1/2" Across	225.00
Birds Figure, 3 Birds, 5" Tall	250.00
Birds Figure, 5 Birds Perched on Branch	1250.00
Bowl, 5", Fish Design	75.00

Bunny Rabbit, 2" Tall *$35.00*
Butterfly, 2³/₄" Tall, Small, Wings Open *50.00*
Butterfly, 6" Tall, Large *30.00*
Cat, 2" Tall, Sleeping *30.00*
Cat, 2¹/₄" Tall, Sitting *45.00*
Cherub, 2" Tall *40.00*
Chick, Baby, 3³/₄" Tall, Jumping, Wings Up *65.00*
Chick, Baby, Drinking, Wings Down *50.00*
Collie, 2" Tall *55.00*
Dove, Small, Head Up *35.00*
Dragonfly, 6" Tall, 5³/₄" Long *150.00*
Elephant *30.00*
Figurine, Isadora Duncan *750.00*
Figurine, Nude with Long Flowing Hair, 6³/₄" Tall *225.00*
Figurine, Venus de Milo, Large *75.00*
Fish, 2" Long *30.00*
Fish, 4" Tall, 4" Long *80.00*
Fox *30.00*
Gazelle *100.00*
German Shepherd, 2" Tall *40.00*
Hand, Either Left or Right *225.00*
Hen *35.00*
Knife Rest, Bee or Fish Design *25.00*
Mockingbird, Large *100.00*
Mouse, 3" Long *60.00*
Owl, 4¹/₂" Tall *70.00*
Pekingese, 1¹/₄" Tall *35.00*
Perfume Bottle, 6" Tall, Loosely Draped Figures around Bottle *75.00*
Perfume Bottle, 6¹/₄" Tall, Frivolities, Opal Women and Swans Design *75.00*
Pigeon, 6¹/₄" Tall *125.00*
Poodle, 1⁴/₄" Tall *35.00*
Rabbit, 1⁷/₈" Long *35.00*
Rooster, 3¹/₂" Tall *40.00*
Rooster, Large *475.00*
Scottish Terrier, 1¹/₂" Tall *95.00*
Snail, 1" Tall, 3" Long *40.00*
Squirrel, 3¹/₂" Tall, Oval Base *45.00*
Stork, 7¹/₄" Tall *140.00*
Tray, Shell, Small *40.00*
Tray, Swallow, Small *35.00*
Turtle *35.00*
Vase, Opal, Colombes Design *500.00*
Vase, Oval and Pearl Design *250.00*
Woodpecker *65.00*
Zebra, 5¹/₂" Tall, 5¹/₂" Long *150.00*

Marius-Ernest Sabino First made a variety of art glass items (mostly figurines) in the 1920s. When the Art Nouveau period in France came to final halt in the 1930s, Sabino stopped production. He resurfaced in the 1960s with his own handmade molds and a special formula for gold opalescent glass. Sabino died in 1971, and his family continued export of the glass but were unable to duplicate his original formula.

St. Louis glass (France).
Photo by Robin Rainwater.

ST. LOUIS   FRANCE, 1840S–EARLY 1900S, 1950S–PRESENT

Object	*Price*

Bear Cub, 5¼" Tall, Frosted, with Clear Ball Base *$90.00*

Paperweight, 2⅜", Hollow White Canes (Honeycomb Effect) with Green Interior, Millifiore Center *2250.00*

Paperweight, 2⅜", 10 Red and Green Spiral Twists Alternating with 10 White Spiral Twists, Blue and White Millefiore Center *550.00*

Paperweight, 2½", 15-Petal Blue Clematis, Red and White Ground *1750.00*

Paperweight, 2½", Dark Pink Camomile with 4 Green Leaves and 1 Bud *375.00*

Paperweight, 2⅝", 2 Strawberries with 5 Blossoms *1500.00*

Paperweight, 2¾", Camomile with 52 Blue Petals, Cane Center *425.00*

Paperweight, 2¾", Double Pink Clematis, Double Swirl on White Lattice Ground . . .*350.00*

Paperweight, 2¾", 45-Petal Dahlia, Star Base, Blue and Amber Cane Stamen *3500.00*

Paperweight, 2¾", 2 Red and 2 White Turnips in Swirled Basket *1500.00*

Paperweight, 2⅞", Multicolored Butterfly with Millifiore Wings and Circular Border .*2500.00*

Paperweight, 2⅞", 9-Petaled Red Clematis with 3 Green Leaves, Millifiore Center, Blue and White Jasper Ground *1750.00*

Paperweight, 2⅞", Marbelized Turquoise and White Swirls *475.00*

Paperweight, 3", Red and White Flower Bouquet *600.00*

Paperweight, 3⅛", 3 Apples and 3 Pears in White Lattice Bowl *1850.00*

Paperweight, 3⅛", Millifiore Mushroom, Green Stem, Blue and White Filigree Base *2000.00*

Paperweight, 3⅛", 5-Petaled Blue, White, and Red Flowers with Millifiore Centers, Green Leaves *750.00*

Paperweight, Sulphide, 2", King Edward VIII Plaque Design *250.00*

Paperweight, Sulphide, 3", Faceted, Marquis de Lafayette Design *250.00*

Paperweight, Sulphide, Faceted, Pope John Paul II Design *150.00*

Seal With Ball, 6" Tall, Frosted with Clear Ball Base and Clear Ball on Seal's Nose .*115.00*

Vase, 13¾" Tall, 3 ¼"-Square base, Cobalt Blue Encased in Crystal *165.00*

Vase, 14" Tall, 3"-Square Base, Crystal or Burgundy *150.00*

The French classic period of paperweight manufacturing ran from about 1845 to 1860. The factories in the town of St. Louis, like Baccarat and Clichy, produced many pieces, then closed during the later Art Nouveau period. A revival of paperweight production occurred in the 1950s in all of these famous French glassmaking towns.

STEVENS AND WILLIAMS   ENGLAND, 1830S–1920S

Object	Price
Bowl, 3³/₄", 2¹/₂" Tall, Ruffled, Pale Orange	*$175.00*
Bowl, 7¹/₂", 6" Tall, Crimped, Amber Rim, Floral Design	*350.00*
Bowl, Rose, 2³/₄", Blue, Thumbprint Pattern	*200.00*
Bowl, Rose, 3¹/₂", Crimped, Opaque White	*150.00*
Bowl, Rose, 4¹/₄", Cranberry	*225.00*
Candlestick, 10" Tall, Moss Agate	*150.00*
Compote, 6", Honeycomb Stem, Engraved Poppies and Pods Design	*225.00*
Ewer, 5¹/₄ Tall, Amber Branch Handle, Cherry Design	*150.00*
Goblet, 7" Tall, Crystal Foot and Stem, Red Cut Overlay Bowl	*225.00*
Goblet, 8¹/₂" Tall, Gold Cut Overlay Floral Design on Green Ground	*250.00*
Perfume Bottle, 13" Tall, Swirled, Blue with Gold and Enameled Berries	*350.00*
Perfume Bottle with Stopper, 4¹/₂" Tall, Moss Agate	*125.00*
Perfume Bottle with Stopper, 9" Tall, Green and Crystal Swirl Design	*200.00*
Salt Dip, White Threading, Enameled Berry Design	*150.00*
Vase, 5" Tall, 3" Diameter, Pink with White Leaves and Engraved Grass	*425.00*
Vase, 5³/₄" Tall, Amber and Gold, Loop and Berry Design	*275.00*
Vase, 5³/₄" Tall, 4" Diameter, Dark Pink with Opal Interior and Ruffled Amber Leaves	*175.00*
Vase, 6¹/₂" Tall, Opaque Cream with Pink Cherries	*175.00*
Vase, 6¹/₂" Tall, 3³/₄" Diameter, 8-Crimped Rim, Pink with Ruffled Leaves Design	*225.00*
Vase, 7¹/₂" Tall, Ruffled, Amber Feet, Pink with Apple Leaves	*250.00*
Vase, 8³/₄" Tall, Silveria Design	*275.00*
Vase, 12" Tall, 5" Diameter, Clear Opal Rim and Leaves, Coral with White Interior	*450.00*
Vase, 13" Tall, Pear Shape, Multicolored Floral Design	*325.00*

Stevens and Williams produced glass in the famous village of Stourbridge, England. Their factory was named the Brierly Hill Glassworks, but many of their products are signed "Stevens & Williams." They made several art styles of glass (Alexandrite, Engraved Crystal, Silver Decorating, etc.), including an inexpensive method of manufacturing cameo glass. See additional listings under English Cameo Glass.

SWEDISH GLASS   20TH CENTURY

Object	Price
Angle Fish Ice Sculpture, 4¹/₄" Tall, Jonasson	*$90.00*
Bear Ice Sculpture, 6³/₄" Long, Grizzly, Jonasson	*250.00*
Bird Figurine, 3" Tall, Ruby Red, Early 1980s	*15.00*
Bowl, 4¹/₂", Crystal, Corona Design, Orrefors	*40.00*
Bowl, Berry, 5", Grand Thistle Pattern, Marigold Carnival	*20.00*
Bowl, Berry, 5", Grand Thistle Pattern, Green, Purple, or Smoke Carnival	*40.00*
Bowl, 5", 3¹/₂" Tall, Bulbous, Flared, Cranberry with White Gridding, Kosta	*200.00*

Bowl, 5¼", 3" Tall, Blue Crystal, Kosta *$525.00*

Bowl, 6", 3⅜" Tall, Crystal Faceted Cuts, Orrefors *70.00*

Bowl, 6¼", 5" Tall, Crystal Cased to Green, Brown Swirls, Etched "Kosta Sweden" . *400.00*

Buffalo Ice Sculpture, 6" Long, Jonasson *125.00*

Cardinals' Ice Sculpture, 6¼" Long, Pair, Jonasson *150.00*

Clock, 3⅛" Octagon, Crystal, Beveled, Orrefors *100.00*

Decanter with Stopper, 11¾" Tall, Crystal with Engraved Underwater Fisherman (Orrefors) *175.00*

Dolphin Ice Sculpture, 2" Long, Jonasson *40.00*

Dolphins Ice Sculpture, 5¾" Long, Pair, Jonasson *130.00*

Elephant Ice Sculpture, 6" Long, Jonasson *55.00*

Elephant Ice Sculpture, 8" Long, Jonasson *120.00*

Foal Ice Sculpture, 4¾" Long, Jonasson *90.00*

Goats Ice Sculpture, 6" Long, Pair of Mountain Goats, Jonasson *160.00*

Golfer Ice Sculpture, 6" Tall, Golfer Swinging, Nybro *90.00*

Ice Sculpture, Jagged Outer Edge, Engraved Reindeer Drinking from a Pool of Water (Kosta) *1750.00*

Kitten Ice Sculpture, 2" Long, Jonasson *40.00*

Kitten Ice Sculpture, 3¾" Long, Jonasson *65.00*

Lion Cub Ice Sculpture, 4¾" Long, Jonasson *90.00*

Lion and Lioness Ice Sculpture, 6¼" Long, Jonasson *325.00*

Loon Ice Sculpture, 5¼" Long, Jonasson *175.00*

Lynx Ice Sculpture, 6" Long, Jonasson *125.00*

Owl Ice Sculpture, 3¾" Long, Owlet, Jonasson *70.00*

Owl Ice Sculpture, 6¼" Long, Barn Owl, Jonasson *130.00*

Owl Ice Sculpture, 7¼" Long, Eagle Owl, Jonasson *235.00*

Owls Ice Sculpture, 5" Long, 5 Owlets, Jonasson *95.00*

Paperweight, 3" Round, Crystal, Cat, Dove, Eagle, Koala, Mouse, or Wren, Jonasson .*45.00*

Pitcher, Water, 38 oz., Crystal, Orrefors *100.00*

Pitcher, Water, Grand Thistle Pattern, Blue Carnival *2500.00*

Plate, 8", Crystal with Copper Wheel Engraved Head of Greek Goddess Helena, 1940s .*550.00*

Polar Bear Cub Ice Sculpture, 2" Long, Jonasson *40.00*

Polar Bear Ice Sculpture, 6" Long, Jonasson *125.00*

Rabbit Ice Sculpture, 3¾" Long, Jonasson *70.00*

Seal Ice Sculpture, 3¼" Long, Baby Seal, Jonasson *75.00*

Seals Ice Sculpture, 8" Tall, Pair, Limited Edition (975), Jonasson *475.00*

Swans Ice Sculpture, 4" Long, Swan and Cygnet, Jonasson *100.00*

Tumbler, Grand Thistle Pattern, Blue Carnival *600.00*

Vase, 4" Tall, Crystal with Etched Woman Viewing Moon and Stars, Orrefors *325.00*

Vase, 5" Tall, Crystal with Engraved Bird in Flight (Orrefors) *125.00*

Vase, 6¾" Tall, Flattened Oval Shape, Blue and Green Spiral Striping, Kosta *450.00*

Vase, 7⅞" Tall, Prism "Thousand Windows" Cut Crystal Pattern, Orrefors *275.00*

Vase, 8¼" Tall, Crystal, Square Base, Orrefors *125.00*

Vase, 8¾" Tall, Crystal with Interior Decoration of Amorphic Figures Playing Games, Inscribed "Orrefors 1938 Graal" *7000.00*

Vase, 10¼" Tall, Frosted Slim Female Archer, Signed "Orrefors" *150.00*

Vase, 12" Tall, Teardrop Form, Cased Crystal to Red, Kosta *300.00*

Vase, 13" Tall, Cut Crystal Twist Design, Black-Lined Interior, Kosta *600.00*

Vase, 14" Tall, Crystal with White Interior, Seaweed Design, Kosta *625.00*

Vase, Crystal with Separate Base, Copper Wheel Engraved Egyptian Dancer, 1940s .*675.00*

Wolf Ice Sculpture, 6" Tall, Jonasson *110.00*

One of the oldest Swedish glass firms noted for quality glass products was the Kosta Company in 1742. Much of their contemporary art forms of the early to mid-20th century are highly collectible. The Eda Glassworks in the Varmland region also produced some glass, including Carnival items in the early 20th century. Other Swedish firms experimented later with crystal art forms and engraving. The Orrefors Glasbruck is noted for engraving, particularly for their spectacular "Graal" line, and Mats Jonasson is a contemporary designer of crystal animal sculptures.

VAL ST. LAMBERT BELGIUM, 1880S–PRESENT

Object	*Price*
Bowl, 6", Blue Rim, Crystal Overlay, Engraved Design, Signed	*$150.00*
Bowl, 8", Scalloped, Applied Teardops	*200.00*
Candlestick, 6¼" Tall, Crystal Elysee Design	*90.00*
Candlestick, 11" Tall, Crystal Elysee Design	*115.00*
Candlestick, 11" Tall, 4-Footed, Bird Design	*75.00*
Perfume Bottle with Stopper, 5" Tall, Embossed Frosted Blue Design	*100.00*
Perfume Bottle with Stopper, 5¼" Tall, Cranberry to Crystal, Signed	*225.00*
Tumble-Up, Cameo Cranberry, Signed (Includes Tumbler and Matching Underplate), Tumbler, 5½" Tall	*775.00*
Translucent Pink, Signed	*100.00*
Vase, 5¾" Tall, Multicolored Enamel Coloring on Cameo Olive Green Base	*750.00*
Vase, 6" Tall, Green, Sweet Gum Leaves and Balls Design	*350.00*
Vase, 6" Tall, Multicolored on Opal Gray Cameo, Sailboat Design	*1250.00*
Vase, 7" Tall, 3 Notches on Collar, Crystal	*150.00*
Vase, 7" Tall, 3" Diameter, Notched Collar, Light Green on Frost Cameo, Floral Design	*750.00*
Vase, 7¾" Tall, Gray with Scrolled Foliage Bands	*325.00*
Vase, 8" Tall, Cameo Cranberry	*475.00*
Vase, 9" Tall, Ovoid Shape, Amber with Embossed Acanthus Leaves	*225.00*
Vase, 10" Tall, Double Gourd Shape, Lavender Floral Design	*600.00*
Vase, 10½" Tall, Red Floral and Branch Cameo Design on White	*1250.00*
Vase, 16½" Tall, Cameo with Multicolored Enameled Floral Design	*925.00*
Vase, 17½" Tall, Silver, Green, and Yellow Cameo Floral Design on Cream Base	*1500.00*

This firm in Belgium followed the French in the Art Nouveau movement in the later 19th century. They produced cameo glass as well as glass styled similarly to that of Lalique. Though their quality was outstanding, they never achieved the reputation of their French counterparts; hence, their products sell for less in sales and auctions today.

VENETIAN GLASS VENICE, ITALY, 13TH CENTURY– PRESENT

Object	*Price*
Bird Figurine, 3½" Tall, Latticino Design, Gold-Flecked Beak	*$75.00*
Birds, Figural Pair, 10" Tall, Ruby Red to Clear Shading	*175.00*
Birds in Tree Sculpture, 20 Birds in Large Tree, 20" Tall	*225.00*
Bottle, Water, 9" Tall, Cranberry, Enameled Decoration	*125.00*

Venetian glass. Photo by Robin Rainwater.

Bowl, 6¹/₂", Green and Gold Ribbons with Latticino Bands, Flower Finial *$200.00*
Bowl, 7", Red and White Stripes *175.00*
Bowl, 9" Oval, 3³/₄" Tall, Cranberry with Opalescent Ribbing *125.00*
Candle Holder, 6" Tall, Ovoid Design, Seated Female Figure *850.00*
Candlestick, 5" Tall, Dolphin Stem, Gold Flecks with Berry Prunts *30.00*
Candlestick, 10¹/₂" Tall, Crystal Angel Shape, Amber Halo *55.00*
Candlestick, 12" Tall, Crystal with Gold Dust *150.00*
Compote, 6" Tall, Green with White and Gold Decorations *150.00*
Creamer, 4" Tall, Pitcher-Style, Red Clover Design *375.00*
Decanter with Stopper, 13" Tall, Silver-Speckled Amber with Star Canes *375.00*
Decanter with Cone-Shaped Stopper, 20" Tall, Multicolored Vertical Bands *300.00*
Fish Figurine, 9³/₄" Tall, Ruby Red with Gold-Flecked Fins *100.00*
Flask with Ruby Red Stopper, 11¹/₂" Tall, Crystal with Enameled Red and Green Floral
Decoration *50.00*
Goblet, Water, 9" Tall, Tall Stem, White and Red Latticino Design *200.00*
Lamp, 8" Tall, Miniature, Millefiore Mushroom-Styled Shade and Base *375.00*
Lamp, 20" Tall, 11" Millefiore Mushroom Shade with Matching Base *275.00*
Lamp, 20" Tall, 4-Arm Stand, 11" Swirled Silver, Gold, and Silver Shade *350.00*
Paperweight, Car Shape, 1¹/₂" Tall, 5¹/₂" Long, Amethyst, Blue, Cobalt Blue, Emerald Green,
or Yellow *35.00*
Paperweight, Dome-Shaped, Millefiore Floral Design *75.00*
Perfume Bottle with Ruby Red Stopper, 3¹/₄" Tall, Crystal with Enameled Red and Green
Floral Design *35.00*
Rooster Figurine, 9³/₄" Tall, Standing Position, Amber with Gold Dust *125.00*
Tumbler, Water, 4" Tall, Millefiore Purple Shades *100.00*
Vase, 6" Tall, Multicolored Spatter on Ruby Red *50.00*
Vase, 8" Tall, Handled, Red and White Floral Design *225.00*
Vase, 8" Tall, Millefiore Floral and Net Design *675.00*
Vase, 8" Tall, Blue with Red Lines and Millefiore Floral Design *650.00*

Vase, 8" Tall, Handled, Millefiore Vertical Bands *$350.00*
Vase, 12" Tall, Scalloped, Inverted Ribbing on Neck, Ruby Red *150.00*
Wine Glass, 4" Tall, Clear with Encrusted Gold Band *100.00*
Wine Glass, 6" Tall, Sea Serpent–Shaped Stem *50.00*

Venetian-style glass is usually characterized by millefiore designs on very fragile or thin soda- or lime-based glass. For centuries, the Venetians dominated the world in glass products, particularly clear glass objects such as mirrors and tableware. The items priced above are from the late 18th century to the present; older items do not surface often (most are in museums or permanent private collections). Newer items are also thicker than the thin cristallo of old. Venetian glass is still made on the island of Murano near Venice today, utilizing many of the same designs and techniques employed for centuries. See Venini for additional listings.

VENINI ART GLASS   MURANO, ITALY, 1950S–PRESENT

Object	*Price*
Bird Figurine, 12" Tall, Transparent Iridescent, Signed "Murano Made in Italy"	..*$1500.00*
Bottle with White Stopper, 13" Tall, White Lower Half, Olive Green Upper Half	...*450.00*
Bowl, 7³/₄", 3¹/₂" Tall, Moss Green with Bubbles	*125.00*
Bowl, 10", Crystal with Colored (Amethyst, Gold, and White) Spiral Stripes	*150.00*
Candy Dish, 2¹/₄" Tall, 5" Diameter, Light Green and White Ribbon Design	*175.00*
Candy Dish with Cover, 6" Tall, Frosted, Pinecone Pattern	*75.00*
Decanter, Clown Figurine Design, 14" Tall, Multicolored Body with Cobalt Blue Hat and Tie	*300.00*
Decanter with Stopper, 8" Tall, Clear Cased Amber with Incised Surface	*1000.00*
Decanter with Stopper, 14" Tall, Clear Cased Amber with Incised Surface	*1500.00*
Hour Glass, 7" Tall, Blue and Green, Signed	*600.00*
Musician Figurine with Gown and Headpiece, 9" Tall	*350.00*
Vase, Handkerchief, 3³/₄" Tall, Pink and White Latticino Design	*275.00*
Vase, 4" Tall, 6" Diameter, Egg Form, 2 Rim Openings, Cameo, 3 Color Layers	...*5000.00*
Vase, Handkerchief, 5³/₄" Tall, Crystal with Blue and White Latticino Design	*300.00*
Vase, Handkerchief, 6" Tall, White, Cased in Crystal	*375.00*
Vase, Handkerchief, 8" Tall, White with Yellow Interior	*600.00*
Vase, Handkerchief, 9" Tall, Tan Cased to White	*625.00*
Vase, Bottle, 10" Tall, Dark Green with Red and White Band	*1100.00*
Vase, 12" Tall, Crystal with Amber and Tan Interior and 2 Holes That Completely Pass through the Body	*925.00*
Vase, 14" Tall, Cylindrical, Red and Blue Swirled Stripes Design	*525.00*
Vase, 24" Tall, Classic Form, Crystal Cased to White	*600.00*

Contemporary art glass is still being made on the famous island of Murano using ancient methods combined with modern technology. Most items listed above are signed "Venini" or "Venini Murano" or even "Murano Made in Italy."

WATERFORD GLASS COMPANY   IRELAND,
1783–1851, 1951–PRESENT

Object	*Price*
Angel Fish Figurine, 3" Tall	*$60.00*

Bell, 4³/₄" Tall, Etched Crest Design *$70.00*
Biscuit Jar with Cover, 6" Tall, Diamond and Slender Leaf Cuts *160.00*
Block, ABC Baby Style, 2" Dimensions, Beveled Crystal *65.00*
Bookends, 5¹/₄"-Diameter ¹/₄ Circle Wedges, 1⁵/₈" Thick, Diamond and Fan Cuts, Pair *175.00*
Bowl, Heart-Shaped, 4¹/₂" Across, Wedge Cut *55.00*
Bowl, Potpourri, 4⁵/₈", 2¹/₄" Tall, Leaf Design *55.00*
Bowl, 6¹/₄" Oblong, 3¹/₂" Wide, 1¹/₂" Tall, Vertical Ribbed Sides and Diamond Base ...*60.00*
Bowl, 7", 3¹/₂" Tall, Leaf and Diamond Design *85.00*
Bowl, 8", Calais Pattern *70.00*
Bowl, 8", 3¹/₂" Tall, Colleen Pattern *135.00*
Bowl, 9", 6¹/₂" Tall, Round Base, Leaf and Diamond Cuts *375.00*
Bowl, 10", 7¹/₂" Tall, Footed, Diamond and Wedge Cuts *1150.00*
Bowl, 11", Cut Apprentice Pattern *625.00*
Bowl, Oval (11" × 7"), Notched, Diamond and Fan Cuts *150.00*
Box with Hinged Lid, Shell-Shaped *95.00*
Brandy Glass, Alana Pattern *95.00*
Brandy Glass, Colleen Pattern *55.00*
Brandy Glass, Kylemore Pattern *60.00*
Brandy Glass, Patrick Pattern *55.00*
Brush, Makeup, 6" Long, Crystal Handle *45.00*
Butter Dish with Cover, ¹/₄-lb. size, 7¹/₄" Long, 2¹/₂" Tall, Open Diamond-Cut Design .*150.00*
Candelabra, 9¹/₄" Tall, 2-Tiered Candle Holder, Diamond and Wedge Cuts with Teardrops
.... *750.00*
Candle Holder, 3⁵/₈" Tall, Scalloped, Round Base *50.00*
Candle Holder, 2-Piece, Base Bowl and Small Shade, Diamond Cuts *150.00*
Candlestick, Globe-Shaped, 2¹/₂" Diameter, Diamond Pattern *40.00*
Candlestick, 4¹/₂" Tall, Palladia Pattern *70.00*
Candlestick, 5¹/₂" Tall, Stemmed, Diamond Cuts *50.00*
Candy Dish, Heart-Shaped, 7³/₄" × 7¹/₂" *65.00*
Centerpiece Stemmed Bowl, 9" Tall, Diamond and Vertical Cuts *825.00*
Champagne Glass, Alana Pattern *45.00*
Champagne Glass, Castletown Pattern *75.00*
Champagne Glass, Colleen Pattern *55.00*
Champagne Glass, Kylemore Pattern *55.00*
Champagne Glass, Patrick Pattern *45.00*
Champagne Glass, Powerscourt Pattern *65.00*
Chandelier, 22" Tall, 15" Wide, 5 Large Teardrops *2150.00*
Chandelier, 23" Tall, 22" Wide, 57 Teardrops *2250.00*
Chandelier, 30" Tall, 30" Wide, 9 Large Teardrops *2850.00*
Claret Glass, Alana Pattern *45.00*
Claret Glass, Castletown Pattern *75.00*
Claret Glass, Colleen Pattern *55.00*
Claret Glass, Kylemore Pattern *55.00*
Claret Glass, Patrick Pattern *45.00*
Claret Glass, Powerscourt Pattern *65.00*
Clock, 2⁵/₈" Tall, 4" Long, Kensington Pattern *70.00*
Clock, 2³/₄" Tall, Crystal Shell Shape *60.00*
Coaster, 5" Diameter, Diamond Cuts *55.00*
Creamer, Pitcher-Style, Cut Ovals, Gold Rim *45.00*
Creamer, Footed, Pitcher-Style, Leaf Cuts *75.00*
Cruet, 4¹/₄" Tall (No Stopper), Diamond Cut *50.00*

Decanter, Cut, with Etched Christmas Tree *$200.00*
Decanter, Claret, with Faceted Stopper, 12½" Tall, Old-Fashioned Style, Diamond Cut .*650.00*
Decanter, Ship's, with Faceted Stopper, 9½" Tall, Diamond Cuts *275.00*
Decanter, Whiskey, Kylemore Pattern *185.00*
Decanter, Whiskey, Patrick Pattern *160.00*
Decanter, Wine, Alana Pattern *225.00*
Decanter, Wine, Castletown Pattern *350.00*
Decanter, Wine, Colleen Pattern *225.00*
Decanter, Wine, Patrick Pattern *175.00*
Decanter, Wine, Powerscourt Pattern *375.00*
Dove Figure, 1¾" Tall, 5" Long *75.00*
Dreidel Spinning Shape, 5" Tall, 2½" Square, Prism-Faceted Cut *125.00*
Duck, Mallard, 2½" Tall, 3¾" Long, Wedge-Cut Feathers *100.00*
Egg, 3½" Tall, 2¼" Wide, Diamond and Sunburst Pattern *100.00*
Egg, 5½" Tall, Pedestal Stand, Diamond Cuts *115.00*
Frame, Photo, Heart-Shaped, 4½" Tall, 4¼" Wide *55.00*
Gavel, 5½" Long *75.00*
Ginger Jar with Cover, 8" Tall, Diamond and Rosette Pattern *175.00*
Globe Sculpture, 6½" Diameter, 14" Tall with Mahogany Base, Diamond-Cut Continents
....*2500.00*
Goblet, Alana Pattern *50.00*
Goblet, Castletown Pattern *75.00*
Goblet, Cut, with Etched Christmas Tree *50.00*
Goblet, Colleen Pattern *55.00*
Goblet, Kylemore Pattern *55.00*
Goblet, Patrick Pattern *50.00*
Goblet, Powerscourt Pattern *65.00*
Harp, 5" Tall, 2" Wide *70.00*
Ice Bucket, 5⅜" Tall, Silver-Plated Handle, Diamond Cut *160.00*
Lamp, 13" Tall, Diamond Pattern *450.00*
Lamp, 18" Tall, Diamond Pattern *775.00*
Lamp, 20" Tall, Brass Base, Crystal Part 8¾" Tall *225.00*
Mug, Christening, 3" Tall *70.00*
Mug, Tankard Style, 4½" Tall, 13 oz., Diamond and Long Slender Leaf Cuts *85.00*
Mustard Pot with Cover, 3" Tall, Perpendicular Cuts *40.00*
Napkin Ring, Oval, Open Diamond Cut Design *40.00*
Paperweight, 2⅜" Tall, Frog Design *70.00*
Paperweight, 2½" Diameter, Golf Ball Design *70.00*
Paperweight, 3" Tall, Golf Head Design *70.00*
Paperweight, 3⅛" Tall, Owl Figure *70.00*
Paperweight, 3½" Diameter, Diamond and Star Cuts *60.00*
Paperweight, 3½" Long, 2¾" Wide, Strawberry Shape *75.00*
Paperweight, 4", Shamrock Design *125.00*
Paperweight, 4½" Long, 1¾" Tall, Open Diamond Cuts, Turtle Design *65.00*
Paperweight, 5" Tall, Number "1" Shape, Diamond Cuts *70.00*
Paperweight, 6¾" Tall, Seahorse Figure *200.00*
Perfume Atomizer, 4" Tall, Diamond Cuts *85.00*
Pitcher, Water, 24 oz., Cut Design with Etched Christmas Tree *135.00*
Pitcher, Water, 32 oz., Long Slender Oval Cuts *150.00*
Plate, 8", Cut Diamonds and Etched Golfer in Center *100.00*
Ram, 2" Tall, 3¼" Long *65.00*

Ring Holder, 2³/₄" Tall, Heart Base (3" Across) *$45.00*
Sail Boat, 5¹/₂" Tall, 4³/₄" Long, Cut Ovals *110.00*
Salt Cellar, 2⁵/₈" Tall, Stemmed, Boat-Shaped, Tiny Diamond Cuts *85.00*
Salt and Pepper Shakers, 6" Tall, Round Feet, Silver-Plated Tops, Diamond and Leaf Cuts
. . . .*100.00*
Sconce, 2-Light, 11¹/₄" Tall, 12¹/₂" Wide, Two 4¹/₂" Diamond-Cut Plates, Each with 8 Tear-drops *800.00*
Sherbet, Alana Pattern *50.00*
Sherbet, Castletown Pattern *85.00*
Stein, 6" Tall, Diamond and Narrow Leaf Cuts *95.00*
Sugar, Cut Ovals, Gold Rim *45.00*
Sugar, Footed, Leaf Cuts *65.00*
Sugar Shaker with Silver-plated Top, 6¹/₂" Tall, Stemmed, Diamond and Leaf Cut
. . . .*65.00*
Tray, Shell-Shaped, 5" × 4¹/₂" Tall *55.00*
Tray, Oval (8" × 6"), Central Star, Vertical Flutes *65.00*
Tumbler, 9 oz., Old-Fashioned Style, Alana Pattern *40.00*
Tumbler, 9 oz., Castletown Pattern *70.00*
Tumbler, 9 oz., Colleen Pattern *45.00*
Tumbler, 9 oz., Old-Fashioned Style, Kylemore Pattern *50.00*
Tumbler, 9 oz., Patrick Pattern *35.00*
Tumbler, 9 oz., Powerscourt Pattern *55.00*
Tumbler, 9 oz., Wide Diamond Pattern *35.00*
Tumbler, 9 or 10 oz., Cut with Etched Christmas Tree *40.00*
Tumbler, 12 oz., Colleen Pattern *55.00*
Tumbler, 12 oz., Old-Fashioned Style, Patrick Pattern *45.00*
Tumbler, 12 oz., Powerscourt Pattern *60.00*
Vase, 4" Tall, Diamond and Flute Design *55.00*
Vase, 7" Tall, Slender, Diamond and Vertical Cuts *60.00*
Vase, 7⁵/₈" Tall, Prism "Thousand Windows" Pattern *250.00*
Vase, 9" Tall, Araglin Pattern *150.00*
Vase, 9" Tall, Calais Pattern *60.00*
Vase, 10" Tall, Round Base, Wide Neck, Wedge and Diamond Cuts *185.00*
Vase, 12" Tall, Round Base, Flared Top, Allover Cut Pattern, Masterpiece Collection *875.00*
Wine Glass, Alana Pattern *40.00*
Wine Glass, Castletown Pattern *75.00*
Wine Glass, Colleen Pattern *50.00*
Wine Glass, Colleen Pattern, Oversize *100.00*
Wine Glass, Kylemore Pattern *50.00*
Wine Glass, Patrick Pattern *40.00*
Wine Glass, Powerscourt Pattern *60.00*

The New Waterford is not unlike the old in style, that is, the production of fine crystal with cut decorations. Original items were made of a fine grade of crystal, as good as any in the world at the time. The new items, including tableware, functional products, and some novelty items, are also made of quality lead crystal and are becoming quite collectible too. The new Waterford has prospered well, and by the 1970s, they became the largest producer of handmade crystal in the world. Of particular note are the handmade limited-edition masterpiece collection items.

More Waterford listings can be found under Lismore.

Webb glass. Photo by Robin Rainwater. Courtesy of the Corning Museum of Glass.

WEBB, THOMAS & SONS STOURBRIDGE, ENGLAND, 1880S–1930S

Object	Price
Biscuit Jar with Cover, 7½" Tall, Pink Satin with Floral Design on Body and Cover	*$550.00*
Biscuit Jar with Cover, 8" Tall, Frosted Yellow, Signed	*1250.00*
Bowl, 3½", Ruffled, Enameled Floral and Butterfly Design, Signed	*350.00*
Bowl, 4⁷⁄₈", Crimped, Mother-of-Pearl, Diamond Quilted Pattern	*625.00*
Bowl, 5¾", Pink with White Lining, Intaglio Flowers and Branches	*800.00*
Bowl, Rose, 6", 5" Tall, Yellow to Cream Satin with White Interior	*350.00*
Bowl, 6¼", Applied Rim, Burmese with Floral Design	*1250.00*
Centerpiece, 12½" Diameter, 7" Tall, Ruffled, Blue Overlay with Enameled Floral Design	*525.00*
Creamer, 2⁵⁄₈" Tall, Fluted, Burmese with Green Leaves Design	*650.00*
Epergne, 21" Tall, Center Trumpet Design with 3 Hanging Baskets, Cranberry and Vaseline	*1000.00*
Ewer, 3¾" Tall, 5¼" Diameter, Ivory Handle, Green to White Satin, Apples and Leaves Design	*525.00*
Perfume Bottle with Silver Top, 6" Tall, Red to Yellow to Dark Amber Shading	*275.00*
Perfume Bottle with Sterling Silver Stopper, 4¾" Tall, Burmese with Gold Branches Design	*750.00*
Perfume Bottle with Stopper, 5½" Tall, Ivory Satin with Gold Bamboo and Multicolored Floral Design	*450.00*
Perfume Bottle with Stopper, Citron, Vine and Floral Decoration	*750.00*
Pitcher, Water, 6½" Tall, Loop Handles, Ivory, Blooming Bamboo Plant Design	*1600.00*
Pitcher, Water, 7½" Tall, Red to White Shading	*575.00*
Plate, 6½", Ruffled, Butterscotch, Diamond Quilted Pattern	*100.00*
Salt Dip, Rectangular, Red	*625.00*

Toothpick Holder, 2⁵/₈" Tall, Hexagonal Collared Top, Burmese *$325.00*

Tumbler, 5" Tall, Red to White Shading *175.00*

Vase, 2¹/₂" Tall, Miniature, Blue with Enameled Butterfly and Floral Design *625.00*

Vase, 3" Tall, Miniature, Red with Carved White Fuchsias *325.00*

Vase, 3³/₄" Tall, Hexagonal Top, Burmese with Lavender Floral and Leaves Design . .*375.00*

Vase, 4¹/₂" Tall, Green with Gold Leaves and Hydrangea Blossoms *350.00*

Vase, 5" Tall, 2³/₄" Diameter, Gold on Coral, Floral and Bees Design *250.00*

Vase, 5" Tall, Pink Interior, Gold Floral and Butterfly Design *375.00*

Vase, 6" Tall, Ruffled, Satin, Diamond Quilted Pattern *325.00*

Vase, 6¹/₂" Tall, Red to Pink Shading *375.00*

Vase, 7" Tall, Urn-Shaped, 2 Applied Handles, Ribbed, Iridescent Gold *1500.00*

Vase, 8¹/₄" Tall, Burmese with Green Leaves and Coral Flower Buds *775.00*

Vase, 8¹/₂" Tall, Ribbed, Fish Scale and Vine Design, Signed *3000.00*

Vase, 8¹/₂" Tall, Amber with Enameled Butterflies and Cattails Design *475.00*

Vase, 10" Tall, Amethyst Cameo Design, Signed *1250.00*

Vase, 10" Tall, Bottle-Shaped, Burmese, with Mums and Leaves Design *1100.00*

Vase, 10¹/₂" Tall, Gourd-Shape, Blue with White Floral Design *2500.00*

Vase, 11" Tall, Gourd Shape, Footed, Yellow Satin with Cream Interior *350.00*

Vase, 12" Tall, Ruffled, Coral Design with Cream Interior *425.00*

Vase, 14" Tall, Red with Enameled Floral Decorations *625.00*

Vase, 15" Tall, Flared, Multicolored Floral Design *600.00*

Webb is simply the most famous English name in the art glass world. They were a major part of the European Art Nouveau movement and followed American trends as well. They borrowed Peachblow and Burmese designs from America but also produced Alexandrite, Burmese, Cameo, and a host of other designs. Additional listings for Webb can be found under Alexandrite, English Cameo, and Peachblow.

CHAPTER 2

PRESSED GLASS

The American glass industry experienced a shaky start, but it was not for lack of ambition. As early as 1607, the Jamestown Colony settlers included glassblowers. America had an abundance of all the necessary ingredients: excellent sources for ash, plenty of sand, and massive forests for fuel. A small glasshouse was built the very next year, but it closed without producing any useful items. The Germans, with very limited success, would be the next immigrants to attempt glassmaking in the New World.

In 1739, a German immigrant named Caspar Wistar built a factory in New Jersey. He hired skilled German glassworkers and became the first commercially successful glass manufacturer in the United States. Just as in the forest glasshouses of Europe, the immediate need or practical use for glass products was bottles and windows. Wistar also made some crude tableware and a few scientific glass vessels for Benjamin Franklin. It was surprising that any glass was made at all, since England had banned the manufacturing of glass in the colonies. The Wistar house, however, did not survive for long.

From 1763 to 1774, another German, by the name of Henry W. Stiegel, operated a glasshouse in Manheim, Pennsylvania. Stiegel acquired some of the former employees of Wistar's business and hired a few additional experienced foreign workers from both Germany and England. He went bankrupt in 1774 but did manage to create some window and bottle glass. The American Revolution forced his glasshouse to shut down permanently.

One year after the Revolution, another German immigrant opened a glass factory in America. In 1784, John Frederick Amelung produced a fair amount of hand-cut tableware, much of it engraved. Amelung's factory also made Benjamin Franklin a pair of bifocals. They too could not operate consistently at a profit and shut down in 1795.

There were many reasons for these failures even though there was a great demand for glass in the colonies. Foreign competition and pressure from the English government were significant reasons for those failures. Glasshouses or manufacturing plants were well established in England and Ireland, producing large quantities of cheap glass. Early Americans lacked the capital and many of the skills necessary to manufacture glass. Transportation problems made shipping across the Alleghenies difficult and costly. People out West used crude bowls, teacups, and bottles to consume food and spirits.

The Alleghenies were a disadvantage to eastern manufacturers but a boom to those living in eastern Ohio, northern West Virginia, and western Pennsylvania. The mountains served as a barrier to foreign and eastern glass before the great canals were built. In 1797, the first frontier glasshouse, about 60 miles south of Pittsburgh, was constructed by Albert Gallatin, an immigrant from Switzerland. Later that year, a bottle factory was built in Pittsburgh by James O'Hara and Isaac Craig. This factory was named the Pittsburgh Glass Works, and in 1798 they merged with Gallatin's New Geneva Glass Works. They managed to produce hand-blown windows, bottles, and a bit of tableware, but they were unable to operate profitably. They sold out to Edward Ensell soon after.

Pittsburgh and the surrounding area was an ideal place to manufacture glassware. Wood for fuel was readily available; later, massive coal deposits were discovered in the region. Large sand or sandstone deposits lay along the numerous riverbeds, and red lead for fine crystal production was available nearby in the Illinois Territory. The commercial markets were wide open in every direction except back East. North to Canada, west to the Pacific, and south to the major trading centers of New Orleans and the Gulf of Mexico—all were available by easy river transport. Even with these strategic advantages, early attempts still ended in failure.

America's early successes in glassmaking can be traced to many individuals, but one figure stands out in particular. Deming Jarves not only founded many companies but obtained knowledgeable foreign workers, the proper ingredients, and good formulas, and he wrote an important trade volume in 1854 titled *Reminiscences of Glassmaking*. Most important, he was able to obtain enough financial backing to keep the businesses operating long enough to achieve long-standing profit margins.

In the 1790s, the Boston Crown Glass Company was chartered to produce window glass but managed to do very little. The only noteworthy contribution worth mentioning is that they were the first to introduce lead crystal in America. Many of the workers left and later formed the Boston Porcelain and Glass Company in 1814. They built a factory in 1815 and made a few limited lead glass products before failing in 1817. Deming Jarves with three associates (Amos Binney, Daniel Hastings, and Edmund Monroe) purchased their holdings and incorporated them into a new company in 1818. This was dubbed The New England Glass Company of East Cambridge, Massachusetts.

From the very beginning, the new company operated profitably, continuously reinvested in new equipment, and recruited skilled workers from Europe. Jarves assumed a leading role as first agent and manager. He was a prosperous businessman and held a monopoly on red lead production early on in America. Red lead is a vital ingredient for making fine lead crystal. Jarves left New England Glass in 1826 and went on to form the Boston & Sandwich Glass Company, another successful operation.

What Jarves accomplished in the East, the team of Bakewell, Ensell, and Pears was working in the West. In 1807, Edward Ensell founded a small glass company in Pittsburgh, which was purchased by Benjamin Bakewell and associates in 1808. Benjamin sent his son Thomas and a trusted clerk named Thomas Pears on numerous trips to Europe to hire experienced glassworkers. Thomas Pears left in 1818 to start a bottle factory, but it failed and he rejoined the Bakewells. He quit again in 1825 and moved to Indiana but came back once more in 1826. He died soon after, but his son, John Palmer Pears, became manager of the glasshouse; the name changed to Bakewell, Pears, and Company.

These early successes were somewhat rare. The first period, referred to as the Early American Period of American glass, lasted from 1771 to 1830. Several glass companies were founded east and west of the Alleghenies, but nearly all ended in failure. Cheap European glass and the lack of protective tariffs hurt eastern glassmakers. Out West, skilled workers were difficult to obtain, and the capital necessary to sustain long-term growth and operation was not available. Economic depressions, such as the one after the War of 1812, were also factors in those shutdowns. Except for a few enterprising men like Jarves, this first period in American glass history was marked by unprofitability and failure.

The Middle Period was the second period in American glass history; it dates from 1830 to about 1880. The Baldwin Bill in 1830 placed import duties and high tariffs on foreign imports. The new tariffs worked, and the glass industry in the United States was given a much needed boost. In addition, the American invention of a mechanical pressing machine in the late 1820s led to the mass production of glassware. The invention of this hand press was America's greatest contribution to glassmaking. It was as important as the discovery of lead crystal, glassblowing, and the invention of glass itself. Hand pressing revolutionized the industry; it was very fast and efficient, and it could be run by less-skilled workers.

Pressed glass was made by forcing melted glass into shape under pressure. A plunger was used to force or press molten glass into iron molds. A mold was made up of two or more parts, and lines or seams occurred where the mold comes apart. With each piece the mold was reassembled and filled once again. Some of the marks left by the mold were hand-finished to remove them. Molds were usually hinged, and might contain patterns within them. They could be full-size, single-piece molds or separate for more complicated objects. Candlesticks, vases, common table items, and especially matched sets of tableware were easily manufactured by hand pressing.

Pressed items were made in great quantities, especially in the factories opened by Jarves. The New England Glass Company, which eventually became Libbey, and the Boston & Sandwich Glass Company were two of the most successful companies in America producing pressed glass. Many others followed in the mid-19th century, such as Adams & Company; Bakewell, Pears and Company; Mckee Brothers; Bryce Brothers; Hobbs, Brocunier & Company; King & Son, and so on.

Individual patterns were rarely patented by any one company. Even when patents were obtained, designs were copied. Ashburton or Hex Optic, Bull's Eye, Cable, Thumbprints, Hamilton, Comet, Grapes, Pineapples, Ribs, Sunbursts, Pillars, Flutes, and so on are at times difficult to distinguish from one company to the next.

Another American invention was the discovery of a cheap lead substitute in 1864 by William Leighton, who was employed by Hobbs, Brocunier and Company at the time. He developed a glass formula that substituted lime for the much more expensive lead. The glass products manufactured with lime still maintained a good degree of clarity. Though the brilliance was not as sharp as lead crystal, the price savings and practicality more than made up for the difference in quality. Most companies were forced to switch to lime in order to remain competitive.

Pressed glass remained somewhat affordable (compared to art and cut glass) in the late 19th and early 20th centuries. Fire polishing, which was developed in England in 1834, was adopted in America. Fire polishing removed mold and tool marks by reheating and gave glass a shinier finish that was a little closer to fine-cut crystal.

Simple, clear pressed-glass articles were combined with other design features and decorating techniques. Pressed glass was made in many colors, flashed, cut occasionally like simple fluting, cased, and enameled and might contain applied blown accessories like handles and feet. All still qualify as pressed-glass items, but the quality and dull colors were far behind cut crystal and art glass items; however, prices for pressed glass were not necessarily out of reach of the average American.

Other makers in the late 19th and early 20th centuries in America included the conglomerate U.S. Glass, George Duncan & Sons, Central Glass Company, Indiana Tumbler & Goblet Company, as well as many others who were engaged in the mass production of pressed-glass items. Many of the later pressed patterns were more elaborate; and they were patented and not as easily copied—a great aid in identification!

ACTRESS   LABELLE GLASS COMPANY, 1870S

Object	Price
Bowl, Flat	$25.00
Bowl, Footed	35.00
Butter Dish with Cover	125.00
Cake Stand, 7" Tall	150.00
Candlestick	100.00
Celery Dish, Pinafore Design	175.00
Cheese Dish with Cover, "The Lone Fisherman" Design	200.00
Compote with Cover, Low	150.00
Compote with Cover, 8" Tall	175.00
Creamer	75.00
Goblet	100.00
Honey Dish with Cover	100.00
Jam Jar with Cover	125.00
Mustard Jar with Cover	75.00
Pickle Dish, Embossed "Love's Request is Pickles"	65.00
Pitcher, Milk (Small)	225.00
Pitcher, Water (Large)	250.00
Platter, Round, "Miss Nielson" Design	175.00
Platter, Oval, Pinafore Design	150.00
Salt and Pepper Shakers	75.00
Sauce Bowl, Flat	35.00
Sauce Bowl, Footed	45.00
Spooner	70.00
Sugar	100.00
Tray Embossed "Give Us This Day"	125.00

Actors and actresses are portrayed in this pattern with light ridges. The pieces are also framed by stippled shell forms rising off the sides of the glass.

 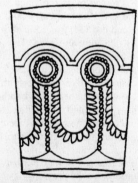

Left: Pressed glass, "Actress" pattern. Drawing by Mark Pickvet. Right: Pressed glass, "Alabama" pattern. Drawing by Mark Pickvet.

ALABAMA   U.S. GLASS COMPANY, EARLY 1890S

Object	*Price*
Butter Dish with Cover	*$75.00*
Cake Stand	*50.00*
Celery Holder, Upright	*50.00*
Compote, Open, 5" Tall	*40.00*
Compote with Cover	*50.00*
Creamer	*45.00*
Honey Dish with Cover	*100.00*
Nappy with Handle	*30.00*
Pitcher, Syrup, with Lid	*75.00*
Pitcher, Milk	*75.00*
Pitcher, Water	*80.00*
Relish Dish, Oblong, 3 Varieties	*25.00*
Spooner	*30.00*
Sugar with Cover	*75.00*
Tumbler	*30.00*

"Alabama" was the first of U.S. Glass's famous state series. It is also known as "Beaded Bull's Eye" (at top) and "Drape" (at bottom) pattern. Green pieces are priced the same as the clear (above) while a few rare ruby-flashed items should be double in price.

AMERICA   AMERICAN GLASS COMPANY AND RIVERSIDE GLASS WORKS, EARLY 1890S

Object	*Price*
Bowl, 8½"	*$20.00*
Butter Dish with Cover, Pedestal Base	*50.00*
Carafe	*35.00*

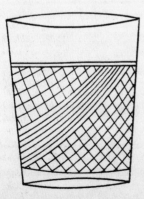

Pressed glass, "America" pattern. Drawing by Mark Pickvet.

Celery Vase *$25.00*
Compote, 8" Tall, 8" Diameter *50.00*
Creamer, Tankard Style, Applied Handle *30.00*
Goblet *20.00*
Pitcher, Tankard Style, 64 oz., Applied Handle *50.00*
Relish Dish *15.00*
Sauce Dish, 4¹/₂", Flat *10.00*
Spooner *15.00*
Sugar with Cover, Individual (Small) *25.00*
Sugar with Cover (Large) *35.00*
Tumbler *15.00*

This pattern is also referred to as "Swirl and Diamond" and is confused with other similar patterns.

AMERICAN   FOSTORIA GLASS COMPANY, 1915–1970S

Object   *Price*
Ashtray, 3⁷/₈" Oval *$15.00*
Ashtray, 5" Square *25.00*
Banana Dish, 9" Oblong, 3¹/₂" Width, 1 Tab Handle *25.00*
Bottle, Water, 9¹/₄" Tall, 44 oz. *75.00*
Bowl, 4¹/₄" *8.00*
Bowl, 5" *10.00*
Bowl, 5", Flared *12.00*
Bowl, 6" *12.00*
Bowl, 7" *14.00*
Bowl, 8" *16.00*
Bowl, 8", 3-Footed *30.00*
Bowl, 9" *18.00*
Bowl, 10" *20.00*
Bowl, 11", Centerpiece *50.00*
Bowl, 16", Centerpiece *125.00*
Butter Dish with Cover, 5³/₄" Dome Diameter, 7¹/₄" Underplate Diameter *50.00*
Cake Salver, 10" Round *75.00*
Cake Salver, 10" Square *100.00*
Candlestick, 3" Tall *15.00*
Candlestick, 6" Tall *45.00*
Celery Vase, 6" Tall, 3¹/₂" Diameter *25.00*
Cigarette Box *50.00*
Coaster, 3¹/₂" *8.00*
Cocktail Glass, 2⁷/₈" Tall, 3 oz., Footed *15.00*
Cologne Bottle with Stopper, 7¹/₂" Tall, 8 oz. *35.00*
Comport, 4", Open *15.00*
Comport, 5¹/₄", Open, No Stem *16.00*
Comport, 8¹/₂", Open, No Stem *20.00*
Comport, 9¹/₂", Open, No stem *22.00*
Compote, 5", Open *15.00*
Compote, 7", Open *17.00*
Cordial, 2⁷/₈" Tall, Footed *8.00*

Cracker Jar with Cover, 8³/₄" Tall, 5³/₄" Diameter *$85.00*
Cracker Jar with Cover, 10" Tall, 5³/₄" Diameter *100.00*
Creamer, Individual, 5 oz. (Small) *10.00*
Creamer, 4¹/₄" Tall (Large) *12.00*
Cruet with Stopper, 6¹/₂" Tall, 5 oz. *55.00*
Cruet with Stopper, 7" Tall, 7 oz. *65.00*
Cup, 8 oz. *5.00*
Cup, Custard, 6 oz., 2 Styles *5.00*
Decanter with Sterling Silver Stopper, 10" Tall *125.00*
Decanter with Stopper, 2 Styles, Metal Holder and Chain, Engraved Tabs ("Scotch" or "Rye") *150.00*
Glove Box with Cover, Rectangular (9¹/₂" × 3¹/₂") *90.00*
Goblet, 5¹/₂" Tall, 9 oz. *12.00*
Goblet, 6³/₄" Tall, 9 oz. *15.00*
Hairpin Box with Cover, Rectangular (3¹/₂" × 1¹/₂") *100.00*
Handkerchief Box with Cover, Rectangular (5¹/₂" × 4¹/₂") *75.00*
Ice Bucket, 7" Tall, 10" Diameter *85.00*
Jelly Dish with Cover, 4¹/₂" Diameter, 7" Tall *100.00*
Jewel Box with Cover, Rectangular (5¹/₄" × 2¹/₄") *75.00*
Mustard Jar with Cover and Spoon, 3³/₄" Tall *40.00*
Napkin Ring *6.00*
Nappy, 4¹/₄", 1 Handle *12.00*
Nappy, 5¹/₄", 1 Handle *14.00*
Nappy, 5¹/₄", 2 Handles *15.00*
Nut Dish, Oval (3³/₄" × 2³/₄") *10.00*
Olive Dish, Oval (6" × 3¹/₂") *12.00*
Pickle Dish, Oval (8" × 4") *15.00*
Pitcher, Syrup with Metal Lid, 5¹/₄" Tall, 6 oz. *80.00*
Pitcher, Syrup with Metal Lid, 6³/₄" Tall, 11 oz. *90.00*
Pitcher, Water, 55 oz. *100.00*
Pitcher, Water, 58 oz., 7¹/₄" Tall *100.00*
Pitcher, 69 oz., Jug-Style *125.00*
Pitcher, Water, 71 oz. *110.00*
Plate, 9" *6.00*
Plate, 10¹/₂" *8.00*
Plate, 11¹/₂" *10.00*
Platter,. 10¹/₂" Oval *50.00*
Platter, 12" Round *100.00*
Puff Box with Cover, Cube-Shaped (3" × 3" × 2⁷/₈") *110.00*
Punch Bowl with Stand, 14", 10" Tall, 2 Gallon *350.00*
Punch Bowl with Stand, 18", 12" Tall, 3³/₄ Gallon *450.00*
Salt and Pepper Shakers, 2 Styles (3" or 3¹/₄" Tall) *25.00*
Saucer, 6" *4.00*
Sherbet, 3¹/₂" Tall, 4¹/₂ oz. *8.00*
Sherbet, 3¹/₂" Tall, 4¹/₂ oz., with Handle *10.00*
Sherbet, 4¹/₄" Tall, Flared, Hexagonal Stem *12.00*
Spooner, 3³/₄" Tall *8.00*
Sugar, Open, Individual, 6 oz., 2-Handled (Small) *12.00*
Sugar with Cover, 6¹/₄" Tall (Large) *15.00*
Sugar Shaker with Chrome Top, 4³/₄" Tall *25.00*
Tidbit, 7" Tall, 3-Footed *22.00*

Toothpick Holder, 2¼" Tall $20.00
Tray, Oval (6¾" × 3") 12.00
Tray, Oval (10" × 5"), 2-Handled 35.00
Tray, Boat, 8½" Oblong, 3½" Width 45.00
Tray, Boat, 12" Oblong, 4½" Width 60.00
Tray, Celery, Oval (10" × 4½") 25.00
Tray, Fruit, 16" Round, 4" Tall 80.00
Tray, Ice Cream, Oval (13½" × 10") 65.00
Tray, Serving, Oval (11½" × 8") 50.00
Tumbler, 4" Tall, 8 oz. 15.00
Tumbler, 4¼" Tall, 8 oz. 16.00
Tumbler, 5¼" Tall, 8 oz. 18.00
Vase, 8" Tall, Cylindrically Shaped, 3½" Diameter 55.00
Vase, 10" Tall, Cylindrically Shaped, 4" Diameter 65.00
Vase, 10" Tall, 6" Diameter 85.00
Vase, 10" Tall, 8" Diameter 95.00
Vase, 12" Tall, Cylindrically Shaped, 4½" Diameter 75.00
Vase, 15" Tall, Narrow 60.00
Vase, 20" Tall, Narrow 75.00
Vase, 25" Tall, Narrow 100.00
Whiskey Tumbler, 2 oz. 15.00
Wineglass, 4¼" Tall, 2½ oz. 12.00

Fostoria's "American" pattern is sometimes confused with block optic or cubist patterns of the Depression. Some colors were added during the Depression, including amber, green, yellow (increase above prices by 50%) and blue (double the above prices).

"American" is a relatively inexpensive pattern because of its long production; however, some pieces were discontinued early on.

APOLLO   ADAMS AND COMPANY, 1870S

Object	Crystal	Frosted	Ruby-Flashed
Bowl, 7"	$25.00	$35.00	$50.00
Bowl, 8"	30.00	40.00	60.00
Butter Dish with Cover	40.00	50.00	75.00
Cake Stand, 10"	65.00	75.00	100.00
Celery with Base, Upright	20.00	30.00	45.00
Cheese Dish with Cover	75.00	100.00	125.00
Compote, Open, 5"	35.00	45.00	65.00
Compote with Cover, 8"	50.00	65.00	85.00
Creamer,	40.00	50.00	70.00
Egg Holder	25.00	35.00	50.00
Goblet	35.00	45.00	65.00
Pickle Dish	25.00	35.00	45.00
Pitcher, Syrup, with Lid	65.00	80.00	100.00
Pitcher, Water	50.00	70.00	90.00
Sauce Dish, Flat	8.00	10.00	15.00
Sauce Dish, Footed	10.00	15.00	20.00
Spooner	25.00	35.00	50.00

Pressed glass, "Arched Grape" pattern. Drawing by Mark Pickvet.

Object	Crystal	Frosted	Ruby-Flashed
Sugar Shaker	$35.00	$45.00	$60.00
Tray	.35.00	45.00	60.00
Tumbler	.25.00	35.00	50.00
Wine	.35.00	45.00	65.00

There was also an "Apollo" pattern made by McKee that is quite different from Adams's.

ARCHED GRAPE   BOSTON & SANDWICH GLASS COMPANY, 1870S–1880S

Object	Price
Butter Dish with Cover	$55.00
Celery Vase	.40.00
Compote with Cover (Low)	.55.00
Compote with Cover (High)	.65.00
Pitcher, Water	.75.00
Sauce Dish, 4"	.10.00
Spooner	.25.00
Stemware, Cordial	.40.00
Stemware, Wine Goblet	.35.00
Sugar Dish	.30.00
Sugar with Cover	.45.00

"Arched Grape" is one of the many typical "Grape" patterns produced throughout the 19th century.

ASHBURTON   VARIOUS COMPANIES, 1840S–1880S

Object	Price
Ale Glass, 5" Tall, Crystal	$60.00
Bitters Bottle	.65.00
Butter Dish with Cover	.150.00
Celery Dish	.85.00
Celery Dish, Scalloped	.95.00

Cordial, 4½" Tall *$65.00*
Creamer *175.00*
Decanter with Stopper, 16 oz. *90.00*
Decanter with Stopper, 32 oz. *100.00*
Decanter with Stopper, 48 oz. *110.00*
Egg Holder *75.00*
Goblet, Barrel-Shaped Cup, Flared, Crystal *35.00*
Goblet, Straight Sides *30.00*
Lamp *125.00*
Mug *15.00*
Pitcher, Syrup, with Lid, 16 oz., Jug Style *200.00*
Pitcher, Milk, 32 oz. *175.00*
Pitcher, Water, 48 oz. *225.00*
Sauce Dish, Small *12.00*
Sauce Dish, Large *15.00*
Spooner *40.00*
Sugar with Cover *100.00*
Toddy Jar with Cover, Matching Underplate *350.00*
Toddy Jar with Cover, Handled, Matching Underplate *400.00*
Tumbler, Water *65.00*
Tumbler, Water, Footed *75.00*
Tumbler, Whiskey, with Handle *75.00*
Wineglass *30.00*

"Ashburton" is a large thumbprint pattern and was made in some quantity by Boston & Sandwich, New England, McKee, and many others. There are a few rare pieces such as the toddy jar, butter dish, and creamer.

The creamer, along with the sugar, wineglass, and goblet have all been reproduced, which is cause for some concern.

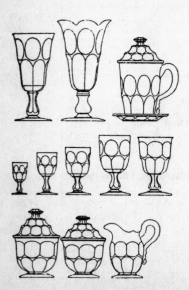

Pressed glass, "Ashburton" pattern.
Reproduced from an 1878 trade catalog.

BALDER   U.S. GLASS COMPANY, 1890S–EARLY 1900S

Object	Crystal	Emerald Green	Ruby Red
Bowl, 8"	$20.00	$30.00	$35.00
Butter Dish with Cover	45.00	55.00	65.00
Carafe	35.00	45.00	60.00
Compote, Ruffled	35.00	45.00	60.00
Creamer, Individual (Small)	20.00	30.00	35.00
Creamer, Large	30.00	40.00	50.00
Cup	10.00	12.00	15.00
Goblet	25.00	35.00	40.00
Pitcher, Syrup, with Metal Lid	50.00	75.00	100.00
Plate, 8"	25.00	35.00	40.00
Sauce Dish	10.00	12.00	15.00
Spooner	20.00	30.00	35.00
Sugar, Handled (Small)	15.00	20.00	25.00
Sugar with Cover (Large)	35.00	45.00	60.00
Tumbler	25.00	35.00	40.00
Whiskey Tumbler	50.00	75.00	100.00
Wineglass	20.00	30.00	35.00

A few pieces of this pattern were trimmed in gold (add 25% to the above prices), but it is difficult to find the gold lining or trim completely intact. Note that gold trim can usually be removed from clear or colored glass with a pencil eraser, but be careful with flashed items; the flashing could easily be scraped or rubbed off too!

BARRED OVAL   GEORGE DUNCAN & SONS AND U.S. GLASS COMPANY, 1890S–EARLY 1900S

Object	Crystal	Frosted	Ruby Red
Bottle, Water	$40.00	$60.00	$100.00
Butter Dish with Cover	75.00	125.00	200.00
Celery Dish	30.00	50.00	75.00
Compote, Open	35.00	60.00	90.00
Creamer	30.00	50.00	75.00
Cruet with Faceted Stopper	60.00	110.00	175.00
Goblet	25.00	40.00	60.00
Pitcher, Water	75.00	125.00	200.00
Plate, 5"	25.00	40.00	60.00
Sauce Dish	15.00	25.00	40.00
Spooner	25.00	40.00	60.00
Sugar with Cover	50.00	75.00	125.00
Tumbler	25.00	40.00	60.00

The frosted items can be found a little more frequently than the rare ruby red. The pattern is characterized by five horizontal bars that pass through the center of the ovals in each object.

BASKET WEAVE   VARIOUS COMPANIES, 1880S–1890S

Object	Crystal	Colors
Bowl, Berry	$20.00	$35.00
Bowl, Finger	25.00	40.00
Bowl with Cover	30.00	50.00
Butter Dish	30.00	50.00
Cake Plate	40.00	60.00
Compote with Cover	40.00	65.00
Cordial	30.00	45.00
Creamer	25.00	35.00
Cup	20.00	30.00
Egg Holder, Double	20.00	35.00
Goblet	25.00	35.00
Lamp	35.00	55.00
Mug	20.00	30.00
Pickle Dish	25.00	35.00
Pitcher, Syrup, with Metal Lid	50.00	75.00
Pitcher, Milk	45.00	70.00
Pitcher, Water	50.00	75.00
Plate, 8¾", 2 Handles	15.00	25.00
Salt Dip	12.00	20.00
Salt and Pepper Shakers	30.00	50.00
Sauce Dish, Round	20.00	35.00
Saucer	10.00	15.00
Spooner	20.00	30.00
Sugar	30.00	40.00
Tray, 12" Diameter	40.00	60.00
Wineglass	20.00	30.00

Colored pieces include amber, blue, green, and yellow. Beware of modern reproductions of pitchers, tumblers, and goblets.

BEADED GRAPE MEDALLION   BOSTON SILVER
GLASS COMPANY, LATE 1860S–1870S

Object	Price
Bowl, Oval, Small	$25.00
Bowl, Oval, Large	35.00
Butter Dish, Acorn Finial	65.00
Castor Bottle	75.00
Celery Vase	45.00
Champagne Glass	50.00
Compote with Cover, Low, Oval	60.00
Compote with Cover, High, Oval (10" × 7")	80.00
Cordial	75.00
Creamer, Applied Handle	50.00
Egg Holder	25.00
Goblet	30.00

Pressed glass, "Beaded Grape Medallion" pattern. Drawing by Mark Pickvet.

Honey Dish	*$25.00*
Lamp, Handled	*80.00*
Pickle Dish	*35.00*
Pitcher, Water	*125.00*
Plate, 6"	*45.00*
Salt Dip, Round, Flat	*30.00*
Salt Dip, Oval, Flat	*30.00*
Salt Dip, Footed	*35.00*
Spooner	*30.00*
Sugar Bowl with Cover, Acorn Finial	*70.00*

The feet of certain objects may be plain or banded. The traditional grape design is in a cameo or medallion form. Color-flashed versions were made during the Depression era.

BEDFORD   FOSTORIA GLASS COMPANY, 1901–1905

Object	*Price*
Bonbon Dish, 5", 1 Handle	*$20.00*
Bonbon Dish, 6", 1 Handle	*25.00*
Bowl, Berry, 7"	*25.00*
Bowl, Berry, 8"	*30.00*
Bowl, 9" Oval	*35.00*
Bowl, 10" Oval	*40.00*
Butter Dish with Cover	*65.00*
Celery Vase	*35.00*
Claret Glass	*35.00*
Compote, 6", Open	*35.00*
Compote with Cover, 6"	*65.00*
Compote, 7", Open	*40.00*
Cracker Jar with Cover	*125.00*
Creamer, Individual (Small)	*25.00*
Creamer (Large)	*35.00*
Cruet with Hollow Stopper	*50.00*
Cup, Custard	*25.00*
Goblet	*35.00*
Ice Cream Tray, Rectangular	*45.00*

Pitcher, Jug-Shaped *$60.00*
Salt Dip, Individual .... *.20.00*
Spooner .... *.35.00*
Sugar (Large) .... *.45.00*
Sugar with Cover, Individual (Small) .... *.50.00*
Sugar Shaker .... *.55.00*
Toothpick Holder .... *.40.00*
Tumbler, Water .... *.25.00*
Whiskey Tumbler .... *.15.00*
Wineglass .... *.30.00*

The "Bedford" was one of Fostoria's first lines of glass and was referred to as "Line No. 1000" by Fostoria.

BELLFLOWER   VARIOUS COMPANIES, 1840S–1880S

Object	*Price*
Bowl, 6"	*$100.00*
Bowl, 8"	*.125.00*
Bowl, Flat with Scalloped Edge	*.125.00*
Bowl, Flat, Scalloped and Pointed Edge	*.150.00*
Bowl, Oval, 7" × 5"	*.45.00*
Bowl, Oval, 9" × 6"	*.55.00*
Butter Dish with Cover, Plain Edge	*.100.00*
Butter Dish with Cover, Beaded Edge	*.125.00*
Butter Dish with Cover, Rayed Edge	*.150.00*
Cake Stand	*.2000.00*
Celery Vase	*.200.00*
Champagne Glass	*.125.00*
Compote, Open, Low	*.100.00*
Compote, Open, High, 8"	*.110.00*
Compote, Open, High, 8½" Tall, 9¾" Diameter	*.125.00*
Compote with Cover, Low, 8"	*.150.00*
Compote with Cover, High, 8"	*.175.00*
Cordial, Several Styles	*.50.00*
Creamer	*.150.00*
Cruet with Stopper	*.75.00*
Decanter with Stopper, 16 oz.	*.250.00*
Decanter with Stopper, 32 oz.	*.300.00*
Decanter with Bellflower-Patterned Stopper, 16 and 32 oz.	*.500.00*
Egg Holder, Straight Sides	*.45.00*
Egg Holder, Flared Sides	*.50.00*
Goblet, Several Styles	*.50.00*
Honey Dish, 3¼" × 2½"	*.25.00*
Lamp, Bracket, All Glass	*.350.00*
Lamp, Marble Base	*.150.00*
Mug, Applied Handle	*.250.00*
Pickle Dish	*.55.00*
Pitcher, Syrup, with Lid, Round	*.800.00*
Pitcher, Syrup, with Lid, 10-Sided	*.1000.00*

Pitcher, Milk	.$750.00
Pitcher, Water (2 Styles)	.300.00
Plate, 6"	.125.00
Salt Dip, Footed	.50.00
Salt Dip with Cover, Footed	.200.00
Sauce Dish, Various Styles	.25.00
Spooner	.45.00
Sugar, Octagonal	.375.00
Sugar with Cover	.150.00
Tumbler, Footed	.250.00
Tumbler, Water	.100.00
Whiskey Tumbler	.200.00
Wineglass, Several Styles	.125.00

Also known as the "Ribbed Leaf and Bellflower," this line boasts some of the oldest, rarest, and most valuable early pattern glass pieces made in America. It is also characterized by fine vertical ribbing. Some pieces may have a single or double vine within the pattern. A few rare colors such as amber and cobalt also exist (double the above prices).

The Boston and Sandwich Glass Company was the original maker of this pattern, but others, like the McKee Brothers, produced it too.

BERRY OR BARBERRY   BOSTON & SANDWICH GLASS
COMPANY, 1860S; MCKEE BROTHERS, 1880S

Object	*Price*
Bowl with Cover, 8"	.$60.00
Bowl, Oval (8" × 5½")	.65.00
Butter Dish with Cover, 8"	.75.00
Cake Stand	.150.00
Celery Dish	.50.00
Compote with Cover, Low	.55.00
Compote with Cover, High	.65.00
Cordial	.50.00
Creamer	.40.00
Egg Holder	.35.00
Goblet	.30.00
Honey Dish, 3½"	.20.00
Pickle Dish	.25.00
Pitcher, Syrup, with Pewter Lid	.150.00
Pitcher, Water, Applied Handle	.125.00
Plate, 6"	.20.00
Salt Dip, Footed	.30.00
Sauce Dish	.25.00
Sauce Dish, Footed	.30.00
Spooner	.30.00
Sugar with Cover	.50.00
Wineglass	.30.00

The berries on this pattern may be round or oval, and their number varies as well (particularly on the goblets). A few pale green pieces have been found (same price as the clear) as well as amber and blue (double the above prices).

BLEEDING HEART   BOSTON & SANDWICH GLASS COMPANY, 1860S–1870S; KING, SON AND COMPANY, 1870S

Object	Price
Bowl, Waste	$45.00
Bowl, Oval	.50.00
Bowl with Cover	.65.00
Butter Dish	.75.00
Cake Plate with Stand, 9½" Tall	.75.00
Compote with Cover, Low-Footed	.85.00
Compote with Cover, High-Footed	.95.00
Compote with Cover, Oval	.110.00
Creamer, Applied Handle	.65.00
Egg Holder, Straight-Sided	.40.00
Egg Holder, Barrel-Shaped	.45.00
Goblet, Knob on Stem (Several Styles)	.35.00
Mug	.50.00
Pickle Dish, Oval	.30.00
Pitcher, Milk	.200.00
Pitcher, Water	.150.00
Plate (Several Styles)	.75.00
Platter, Oval	.80.00
Relish Dish, 4 Divisions	.100.00
Salt Dip, Round, Footed	.30.00
Salt Dip, Oval	.40.00
Sauce Dish, Round, Flat	.20.00
Sauce Dish, Oval	.25.00
Spooner	.35.00
Sugar	.75.00
Tray, Oval	.50.00
Tumbler, Footed	.50.00
Tumbler, Water	.75.00
Wineglass	.100.00

This patten was originally known as "Floral" and the floral design is usually separated by a vertical line above the halfway point of each object. King and Son also produced this pattern in white opaque (milk) glass (increase the above prices by 25%).

BLOCK AND FAN   RICHARDS & HARTLEY GLASS COMPANY, 1880S

Object	Price
Bowl, 8"	$35.00
Butter Dish with Cover	.70.00
Cake Stand, 10"	.50.00

*Left: Pressed glass,
"Bleeding Heart" pattern.
Drawing by Mark Pickvet.
Right: Pressed glass,
"Block and Fan" pattern.
Drawing by Mark Pickvet.*

Celery Vase $25.00
Compote, Open 45.00
Cordial 50.00
Creamer 45.00
Cruet without Stopper, Small 35.00
Cruet without Stopper, Large 45.00
Goblet 50.00
Jam Jar without Cover 75.00
Lamp 125.00
Pickle Dish 30.00
Pitcher, Water, Pedestal Base 75.00
Plate, 10¹/₂" 30.00
Salt and Pepper Shakers 50.00
Sauce Dish, Square, Flat 20.00
Sauce Dish, 4", Circular, Footed 25.00
Spooner 35.00
Sugar, Open 40.00
Sugar with Cover 50.00
Tumbler 45.00
Wineglass 50.00

This pattern is characterized by horizontal bands of fans that circle the top and bottom of each object. Between the fans are horizontal rows of blocks. There are a few rare ruby-flashed pieces (double the above-listed prices).

BROKEN COLUMN   VARIOUS COMPANIES, 1880S–1890S

Object	Price
Banana Dish, Flat	.$50.00
Basket with Handle 13¹/₂" Long	.100.00
Bottle, Water	.75.00
Bowl, Finger	.25.00
Bowl, 6", with Cover	.40.00
Bowl, 7", with Cover	.45.00
Bowl, 8", with Cover	.50.00

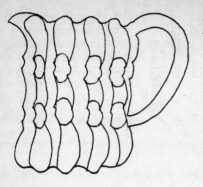

Pressed glass, "Broken Column" pattern. Drawing by Mark Pickvet.

Bowl, 8½"	.$40.00
Butter Dish with Cover	.75.00
Cake Stand	.70.00
Celery Dish	.45.00
Celery Tray	.40.00
Compote, Open	.50.00
Compote with Cover	.70.00
Creamer	.45.00
Cruet with Stopper	.75.00
Cup, Custard	.25.00
Goblet	.45.00
Pitcher, Syrup, with Lid, Jug-Shaped	.80.00
Pitcher, Water	.70.00
Plate, 7¾"	.35.00
Salt and Pepper Shakers	.40.00
Sauce Dish, Flat	.20.00
Spooner	.35.00
Sugar	.45.00
Sugar Shaker	.70.00
Tumbler	.40.00
Wineglass	.45.00

This pattern is also referred to as "Irish Column" or "Notched Rim" and is characterized by raised columns that project outward from the object. Known producers were the Colombia Glass Company, the Portland Glass Company, the U.S. Glass Company, and possibly others.

Some pieces have ruby notches or flashing (increase the above prices by 50%); others are trimmed in gold (increase the above prices by 25%). Beware of reproductions—the goblet and compotes have been reproduced.

BUCKLE   VARIOUS COMPANIES, 1850S–1870S

Object	Price
Bowl, 6", Rolled Rim	.$60.00
Bowl, 7", Rolled Rim	.65.00
Bowl, 8", Rolled Rim	.70.00

Bowl, 6", with Band, Flat Rim *$25.00*
Bowl, 7", with Band, Flat Rim *30.00*
Bowl, 8", with Band, Flat Rim *35.00*
Butter Dish with Cover *100.00*
Champagne Glass *50.00*
Compote, Open *40.00*
Compote, Open, with Band *40.00*
Compote with Cover, with Band *50.00*
Cordial, with Band *40.00*
Creamer, Pedestal Foot, Applied Handles *50.00*
Creamer, with Band *40.00*
Egg Holder *30.00*
Egg Holder, with Band *30.00*
Goblet *30.00*
Goblet, with Band *30.00*
Pickle Dish, Oval *35.00*
Pitcher, Water, Applied Handle *750.00*
Pitcher, Water, with Band *500.00*
Salt Dip, Oval, Flat, Pattern in Base Only *15.00*
Salt Dip, Footed *20.00*
Salt Dip, Footed, with Band *15.00*
Spooner, Scalloped *35.00*
Spooner, with Band *25.00*
Sugar with Cover *60.00*
Sugar with Cover, with Band *50.00*
Tumbler *50.00*
Tumbler, with Band *40.00*
Wineglass *40.00*

The original "Buckle" pattern is attributed to Boston & Sandwich, but others followed. Those listed "with Band" are identical in pattern except for an extra horizontal band at the top of each piece.

Some pieces were made in a finer grade of crystal (add 25% to the above prices); also, a few light blue pieces have been found (double the above prices). Water pitchers are very rare in this pattern.

Pressed glass, "Buckle" pattern. Courtesy of the Sandwich Glass Museum.

BULL'S EYE   VARIOUS COMPANIES, 1850S–1870S

Object	Price
Bitter's Bottle	$75.00
Bottle, Water, Tumble-Up	175.00
Butter Dish with Cover	150.00
Castor Bottle with Stopper	60.00
Celery Vase	90.00
Champagne Glass	125.00
Cologne Bottle with Stopper	100.00
Compote, Open, Low Footed	60.00
Compote, Open, High	80.00
Creamer	135.00
Decanter with Stopper, 16 oz.	150.00
Decanter with Stopper, 32 oz.	175.00
Egg Cup with Cover	200.00
Egg Holder	50.00
Goblet	65.00
Goblet, with Knobbed Stem	85.00
Jam Jar with Cover	90.00
Lamp	100.00
Pickle Dish, Oval	45.00
Salt Dip, Footed	40.00
Salt Dip with Cover, Oblong, Footed	125.00
Spooner	45.00
Sugar with Cover	125.00
Tumbler, Water	100.00
Wineglass	50.00

The original "Bull's Eye" was made by both the New England Glass Company and the Boston and Sandwich Glass Company. A few pieces were produced in green, red, milk white, etc. (double the above prices).

Several variations of the basic "Bull's Eye" design were produced by the U.S. Glass Company; the Union Glass Company; Dalzell, Gilmore & Leighton; and others. These included "Bull's Eye and Daisy," "Bull's Eye and Fan," "Bull's Eye with Fleur-de-Lys," and others.

Pressed glass, "Bull's Eye" pattern. Drawing by Mark Pickvet.

CABBAGE ROSE CENTRAL GLASS COMPANY,
1880S-1890S

Object	Price
Butter Dish with Cover	$75.00
Cake Stand, 11"	.70.00
Cake Stand, 12½"	.80.00
Celery Vase	.50.00
Compote with Cover, 6"	.60.00
Compote with Cover, 7"	.65.00
Compote with Cover, 8"	.70.00
Compote with Cover, 9"	.75.00
Cordial	.45.00
Creamer, Applied Handle	.55.00
Egg Holder	.40.00
Goblet	.35.00
Pickle Dish	.25.00
Pitcher, 32 oz.	.125.00
Pitcher, 48 oz.	.150.00
Salt Dip, Footed, Beaded Rim	.35.00
Sauce Dish (Several Varieties)	.20.00
Spooner	.35.00
Sugar	.40.00
Sugar with Cover	.65.00
Tumbler, Water	.50.00

The pattern is usually on the lower half to two-thirds of each object and is separated from the clear unpatterned portion by a horizontal band.

CABLE BOSTON AND SANDWICH GLASS COMPANY, 1850S

Object	Crystal	Colors
Butter Dish with Cover	$100.00	$225.00
Compote, 5¾" Tall, 11" Diameter	.90.00	200.00
Compote, 9¾" Tall, 10" Diameter	.100.00	225.00
Cordial	.125.00	250.00
Creamer	.350.00	550.00
Decanter with Stopper, 16 oz.	.200.00	375.00
Decanter with Stopper, 32 oz.	.250.00	450.00
Egg Holder	.50.00	100.00
Goblet	.60.00	125.00
Honey Dish	.50.00	90.00
Lamp, All Glass	.125.00	250.00
Lamp, with Marble Base	.100.00	225.00
Mug	.100.00	225.00
Pitcher, Water	.500.00	1250.00
Plate, 6"	.100.00	225.00
Salt Dip, Individual, Flat	.25.00	60.00
Salt Dip, Footed	.35.00	70.00

Object	Crystal	Colors
Sauce Dish	$35.00	$70.00
Spooner	.40.00	75.00
Sugar with Cover	.100.00	225.00
Tumbler, Footed	.175.00	400.00
Wineglass	.50.00	90.00

Color pieces, which are very rare, include opaque blue and opaque green. Some pieces can also be found with amber panels. "Cable" was produced to commemorate the laying of the Transatlantic Cable linking Europe to America. A few pattern variations were introduced later by others.

CALIFORNIA   U.S. GLASS COMPANY, 1880S–1890S

Object	Crystal	Green
Bowl, Oblong	$25.00	$40.00
Bowl, 5¹/₄" Square	.20.00	35.00
Bowl, 6¹/₄" Square	.25.00	40.00
Bowl, 7¹/₄" Square	.30.00	45.00
Bowl, 8¹/₄" Square	.35.00	50.00
Butter Dish with Cover	.60.00	80.00
Cake Stand	.50.00	70.00
Celery Tray, Oblong	.25.00	35.00
Compote, Open, 4" Tall	.25.00	35.00
Compote with Cover, 7" Tall	.40.00	55.00
Compote with Cover, 8" Tall	.45.00	60.00
Compote with Cover, 9" Tall	.50.00	65.00
Cordial	.45.00	65.00
Creamer	.40.00	55.00
Cruet with Swirl Stopper	.75.00	100.00
Goblet	.30.00	45.00
Jelly Dish with Cover, 4" Tall	.40.00	55.00
Pickle Dish	.25.00	35.00
Pitcher, 32 oz. (Round)	.60.00	80.00
Pitcher, 32 oz. (Square)	.70.00	100.00
Pitcher, 48 oz. (Round)	.70.00	90.00
Pitcher, 48 oz. (Square)	.80.00	110.00
Pitcher, 64 oz. (Round)	.100.00	125.00
Plate, 8¹/₂" Square	.25.00	35.00
Platter, 10¹/₄" × 7¹/₄" Oblong	.50.00	65.00
Salt and Pepper Shakers with Metal Tops	.55.00	75.00
Sauce Dish, 3¹/₂"	.10.00	14.00
Sauce Dish, 4"	.12.00	16.00
Sauce Dish with 2 Handles	.15.00	20.00
Salt Dish, 4¹/₂"	.14.00	18.00
Salt and Pepper Shakers	.50.00	75.00
Spooner	.25.00	35.00
Sugar with Cover	.50.00	70.00
Sugar Shaker	.55.00	80.00
Toothpick Holder	.40.00	55.00
Tumbler, Water	.35.00	50.00

Object	Crystal	Green
Vase, 6" Tall	.25.00	35.00
Wineglass	.30.00	45.00

The "California" pattern is also known as "Beaded Grape." There is a horizontal line of beading at the top as well as vertical bands that frame the grape design.

Some pieces were trimmed in gold (add 25% to the above prices if the gold is completely intact).

COLORADO   U.S. GLASS COMPANY, 1890S–EARLY 1900S

Object	Price
Bowl, Triangular	.$20.00
Butter Dish with Cover	.60.00
Cheese Dish, Footed	.35.00
Creamer	.40.00
Pitcher, Water	.50.00
Salt and Pepper Shakers, 3-Footed	.45.00
Spooner	.30.00
Sugar, Individual, 2 Open Handles (Small)	.25.00
Sugar with Cover (Large)	.50.00
Toothpick Holder	.40.00
Tray, 4", Crimped	.20.00
Tray, 4", Flared	.15.00
Tray, 8", Crimped	.30.00
Tray, 8", Flared	.25.00
Tumbler	.30.00

The state series of U.S. Glass continues with the "Colorado" pattern. There are several color variations associated with the "Colorado." For green, cobalt blue, and ruby red, increase the above prices by 50%. For clambroth, double the above prices. For the rare amethyst-stained glass in this pattern, triple the above prices. Finally, increase the above prices by 25% for engraved pieces. Note that some pieces may also contain enameled decorations (same prices).

CORD AND TASSEL   CENTRAL GLASS COMPANY, 1870S

Object	Price
Bowl, Oval	.$30.00
Butter Dish with Cover	.65.00
Cake Stand	.45.00
Celery Vase	.40.00
Compote	.60.00
Cordial	.25.00
Creamer	.40.00
Cruet with Stopper	.50.00
Egg Holder	.35.00
Goblet	.35.00
Lamp, Low Pedestal	.75.00
Mug	.40.00

Pitcher, Water *$100.00*
Sauce Dish, Flat *15.00*
Spooner *25.00*
Sugar with Cover *50.00*
Wineglass *35.00*

Several objects contain handles (Creamer, Cruet, Lamp, Mug, Pitcher, and Sugar) that were either applied or pressed. The price is the same for either method.

CORD DRAPERY   INDIANA TUMBLER AND GOBLET COMPANY, 1890S–EARLY 1900S

Object	Crystal	Colors
Bowl, Berry	*$25.00*	*$40.00*
Bowl, Oval, Deep	*35.00*	*50.00*
Butter Dish	*50.00*	*85.00*
Cake Stand	*50.00*	*80.00*
Compote, Open, Fluted	*65.00*	*110.00*
Compote with Cover	*75.00*	*125.00*
Creamer	*50.00*	*80.00*
Cruet with Dewey Stopper (Amber Only)		*325.00*
Goblet	*45.00*	*75.00*
Jelly Dish with Cover	*55.00*	*85.00*
Pitcher, Syrup, with Lid	*75.00*	*125.00*
Pitcher, Water	*75.00*	*125.00*
Plate, 6"	*40.00*	*75.00*
Salt and Pepper Shakers	*50.00*	*85.00*
Sauce Dish	*25.00*	*40.00*
Spooner	*35.00*	*55.00*
Sugar	*50.00*	*80.00*
Tumbler	*40.00*	*70.00*
Wineglass	*45.00*	*75.00*

Colors include amber, canary yellow, cobalt blue, emerald and opaque nile green, and white. Chocolate pieces are far more valuable than these colors (2–3 times) and are listed under "Chocolate" in the Art Glass section.

Left: Pressed glass, "Cord and Tassel" pattern. Drawing by Mark Pickvet. Right: Pressed glass, "Cord Drapery" pattern. Drawing by Mark Pickvet.

CUPID AND VENUS RICHARDS & HARTLEY GLASS COMPANY, 1870S–1880S

Object	Price
Bowl, Oval	$70.00
Butter Dish with Cover	.85.00
Cake Plate, 11"	.55.00
Celery Vase	.65.00
Champagne Glass	.125.00
Compote, Open	.50.00
Compote with Cover, Low	.65.00
Compote with Cover, High	.75.00
Cordial	.80.00
Creamer	.50.00
Goblet	.75.00
Marmalade Jar with Cover	.125.00
Mug, 2"	.25.00
Mug, 2¹/₂"	.30.00
Mug, 3¹/₂"	.35.00
Pickle Castor	.25.00
Pickle Castor in Frame, Metal Lid	.200.00
Pitcher, Milk	.75.00
Pitcher, Water	.90.00
Plate, 10¹/₂"	.45.00
Plate, 10¹/₂", Handled	.50.00
Sauce Dish, Round, Flat	.12.00
Sauce Dish, 3¹/₂", Footed	.15.00
Sauce Dish, 4", Footed	.17.00
Sauce Dish, 5", Footed	.20.00
Spooner	.40.00
Sugar with Cover	.80.00
Wineglass	.100.00

This pattern is sometimes referred to as "Guardian Angel," and the mythological figures appear in beaded medallion form. Amber and vaseline items have been found (double the above listed prices).

Pressed glass, "Cupid and Venus" pattern. Drawing by Mark Pickvet.

DIAMOND HORSESHOE   THE BRILLIANT GLASS
WORKS, LATE 1880S; GREENSBURG GLASS COMPANY, 1880S–1890S

Object	Price
Butter Dish with Cover	*$75.00*
Cake Stand	*.50.00*
Compote, Open	*.30.00*
Compote with Cover	*.45.00*
Creamer	*.40.00*
Decanter with Stopper	*.65.00*
Goblet	*.35.00*
Pitcher, Water	*.60.00*
Salt and Pepper Shakers	*.30.00*
Spooner	*.25.00*
Sugar	*.40.00*
Wineglass	*.25.00*

This "Diamond Horseshoe" design is sometimes referred to as "Aurora." A few were engraved (increase the above prices by 25%) and ruby-flashed (double the above prices).

DIAMOND POINT   VARIOUS COMPANIES, 1830S–1880S

Object	Prices
Ale Glass	*$60.00*
Bowl, 7" Oval	*.35.00*
Bowl, 8" Oval	*.40.00*
Bowl, 9" Oval	*.45.00*
Bowl, 10" Oval	*.50.00*
Butter Dish with Cover	*.125.00*
Celery Vase	*.75.00*
Champagne Glass	*.70.00*
Compote, 6", Open	*.65.00*

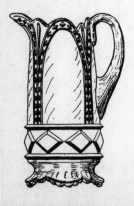 

Left: Pressed glass, "Aurora" or "Diamond Horseshoe" pattern. Drawing by Mark Pickvet.
Right: Pressed glass, "Diamond Point" pattern. Drawing by Mark Pickvet.

Compote, 7", Open $70.00
Compote, 8", Open ....*.75.00*
Compote with Cover, 6" ....*.110.00*
Compote with Cover, 7" ....*.125.00*
Compote with Cover, 8" ....*.150.00*
Cordial ....*.65.00*
Creamer, Scalloped, Footed ....*.150.00*
Cruet with Stopper ....*.125.00*
Decanter with Stopper, 16 oz. ....*.200.00*
Decanter with Stopper, 32 oz. ....*.250.00*
Egg Holder ....*.40.00*
Goblet, Knob Stem ....*.55.00*
Honey Dish ....*.35.00*
Lamp ....*.175.00*
Mug ....*.80.00*
Pitcher, Syrup, 16 oz. ....*.250.00*
Pitcher, Syrup, 16 oz., Footed ....*.275.00*
Pitcher, Milk, 32 oz. ....*.175.00*
Pitcher, Milk, 32 oz., Footed ....*.200.00*
Pitcher, Water, 48 oz. ....*.275.00*
Pitcher, Water, 48 oz., Footed ....*.300.00*
Plate, 3" ....*.30.00*
Plate, 5½" ....*.40.00*
Plate, 6" ....*.45.00*
Plate, 7" ....*.50.00*
Plate, 8" ....*.55.00*
Plate, Pie, 6" (Deep) ....*.65.00*
Plate, Pie, 8" (Deep) ....*.75.00*
Salt Dip with Cover, Footed ....*.90.00*
Sauce Dish ....*.40.00*
Spooner ....*.45.00*
Sugar with Cover ....*.125.00*
Tumbler, Water ....*.75.00*
Whiskey Tumbler ....*.75.00*

The original "Diamond Point" was produced by the Boston & Sandwich Glass Company as early as 1930. Bryce, Richards & Company produced it in the 1850s, and others followed later. There are many rare pieces, and some colors were produced (triple the above-listed prices for color).

DOT   BRYCE BROTHERS, 1870S–1880S

Object	*Price*
Bowl, 6¼"	$25.00
Bowl, 8"	.30.00
Butter Dish with Cover	.55.00
Cake Stand	.40.00
Compote, Open	.35.00
Compote with Cover	.45.00
Cordial	.35.00

Pressed glass, "Dot" or "Beaded Oval and Scroll" pattern. Drawing by Mark Pickvet.

Creamer . . . . *.$30.00*
Goblet . . . . *.30.00*
Pickle Dish . . . . *.25.00*
Pitcher, Water . . . . *.55.00*
Salt and Pepper Shakers . . . . *.40.00*
Sauce Dish, Flat . . . . *.12.00*
Spooner . . . . *.25.00*
Sugar, Open . . . . *.25.00*
Sugar with Cover . . . . *.40.00*
Wineglass . . . . *.30.00*

"Dot" is also known as "Beaded Oval and Scroll" because of the large beaded vertical ovals that alternately enclose the scroll design.

EXCELSIOR   VARIOUS COMPANIES, 1850S–1870S

Object	*Price*
Ale Glass	*.$75.00*
Bitters Bottle	*.55.00*
Bowl, 10"	*.45.00*
Bowl with Cover	*.65.00*
Butter Dish with Cover	*.125.00*
Butter Dish with Cover (McKee Pattern Variant)	*.75.00*
Candlestick	*.150.00*
Celery Vase (McKee Pattern Variant)	*.50.00*
Celery Vase, Scalloped (McKee Pattern Variant)	*.65.00*
Champagne Glass	*.60.00*
Cordial (McKee Pattern Variant)	*.60.00*
Creamer, 2 Styles	*.125.00*
Creamer (McKee Pattern Variant)	*.125.00*
Decanter, 16 oz., with or without Foot	*.60.00*
Decanter, 32 oz.	*.75.00*
Egg Holder, Single	*.40.00*

Egg Holder, Double *$50.00*
Goblet, Barrel-Shaped Bowl, Maltese Cross Design (Boston & Sandwich) .... *.75.00*
Goblet (McKee Pattern Variant) .... *.50.00*
Lamp, Whale Oil, Maltese Cross Design (Boston & Sandwich) .... *.200.00*
Pitcher, Syrup, with Lid .... *.350.00*
Pitcher, Milk .... *.350.00*
Pitcher, Water (McKee Only) .... *.400.00*
Salt Dip, Footed .... *.35.00*
Spooner .... *.40.00*
Spooner (McKee Pattern Variant) .... *.40.00*
Sugar, 2 Styles .... *.125.00*
Sugar with Cover (McKee Pattern Variant) .... *.75.00*
Tumbler, Bar .... *.50.00*
Tumbler, Water, Various Styles .... *.35.00*
Tumbler, Footed (McKee Pattern Variant) .... *.40.00*
Wineglass .... *.50.00*

"Excelsior" was primarily made by the Boston & Sandwich Glass Company, McKee Brothers, and C. Ihmsen and Company. A few others produced it as well. A few pale green items are occasionally found (increase above prices by 25%).

The pattern variant referred to above was produced exclusively under McKee Brothers and is sometimes referred to as "Tong." The ovals have a wider diameter (nearly circular) but converge at the bottom to what is nearly a point. In short, they are somewhat heart-shaped on the variant.

FAN AND FLUTE   U.S. GLASS COMPANY, 1890S

Object	*Price*
Bowl, 7"	*$15.00*
Bowl, 8"	*.18.00*
Bowl, 9"	*.20.00*
Butter Dish	*.40.00*
Cake Stand	*.40.00*
Celery Tray	*.20.00*
Celery Vase	*.25.00*
Compote, 6", Open	*.20.00*
Compote, 7", Open	*.22.00*
Compote, 8", Open	*.25.00*
Compote, 9", Open	*.30.00*
Creamer	*.25.00*
Cruet with Stopper	*.40.00*
Cup	*.15.00*
Goblet	*.25.00*
Pitcher, Syrup with Lid	*.55.00*
Pitcher, Milk	*.45.00*
Plate, 7"	*.15.00*
Plate, 9"	*.18.00*
Plate, 10"	*.20.00*
Salt Shaker	*.20.00*
Sauce Dish, 4", Flat	*.10.00*

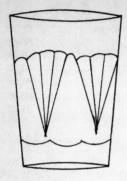

Pressed glass, "Fan and Flute" pattern. Drawing by Mark Pickvet.

Sauce Dish, 4", Footed	*$12.00*
Sauce Dish, 4½", Flat	*12.00*
Sauce Dish, 5"	*15.00*
Spooner	*20.00*
Sugar	*25.00*
Toothpick Holder	*35.00*
Tray, 7" Oblong	*15.00*
Tray, 8" Oblong	*18.00*
Tray, 9" Oblong	*20.00*
Tray, 10" Oblong	*22.00*
Tumbler, Water	*20.00*
Wineglass	*25.00*

This pattern was also referred to as "Millard." The fluted panels may be stained with amber (increase the above-listed prices by 50%) or with ruby red (double the above prices). The panels might also be engraved rather than pressed (increase prices by 25%).

FEATHER   MCKEE GLASS COMPANY, 1890S

Object	*Price*
Banana Dish	*$65.00*
Bowl, 7½"	*25.00*
Bowl, 8½"	*30.00*
Bowl, Berry, Square	*30.00*
Bowl, Oval	*25.00*
Butter Dish with Cover	*65.00*
Cake Stand, 8½"	*50.00*
Cake Stand, 11"	*65.00*
Celery Vase	*40.00*
Compote, Open	*50.00*
Compote with Cover	*65.00*
Cordial	*75.00*
Creamer, Scalloped	*40.00*
Cruet with Stopper	*75.00*

Goblet	*$35.00*
Jam Jar with Cover	*90.00*
Pickle Dish	*30.00*
Pitcher, Milk	*60.00*
Pitcher, Water	*75.00*
Plate, 7"	*25.00*
Plate, 8"	*30.00*
Plate, 9½"	*35.00*
Plate, 10"	*40.00*
Platter	*40.00*
Relish Dish	*35.00*
Sauce Dish, Flat	*15.00*
Sauce Dish, Footed	*22.00*
Spooner, Scalloped	*30.00*
Sugar with Cover	*60.00*
Toothpick Holder	*60.00*
Tumbler, Water	*50.00*
Wineglass, Scalloped Band	*45.00*

"Feather" has many names, including the original "Doric" as well as "Finecut and Feather" and "Indiana Swirl." Like so many pressed designs, this one resembles cut glass with alternating panels of rosette points and beaded flutes.

Colors are very scarce and valuable. For green, double the above prices; for amber or ruby red, triple the above prices; for chocolate, quadruple the above prices.

Wineglasses made in cranberry or pink stain were reproduced in the 1950s by the Jeannette Glass Company (they purchased McKee).

FINE RIB   NEW ENGLAND GLASS COMPANY, 1850S–1870S

Object	Price
Ale Glass	*$60.00*
Bitters Bottle	*65.00*
Bottle, Water, Tumble-Up	*75.00*
Bowl, 7" Oval	*45.00*
Bowl, 8" Oval	*50.00*
Bowl, 9" Oval	*55.00*
Bowl, 10" Oval	*60.00*
Bowl with Cover, 7"	*60.00*
Butter Dish with Cover	*125.00*
Celery Vase	*70.00*
Champagne Glass	*55.00*
Compote, Open, 7", Footed	*75.00*
Compote, Open, 8", Footed	*80.00*
Compote, Open, 9", Footed	*85.00*
Compote, Open, 10", Footed	*90.00*
Compote with Cover, 7", Footed	*120.00*
Compote with Cover, 8", Footed	*140.00*
Creamer	*100.00*
Cruet with Stopper	*100.00*
Cup, Custard,	*65.00*

 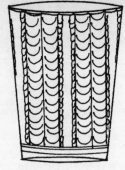

Left: Pressed glass, "Fine Rib" pattern. Drawing by Mark Pickvet. Right: Pressed glass, "Fishscale" pattern. Drawing by Mark Pickvet.

Decanter with Stopper, 16 oz.	*$100.00*
Decanter with Stopper, 32 oz.	*125.00*
Egg Holder	*50.00*
Goblet	*55.00*
Honey Dish	*30.00*
Lamp, Handled	*175.00*
Mug	*65.00*
Pitcher, Syrup, with Lid, 16 oz.	*300.00*
Pitcher, Milk, 32 oz.	*200.00*
Pitcher, Water, 48 oz.	*250.00*
Plate, 6"	*60.00*
Plate, 7"	*70.00*
Salt Dip, Flat	*45.00*
Salt Dip with Cover, Footed	*125.00*
Sauce Dish	*35.00*
Tumbler, Water	*60.00*
Whiskey Tumbler	*50.00*
Wineglass	*55.00*

There were many ribbed designs created by other companies, but this New England pattern has some distinction. The ribbing is very fine and extends from the top to bottom of each piece. Nearly all of the pieces have scalloped bottom panels. Some bowls and compotes also have wavy rims.

FISHSCALE   BRYCE BROTHERS, 1880S–1890S

Object	*Price*
Ashtray, Daisy and Button Slipper Design (Slipper Is Amber, Blue, Crystal, or Topaz) Attached to Rectangular Tray (Tray Contains the Fishscale Pattern)	*$50.00*
Bowl, 6"	*20.00*
Bowl, 7"	*25.00*
Bowl, 8"	*30.00*
Bowl with Cover, 7" Square, Round Base	*45.00*
Bowl with Cover, 8" Square, Round Base	*55.00*
Butter Dish with Cover	*65.00*

Cake Stand, 9"	.$30.00
Cake Stand, 10"	.35.00
Cake Stand, 11"	.40.00
Celery Vase	.50.00
Compote, Open, 7"	.25.00
Compote, Open, 8"	.30.00
Compote, Open, 9"	.35.00
Compote, Open, 10"	.40.00
Compote with Cover, 6"	.50.00
Compote with Cover, 7"	.60.00
Compote with Cover, 8"	.70.00
Creamer	.35.00
Goblet	.35.00
Lamp, Handled	.75.00
Mug	.35.00
Pickle Dish	.20.00
Pitcher, 32 oz.	.60.00
Pitcher, 64 oz.	.80.00
Plate, 7"	.25.00
Plate, 8"	.30.00
Plate, 8" Square	.35.00
Plate, 9" Square, Round Corners	.40.00
Salt and Pepper Shakers	.65.00
Sauce Dish, 4", Flat	.12.00
Sauce Dish, 4", Flared, Footed	.15.00
Spooner	.25.00
Sugar with Cover	.50.00
Tray, Oblong, Scalloped Edge (for Shakers)	.40.00
Tray, Water, Round	.45.00
Tumbler	.30.00

"Fishscale" is also known as "Coral." It contains vertical bands of half-circles from top to bottom of each object, resembling the scales of fish.

FLEUR-DE-LYS ADAMS AND COMPANY, 1880S–1890S

Object	*Price*
Bottle, Water	.$55.00
Butter Dish with Cover	.65.00
Cake Stand	.50.00
Celery Vase	.35.00
Claret Glass	.45.00
Compote, Open	.45.00
Compote with Cover	.60.00
Cordial	.50.00
Creamer	.35.00
Goblet	.35.00
Lamp	.125.00
Mustard Jar with Ribbed Cover	.75.00
Pitcher, Syrup, with Lid	.75.00

Pitcher, Milk . . . . *.$60.00*
Pitcher, Water . . . . *.75.00*
Sauce Dish, 4", Flat . . . . *.15.00*
Sauce Dish, 4¹/₂", Flat . . . . *.18.00*
Spooner . . . . *.20.00*
Sugar with Cover . . . . *.50.00*
Tumbler . . . . *.35.00*
Wineglass . . . . *.45.00*

"Fleur-de-Lys" is also referred to as "Fleur-de-Lys and Drape" or "Fleur-de-Lys and Tassel." For green and opal colors, increase the above prices by 50%.

The basic design is in relief and includes upright fleur-de-lys with upside down tassels (or drapes).

FLUTE   VARIOUS COMPANIES, 1850S–1880S

Object	*Price*
Ale Glass	*.$35.00*
Bitters Bottle	*.45.00*
Bowl Scalloped	*.40.00*
Candlestick	*.30.00*
Champagne Glass	*.30.00*
Compote, 8" Diameter	*.45.00*
Creamer	*.35.00*
Cup, Custard	*.40.00*
Decanter, 32 oz.	*.65.00*
Egg Holder, Single	*.25.00*
Egg Holder, Double	*.35.00*
Goblet	*.30.00*
Honey Dish	*.25.00*
Lamp, Whale Oil	*.100.00*
Mug, Applied Handle	*.40.00*
Mug, Toy, 2 oz., with Handle	*.20.00*
Pitcher, Water	*.80.00*
Salt Dip, Footed	*.25.00*
Sauce Dish, Flat	*.20.00*
Spooner	*.25.00*
Tumbler, 4 oz.	*.20.00*
Tumbler, 6 oz.	*.25.00*
Tumbler, 8 oz.	*.30.00*
Tumbler, Bar, 12 oz.	*.40.00*
Whiskey Tumbler, 2 oz.	*.15.00*
Wineglass	*.30.00*

The original "Flute" patterns usually had six or eight large rounded flutes that encompassed most of the object. Most pieces contain a plain band across the top. Many companies had their own individual names, such as "Bessimer Flute," "Brooklyn Flute," "New England Flute," "Reed Stem Flute," "Sandwich Flute," "Sexton Flute," and so on.

Some "Flute" pieces were made in colors (double the above-listed prices).

HAMILTON BOSTON & SANDWICH GLASS COMPANY, 1860S–1880S

Object	Price
Butter Dish with Cover	$100.00
Butter Dish with Cover (Leaf Pattern Variant)	125.00
Castor Bottle with Stopper	60.00
Celery Vase	55.00
Celery Vase (Leaf Pattern Variant)	60.00
Compote, Open, Low Foot	45.00
Compote, Open, High Foot	50.00
Compote, Open (Leaf Pattern Variant)	55.00
Compote with Cover, 6"	75.00
Cordial (Leaf Pattern Variant)	50.00
Creamer	50.00
Creamer, Molded Handle (Leaf Pattern Variant)	65.00
Decanter with Stopper	175.00
Egg Holder	40.00
Egg Holder (Leaf Pattern Variant)	65.00
Goblet	40.00
Honey Dish	25.00
Lamp, 7" Tall, 2 Styles (Leaf Pattern Variant)	150.00
Pitcher, Syrup, with Metal Lid	250.00
Pitcher, Water	225.00
Pitcher, Water (Leaf Pattern Variant)	175.00
Plate, 6"	100.00
Salt Dip, Footed (Leaf Pattern Variant)	40.00
Sauce Dish, 4"	15.00
Sauce Dish, 5"	20.00
Spooner	35.00
Spooner (Leaf Pattern Variant)	45.00
Sugar, Open	50.00
Sugar with Cover (Leaf Pattern Variant)	100.00
Tumbler, Bar (Leaf Pattern Variant)	100.00
Tumbler, Water	90.00

Pressed glass, "Hamilton" pattern. Drawing by Mark Pickvet.

Whiskey Tumbler *$125.00*
Wineglass .... *.90.00*
Wineglass (Leaf Pattern Variant) .... *.100.00*

The leaf pattern variant is sometimes referred to as "Hamilton with Leaf." The horizontal diamond band in the middle of each piece in the original "Hamilton" is replaced by leaves in the pattern variant.

The "Hamilton with Leaf" pattern was also produced by others in the 1890s. Occasionally the leaves can be found frosted (add 25% to the above prices).

HONEYCOMB   VARIOUS COMPANIES, 1860S–1880S

Object	*Price*
Ale Glass	*$50.00*
Bitters Bottle	*.65.00*
Bowl, 6"	*.25.00*
Bowl, 7"	*.28.00*
Bowl, 8"	*.30.00*
Bowl, 9"	*.32.00*
Bowl, 10"	*.35.00*
Bowl, Oval	*.30.00*
Bowl with Cover, 6"	*.35.00*
Bowl with Cover, 7"	*.40.00*
Bowl with Cover, 8"	*.45.00*
Butter Dish	*.40.00*
Castor Bottle with Stopper	*.55.00*
Celery Vase	*.65.00*
Champagne Glass	*.40.00*
Compote, Open, 7"	*.35.00*
Compote, Open, 7", Low Foot	*.30.00*
Compote, Open, 8"	*.40.00*
Compote, Open, 8", Low Foot	*.35.00*
Compote, Open, 9"	*.45.00*
Compote, Open, 10"	*.50.00*
Compote with Cover, 7"	*.55.00*
Compote with Cover, 7", Low Foot	*.50.00*
Compote with Cover, 8"	*.65.00*
Compote with Cover, 8", Low Foot	*.60.00*
Cordial	*.50.00*
Creamer, 5¹/₂" Tall	*.40.00*
Cup, Custard	*.40.00*
Decanter with Stopper, 16 oz.	*.55.00*
Decanter with Stopper, 32 oz.	*.70.00*
Egg Holder	*.35.00*
Goblet, Barrel-Shaped Bowl	*.45.00*
Honey Dish	*.20.00*
Jelly Glass, Pedestal Base	*.65.00*
Jug, 8 oz.	*.40.00*
Jug, 16 oz.	*.45.00*

*Left: Pressed glass,
"Honeycomb" pattern.
Drawing by Mark Pickvet.
Right: Pressed glass, "Horn of
Plenty" pattern. Drawing by
Mark Pickvet.*

Jug, 32 oz. *$50.00*
Jug, 48 oz. *55.00*
Lamp, All Glass *75.00*
Lamp, Marble Base *95.00*
Mug, 8 oz. *50.00*
Pitcher, Water, Applied Handle *100.00*
Plate, 6" *40.00*
Plate, 7" *50.00*
Salt and Pepper Shakers *50.00*
Salt Dip, Footed *20.00*
Salt Dip with Cover, Footed *55.00*
Sauce Dish *20.00*
Spooner *30.00*
Sugar *50.00*
Tumbler, 5¹/₂ oz. *45.00*
Tumbler, 8 oz. *55.00*
Tumbler, 8 oz., Footed *65.00*
Wineglass *30.00*

"Honeycomb" has been referred to as "Cincinnati," "Vernon," "Hex Optic," and others. Bakewell, Pears, & Company, Lyons Glass Company, McKee Brothers, and others all made this pattern. Colors include amber, cobalt blue, green, opal, and topaz (double the above-listed prices).

"Honeycomb" variations were later made during the Depression.

HORN OF PLENTY   VARIOUS COMPANIES, 1830S–1870S

Object	*Price*
Bowl, 8¹/₂"	*$200.00*
Bowl, Oval (8" × 5¹/₂")	*175.00*
Butter Dish with Cover, 6" Diameter	*150.00*
Butter Dish with Cover, George Washington's Head Finial	*750.00*
Cake Stand	*1000.00*
Celery Vase	*175.00*
Champagne Glass	*150.00*
Compote, 8" Tall, Open	*125.00*

Compote, 12" Tall, Open *$150.00*
Compote with Cover, 6" *125.00*
Cordial *150.00*
Creamer, 5½" Tall *200.00*
Creamer, 7" Tall *225.00*
Creamer ("Comet" Pattern, Boston & Sandwich) *225.00*
Decanter with Stopper, 16 oz. *125.00*
Decanter with Stopper, 32 oz. *150.00*
Decanter with Stopper, 64 oz. *175.00*
Egg Holder *60.00*
Goblet ("Comet" Pattern, Boston & Sandwich) *125.00*
Honey Dish, 3¼" *20.00*
Lamp, All Glass *200.00*
Lamp, Marble Base *225.00*
Mug, Applied Handle *175.00*
Pickle Dish *110.00*
Pitcher, Milk *750.00*
Pitcher, Water *600.00*
Pitcher, Water ("Comet" Pattern, Boston & Sandwich) *600.00*
Plate, 6" *100.00*
Salt Dip, Oval *55.00*
Sauce Dish, 4½" *20.00*
Sauce Dish, 5" *25.00*
Sauce Dish, 6" *35.00*
Spooner *50.00*
Spooner ("Comet" Pattern, Boston & Sandwich) *75.00*
Sugar with Pagoda Cover *200.00*
Tumbler, Water ("Comet" Pattern, Boston & Sandwich) *175.00*
Whiskey Tumbler *100.00*
Whiskey Tumbler ("Comet" Pattern, Boston & Sandwich) *150.00*
Wineglass *150.00*

"Horn of Plenty" and "Comet" are virtually identical; however, "Comet" is attributed solely to the Boston & Sandwich Glass Company. "Horn of Plenty" was also made by Boston & Sandwich as well as Bryce Brothers, McKee Brothers, and possibly others.

This is a rare and valuable pattern. A few pieces were made in amber, canary yellow, cobalt blue, and an opalescent white (double the above-listed prices).

The lamp is completely glass. The water tumbler and goblet have been reproduced in amber and crystal.

JACOB'S LADDER   BRYCE BROTHERS, 1870S–1880S

Object	*Price*
Bowl, 6"	*$30.00*
Bowl, 7" Oval	*35.00*
Bowl, 8" Oval	*40.00*
Bowl, 9" Oval	*45.00*
Bowl, 10" Oval	*50.00*
Butter Dish with Cover, Maltese Cross Finial	*80.00*

Cake Stand, 8" *$45.00*
Cake Stand, 9" .... *.50.00*
Cake Stand, 11" .... *.60.00*
Cake Stand, 12" .... *.65.00*
Castor Bottle with Stopper .... *.45.00*
Celery Vase .... *.40.00*
Compote, Open, Scalloped Edge .... *.55.00*
Compote, Open, with Silverplated Holder .... *.125.00*
Compote, Dolphin .... *.325.00*
Compote with Cover .... *.90.00*
Cordial .... *.65.00*
Creamer, Footed .... *.45.00*
Cruet with Maltese Cross Stopper .... *.100.00*
Goblet .... *.60.00*
Marmalade Dish, Maltese Cross Finial .... *.75.00*
Mug .... *.55.00*
Pickle Dish .... *.40.00*
Pitcher, Syrup, with Metal Lid, 2 Styles .... *.100.00*
Pitcher, Water, Applied Handle .... *.150.00*
Plate, 6" .... *.30.00*
Salt Dip, Master, Round, Flat .... *.40.00*
Salt Dip, Master, Footed .... *.50.00*
Sauce Dish, 3¹/₂", Flat, Footed .... *.15.00*
Sauce Dish, 4", Flat, Footed .... *.18.00*
Sauce Dish, 4¹/₂", Footed .... *.18.00*
Sauce Dish, 5", Flat, Footed .... *.20.00*
Spooner .... *.40.00*
Sugar with Cover, Maltese Cross Finial .... *.75.00*
Tray, Oval .... *.35.00*
Tumbler, 8 oz. .... *.50.00*
Wineglass .... *.45.00*

The original name for "Jacob's Ladder" was "Maltese" because of the cross design on many pieces. A few rare amber and yellow pieces were also made (double the above-listed prices).

Pressed glass, "Jacob's Ladder" pattern. Drawing by Mark Pickvet.

LATTICE   KING, SON & COMPANY, 1880S

Object	Price
Bowl, 8" Oval	$25.00
Butter Dish with Cover	55.00
Cake Stand, 8"	40.00
Celery Vase	35.00
Compote with Cover, 8"	55.00
Cordial	50.00
Creamer	30.00
Goblet	35.00
Lamp	100.00
Marmalade Jar	125.00
Pickle Dish	25.00
Pitcher, Syrup, with Lid	65.00
Pitcher, Water	75.00
Plate, 6¼"	20.00
Plate, 7¼"	25.00
Plate, 10"	35.00
Platter, Oval (11½" × 7½"), Embossed "Waste not, want not"	55.00
Salt and Pepper Shakers	50.00
Sauce Dish, Flat	12.00
Sauce Dish, Footed	15.00
Spooner	20.00
Sugar with Cover	45.00
Tray	65.00
Wineglass	35.00

"Lattice" is also known as "Diamond Bar" and is characterized by occasional vertical diamond bands that resemble latticework. There are usually horizontal diamond bands at the top and bottom of each object as well.

MADORA   HIGBEE GLASS COMPANY, 1880S–1890S

Object	Price
Basket, 7" Long	$50.00
Bowl, Rose, with Foot and Stem	35.00
Cake Stand	40.00
Celery Dish with Handles	35.00
Children's Miniatures:	
Butter Dish with Cover	40.00
Creamer	25.00
Spooner	25.00
Sugar with Cover	35.00
Complete Set of 6 Pieces	130.00
Creamer	25.00
Plate, 7" Square	20.00
Punch Cup	15.00
Salt Dip, Individual	15.00

Left: Pressed glass, "Lattice" pattern. Drawing by Mark Pickvet. Center: Pressed glass, "Madora (Arrowhead in Oval)" pattern. Drawing by Mark Pickvet. Right: Pressed glass, "New England Pineapple" pattern. Drawing by Mark Pickvet.

Salt and Pepper Shakers	*$40.00*
Sherbet	*20.00*
Sugar with Cover	*35.00*
Wine Goblet	*25.00*

"Madora" is sometimes referred to as "Arrowhead" or "Arrowhead in Oval" because of the large arrowhead design in the center of the pattern. A few pieces were embossed with a "bee" (the company trademark) and are a little more valuable than those without it.

NEW ENGLAND PINEAPPLE BOSTON & SANDWICH GLASS COMPANY, 1860S

Object	*Price*
Bowl, Fruit	*$175.00*
Butter Dish with Cover	*200.00*
Castor Bottle	*85.00*
Celery Vase	*225.00*
Champagne Glass	*175.00*
Compote, Open	*75.00*
Compote with Cover, 6"	*225.00*
Cordial	*150.00*
Creamer	*200.00*
Cruet with Stopper	*125.00*
Decanter with Stopper, 16 oz.	*250.00*
Decanter with Stopper, 32 oz.	*300.00*
Egg Holder	*50.00*
Goblet, 2 Styles	*75.00*
Honey Dish	*25.00*
Mug	*150.00*
Pitcher, Water	*325.00*

Plate, 6"	*$150.00*
Salt Dip, Footed	*.85.00*
Sauce Dish	*.25.00*
Spooner	*.50.00*
Sugar with Cover	*.225.00*
Tumbler, Water	*.100.00*
Tumbler, Water, Footed	*.125.00*
Whiskey Tumbler, 2 oz.	*.100.00*
Wineglass	*.75.00*

The pineapples of this pattern are pressed into large oval shapes that encompass the majority of each object. There are many pieces that are quite scarce and valuable in this pattern.

OREGON U.S. GLASS COMPANY, EARLY 1900S

Object	*Price*
Bowl with Cover, 6"	*$25.00*
Bowl with Cover, 7"	*.35.00*
Bowl with Cover, 8"	*.45.00*
Butter Dish (2 Styles)	*.50.00*
Cake Stand, 6" (Small)	*.35.00*
Cake Stand, 9½" (Large)	*.50.00*
Celery Vase	*.35.00*
Compote with Cover	*.50.00*
Cordial	*.35.00*
Creamer	*.30.00*
Goblet	*.40.00*
Jelly Dish	*.35.00*
Mug	*.35.00*
Pickle Dish, Boat-Shaped	*.35.00*
Pitcher, Syrup, with Lid	*.75.00*
Pitcher, Milk	*.55.00*
Pitcher, Water, 64 oz.	*.75.00*
Sauce Dish, 3½"	*.15.00*
Sauce Dish, 4"	*.20.00*
Salt and Pepper Shakers	*.40.00*
Sugar, Open	*.30.00*
Sugar with Cover	*.45.00*
Sugar Shaker	*.35.00*
Toothpick Holder	*.75.00*
Tray, 7½" Oval	*.25.00*
Tray, 9½" Oval	*.40.00*
Tray, 10½" Oval	*.45.00*
Tray, Bread	*.50.00*
Tumbler, Water	*.40.00*
Vase	*.35.00*
Wineglass	*.45.00*
Wineglass, Pedestal Base	*.55.00*

"Oregon" is also known as "Beaded Loop" and is characterized by oval beading and diamonds that resemble cut glass. The beading intersects, as do the horizontal band of ovals at the top. Prices should be increased by $^1/_3$ to $^1/_2$ for green. Flashed pieces were made during the Depression years.

PANELLED DEWDROP CAMPBELL, JONES & COMPANY, 1870S–1880S

Object	*Price*
Butter Dish with Cover	*$60.00*
Celery Vase	*.40.00*
Champagne Glass	*.35.00*
Cheese Dish with Cover	*.75.00*
Compote, Open, 8", Footed	*.65.00*
Cordial	*.35.00*
Creamer, Applied Handle	*.40.00*
Goblet, Plain Base	*.30.00*
Goblet, Dewdrops on Base	*.35.00*
Honey Dish with Cover, 11"	*.125.00*
Marmalade Jar	*.65.00*
Mug, Applied Handle	*.35.00*
Pickle Dish	*.60.00*
Pitcher, Water	*.60.00*
Plate, 7"	*.35.00*
Plate, 11"	*.65.00*
Platter, Oval	*.40.00*
Platter, Oblong, Handles	*.55.00*
Relish	*.20.00*
Sauce Dish, Flat	*.12.00*
Sauce Dish, Footed	*.15.00*
Spooner	*.20.00*
Sugar with Cover	*.50.00*
Tumbler, Water	*.35.00*
Wineglass	*.35.00*

This pattern is sometimes referred to as "Striped Dewdrop" and is characterized by vertical strips or panels of dewdrops. Some pieces may or may not have rows of dewdrops on the base.

Pressed glass, "Panelled Dewdrop" pattern. Drawing by Mark Pickvet.

PANELLED GRAPE   D. C. JENKINS GLASS COMPANY, EARLY 1900S

Object	Price
Ale Glass	$70.00
Bowl, Oval	.35.00
Bowl with Cover	.55.00
Butter Dish	.60.00
Celery Vase	.50.00
Compote, Open	.55.00
Compote with Cover	.75.00
Cordial	.60.00
Creamer, 4½" Tall	.55.00
Cup	.45.00
Goblet	.75.00
Pitcher, Syrup	.150.00
Pitcher, Milk	.125.00
Pitcher, Water	.150.00
Sauce Dish, 4¼" Round	.25.00
Sauce Dish, Oval	.25.00
Sauce Dish, Footed	.35.00
Spooner	.30.00
Sugar Dish, Open	.40.00
Sugar with Cover	.60.00
Toothpick Holder	.60.00
Tumbler, Water	.65.00
Wineglass	.75.00

This pattern is also known as "Heavy Panelled Grape." Note that the above-listed prices are for clear glass only. This pattern was heavily reproduced in milk glass, Carnival glass, and other colors.

PANELLED THISTLE   VARIOUS COMPANIES, 1910S–EARLY 1920S

Object	Price
Basket, Various Styles	$100.00
Bowl, 6½"	.35.00
Bowl, 7"	.40.00
Bowl, 8½"	.50.00
Bowl, 9"	.55.00
Bowl, Footed	.50.00
Butter Dish, Flanged	.60.00
Cake Stand, 9¾" Diameter	.40.00
Celery Vase, Handled	.40.00
Celery Dish	.30.00
Compote, 5", Open	.35.00
Compote, 8", Open	.45.00
Cordial	.35.00

Left: Pressed glass, "Panelled Grape" pattern. Drawing by Mark Pickvet.
Right: Pressed glass, "Panelled Thistle" pattern. Drawing by Mark Pickvet.

Creamer, Knob Feet *$45.00*
Cruet (without Stopper) *40.00*
Cup, Custard *35.00*
Goblet, Straight *35.00*
Goblet, Flared *40.00*
Honey Dish with Cover, Square, Footed *75.00*
Pickle Dish, 8¼" *25.00*
Pitcher, Milk, 32 oz. *65.00*
Pitcher, Water, 64 oz. *75.00*
Plate, 7¼" *20.00*
Plate, 8¼" *25.00*
Plate, 9½" *30.00*
Plate, 10¼" *35.00*
Salt Dip, Individual, 1" Tall, Footed *20.00*
Salt and Pepper Shakers *65.00*
Sauce Dish, Several Styles *20.00*
Spooner, 2-Handled *30.00*
Sugar Bowl with Cover, 2-Handled *55.00*
Toothpick Holder *55.00*
Tray, Celery *35.00*
Tumbler, Water *35.00*
Wineglass, Straight *30.00*
Wineglass, Flared *35.00*

The Higbee Glass Company was the original maker of this pattern, which they referred to as "Delta." The Jefferson Glass Company of Toronto, Canada, and the Dominion Glass Company also produced items in this pattern. Some pieces have Higbee's "bee" mark (increase above prices by 25%).

A few reproductions have been made, including colored salt dips, clear salt dips that are taller than 1", and a slim, flared toothpick holder.

PINEAPPLE AND FAN   ADAMS & COMPANY, 1880S; U.S. GLASS COMPANY, 1890S

Object   *Price*
Bowl 8" *$25.00*

Left: Pressed glass, "Pineapple and Fan" pattern. Drawing by Mark Pickvet. Right: Pressed glass, "Primrose" pattern. Drawing by Mark Pickvet.

Bowl, 9"	.$30.00
Butter Dish with Cover	.55.00
Cake Stand	.45.00
Celery Vase	.40.00
Creamer	.35.00
Custard Cup	.15.00
Goblet	.30.00
Mug	.15.00
Piccalilli Jar with Cover	.50.00
Pitcher, 16 oz.	.40.00
Pitcher, 32 oz.	.50.00
Pitcher, 64 oz., Tankard Style	.60.00
Pitcher, 96 oz., Tankard Style	.75.00
Salt Dip, Individual	.12.00
Sauce Dish, 4"	.8.00
Sauce Dish, 4¹/₂"	.10.00
Spooner	.30.00
Sugar with Cover	.45.00
Tumbler, Water	.20.00
Wineglass	.25.00

This pattern is also referred to as "Cube with Fan" because of the cube or pineapple-like design on the lower half of each piece. The fan design is on the top portion, and the cubes are flat beveled squares.

A few objects have been found in color; for green increase the above-listed prices by 50%; for ruby-stained, double the prices.

POINTED THUMBPRINT BAKEWELL, PEARS & CO., 1860S; BRYCE BROS., 1890S

Object	*Price*
Butter Dish with Cover, Cable Edge	.$125.00
Celery Vase	.60.00
Compote with Cover, 4³/₄" Tall	.50.00
Compote with Cover, 7" Tall	.60.00
Compote with Cover, 10" Tall	.75.00

Creamer	.$50.00
Egg Holder	.35.00
Goblet	.35.00
Pitcher, Water	.100.00
Sugar with Cover	.65.00
Tumbler	.50.00

The thumbprints on this pattern are pointed on the ends, resembling almonds. The pattern was also referred to as "Fingerprint." Bryce Brothers produced a cheaper lime glass in the early 1890s in the same pattern; the prices above are for lead glass (reduce by ²/₃ for non-lead).

PRIMROSE   CANTON GLASS COMPANY, 1880S

Object	*Price*
Bowl, Berry	.$25.00
Bowl, Waste	.30.00
Butter Dish with Cover	.55.00
Cake Stand	.45.00
Celery Vase	.30.00
Compote with Cover, 6"	.35.00
Compote with Cover, 7¹/₂"	.45.00
Compote with Cover, 8"	.50.00
Compote with Cover, 9"	.60.00
Cordial	.40.00
Creamer	.35.00
Egg Holder	.35.00
Goblet, Plain Stem	.30.00
Goblet, Knob Stem	.35.00
Marmalade Jar	.55.00
Pickle Dish	.20.00
Pitcher, 7¹/₂" Tall	.55.00
Plate, 4¹/₂"	.18.00
Plate, 6"	.20.00
Plate, 7"	.22.00
Plate, 8³/₄", Cake, Handled	.35.00
Platter, Oval (12¹/₂" × 8"), Flower Handles	.40.00
Sauce Dish, Flat	.10.00
Sauce Dish, 4", Footed	.12.00
Sauce Dish, 5¹/₂", Footed	.15.00
Spooner	.25.00
Sugar with Cover	.45.00
Tray, Water	.45.00
Wineglass	.30.00

This flower and leaf design also includes vertical panels and horizontal ribbing. Several items were made in a variety of colors aside from the usual crystal. For amber, green, and yellow, increase the above-listed prices by 50%. For amethyst (slag), cobalt blue, vaseline, and black, double the above-listed prices.

RIBBED GRAPE BOSTON AND SANDWICH GLASS COMPANY, 1850S–1860S

Object	Price
Bowl, Berry	$75.00
Butter Dish with Cover	125.00
Celery Vase	80.00
Compote, 8", Open, Footed	85.00
Compote with Cover, 6"	175.00
Cordial	125.00
Creamer	150.00
Goblet, 2 Styles	75.00
Pitcher, Water	225.00
Plate, 6"	45.00
Plate, 7½"	55.00
Sauce Dish, Flat	25.00
Spooner	50.00
Sugar with Cover	125.00
Tumbler, Water	80.00
Whiskey Tumbler	100.00
Wineglass	50.00

This pattern is characterized by grape clusters, leaves, vines, and vertical ribbing. Colors include an aqua or bluish green and opaque white (double the above-listed prices).

RIBBED PALM MCKEE BROTHERS, 1860S–1870S

Object	Price
Bowl, 6", Flat Rim	$40.00

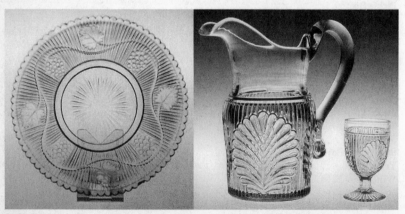

Left: Pressed glass, "Ribbed Grape" pattern. Courtesy of the Sandwich Glass Museum. Right: Pressed glass, "Ribbed Palm" pattern. Courtesy of the Sandwich Glass Museum.

Bowl, 6" Oblong, Scalloped *$50.00*
Bowl, 7" Oblong, Scalloped .... *.55.00*
Bowl, 8" Oblong, Scalloped .... *.60.00*
Bowl, 9" Oblong, Scalloped .... *.65.00*
Butter Dish with Cover .... *.100.00*
Celery Vase .... *.75.00*
Champagne Glass .... *.100.00*
Compote, 7", Open, Scalloped .... *.80.00*
Compote, 8", Open, Scalloped .... *.100.00*
Compote, 10", Open, Scalloped .... *.150.00*
Compote with Cover, 6" .... *.150.00*
Cordial .... *.100.00*
Creamer, Applied Handle .... *.200.00*
Egg Holder .... *.40.00*
Goblet .... *.50.00*
Lamp, 3 Styles .... *.125.00*
Pickle Dish .... *.55.00*
Pitcher, 9" Tall, Applied Handle .... *.225.00*
Plate, 6" .... *.45.00*
Salt Dip, Pedestal Base .... *.45.00*
Sauce Dish, 4" .... *.20.00*
Spooner .... *.35.00*
Sugar with Cover .... *.100.00*
Tumbler, 8 oz. .... *.100.00*
Whiskey Tumbler .... *.100.00*
Wineglass .... *.75.00*

The palm leaves in this pattern are quite large, usually beginning at the bottom and nearly reaching the top. The remaining portion consists of vertical ribbing. There are quite a few rare pieces, such as the creamer and pitcher.

A few odd colors, such as green and ruby-stained, have been found (double the above-listed prices).

ROMAN ROSETTE   BRYCE, WALKER & COMPANY, 1870S; U.S. GLASS COMPANY, 1890S

Object	*Price*
Bowl, 5"	*$18.00*
Bowl, 6"	*.20.00*
Bowl, 7"	*.25.00*
Bowl, 8"	*.30.00*
Bowl with Cover, 9"	*.65.00*
Butter Dish with Cover	*.60.00*
Cake Stand, 9"	*.45.00*
Cake Stand, 10"	*.55.00*
Castor Bottle with Stopper	*.40.00*
Castor Stand (Holds 3 Castor Bottles)	*.25.00*
Celery Vase	*.35.00*
Compote with Cover, 5"	*.50.00*
Compote with Cover, 6"	*.60.00*

Pressed glass, "Roman Rosette" pattern. Drawing by Mark Pickvet.

Compote with Cover, 7"	$70.00
Compote with Cover, 8"	.80.00
Cordial	.50.00
Creamer, 16 oz.	.40.00
Goblet	.35.00
Mug	.40.00
Mustard Jar	.55.00
Pickle Dish	.25.00
Pitcher, Syrup, with Metal Lid	.75.00
Pitcher, Milk, 32 oz.	.150.00
Plate, 7¼"	.70.00
Platter, Oval (11" × 9")	.40.00
Salt and Pepper Shakers	.45.00
Sauce Dish, Flat, 4"	.12.00
Sauce Dish, Flat, 4½"	.15.00
Sauce Dish, Footed	.20.00
Spooner	.25.00
Sugar with Cover	.50.00
Tumbler, Water	.75.00
Wineglass	.70.00

The rosettes in this pattern are quite large and circle around each object. The pattern is a typical "Sandwich" design in that many similar patterns have been reproduced and referred to as "Old Sandwich" glass.

A few odd colors and ruby decorations have been found in the original pattern (double the above-listed prices).

SAWTOOTH   BOSTON AND SANDWICH GLASS COMPANY, 1860S; NEW ENGLAND GLASS COMPANY, 1860S

Object	*Price*
Bowl, Berry, 8"	$45.00
Bowl, Berry, 9"	.50.00
Bowl, Berry, 10"	.55.00
Bowl with Cover, 7"	.60.00
Butter Dish, Miniature (Children's)	.75.00
Butter Dish	.60.00

Cake Stand, 9" *$100.00*
Cake Stand, 10" *110.00*
Celery Vase, Pointed Edge *60.00*
Celery Vase, Rolled Edge *75.00*
Champagne Glass *75.00*
Compote, 6", Open *40.00*
Compote, 7", Open *50.00*
Compote, 8", Open *60.00*
Compote, 10", Open *75.00*
Compote with Cover, 6" *65.00*
Compote with Cover, 7" *70.00*
Compote with Cover, 8" *75.00*
Compote with Cover, 9" *80.00*
Compote with Cover, 10", Knob on Stem *150.00*
Compote with Cover, 11", Knob on Stem *175.00*
Compote with Cover, 12", Knob on Stem *200.00*
Cordial *50.00*
Creamer, Miniature (Children's) *75.00*
Creamer *60.00*
Cruet with Stopper *125.00*
Decanter with Stopper, 32 oz. *75.00*
Egg Holder *40.00*
Goblet, Knob on Stem *45.00*
Honey Dish *25.00*
Lamp *100.00*
Pitcher, Water, 64 oz. *125.00*
Salt Dip *25.00*
Salt Dip with Cover, Footed *45.00*
Sauce Dish, 4" *15.00*
Sauce Dish, 5" *18.00*
Spooner *40.00*
Spooner, Octagonal *55.00*
Spooner, Miniature (Children's) *50.00*
Sugar Dish *60.00*
Sugar Dish, Miniature (Children's) *75.00*
Tray, 10" Oval *45.00*
Tray, 11" Oval *50.00*
Tray, 12" Oval *60.00*

Pressed glass, "Sawtooth" pattern. Drawing by Mark Pickvet.

Tray, 14" Oval $75.00
Tumbler, Water 40.00
Tumbler, Water, Footed 50.00
Wineglass, Knob on Stem 40.00

The sawteeth are a little sharp for a pressed pattern but still easily distinguished from cut glass. The teeth usually begin at the bottom of each object and proceed about ¾ of the way up. Original pieces usually have sawtooth rims, knobbed stems, and applied handles (reduce the above prices by 25% if any of these are lacking). For any colored pieces, double the above-listed prices.

STAR-IN-BULL'S EYE   U.S. GLASS COMPANY, EARLY 1900S

Object	Price
Bowl, Berry	$30.00
Butter Dish	45.00
Cake Stand	45.00
Celery Vase	35.00
Compote, 6", Open, Flared	35.00
Compote with Cover	50.00
Creamer	30.00
Cruet with Stopper, 4" Tall	40.00
Goblet	25.00
Pickle Dish, Diamond-shaped	20.00
Pitcher, Water	60.00
Spooner	25.00
Sugar with Cover	40.00
Toothpick Holder, Single	35.00
Toothpick Holder, Double	45.00
Tumbler, Water, Gold Band	25.00

Left: Pressed glass, "Star-in-Bull's Eye" pattern. Drawing by Mark Pickvet. Center: Pressed glass, "Sunburst" pattern. Drawing by Mark Pickvet. Right: Pressed glass, "Teardrop and Thumbprint" pattern. Drawing by Mark Pickvet.

Whiskey Tumbler, 2 oz. *$50.00*
Wineglass ....*.25.00*

The eyes of this "Bull's Eye" pattern are large, and the circles overlap at the edges. The star pattern is within the bull's eyes, as the pattern name suggests. A few other pieces besides the water tumbler may also be found trimmed in gold (add 25% to the above-listed prices if the gold is completely intact). For ruby-stained pieces, double the above-listed prices.

SUNBURST   D. C. JENKINS GLASS COMPANY, EARLY 1900S

Object	*Price*
Bowl, Oblong (Deep)	*$30.00*
Butter Dish	*30.00*
Cake Plate	*35.00*
Celery Vase	*30.00*
Compote with Cover	*50.00*
Cordial	*30.00*
Creamer, Individual (Small)	*15.00*
Creamer, 4½" Tall (Large)	*20.00*
Cup	*15.00*
Egg Holder	*20.00*
Goblet	*20.00*
Marmalade Jar	*50.00*
Pickle Dish, Single	*25.00*
Pickle Dish, 8", 2 Divisions	*35.00*
Pickle Dish, 10", 2 Divisions	*45.00*
Pitcher, Milk	*35.00*
Pitcher, Water	*40.00*
Plate, 6"	*25.00*
Plate, 7"	*30.00*
Plate, 11"	*40.00*
Salt Shaker	*25.00*
Sauce Dish, 1 Handle	*20.00*
Spooner	*15.00*
Sugar, Open, Individual (Small)	*15.00*
Sugar with Cover (Large)	*25.00*
Tumbler, Water	*15.00*

The original "Sunburst" pattern by Jenkins was also referred to as "Squared Sunburst." It is a fairly common pattern.

TEARDROP   RIPLEY & COMPANY, 1870S–1880S; U.S. GLASS COMPANY, 1890S

Object	*Price*
Bowl, Oval	*$25.00*
Butter Dish with Cover	*55.00*
Cake Stand	*50.00*

Celery Dish	*$35.00*
Compote, Open	*.45.00*
Creamer	*.35.00*
Goblet	*.25.00*
Pitcher, Syrup, with Metal Lid	*.75.00*
Pitcher, Water	*.75.00*
Salt Shaker	*.35.00*
Sauce Dish, 4", Flat	*.12.00*
Sauce Dish, Footed	*.15.00*
Spooner	*.25.00*
Sugar, Open	*.30.00*
Sugar with Cover	*.45.00*
Tumbler, Water	*.25.00*
Wineglass	*.20.00*

The basic "Teardrop" is sometimes referred to as "Teardrop and Thumbprint" because of the band of thumbprints that usually rests above the teardrops. There are many variations of teardrop and thumbprint patterns.

Some pieces may be engraved (increase prices by 25%). Other colors include ruby-flashed and cobalt blue (double the above-listed prices). A few ruby-flashed items in this pattern were produced as well and may contain engraving or enameling.

TEARDROPS AND DIAMOND BLOCK ADAMS & COMPANY, 1870S; U.S. GLASS COMPANY, 1890S

Object	*Price*
Banana Dish, Oblong, Flat	*$40.00*
Basket, 10" Tall	*.60.00*
Bowl, 8"	*.50.00*
Butter Dish with Cover	*.75.00*
Cake Stand 10"	*.65.00*
Compote, 8", Open	*.45.00*
Compote, 9", Open	*.50.00*
Compote, 10", Open	*.55.00*
Compote with Cover, 7", Footed	*.70.00*

Pressed glass, "Teardrops and Diamond Block" pattern. Drawing by Mark Pickvet.

Cracker Jar with Cover	.$75.00
Creamer, 2 Styles	.45.00
Cruet with Stopper	.65.00
Goblet	.35.00
Mug	.30.00
Pitcher, Water, 64 oz.	.70.00
Relish Dish	.30.00
Sauce Dish, 4", Shallow	.20.00
Spooner	.30.00
Sugar with Cover	.55.00
Tumbler	.35.00
Wineglass	.35.00

This pattern is characterized by large teardrops at the bottom of each object. The remaining portion is in block diamonds. It is also referred to as "Job's Tears" and "Art." Some pieces that may have been found with ruby flashing are a bit more valuable (increase the above-listed prices by 50%).

TEXAS   U.S. GLASS COMPANY, LATE 1890S–EARLY 1900S

Object	*Price*
Bowl, Berry	.$40.00
Bowl with Cover, 6"	.55.00
Bowl with Cover, 7"	.65.00
Bowl with Cover, 8"	.75.00
Butter Dish with Cover	.150.00
Celery Dish	.65.00
Celery Vase	.75.00
Compote, 5½" Diameter, Open	.50.00
Creamer, Individual (Small)	.30.00
Creamer (Large)	.65.00
Cruet with Stopper, Inverted Pattern	.200.00
Goblet	.85.00
Horseradish Dish with Opening for Spoon	.75.00
Pitcher, Syrup with Metal Lid	.325.00
Pitcher, 48 oz., Inverted Pattern	.250.00
Pitcher, Pattern Variant	.400.00
Plate, 8¾"	.65.00
Preserve Dish, Oval	.55.00
Salt Shaker	.75.00
Salt and Pepper Shakers, Small	.125.00
Salt and Pepper Shakers, Large	.150.00
Spooner	.60.00
Sugar, Open	.30.00
Sugar with Cover, Individual (Small)	.100.00
Sugar with Cover, Individual (Large)	.125.00
Toothpick Holder	.45.00
Tumbler, Water, Inverted Pattern	.55.00
Tumbler, Water, Pattern Variant	.55.00
Vase, 6½" Tall (Straight or Cupped)	.25.00

Vase, 8" Tall (Straight or Cupped) *$40.00*
Vase, 9" Tall (Straight or Cupped) *50.00*
Vase, 10" Tall (Straight or Cupped) *60.00*
Wineglass *75.00*

One of the rarest of U.S. Glass's state patterns, "Texas" is also referred to as "Loop with Stippled Panels." For ruby- or red-stained items, double the above-listed prices. For crystal pieces with gilded tops, increase the above prices by 25%; for colored pieces with gilded tops, increase the prices by 150%.

THUMBPRINT   BAKEWELL, PEARS & COMPANY, 1860S

Object	*Price*
Ale Glass, 7½" Tall	*$150.00*
Bowl with Cover	*175.00*
Butter Dish, 2 Styles	*125.00*
Cake Plate	*100.00*
Castor Bottle	*125.00*
Celery Vase, 2 Styles	*135.00*
Champagne Glass	*90.00*
Claret Glass	*150.00*
Compote, Open, 6"	*75.00*
Compote, Open, 8"	*85.00*
Compote, Open, 9"	*95.00*
Compote with Cover, 6", Hexagonal	*100.00*
Compote with Cover, 7", Hexagonal	*125.00*
Compote with Cover, 8", Hexagonal	*150.00*
Compote with Cover, 10", Hexagonal	*200.00*
Cordial	*85.00*
Creamer, Applied Handle	*100.00*
Decanter with Stopper, 32 oz.	*125.00*
Egg Holder	*55.00*
Goblet, Barrel-Shaped	*60.00*
Goblet, Ring Stem	*75.00*
Honey Dish	*30.00*
Mug, Applied Handle, 8 oz.	*100.00*
Pickle Dish	*45.00*
Punch Bowl with Stand, 12" Diameter, 23½" Tall	*1250.00*
Salt Dip, Individual (Small)	*20.00*
Salt Dip, Master (Large)	*35.00*
Sauce Dish, 4", Flat	*25.00*
Sauce Dish, 4½", Flat	*30.00*
Spooner	*50.00*
Sugar with Cover	*125.00*
Tumbler, Bar	*90.00*
Tumbler, Footed	*65.00*
Whiskey Tumbler, 2 oz.	*75.00*
Wineglass	*65.00*

The original "Thumbprint" pattern was first named "Argus" by Bakewell & Pears.

It has also been referred to as "Early Thumbprint." Colors in this pattern are extremely scarce (triple the above-listed prices).

TULIP WITH SAWTOOTH BRYCE, RICHARDS AND COMPANY, 1850S

Object	Price
Bowl, Berry	*$65.00*
Butter Dish with Cover	*125.00*
Celery Vase	*85.00*
Champagne Glass	*125.00*
Compote, 8", Open	*55.00*
Compote with Cover (Low)	*75.00*
Compote with Cover, Small	*85.00*
Compote with Cover, Large	*100.00*
Cordial	*75.00*
Creamer	*125.00*
Decanter with Stopper, 8 oz.	*125.00*
Decanter with Stopper, 16 oz.	*175.00*
Decanter with Patterned Stopper, 32 oz., Handled	*250.00*
Egg Holder with Cover	*200.00*
Goblet, 7" Tall, Knob Stem	*75.00*
Honey Dish	*45.00*
Pitcher, Water	*275.00*
Plate, 6"	*75.00*
Pomade Jar	*80.00*
Salt Dip, Master	*40.00*
Salt Dip, Petal Rim, Pedestal Base	*55.00*
Spooner	*50.00*
Sugar Dish, Open	*75.00*
Tumbler, Bar	*75.00*
Tumbler, Water	*70.00*
Tumbler, Water, Footed	*75.00*
Whiskey Tumbler	*75.00*
Wineglass	*75.00*

The original pattern name was simply "Tulip"; the "Sawtooth" was added because

Pressed glass, "Tulip with Sawtooth" pattern. Drawing by Mark Pickvet.

of that design patterned at the bottom of the tulips. The original pieces were made primarily in crystal, but some cheaper lime substitutes have been found (reduce the above prices by 50% for noncrystal).

VERMONT   U.S. GLASS COMPANY, LATE 1890S–EARLY 1900S

Object	Price
Basket (Several Varieties)	$40.00
Bowl	35.00
Bowl, Waste	40.00
Butter Dish with Cover	60.00
Candlestick (Custard Only)	75.00
Celery Vase	35.00
Celery Tray	25.00
Compote, Open	45.00
Compote with Cover	55.00
Creamer	30.00
Goblet	35.00
Pickle Dish	20.00
Pitcher, Water	75.00
Salt Shaker	25.00
Sauce Dish	20.00
Spooner	25.00
Sugar	30.00
Sugar with Cover	40.00
Toothpick Holder	40.00
Tumbler, Water	35.00
Vase	25.00

Another of U.S. Glass's state patterns, "Vermont" is also known as "Honeycomb with Flower Rim" and "Inverted Thumbprint with Daisy Band."

There are quite a few color variations. For amber and green, increase the prices by 50%; for cobalt blue and decorated custard, double the above prices; and for the reproduced toothpick holder in chocolate or opalescent, $60.00.

The candlestick that was produced in custard only was originally referred to as "Jewelled Vermont."

VIRGINIA OR BANDED PORTLAND   U.S. GLASS COMPANY, 1901

Object	Price
Bottle, Water	$50.00
Bowl, 6"	25.00
Bowl, 8"	35.00
Butter Dish with Cover	75.00
Celery Dish	40.00
Compote with Cover	90.00
Cup	15.00
Creamer	40.00

Cruet with Stopper	.$60.00
Dish, Sardine, Oblong	.20.00
Goblet	.35.00
Jelly Dish with Cover	.100.00
Pitcher, Syrup, with Lid	.50.00
Relish Dish	.25.00
Salt and Pepper Shakers	.60.00
Sugar with Cover	.50.00
Sugar Shaker	.40.00
Toothpick Holder	.40.00
Tumbler	.35.00
Wineglass	.40.00

Another of U.S. Glass's state series. Aside from "Banded Portland," it was also referred to as "Maiden Blush." Flashed-on colors of blue, green, ruby red, and yellow
have also been discovered (double the above prices).

WAFFLE BOSTON & SANDWICH GLASS COMPANY,
1850S–1860S; BRYCE, WALKER & COMPANY, 1850S–1860S

Object	*Price*
Butter Dish with Cover	.$125.00
Celery Vase, 9" Tall	.85.00
Champagne Glass	.125.00
Claret Glass	.130.00
Compote, 6", Open	.75.00
Compote, 8", Open	.85.00
Compote with Cover, 7"	.125.00
Compote with Cover, 9"	.150.00
Cordial	.55.00
Creamer, 6¾" Tall	.150.00
Decanter with Stopper, 16 oz.	.100.00
Decanter with Stopper, 32 oz.	.150.00
Egg Holder	.55.00
Goblet, Knob Stem	.65.00
Lamp, Complete Glass	.175.00
Lamp, Applied Handle, Marble Base	.150.00
Pitcher, Water, 9½" Tall	.450.00
Plate, 6"	.90.00
Relish Dish, Oval *(6" × 4")*, Scalloped	.60.00
Salt Dip, Footed	.50.00
Salt Dip with Cover	.125.00
Sauce Dish, 4"	.20.00
Spooner	.75.00
Sugar with Cover	.175.00
Toy Mug, Applied Handle	.125.00
Tumbler, Water	.85.00
Whiskey Tumbler	.75.00
Wineglass	.60.00

There is some confusion as to which company produced the pattern first, but records are sketchy. A few colors, including opaque white, have been found (double the above-listed prices). The simple square "Waffle" design has been reproduced in a variety of forms.

WAFFLE AND THUMBPRINT   VARIOUS COMPANIES, 1850S–1870S

Object	Price
Bowl, Rectangular (7" × 5")	*$40.00*
Bowl, Rectangular (8" × 6")	*.50.00*
Butter Dish with Cover	*.125.00*
Celery Vase	*.95.00*
Champagne Glass	*.80.00*
Claret Glass	*.80.00*
Compote with Cover, 6"	*.110.00*
Compote with Cover, 7"	*.125.00*
Compote with Cover, 8"	*.140.00*
Cordial	*.75.00*
Creamer	*.150.00*
Decanter with Stopper, 16 oz.	*.125.00*
Decanter with Stopper, 32 oz. (Pointed Paneled Stopper)	*.175.00*
Egg Holder	*.60.00*
Goblet	*.65.00*
Goblet, Knob Stem	*.80.00*
Lamp	*.125.00*
Pitcher, Water	*.500.00*
Spooner	*.65.00*
Sugar with Cover	*.175.00*
Tumbler, Water	*.100.00*
Tumbler, Water, Footed	*.110.00*
Whiskey Tumbler	*.90.00*
Wineglass	*.75.00*

Here is one variation of the "Waffle" where the rectangles are interspersed with thumbprints. For noncrystal pieces, reduce the above-listed prices by 50%. The Boston and Sandwich Glass Company, the New England Glass Company, and Curling, Robertson & Company were the primary producers of this pattern.

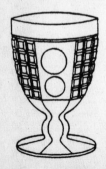

Pressed glass, "Waffle and Thumbprint" pattern. Drawing by Mark Pickvet.

WILDFLOWER ADAMS & COMPANY, 1870S; U.S. GLASS COMPANY, 1890S

Object	Price
Bowl, Waste	$60.00
Butter Dish with Cover	.55.00
Butter Dish with Cover, Footed	.65.00
Cake Plate with Metal Handle	.100.00
Cake Stand, Small	.50.00
Cake Stand, Large	.60.00
Celery Dish	.40.00
Compote, Open	.45.00
Compote, Open, 8" (Low)	.35.00
Compote with Cover, 6"	.50.00
Compote with Cover, 8"	.60.00
Cordial	.60.00
Creamer	.35.00
Goblet	.30.00
Pickle Dish, 5³/₄" Square	.25.00
Pickle Dish, 6¹/₄" Square	.30.00
Pickle Dish, 7³/₄" Square	.35.00
Pickle Dish with Cover, 7³/₄" Square	.55.00
Pitcher, Syrup, with Metal Lid	.100.00
Pitcher, Water	.65.00
Plate, 10"	.75.00
Platter, 10" Oblong	.75.00
Salt and Pepper Shakers	.60.00
Sauce Dish, Round, Flat	.10.00
Sauce Dish, Square, Flat	.15.00
Sauce Dish, 3¹/₂", Round, Footed	.30.00
Sauce Dish, 4", Round, Footed	.35.00
Spooner	.20.00
Sugar with Cover	.45.00
Tray, Round	.40.00
Tray, Oval (13" × 11")	.50.00
Tumbler, Water	.35.00
Wineglass	.40.00

This pattern is characterized by six-petaled flowers with leaves, stems, and berries that form a continuous design around each object. There are also vertical flutelike ribbing at the bottom and vertical trapezoidal bands at the top.

Colors include amber, cobalt blue, green, and yellow (double the above-listed prices). The goblet, flat sauce dish, water tumbler, wineglass, and a 10" diameter plate have all been reproduced in this pattern.

WISCONSIN U.S. GLASS COMPANY, 1898–EARLY 1900S

Object	Price
Bowl, 7"	$35.00

Bowl, 8" *$40.00*
Butter Dish with Cover . . . . *.75.00*
Cake Stand . . . . *.60.00*
Candy Dish . . . . *.25.00*
Celery Dish . . . . *.35.00*
Celery Vase . . . . *.40.00*
Compote, Open, 5" . . . . *.40.00*
Compote with Cover, 6" Tall . . . . *.50.00*
Compote with Cover, 7" Tall . . . . *.60.00*
Compote with Cover, 8" Tall . . . . *.70.00*
Creamer, Individual (Small) . . . . *.35.00*
Creamer (Large) . . . . *.45.00*
Cruet with Stopper . . . . *.50.00*
Goblet . . . . *.40.00*
Jelly Dish, Handled . . . . *.30.00*
Lamp . . . . *.85.00*
Marmalade Jar . . . . *.75.00*
Mug . . . . *.35.00*
Pickle Dish . . . . *.30.00*
Pitcher, Syrup, with Lid . . . . *.75.00*
Pitcher, 32 oz. . . . . *.50.00*
Pitcher, 48 oz. . . . . *.60.00*
Salt and Pepper Shakers, Short . . . . *.40.00*
Salt and Pepper Shakers, Tall . . . . *.50.00*
Sauce Dish, 4", Flat . . . . *.15.00*
Spooner . . . . *.35.00*
Sugar with Cover . . . . *.60.00*
Sweetmeat Dish . . . . *.30.00*
Toothpick Holder, 3-Footed Base . . . . *.45.00*
Tray, 6" Oval, Handled, with Cover . . . . *.45.00*
Tumbler . . . . *.45.00*
Wineglass . . . . *.40.00*

The last of U.S. Glass's state patterns, "Wisconsin" is also known as "Beaded Dewdrop." It is characterized by vertical tears or drops that section off oval beaded designs.

CHAPTER 3

CUT GLASS

The Brilliant Period of American glassmaking lasted from 1880 to 1915. It was characterized by deep cutting, exceptional brilliance or sparkle, heavy lead crystal formulas, and very elaborate and ornate design. Cut glass is completed by steel or iron wheels revolving in a trough while a stream of water mixed with abrasives drips down upon the wheel from above. This initial process is known as roughing and is responsible for the first cut. Heavier wheels were used to make deeper and sharper cuts. The glass then proceeded to a hard stone wheel, where the rough cut was smoothed out. At this point a polisher polished it on a softer wooden wheel, and then a buffer further smoothed it out on a buffing wheel. Buffing was eventually replaced with acid polishing in the 1890s, but true craftsmen argued that acid polishing was inferior since it wasn't permanent and gradually wore away. Acid polishing also left a somewhat dull finish obstructing the brilliance of the piece to a small degree.

The aim of a cutter was to remove imperfections and impart facets to capture a good deal of light (the prismatic effect). American inventions improved on cutting. Flat-edged wheels made square-ended cuts, and convex-edged wheels made hollowed cuts. Americans added mitre-edged wheels, which made curved or V-shaped cuts. Mitre-edged wheels were invented in the late 1870s and freed cutters from dependence on straight-line cuts. Wheels were made not only of stone and steel but also copper and carborundum. Electricity, when available, was used to power the wheels as well as to provide the craftsmen with better lighting to see by; of course, it may have added more hours to their workday too! Additional steps were added to the cutting process as finer wheels and milder abrasives made cutting more precise.

Copper wheel cutting or engraving was the end in the evolutionary process for the finest cut glass. Up to 150 wheels of various diameters, from very large down to those the size of a pin, were utilized. A copper wheel engraver held the final pattern in his mind without outlining it on the glass. A glass object was pressed to the revolving wheel, which instantly cut through or roughened the surface. It was then rubbed repeatedly with oils, using one's fingers, as the object was placed on and off the wheel. Prior to electricity, lathes were operated by foot-powered treadles and were somewhat limited in size. An electrically operated lathe made heavier wheels possible, including large diamond-point cutting wheels. It might take weeks, months, and even years to finish a single piece on copper wheels.

Elaborate carving such as cameo engraving was also completed on copper wheels. Stone wheels were primarily used for depth, while copper was best for fine detailed work. Copper wheel engravers were compensated more than cutters and were among the most highly skilled artisans in the glassmaking business.

Along with blowers, copper wheel engravers commanded salaries as high as $6.00 a day in the 1880s; common cutters about, $3.50 to $4.00 a day; and ordinary general workmen, about $14.00 to $20.00 a week based on a six-day work week.

The higher wages provided incentive to foreign workers to emigrate to America. In Europe, English and Irish glassmakers earned $7.00 to $9.00 per week; Germans and Austrians, much less at $3.00 a week. American wages were typically three to four times greater than those of their European counterparts. One disadvantage was that European glassmakers produced cheaper glass products. Even after a 45 percent tariff was placed on imported glass in 1888, European glassware was still highly competitive. America's advantages included an abundance of cheap fuel (a problem in Europe) and advanced mechanization.

To make fine cut glass, a quality hand-blown blank was necessary. Many decorating companies purchased blanks of high-quality lead glass from major glass companies for their cutters to work. Traditionally, blowers had to be very skilled artisans. Years of training, hard work, and the ability to perform effectively under pressure as well as in poor working conditions were all prerequisites for a successful blower. A blower typically had to work near a blinding furnace with roasting heat and eye-watering smoke; his hands were constantly scorched and dirtied with coal dust. It was surprising indeed that such exquisite objects could be blown from these stoke-hole-like conditions. Under such pressures, the glassblower had to exercise the utmost skill, control, patience, steady nerves, and judgment mixed with creativity and occasional bouts of spontaneity. In short, glassblowing was an art.

There were many other positions in the glassmaking trade. A gatherer was one who gathered a blob of molten glass at the end of a blowpipe, pontil, or gathering iron for the blower. Cutters ordinarily apprenticed for three years at a small salary, usually after completing eight grades of formal education. The best cutters might work up to copper wheel engraving after years of practice.

At the turn of the 20th century, women held some jobs, though glassmaking was primarily a man's business. Women dusted glass in showrooms and salesrooms, distributed glass to cutters, updated catalogs, made drawings of blanks, waxed the glass before an acid dip, and washed or dried glass before packaging it. A rare enameler or cutter might have been female.

The production of glass itself was not an easy, inexpensive, or safe practice. The basic ingredients—sand, potash, and lead for the best crystal, plus a few other additions—were mixed in a huge clay pot and heated to extreme temperatures. A batch was termed "metal" by chemists, and the best metal batch always contained the highest lead content. Cut glass was usually made with a company's best metal formula.

Molten glass had to be gathered by a worker to press into a mold or simply for the blower to work. Several tools were available for them, including a pontil, which was used to remove expanded glass objects from the blowing iron. However, it did leave a mark; it was later replaced with a special rod called a gadget. A gadget had a spring clip on one end to grip the foot of a glass piece and hold it while another worker trimmed the rim and applied what finishing touches were needed.

Ovens were important, especially those with a special opening called a "glory hole." A glory hole was a small opening in the side of the oven where objects could be reheated and reworked without destroying the original shape. A lehr was an annealing oven that toughened glass through gradual cooling. A muffle kiln was a low-temperature oven used for firing on or permanently fusing enamels.

A variety of technical terms and tools were associated with the glassmaking process. Moil was waste glass left on the blowpipe or pontil. Pucellas were similar to tongs and were used to grip or grasp glass objects. Arrissing was the process of removing sharp edges from glass. Cracking-off involved removing a piece of glass from the pontil by cooling, gently tapping, and then dropping it into a soft sand tray. Fire polishing was the art of reheating objects at the glory hole to remove tool marks.

Glass did not always turn out perfectly, and "sickness" resulted. Sick glass was usually not tempered or annealed properly and showed random cracks, flaking, and possible disintegration. Seeds were tiny air bubbles in glass, indicating an under-heated furnace or impurities caused by flecks of dirt.

The techniques of American glassmaking included a good deal of originality. Cutting was primarily done in geometrical patterns. Pictorial, cameo, and intaglio (heavily engraved) designs were all cut regularly. Acid etching was the process of covering glass with an acid-resistant layer, scratching on a design, and then perma-nently etching the design with acids. Acid polishing—dipping the entire object into a mild solution of sulfuric or hydrofluoric acid—gave cut glass a polished surface. Hand painting and firing on enamels were two additional techniques.

Sandblasting was a distinct American process. A design was coated with a protec-tive layer, and then the exposed surfaces were sandblasted with a pressurized gun. Trimming with enamels like silver, gold, platinum was common in the early 1900s prior to World War I. Staining, gilding, monogram imprinting, rubber stamping, and silk screening were other, cheaper methods of decorating glass in that period.

In 1913, a gang-cut wheel was invented in America to make several parallel inci-sions at once. It made rapid and inexpensive cutting possible, such as for cross-hatching and blunt-edged flower petals. For the most part cut glass was simply that, undecorated crystal except for the elaborate cutting.

The decline of superb cut crystal reached its lowest point as World War I neared. The exclusive market it catered to disappeared as the wealthy preferred Art Deco styles and European imports. Cheaper glass formulas, labor troubles, increased im-ports, more and more machine-made glass, and scarcity of lead, which was needed for the war effort, were all factors leading to the end of the Brilliant Period in American glass history.

Some of the biggest names in the cut-glass world included Libbey, T. J. Hawkes, C. Dorflinger, Mt. Washington/Pairpoint, John Hoare, T. B. Clark, H. P. Sinclaire, and Tuthill. Hundreds of cut-glass patterns were made, and though many were patented, they were still copied or similar variations of them were produced by oth-ers. There were also many common designs or combinations of them shared by all, including rosettes, hobstars, fans, strawberry diamonds, geometric cuts, flutes, buzz-stars, cross-hatching, blocks, hobnails, and so on. Fortunately, more distinct marks and signatures were applied to cut-glass products than any other category of glass (see Appendix 4 on Manufacturers' Marks).

ALFORD, C. G. & CO. 1872–1918

Object	Price
Bonbon Dish, Hobstar Bottom, Signed "Alford"	$175.00
Celery Dish, 12" Oval, 4 Hobstars in Each Corner, Signed "Alford"	275.00
Cruet with Faceted Ball Stopper, Brunswick Pattern	250.00
Decanter with Faceted Stopper, 9½" Tall, 32 oz., No Handle, Hobstar and Fan Design, Viola Pattern	750.00
Nappy, 6", Trieste Pattern	225.00
Plate, 7¼", Large Center Hobstar Surrounded by 8 Smaller Hobstars, Signed "Alford"	150.00
Vase, 14" Tall, Brunswick Pattern, Signed "Alford"	375.00

Alford was a jeweler and watch repairman operating in the city of New York. There is some debate as to whether the company cut any glass or simply applied their mark to what was completed by others and then sold the glass in their store.

ALMY & THOMAS   1903–1918

Object	Price
Bowl, 8", Notched Rim, Alternating Star and Hobstar Design	$225.00
Decanter with Faceted Stopper, 7" Tall, Notched Handle, Fan and Star Pattern	675.00
Decanter with Faceted Stopper, 8¾" Tall, Brunswick Pattern	775.00
Whiskey Tumbler, 3" Tall, Fan and Star Pattern	125.00

Although they were not a large maker of cut glass, the team of Charles H. Almy and G. Edwin Thomas cut good-quality blanks provided by the Corning Glass Works.

AVERBECK CUT GLASS COMPANY   1892–1923

Object	Price
Bowl, 6" Nappy; Boston, Frisco, Occident, Paris, Puck, Saratoga, or Spruce Pattern	$175.00
Bowl, 7" Nappy; Boston, Frisco, Occident, Paris, Puck, Saratoga, or Spruce Pattern	200.00
Bowl, 8", Azalia Pattern	250.00
Bowl, 8" Nappy; Boston, Frisco, Occident, Paris, Puck, Saratoga, or Spruce Pattern	225.00
Bowl, 9" Nappy; Boston, Frisco, Occident, Paris, Puck, Saratoga, or Spruce Pattern	250.00
Bowl, 10" Nappy; Boston, Frisco, Occident, Paris, Puck, Saratoga, or Spruce Pattern	275.00
Decanter with Stopper, 9¼" Tall, Acme Pattern	775.00
Decanter with Stopper, 10" Tall, Electric Pattern	1000.00
Decanter with Stopper, 12" Tall, Alabama Pattern	1100.00
Jug with Stopper, 6" Tall, Liberty Pattern	300.00
Jug with Stopper, Genoa Pattern	325.00
Spoon Holder, 4" Tall, Prism	150.00
Tray, 7" Oval; Canton, Lady Curzon, Marietta, Priscilla, Ruby, or Saratoga Pattern	325.00
Tray, 8" Oval; Canton, Empress, Marietta, Royal, Ruby, or Saratoga Pattern	375.00
Tray, 12" Oblong; Diamond, Frisco, or Liberty Pattern	425.00
Tray, 14" Oblong, Ruffled Edge, Acme Pattern	450.00
Tray, 14½" Oval, Cape Town Pattern	500.00

Averbeck first operated as a jewelry store. In 1892, they began selling cut glass by mail order. Their name appeared on some of what they shipped, and it is possible that they owned a small cutting shop in Honesdale, Pennsylvania; however, they most likely purchased glass wholesale from small, relatively unknown cutting shops.

BERGEN, J. D., COMPANY   1880–1916

Object	Price
Basket, Small, Straight Cuts	$50.00
Basket, Large, Straight Cuts	75.00
Bonbon Dish, 6", Pilgrim Pattern	125.00
Bonbon Dish, Heart-Shaped, Emblem Pattern	350.00

Bottle, Wine with Straight-Cut Stopper, 12¾" Tall, Tasso Pattern *$550.00*
Bowl, 6" Oval, Ripple Pattern *175.00*
Bowl, 7" Oval, Caprice Pattern *200.00*
Bowl, 7" Oblong, Keystone Pattern *225.00*
Bowl, 8", 6 Circles, Notched Edge, Azalia Design *300.00*
Bowl, 8", Goldenrod Pattern *200.00*
Bowl, 9", Bermuda Pattern *225.00*
Celery Dish, 2-Handled, Logan Pattern *500.00*
Cheese Dish with Domed Cover, 9" Tall, Glenwood Pattern *750.00*
Compote with Cover, Arcadia Pattern *2000.00*
Decanter with Stopper, 8" Tall, Bedford Pattern *425.00*
Goblet, Star Base, 3 16-Point Hobstars, Strawberry Diamond and Fan Vesicas, Signed .*100.00*
Hairpin Box with Cover, 3 Applied Feet, Chair Bottom Design, Harvard Pattern, Signed
"Bergen" *1400.00*
Plate, 7", Sunflower Pattern *150.00*
Plate, 7", White Rose Pattern *175.00*
Powder Jar with Cover, Swirled Comet Pattern, Signed "Bergen" *475.00*
Punch Bowl with Stand, 14", Glenwood Pattern *2500.00*
Punch Bowl with Stand, Wabash Pattern *2250.00*
Saucer, 5"; Bedford, Bermuda, Corsair, Frisco, Golf, Kenwood, Magnet, Progress, and Web-
ster Patterns *75.00*
Saucer, 6"; Bedford, Bermuda, Corsair, Frisco, Golf, Kenwood, Magnet, Progress, and Web-
ster Patterns *100.00*
Tray, 6" Oblong, Slanted, Key West Pattern *150.00*
Tray, 6½" Oblong, Straight Sides, Magnet Pattern *175.00*
Tray, 7" Oval, Laurel Pattern *175.00*
Tray, 7½" Oblong, Short Handle, Emblem Pattern *250.00*
Tray, 9" Oblong, Circular Center, 5" Wide, Dariel Pattern *450.00*
Tray, Oval, 9" × 5", Hawthorne Pattern *300.00*
Tray, Rectangular (11½" × 7"), Hobstars and Diamonds *400.00*
Vase, 6" Tall, Notched Prism *200.00*
Vase, 21" Tall, 9" Diameter, 2-Part, Sunbeam Pattern *525.00*

James D. Bergen operated a cut-glass business under a variety of names, and like so
many others in the 19th and early 20th centuries, he recruited relatives to work in
his cutting shop. Other names included the Bergen Cut Glass Company, Bergen-
Phillips Cut Glass Company, Bergen & Son, Bergen Glass Works, and the Bergen
Glass Company.

BLACKMER CUT GLASS COMPANY   1894–1916

Object	*Price*
Bowl, 7", Starling Pattern	*$175.00*
Bowl, 7", Troy Pattern	*150.00*
Bowl, 9", Columbia Pattern	*250.00*
Cruet with Faceted Stopper, 6" Tall, Oregon Pattern	*275.00*
Decanter with Cut Stopper, Concord Pattern	*450.00*
Ice Tub, Angled Cradle Shape, Columbia Pattern	*775.00*
Nappy, 6", Regal Pattern	*225.00*
Nappy, 6", Notched Edge, Troy Pattern	*125.00*

Plate, 7", Newport Pattern $150.00
Plate, 8", Doris Pattern 175.00
Platter, 12" Round, Crescendo Pattern 575.00
Relish Dish, 7" Across, Tab Handle, Sultana Pattern 200.00
Tray, 10" Round, Emerson Pattern 250.00
Tray, 12" Oval, Plymouth Pattern 375.00
Tumbler, 8" Tall, Constellation Pattern 175.00

Arthur L. Blackmer was a businessman and salesman for his company and employed others to make the glass. Like so many others, the business did not survive World War I.

CLARK, T. B. & COMPANY   1884–1930

Object	Price
Bonbon Dish, Adonis, Arbutus, Dorrance, Jewel, Manhattan, St George, Venus, or Winola Pattern	$100.00
Bonbon Dish with Handle, Irving, Jefferson, or St. George Pattern	125.00
Bowl, 6", Footed, Manhattan Pattern	225.00
Bowl, Rose, 7", Manhattan Pattern	250.00
Bowl, 8", Prima Donna Pattern, Signed "Clark"	400.00
Bowl, 8" Square, Corinthian Pattern	275.00
Bowl, 8", Adonis, Arbutus, Desdemona, Magnolia, Manhattan, Priscilla, Venus, or Winola Pattern	250.00
Bowl, 9", Adonis, Arbutus, Desdemona, Magnolia, Manhattan, Priscilla, Venus, or Winola Pattern	275.00
Bowl, 10", Adonis, Arbutus, Desdemona, Magnolia, Manhattan, Priscilla, Venus, or Winola Pattern	300.00
Bowl, 12", Notched Edge, Strawberry Diamond Pattern, Signed "Clark"	350.00
Bowl, Oval (11½" × 9"), Quatrefoil Rosette Pattern, Signed "Clark"	475.00
Cheese Dish with Dome Cover, Manhattan Pattern	750.00
Claret Jug with Sterling Silver Stopper, Arbutus Pattern, Signed "Clark"	1250.00
Cologne Bottle with Stopper, 6 oz., Globe-Shaped, Jewel or Venus Pattern	450.00
Compote, 5" Diameter, 5½" Tall, Hobstars, Signed "Clark"	325.00
Compote, 8" Tall, Harvard Pattern Variant	450.00
Compote, 10" Diameter, Arbutus Pattern	375.00
Creamer, 4" Tall, Strawberry Diamond and Star Pattern	350.00
Decanter with Stopper, 32 oz., No Handle, Winola Pattern	450.00
Decanter with Stopper, 32 oz., with Handle, Winola Pattern	500.00
Decanter with Stopper, 32 oz., with Handle, Strawberry Diamond and Fan Pattern	425.00
Goblet, Winola Pattern	100.00
Mug, Jewel or Winola Pattern	150.00
Nappy, 5", Jewel, Manhattan, or Winola Pattern	125.00
Nappy, 6", Jewel, Manhattan, or Winola Pattern	150.00
Nappy, 7", Arbutus, Desdemona, Jewel, Manhattan, or Winola Pattern	175.00
Nappy, 8", Arbutus, Desdemona, or Manhattan Pattern	200.00
Nappy, 9", Arbutus, Desdemona, or Manhattan Pattern	225.00
Nappy, 10", Arbutus, Desdemona, or Manhattan Pattern	250.00
Pitcher, Milk, 32 oz., Venus Pattern	375.00
Pitcher, Water, 48 oz., Venus Pattern	425.00

Pitcher, Water, Triple Square Pattern, Signed "Clark" *$500.00*
Plate, 6", Harvard Pattern Variant *100.00*
Plate, 7", Prima Donna Pattern, Signed "Clark" *175.00*
Plate, 7", Venus Pattern *150.00*
Plate, 12", Pinwheel Pattern, Signed "Clark" *450.00*
Platter, 12" Round, Waldorf Pattern *425.00*
Punch Bowl, 12", Desdemona Pattern *900.00*
Punch Bowl with Stand, 14" Diameter, Desdemona Pattern *1500.00*
Relish, 9" Diameter, 4-Part, 2-Handled, 4 Hobstars *250.00*
Sugar with Cover, 4¹/₂" Tall, Strawberry Diamond and Star Pattern *425.00*
Sugar Shaker with Sterling Silver Top, Henry VIII Pattern *250.00*
Tray, Celery, 11", Adonis, Desdemona, Dorrance, Manhattan, Nordica, or Winola Pattern
.... *325.00*
Tray, Celery, Pinwheel Design, Signed "Clark" *225.00*
Tray, Celery, 11⁷/₈" Oval, Pinwheels and Hobstars Design *200.00*
Tray, 12", Oval, Baker's Gothic Pattern *350.00*
Tray, 13", Adonis, Manhattan, Venus, or Winola Pattern *425.00*
Tumbler, 8 oz., Strawberry Diamond and Fan Design *100.00*
Tumbler, 8 oz., Coral Pattern *150.00*
Vase, 4" Tall, Notched Rim, Wide Style, Henry VIII Pattern *200.00*
Vase, 8" Tall, Circular Base, Jewel Pattern *175.00*
Vase, 10" Tall, Circular Vase, Jewel Pattern *225.00*
Vase, 12" Tall, Circular Base, Jewel Pattern *275.00*
Vase, 18" Tall, Circular Base, Palmetto Pattern *525.00*
Whiskey Tumbler, Strawberry Diamond and Fan Design *75.00*
Wineglass, Winola Pattern *75.00*

Thomas Byron Clark operated the second-largest cut-glass operation in all of Pennsylvania (Dorflinger was first). Clark actually used Dorflinger's blanks early on, and the quality of Clark's products rank with the best.

DITHRIDGE AND COMPANY   1881–1891

Object	*Price*
Pitcher, 10" Tall, Corset-Shaped, Scalloped, Sunburst and Geometric Design	*$400.00*
Tray, Oval, 6⁷/₈" Long, Angled Cut Squares Alternating with Diamond Cross-Cut Squares	*175.00*
Wineglass, 4³/₄" Tall, Strawberry Diamond and Fan Pattern	*150.00*

Dithridge was a large supplier of lead blanks and did a little cutting of their own too.

DORFLINGER, CHRISTIAN, & SONS   1852–1921

Object	*Price*
Bowl, Finger, with Underplate, Picket Fence Pattern	*$85.00*
Bowl, 6¹/₂" Square, Strawberry Diamond Pattern	*150.00*
Bowl, 8", Notched Edge, Amore Pattern	*175.00*
Bowl, 8", Gladys Pattern	*225.00*

Bowl, 9", Alternating Small and Large Diamond-Checkered Pattern (#28 Pattern) ..*$250.00*

Bowl, 9", Large Leaf (6 Leaves) Design, Paola Pattern *150.00*

Bowl, 9" Diameter, 7" Tall, Prince of Wales Design, Plumes Pattern with Hobstar Foot
....*500.00*

Bowl, 10" Oval, Strawberry Pattern *225.00*

Carafe, 8¼", Tall, Split Pattern *225.00*

Cheese Dish with Dome Cover, 7", Russian Pattern *775.00*

Cookie Jar with Cover, 6¼" Tall, Hobstar Base, Sterling Silver Cover Marked "Gorham,"
Sussex Pattern *500.00*

Cruet, Fan and Star Design, Pattern #80 ....*175.00*

Cruet with Stopper, 8" Tall, Globe-Shaped, Gladys Pattern *350.00*

Decanter with Silver Stopper, 12" Tall, Parisian Pattern *750.00*

Decanter, Renaissance Pattern *225.00*

Fernery, Picket Fence Pattern *75.00*

Goblet, 5½" Tall, Mitred Stem, Parisian Pattern *250.00*

Ice Bucket with Underplate, Handle Tabs, Marlboro Pattern *1750.00*

Lamp, Banquet Oil, 4-Part, Matching Cut Chimney, Paper Label *650.00*

Lamp, Gone with the Wind, 20" Tall, 12" Base Diameter, Hobstar and Diamond Design
....*1250.00*

Parfait, 6" Tall, Kalana Lily Pattern *125.00*

Perfume with Stopper, Hobstar Base, Marlboro Pattern *200.00*

Pitcher, Cream, 4½" Tall, Parisian Pattern *225.00*

Pitcher, Cream, 6" Tall, Parisian Pattern *275.00*

Pitcher, Cereal, 5" Tall, Diamond and Fern Cuts (Dorflinger's #80 Pattern) *200.00*

Pitcher, Water, 7¼" Tall, Globe-Shaped, Applied Handle, Strawberry Diamond and Fan
Pattern *250.00*

Pitcher, Water, 7½" Tall, Colonial Pattern *275.00*

Pitcher, Water, 8" Tall, Colonial Pattern *300.00*

Pitcher, Water, 8½" Tall, Globe-Shaped, Scalloped, Sunburst Base, Paneled Neck, Strawberry Diamond and Fan Pattern *400.00*

Plate, 6¼", Picket Fence Pattern *75.00*

Plate, 7", Parisian Pattern *125.00*

Plate, 7½", Scalloped and Serrated Rim, American Pattern *100.00*

Plate, 8", Gladys Pattern *175.00*

Punch Bowl with Stand, 14⅛" Diameter, 11½" Tall, 24-Point Hobstar on Center and Base,
Twelve 8-Point Hobstars, Marlboro Pattern *2000.00*

Punch Bowl Ladle, Cranberry to Clear, Montrose Pattern *3000.00*

Salad Set, 3-Piece, 10" Handled Square Bowl, Parisian Pattern, Sterling Silver Fork and
Spoon *2000.00*

Salt Dip, Paperweight Style, Parisian Pattern *125.00*

Tray, 11" Oval, Middlesex Pattern *275.00*

Tray, 12½" Oval, Ice Cream, Pinwheels *550.00*

Tumbler, Juice, 3¾" Tall, Old Colony Pattern *175.00*

Tumbler, Juice, 3⅞" Tall, Parisian Pattern *200.00*

Vase, 6" Tall, Kalana Pansy Pattern *100.00*

Vase, 7½" Tall, Kalana Geranium Pattern *125.00*

Vase, 10" Tall, Hobstars with 5 Large Bull's Eyes *275.00*

Vase, 10" Tall, Kalana Wild Rose Pattern with Amethyst Flowers Design *300.00*

Vase, 10" Tall, 7" Diameter, Russian Pattern *350.00*

Vase, 12" Tall, Flared Top and Bottom, Kalana Pansy Design *275.00*

Vase, 14" Tall, Cosmos Pattern *350.00*

Vase, 14" Tall, Circular Base, Notched Top Edge, Parisian Pattern *425.00*

Vase, 15" Tall, Inverness Pattern *$225.00*
Wineglass, Knobbed Stem, Colonial Pattern *100.00*

Fine cut glass by Christian Dorflinger and his sons graced the table of many a president. Dorflinger spared no expense in finding excellent workmen; obtaining the best lead and other ingredients, and above all else, demanding quality workmanship. Dorflinger was one of the largest producers of cut-crystal glassware up until World War I.

EGGINTON, O. F., COMPANY 1899–1920

Object	*Price*
Bowl, Finger, 5", Bull's Eye and Hobstar Pattern, Signed "Egginton"	*$75.00*
Bowl, 5³/₄", Notched Edge, Cluster Pattern	*125.00*
Bowl, 8", Chain of Hobstars, Triple Bands	*225.00*
Bowl, 8", Cluster Pattern	*250.00*
Bowl, 10", Calve Pattern, Signed	*200.00*
Butter Dish with Cover, 5" Dome Cover, 7" Plate, Lotus Pattern, Signed	*550.00*
Celery Dish, 11³/₄ × 4³/₄" Oval, Arabian Pattern	*375.00*
Creamer, 4" Tall, Trellis Pattern Variation, Signed	*225.00*
Decanter with Matching Stopper, Creswick Pattern	*3000.00*
Ice Bucket, 8" Tall, Tab Handles, Creswick Pattern	*425.00*
Nappy, 6", Notched Edge, Lotus Pattern	*100.00*
Nappy, 7", Notched Edge, 1 Handle, Lotus Pattern	*150.00*
Pitcher, Water, 10" Tall, Thistle Pattern, Signed "Egginton"	*225.00*
Plate, 7", Lotus Pattern, Signed	*125.00*
Plate, 7", Prism Pattern	*150.00*
Plate, 8", Magnolia Pattern, Signed "Egginton"	*175.00*
Platter, 12" Diameter, Trellis Pattern, Signed "Egginton"	*450.00*
Platter, 14" Diameter, Cluster Pattern, Signed	*525.00*
Punch Bowl with Stand, 14" Diameter, 13" Tall, Arabian Pattern, Signed	*1250.00*
Punch Cup, Stemmed, Arabian Pattern	*125.00*
Relish, 8" Oval, Arabian Pattern	*200.00*
Spooner, Oval, 8" × 4", Flat, Lotus Pattern	*100.00*
Sugar, 4" Tall, Rose Bowl Shape, Trellis Pattern Variation, Signed	*225.00*
Tray, Celery, 12" Oval, Lotus Pattern	*225.00*
Tray, Ice Cream, 12" Oval, Calve Pattern	*225.00*
Tumbler, Thistle Pattern, Signed "Egginton"	*125.00*
Vase, 14" Tall, Urn-Shaped, 4 Hobstars with Comet Swirls Design	*2250.00*

Oliver F. Egginton was once manager of T. G. Hawkes's cutting department and went on to establish the Egginton Rich Cut Glass Company with Walter F. Egginton. Egginton purchased their blanks from the Corning Glass Works and patented a few patterns such as the Magnolia and Trellis.

EMPIRE CUT GLASS COMPANY 1890S–1925

Object	*Price*
Bowl, 6", Notched Edge, Saxonia Pattern	*$150.00*

Bowl, 8", Dupont, Isabella, Manhattan, Nelson, or Typhoon Pattern *$225.00*
Bowl, 8", Shallow, Japan Pattern . . . .*.200.00*
Bowl, 8", Kremlin Pattern . . . .*.250.00*
Bowl, 9", Berkshire or Iorio Special Patterns . . . .*.275.00*
Decanter with Faceted Ball Stopper, Diamond and Fan Design . . . .*.300.00*
Nappy, 6", Notched Edge, Prince Pattern . . . .*.125.00*
Plate, 8", Notched Edge, Plymouth Pattern . . . .*.175.00*
Tray, 12" Oblong, Notched Edge, Atlantic Pattern . . . .*.350.00*
Tray, 14" Oblong, Notched Edge, Elsie Pattern . . . .*.375.00*
Vase, 9" Tall, Waldorf Pattern . . . .*.275.00*

Empire was founded in the early 1890s by Harold Hollis in New York City. In 1902, he sold it to his employees, who operated it as a cooperative until 1904. It was sold to Henry C. Fry who continued producing cut glass under the Empire name into the 1920s.

ENTERPRISE CUT GLASS COMPANY   1905–1917

Object	*Price*
Bowl, 7½", Buzz Star Pattern	*$150.00*
Bowl, 7½", Notched Edge, Star Pattern	*175.00*
Decanter with Stopper, 13" Tall, Large Hobstar on Globe-Shaped Base, Vertically Cut Neck	*575.00*
Pitcher, 7" Tall, Tankard Style, Daisy Pattern	*300.00*
Pitcher, Milk, 8" Tall, Sunburst Pattern	*325.00*
Pitcher, Water, 13½" Tall, Imperial Pattern	*475.00*
Plate, 8¼", Notched Edge, Daisy Pattern	*150.00*
Punch Bowl with Stand, 11" Diameter, 10" Tall, Majestic Pattern	*2750.00*
Punch Bowl with Stand, 14" Diameter, 16½" Tall, 8½" Deep, Royal Pattern	*4000.00*
Tray, Celery, 12½" Oval, Notched Edge, Rose Pattern	*475.00*
Tray, Ice Cream, 14" × 7½" Oval, Buzz Star Pattern	*575.00*
Vase, 13" Tall, Circular Diamond-Cut Base, Large Hobstar Design	*1250.00*

Enterprise actually obtained a good deal of their blanks for cutting from Belgium; others were purchased from the Union Glass Works. As with so many others, the advent of World War I cut off supplies of both, and they were out of business in 1917.

FRY, H. C., AND COMPANY   1901–1934

Object	*Price*
Bonbon Dish, 5" Square, King George Pattern	*$150.00*
Bowl, 4", Wheat Pattern	*100.00*
Bowl, 6", 4 Ovals with Crosscuts and Chains of Stars	*150.00*
Bowl, 6", Wheat Pattern	*150.00*
Bowl, 8", Cleo Pattern, Signed "Fry"	*200.00*
Bowl, 8", Nelson or Wheat Pattern	*175.00*
Bowl, 8", 2 Circular Handles, Trojan Pattern	*275.00*
Bowl, 9", Rayed Base, Chain Hobstars and Fans, Signed "Fry"	*275.00*

Bowl, 10", Wheat Pattern $225.00
Decanter with Faceted Stopper, 10" Tall, Genoa Pattern 575.00
Lamp, 20" Tall, Notched Prism Pattern with Hobstars 1250.00
Mayonnaise Bowl, 5" Diameter, Circular Pedestal Base, Swirled Wheat Pattern 200.00
Plate, 7", Brighton Pattern 200.00
Plate, 8", Wheat Pattern 150.00
Platter, 12" Round, Frederick Pattern, Signed "Fry" 675.00
Platter, 12" Oblong, Atlantic Pattern 450.00
Serving Dish, 9³/₄", Tri-Cornered, Flaring Notched Prism Pattern 700.00
Tray, Bread, 12" Oval, Typhoon Pattern 450.00
Tray, 14" Oblong, Notched Edge, Elsie Pattern 375.00
Tray, 14" Oval, Sciota Pattern 475.00
Tray, 14" Rectangular, Leman Pattern 550.00
Tumbler, Highball, 5¹/₂" Tall, Pinwheel Center, Hobstar on Base 125.00
Tumbler, 6" Tall, Georgia Pattern 125.00
Wineglass, Supreme Pattern, Signed "Fry" 75.00

Henry C. Fry worked for a variety of glass firms before finally establishing his own business in 1901. Fry was diversified in his product line, which included not only cut glass but also pressed and etched glass, his famous ovenware, and blown blanks.

HAWKES, T. G., COMPANY 1880–1903

Object	*Price*

Basket, 9" Tall, 8" Diameter, 3 Thumbprints on Applied Handle, Hobstar Base, Hobstar and Fans $1000.00
Basket, 12" Tall, 8¹/₂" Diameter, Barrel-Shaped, Notched Handle, Cut Horizontal Rows with Vertical Divisions 750.00
Basket, 10" Diameter, Russian Pattern 550.00
Bonbon Dish, 5", Strawberry Diamond and Fan Pattern 100.00
Bonbon Dish, 5" Round, Russian Pattern 125.00
Bowl, 4¹/₂", Harvard Pattern 100.00
Bowl, 6", Festoon Pattern 150.00
Bowl, 7", Gladys Pattern 175.00
Bowl, 7", 2" Tall, Kohinoor and Hobstar Pattern, Signed "Hawkes" 325.00
Bowl, 7", Oblong, Panel Pattern 300.00
Bowl, 7", Straight Sides, Venetian Pattern 275.00
Bowl, Rose, 7¹/₂", 8" Tall, Queen's Pattern, Signed "Hawkes" on Bottom and Liner ..675.00
Bowl, 8", Nautilus Pattern 525.00
Bowl, 8", Crimped, Russian Pattern 350.00
Bowl, 8", Footed, Russian Pattern 375.00
Bowl, 8" Square, Notched Edge, Festoon Pattern 200.00
Bowl, Fruit, 9", Millicent Pattern 325.00
Bowl, 9", Hobstars and Bull's Eye Clusters (Queen's Pattern Variant) 525.00
Bowl, 9" Russian Pattern 375.00
Bowl, Centerpiece, 9" Diameter Base, 4" Diameter Bowl, Scalloped, 24-Point Hobstar Bottom, Hobstar Pattern, Signed "Hawkes" 550.00
Bowl, 9¹/₄", Scalloped, Engraved Dahlias and Swirls 475.00
Bowl, 10", Comet Pattern, Signed "Hawkes" 425.00
Bowl, 10", Devonshire Pattern 450.00

Bowl, 10", Harvard Pattern *$300.00*
Bowl, 10", Footed, Russian Pattern ....*.425.00*
Bowl, 12", Chrysanthemum or Russian Pattern, Signed "Hawkes" ....*.775.00*
Butter Dish with Cover, 5" Cover Diameter, Jersey Pattern ....*.650.00*
Candelabra, 17" Tall, 3-Light, Brazilian Pattern *3000.00*
Candle Holder, 3½" Tall, Hollow Bulb Stem, Intaglio Floral Design ....*.85.00*
Candlestick, 12" Tall, Swirled Pillar Stem, Russian Patterned Square Foot ....*.350.00*
Candlestick, Rayed Base, Faceted Ball, Paneled Stem ....*.275.00*
Carafe, Water, Devonshire Pattern ....*.750.00*
Celery Dish, Boat-Shaped, Harvard Pattern ....*.550.00*
Cheese Dish with Cover, Aberdeen Pattern ....*.400.00*
Compote, 7" Diameter, 7" Tall, Open, Venetian Pattern ....*.250.00*
Compote, 13" Diameter, 10" Tall, Panel Pattern, Signed "Hawkes" ....*.625.00*
Compote, Large, Hobstar and Thumbprints Enclosed in Diamonds ....*.550.00*
Cruet with Stopper, 6" Tall, Venetian Pattern ....*.500.00*
Cruet with Stopper, 9" Tall, Dundee Pattern *1200.00*
Decanter with Stopper, 12" Tall, Brunswick Pattern ....*.650.00*
Decanter with Silver-Hinged Stopper, Chrysanthemum Pattern ....*.600.00*
Decanter with Stopper, 12" Tall, Grecian Pattern ....*.650.00*
Globe, Rose, 6½" Tall, Circular Pedestal Base, Brunswick Pattern ....*.175.00*
Goblet, 5¾" Tall, Gravic Floral Design, Signed "Hawkes" ....*.125.00*
Goblet, 6¾" Tall, Intaglio 3-Fruit Design ....*.175.00*
Humidor, Tobacco, 8" Tall, Large Cut Oval Ball on Cover, Brunswick Pattern ....*.750.00*
Humidor, Tobacco, 8½" Tall, Large Cut Oval Ball on Cover, Marlboro Pattern ....*.850.00*
Ice Cream Tray, Oval (15½" × 10½"), Chrysanthemum Pattern ....*.775.00*
Ice Tub, 5" Tall, 6" Across, Rayed Base, Strawberry Diamond and Fan Pattern ....*.325.00*
Nappy, 6", Handled, Engraved Flowers between Hobstars ....*.75.00*
Nappy, 8", Russian Pattern, Signed "Hawkes" ....*.275.00*
Olive Dish, 9" Acorn-Shaped, Strawberry Diamond Pattern ....*.375.00*
Pitcher, Syrup, with Sterling Silver Lid, 7" Tall, Brunswick Pattern, Signed *1250.00*
Pitcher, Milk, 6½" Tall, 7½" Wide, Intaglio and Chrysanthemum Pattern, Signed "Hawkes"
....*1750.00*
Pitcher, Water, 10" Tall, Panel Pattern, Signed "Hawkes" ....*.950.00*
Pitcher, Water, 11" Tall, Pedestal Base, Queen's Pattern, Signed "Hawkes" *1350.00*
Pitcher, Water, 11½" Tall, Chrysanthemum Pattern *1000.00*
Pitcher, Water, 12" Tall, Intaglio Cut and Chrysanthemum Pattern, Signed "Hawkes"
....*1500.00*

Left: T. G. Hawkes cut glass. Photo by Mark Pickvet. Right: T. G. Hawkes cut glass. Photo by Mark Pickvet.

T. G. Hawkes cut glass. Courtesy of the Corning Museum of Glass.

Pitcher, Cocktail, 16" Tall, Silverplated Stirrer, Cut Band Design $200.00
Plate, 7" Astor, Cambridge, Grecian, or Venetian Patterns 225.00
Plate, 7", Chrysanthemum Pattern 250.00
Plate, 7¹/₂", Queens' Pattern 375.00
Plate, 7¹/₂", Napoleon Pattern 275.00
Plate, 8", Notched Edge, Russian Pattern 300.00
Plate, 9", Venetian Pattern, Signed "Hawkes" 325.00
Plate, 10", Constellation or Holland Pattern 225.00
Plate, 8¹/₂", Venetian Pattern 300.00
Plate, 11", Cardinal Pattern, Signed "Hawkes" 350.00
Plate, 12", Constellation or Panel Pattern 275.00
Plate, 12", Venetian Pattern, Signed "Hawkes" 425.00
Plate, 13", Kensington Pattern 1200.00
Plate, 13¹/₂", Scalloped, 8-Point Hobstar, Stamped "Hawkes" 1250.00
Platter, 11¹/₂" Round, Panel Pattern, Signed "Hawkes" 650.00
Platter, 12¹/₂" Oval, Albany Pattern 525.00
Platter, 13" Round, Venetian Pattern 675.00
Platter, 14" Round, Constellation Pattern 325.00
Platter, 14" Round, North Star Pattern 875.00
Platter, 15¹/₂" Round, Kings Pattern 850.00
Platter, 16" Round, Constellation Pattern 400.00
Powder Box with Hinged Cover, Chrysanthemum Pattern, Signed 525.00
Punch Bowl with Stand, 12" Diameter, 12" Tall, Queen's Pattern, Signed "Hawkes"
.... .2750.00
Salt and Pepper Shakers, Alberta Pattern 250.00
Tray, Dresser, 10" Oval, Sheraton Pattern 275.00
Tray, 11" Oval, Devonshire, Naples, or Wild Rose Pattern 450.00
Tray, Ice Cream, 14" (Nearly Rectangular), Ruffled Edge, Mars Pattern 400.00
Tray, Ice Cream, 14" Oval, Russian Pattern 675.00
Tray, Oblong, 15" × 8", Nautilus Pattern, Signed "Hawkes" 1375.00
Vase, 4¹/₂" Tall, 3 Engraved Medallions, Gracia Pattern, Signed "Hawkes" 250.00
Vase, 11" Tall, Globe-Holder, Globe Knob Stem, Circular Base, Russian Pattern 425.00
Vase, 11¹/₂" Tall, Sterling Silver Foot, Knob Stem, Millicent Pattern 275.00
Vase, 12" Tall, Brunswick Pattern 350.00

Vase, 12" Tall, Globe Top, Circular Base, Franklin Pattern *$425.00*
Vase, 12" Tall, Engraved Ferns and Roses with Bands of Hobstars *375.00*
Vase, 13" Tall, Globe Holder, Globe Knob Stem, Circular Base, Russian Pattern *500.00*
Vase, 14" Tall, Flared, Notched Rim, Circular Base, Brighton Pattern *750.00*
Vase, 14" Tall, 6" Diameter, Lattice and Rosette Pattern, Signed "Hawkes" *775.00*
Vase, 18" Tall, Pedestal Base, Queen's Pattern, Signed "Hawkes" *875.00*
Whiskey Tumbler, 2³/₄" Tall, Monarch Pattern, Signed "Hawkes" *110.00*
Wineglass, 5¹/₂" Tall, Double Knob, Circular Foot, Engraved Irish Design *75.00*
Wineglass, 6¹/₂" Tall, Square Base, Queen's Pattern *100.00*

A big name in the cut-glass world, Thomas Gibbon Hawkes was an Irish immigrant with a long family history of glass artistry. He was a direct descendant of the Hawkes family of Dudley, England, and the Penrose family of Waterford, Ireland.

He came to America in 1863 and fell in with such famous cut-glass makers as John Hoare, Henry Sinclaire, and Oliver Hawkes. He purchased his blanks from the Corning Glass Works through 1904. He then teamed up with various relatives and Frederick Carder to form the Steuben Glass Works.

Hawkes's painstaking details and such famous patents as the Russian, Louis XIV, Brazilian, Nautilus, and many others established him as one of the elite of America's cut-glass manufacturers.

HOARE, J., & COMPANY   1853–1890s

Object   *Price*
Basket, Small, 2³/₄" Diameter, 5" Tall, Applied Thumbprint Handle, Crosby Pattern .*$150.00*
Basket, 18" Tall, Flared Top, Diamond, Fan, and Hobstar Cuts *850.00*
Bell, 6" Tall, Monarch Pattern *125.00*
Bonbon Dish, 5" Round, Croesus Pattern *100.00*
Bowl, 7", Rolled Side, Creswick Pattern *250.00*
Bowl, Rose, 7", 6" Tall, Wedding Ring Pattern *675.00*
Bowl, 8", Croesus Pattern *225.00*
Bowl, 8" Square, Pebble Pattern *350.00*
Bowl, 8", Strawberry Diamond and Fan Pattern, Signed "Hoare" *200.00*
Bowl, 8¹/₄" Diameter, 2¹/₂" Tall, Scalloped, Serrated Rim, 8 Oval Mitres with 6 Rows of Hob-
stars between the Ovals, Marked "J. Hoare & Co./1853/Corning" *600.00*
Bowl, 9", Footed, Corning Pattern *275.00*
Bowl, 9" Square, Croesus Pattern *325.00*
Bowl, 10" Square, Corning Pattern *375.00*
Bowl, 11" Square, Marquise Pattern *450.00*
Bowl, Centerpiece, 11¹/₂" Diameter, 5¹/₂" Tall, Scalloped and Swirled Leaves with Alternating
Strawberry and Diamond Pattern *1250.00*
Bowl, 14", Shallow, Diamond and Bar Design, #5336 Pattern *675.00*
Butter Pat, Hobstar and Crossed Oval Pattern, Signed "Hoare" *50.00*
Candlestick, 10" Tall, Colonial Pattern *175.00*
Carafe, Queens Pattern, Signed "J. Hoare and Company" *500.00*
Celery Dish, 11¹/₄" Long, Harvard Pattern, Signed "Hoare" *200.00*
Centerpiece, Canoe-Shaped, 12¹/₂" Long, 4" Tall, Scalloped, Quarter Diamond Pattern
. . . .*1100.00*

Champagne Glass, Sunburst Base, Circular Foot, Fluted and Notched Hour Glass Stem, Hobstars between Mitre Cuts *$100.00*

Cruet with Stopper, 6" Tall, Strawberry Diamond and Fan Pattern, Signed "Hoare" *.375.00*

Decanter with Stopper, 8" Tall, 16 oz., Hindoo Pattern .... *.325.00*

Decanter with Stopper, 13½" Tall, Wedding Ring Pattern .... *.775.00*

Handkerchief Box with Hinged Cover, Nassau Pattern, Silver Overlay by Birks . *.1250.00*

Ice Cream Tray, 13" Long, Scalloped Hobstar and Strawberry Diamond Border, Oval Hobstar and Fans on Center, Marked "J. Hoare and Company" .... *.800.00*

Jug, Whiskey with Stopper, 10" Tall, 7" Diameter, 1 Gallon, Monarch Pattern, Signed .... *.2500.00*

Pitcher, Water, 9¼" Tall, Applied Handle, Notched Rim, Hindoo Pattern .... *.450.00*

Pitcher, Water, 9¼" Tall, Flared Bottom, Sunburst Base, Scalloped, Large Hobstars, Signed "J. Hoare & Co./1853/Corning" .... *.500.00*

Pitcher, Water, 12" Tall, Eleanor Pattern .... *.2500.00*

Pitcher, Water, 12" Tall, Wheat Pattern .... *.625.00*

Plate, 6", Acme Pattern .... *.150.00*

Plate, 7" Square, Corning Pattern .... *.175.00*

Plate, 7", Hexagonal, Nassau Pattern .... *.175.00*

Plate, 8" Square, Corning Pattern .... *.200.00*

Platter, 12", Circular, Carolyn Pattern .... *.475.00*

Platter, 14", Circular, Creswick Pattern .... *.550.00*

Platter, 14", Circular Hindoo Pattern .... *.600.00*

Punch Bowl with Stand, 12" Diameter, 13" Tall, Limoge Pattern .... *.3500.00*

Punch Bowl, 12", 6" Tall, Wheat Pattern .... *.2750.00*

Punch Bowl, 12½", Newport Pattern .... *.2500.00*

Punch Bowl with Base, Oval (20" × 13"), 10" Tall, Croesus Pattern .... *.4000.00*

Punch Cup, Handled, Croesus Pattern .... *.125.00*

Relish Dish, 6" Long, 3-Lobed, Hobstar and Facets Design .... *.100.00*

Relish Dish, 7" Long, Brighton Pattern .... *.125.00*

Sachet jar with Cover, 4" Tall, Hindoo Pattern .... *.450.00*

Tobacco Jar with Cover, 7⅛" Tall, Hobstars, Swags, and Facets .... *.675.00*

Tray, Celery, Oval (9½" × 4"), Strawberry Diamond and Fan Pattern .... *.275.00*

Tray, Celery, Oval (10½" × 5"), Large Hobnail Design .... *.375.00*

Tray, Celery, Oval (11" × 5"), Eclipse Pattern .... *.400.00*

Tray, Celery, Oval (12" × 4½"), Victoria Pattern .... *.450.00*

Tray, Ice Cream, 13½" Oval, Wheat Pattern .... *.850.00*

Tray, Ice Cream, 17" Oval, Meteor Pattern .... *.1250.00*

Vase, 12" Tall, Trumpet Shape, Prism with Button Squares, 5" Diameter .... *.350.00*

Vase, 14" Tall, 6½" Diameter, Comet Pattern, Signed .... *.1750.00*

Whiskey Tumbler, 2¾" Tall, Monarch Pattern .... *.100.00*

Wineglass, Monarch Pattern .... *.75.00*

John Hoare was one of the early leaders of America's Brilliant Period in glassmaking. He and his father, James, were both born in the famous glassmaking town of Cork, Ireland. The Hoare family was also associated with Thomas Webb & Sons and other firms in England. John Hoare also paid the boat fare for Thomas G. Hawkes, who was employed briefly with the Hoare's.

Hoare's quality also elevated the company's cut-glass products to some of the best ever produced. This is evidenced by the numerous awards they received at various expositions (i.e., gold medal award at the Columbian Exposition in Chicago in 1893).

HOPE GLASS WORKS 1872–1923

Object	Price
Bowl, 7", Shallow, Notched Edge, Large Star Cut Surrounded by 6 Small Hobstars	.$150.00
Creamer, 4½" Tall, Handle and Spout (Pitcher Style), Notched Rim, Applied Notched Handle, Vertically Cut, with Mitred Diamond Band at Top	.225.00
Cruet with Stopper, 5" Tall, Hobstar and Diamond Pattern	.475.00
Plate, 7", Cut Star in Center Surrounded by Engraved Carnations	.550.00
Sugar, 4¼" Tall, 2 Notched Handles, Notched Rim, Vertically Cut, with Mitred Diamond Band at Top	.175.00

This small manufacturer of cut glass had trouble operating profitably and went through several changes in ownership though the company name itself was not altered. They made glass globes, knobs, and shades along with some tableware.

IDEAL CUT GLASS COMPANY 1904–1934

Object	Price
Lamp, 18" Tall, Hobstar and Fluted Design	.$1250.00
Pitcher, 14½" Tall, Corset-Shaped, Serrated Lip, Cut Vertical Rows Alternating with Hobstars	.800.00
Plate, 8", Engraved Sailing Ship (*Constitution*)	.1500.00
Tumbler, Diamond-Poinsettia Pattern	.275.00
Vase, 12" Tall, Notched Edge, Diamond Poinsettia Pattern	.1100.00

Ideal was another tiny company that made very few products. They patented a six-petaled flower and a sailing ship pattern.

IRVING CUT GLASS COMPANY 1910–1933

Object	Price
Bowl, 8", Pinwheel Pattern	.$175.00
Butter Dish with Cover, 6" Diameter Dome, 8" Diameter Underplate, Rose Combination Pattern	.650.00
Butter Dish with Cover, 8" Diameter, 5½" Tall, Zella Pattern	.675.00
Creamer, Pitcher-Style, Applied Handle, Notched Rim, Large Hobstar Design	.250.00
Goblet, 4½" Tall, White Rose Pattern	.150.00
Lamp, 22" Tall, Dome Shade, Zella Pattern	.2650.00
Nappy, 11" Diameter, 6" Tall, 2-Sectioned, Center Top Handle, Hobstar and Diamond Cut Design	.475.00
Plate, 7", White Rose Pattern	.150.00
Plate, 10", Victrola Pattern	.450.00
Pitcher, Water, 9" Tall, Applied Handle, Carnation Pattern	.525.00
Sugar, 2 Applied Handles, Notched Rim, Large Hobstar Design	.250.00
Tray, Boat-Shaped, 9" Oblong, Iowa Pattern	.575.00

Irving was formed by six glass cutters who had previously worked for others (George Reichenbacher, Eugene Coleman, William Hawken, William Seitz, George

Roedine, and John Gogard). The firm survived World War I but closed during the Depression.

JEWEL CUT GLASS COMPANY 1907–1928

Object	Price
Bonbon Dish, 6", 2 Tab Handles, Engraved Floral Design	$275.00
Bowl, 8", Shallow, Notched Edge, Engraved Primrose Pattern	350.00
Bowl, 11", Rolled Rim, Bishop's Hat Design, Aberdeen Pattern	425.00
Creamer, 3¹/₂" Tall, Aberdeen Pattern	275.00
Handkerchief Box with Cover, 7" Square, Aberdeen Pattern	1250.00
Plate, 7", Regency Pattern	125.00
Plate, 8", Fluted and Hobnail Design	150.00
Plate, 8", Empire Pattern	200.00
Platter, 16" Circular, Aberdeen Pattern	1250.00
Punch Bowl with Stand, 14" Diameter, 14" Tall, Aberdeen Pattern	2750.00
Sugar, Open, 3¹/₂" Tall, Aberdeen Pattern	275.00
Tray, Oval (15¹/₄" × 9¹/₂"), Aberdeen Pattern	475.00

The firm began as the C. H. Taylor Glass Company in 1906 but changed the name to Jewel the following year. The company patented a few patterns, and as the market for fine cut glass declined, they stopped cutting glass and began selling greeting cards in 1928.

KEYSTONE CUT GLASS COMPANY 1902–1918

Object	Price
Bowl, 9", 4¹/₂" Tall, Notched Edge, Rose Pattern	$325.00
Butter Dish with Cover, 6" Tall, Rose Pattern	875.00
Creamer, 2-Handled, Double Spout, Signed "Keystone Cut Glass Company"	500.00
Creamer, 2 Applied Handles, Double Spout, Romeo Pattern	475.00
Goblet, 6" Tall, Pluto Pattern	150.00
Lamp, 22" Tall, Branning's Fan Scallop Pattern	2750.00
Pitcher, Water, 10¹/₄" Tall, Applied Handle, Pluto Pattern	425.00
Sugar, 2-Handled, Signed "Keystone Cut Glass Company"	500.00
Sugar, 2 Applied Handles, Notched Edge, Romeo Pattern	475.00

Keystone was a small company that purchased their blanks from the Corning Glass Works and Dorflinger. As blanks were harder and harder to come by, the business closed just after the end of World War I.

LAUREL CUT GLASS COMPANY 1903–1920

Object	Price
Bowl, 8", Everett Pattern	$200.00
Compote, 8" Tall, 8" Diameter, Notched Edge, Hobstar Design	225.00
Creamer, Single Handle and Spout, Eunice Pattern	175.00
Plate, 8", Central Hobstar Surrounded by 6 Smaller Hobstars	175.00

Sugar, 2-Handled, Eunice Pattern $175.00
Tray, 8" Oblong, Ruffled Edge, Audrey Pattern 275.00

Laurel was another of those small companies with a limited distribution network. They produced some cut-glass products and briefly joined with Quaker City directly after World War I. The two separated by 1920, and Laurel ended cut-glass production.

LIBBEY GLASS COMPANY 1888–1936

Object	*Price*
Basket, Oval (12¼" × 7¼"), 17" Tall, Intaglio and Brilliant Pattern, Signed "Libbey"	$975.00
Bell, 4½" Tall, Faceted Handle, Puritana Pattern	525.00
Bottle, Water, Imperial Pattern, Signed "Libbey"	275.00
Bottle, Whiskey, 14" Tall, Cut Stopper, Intaglio Rye	275.00
Bowl, 4½", Flared, Ruffled, Foliage Design, Signed "Libbey"	200.00
Bowl, Finger, 5", Etched Floral Design	125.00
Bowl, Finger, 5", Intaglio Grape and Leaf Design	200.00
Bowl, 7", Colonna Pattern, Signed "Libbey"	250.00
Bowl, 8", Star and Feather Pattern	225.00
Bowl, 8", 2 Tab Handles, Sunset Pattern	350.00
Bowl, 8", Corinthian Pattern	250.00
Bowl, 8", Delphos Pattern, Signed "Libbey"	325.00
Bowl, 8", Gloria or Isabella Pattern	225.00
Bowl, 8½", Hobstars with Fans and Diamond Panels, Signed "Libbey	250.00
Bowl, 9", Columbia Pattern	250.00
Bowl, 9", Colonna or Greek Key Pattern	250.00
Bowl, 9", Empress Pattern	300.00
Bowl, 9", Glenda Pattern, Signed "Libbey"	300.00
Bowl, 9", Senora Pattern	425.00
Bowl, 9", Finely Detailed Snowflake Pattern, Signed "Libbey"	1000.00
Bowl, 10", 5" Tall, Intaglio and Leaves Pattern, Signed "Libbey"	450.00
Bowl, 10", Aztec or Florence Pattern	300.00
Bowl, 10", Fluted, Kimberly Pattern	400.00
Bowl, 10", Tri-Cornered, Marcella Pattern, Signed "Libbey"	725.00
Bowl, 10", 16 Point Hobstar on Base, Sultana Pattern, Signed "Libbey"	400.00
Bowl, 10⅛", Stratford Pattern	600.00
Bowl, 11½" × 4½" Oval, Russian Ambassador Pattern	900.00
Bowl, 14", Shallow, Libbey Pattern, Signed "Libbey"	600.00
Bowl, Fruit, Hat-Shaped, Thistle Pattern, Signed "Libbey"	550.00
Bowl, Fan and Hobstars, Eulalia Pattern	500.00
Bowl, Rose, 6½" Tall, 4½" Top Opening, Ribbed, Signed "Libbey" in Circle	175.00
Box, Powder, 6" Diameter, Hinged Lid, Florence Pattern	600.00
Butter Dish with Domed Cover, Matching Underplate, Columbia Pattern	750.00
Butter Dish with Domed Cover, Matching Underplate, Hobstar and Strawberry Diamond Design, Gloria Pattern	750.00
Butter Dish with Domed Cover, Rajah Pattern	750.00
Cake Plate, 12", Aztec Pattern, Signed "Libbey"	475.00
Candlestick, 6" Tall, Fluted, Teardrop Stem, Signed "Libbey"	200.00

Carafe, Elsmere Pattern, Signed "Libbey" on Flute *$250.00*
Carafe, Fan, Hobstar, and Mitre Cut, Signed "Libbey" *200.00*
Carafe, New Brilliant Pattern *225.00*
Celery Dish, 11" Long, Harvard Pattern *175.00*
Chalice, 11" Tall, Colonna Pattern *950.00*
Champagne Glass, Embassy Pattern, Signed "Libbey" *75.00*
Champagne Glass, Fern and Flower Design, Signed "Libbey" *75.00*
Champagne Glass, Imperial Pattern, Signed "Libbey" *75.00*
Cheese Dish with Dome Cover, Matching Underplate, Columbia Pattern, Signed "Libbey"
. . . .*850.00*
Cologne Bottle with Stopper, 6" Tall, 6" Diameter, Globe-Shaped, Columbia Pattern *575.00*
Cologne Bottle with Stopper, 8" Tall, Globe-Shaped, Columbia Pattern *625.00*
Compote, 8½" Diameter, Ozella Pattern *550.00*
Compote, 10½" Diameter, Knobbed Stem with Teardrop, Geometric Design, Signed "Libbey" *825.00*
Cordial, 24-Ray Base, Fluted, Faceted Knob, Harvard Pattern, Signed "Libbey" *100.00*
Cordial, Princess Pattern, Signed "Libbey" *100.00*
Cordial, 3½" Tall, Sultana Pattern, Signed "Libbey" *100.00*
Creamer, Hobstars and Strawberry Diamond, Signed "Libbey" *150.00*
Creamer, Raised Lip, Eulalia Pattern *125.00*
Decanter, Side Handle, Corinthian Pattern *425.00*
Decanter with Stopper, 18" Tall, Pedestal Base, Herringbone Pattern, Signed "Libbey"
. . . .*3250.00*
Decanter with Stopper, 19⅛" Tall, Cut Circular Foot, Applied Cut Handle, Tapering Shape, Small Pouring Lip, Sunburst Pattern Variant, Signed "Libbey" *5000.00*
Goblet, Columbia Pattern *150.00*
Goblet, Water, Princess Pattern, Signed "Libbey" *75.00*
Ice Cream Dish, 17½" Long, Sonora Pattern *1250.00*
Ice Cream Tray, 12" Diameter, Somerset Pattern *225.00*
Ice Cream Tray, 14" × 7½", Kimberly Pattern *350.00*
Ice Cream Tray, 16" × 9¾", 4-Sectioned Cut Flowers, Flashed, Ivernia Pattern, Signed "Libbey" *1250.00*
Ice Cream Tray, 18" Diameter, Princess Pattern *750.00*
Jug, 7" Tall, with Handle, Stopper on Side Spout, Sultana Pattern, Signed "Libbey" .*2500.00*
Nappy, 7", Heart-Shaped Heart Pattern, Signed "Libbey" *175.00*
Nappy, Hobstars, Strawberry Diamond, and Fan Design, Signed "Libbey" *125.00*
Pitcher, Milk, Harvard Pattern *350.00*
Pitcher, Water, 8" Tall, Tankard-Style, Rayed Base, Sunburst with Bands of Hobstars . .*325.00*
Pitcher, Water, 8½" Tall, Corinthian Pattern *425.00*
Pitcher, Water, 9" Tall, Columbia Pattern, Signed "Libbey" *525.00*
Pitcher, Water, 9" Tall, Kingston Pattern *450.00*
Pitcher, Water, 11" Tall, Imperial Pattern, Signed "Libbey" *625.00*
Pitcher, Champagne, 11½" Tall, Iola Pattern *650.00*
Pitcher, Water, 12" Tall, Aztec Pattern, Signed "Libbey" *725.00*
Pitcher, Water, 13" Tall, Kingston Pattern *625.00*
Pitcher, Water, Scotch Thistle Pattern *400.00*
Plate, 6", Columbia Pattern *125.00*
Plate, 6¾", Ellsmere Pattern, Signed "Libbey" with Saber *175.00*
Plate, 6¾", Ice Cream, Prism Pattern, Signed "Libbey" *200.00*
Plate, 7", Aztec Pattern, Signed "Libbey" *175.00*
Plate, 7", Colonna or Kimberly Pattern *175.00*

Plate, 7", Prism Pattern, Signed "Libbey" $150.00
Plate, 7", Spillane Pattern, Signed "Libbey" 150.00
Plate, 10", Columbia or Corinthian Pattern 250.00
Plate, 10", Kingston Pattern, Signed Libbey 275.00
Plate, 11½", 6-Paneled, Thistle Design, Signed "Libbey" 350.00
Plate, 11¾", Sultana Pattern, Signed "Libbey" 400.00
Platter, 12", Circular, Ozella Pattern 600.00
Platter, 12", Circular, Neola Pattern 775.00
Platter, 16", Circular, Diana Pattern, Signed 1750.00
Punch Bowl with Stand, Spillane Pattern, Signed "Libbey" 4000.00
Relish, 6" Diameter, 2½" Tall, Signed "Libbey" 225.00
Salt Dip, Pedestal Base, Signed "Libbey" 150.00
Sherry Glass, Moonbeam Pattern, Signed "Libbey" 50.00
Spooner, 6" Tall, Sultana Pattern 175.00
Sugar, Hobstars and Strawberry Diamond, Signed "Libbey" 150.00
Sugar, Flared Rim on 2 Sides, Eulalia Pattern 125.00
Tankard, 11½" Tall, Hobnail and Cross Cutting, Signed "Libbey" 750.00
Tray, Pickle, 8" Oval, Regis Pattern 175.00
Tray, 10" Oval, Senora Pattern, Signed "Libbey" 500.00
Tray, 10½" Oblong, Puritan Pattern, Signed "Libbey" 625.00
Tray, 11¼" × 4½", Wisteria and Lovebird Pattern 1500.00
Tray, 12" Diameter, Senora Pattern, Signed "Libbey" 700.00
Tray, 12" Diameter, Scalloped, 6-Paneled, Diamond Point with Star 1250.00
Tray, Celery, 12" × 4⅜", 8 12-Pointed Hobstars, Fan Center, Diamond and Fan Cuts, Gem
Pattern 200.00
Tray, 14" Oval, Ice Cream, 2 Tab Handles, Prism Pattern, Signed "Libbey" 775.00
Tray, 15¾" Oblong, 9½" Wide, Fishtail-Shaped, Prism Pattern, Signed "Libbey" 975.00
Tray, 17½" Oval, Wedgemere Pattern, Signed "Libbey" 1750.00
Tray, Heart-Shaped, Florence Star Pattern 550.00
Tumbler, Juice, Corinthian Pattern 75.00
Tumbler, Scotch Thistle Pattern 75.00
Tumbler, Strawberry Diamond Design, Signed "Libbey" 75.00
Vase, 5½" Tall, Sawtooth Rim, Bull's Eyes and Fern Design 175.00
Vase, 10" Tall, Fine Ribbed Cuts 175.00
Vase, 12" Tall, Corset-Shaped, Signed "Libbey" 625.00
Vase, 12" Tall, Radiant Pattern 400.00
Vase, 16" Tall, Rose Cutting, Signed "Libbey" 225.00
Vase, 16" Tall, Star and Feather Pattern, Signed "Libbey" 1250.00
Vase, 18" Tall, 2 Notched Handles, Hobstars and Hobnails' Design 2500.00
Vase, 18" Tall, Wedgemere Pattern 2400.00
Vase, 20" Tall, 7½" Diameter, Pedestal Base, Kensington Pattern Variation, Signed "Libbey"
.... .2250.00
Wineglass, 5¾" Tall, Circular Foot, Double Knob, Signed "Locke Art" 125.00
Wineglass, 7¼" Tall, Cornucopia Pattern 75.00
Wineglass, Embassy Pattern, Signed "Libbey" 75.00
Wineglass, Cut Stem Only, Signed "Libbey" 175.00

You will find more listings for Libbey than any other cut-glass manufacturer and
for good reason; Libbey was simply the largest producer of cut glass in the world.
Their products rivaled the best anywhere, and they won numerous awards at various expositions.

LUZERNE CUT GLASS COMPANY 1910S–LATE 1920S

Object	Price
Tray, 14" Oblong, Notched Edge, 2 Tab Handles, Myron Pattern	*$325.00*
Tray, 14½" Oval, Notched Edge, Electra Pattern	*375.00*

Luzerne, like countless others, was a small obscure company with few surviving products. They were established sometime before World War I and were out of business by 1930.

MAPLE CITY GLASS COMPANY 1910–1920S

Object	Price
Bowl, 7", Crossed Oval Design	*$175.00*
Bowl, 8", Fenmore Pattern	*175.00*
Bowl, 9", Notched Edge, Emerald Pattern	*200.00*
Celery Dish, Boat-Shaped, Marked Inside with Maple Leaf	*1000.00*
Ice Cream Tray, 14½" × 8", Cane, Fan, Hobstar, and Strawberry Design, Marked with Maple Leaf	*700.00*
Mustard Dish with Cover and Matching Underplate, 3½" Tall, Panel and Notched Prism Design, Signed	*250.00*
Punch Bowl, 12¼" Diameter, 11½" Tall, Temple Pattern	*3500.00*
Tobacco Jar with Cover, 6" Tall, 5" Diameter, Hemispherical Cut Finial, Hobstar and Fan Design	*1250.00*
Tray, 12" Oval, Notched Edge, Manchester Pattern	*275.00*
Tray, 14" Oval, Notched Edge, Gloria Pattern	*325.00*
Vase, 7½" Tall, Pansy Pattern	*350.00*

Maple City purchased a factory formerly run by John S. O'Connor in Hawley, Pennsylvania. What few cut-glass products they made were marked with an etched maple leaf.

MERIDEN CUT GLASS COMPANY 1895–1923

Object	Price
Bottle, Worcester with Stopper, 8" Tall, Alhambra Pattern	*$700.00*
Cake Salver, 10" Diameter, Stemmed, Alhambra Pattern	*475.00*
Cheese Dish with Domed Cover, Plymouth Pattern	*400.00*
Cruet with Stopper, 9½" Tall, Alhambra Pattern	*750.00*
Decanter with Stopper, 12½" Tall, Alhambra Pattern	*1250.00*
Decanter with Stopper, Plymouth Pattern	*650.00*
Decanter with Stopper, 6" Tall, Wheeler Pattern	*500.00*
Pitcher, Water, 9" Tall, Large Heavy Sterling Silver Top, Including Pouring Lip, Alhambra Pattern	*1250.00*
Pitcher, Water, 12½" Tall, Tankard-Style, Sterling Silver Top, Alhambra Pattern	*1750.00*

C. F. Monroe cut glass. Reproduced from a 1902 patent.

Plate, 7", Alhambra Pattern *$150.00*
Plate, 7" Square, Notched Edge, Hobstars and Circles Inscribed in Squares *225.00*
Plate, 10", Alhambra Pattern *300.00*
Tray, 13" Oval, Alhambra Pattern *1250.00*
Tumbler, 4½" Tall, Thalia Pattern *375.00*

Meriden, Connecticut, was a small, relatively unknown glassmaking town that featured several small companies. The Meriden Cut Glass Company was one such business that produced blanks for cutting as well as some cut products of their own. They were noted most for the "Alhambra" pattern, which is also known and more familiar as "Greek Key."

MONROE, C. F., COMPANY   1880–1916

Object   *Price*
Bowl, 7", Rockmere Pattern *$225.00*
Bowl, 8", Notched Edge, Monroe Pattern *175.00*
Bowl, 9½", Footed, Central Hobstar with Chain of Smaller Hobstars, Silver Rim *575.00*
Fernery, 8" Tall, Silver Rim, Allover Hobstar and Fan Pattern *525.00*
Hairpin Box with Lid, 4" Diameter, Brass Rim at Top of Box and Bottom of Lid, Fluted Base, Hobstar and Fan Design on Lid *500.00*
Pitcher, Syrup, with Silverplated Lid and Handle, Hobstar and Fan Pattern *750.00*
Powder Box with Cover, 5½" Diameter, Silver Rim at Top of Box and Bottom of Cover; Hobstar, Fan, and Strawberry Diamond Design on Base and Cover *675.00*
Powder Box with Cover, 6" Diameter, Brass Rim at Top of Box and Bottom of Cover; Central Hobstar with Star and Fan Design on Base and Cover *700.00*
Powder Box with Cover, 6" Diameter, Silver Rim at Top of Box and Bottom of Cover, Fluted Base, Large Center Hobstar on Cover *600.00*
Powder Box with Cover, 8" Diameter, Silver Rim at Top of Box and Bottom of Cover, Fluted Base, Central Hobstar with Several Small Hobstars on Cover *725.00*
Watch Box with Cover, 3" Diameter, Brass Rim at Top of Box and Bottom of Cover, Fluted Base, Pinwheel Design on Cover *425.00*

C. F. Monroe was better known as an art glass company; however, they employed glass cutters too (see the Art Glass chapter for additional Monroe listings).

MOUNT WASHINGTON GLASS WORKS
1837–1894

Object	*Price*
Bonbon Dish, 5", Finger-Hold Handle, Priscilla Pattern	*$175.00*
Bowl, 6", Bedford Pattern	*150.00*
Bowl, 8", Magnolia Pattern	*225.00*
Bowl, 8", Russian Pattern	*275.00*
Bowl, 8¾", Picket Fence with 24-Point Star Base, Acid Finish	*250.00*
Bowl, 10", Princess Pattern	*375.00*
Butter Tub with Cover, 2-Handled (Cover Has Indentation for Handles), 5" Diameter, 8" Diameter Matching Underplate, Diamond and Star Pattern	*2750.00*
Champagne Glass, 5" Tall, Diamond and Star Pattern with Hobstar Base	*125.00*
Cracker Jar with Cover, Strawberry Diamond and Fan Pattern	*750.00*
Creamer, Bedford, Corinthian, Regent, Strawberry Diamond and Fan, and West Patterns	*150.00*
Decanter with Stopper, Right-Angle Handle, Bedford Pattern	*550.00*
Decanter with Stopper, No Handle, Corinthian Pattern	*600.00*
Decanter with Stopper, Westminster Pattern	*650.00*
Jam Jar with Hinged Cover, Handled, Strawberry Diamond and Hobstar Pattern, Marked "M.W." on Cover	*400.00*
Mug, 8 oz., Regent, Westminster, or Wheeler Pattern	*150.00*
Mustard Jar with Cover, 1 Handle, Strawberry Diamond and Fan and Westminster Patterns	*300.00*
Pitcher, Water, Corinthian Pattern	*250.00*
Pitcher, Water, Regent, Strawberry Diamond and Fan, and West Patterns	*350.00*
Pitcher, Water, 8" Tall, Radiant Pattern	*350.00*
Plate, 5½", Hortensia Pattern	*100.00*
Plate, 6", Corinthian, Priscilla, Strawberry Diamond and Fan, and West Patterns	*125.00*
Plate, 7", Bedford, Corinthian, Priscilla, Regent, and Westminster Patterns	*150.00*
Plate, 7" Square, Madora Pattern	*225.00*
Plate, 8", Bedford, Butterfly and Daisy, Corinthian, and Westminster Patterns	*175.00*
Platter, 14½" Circular, Silver Rim, Daisy Pattern	*1500.00*
Platter, 15" Oval, Large Diamond with Octagon Cuts	*500.00*
Punch Bowl with Base, 14" Diameter, Regent Pattern	*3500.00*
Punch Ladle, Regent Pattern	*550.00*
Relish Dish, 3 Divisions, Strawberry Diamond and Fan Pattern	*200.00*
Salt and Pepper Shakers, Ribbed, Pillar Pattern, Metal Holder with Handle	*350.00*
Spoon Holder, 6" Oblong, Strawberry Diamond and Fan Pattern	*75.00*
Spoon Holder, 7" Oblong, Strawberry Diamond and Fan Pattern	*100.00*
Sugar, Bedford, Corinthian, Regent, Strawberry Diamond and Fan (without Cover), and West Patterns	*150.00*
Sugar with Cover, Strawberry Diamond and Fan Pattern	*200.00*
Sugar Shaker, Egg-Shaped, Metal Top, Corinthian, Strawberry Diamond and Fan, and Wheeler Patterns	*500.00*
Tray, Dresser, Tulip Pattern	*225.00*
Tray, 9" Square, Corinthian Pattern	*450.00*
Tray, 12" × 5½" Rectangular, Block Diamond and Strawberry Diamond and Fan Patterns	*250.00*
Tray, 14" Oblong, Strawberry Diamond and Fan Pattern	*275.00*

Tray, Irregular, 1 Large Semicircle for Pitcher, 2 Smaller Semicircles for Tumblers, Strawberry Diamond and Fan Pattern *$400.00*
Whiskey Tumbler, 2¹/₂" Tall, Westminster Pattern *100.00*
Wineglass, 6¹/₈" Tall, Fluted Stem, Angular Ribbon Pattern with Star Base *125.00*

Mount Washington is noted more for its famous art glass products but were also a significant producer of cut glass. They patented many designs, including several floral patterns such as Rose, Rose variations, Daisy, and others. Mount Wasington eventually became part of the Pairpoint Manufacturing Company in 1894, which continued with several of Mount Washington's cut lines.

PAIRPOINT GLASS CORPORATION   1880–1938

Object	*Price*
Bonbon Dish, 5", 2 Tab Handles, Salem Pattern	*$175.00*
Bottle, Whiskey, with Stopper, 10" Tall, 1 Quart, Old English Pattern	*1750.00*
Bowl, 8", Notched Edge, Montrose or Wisteria Pattern	*350.00*
Bowl, 9", Notched Edge, Montrose Pattern	*375.00*
Bowl, 11", Myrtle Pattern	*525.00*
Bowl, 12", Berwick Pattern	*650.00*
Bowl, 12", Notched Edge, Wisteria Pattern	*650.00*
Bowl, 14", Notched Edge, Wisteria Pattern	*850.00*
Cheese Dish with Cover, Strawberry Diamond Pattern	*1250.00*
Cologne Bottle with Stopper, 2 oz., Arbutus Pattern	*200.00*
Comport, 6¹/₂" Tall, Diamond-Hob Design	*200.00*
Comport, 8" Tall, Diamond-Hob Design	*250.00*
Compote, 10" Tall, Teardrop Stem, Hobstar Base, Avila Pattern	*350.00*
Compote, 10" Tall, Hobstar and Fan Design, Uncatena Pattern	*350.00*
Creamer, Domed Base, Colias Pattern	*75.00*
Cruet with Flower Cut Stopper, Ramona Pattern	*275.00*
Flower Holder, 13¹/₂" Diameter, Butterfly and Daisy Pattern	*475.00*
Mug, 4" Tall, Tyrone Pattern	*275.00*
Nappy, 5", "+"-Shaped, Block Diamond Design	*100.00*
Nappy, 5¹/₂" Heart-Shaped, Fairfax Pattern	*200.00*
Nappy, 7³/₄", Essex Pattern	*125.00*
Nappy, 8", Bombay and Montank Patterns	*150.00*
Plate, 8", Clarina Pattern	*75.00*
Spoon Holder, 7³/₄" Oval, Canton Pattern	*125.00*
Spoon Holder, 2 Handles, Malden Pattern	*150.00*
Sugar, Domed Base, Colias Pattern	*75.00*
Sugar Tray, Domino, Rectangular with Tab Handles	*200.00*
Tray, 8¹/₂" × 4" Rectangular, Wakefield Pattern	*225.00*
Tray, 9" Oval, Essex Pattern	*250.00*
Tray, 9¹/₄" Oval, Kingston Pattern	*250.00*
Tray, 10", Triangular, Russian Pattern	*375.00*
Tray, 10" Oval, Russian Pattern (Persian Variation)	*325.00*
Tray, 14" Oblong, Ruffled Edge, Silver Leaf Pattern	*475.00*
Vase, 6" Tall, Fan Scroll Pattern	*175.00*
Vase, 8" Tall, Fan Scroll Pattern	*200.00*

Vase, 12" Tall, Fan Scroll Pattern *$250.00*
Whiskey Tumbler, 2½" Tall, Butterfly and Daisy Pattern *75.00*

As noted under listing for Mount Washington, Pairpoint purchased that company in 1894 and continued production of cut glass. They also patented several lines, including Tulip and Anemone.

PITKIN & BROOKS 1870S–1920

Object	Price
Bowl, 8", Athole Pattern	*$200.00*
Bowl, 8", Shallow, Belmont Pattern	*150.00*
Bowl, 8", 3½" Tall, Notched Edge, Hobstar and Diamond Pattern	*175.00*
Bowl, 8", Plymouth Pattern	*200.00*
Bowl, 9", Notched Edge, Heart Pattern	*275.00*
Candlestick, 14" Tall, Heart Pattern	*375.00*
Compote, 7" Tall, Border Pattern	*425.00*
Compote, 11¾" Tall, 10½" Diameter, 2-Part, Floral Design, Plymouth Pattern, Signed .	*775.00*
Creamer, Rajah Pattern	*150.00*
Fernery, 7¾" Diameter, Paneled Floral and Diamond Design, Signed	*175.00*
Lamp, 23" Tall, 12" Diameter Shade, Plymouth Pattern, Signed	*1750.00*
Nappy, 6", Tab Handle, Heart Pattern	*225.00*
Nappy, 6", Seymour Pattern	*125.00*
Nappy, 7", Corsair, Meadville, Mikado, or Myrtle Pattern	*200.00*
Nappy, 7½", 2 Tab Handles, Phena Star Pattern	*225.00*
Nappy, 8", Corsair, Meadville, or Myrtle Pattern	*225.00*
Nappy, 9", Corsair or Meadville Pattern	*250.00*
Pickle Dish, 7", Nellore Pattern	*175.00*
Pitcher, 12" Tall, Heart Pattern	*975.00*
Plate, 7", Rosette and Buzz Star Pattern	*125.00*
Plate, 7", Hexagonal, Star Pattern	*225.00*
Plate, 7", Mars or Wild Daisy Pattern	*100.00*
Plate, 9", Roland Pattern	*150.00*
Plate, 12", Roland Pattern	*200.00*
Plate, 14", Roland Pattern	*225.00*
Relish Tray, 7", Osborn Pattern	*250.00*
Saucer, 5", Corsair, Meadville, Mikado, or Myrtle Pattern	*150.00*
Saucer, 6", Corsair, Meadville, Mikado, or Myrtle Pattern	*175.00*
Spoon Tray, 7½" Oblong, Cortez Pattern	*250.00*
Sugar, 2-Handled, Rajar Pattern	*200.00*
Tray, 10", Hobstar Center, Myrtle Pattern	*275.00*
Tray, 10", Oval, Nellore Pattern	*275.00*
Tray, 11" Oblong, 5 Large Hobstars, Cortez Pattern	*350.00*
Tray, 12" Oval, Athole Pattern	*275.00*
Tray, 12" Oval, Notched Edge, Bowa Pattern	*225.00*
Tray, 13½" Across, Oak Leaf Shape, Notched Prisms and Vesicas	*750.00*

Edward Pitkin and Jonathan Brooks, Jr., formed a wholesale glass and china business in 1872. They later opened up various cutting shops and employed cutters to produce products with their P & B mark. They sold the glass in their whole-sale business and patented several lines (e.g., Korea, Wild Daisy, and Heart and Hobstar).

QUAKER CITY CUT GLASS COMPANY
1902–1927

Object	Price
Bonbon Dish, 5½" Oval, Notched Edge, Mystic Pattern	*$150.00*
Bowl, 4" Tall, Footed, Ruffled Edge, Berlyn Pattern	*300.00*
Bowl, 4½" Tall, Footed, Notched Edge, Whirlwind Pattern	*225.00*
Bowl, 9", Notched Edge, Marlborough Pattern	*175.00*
Compote, Angora Pattern	*575.00*
Plate, 11", Du Barry Pattern	*325.00*
Vase, 20" Tall, 3-Part, Empress Pattern	*5500.00*
Vase, 36" Tall, 3-Part, Riverton Pattern	*7500.00*

Quaker City was also known as the Cut Glass Corporation of America. Few examples of their products have been found that are easily identified. They did use paper labels with a bust of William Penn, but the gummed labels easily fell off or were removed. The most impressive and valuable pieces are the vases typically made in three separate pieces that screw together.

SINCLAIRE, H. P., COMPANY   1904–1930S

Object	Price
Bonbon Dish, 7" Rectangular, Strawberry Diamond or Assyrian Pattern	*$175.00*
Bowl, Fruit, 8" Diameter, 5" Tall	*350.00*
Bowl, 9", 2¾" Tall, Hobstar and Mitred Cuts, Signed "Sinclaire"	*275.00*
Bowl, 9" Top Diameter, 4" Tall, Assyrian Pattern	*425.00*
Butter Dish, 6" Rectangular, Open, Strawberry Diamond Pattern	*150.00*
Champagne Glass, Ivy Pattern, Signed "Sinclaire"	*75.00*
Children's Miniature Cereal Set, 2-Piece, Pitcher and Bowl, Queen Louise Pattern, Signed "Sinclaire"	*425.00*
Clock, Mantel, 8" Tall, Copper Wheel Engraved, Signed "Sinclaire"	*500.00*
Cologne Bottle with Stopper, 6" Tall, Floral Design, Signed "Sinclaire"	*225.00*
Cordial, Star Base, Greek Key Pattern, Signed "Sinclaire"	*75.00*
Creamer, Queen Louise Pattern, Signed "Sinclaire"	*150.00*
Creamer, 6" Tall, Vintage Pattern, Signed "Sinclaire"	*225.00*
Cup, Loving, 9¼" Tall, 8½" Diameter, 2-Handled, Signed "Sinclaire"	*1500.00*
Decanter with Stopper, 5" Tall, Bengal Pattern, Signed "Sinclaire"	*300.00*
Decanter with Stopper, Queens Pattern, Signed "Sinclaire"	*550.00*
Epergne, 2-Part, 14" Tall, 10½" Diameter, Engraved Floral and Foliage Design, Signed "Sinclaire"	*1250.00*
Flowerpot, Intaglio Border, Geometric Design, Signed "Sinclaire"	*275.00*
Ice Cream Tray, Rectangular (14" × 9"), Assyrian Pattern, Signed "Sinclaire"	*1100.00*
Lamp, 17" Tall, Flower Basket Pattern	*1250.00*
Nappy, 3¼" Triangular-Shaped, Cumberland Pattern	*150.00*

Oliver Dish, 7¼" × 4", 16 12-Point Hobstars in a Chain, Etched Floral and Foliage Design
....*$150.00*

Pitcher, 7" Tall, Westminster Pattern, Signed "Sinclaire" *275.00*

Pitcher, 8½" Tall, Barrel-Shaped, Scalloped, Strawberry and Diamonds above Vertical
Panels *425.00*

Pitcher, 9" Tall, Pedestal Base, Signed "Sinclaire" *2500.00*

Plate, 5", 32-Point Star on Base, Diamond Cross Cut, Signed "Sinclaire" *100.00*

Plate, 7", Assyrian Pattern, Signed "Sinclaire" *275.00*

Plate, 10", Adam Pattern *375.00*

Plate, 12", Stars and Garlands, Signed "Sinclaire" *425.00*

Platter, 13¼", Circular, Assyrian Pattern, Signed "Sinclaire" *675.00*

Platter, 15", Circular, Hiawatha Pattern, Signed "Sinclaire" *725.00*

Sugar, Open, Vintage Pattern, Signed "Sinclaire" *225.00*

Sugar with Cover, Queen Louise Pattern, Signed "Sinclaire" *200.00*

Teapot with Lid, 8" Tall, Intaglio and Damascus Pattern, Signed "Sinclaire" *2750.00*

Tray, 7" × 4¾", Hobs in Chain Design, Engraved Border, Signed "Sinclaire" *150.00*

Tray, 12" × 5", Assyrian Pattern *350.00*

Tray, 12" × 5", Flared Ends, Scalloped Sides, Geometric Cutting with Hobstars, Signed
"Sinclaire" *325.00*

Tray, Rectangular (12" × 5"), Adam Pattern, Signed "Sinclaire" *425.00*

Tray, Oval (10" × 7"), Crosscut, Fans and Hobstars *275.00*

Tray, 14" Oval, Two Tab Handles, Diamond and Threading with Engraved Floral Design in
Center *750.00*

Vase, 6½" Tall, Flower Center, Bengal Pattern *900.00*

Vase, 11" Tall, Flower Center, Flute and Panel Border *375.00*

Vase, 12" Tall, 5" Diameter, Assyrian Pattern, Signed "Sinclaire" *475.00*

Vase, 14" Tall, 5" Diameter, Assyrian Pattern, Signed "Sinclaire" *775.00*

Vase, 15½", Queen Louise Pattern, Signed "Sinclaire" *225.00*

Vase, 16" Tall, Stratford Pattern, Signed "Sinclaire" *450.00*

Wineglass, Ivy Pattern, Signed "Sinclaire" *75.00*

The Sinclaires were associated with several famous glassmakers. Henry P. Sinclaire, Sr., was the secretary of the Corning Glass Works from 1893 until he died in
1902. Henry P. Sinclaire, Jr., was the secretary of T. J. Hawkes from roughly the
same time (1893–1903) and went on to establish his own business. He purchased
blanks from the Corning Glass Works and patented several cut patterns before forcing to close during the Depression.

STERLING CUT GLASS COMPANY 1904–1950

Object   *Price*
Plate, 10", Fruits and Butterfly Design, Eden Pattern *$1750.00*
Plate, 10", Engraved Floral Border, Regal Pattern *1250.00*

The Sterling Glass Company was established in 1904 by Joseph Phillips and was
joined in 1913 by Joseph Landenwitsch. The company was briefly known as Joseph
Phillips & Company. Apparently, what little cut glass they produced was in the
early teens, for in 1919, Phillips became a salesman for the Rookwood Pottery
Company and Landenswitsch became president of Phillips Glass Company, another
offshoot.

Later, the company reorganized as the Sterling Cut Glass Company. Pieces made by Sterling are scarce; however, those that exist contain cutting as well as elegant engraving and are quite valuable.

STRAUS L., & SONS 1888–EARLY 1900S

Object	Price
Bowl, 6", Bijoux Pattern	*$125.00*
Bowl, 8", Notched Ovals Edge, Daisies and Diamonds Pattern	*175.00*
Bowl, 9", Notched Edge, Americus Pattern	*175.00*
Bowl, 9", Tassel Pattern	*200.00*
Bowl, 10", Warren Pattern	*250.00*
Bowl, 11½" Oval, Imperial Pattern	*300.00*
Bowl, 12" Square, Venetian Pattern	*325.00*
Carafe, Water, Drape Pattern, Signed "Straus"	*250.00*
Celery Dish, Encore Pattern, Signed "Straus"	*225.00*
Cheese Dish with Dome Cover, 9" Diameter Underplate, 6" Diameter Dome, Corinthian Pattern	*675.00*
Compote, 12" Tall, Corinthian Pattern	*750.00*
Decanter with Cut Stopper, 11" Tall, Americus Pattern	*425.00*
Pitcher, Water, 12" Tall, Drape Pattern	*1250.00*
Plate, 7", Inverted Kite Pattern	*125.00*
Plate, 8", Notched Edge, Lily of the Valley and Pansy Pattern	*150.00*
Plate, 8", Venetian Pattern	*175.00*
Platter, 12" Round, Maltese Urn Pattern	*625.00*
Punch Bowl, 12½" Diameter, Corinthian Pattern	*750.00*
Tray, Celery, 11" Oblong, 2 Hobstars and Crosscuts	*325.00*
Tray, Celery, Acorn-Shaped, Rosettes and Crosscuts	*450.00*
Wineglass, Encore Pattern	*100.00*

A Bavarian immigrant, Lazarus Straus came to America along with his wife (Sara) and two sons (Isidor and Nathan) in 1852. He opened an import business selling china and glassware. Lazarus and his sons began cutting their own glass products around 1888 and usually marked every piece with "Straus Cut Glass" with a faceted gem within a circle.

TAYLOR BROTHERS COMPANY, INCORPO-RATED 1902–1915

Object	Price
Bowl, 9" Diameter, 4½" Tall, Ferns, Hobstars, and Stars	*$325.00*
Bowl, 9", Pentagonal, Palm Pattern	*500.00*
Casserole Dish with Cover, 8½", 7" Tall, Palm Pattern, Signed	*1750.00*
Casserole Dish with Hobstar Cover, 9", 2 Handles, Palm Pattern, Signed	*2000.00*
Casserole Dish with Cover, 2 Handles, Pedestal Base, Hobstar and Diamond Pattern, Signed	*2250.00*
Compote, 13½" Tall, 10" Diameter, Fine Diamond and Fan Pattern	*1350.00*
Nappy, 5", 1 Handle Tab, Large Fluted Star in Center, Small Hobstars and Crosscuts	*250.00*
Nappy, 6", 1 Tab Handle, Large Star Surrounded by Six Smaller Stars	*175.00*

Platter, 12" Round, Ruffled Edge, Palm Pattern, Signed *$375.00*
Tray, Ice Cream, 10" Oval, Scalloped, Hobstar Rings within a Crystal Band . . . . *.625.00*
Tray, 10½" Oval, Ruffled Edge, Arcadia Pattern . . . . *.500.00*
Tray, Oval, 11½" × 6½", Hobstars, Stars and Diamonds . . . . *.400.00*

The Taylor brothers, Albert and Lafayette, first formed Taylor Brothers and Williams along with John H. Williams in 1902. Williams moved on soon after and was dropped from the title. The company managed to stay afloat for only a short time and filed for bankruptcy in 1911. They hung on a little longer until World War I forced them out permanently. One of the most intersting designs of the company was that of cut casserole dishes; not many produced this particular object.

THATCHER BROTHERS   1886–1907

Object	*Price*

Bowl, 8¼", Notched Edge, Rosette and Foliage Design *$150.00*
Vase, 10½" Tall, Cylindrical, Diamond and Fan Design (Alternating Large Diamonds and Tiny Diamond Sections) *375.00*
Vase, 13" Tall, Circular Base, Stemmed, Vertically Ribbed Bulbous Midsection, Rosette and Foliage Design *525.00*

George Thatcher, who worked at the Boston & Sandwich Glass Company, the Mt. Washington Glass Company, and in the cutting department of Smith Brothers, joined his brother Richard to form Thatcher Brothers. They produced some cut glass before going out of business during the Panic of 1907.

TUTHILL CUT GLASS COMPANY   1900–1923

Object	*Price*

Basket, Oval, 9" Long, 5" Tall, Poppy Pattern *$875.00*
Basket, Rectangular, Intaglio and Brilliant Pattern *1050.00*
Basket, 21" Tall, Vintage Pattern *2800.00*
Bowl, 8", Rose Pattern *400.00*
Bowl, 8", Hobstar and Fan Design *450.00*
Bowl, 8", 2½" Tall, Rolled Rim, Bishop's Hat Design, Vintage Pattern *1350.00*
Bowl, 9½", Rex Pattern *350.00*
Candlestick, 12" Tall, Rosemere Pattern, Signed "Tuthill" *625.00*
Candy Box with Cover, 6" Round, 3" Tall, Vintage Pattern *1600.00*
Charger, 12½", Intaglio Strawberry Leaf and Fine Design *450.00*
Cologne Bottle with Sterling Silver Stopper, Wild Rose Pattern, Signed "Tuthill" . .*475.00*
Compote, 8¼" Top Diameter, 3½" Tall, Rosemere Pattern *325.00*
Compote, 6½" Diameter, 14½" Tall, Intaglio Vintage Pattern *225.00*
Cruet with Stopper, 8" Tall, Poppy Pattern, Signed "Tuthill" *450.00*
Cruet with Stopper, 10" Tall, Pedestal Base, Vintage Pattern, Signed "Tuthill" . . . . *.500.00*
Decanter with Stopper, 11" Tall, 6" Diameter, Intaglio and Brilliant Pattern, Signed "Tuthill" *900.00*
Decanter, with Stopper, 12" Tall, Handled, Primrose Pattern *525.00*
Lamp, 22" Tall, 12" Diameter Shade, Rex Pattern, Signed "Tuthill" *5500.00*
Mayonnaise Set, 2-Piece, 6" Hexagonal Bowl with Matching 6" Hexagonal Underplate, Phlox Pattern, Signed "Tuthill" *675.00*

Mayonnaise Set, 2-Piece, 5" Bowl with 6" Matching Underplate, Stars and Arcs Pattern, Signed "Tuthill" $475.00

Pitcher, 9" Tall, Rose Pattern, Signed "Tuthill" *1000.00*

Plate, Oval (5⅛" × 4½"), Rosemere Pattern, Signed "Tuthill" *275.00*

Plate, 7", Rex Pattern, Signed "Tuthill" *325.00*

Plate, 9", Quilted Diamond Pattern *350.00*

Plate, 10", Rosemere Pattern *700.00*

Plate, 10", Silver Rose Pattern *750.00*

Plate, 10", Wild Rose Pattern *400.00*

Platter, 12", Circular, Vintage Pattern, Signed "Tuthill" *675.00*

Platter, 13", Circular, Wild Rose Pattern, Signed "Tuthill" *750.00*

Platter, 14¼", Circular, Wild Rose Pattern, Signed "Tuthill" *850.00*

Punch Bowl, 13" Diameter, 16" Tall, Scalloped, Footed, and Engraved Grape Clusters and Leaves, Alternating Cross Cuts and Hobstars, Signed "Tuthill" *6000.00*

Punch Cup, 3½" Tall, Flared, Circular Foot, Stemmed, Vintage Pattern *150.00*

Toothpick Holder, 4" Tall, Stemmed, Wild Rose Pattern, Signed "Tuthill" *175.00*

Tray, 8½" Oval, Scalloped, Intaglio Floral Design *275.00*

Tray, Celery, Pinwheel Design, Signed "Tuthill" *450.00*

Vase, 10" Tall, Cylindrically Shaped (4" Diameter from Top to Bottom), Rex Pattern, Signed "Tuthill" *3000.00*

Vase, 11" Tall, Urn Shape, 2 Handles, Vintage Pattern *850.00*

Vase, 16½" Tall, Slender Form, Vintage Pattern *475.00*

Charles Guernsey Tuthill formed C. G. Tuthill & Company in 1900. His brother James and sister-in-law Susan joined him in 1902, and the name was amended to the Tuthill Cut Glass Company. The quality of their products was outstanding, and much of it was attributed to Susan, who served as somewhat of an inspector, constantly measuring depth, observing details, and not allowing glass that was in less than perfect condition to leave the factory.

As a result, Tuthill won numerous awards, and their products rivaled those of the best cut-glass producers in the country. They patented many patterns, including several floral and fruit designs: Tomato, Tiger Lily, Grape, Cosmos, Orchid, Grapefruit, etc.

UNGER BROTHERS   1901–1918

Object   *Price*

Bowl, 8", Shallow, Notched Edge, Fontenoy Pattern $175.00

Perfume Bottle with Sterling Silver Screw Top, 4" Tall, Russian Pattern *875.00*

Pitcher, Water, Notched Handle, Ruffled Ridge, Hobart Pattern *525.00*

Plate, 7", Six Hobstars in a Circular Pattern *125.00*

Plate, 12", Notched Edge, La Voy Pattern *375.00*

Tray, 14", Rectangular, Duchess Pattern *350.00*

Another small company with limited production, the two Unger brothers produced some silver housewares and cut glass before closing for good just after World War I.

CHAPTER 4

AMERICAN ART GLASS

In the midst of America's Brilliant Period, a new form of glass arose. This new "Art Nouveau" or "art glass" period began in the 1880s and lasted well into the early 20th century. Artists, designers, and other creative people who had not previously worked in glass turned their talents to some of the most unique and spectacular glass objects ever composed. Some make a legitimate argument that the Brilliant Period, coupled with the introduction of art glass, began in America with the Philadelphia Centennial Exhibition in 1876.

Like the expositions taking place in Europe, these events allowed glassmakers to display some of their finest pieces to date. The Philadelphia event featured a massive cut chandelier and a glass fountain that was 17 feet in height. The fountain was an ornamental design with cut-crystal prisms lit by 120 gas jets and surmounted by a glass figure of Liberty.

The Art Nouveau movement had its beginnings in France with Rousseau and Gallé (see Chapter 1, "Foreign Glass and Glassmaking"); however, America produced its own share of world-class designers. Two of the most famous American art glass sculptors were Louis Comfort Tiffany and Frederick Carder.

Tiffany was an American painter who visited Paris in 1889 and observed Gallé's work in person at the Exposition Universelle. He was also the son of the jewelry magnate who had founded Tiffany & Co., the famous jewelry store. Louis Comfort Tiffany began his work in glass by producing stained-glass windows without using stains or paints. The color, detail, and illusion were created within the glass itself by plating one layer of glass over another. He broadened his work to include lamps and was one of the first to experiment with iridescent glass. He named his iridescent products "Favrile" or "Tiffany Favrile." The word was derived from the English "fabrile," which means "belonging to a craftsman or his craft."

Iridescence is produced by firing on combinations of metallic salts that in turn create a wide variety of coloring effects. Luminous colors and metallic luster produced a silky smooth or delicate patina on Tiffany's glass. According to Tiffany, his main inspiration was the decayed objects made of Roman glass discovered in archaeological excavations.

With the great success of his works at the World's Exposition in Chicago in 1893, orders poured in and he further expanded his work to other art forms. Tableware, vases, flowers, and many other unique shapes were blown by Tiffany's skilled hands. His designs were never decorated or painted; they were made by combinations of different-colored glass during the blowing operation. His goods were displayed throughout Europe, including the 1900 Paris Exposition, which inspired young European artists to copy his style.

Frederick Carder was an apprentice of the famous English glass artisan John Northwood. Carder emigrated from Stourbridge, England, and founded the Steuben Glass Works in Corning, New York. Carder created several varieties of lustrous lead glass such as Aurene, an ornamental iridescent form. He sold Steuben to the

Corning Glass Works in 1918 but continued to produce some of the finest crystal forms in the world for Corning through 1936. Carder's glass was also exhibited at numerous national and international expositions, galleries, and museums.

Many others followed in the footsteps of Tiffany and Carder. So much experimentation took place that America invented more distinctive styles than all of Europe combined. Many American firms copied or attempted to reproduce popular designs of others, and at times the experimentation led to new creations.

In 1883, Joseph Locke, an Englishman employed by the New England Glass Company, was the first to obtain a patent for Amberina. In 1885, another Englishman, named Frederick Shirley, patented Burmese for the Mount Washington Glass Company. Burmese products were sent to Queen Victoria of England as gifts, and she was so impressed with the style that she ordered more. Mount Washington shared the formula with Thomas Webb & Sons of England, which also produced Burmese products. In 1886, Shirley also patented Pearl Satin Glass for Mount Washington. In 1887, Locke patented Agata Glass for New England Glass Co.

More patents followed for a huge variety of art styles, including Amethyst, Aurora, Cintra, Cluthra, Cranberry, Crown Milano, Custard, Intarsia, Lava, Mercury, Peach Blow, Slag, Rubina, Satin, and Spatter, to name just a few. See the individually priced categories as well as the Glossary for descriptions of these particular designs.

AMBERINA   NEW ENGLAND, LIBBEY, MOUNT WASHINGTON, TIFFANY, AND OTHERS; 1880S–1920

Object	Price
Basket, 7¹/₂" Tall, signed "Libbey"	.$1925.00
Bonbon Dish, 7" Oval, Shallow, Daisy and Button Pattern (Hobbs Brocunier)	.500.00
Bottle, Perfume, with Stopper, Signed "Libbey"	.875.00
Bowl, 2³/₄", 4¹/₂" Tall, Plated Amberina	.3500.00
Bowl, 3", Fluted, Plated Amberina	.3500.00
Bowl, 3", Scalloped, Fine Coloring, Plated Amberina	.5000.00
Bowl, 5¹/₄", Plated Amberina, Ruffled Top (New England Glass Co.)	.2100.00
Bowl, Finger, 5³/₈", 2¹/₂" Tall (New England Glass Co.)	.225.00
Bowl, 5³/₈", 2³/₄" Tall, with Scalloped Rim	.250.00
Bowl, Rose, 6", Hobnail	.350.00
Bowl, Melon, 7" Tall, Ribbed, 4–Footed	.450.00

"Amberina" art glass. Photo by Mark Pickvet.

Bowl, 7½", 3½" Tall, Plated Amberina, Scalloped Rim, White Lining, Paper Label "Aurora/NEGW" (New England Glass Co.) *$2800.00*

Bowl, 8", Scalloped, Plated Amberina *5500.00*

Bowl, Footed, Lustrous Rose, Old Iron Cross Mark (Imperial) *225.00*

Butter Dish, 4¾", Ribbed, Silverplated Base with Unicorn in Center, Plated Amberina .*2600.00*

Carafe, 6¼" Tall, Ruffled Tri-Cornered Top (New England Glass Co.) *325.00*

Carafe, 8" Tall, Hobnail *350.00*

Castor Set, 2 Cruets with Stoppers, Salt and Pepper Shakers with Pewter Tops, and Silverplated Tray (New England Glass Co.) *1500.00*

Celery Vase, 6½" Tall, Light Color, Diamond Quilted Pattern *250.00*

Champagne Glass, 6" Tall, with Hollow Stem (New England Glass Co.) *300.00*

Cheese Dish with Cover, 9½" Diameter, 8" Tall, Large Circles in Cover and Round Knob, Flared Rim (New England Glass Co.) *650.00*

Compote, 4¼" Diameter, 7" Tall, Crimped Rim, Diamond Quilted Pattern (New England Glass Co.) *700.00*

Compote, 5" Diameter, Signed "Libbey" *750.00*

Cordial (Gunderson-Pairpoint) *50.00*

Creamer, 4¾" Tall, Ribbed, Ribbed Feet, Hollow Knobby Stem, Signed "Libbey" .*1250.00*

Creamer, 2½" Tall, Plated Amberina (New England Glass Co.) *3500.00*

Creamer, 2⅝" Tall, Amber Handle, Scalloped, Inverted Thumbprint Pattern (New England) *425.00*

Creamer, 5" Tall, Pitcher-Style, Ribbed, Plated Amberina *5000.00*

Cruet, 6½" Tall with Faceted Stopper, Amber Handle, Plated Amberina *2600.00*

Cup, Punch, Diamond Quilted Pattern (New England Glass Co.) *325.00*

Cup, Punch, Plated Amberina (New England Glass Co.) *1800.00*

Dish, Canoe-Shaped, 8" Long, Daisy and Button Pressed Design *850.00*

Goblet, Rose Amber (Mt. Washington Glass Co.) *250.00*

Hat, 6" Wide *100.00*

Lamp Shade, 14", Plated Amberina (New England Glass Co.) *3750.00*

Lemonade, Plated Amberina *1400.00*

Mug, Barrel-Shaped, 2½" Tall with Thumbprint Pattern *200.00*

Mug, 7½" Tall, Reverse Color, Inverted Thumbprint Pattern *400.00*

Mug, Amber Handle, Ribbed, Plated Amberina *2250.00*

Parfait, Plated Amberina (New England Glass Co.) *1400.00*

Pitcher, Syrup, with Pewter Top, Inverted Thumbprint Pattern (New England Glass Co.) *450.00*

Pitcher, Syrup, with Top, 6" Tall, Plated Amberina (New England Glass Co.) *7000.00*

Pitcher, 7" Tall, Square Top, Inverted Thumbprint Pattern (New England Glass Co.) .*275.00*

Pitcher, 7" Tall, Cornered Spout, Plated Amberina (New England Glass Co.) *7250.00*

Pitcher, 7½" Tall, Ribbed, Inverted Thumbprint Pattern, Reverse Amberina Color, Signed "Libbey" *700.00*

Pitcher, Water, 8" Tall, Reverse Color Design *450.00*

Pitcher, 9½" Tall, Ruffled, Amber Handle, Inverted Thumbprint Pattern *325.00*

Pitcher, 10" Tall, Amber Handle, Inverted Thumbprint Pattern, Signed "Libbey" *425.00*

Pitcher, 12", Engraved Otus and Ephialtes Holding Mars Captive, Title Panel, Signed "J. Locke" *1100.00*

Punch Cup, 2½" Tall, Diamond Quilted Pattern (New England) *150.00*

Punch Cup, 2¾" Tall, Ribbed, Amber Handle, Plated Amberina *2000.00*

Salt and Pepper Shakers, Inverted Thumbprint Pattern (Mt. Washington Glass Co.) .*375.00*

Salt and Pepper Shakers, Diamond Quilt Pattern *225.00*

Salt and Pepper Shakers, Plated Amberina *5250.00*

Salt Shaker, Pewter Top, Reverse Amberina Color Pattern *200.00*

Sauce Dish, 5¹/₂" Square, Daisy and Button Pattern (Hobbs Brocunier) *$275.00*

Spittoon, Hourglass-Shaped with Ruffled Edge *350.00*

Spooner, Round with Scalloped Top and Square Mouth, Venetian Diamond Pattern (New England Glass Co.) *550.00*

Spooner, 5" Tall, Plated Amberina *2100.00*

Sugar, 4¹/₂" Tall, Ribbed, Ribbed Feet, Hollow Knobby Stem, Signed "Libbey" *1250.00*

Sugar, 2¹/₂" Tall, Plated Amberina (New England Glass Co.) *3500.00*

Sugar Shaker, 4" Tall, Butterfly on Lid, Inverted Thumbprint Pattern *450.00*

Swan, 5" Tall (Pairpoint-Bryden) *60.00*

Toothpick Holder, Reversed Color Pattern *175.00*

Toothpick Holder, 2" Tall, Ribbed, Plated Amberina *2750.00*

Toothpick Holder, 2¹/₂" Tall, Round with Square Rim, Diamond Quilted Pattern (New England Glass Co.) *150.00*

Tumbler, Inverted Thumbprint Pattern *100.00*

Tumbler, Inverted Thumbprint Pattern, Signed "Libbey" *125.00*

Tumbler, Ribbed, 5" Tall, Plated Amberina *2000.00*

Tumbler, Swirled *125.00*

Tumbler, Swirled, 3³/₄" Tall, Gold Amber (New England Glass Co.) *150.00*

Tumbler, Diamond Pattern, Fuchsia Shading at the Top (New England Glass Co.) . . .*225.00*

Tumbler, Plated Amberina (New England Glass Co.) *2100.00*

Vase, 4" Tall, Cylindrically Shaped (New England) *150.00*

Vase, 4¹/₈" Tall, Plated Amberina (New England Glass Co.) *2750.00*

Vase, 4⁵/₈" Tall, Pressed Stork Pattern, Scalloped Top (New England Glass Co.) *600.00*

Vase, Lily, 6¹/₄" Tall, Plated Amberina (New England Glass Co.) *2300.00*

Vase, Swirled, Satinized, Reverse Amberina Color Pattern, Enameled Gold Flowers *1500.00*

Vase, 7" Tall, with Tri-Cornered Top (New England Glass Co.) *500.00*

Vase, 7" Tall, Cylindrically Shaped, Ruffled, Inverted Thumbprint Pattern *150.00*

Vase, 7" Tall, Jack-in-the-Pulpit Style, Fuchsia to Amber Shading *475.00*

Vase, Lily, 7¹/₂" Tall, Signed "Libbey" *600.00*

Vase, 7³/₄" Tall, Applied Swirled Circular Domed Foot, Drinking Horn Shaped with Coiled Tail (Libbey) *1250.00*

Vase, 8" Tall, Lily Shaped, Plated Amberina *2500.00*

Vase, 8¹/₈" Tall, Applied Crystal Spiral Stem *250.00*

Vase, 8³/₄" Tall, Cylindrically Shaped, Swirled *175.00*

Vase, 9¹/₂" Tall, 2-Handled, Signed "Libbey" *725.00*

Vase, 10" Tall, Jack-in-the-Pulpit Style, Signed "Libbey" *750.00*

Vase, 10¹/₂" Tall, Swirled, Amber Rigaree, Footed *225.00*

Vase, 10¹/₂" Tall, Lily-Shaped, Metal Stand, Plated Amberina *4250.00*

Vase, 11" Tall, Signed "Libbey" *1150.00*

Vase, 23¹/₂" Tall, Ribbed, Knob Stem (New England) *1600.00*

Whiskey Glass, 2⁵/₈" Tall, Diamond Quilted Pattern (New England Glass Co.) *125.00*

"Amberina" is a single-layered style of glass created by the New England Glass Company in 1883. Joseph Locke was responsible for much of its development. "Amberina" is characterized by an amber color at the bottom of an object that gradually shades into red at the top. The shading could very well change with each new object. The red might be a brilliant ruby red, a deep violet or purple sometimes was referred to as fuchsia, and genuine gold was at times mixed with the transparent amber. The New England Glass Company did place a high-quality, vibrantly colored, thick Amberina plating on some of their wares. These particular items are very rare and valuable.

"Amberina" was made in both art objects and functional tableware. The style was continued under Edward Libbey when the company was purchased by him and moved to Toledo, Ohio. Both the New England Glass Works and Libbey can be found on many examples. "Amberina" was most popular in the 1880s and was revived by Libbey from 1917 to 1920, but it flopped after World War I.

In the meantime, Libbey sold some patent rights, including "Amberina" to others, such as Tiffany. Varieties of "Amberina" have been reproduced by several companies and individuals. Reproductions exist too, as well as less valuable flashed-on and enameled examples. Flashed-on and enameled items usually include metal oxides that produce an iridescent finish or enamel that flecks or eventually peels.

The original "Amberina" has no such iridescence and was rarely enameled.

AURENE   STEUBEN GLASS WORKS, 1904–1933

Object	Price
Atomizer, 5", Ribbed, Iridescent Gold	$250.00
Basket, 5" Tall, Ruffled, Gold with Light Green Highlights	1250.00
Bowl, Finger 3", Red, Signed, "F. Carder"	5000.00
Bowl, 9", 3½" Tall, Footed, Gold	475.00
Bowl, 10", Blue	525.00
Bowl, Oval (4" × 2"), Calcite and Gold	150.00
Candlestick, 4¾" Tall, Gold	500.00
Candlestick, 8" Tall, Gold, Marked "Aurene 686"	550.00
Candlestick, 10" Tall, Air Twist Stem, Blue	800.00
Candlestick, 12" Tall, Tulip Shape, Gold	750.00
Cologne Bottle with Stopper, 5½" Tall, Bell-Shaped, Iridescent Gold, Marked "Aurene 1818"	650.00
Cologne Bottle with Stopper, 6½" Tall, Ribbed, Iridescent Gold	850.00
Compote, 6", Blue	1150.00
Compote, 8", Gold	1000.00
Cordial, 7" Tall, Blue	525.00
Darner, Stocking, Blue	750.00
Darner, Stocking, Gold	600.00
Decanter with Stopper, 10¾" Tall Dimpled Body, Circular Foot, Gold, Marked "Aurene 2759"	650.00
Goblet, 8" Tall, Venetian Style, Gold	500.00
Perfume Bottle with Stopper, 5⅞" Tall, Blue	725.00
Perfume Bottle with Stopper, 8" Tall, Blue, Signed	750.00
Salt Dip, 2" Tall, Pedestal Foot, Gold, Signed	250.00
Salt Dip, 8 Ribs, Blue	400.00
Shade, 4½" Tall, Iridescent Green with Calcite Interior, Platinum Foliage Design	1150.00
Shade, 4½" Tall, Tulip-Shaped, Gold	250.00
Shade, 6½" × 6", Green with Calcite Interior, Platinum Foliage Design	1200.00
Shade, Iridescent Brown with Calcite Lining, Blue Drape Design	500.00
Shade, Iridescent Light Brown with Gold Leaves and Threading, Gold Lining	350.00
Sherbet with Matching Underplate, Gold	400.00
Tray, Oblong Stretched Border, Footed, Blue, Signed "Carder"	800.00
Vase, 5" Tall, Blue, Signed	600.00
Vase, 5½" Tall, Iridescent Gold with Green and White Floral Design	2000.00

GLASSWARE

"Aurene" art glass. Courtesy of the Corning Museum of Glass.

Vase, 6" Tall, Jack-in-the-Pulpit Style, Gold *$1350.00*
Vase, 6" Tall, Stick Style, Iridescent Blue *475.00*
Vase, 6" Tall, Iridescent Gold *450.00*
Vase, 6¼" Tall, Stump-Shaped, 3-Pronged, Gold, Signed *625.00*
Vase, 6½" Tall, 3-Stemmed, Blue *1000.00*
Vase, 6¾" Tall, Iridescent Gold with Calcite Interior *500.00*
Vase, 7" Tall, Gold with Green Foliage and White Flowers *3350.00*
Vase, 9" Tall, 9" Top Diameter, Ruffled, Iridescent Gold *1100.00*
Vase, 9" Tall, 3-Handled, Gold *825.00*
Vase, 10" Tall, Blue Button Design, Signed "F. Carder" *1500.00*
Vase, 10" Tall, Blue, Paneled Design *1250.00*
Vase, 10½" Tall, Green with Gold Interior, Rim, and Heart and Vine Decoration ...*3600.00*
Vase, 11" Tall, Fan-Shaped, Iridescent Gold *1250.00*
Vase with Holder, 4" Tall, Gold *525.00*
Wineglass, 6" Tall, Air Twist Stem, Gold *550.00*

"Aurene" was produced in five basic colors: blue, brown, gold, green, and red. It remains as Steuben's most desirable and popular colored-glass design; however, it is quite scarce today. "Aurene" is characterized by an iridescent sheen applied by spraying on various metallic salts and other chemical mixtures. Base colors were ordinarily clear, amber, or topaz. Matte finishes were applied by spraying on tin or iron chloride solutions. Alabaster and calcite were necessary for the green and red colors.

BOSTON & SANDWICH GLASS COMPANY
1820S–1880S

Object	*Price*
Basket, Bride's, 9" Diameter, Overshot, Twisted Handle, Crystal	*$225.00*
Bottle with Screw-on Cap, 2½" Tall, Marbleized Cobalt and White	*125.00*

Bottle, 8" Tall, Triple Cased, with Cut Windows *$175.00*
Bowl, 9", Lacy Design, Peacock Eye Coloring *125.00*
Bowl with Matching Underplate, 3" Tall, Ruffled, Canary Yellow *125.00*
Candlestick, 1⅞" Tall, Miniature, Crystal *30.00*
Candlestick, 6¾" Tall, Hexagonal Base, Clambroth, Dolphin Design *450.00*
Candlestick, 7" Tall, Circular Base, Petal Socket, Canary Yellow *250.00*
Candlestick, 7" Tall, Circular Diamond Point Base, Petal Socket, Canary Yellow ...*300.00*
Candlestick, 7" Tall, Clambroth, Petal and Loop Design *175.00*
Candlestick, 7" Tall, Hexagonal, Amber *350.00*
Candlestick, 7¼" Tall, Hexagonal Base, Green Socket, Clambroth Foot and Stem ...*650.00*
Candlestick, 7½" Tall, Hexagonal, Amber *375.00*
Candlestick, 7½" Tall, Hexagonal Base, Amethyst *475.00*
Candlestick, 9" Tall, Cobalt Petal Socket, Clambroth Column *250.00*
Candlestick, 9¼" Tall, Hexagonal Base, Light Blue *350.00*
Candlestick, 9¾" Tall, Cobalt Socket, Clambroth Base and Stem, Acanthus Leaf Design
....*400.00*
Candlestick, 10¼" Tall, Single Step Base, Clambroth, Dolphin Design *450.00*
Candlestick, 10¼" Tall, Single Step Base, Green, Dolphin Design *650.00*
Candlestick, 10¼" Tall, Single Step Base, Blue Socket, Gilded, Clambroth, Dolphin Design
....*750.00*
Candlestick, 10¾" Tall, Double Step Base, Clambroth, Dolphin Design *400.00*
Candlestick, 11½" Tall, Crucifix Design, Canary Yellow *350.00*
Candlestick, 11½" Tall, Crucifix Design, Green *550.00*
Candlestick, 12" Tall, Hexagonal, Dark Blue *400.00*
Candlestick, Clambroth with Translucent Blue Acanthus Leaves *600.00*
Cheese Dish with Cover, 8", Crystal Overshot *300.00*
Claret Glass, 4½" Tall, Craquelle Finish with Ruby Threading *75.00*
Claret Glass, 5" Tall, Canary Yellow with Threading *150.00*
Cologne Bottle with Ball Stopper, 8" Tall, Square, Crystal Overshot *200.00*
Epergne, 12" Tall, Ruffled Bowl with Ruby Threading, Cut Circular Tray *250.00*
Fishbowl, 16½" Tall, Ruffled Crystal Base with Dolphin's Tail, Crystal Bowl with Etched
Fish and Plants *650.00*
Ice Cream Dish, 4¼" Diameter, 4¼" Tall, Circular Pedestal Base, White Casing with Ruby
Threads *175.00*
Ice Cream Tray, 13" Long, Crystal Overshot *150.00*
Jam Jar, 3½" Tall, Opaque Blue, Bear Design *400.00*
Jug, 6¾" Tall, Barrel-Shaped, Etched Bees and Floral Design, Crystal with Ruby Threading
....*175.00*
Lamp, Kerosene, Jade Green with White Overlay *5000.00*
Paperweight, 2⅜" Diameter, Latticino with Pears, Cherries and Green Leaves *550.00*
Paperweight, 2½" Diameter, Blue Poinsettia, Green Stem, Jeweled Leaves on White
Latticino *750.00*
Paperweight, 2½" Diameter, White Latticino Basket with Multicolored Flowers and Green
Leaves *1000.00*
Paperweight, 2⅝" Diameter, White Latticino with Flowers, Green Leaves, Blue and White
Canes *400.00*
Paperweight, 2⅝" Diameter, Latticino with Pink Poinsettia and Green Leaves *300.00*
Paperweight, 2¾" Diameter, 12-Ribbed Blue Dahlia Petals, Latticino Basket, Yellow Cane,
Emerald Green Stem *350.00*
Paperweight, 2¾" Diameter, 6-Petaled Flower and Leaves *650.00*
Paperweight, 2⅞" Diameter, Candy Cane Design *175.00*
Paperweight, 3" Diameter, Jasper with Jenny Lind Sulphide Bust *225.00*

Left: Boston and Sandwich Co. art glass. Photo by Mark Pickvet. Right: Boston and Sandwich Co. art glass. Courtesy of the Sandwich Glass Museum.

Paperweight, 3" Diameter, Sulphide Bird Design, Red, White, and Blue $275.00

Pipe, 15" Long, Crystal with White Loopings *400.00*

Pitcher, 6½" Tall, Amber Overshot, Green Reeded Handle *250.00*

Pitcher, 8½" Tall, Tortoiseshell Design, Amber Handle *375.00*

Pitcher, 10½" Tall, Blue Overshot, Amber Lip and Handle *450.00*

Pitcher, 11" Tall, Pink Overshot with Crystal Handle *500.00*

Pitcher, 12" Tall, Pear-Shaped, Fluted Rim, Crystal Crackle Design *350.00*

Punch Bowl with Cover, 11" Tall, Overshot, Globe-Shaped, Fruit Stem Finial *500.00*

Salt Dip, Boat-Shaped, 3½" Long, Blue Paddle Wheeler, Marked "Lafayet" on Wheels, Signed "B. & S. Glass Co." *550.00*

Salt Dip, Rectangular (2⅞" × 1⅞"), Oval Knobs on Base, Scrolled, Stippled, Transparent Green, French Lacy Design *225.00*

Salt Dip, Rectangular (2⅞" × 1⅞"), 4-Footed, Gothic Arches on Feet, Opalescent Blue *225.00*

Salt Shaker, 2¼" Tall, Barrel-Shaped, Threaded Rim with Pewter Top, Dark Blue, Sunburst on Base, Marked "patented December 25, 1877" *175.00*

Tankard, 7¼" Tall, Engraved Cattails and Lilies, Amber with Threading *325.00*

Tankard, 7½" Tall, Engraved Cattails, Water Lilies, and Crane, Crystal with Ruby Threading *300.00*

Tankard, 9" Tall, Dark Amber Overshot *500.00*

Tankard, 11" Tall, Crystal Overshot, Reeded Handle *150.00*

Tieback Knob, Cobalt to Clear Coloring over Mercury *100.00*

Tieback Knob, Cranberry to Clear Coloring over Mercury *100.00*

Tumbler, 3¼" Tall, Engraved Cattails and Lilies, Crystal with Ruby Threading *125.00*

Tumbler, 3¾" Tall, Engraved Foliage, Crystal with Ruby Threading *125.00*

Tumbler, 5½" Tall, Canary Yellow with Threading *175.00*

Tumbler, 5½" Tall, Crystal with Blue Threading *175.00*

Tumbler, 6" Tall, Engraved Floral Design on Top, Cranberry Threading on Bottom . .*125.00*

Vase, 4" Tall, Enameled Floral Design *125.00*

Vase, 6½" Tall, Bluerina (Blue to Amber Shading), Floral Design *300.00*

Vase, 8¹/₂" Tall, Celery, Scalloped, Hour Glass *$100.00*
Vase, 9¹/₄" Tall, Flared, 3 Scrolled Gilded Feet, Opaque White with Red Enameled Leaves
....*300.00*
Vase, 10" Tall, Cranberry Cut to Clear Roundels *350.00*

One of America's early successful firms, Boston and Sandwich was noted most for "Sandwich" or pressed glass from which its name is derived. They manufactured large amounts of this new hand-pressed glass but occasionally created objects of art in the form of lacy glass in the French style, paperweights, opal wares, engraved glass, and so on.

See additional listings under "Mary Gregory."

BURMESE MOUNT WASHINGTON WORKS AND PAIRPOINT
MANUFACTURING COMPANY, 1880S–1950S

Object	*Price*
Basket, Thorn Handle, 1950s (Gunderson)	*$325.00*
Bell, 11³/₄" Tall, Emerald Green Handle	*2500.00*
Biscuit Jar, Barrel-Shaped, Silverplated Top, Oak Leaves and Acorn Design, Paper Label	*1200.00*
Bowl, 4", Fluted Edge	*275.00*
Bowl, 4³/₄", Ice Cream, Ruffled	*300.00*
Bowl, 6¹/₂", Footed, Applied Burmese Decoration	*1500.00*
Bowl, 7", Curled Feet (Gunderson)	*325.00*
Bowl, 12", Scalloped	*950.00*
Bowl, Rose, Gold Handles, Ivy Decor, Dickens Verse	*2500.00*
Bowl, Rose, 2¹/₂", Hexagonal Top	*225.00*
Castor Set, 5-Piece, Salt and Pepper Shakers with Silverplated Tops, 2 Globe-Shaped Cruets with Pointed Stoppers, Footed Silverplated Stand	*2750.00*
Cracker Jar with Cover, 6¹/₂" Tall, Acidized Finish, Applied Handles	*1250.00*
Creamer, 4" Tall, 3¹/₂" Diameter, Footed	*1200.00*
Creamer, 5¹/₂" Tall, Pitcher Style, Hobnail Pattern	*2000.00*
Cruet with Stopper, 7" Tall, Acid or Gloss Finish	*1100.00*
Cup, Satin Shading	*225.00*
Epergne, 2 Circular Bowls, 4" Tall, Ruffled, Enameled Flowers, 4-Footed Silverplated Stand	*3500.00*
Ewer, 9" Tall, Squat Dome, Enameled Decoration	*1750.00*
Hat, 3¹/₂" × 2³/₄", Upside Down (Bryden)	*125.00*
Lamp, Crimped Top and Plate, Fairy (Gunderson)	*500.00*
Mustard Pot, Silver Cover, Acidized, Ribbed	*250.00*
Perfume Bottle with Cut Stopper	*275.00*
Pig, Miniature, ⁷/₈" Long (Gunderson)	*150.00*
Pitcher, 4³/₄" Tall, Square Lip, Yellow Reeded Handle, Enameled Mums	*700.00*
Pitcher, 5" Tall, Inverted Thumbprint Pattern, Egyptian with Bow in Chariot Design	*1250.00*
Pitcher, Syrup, with Silver Lid, 6" Tall, Enameled Decoration	*1500.00*
Pitcher, 6³/₄" Tall, Acidized, Ivy Design, Dickens Verse	*3500.00*
Pitcher, 9" Tall, Acidized, Gold-Outlined Foliage Design	*3500.00*
Pitcher, Tankard Style, Acidized, Gloss Finish	*1000.00*
Pitcher, Water, Satin Finish	*2000.00*
Plate, 6"	*125.00*

Plate, Acidized, Floral Design *$325.00*
Salt and Pepper Shakers, Barrel-Shaped, Pewter Tops *450.00*
Saucer, Satin Shading *175.00*
Shade, 5¼" × 3¾", Satin Finish *250.00*
Sugar Shaker, 4" Tall, Globe-Shaped, Leaves and Berries Design *850.00*
Toothpick Holder, Circular Base, Square Top, Enameled Floral Design *550.00*
Toothpick Holder, Bowl-Shaped, Hexagonal Top, Satin Finish *325.00*
Toothpick Holder, Diamond Quilted Pattern *425.00*
Top Hat, 1⅝" Tall, Gloss Finish *600.00*
Tumbler, 3⅞" Tall, Satin Finish *200.00*
Tumbler, 4" Tall, Dull or Shiny Finish (Gunderson) *200.00*
Tumbler, Thomas Hood Versed *1500.00*
Vase, 3" Tall, Bulbous, 3-Petal Folded Rim *250.00*
Vase, 4" Tall, Ruffled, Fluted Base *325.00*
Vase, 4" Tall, Ruffled, Acidized, Enameled Foliage Design, 4-Footed Silverplated Holder
....*800.00*
Vase, 5" Tall, Ruffled, Footed *325.00*
Vase, 5" Tall, Enameled Yellow Handles, Pink and Yellow Enameled Floral Design .*2000.00*
Vase, 6" Tall, Lily-Shaped, Paper Label *750.00*
Vase, 6¼" Tall, Jack-in-the-Pulpit Design, Enameled *700.00*
Vase, 7" Tall, Lily-Shaped, Paper Label *800.00*
Vase, 7" Tall, Acidized, Hobnail Pattern (Gunderson) *300.00*
Vase, 8" Tall, Lily-Shaped, Paper Label *850.00*
Vase, 9" Tall, Crimped, Jack-in-the-Pulpit Design *750.00*
Vase, 10" Tall, Lily-Shaped, Paper Label *900.00*
Vase, 10¾" Tall, Enameled Daisy and Butterfly Design, Versed (Poetry) *2500.00*
Vase, 11¾" Tall, Enameled Daisy and Butterfly *2750.00*

Burmese art glass. Photo by Mark Pickvet.

Vase, 11³/₄" Tall, Acidized, Enameled, Scroll and Floral Design *$2200.00*
Vase, 11³/₄" Tall, Enameled Daisy and Butterfly Design, Montgomery Verse *2750.00*
Vase, 12" Tall, Gloss Finish, Jack-in-the-Pulpit Design *1400.00*
Vase, 12" Tall, Enameled Daisy and Butterfly Design Montgomery Verse *3000.00*
Vase, 12" Tall, Ibis and Pyramid Design *4000.00*
Vase, 12" Tall, Crimped, Folded Rim, Floral Stem, Jack-in-the-Pulpit Design *1000.00*
Vase, 12" Tall, Lily-Shaped, Paper Label *950.00*
Vase, 13¹/₂" Tall, Ruffled Foot and Top *1250.00*
Vase, 14" Tall, Lily-Shaped, Paper Label *1000.00*
Vase, 15" Tall, 2-Handled, Enameled Yellow to Pink *6000.00*
Vase, 17¹/₂" Tall, Egyptian Man with Staff Design *5500.00*
Vase, 24" Tall, Lily-Shaped, Paper Label *1500.00*
Vase, 26" Tall, Slender, Yellow to Pale Pink Coloring *1250.00*

"Burmese" is characterized by a gradual shading of bright or canary yellow at the base to salmon pink at the top. It is also thin and rather brittle. The colors were created by the addition of expensive elements, namely, gold and uranium. The most common decorations applied were gold enamels (real gold mixed with acid) and popular cut patterns.

Mount Washington actually obtained an exclusive patent on this pattern in 1885. The technique of creating "Burmese" continued when Pairpoint purchased Mount Washington, including reissues in the 1950s. Reproductions are difficult if not impossible to make because of the federal government's restrictions on the use of uranium.

CHOCOLATE INDIANA TUMBLER AND GOBLET COMPANY, 1900–1903

Object   *Price*
Berry Set, 8" Diameter Fruit Bowl with 6 Sauce Dishes, Leaf Pattern *$550.00*
Bowl, Fruit, 8" Diameter *150.00*
Bowl, Fruit, 9¹/₄" Diameter, Cactus Pattern *110.00*
Bowl, Oval, 8¹/₄" × 5¹/₄", Geneva Pattern *100.00*
Butter Dish with Cover, Cactus Pattern *250.00*
Butter Dish with Cover, Pedestal, Cactus Pattern *450.00*
Butter Dish with Cover, 4" Diameter, Dewey Pattern *200.00*
Compote, 4¹/₂" Diameter, 3¹/₂" Tall, Geneva Pattern *190.00*
Compote, 5¹/₄" Diameter, 5" Tall, Cactus Pattern *200.00*
Compote, 6" Diameter, Melrose Pattern with Scalloped Rim *350.00*
Compote, 8¹/₄" Diameter, Cactus Pattern *250.00*
Creamer, Cactus Pattern *110.00*
Creamer, Cord Drapery Pattern *125.00*
Creamer, Leaf Pattern *100.00*
Creamer, Shuttle Pattern *90.00*
Creamer, Stirgil Pattern, Large (6" Tall) *125.00*
Cruet with Stopper, Cactus Pattern *230.00*
Cruet with Stopper, Leaf Pattern *215.00*
Fernery, 3-Footed, Fenton Village Pattern *225.00*

Hatpin Box, Orange Tree Pattern *$325.00*
Jelly Dish with Cover, Cord Drapery Pattern *200.00*
Lamp, Kerosene, Wild Rose Pattern *300.00*
Mug, Cactus Pattern *100.00*
Mug, Herringbone Pattern *90.00*
Mug, Shuttle Pattern *110.00*
Nappy, Triangular, Handled, Leaf Pattern *90.00*
Nappy, Handled, Masonic Pattern *125.00*
Pitcher, Syrup, with Lid, Cactus Pattern *175.00*
Pitcher, Syrup, with Lid, Cord Drapery Pattern *350.00*
Pitcher, Water, Cord Drapery Pattern *350.00*
Pitcher, Water, Deer Pattern *500.00*
Pitcher, Water, Feather Pattern *800.00*
Pitcher, Water, Heron Pattern *350.00*
Pitcher, Water, Ruffled Eye Pattern *550.00*
Pitcher, Water, Squirrel Pattern *450.00*
Pitcher, Water, Wild Rose Pattern *475.00*
Relish, Oval (8" × 5"), Leaf Pattern *100.00*
Salt Shaker, Leaf Pattern *150.00*
Sauce Dish, Cactus Pattern *75.00*
Sauce Dish, Dolphin Pattern *375.00*
Sauce Dish, Geneva Pattern *70.00*
Sauce Dish, Leaf Pattern *60.00*
Sauce Dish, Tassel Pattern *200.00*
Sauce Dish, Wild Rose Pattern *125.00*
Spooner, Austrian Pattern *225.00*
Spooner, Cactus Pattern *125.00*
Spooner, Cord Drapery Pattern *110.00*
Spooner, Dewey Pattern *110.00*
Spooner, Leaf Pattern *150.00*
Spooner, Wild Rose Pattern *175.00*
Sugar, Cord Drapery Pattern *125.00*
Sugar with Cover, Cactus Pattern *200.00*
Sugar with Cover, Chrysanthemum Pattern *450.00*
Sugar with Cover, Leaf Pattern *150.00*
Sweetmeat Dish with Cover, Cactus Pattern *500.00*
Toothpick Holder, Cactus Pattern *125.00*
Toothpick Holder, Geneva Pattern *175.00*
Toothpick Holder, Picture Frame Design *850.00*
Tray, 11" Long, Leaf Pattern *150.00*
Tray, Oval (10¾" × 5½"), Leaf Pattern *125.00*
Tray, Serpentine, Dewey Pattern *75.00*
Tumbler, Biscuit Pattern *225.00*
Tumbler, Cactus Pattern *100.00*
Tumbler, Cord Drapery Pattern *350.00*
Tumbler, Leaf Pattern *90.00*
Tumbler, Sawtooth Pattern *110.00*
Tumbler, Shuttle Pattern *125.00*
Tumbler, Wild Rose Pattern *150.00*
Vase, 5¾" Tall, Fleur-de-lis Pattern *300.00*
Vase, Scalloped Flange Pattern *100.00*

"Chocolate" refers to the color of this earthy opaque glass. Variances are from a light tan to caramel to a deep chocolate brown. The dark chocolate color is most desirable and may sell for a 10–20% premium above lighter colors. Lighter "Chocolate" articles are sometimes incorrectly referred to as "Caramel Slag Glass."

Aside from a few novelty items such as glass animals, "Chocolate" was produced in numerous patterns, such as "Austrian," "Cactus," "Dewey," "Geneva," "Melrose," "Shuttle," and many others, including several floral and leaf designs.

COIN GLASS   CENTRAL GLASS COMPANY, 1890S

Object	Price
Bowl, 8", Oval, Frosted Coins	*$325.00*
Bread Tray, Frosted Half Dollars and Silver Dollars	*425.00*
Butter Dish, Half Dollars and Silver Dollars	*675.00*
Cake Stand, 10" Diameter, Frosted Silver Dollars	*500.00*
Cake Stand, 10" Diameter, Clear Silver Dollars	*350.00*
Champagne Glass, Frosted Dimes	*425.00*
Compote, 5½" Diameter, 5½" Tall, Frosted Dimes and Quarters	*300.00*
Compote, 6½" Diameter, 8" Tall, Frosted Dimes and Quarters	*325.00*
Compote, 7" Diameter, 5¾" Tall, Frosted Dimes and Quarters	*500.00*
Compote, 8" Diameter, 11¼" Tall, Frosted Coins	*675.00*
Compote with Cover, 6" Diameter, 9½" Tall, Silver Dollar	*475.00*
Compote with Cover, 6⅞" Tall, Frosted Coins	*600.00*
Compote with Cover, 8" Diameter, 11½" Tall, Frosted Coins	*700.00*
Compote with Cover, 8" Diameter, High Pedestal, 1892 Quarters and Half Dollars	*500.00*
Compote with Cover, 9" Diameter, Frosted Coins	*700.00*
Cruet with Stopper, 5½" Tall, Frosted Coins	*675.00*
Epergne, Frosted Silver Dollars	*1600.00*
Goblet, Frosted Dimes	*350.00*
Lamp, Kerosene, Handled, Clear Quarters in Base	*450.00*
Lamp, Kerosene, Pedestal Base, Frosted Quarters	*650.00*
Lamp, Milk Glass, 8" Tall, Columbian Coin	*425.00*
Mug, Frosted Coins	*450.00*
Pickle Dish, Oval, 7½" × 3¾", Clear Coins	*275.00*
Pitcher, Water, Frosted Coins	*650.00*
Relish, Frosted Coins	*275.00*
Salt Shaker with Top	*175.00*
Sauce Dish, 4" Diameter, Frosted Quarters	*225.00*
Spooner, Frosted Quarters	*400.00*
Sugar with Cover, Frosted Coins	*500.00*
Toothpick Holder, Clear Coins	*250.00*
Tumbler, Frosted Dollar in Base	*225.00*
Vase, Clear Dimes	*200.00*
Vase, Frosted Quarters	*375.00*
Vase, Clear Quarters	*325.00*
Wineglass, Frosted Half Dimes	*600.00*

The first "Coin Glass" was made in 1892, the centennial year of the United States Mint. Silver dollars, half dollars, quarters, twenty-cent pieces, dimes, and half dimes were reproduced in glass relief and then placed on each article. The coins in relief were usually frosted on clear crystal glass but clear, amber, red, and gold examples were also produced.

The patterns were not identical to the actual minted coins; however, five short months after production, they were outlawed by the U.S. government as being a form of counterfeiting. Other medallions were allowed, such as Christopher Columbus ("Columbian Coin Glass"), coats-of-arms, and other foreign explorers ("Foreign Coin Glass"). Numerous coin examples have been made since by such makers as Fostoria, Avon, and others (see the chapter on Modern Glassware).

CONSOLIDATED LAMP AND GLASS COMPANY   1890S–EARLY 1900S

Object	Price
Butter Dish with Cover, White with Gold Trim	$100.00
Butter Dish with Cover, Pink, Florette Pattern	200.00
Candlestick, Hummingbird Design	100.00
Cookie Jar, Pink with Silverplate	275.00
Cruet with Stopper, White	225.00
Lamp, Miniature, Enameled Floral Design	325.00
Lamp, Miniature, Various Leaf and Scrolling	375.00
Lamp, 8½" Tall, Pink, Guttate Pattern	375.00
Lamp, 10½" Tall, Enameled Daisies	450.00
Lamp, 11" Tall, Milk Glass with Blue Floral Design	475.00
Lamp, 11" Tall, Avocado Green with Yellow Scrolling	450.00
Lamp, Oil, 12" Tall, Florette Pattern	500.00
Lamp, 14" Tall, Apricot with Gilded Edging, Enameled Blue Floral Design	650.00
Lamp, 15" Tall, Pink with White Floral Design, Gilded Edging	750.00
Mustard Dish, Pink, Florette Pattern	125.00
Pitcher, Syrup, with Silverplated Rim, Blue	275.00
Pitcher, Water, White, Guttate Pattern	100.00
Pitcher, Water, White with Gold Trim, Guttate Pattern	125.00
Pitcher, Water, Yellow Casing, Guttate Pattern	350.00
Pitcher, Water, 7¼" Tall, Pink, Florette Pattern	300.00
Salt and Pepper Shakers with Tops, Pink Casing, Guttate Pattern	125.00
Salt and Pepper Shakers with Tops, Pink, Florette Pattern	150.00
Spooner, Pink, Florette Pattern	175.00
Sugar Dish, Pink, Florette Pattern	125.00
Sugar Shaker with Top, Pink Casing, Guttate Pattern	175.00
Sugar Shaker with Top, Pink, Florette Pattern	200.00
Toothpick Holder, Yellow, Florette Pattern	100.00
Tumbler, Pink Casing, Guttate Pattern	60.00
Vase, Florentine, Milk White Color	90.00
Vase, 8¼" Tall, Frosted Grasshoppers on Green Background	100.00
Vase, Pinecone Design, Opal Blue Color	110.00

Consolidated is noted most for lamps and glass blown under the "Florette" and "Guttate" pattern names. Several color styles are apparent on much of their wares, including blue, green, pink, white, and yellow; many are in opaque art styles, some are trimmed in gold, and others have either satin or gloss finishes. A few articles were even made in apricot, pigeon blood, and gilded forms. Nearly everything the company produced was functional tableware or lighting.

CORALENE MOUNT WASHINGTON GLASS WORKS, 1880S–1890S

Object	Price
Bowl, Rose, 3" Tall, 4½" Diameter, Crimped, Amber Foot, Pink with Yellow Seaweed Design	$400.00
Decanter with Stopper, 10" Tall, Yellow Seaweed Decoration	450.00
Mug, 2" Tall, Orange Seaweed with Turquoise Handle	125.00
Pitcher, 7½" Tall, Orange and Green Coral, Orange Handle	275.00
Pitcher, 8" Tall, Blue and Yellow Coral Design	600.00
Pitcher, Water, 9½" Tall, Blue and Yellow Seaweed, White Handle, Blue Inner Casing	750.00
Toothpick Holder, Yellow Seaweed with White Shading	300.00
Tumbler, 4" Tall, Yellow Seaweed with Pink Shading	225.00
Tumble-Up, Carafe with Lid, White Coral on Light Pink Cranberry	325.00
Vase, 5" Tall, Yellow and Green Coral on a Dark Brown Background	250.00
Vase, 5¾" Tall, Blue with Beaded Yellow Seaweed, White Inside	575.00
Vase, 6" Tall, Ruffled, Blue Coral Design with White Floral Beading	175.00
Vase, 6" Tall, Mother-of-Pearl, Floral and Sprayed Beading Design	550.00
Vase, 7" Tall, Footed, Tan Satin Design	750.00
Vase, 8½" Tall, Flared Rim, Yellow Seaweed	375.00
Vase, 9" Tall, Urn-Shaped, Vertical Rainbow Colors	850.00
Vase, 9" Tall, Orange on White Coloring	1000.00
Vase, 10¼" Tall, Reeded and Scrolled Feet, Gold Rim, Green Leaves and Pink and Blue Floral Beading on a Cranberry Background	400.00

"Coralene" is sometimes referred to as "Mother-of-Pearl" for its pearly or coral-like sheen. Small glass beads of clear, colored, or opalescent glass are applied to an object, then fired on. There were several pattern styles, but most include coral, seaweed, and floral designs. Beware of reproductions or remakes where the beading is not fired on; it chips and flakes very easily.

CRANBERRY VARIOUS PRODUCERS, 1820S–1880S

Object	Price
Basket, 6" Tall, Vertical Ribbing, Scalloped, Clear Handle, Circular Foot	$175.00
Basket, 8" Tall, Ruffled, Crystal Handle	175.00
Bell, 5" Tall, Dark Coloring	100.00
Bell, 7" Tall, Gold Tracing	500.00
Bell, 7½" Tall, Swirled, with Crystal Handle	325.00
Bell, 12" Tall, Clear Handle, Green Clapper	250.00
Bottle, Perfume, with Stopper, 3¼" Tall	100.00
Bottle, Perfume, with Cut Stopper, 8¼" Tall, Brass Ormolu at Base	225.00
Bottle, Square, 8½" Tall, Vertical Ribbing	125.00
Bowl, Finger, 3¼" Diameter, Ruffled	100.00

Bowl, 4" Diameter with Hinged Cover *$150.00*
Bowl, 7½" Diameter, Enameled Flowers *175.00*
Bowl, Flower, Ruffled, 3" Tall *90.00*
Box with Hinged Lid, 3" Tall, 3½" Square, Ribbed, Gold Decoration *250.00*
Castor Set, Pickle Dish in Silverplated Frame with Lid and Tongs (Several Designs) *.375.00*
Chalice with Cover, 16" Tall, Gilded, with Enameled Figure of Girl *250.00*
Cologne Bottle with Stopper, 6" Tall, Silver Overlay *400.00*
Cordial, 4" Tall, Gold Paneled, Clear Stem and Base *75.00*
Creamer, 4¼" Tall, Ruffled, Clear Handle, Shell Feet *125.00*
Creamer and Sugar Set in Silverplated Holder (Several Varieties) *300.00*
Cruet with Silverplated Stopper, 5½" Tall *100.00*
Cruet with Stopper, 6" Tall, Clear Handle *225.00*
Cruet with Cut Crystal Stopper, 6½" Tall, Clear Handle *275.00*
Cup, Loving, 3½" Tall, 3-Handled, Silver Overlay *750.00*
Cup, Punch, Clear Handle, Enameled Flowers *50.00*
Decanter with Crystal Cut Stopper, 10" Tall *200.00*
Decanter with Clear Stopper, 10½" Tall, Clear Handle, Enameled Floral Design ...*225.00*
Decanter with Clear Stopper, 11" Tall, Clear Handle, Inverted Thumbprint Pattern *.250.00*
Decanter without Stopper, 6" Tall *100.00*
Epergne, 12" Tall, Double Trumpet Style *325.00*
Epergne, 13½" Tall, 3 Trumpets, Crystal Base, Enameled Floral Design *375.00*
Hat, 2½" Tall *150.00*
Lamp, Kerosene, 8½" Tall, Brass Base with Cranberry Shade *400.00*
Lamp, Kerosene, Swirled Shade, Brass Frame for Hanging *400.00*
Lamp, Oil, 18" Tall, Thumbprint Patterned Globe, Enameled Design *600.00*
Mug, 4" Tall, Clear Handle, Inverted Thumbprint Pattern *100.00*
Nappy, 6½", Cut Strawberry and Diamond (C. Dorflinger & Sons) *600.00*
Pitcher, Syrup, 6¾" Tall, Silverplated Handle and Spout *350.00*
Pitcher, 7½" Tall, Ruffled, Clear Handle, Enameled Floral Design *275.00*
Pitcher, Square Top, Bull's Eye Pattern *325.00*
Pitcher, Water, 8" Tall, Inverted Thumbprint Pattern *175.00*
Pitcher, 8½" Tall, Tankard, Inverted Thumbprint Pattern *400.00*
Pitcher, 9" Tall, Swirl Pattern with Enameled Flowers *250.00*
Plate, 6" Diameter *50.00*
Plate, 8" Diameter *55.00*

Cranberry art glass. Photo by Mark Pickvet.

Salt and Pepper Shakers, Metal Tops, Enameled Floral Design *$175.00*
Sugar Bowl with Cover, Guttate Pattern (Consolidated) *175.00*
Sugar Bowl with Cover, Shell Feet *150.00*
Sugar Shaker with Silver Top, 6½" Tall, Drape Pattern *125.00*
Toothpick Holder, Barrel-Shaped, Inverted Thumbprint Pattern *150.00*
Tumbler, 3½" Tall, Clear Pedestal Foot, Enameled Floral Design with Gold Decoration
. . . .*75.00*
Tumbler, 4¾" Tall, Small Thumbprint Pattern *75.00*
Vase, 5¼" Tall, 5¼" Diameter, Footed, Silver Leaves and Gold Floral and Butterfly Design
. . . .*425.00*
Vase, 6¾" Tall, Flared, Clear Pedestal Base *100.00*
Vase, 7½" Tall, Enameled Gold and White Flowers *125.00*
Vase, 7½" Tall, Ruffled, Clear Circular Foot *150.00*
Vase, 8" Tall, Ruffled *125.00*
Vase, 8½" Tall, Enameled Gold and White Flowers *150.00*
Vase, 10" Tall, Slender Form, Enameled Floral Design *175.00*
Vase, 12" Tall, Bubble Connector (Pairpoint) *225.00*
Vase, 12" Tall Cylindrical, 3-Footed *175.00*

"Cranberry" is sometimes referred to as a light ruby or rose-red colored glass. It is a transparent glass the color of dark pink or light red cranberries. It was created by adding tiny amounts of gold oxide as the primary coloring agent. Larger amounts of gold produce a darker, true ruby red.

"Cranberry" glass was a popular item with many glass and decorating companies, including T. B. Clark, T. G. Hawkes, Mount Washington, New England, Northwood, Steuben, etc. It is also one of the oldest forms of art glass produced in America.

Beware of cheaper flashed, coated, and stained articles in the identical or similar color. They chip and scratch easier if the color is not consistent throughout the entire glass inside and out. "Cranberry" has been reproduced by several modern companies in a wide variety of items.

CROWN MILANO MOUNT WASHINGTON GLASS WORKS, 1890S

Object	*Price*
Basket, Bride's, 9" Tall, Folded Rim, White with Enameled Floral Design	*$500.00*
Basket, Bride's, 14¼" Tall, Ruffled, Yellow with Enameled Floral Design, Footed Silver-plated Stand, Signed	*1000.00*
Biscuit Jar with Cover, 6" Tall, Thistle and Gold Enameled Design, Signed on Bottom and Cover	*1750.00*
Biscuit Jar with Cover, 8¼" Tall, White, Enameled Desert Scene, Cover Contains Silver Decoration, Pairpoint Stamp	*1200.00*
Biscuit Jar with Cover, 9" Tall, Floral and Foliage Design, Signed	*850.00*
Bowl, 6", Crimped, Gold Rim, Pansy Design	*150.00*
Bowl, 8", Fan-Shaped, Shallow, White Pansy Design	*175.00*
Bowl, Rose, 4", Yellow with Gold Lines and Enameled Floral Design	*225.00*
Cracker Jar with Cover, Gold and Green Foliage Design, Signed	*750.00*
Creamer, 3¼" Tall, Ribbed, White with Gold Decoration, Signed	*450.00*
Ewer, Shepherd, Flock and Church Enameled Design	*3200.00*

Crown Milano art glass. Photo by Robin Rainwater.

Ewer, 10" Tall, Twisted Handle, Paneled Design *$1500.00*
Jar with Cover, White Opal with Gold Beading *750.00*
Lamp, 16³/₄" Tall, Asian Man and Camel Design on Shade, Elephants on Base Globe, Metal Base *5500.00*
Pitcher, Water, 12" Tall, White Floral Design, Signed *1500.00*
Pitcher, Water, 13¹/₂" Tall, Bulbous, Rural Scene, Gold Decoration *1750.00*
Powder Jar with Cover, 3" Tall, Ribbed, Enameled Floral Design, Signed *700.00*
Sugar with Cover, 6" Tall, Ribbed, Handled, White with Gold Decoration *500.00*
Sugar Shaker, 3" Tall, Ribbed, Orange to Yellow Shading, Foliage Design *550.00*
Sweetmeat Jar with Cover, 5" Tall, Embossed, Gold Wash Design, Signed *750.00*
Tumbler, Gloss Finish, 3³/₄" Tall, Enameled Floral and Wreath Design *1000.00*
Urn with Crown-Shaped Cover, 16¹/₂" Tall, Foliage Decoration *3750.00*
Vase, 3" Tall, Enameled Leaf Design *625.00*
Vase, 5¹/₂" Tall, Scroll and Floral Design, Signed *1750.00*
Vase, 7" Tall, Swirled, Bulbous, Cactus, and Foliage Design *3250.00*
Vase, 8¹/₂" Tall, Swirled, Wild Fowl Design, Signed *2750.00*
Vase, 9" Tall, Globular, Scrolls on Neck, Gold and Tan Fern Design *1000.00*
Vase, 10¹/₂" Tall, Duck Design *3000.00*
Vase, 11" Tall, Baluster-Shaped, Gloss Finish, Gilded Handles, "The Courting Couple" Design, Scrolled Ribbons, Signed *2250.00*
Vase, 11" Tall, Bulbous, Chrysanthemum Design, Signed *1350.00*
Vase, 13" Tall, Angel Design *2500.00*
Vase, 13" Tall, White to Green Shading, Gold Enamel *1250.00*
Vase, 14" Tall, Handled, Floral Design *1500.00*
Vase, 14" Tall, Handled, Acorn Design with Gold Trim, Signed *1750.00*
Vase, 15" Tall, Gold Dragon Design, Signed *2000.00*
Vase, 17" Tall, Duck Design, Signed "Frank Guba" *4750.00*

"Crown Milano" is another of Mount Washington's patented art glass patterns. "Crown Milano" is characterized by heavy gold enameling upon an opal or earth-toned background. Some contain jewel work or settings for glass beads. The name was derived from the signature that is typically a crown within a wreath. For the most part, "Crown Milano" is identical in design to that of the older but less popular "Albertine" glass (originally created by Albert Steffin).

CUSTARD   VARIOUS PRODUCERS, 1890S–1915

Object	Price
Bowl, 8", Banded Ring Pattern	*$150.00*
Bowl, 8½", Maple Leaf Pattern	*150.00*
Bowl, 10½", Argonaut Shell Pattern	*250.00*
Bowl, 11", Ruffled, Footed, Grape Pattern	*550.00*
Bowl, 11½", Fan and Feather Pattern	*400.00*
Bowl, 12", 3-Footed, Maple Leaf Pattern	*500.00*
Butter Dish with Cover, Gold Decoration, Argonaut Shell Pattern	*350.00*
Butter Dish with Cover, Beaded Circle, Cherry and Scale, Diamond, Grape, or Maple Leaf Pattern	*300.00*
Butter Dish with Domed Cover, Gold Louis XV Pattern, Northwood	*325.00*
Cologne Bottle with Stopper, 5½" Tall, Grape Pattern	*650.00*
Cologne Bottle with Stopper, 6¼" Tall, Scrolled Design	*350.00*
Compote, Footed, Gold Louis XV Pattern, Northwood	*150.00*
Creamer, Argonaut Shell, Banded Ring, Beaded Circle, Chrysanthemum, Maple Leaf, Scrolled, or Victoria Pattern	*175.00*
Creamer, Gold Louis XV Pattern, Northwood	*200.00*
Cruet with Stopper, 5½" Tall, Banded Ring, Chrysanthemum, Grape, or Scrolled Pattern	*400.00*
Cruet with Stopper, 6" Tall, Beaded Circle Pattern	*800.00*
Cruet with Stopper, 6¼" Tall, Intaglio Design	*425.00*
Cruet with Stopper, Gold Louis XV Pattern, Northwood	*400.00*
Humidor with Cover, 8" Tall, Grape Design	*700.00*
Jelly Dish, Everglade or Maple Leaf Pattern	*450.00*
Jelly Dish, Inverted Fan and Feather Pattern	*500.00*
Mug, Souvenir (Several Varieties)	*75.00*
Napkin Ring, Souvenir (Several Varieties), Diamond Pattern	*175.00*
Nappy, 6½", Ruffled	*75.00*
Pickle Dish, 7½" Long, Beaded Swag Pattern	*300.00*
Pitcher, Syrup, with Lid, Scroll Pattern	*450.00*
Pitcher, Water, 8–10" Tall, Argonaut Shell, Beaded Circle, Chrysanthemum, Diamond, Grape, Maple Leaf, Drape, or Scrolled Pattern	*425.00*
Pitcher, Water, Gold Louis XV Pattern, Northwood	*475.00*
Punch Bowl, Footed, Fan and Feather Pattern	*3500.00*
Salt and Pepper Shakers, with Tops, Geneva Pattern	*175.00*
Salt and Pepper Shakers, with Pewter Tops, Fan and Feather Pattern, Pink and Gold Trim	*550.00*
Sauce Dish, Various Styles and Patterns	*75.00*
Spooner, Argonaut Shell, Banded Ring, Beaded Circle, Everglade, Fan and Feather, Geneva, Grape, Maple Leaf, or Scrolled Pattern	*150.00*
Sugar with Cover, Argonaut Shell, Banded Ring, Beaded Circle, Chrysanthemum, Maple Leaf, Scrolled, or Victoria Pattern	*200.00*
Sugar with Cover, Gold King Louis XV Pattern, Northwood	*250.00*
Toothpick Holder, 2¾" Tall, Chrysanthemum or Fan and Feather Pattern	*550.00*
Toothpick Holder, Wild Bouquet Pattern	*750.00*
Toothpick Holder, 3" Tall, Ribbed Drape Pattern	*200.00*
Tumbler, Banded Ring, Beaded Circle, Chrysanthemum, Everglade, Intaglio, Maple Leaf, Prayer Rug, Scrolled, or Victoria Pattern Tumbler, Gold Louis XV Pattern, Northwood	*150.00*

Vase, 6" Tall, Georgia Gem Pattern *$375.00*
Vase, 7¹/₂" Tall, Banded Ring or Scrolled Pattern *225.00*
Vase, Hat-Shaped, Ruffled, Grape and Arch Pattern *100.00*
Vase, Souvenir (Several Varieties) *100.00*
Wineglass, Diamond Pattern *80.00*

"Custard" refers to the milky white to deep yellow opaque coloring like that of custard pudding. It is sometimes referred to as "Buttermilk" because the color also resembles yellow buttermilk. Uranium salts are often added to produce a vibrant yellow opalescence that is very mildly radioactive (safe for one to handle!) and reacts to black light.

As with most art glass, a variety of decorations and colors were applied to the base custard-colored glass. These include flashing or enameling of blue, brown, green, pink, red, and even gold gilding or painting. Flower enameling is the most common, but the basic glass itself was produced in numerous patterns by a host of companies. Northwood is recognized as the most prolific producer of "Custard" glass, but a good deal was also made by Adams, Cambridge, Diamond, Dugan, Fenton, Greenberg, Heisey, Jefferson, LaBelle, McKee, and many others.

CUT VELVET VARIOUS PRODUCERS, 1880S–EARLY 1900S

Object	*Price*
Bottle, 8¹/₄" Tall, Blue with White Lining, Diamond Quilted Pattern	*$225.00*
Bowl, Finger, 3¹/₂" Diameter, Pink with White Lining	*200.00*
Bowl, Flower, 4" Diameter, Blue with White Lining	*200.00*
Bowl, Flower, 4¹/₄" Tall, Pink and White or Blue and White Shading, Diamond Quilted Pattern	*225.00*
Bowl, 7", Ribbed, Tan	*325.00*
Bowl, Rose, 3¹/₂", Crimped (4 or 6), Blue or Pink, Diamond Quilted Pattern	*200.00*
Creamer, 3¹/₂" Tall, Diamond Quilted Pattern	*300.00*
Cup, Punch, Pink with White Lining, Diamond Quilted Pattern	*125.00*
Ewer, 12" Tall, Pink and White Shading, Diamond Quilted Pattern	*325.00*
Pitcher, 4¹/₂" Tall, Pink with White Lining, Amber Handle, Honeycomb Pattern	*450.00*
Pitcher, Water, Yellow, Diamond Quilted Pattern	*600.00*
Pitcher, 7¹/₂" Tall, Blue, Diamond Quilted Pattern	*350.00*
Tumbler, 3¹/₂" Tall, Pink, Diamond Quilted Pattern	*325.00*
Tumbler, 5" Tall, Pink or Blue, Diamond Quilted Pattern	*100.00*
Vase, 6" Tall, Ribbed, Butterscotch Color	*325.00*
Vase, 6¹/₄" Tall, Green with White Lining, Diamond Quilted Pattern	*150.00*
Vase, 6¹/₂" Tall, Pleated Top, Dark Blue, Diamond Quilted Pattern	*525.00*
Vase, 7" Tall, Ruffled, Footed, Pink to White Shading, Diamond Quilted Pattern	*250.00*
Vase, 8" Tall, Blue with Vertical Ribbing	*225.00*
Vase, 8" Tall, Blue Satin, Diamond Quilted Pattern	*450.00*
Vase, 9" Tall, Ruffled, Blue, Diamond Quilted Pattern	*500.00*
Vase, 9¹/₄", Flared, Ruffled, Diamond Quilted Pattern	*200.00*
Vase, 11" Tall, Pink, Herringbone Pattern	*275.00*
Vase, 11" Tall, Amethyst, Diamond Quilted Pattern	*500.00*

"Cut Velvet" is characterized by two separate layers fused together that are blown into a mold. "Cut Velvet" comes in a variety of colors and was made by many manufacturers in several patterns. It is most often found in the "Diamond Quilted" pattern.

DE VILBISS 1880S–1920S

Object	Price
Bottle, Perfume, 5" Tall, Footed, Gold Trim	*$175.00*
Bottle, Perfume, 7" Tall, Gold Crackle with Black Trim	*125.00*
Bottle, Perfume, Metallic Black with Chrome Neck	*100.00*
Dresser Set, 7-Piece, Gold Trim with Enameled Flowers, Signed "De Vilbiss"	*900.00*
Hairpin Box, Hinged Lid, Iridescent with Gilding	*125.00*
Lamp, Perfume, 7" Tall, Glass Insert with Nude Figure	*250.00*
Lamp, Perfume, 12" Tall, Glass Insert with Nude Figure	*325.00*
Perfume Atomizer, 4³/₄" Tall, Gold Crackle Design with Beaded Flower at Top	*75.00*
Perfume Atomizer, 6" Tall, Crystal Base, Orange Stain	*85.00*
Perfume Atomizer, 6¹/₄" Tall, Tasseled Bulb, Black	*100.00*
Perfume Atomizer, 6¹/₂" Tall, Cranberry, Signed	*100.00*
Perfume Atomizer, 7¹/₄" Tall, Crystal, Gold Draped Woman on Stem	*275.00*
Perfume Atomizer, 7³/₄" Tall, Iridescent Orange, Signed "De Vilbiss"	*325.00*
Perfume Atomizer, 9¹/₄" Tall, Black and Gold	*175.00*
Perfume Atomizer, Blue with Black Enameling	*100.00*
Perfume Atomizer, Green with Cut Leaves, Signed "De Vilbiss"	*175.00*
Perfume Atomizer, Gilded with Black Enameling	*125.00*
Perfume Atomizer, Iridescent Amber, Signed "De Vilbiss"	*250.00*
Perfume Atomizer, Gilded, Tapered Top, Amber Jewel Set in Cap	*300.00*
Pin Tray, Black with Gold Trim	*50.00*
Pin Tray, Rectangular (5¹/₂" × 3¹/₄"), Black and Gold Decoration, Orange Stain	*50.00*
Tray, Iridescent with Gilding	*75.00*

The De Vilbiss Company purchased the actual vases from others such as Cambridge, Fenton, and Steuben. They added pieces such as bulbs, collars, decorations, gilding, etc. Many were signed, stamped, or labeled with the "De Vilbiss" or "De Vilbiss—Made in U.S.A." trademark. They were most famous for perfume spray bottles referred to as atomizers.

DURAND ART GLASS COMPANY 1924–EARLY 1930S

Object	Price
Bowl, Flower, 7¹/₂" Diameter, Iridescent Blue, Signed "Durand"	*$950.00*
Bowl, 10" Diameter, Orange and Gold	*600.00*
Bowl, Blue and Silver, King Tut Pattern, Signed "Durand"	*700.00*
Bowl with Cover, Red and White, Moorish Crackle Pattern	*300.00*
Box with Cover, Green and Gold, King Tut Pattern, Signed "Durand"	*1200.00*
Candlestick, 9" Tall, Amber with Blue Feathering	*150.00*
Candlestick, 10" Tall, Green, King Tut Pattern	*725.00*
Compote, 5¹/₂", Amethyst	*375.00*
Compote, 7" Diameter, Gold and Iridescent, Numbered and Signed "Durand"	*500.00*
Cup, Iridescent Gold, Signed "Durand"	*225.00*
Jar with Cover, 7" Tall, Iridescent Red with Silver Threading	*3500.00*
Jar with Cover, 11" Tall, Green with White Iridescence, Signed "Durand 1994–8"	*1500.00*
Jar with Cover, 11" Tall, Calcite with Gold Feathers, Signed	*1600.00*

Jar with Cover, Vertical Ribs, Green Triple Overlay, Signed "Durand" *$2750.00*
Lamp, Electric, 7½" Tall *800.00*
Light with Iron Holder, 9¾" Tall, Green, King Tut Pattern *650.00*
Perfume with Stopper, 6" Tall, Gold *750.00*
Plate, 8", Blue with Feathering *350.00*
Plate, 8", Red with White Feathers *400.00*
Plate, 8", Red and White, Engraved "Bridgeton Rose" *425.00*
Saucer, Iridescent Gold, Signed "Durand" *175.00*
Shade, 5½" Tall, Blue, White, and Gold Design (2 Styles) *175.00*
Sherbet, Green with White Feathering, Signed "Durand" *325.00*
Sherbet with Matching Underplate, 2-Piece Set, King Tut Pattern *425.00*
Tazza, 7¾" × 6¾", Iridescent Gold, Signed "Durand" *900.00*
Tumbler, Amber, Signed, "Durand" *125.00*
Vase, 4" Tall, Iridescent Amber, Signed "Durand" *200.00*
Vase, 4" Tall, Iridescent Blue Feathering *375.00*
Vase, 5½" Tall, Green and Gold on Opal, Egyptian Crackle Pattern *800.00*
Vase, 6" Tall, Green with Iridescent Gold and Platinum *950.00*
Vase, 6" Tall, Inverted Rim, Transparent Yellow, Raindrop Pattern, Signed "Durand 1968–6"
. . . .*700.00*
Vase, 6⅛" Tall, Flared, Iridescent Blue with Silver Threading, Signed "Durand 1710–6"
. . . .*925.00*
Vase, 6¼" Tall, Gold Luster, Heart and Vine Design *550.00*
Vase, 6½" Tall, Blue and Black Cameo, Signed "Durand" *2250.00*
Vase, 7" Tall, Iridescent Blue *500.00*
Vase, 7" Tall, Oiled Luster with Opal, Signed "Durand" *475.00*
Vase, 7" Tall, Intaglio Cut, Signed "Durand" *1750.00*
Vase, 7½" Tall, Iridescent Blue with White Hearts and Vines *1400.00*
Vase, 8" Tall, Iridescent Green with Silver, King Tut Pattern, Signed "Durand" *1500.00*
Vase, 8" Tall, Intaglio Cut with Iridescent Gold, Signed "Durand 20161–8" *1200.00*
Vase, 8" Tall, Urn-Shaped, Green and Gold, King Tut Pattern *1000.00*
Vase, 8" Tall, Handled, Iridescent Yellow and Gold with Blue Edge, Engraved "Durand
1974–15" *1400.00*
Vase, 9", Green and Gold, King Tut Pattern *850.00*
Vase, 9" Tall, Green with White Interior and Silver Swirls, King Tut Pattern, Signed
"Durand" *1200.00*
Vase, 9¼" Tall, Blue and Ivory with Gold Interior *1000.00*
Vase, 9¼" Tall, Urn-Shaped, White Exterior with Blue Color and Gold Threading, Yellow
Interior, Signed "Durand" *750.00*
Vase, 9¾" Tall, White with Red Collar and Foot *1200.00*
Vase, 9¾" Tall, Cut Vertically, Red and Clear Overlay *900.00*
Vase, 10" Tall, Iridescent Cobalt Blue, Signed *1500.00*
Vase, 10" Tall, Intaglio Cut, Crystal with Red Casing, Signed "Durand" *900.00*
Vase, 10" Tall, Iridescent Gold with Silver, King Tut Pattern, Signed "Durand 1910" .*800.00*
Vase, 10" Tall, White, Orange, and Gray with Heart-Shaped Leaves *650.00*
Vase, 10½" Tall, Frosted Glass with Blue and White Overlay, Signed "Durand" *900.00*
Vase, 10¾" Tall, Intaglio Cut with 4 Layers, Signed "Durand 1911–70" *1100.00*
Vase, 11½" Tall, Blue Exterior with Silver Interior, Signed "Durand" *1000.00*
Vase, 12" Tall, Iridescent Blue with Gold Crackle, Signed "Durand" *700.00*
Vase, 12½" Tall, Red with Silver Exterior, Gold Interior, King Tut Pattern, Signed "Durand"
. . . .*1250.00*
Vase, 12½" Tall, Green with Pink Highlights, King Tut Pattern, Signed "Durand" . .*1250.00*

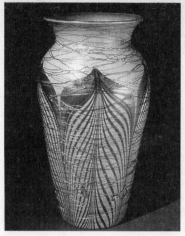 

Left: Durand art glass. Photo by Robin Rainwater. Right: Favrile art glass. Photo by Mark Pickvet.

Vase, 13" Tall, Green with White Feathers *$550.00*
Vase, 15¹/₂" Tall, Ivory on Gold, King Tut Pattern, Signed "Durand 1974–15" *1100.00*
Wineglass, Yellow with Feathering *275.00*

Victor Durand was from the famous glass town of Baccarat, France, and began producing art glass in America in 1924. It was one of the few companies (like Steuben and Tiffany) to make fancy blown art glass during the Depression years.

They made a variety of objects in various colors and patterns but are noted most for vases. Most of their products either contain a silver and black label "Durand" or an engraved silver signature in script. The script may also contain a wide "V" shape beneath it.

FAVRILE LOUIS COMFORT TIFFANY, 1892–1920S

Object	*Price*
Candlestick, 20" Tall, Gold with Bronze Base, Lily Pad Design, Stamped "27466"	.*$925.00*
Candy Jar with Cover, 9³/₄" Tall, Circular Foot, Iridescent Blue, Marked "X236 L.C. Tiffany—Favrile"	.*2000.00*
Chandelier, 50" Tall, Alamander Leaded Glass, 6 Chains, 6 Gold Favrile Shades Marked "L.C.T.," Multicolored Floral Design	.*30,000.00*
Compote, 5" Tall, Blue, Signed "L.C.T. Favrile"	.*1250.00*
Compote, 5¹/₄" Tall, Ruffled, Gold, Signed "L.C. Tiffany—Favrile"	.*650.00*
Floriform, 11¹/₄" Tall, Gold Ribbing, Signed "L.C. Tiffany Favrile—455 H"	.*1100.00*
Flower Bowl with Frog, 10³/₄" Diameter, Blue Floral Design, Bowl Signed "Louis C. Tiffany—Furnaces Inc. Favrile," Frog Signed "L.C. Tiffany—Favrile"	.*2250.00*
Frog, Flower, 3³/₄" Tall, Double, Signed "L.C. Tiffany Favrile—5678K"	.*550.00*

Jar, Ginger, with Cover, 8½" Tall, Yellow with Green Glaze, Signed "L.C. Tiffany—Favrile" *$2250.00*

Jug with Handle, 4" Tall, Blue, Signed "L.C. Tiffany—Favrile" *850.00*

Lamp, 17¾" Tall, Venetian Style, Gilded Shade in Bronze Mount, Iridescent Gold, Signed "L.C.T." *3500.00*

Lamp, 28" Tall, 22" Diameter, Cabochon Jewels, Iridescent Amber, Blue, and Green, Dragonfly Border *42,000.00*

Perfume with Stopper, 4¼" Tall, Iridescent Blue with Blue Highlights, Signed "L.C. Tiffany Favrile—9230G" *750.00*

Sherbet, 3½" Tall, Gold, Intaglio Engraved Grapes, Signed "1225 L.C.T. Favrile" . . .*750.00*

Vase, 2½" Tall, Urn-Shaped, Red Exterior, Yellow Interior, Signed "1611K L.C. Tiffany Favrile" *1500.00*

Vase, 4" Tall, Flared, Iridescent Gold, Signed "1027–883 GM—L.C. Tiffany Favrile" *400.00*

Vase, 5" Tall, Ovoid Form, Yellow with Cobalt, Signed *15,000.00*

Vase, 6" Tall, Crystal with Multicolored Morning Glories, Signed "L.C. Tiffany—Favrile" *3000.00*

Vase, 6¼" Tall, Inverted Rim, Multicolored Cameo Floral Design, Signed "L.C. Tiffany—Favrile" *4000.00*

Vase, 7¼" Tall, Flask-Shaped, Lava, Signed "L.C. Tiffany—Favrile" *20,000.00*

Vase, 9" Tall, Urn-Shaped, Iridescent Gold, Cameo Foliage, Signed "Louis C. Tiffany Favrile 6368N" *2500.00*

Vase, 9¼" Tall, Floriform, Gold with Green Lily Pads, Signed "L.C. Tiffany—Favrile" *1250.00*

Vase, 10" Tall, Iridescent Gold, Intaglio Floral Design, Signed "1153—3643K L.C. Tiffany Favrile" *$2250.00*

Collection of Favrile art glass vases. Courtesy of the Corning Museum of Glass.

Vase, 11¼" Tall, Jack-in-the-Pulpit Style, Blue, Signed "L.C. Tiffany—Favrile" . . .*3250.00*
Vase, 12" Tall, Floriform, Blue with Trailing Green, Lily Pads, Signed "L.C. Tiffany—Favrile" *3000.00*
Vase, 15½" Tall, Green with Amber Lily Pads and Millefiore Flowers, Signed "L.C. Tiffany—Favrile" *4250.00*
Vase, 16½" Tall, Jack-in-the-Pulpit, Iridescent Gold, Foot Inscribed "7841B L.C. Tiffany Favrile" *4000.00*
Vase, 19¼" Tall, Urn-Shaped, Gold Foot, Iridescent Blue on Gold with Blue and Amber Bands, Signed "5622G L.C. Tiffany—Favrile" *4000.00*
Vase, 19½" Tall, Jack-in-the-Pulpit Style, Blue Signed "L.C. Tiffany—Favrile" . .*35,000.00*
Wineglass, 8" Tall, Circular Foot, Opalescent Pink Bowl, Green Stem, Signed "L.C.T. Favrile" *425.00*

Developed and patented in 1892, "Favrile" is characterized by multicolored iridescent base colors decorated with applied or embedded designs. "Favrile" was one of the major movements in the Art Nouveau period as others sought to copy or create similar color effects.

FRY, H.C., GLASS COMPANY 1900–1934

Object	*Price*
Basket, 7½" Tall, 7½" Diameter, Opal with Blue Handle	*$375.00*
Bowl, 10", White Opal with Blue Trim	*275.00*
Bowl, 12", Centerpiece, Green Base, Opalescent	*350.00*
Bread Pan, Fry Ovenware, Opalescent	*30.00*
Candlestick, 10", White Opal with Blue Threading	*125.00*
Candlestick, 12" Tall, White Opal with Blue Handle	*150.00*
Casserole Dish, Miniature (Children's), 4" Diameter, Fry Ovenware	*75.00*
Casserole Dish with Cover, 1½ qt., Oval, Blue Finial, Fry Ovenware, Dated 1925–6	*60.00*
Coffeepot with Cover, White Opal with Blue Handle and Finial	*525.00*
Compote, 7", Opalescent White with Blue Threading	*350.00*
Creamer, Opal with Blue Handle	*200.00*
Cruet, Opal with Cobalt Blue Handle and Cobalt Blue Stopper	*375.00*
Cup, White Opal with Cobalt Blue Handle	*85.00*
Cup, Opal with Jade Green	*75.00*
Cup with Underplate, Handled, Opaque Blue	*100.00*
Custard Cup, Fry Ovenware, Dated 1919	*15.00*
Measuring Cup, ½ Cup, 3-Spout, Fry Ovenware	*100.00*
Nappy, Handled, Opaline	*75.00*
Pie Plate, Fry Ovenware	*30.00*
Pitcher, Water, 8" Tall, Blue and White Opal with Amethyst Handle	*400.00*
Pitcher with Cover, Clear Craquelle with Jade Green Handle	*150.00*
Reamer, Juice, Opaline	*60.00*
Saucer, White Opal	*35.00*
Saucer, Opal with Jade Green	*50.00*
Sherbet, Opal with Blue Stem and Foot	*100.00*
Sugar, Opal with Blue Handles	*100.00*
Teapot with Cover, Opaline with Green Spout and Handle	*250.00*
Toothpick Holder, 2¼" Tall, Opal with Blue Handles	*75.00*

Vase, 8", White Opal with Lavender Top, Signed "Fry" *$250.00*
Vase, 11" Tall, Opaline with Blue Spiral Twist and Blue Rim *225.00*
Vase, Clear Craquelle with Applied Amethyst Rosettes *75.00*
Vase, Opal with Blue Pedestal Vase *350.00*

Fry glass is usually found in fine-cut and ovenware examples; however, as with many others, they experimented with color effects. Their most noteworthy artistic products were opal or opaline "Foval" and "Pearl Art" styles. Both are character-ized by a white opalescence with color accents. Some of their products were also decorated with silver and colored threading.

GILLINDER & SONS   1870S–EARLY 1890S

Object   *Price*
Bowl with Cover, Oval (6⁷/₈" × 3⁷/₈"), Frosted Lion *$150.00*
Bowl with Cover, Oval (7¹/₂" × 4³/₄"), Frosted Lion *175.00*
Bowl with Cover, Oval (9" × 5¹/₂"), Frosted Lion *200.00*
Bust, Abraham Lincoln, 6" Tall, Opaque White *525.00*
Bust, William Shakespeare, 5" Tall, Frosted Bust *250.00*
Bust, George Washington, 5" Tall *350.00*
Butter Dish with Cover, Lion *150.00*
Celery Vase, Etched Lion Design *100.00*
Cheese Dish with Cover, Lion *400.00*
Children's Miniature Set, 5-Piece Lion (Creamer and Sugar, Covered Compote, Stemmed Glass, Stemmed Covered Compote) *525.00*
Compote, 7³/₄" Diameter, Frosted Lion *125.00*
Compote, 8" Oval, Frosted Lion *150.00*
Compote, 9" Oval, Frosted Lion *175.00*
Compote with Cover, 6³/₄" Oval, 7" Tall, Lion *175.00*
Compote with Cover, 7" Diameter, 11" Tall, Lion *175.00*
Compote with Cover, 7³/₄" Oval, Lion *175.00*
Compote with Cover, 8" Diameter, 13" Tall, Lion *200.00*
Creamer, Frosted Lion *100.00*
Duck Dish (Duck Cover), Amber *75.00*
Egg Cup, Frosted Lion *100.00*
Figurine, Buddha, 5³/₄" Tall, Orange, Signed "Gillinder" *125.00*
Figurine, Buddha, 6" Tall, Amber *60.00*
Goblet, 6¹/₄" Tall, Frosted Lion *100.00*
Jar, Marmalade, with Cover, Lion *125.00*
Paperweight, Challinor, 3" Diameter, Faceted, Concentric Colored Rings *325.00*
Paperweight, Frosted Lion *175.00*
Paperweight, Intaglio Portrait of Abraham Lincoln *125.00*
Paperweight, Ruth the Gleaner *150.00*
Pitcher, Syrup with Metal Lid, Frosted Lion *300.00*
Pitcher, Milk, 6¹/₂" Tall, Frosted Lion *450.00*
Pitcher, Water, 8¹/₄" Tall, Frosted Lion *300.00*
Pitcher, Water, Hexagonal, Alternating Draped Women in Gothic Arches *450.00*
Plate, 10", Blaine Design, Signed "Jacobus" *250.00*
Plate, 10", Warrior, Signed "Jacobus" *175.00*
Plate, 10¹/₂", Handled, Frosted Lion *100.00*

Platter, Oval (10½" × 9"), Lion Handles $125.00
Platter, 12¼" Oval, Frosted Lion Center *125.00*
Relish Dish, 8½" Long, Frosted Lion *75.00*
Salt Dip, Rectangular, 3½" Long, Frosted Lion *450.00*
Sauce Dish, 5" Diameter, Footed, Frosted Lion *40.00*
Slipper, Lady's Glass, Marked "Gillinder & Sons Centennial Exhibition" *60.00*
Spooner, Frosted Lion *90.00*
Sugar Dish, 3½" Tall, Frosted Lion *100.00*
Toothpick Holder, 2½" Tall, Baby Chick *125.00*
Vase, 6½" Tall, Frosted Lion *125.00*
Vase, Frosted, Pressed "Gillinder Centennial" *75.00*
Vase, Cameo, 6¾" Tall, White Leaves on Blue Background *2100.00*
Vase, Cameo, Ruffled, Footed, Floral Design on a Ruby Red Background *2300.00*
Vase, Cameo, 7¾" Tall, Floral Design on Yellow Background, Flared *2000.00*
Vase, Cameo, 8½" Tall, Floral Design on Blue Background, Flared *2500.00*
Wineglass, 5¾" Tall, Frosted Lion *225.00*

The Gillinders built a small glasshouse and presented many of their products during the 1876 Centennial Exposition in Philadelphia. Some are even marked "Centennial 1876" or "Gillinder and Sons, Centennial Exhibition." They also gave away small novelty items as souvenirs, such as glass hats and slippers. Many of their products are frosted, cut, and pressed into many shapes.

"Lion" above refers to a head finial, while the "frosted lion" appears on the object as a frosted design. The cameo vases are particularly rare and valuable (beautiful too!).

HANDEL AND COMPANY 1890S–1930S

Object	*Price*
Bowl, 8", Enameled Trees Design, Signed	$200.00
Candlestick, 8½" Tall, Footed, Frosted with Enameled Landscape and Windmills ...	*750.00*
Candlestick, 9" Tall, Amber with Etched Floral Design	*300.00*
Cigar Holder with Hinged Lid, 6" × 3¼", Bear Design	*275.00*
Humidor with Cover, Shriner's Fez and Printed "Cigars" on Cover, Brown and Green, Gold and White Trim, Man Riding Camel Design	*750.00*
Humidor with Pewter Cover, 5" Tall, Opal, Owl and Branch Design, Signed and Numbered	*425.00*
Humidor with Pewter Cover, Opal with Brown and Green, Horse and Dog Design, Signed "Braun"	*500.00*
Humidor with Silverplated Cover, Green Ground, Indian Design, signed	*450.00*
Lamp, 6¾" Tall, Double Green and Yellow Mica Shades	*1250.00*
Lamp, 7" Tall, Crystal Flecked Design, Bronze Base, Signed	*1200.00*
Lamp, 7¼" Tall, Cone Shade, Blue and White Globe, Metal Base	*600.00*
Lamp, 8½" Tall, Glass Base, Blue Floral Design	*1300.00*
Lamp, 9" Tall, Multicolored Floral Design on Red Background	*6500.00*
Lamp, 9" Tall, Multicolored Parrots and Tropical Foliage Design	*4500.00*
Lamp, 9¼" Tall, 3-Footed, Shaded Amber to Blue	*1100.00*
Lamp, 9½" Tall, Brass Base, Amber and Brown Swirled Shade	*1000.00*
Lamp, 10" Tall, Green and Yellow Floral Design on White Background, Brass Base, Signed	*2200.00*

Lamp, 10½" Tall, Green and Red Floral Design on Yellow Background, Signed . .*$1200.00*

Lamp, 11" Tall, Red and White Floral Design on Brown Background, Signed *4000.00*

Lamp, 11¼" Tall, Green and White Lily Design, Signed "Handel" *6500.00*

Lamp, 12" Tall, Multicolored Lake and Trees on Yellow Background, Signed *6500.00*

Lamp, 12" Tall, Windmill Design, Dark Bronze Base *2200.00*

Lamp, 12" Tall, Light Ice Blue Mica Shade with Birds and Foliage, Brass Base . .*10,000.00*

Lamp, Wall Globe, Cobalt Blue Bird on Floral Background *600.00*

Lamp, 22½" Tall, Green Domed Shade, Multicolored Storm at Sea Design *3250.00*

Lamp, 28" Tall, Leaded Blue Domed Shade, Bronze Base, Egyptian (Sphinx) Design
. . . .*10,500.00*

Lamp, Wall Globe, Cobalt Blue Bird on Floral Background *600.00*

Lamp, 22½" Tall, Green Domed Shade, Multicolored Storm at Sea Design *3250.00*

Lamp, 28" Tall, Leaded Blue Domed Shade, Bronze Base, Egyptian (Sphinx) Design
. . . .*10,500.00*

Lamp, 29" Tall, Leaded Blue Domed Shade, Metal Base, Tree and Foliage Design .*12,500.00*

Pitcher, 9½", Pink Roses and White Carnations *350.00*

Plate, Cake, 10", 2 Handles, Pink Floral Design with Gold Edge *125.00*

Vase, 5½" Tall, 4" Diameter, White Floral Design on Green Background *425.00*

Vase, 7½" Tall, Green Trees and Foliage on Yellow Background *675.00*

Vase, 10" Tall, Green and Brown Forest Design, Signed *2000.00*

Vase, 12" Tall, Multicolored Floral and Scrolled Design, Signed *750.00*

Some of the most exquisite lamps ever made in America were fabricated by Handel and signed by numerous individual artists working in the company. Chipped-glass effects, hand-decorated interiors, bent inserts, metal or leaded shades, fired-on metallic stains, gilding, cameo engraving, and etchings can all be found on these famous lamps. Even the bases were quite elaborate; copper, brass, bronze, and white plated metals were used and decorated as well.

Handel also produced some opal glass as well as nonglass products (wood, metal, porcelain, and pottery items).

HOBBS, BROCUNIER AND COMPANY
1860S–1891

Object	Price
Bonbon Dish with Cover, 6", Amber Finial "Frances Ware"	*$175.00*
Bowl, 4", "Frances Ware", Hobnail Pattern	*50.00*
Bowl, 7½", "Frances Ware", Hobnail Pattern	*75.00*
Bowl, 8" Square, "Frances Ware"	*125.00*
Bowl, 9", "Frances Ware"	*100.00*
Bowl, 14¼" × 4¾" Boat-Shaped, Daisy and Button Pattern	*475.00*
Butter Dish with Cover, Amber Rim, Frosted, Hobnail Pattern	*150.00*
Butter Dish with Cover, Frosted, "Frances Ware"	*150.00*
Carafe, Water, Frosted with Amber Flashing, Block Design	*175.00*
Creamer, Amber Rim, Hobnail Pattern	*75.00*
Creamer, Amber Rim, Frosted, Hobnail Pattern	*125.00*
Creamer, Amber Rim, Frosted, "Frances Ware," Hobnail Pattern	*100.00*
Pitcher, Syrup, with Pewter Lid, Frosted, "Frances Ware," Hobnail Pattern	*200.00*
Pitcher, Milk, 5" Tall, Amber Rim, Hobnail Pattern	*225.00*

Pitcher, Milk, 5¹/₂" Tall, Frosted, "Frances Ware" *$250.00*
Pitcher, Water, 8" Tall, Globe-Shaped, Amber Neck and Rim, Hobnail Pattern *300.00*
Plate, 5³/₄" Square, Frosted, "Frances Ware," Hobnail Pattern *35.00*
Sauce Dish, "Frances Ware" *50.00*
Spooner, Amber Rim, Frosted, Hobnail Pattern *75.00*
Sugar with Cover, Amber Rim, Hobnail Pattern *100.00*
Sugar with Cover, Amber Rim, Frosted, Hobnail Pattern *150.00*
Toothpick Holder, Daisy and Button Pattern *250.00*
Toothpick Holder, 2" Tall, "Frances Ware" *100.00*
Tray, 12" × 7", "Frances Ware" *125.00*
Tray, 14" × 9¹/₂", Frosted, "Frances Ware" *300.00*
Tumbler, Amber Ribbon, Hobnail Pattern *450.00*
Tumbler, 4" Tall, Frosted, "Frances Ware" *75.00*
Vase, 7" Tall, Fluted Rim, Opalescent Pink with White Hobnails *350.00*

The most popular art form created by this company was that of "Frances Ware." It is characterized by an amber color, fluted rims, hobnails on the object, and an allover camphor staining. The purpose of the stain is to invoke a somewhat dull finish.

HOLLY AMBER   INDIANA TUMBLER AND GOBLET COMPANY, 1903

Object	*Price*
Bowl, Berry, 7¹/₂" Oval, 4¹/₂" Tall	*$625.00*
Bowl, Berry, 8¹/₂", 3¹/₂" Tall	*750.00*
Bowl, 10" Rectangular	*800.00*
Butter Dish with Cover, Domed, with Tapered Top	*1250.00*
Cake Salver, 9¹/₂" Diameter	*1750.00*
Compote with Cover, 6¹/₂" Diameter	*1350.00*
Compote with Cover, 8¹/₂" Diameter	*1200.00*
Creamer, 3" Tall	*900.00*
Cruet with Stopper, 6¹/₄" Tall	*1750.00*
Cup, Handled, 5" Tall	*550.00*
Dolphin Dish with Cover, 7"	*1250.00*
Mug, Handled, 4" Tall, Amber White Handle	*500.00*
Mug, Handled, 4¹/₂" Tall, Amber White Handle	*550.00*
Parfait, 6" Tall	*625.00*
Pickle Dish, 6¹/₂" × 4", 2-Handled	*450.00*
Pitcher, Syrup with Tin Lid	*1000.00*
Pitcher, Water, 8³/₄" Tall	*2500.00*
Plate, 9¹/₄"	*2250.00*
Relish Dish, 7¹/₂" Oblong	*650.00*
Sauce Dish	*250.00*
Sugar Dish with Cover	*1000.00*
Toothpick Holder, 2¹/₂" Tall	*350.00*
Toothpick Holder, 5" Tall, Pedestal Base	*750.00*
Tumbler, 4" Tall, Holly Branch Panels, Transparent Amber Rim	*425.00*
Tumbler, Water, Wreath in Base	*425.00*
Vase, 6" Tall, Footed	*675.00*

Holly Amber is a rare pressed art design featuring holly leaves on colored glass that shades from a light creamy opalescent to a darker brown-amber. The color is sometimes referred to as golden agate. It was made only from January 1, 1903 to June 13, 1903.

HONESDALE DECORATING COMPANY EARLY
1900S–MID-1930S

Object	Price
Bowl, 8", Cameo Design with Green Scrolls	*$325.00*
Goblet, 7" Tall, Gold Design and Border (Heisey Blank)	*75.00*
Plate, 8½", Amethyst with Gold Rim	*110.00*
Tumbler, 6¼" Tall, Crystal with Gold Trim	*50.00*
Vase, 5" Tall, Light Iridescent with Blue Cameo Scrolls	*350.00*
Vase, 6½" Tall, Multicolored Floral Design on a Blue Base	*425.00*
Vase, 7" Tall, Flared, Yellow Cameo Mums Outlined in Blue	*375.00*
Vase, 8½" Tall, Green, Purple, and Red Floral Design Outlined in Gold, Gold Beaded Rim, Signed	*500.00*
Vase, 9" Tall, Green Acid Cutback Design, Crystal Base with Gold Trim, Signed	*475.00*
Vase, 9" Tall, Green Cameo Scrolls with Gold	*450.00*
Vase, 10" Tall, Green and Gold Cameo, Signed	*525.00*
Vase, 10" Tall, Yellow Cameo Outlined in Crystal	*475.00*
Vase, 10¾" Tall, Blue Cameo with Gold, Gilded Rim	*575.00*
Vase, 11" Tall, Amethyst Cameo on Crystal, Gilded, Signed	*450.00*
Vase, 11" Tall, Red Cameo with Hunting Scene	*1250.00*
Vase, 11½" Tall, Blue Cameo on Crystal Base, Gilded, Signed	*800.00*
Vase, 12" Tall, Red Cameo on Frosted Crystal, Gold Outline, Flared	*750.00*
Vase, 12" Tall, Green Cameo with Gold Outline, Geese and Cattails Design	*700.00*
Vase, 12½" Tall, Blue Cameo on Frosted Crystal, Gilded Outline, Etched Floral and Scroll Designs, Signed "Honesdale"	*800.00*
Vase, 13½" Tall, Blue and Yellow Floral Design on a Crystal Base, Gilded Outline	*400.00*
Vase, 14" Tall, Crystal with Gilding, Signed "Honesdale"	*350.00*
Vase, 14" Tall, Emerald Green Background with Gilding, Floral Design	*200.00*
Vase, 14½" Tall, Gilded, Etched, Versailles Pattern	*250.00*
Vase, 17½" Tall, Crystal with Gold Tracing, Basketweave Design	*1100.00*

Honesdale was a branch of C. Dorflinger and Sons, and they decorated glass vases and other articles by enameling, engraving, etching, gilding, and using silver and gold trims. They fired on some iridescent colors as well.

IMPERIAL GLASS COMPANY 1901–1920S

Object	Price
Bowl, 9", Ribbed, Amber, Signed	*$175.00*
Bowl, Rose, Amethyst, Jewels, Signed	*150.00*
Candlestick, 10" Tall, Crystal with Ruby Red Holder and Base	*100.00*
Candy Dish with Cover, Pink, Jewels	*50.00*
Pitcher, Water, 8½" Tall, Cobalt Blue, Hobnail Pattern	*375.00*
Sweetmeat Jar with Cover, Blue, Jewels	*125.00*

Vase, 6" Tall, Iridescent Blue with White Foliage *$250.00*
Vase, 6" Tall, Amethyst, Jewels *175.00*
Vase, 6" Tall, Ruffled, Ruby Red *200.00*
Vase, 7" Tall, Iridescent White, Gold Loops *300.00*
Vase, 7³/₄" Tall, Flared, Footed, Iridescent Green Ground, Silver Designs *425.00*
Vase, 8" Tall, Frosted Ground, Iridescent Blue Designs *175.00*
Vase, 8¹/₂" Tall, Blue, Imperial Jewels *375.00*
Vase, 9" Tall, Blue Loops on Opal *350.00*
Vase, 9" Tall, White Foliage on Green Background, Orange Neck *200.00*
Vase, 9¹/₂" Tall, 3-Handled, Green Floral Design with Orange Interior *375.00*
Vase, 10" Tall, Opaque White, Blue Loops *275.00*
Vase, 10" Tall, Green Scrolling, Orange Interior *175.00*
Vase, 11¹/₄" Tall, Green Leafing on White, Orange Interior *425.00*

Imperial was a major manufacturer of Carnival and Depression glass but experimented early with iridescent art forms such as vases. "Imperial Jewels" was a pressed and blown colored glass introduced in 1916.

KEW BLAS   UNION GLASS COMPANY, 1893–EARLY 1900S

Object	*Price*
Bowl, 6", Light Blue Opal, 3-Footed, Flared, White Interior, Signed	*$400.00*
Bowl, 6¹/₂", Iridescent Gold and Green, Zipper Pattern, Signed	*750.00*
Candlestick, 8" Tall, Iridescent Gold with Swirled Stem, Signed	*300.00*
Candlestick, 9" Tall, Calcite and Gold with Green Feather Design, Signed	*350.00*
Compote, 5" Tall, 4" Diameter, 3-Footed, Iridescent Gold	*350.00*
Compote, 6" Tall, 4¹/₂" Diameter, Iridescent Gold Design	*425.00*
Creamer, 3¹/₄", Iridescent Gold, Signed	*475.00*
Cup, Iridescent Green, Gold, and Ivory, Applied Handle, Feather Design, Signed	*450.00*
Decanter with Enameled Stopper, 15" Tall, Ribbed, Gold	*1000.00*
Pitcher, 4¹/₂" Tall, Gold with Green Feather Design, Gold Interior, Swirled Handle ..	*750.00*
Saucer, Iridescent Green, Gold, and Ivory, Feather Design, Signed	*250.00*
Tumbler, 3¹/₂" Tall, 4-Sided, Iridescent Gold	*500.00*
Tumbler, 4" Tall, Gold with Feather Design	*450.00*
Vase, 5¹/₂" Tall, Iridescent Gold on White	*500.00*
Vase, 5³/₄" Tall, Flared, Ruffled, Iridescent Amber, Fishscale Pattern	*500.00*
Vase, 6" Tall, Calcite, Wavy Gold Design, Gold Interior	*600.00*
Vase, 6¹/₂" Tall, Green and Gold Feathers on an Iridescent Gold Background, Signed	*1000.00*
Vase, 8¹/₂" Tall, Iridescent Gold	*350.00*
Vase, 9" Tall, Calcite, Gold and Green Feather Design, Signed	*950.00*
Vase, 12" Tall, Iridescent Gold, Cat Tail Design	*1250.00*
Wineglass, 4³/₄" Tall, Twisted Stem, Iridescent Gold, Signed	*200.00*

W. S. Blake (superintendent at Union Glass) created the name "Kew Blas" by rearranging the letters of his name. "Kew Blas" was made in a variety of colors, such as brown, cream, green, tan, white, and several shades of these basic colors.

"Kew Blas" is fairly scarce and is often confused with other art glass produced in the same colors by other companies. "Kew-Blas" is sometimes found etched or signed on the underside of the company's glassware.

KIMBLE GLASS COMPANY   1930S

Object	Price
Bowl, Globe-Shaped, Blue with Streaked Orange and Brown, Cluthra Design, Signed, Numbered	.$250.00
Vase, 4¼" Tall, Light Blue and Orange, Cluthra Design, Signed	.250.00
Vase, 5" Tall, Green to White Shading, Cluthra Design	.350.00
Vase, 5" Tall, Blue, Cluthra Design, Signed	.450.00
Vase, 6" Tall, White, Cluthra Design, Signed	.175.00
Vase, 6½" Tall, Green, Orange, White, and Yellow, Cluthra Design, Signed	.1000.00
Vase, 6½" Tall, Flared, Triple-Hued, Cluthra Design	.700.00
Vase, 7¾" Tall, White, Signed	.225.00
Vase, 8" Tall, Green with White Enameling, Signed	.225.00
Vase, 8½" Tall, Footed, Orange and White, Cluthra Design	.250.00
Vase, 10" Tall, Crystal with Green to White Shading, Enameled Floral Design, Signed	.175.00
Vase, 10" Tall, Blue, Cluthra Design	.325.00
Vase, 11½" Tall, Blue and White, Cluthra Design, Signed	.350.00
Vase, 12" Tall, White with Enameled Design, Signed "Durand-Kimball"	.425.00
Vase, 12" Tall, Jade Green and White, Cluthra Design, Signed, Numbered	.400.00
Vase, 18" Tall, Blue and Yellow, Cluthra Design, Signed	.575.00

"Cluthra" art glass was Kimble's only popular product. It is characterized by brilliant gloss-finished colors with cloud formations and multiple air bubbles of varying sizes. It is often confused with Steuben's "Cluthra," which usually has a higher concentration of bubbles.

Some pieces are signed in silver with the "Kimble" name or a "K" with a date and number code. Also, a few can be found with the "Durand-Kimble" signature, indicating a brief partnership between the two companies.

LIBBEY ART GLASS   1870S–1930S

Object	Price
Bowl, Flared, Pink with Trapped Bubbles, Swirl Pattern, Signed	.$275.00
Bowl, 2½", Cream-Colored Satin, Signed	.900.00
Bowl, 8¾", Opaque White with Green Leaves, "Maize" Pattern	.225.00
Box, 4¼", Cream Satin Finish, Enameled Daisies, Marked "World's Fair 1893," Signed "Libbey Cut"	.425.00
Candlestick, 6" Tall, Crystal Stem and Foot, Red Feather Top, Signed	.850.00
Candlestick, 6" Tall, Crystal Foot and Stem, Opalescent Cup with Pink Interior, Signed "Libbey"	.900.00
Candlestick, 8" Tall, Air Twist Stem	.200.00
Champagne Glass, Squirrel Stem, Signed "Libbey"	.200.00
Cocktail Glass, Crow Stem, Signed "Libbey"	.100.00
Cocktail Glass, Opalescent Kangaroo Stem, Signed "Libbey"	.175.00
Compote, 3⅜" Tall, 5¾" Diameter, Circular Foot, Gold Knob, Blue to Iridescent Gold Shading	.550.00
Cup, Marked "World's Fair 1893"	.75.00
Cup, Vaseline, Marked "World's Fair 1893"	.100.00

Goblet, 6¼" Tall, Raised Blown Oplescent Drops over Bowl, Low Circular Foot, Morning Mist Pattern *$175.00*

Goblet, 9⅛" Tall, Circular Foot, 4 Globe-Shaped Bubbles in Stem, Ruby-Flashed Bowl with Engraved Scroll, Foliage, and Ribbons, Campanille Pattern *750.00*

Goblet, 9¼" Tall, Cut Circular Foot, Rub Knob on Stem, Cased Pink and White Victorian Cameo Cut Design, 4 Lady Cameos Separated by Columns *5500.00*

Goblet, 10¾" Tall, Engraved Circular Foot, Spiral Engraved Stem with Ruby Threading, Engraved Fruit Baskets and Scrolls on Bowl *750.00*

Paperweight, Lady's Head, Marked "World's Fair 1893" *250.00*

Paperweight, Frosted, Lady's Head Design, Marked "Columbian Exposition 1893" .*350.00*

Pitcher, Syrup with Pewter Lid, 6" Tall, Iridescent Gold Corn Cob, Blue Husks, "Maize" Pattern *500.00*

Plate, 7¾", Ship ("Santa Maria"), Sepia-Hued *500.00*

Salt and Pepper Shakers, Blue, Egg Design, Marked "1893 Exposition" *275.00*

Salt and Pepper Shakers, Brass Tops, "Maize" Pattern *250.00*

Saucer, Leaf-Shaped, Marked "World's Fair 1893" *60.00*

Saucer, Vaseline, Marked "World's Fair 1893" *75.00*

Tazza, 6" Tall, Opalescent Bowl and Foot, Crystal Stem, Blue-Swirled Threading . . .*850.00*

Toothpick Holder, Pink Shading to White, Blue and Green Floral Pattern, Gold Inscribed "Little Lob" *125.00*

Toothpick Holder, Yellow with Green Leaves Outlined in Gold, "Maize" Pattern . . .*425.00*

Tumbler, 3" Tall, Crystal Foot, Dark Green Prunts, Signed "Libbey" *175.00*

Tumbler, Iridescent Gold Ear with Blue Leaves, "Maize" Pattern *250.00*

Vase, 4½" Tall, Mushroom-Shaped, Signed "Libbey" *900.00*

Vase, 6½" Tall, Domed Circular Foot, Engraved Sitting Gazelle, Modern American Series *200.00*

Vase, 10" Tall, Opalescent Rabbit Base *225.00*

Vase, 10⅞" Tall, Flared, 3 Bubble Round Strawberry-Shaped Feet, Crystal, Modern American Series *250.00*

Vase, 11¼" Tall, Circular Foot, Amber Stem, Signed "Libbey" *650.00*

Vase, 12½" Tall, Circular Foot, Ribbed, Signed "Libbey" *900.00*

Vase, Opaque White with Green Husks, "Maize" Pattern *200.00*

Wineglass, 5" Tall, Opalescent Monkey Stem, Crystal Bowl, Signed "Libbey" *150.00*

Wineglass, 6" Tall, Kangaroo Stem, Crystal, Signed "Libbey" *125.00*

Wineglass, Opalescent Polar Bear Stem, Crystal Bowl, Signed "Libbey" *150.00*

Although Libbey is noted more for brilliant cut crystal, they continued some of the traditions of the New England Glass Company, which William L. Libbey purchased. "Amberina" was their most popular form of art glass, but they also produced a few other lines, such as souvenir items (from the 1893 World's Fair), "Maize" (corn cob designs), ornamental glassware, and experiments with shading (see additional entries under "Amberina" and "Peach Blow").

LOCKE ART GLASS   1891–1920S

Object	*Price*
Brandy Glass, 3¼" Tall, Etched Floral Design, Paper Sticker	*$125.00*
Champagne Glass, 6" Tall, Poppy Pattern	*125.00*
Goblet, 6¼" Tall, Etched Vines, Signed	*150.00*
Goblet, 6¾" Tall, Etched Floral Design, Signed	*125.00*

Parfait, Footed, Etched Kalana Poppy, Signed *$150.00*
Pitcher, 8" Tall, Etched Vintage Pattern, Signed *500.00*
Pitcher, 8" Tall, Etched Rose Pattern, Signed *300.00*
Pitcher, 8½" Tall, Tankard-Style, Ornate Handle, Grape and Line Design *1000.00*
Pitcher, 13½" Tall, Tankard-Style, Etched Vintage Pattern, Signed *1250.00*
Plate, 7", Etched Poinsettias, Signed *225.00*
Punch Cup, Poppy Pattern, Signed "Locke Art" *90.00*
Salt Dip, Rectangular (2¼" × 1¼"), Pedestal Foot, Vintage Pattern *100.00*
Sherbet, Etched with Various Fruit, Signed *225.00*
Sherbet, 3½" Tall, Etched Grapes and Vines *100.00*
Sherbet, 3¾" Tall, Etched Vines, Signed *225.00*
Tray, Rectangular, 15¾" × 8", Etched Floral Design *375.00*
Tumbler, 5¼" Tall, Ribbed, Etched Vintage Pattern *150.00*
Tumbler, 5¾" Tall, Etched Grape and Vine Design Signed *100.00*
Vase, 5" Tall, Ruffled, Etched Floral Design, Signed *700.00*
Vase, 5" Tall, Flared, Poppies and Flower Buds *525.00*
Vase, 6" Tall, Engraved Poppies *250.00*
Vase, 6¼" Tall, Flared, Etched Roses, Signed *575.00*
Vase, 10½" Tall, Crimped Folded Rim, Ribbed, Etched Fern Design *150.00*
Vase, 10¾" Tall, Gold Tinted Roses and Leaves, Signed "Locke Art—Mount Oliver, Pennsylvania" *1200.00*
Whiskey Tumbler, 2⅝" Tall, Engraved Wheat Pattern *150.00*

After leaving the New England/Libbey Glass companies in 1891, Locke founded his own cutting and decorating shop. Blanks were purchased from Dorflinger, and as a result, some of Locke's art glass is similar to Dorflinger's Kalana designs. Locke's knowledge and original designs were instrumental in New England/Libbey's production of Amberina, Pomona, Peach Blow, and so on. He continued those fine traditions with his own company.

MARY GREGORY GLASS BOSTON & SANDWICH GLASS COMPANY, 1870S–1910

Object *Price*
Bottle, Wine, with Crystal Bubble Stopper, 7⅛" Tall, Cranberry, Boy Design *$210.00*
Bottle, Wine, with Amber Faceted Stopper, 9" Tall, Amber, Boy Design *220.00*
Bottle, Wine, with Crystal Bubble Stopper, 10" Tall, Cranberry, Girl Design *225.00*
Box with Hinged Cover, 3¾" × 3¾", Brass Foot, Lime Green, Boy Design *250.00*
Box with Hinged Cover, 4" × 3⅝", Amber, Girl with Scarf *325.00*
Box with Hinged Cover, 6" × 5⅝", Blue, Girl Feeding Bird *475.00*
Cookie Jar with Cover, Cranberry, Girl Sitting on Fence *500.00*
Cruet with Crystal Stopper, Blue with Crystal Handle, Boy with Flower *350.00*
Cruet with Amber Stopper, 9½" Tall, 3-Petal Top, Amber, Boy Design *275.00*
Decanter with Stopper, 10" Tall, 3-Petal Top, Lime Green, Young Girl *175.00*
Decanter with Stopper, 13½" Tall, Amber, Boy in Riding Outfit *325.00*
Goblet, 4¾" Tall, Cranberry with Crystal Pedestal Foot, Girl with Hat *115.00*
Goblet, 5¾" Tall, Cranberry, Boy Feeding Birds *125.00*
Mug, 3⅞" Tall, Amber, Boy and Girl Design *125.00*
Mug, 4" Tall, Blue, Boy with Balloons *100.00*
Pitcher, Water, 9" Tall, Cranberry with Crystal Spout, Boys Design *425.00*

Mary Gregory art glass. Photo by Mark Pickvet.

Pitcher, Water, 9¹/₂" Tall, Crimped, Crystal, Girl Chasing Butterfly *$150.00*
Pitcher, Water, 10" Tall, Tankard-Style, Blue, Girl Tending Sheep .... *.275.00*
Plate, 8", Black, Girl in Swing .... *.50.00*
Tumbler, 2¹/₂" Tall, Cranberry, Girl and Boy Design .... *.110.00*
Tumbler, 3¹/₂" Tall, Green, 2 Girls, 1 Boy, and 3 Trees Design .... *.85.00*
Vase, 4" Tall, Blue, Boy in Garden .... *.100.00*
Vase, 4¹/₄" Tall, Cranberry with Crystal Pedestal Foot, Girl .... *.100.00*
Vase, 4³/₄" Tall, Cobalt Blue, Girl Sitting with Flower Basket .... *.175.00*
Vase, 6¹/₄" Tall, Cranberry, Boy or Girl .... *.225.00*
Vase, 7¹/₂" Tall, Cobalt Blue, Boy with Hat and Oars .... *.125.00*
Vase, 7³/₄" Tall, Pink with White Interior, Girl with Butterfly Net .... *.150.00*
Vase, 9" Tall, Pedestal Foot, Cranberry, Boy Blowing Bubbles .... *.300.00*
Vase, 9¹/₈" Tall, Cranberry, Girl with Umbrella .... *.250.00*
Vase, 10" Tall, Scalloped, Amber, Boy or Girl .... *.250.00*
Vase, 10³/₄" Tall, Black Amethyst, Boy or Girl .... *.250.00*
Vase, 11¹/₄" Tall, Scalloped, Pedestal Base, Gold Trim .... *.300.00*
Vase, 11³/₄" Tall, Blue, Boy Kneeling Offering Heart to Girl .... *.475.00*
Vase, 12" Tall, 5¹/₂" Diameter, Pink, Girl Sitting on Branch .... *.275.00*
Vase, 17" Tall, Cranberry, Boys and Girls Gathering Apples .... *.550.00*
Vase, 17" Tall, Black Amethyst, Girl with Hat, Umbrella, and Basket .... *.525.00*

Mary Gregory glass is characterized by crystal and colored glassware (most commonly pastel pink) decorated with white enameled designs of one or more boys and/or girls playing in Victorian scenes. Mary Gregory actually worked as a decorator for the Boston & Sandwich Glass Company from 1870 to 1880, but it is a mystery whether or not she painted the glass of her namesake.

MONROE, C. F., COMPANY   KELVA, NAKARA, AND
WAVE CREST, 1880–1916

Object	Price
Ashtray, 4¹/₂", Opal Scrolls and Pink Apple Blossoms	*$275.00*
Bonbon Tray, Swirled with Beading, Signed "NAKARA"	*.425.00*

Box, Glove, Rectangular, 8¹/₂" × 4¹/₂", Hinged Cover, Signed "WAVE CREST" $825.00

Box, Hexagonal, 4" Across, Hinged Cover, Signed "NAKARA" 400.00

Box, Hexagonal, 4" Tall, Hinged Cover, Signed "NAKARA" .400.00

Box, Octagonal, Hinged Cover, Signed "KELVA" 700.00

Box, Jewelry, 7", Signed "WAVE CREST" 275.00

Box, Ring, 3¹/₂", Signed "WAVE CREST" 200.00

Box, Round, 6" Diameter, Hinged Cover, Signed "NAKARA" 550.00

Box, Hexagonal, 8" Across, Hinged Cover, Pink and White, Signed "KELVA" 425.00

Box, Round, 8¹/₄" Diameter, Hinged Cover, Woman's Picture on Cover, Signed "NAKARA"
. . . . .1000.00

Box, Trinket, Signed, "NAKARA" 250.00

Box, 8¹/₂" Wide, Picture of 2 Women in Garden, Signed "NAKARA" 900.00

Box, Hinged Lid, Gold Decoration and Opal Flowers, Signed "WAVE CREST" 850.00

Cigarette Holder, Hexagonal 475.00

Cracker Jar with Silverplated Cover, 6" Tall, Silverplated Handle, Enameled Scroll Design, Wave Crest 375.00

Creamer, Swirl Pattern with Silverplated Mounts 150.00

Cruet with Brass Handle and Stopper, Angel Design Wave Crest 425.00

Ewer, 14" Tall 175.00

Ewer, Melon, 15¹/₂" Tall, Ribbed 250.00

Fernery, 7" Wide, Gold and White Design, Wave Crest (Unsigned) 375.00

Hairpin Dish, 3¹/₄" Diameter, Signed "WAVE CREST" 135.00

Hair Receiver with Cover, 4" Tall, Small Floral Decoration, Signed "KELVA" 325.00

Hair Receiver, Diamond-Shaped with Cover, White Beading and Blue Enamel, Signed "NAKARA" 500.00

Humidor with Cover, 6" Tall, Tan with Floral Design, Signed "KELVA" 725.00

Humidor with Cover, 6" Tall, Brass Rim on Top of Base and Bottom of Cover, Floral Design, Embossed "Cigars," Wave Crest 875.00

Ice Bucket, 11" Tall, 6" Diameter, Silver Cover and Handle, Wild Rose Design, Wave Crest
. . . . .675.00

Jar, Biscuit with Silverplated Cover and Handle, 8" Tall, Lilac Design, Wave Crest . .500.00

Jar, Biscuit with Silverplated Cover, 10" Tall, Swirl Pattern .550.00

Jar, Blown-Out, with Cover, 3" Tall, Wave Crest (Unsigned) 350.00

Jar, Tobacco, with Metal Cover, 6³/₄" Tall, Lettered "Tobacco," Signed "NAKARA" .900.00

Jar, Toothpowder, with Embossed Brass Cover, Signed "WAVE CREST" 500.00

Jardiniere, 7" Tall, Straight Sides, Ring Feet, Enameled Floral Design with Gold Trim, Wave Crest 500.00

Jardiniere, 12" Tall, White, Gold Decoration, Nakara 600.00

Lamp, Table, Signed "WAVE CREST" 450.00

Lamp Base, Blown-Out, 17" Tall, Frosted Crystal Shade, Wave Crest (Unsigned) . . .800.00

Letter Holder, Footed Base, Wave Crest (Unsigned) 375.00

Perfume Bottle with Brass Stopper and Double Handles, 3¹/₂" Tall, Pink and Purple Floral Design, Wave Crest 250.00

Pitcher, Syrup, with Silverplated Lid, 4" Tall, Raised Paneled Floral Design, Wave Crest
. . . . .750.00

Pitcher, Syrup, Swirled with Silverplated Top and Handle, Enameled Pink Roses . .600.00

Planter, 7¹/₂" Tall, Beaded Brass Rim, Signed "WAVE CREST" 450.00

Platter, Rectangular (11" × 8"), Scrolled Edge, Enameled Roses, Wave Crest 550.00

Salt Dip, Brass Rim, 2 Brass Handles, Floral Design, Wave Crest 100.00

Salt and Pepper Shakers with Pewter Tops, 3" Tall, Moss Green, Enameled Floral Design, Kelva 400.00

Salt and Pepper Shakers with Pewter Tops, Signed "WAVE CREST" 450.00

C. F. Monroe art glass. Photo by Mark Pickvet.

Sugar, Swirl Pattern with Silverplated Mounts *$150.00*
Sugar Shaker with Silverplated Top, 4" Tall, Floral Design, Wave Crest *175.00*
Toothpowder Jar with Brass Cover, 3½" Tall, White and Pink Floral Design *325.00*
Vase, 5" Tall, with Bronze-Footed Holder *200.00*
Vase, 11¼" Tall, Blue with Burmese Shading, Enameled Orchids, Nakara *1000.00*
Vase, 12" Tall, 9" Wide, Handled, Footed, Signed "WAVE CREST" *700.00*
Vase, 13" Tall, Hexagonal, Marbled Background with White Rim, Signed "KELVA" *675.00*
Vase, 14" Tall, Green Background with Silverplated Feet, Signed, "KELVA" *825.00*
Vase, 17½" Tall, 4-Footed Brass Base, 2 Brass Handles Connected with Brass Rim, Cartouche Hand-Painted Maiden Outlined in Gold and Mauve, Wave Crest *1500.00*
Whisk Broom Holder, 8½", Signed "WAVE CREST" *800.00*

C. F. Monroe was a small art decorating company in Meriden, Connecticut. They primarily applied opal enamels in both satin and brightly colored finishes to blanks provided to them by Pairpoint as well as by French factories. C. F. Monroe produced only three products, and none is easily distinguished from the others except by name. Most are either signed or stamped "KELVA," "NAKARA," or "WAVE CREST."

MOTHER-OF-PEARL VARIOUS COMPANIES, 1880S–EARLY 1900S

Object	*Price*
Basket, 5½" Tall, Ruffled, Pink with Frosted Handle, Herringbone Pattern	*$250.00*
Basket, 12" Tall, Thorn Handle, Moire Pattern with Enameled Decoration	*700.00*
Bottle, Cologne, 4½" Tall, Apricot with Silver Stopper, Drape Design	*200.00*
Bowl, Rose or Flower, 4" Tall, 3½" Diameter	*625.00*
Bowl, 4" Tall, Ruffled, Frosted Feet, Blue, Ribbon Pattern	*475.00*
Bowl, Bride's, 10" Diameter, Scalloped, Ribbed, Amber with Gold Floral Design, Diamond Quilted Pattern	*950.00*
Bowl, Bride's, 11" Diameter, Ruffled, Blue and White with Gold Highlights, Herringbone Pattern	*450.00*
Box with Hinged Cover, 4¼" Tall, Brass Handle, Blue with White Lining, Gold Leaves and Scrolls	*300.00*
Cookie Jar with Cover, Green with Silverplated Cover, Handle, and Rim, Enameled Chrysanthemums	*200.00*
Creamer, Frosted Handle, Apricot, Raindrop Pattern	*150.00*

Creamer, 4½" Tall, Blue Frosted Handle and White Lining, Teardrop Pattern *$300.00*
Creamer, 5" Tall, Blue with Frosted Handle, Diamond Quilted Pattern *325.00*
Cruet with Stopper, 6" Tall, Pink with White Interior, Diamond Quilted Pattern *175.00*
Cruet with Stopper, 6½" Tall, Blue with Frosted Handle *575.00*
Ewer, 10½" Tall, 2 Frosted Handles, Pink with White Interior *1200.00*
Ewer, 12" Tall, Shaded Rose, Swirl Pattern *750.00*
Lamp, 9¾" Tall, 3-Footed, Brass Base, Raindrop Patterned Shade *800.00*
Lamp, 12¼" Tall, Brass Base, Pink and White Floral Design, Signed *1000.00*
Lamp, 20½" Tall, Brown, Brass Foots and Mounts, Swirl Pattern *1250.00*
Mug, 3½" Tall, Frosted Handle, Pink to White Floral Design, Diamond Quilted Pattern *300.00*
Perfume Bottle with Stopper, 5" Tall, Blue, Diamond Quilted Pattern *375.00*
Pitcher, Cream, 5½" Tall, Ruffled, Frosted Handle, Herringbone Pattern *450.00*
Pitcher, Syrup with Lid, Red, Beaded Drape Pattern *475.00*
Pitcher, Water, 9¼" Tall, Oval Top, Frosted Handle, Enameled Blue Foliage Design .*325.00*
Salt and Pepper Shakers with Pewter Tops, 3½" Tall, Pink to White Shading, Raindrop Pattern *325.00*
Sugar with Dome Cover, Apricot, Raindrop Pattern *200.00*
Sugar Shaker, 5" Tall, Cranberry Floral and Stork Design, Inverted Thumbprint Pattern *750.00*
Tumbler, 3¾" Tall, Apricot, Herringbone Pattern *150.00*
Tumbler, 4" Tall, Enameled Daisies and Leaves, Diamond Quilted Pattern *250.00*
Vase, 3" Tall, Miniature, Salmon, Diamond Quilted Pattern *225.00*
Vase, 4¾" Tall, Blue, Enameled Floral Design, Diamond Quilted Pattern *225.00*
Vase, 5" Tall, Ruffled, Pink, Diamond Quilted Pattern *300.00*
Vase, 5½" Tall, Folded-In Square Top, Blue, Hobnail Pattern *625.00*
Vase, 5¾" Tall, Rose Design, Acorn Pattern *500.00*
Vase, 6" Tall, Yellow to White Shading, Hobnail Pattern *750.00*
Vase, 6½" Tall, White Ground with Gold Design, Ribbon Pattern *1150.00*
Vase, 6¾" Tall, Ruffled, Rose, Herringbone Pattern *250.00*
Vase, 7¼" Tall, Dark Pink, Drape Pattern *250.00*
Vase, 7¼" Tall, Ruffled, Light Caramel, Ribbed, Raindrop Pattern *275.00*
Vase, 8" Tall, White, Enameled Peacock Tail (Eye) Design *625.00*
Vase, 9" Tall, Triple-Ring Neck, Peach, Diamond Quilted Pattern *225.00*
Vase, 9" Tall, Ruffled, Yellow with White Lining, Enameled Floral Design, Silverplated Holder, Ribbon Handles *300.00*
Vase, 10" Tall, Ruffled, Green with White Lining, Diamond Quilted Pattern *550.00*
Vase, 11" Tall, Shaded Apricot, Raindrop Pattern *500.00*
Vase, 11½" Tall, Ruffled, Blue, Loop and Teardrop Pattern *400.00*
Vase, 13" Tall, Ruffled, Blue, Herringbone Pattern *300.00*
Vase, 16" Tall, Ribbed, Chartreuse Lining, Zipper Pattern *575.00*

"Mother-of-Pearl" is characterized by two or more layers of glass in a satin, pearl-like finish and by internal indentations that purposely trap air bubbles. The two major producers of this pearl glass were the Mount Washington Glass Works and the Phoenix Glass Works, but others, like Steuben, Tiffany, and Libbey, also created glass in this manner.

A host of decorating techniques and coloring effects were applied to this art glass. Decorations include applied, beading, cameo engraving, enameling, and gold leafing. Colors are much like those of pearls: shaded light blues, light pinks, light purples, light yellows, and sparkling off-whites. These techniques were also applied to numerous popular cut patterns of the 19th century, including "Diamond Quilted," "Herringbone," "Raindrops," "Ribbed," "Thumbprints," and so on.

MOUNT WASHINGTON GLASS WORKS
1870–1894

Object	*Price*
Basket, Bride's, 6" Tall, 5½" Diameter, Cameo, Blue and White Floral Design, Silverplated Holder	*$850.00*
Basket, Bride's, 12" Tall, Cameo, Flared, 4-Footed, Pink and White Design, Silverplated Holder	*1250.00*
Bowl, 7½" Cameo, Red and White, Floral Design with Winged Griffins	*1000.00*
Bowl, 8½", Cameo, Blue and White Floral Design	*600.00*
Bowl, 9½" Cameo, Pink and White Floral Design	*1000.00*
Bowl, Rose, Cameo, White and Yellow Daisies	*350.00*
Bowl, Rose, 6", 5¼" Tall, Pink and Blue Enameled Floral Design	*300.00*
Candlestick, 7¼" Tall, Silver Holder, Enameled Pink Floral Design	*250.00*
Cookie Jar with Cover, 6" Tall, Pink, Royal Flemish Design	*1750.00*
Cookie Jar with Cover, 6¼" Tall, Gold Thistle Design	*800.00*
Cracker Jar, 6" Tall, Crystal with Enameled Brownies, Signed "Napoli"	*1000.00*
Cracker Jar, 6½" Tall, Pastel Floral Pattern, Albertine	*750.00*
Cracker Jar with Cover, 6½" Tall, Royal Flemish Leaf Design	*750.00*
Cruet with Stopper, 5¾" Tall, Rose Amber, Inverted Thumbprint Pattern	*550.00*
Ewer, 11⅜" Tall, Twisted Handle and Neck, Royal Flemish Design	*450.00*
Ewer, 15½" Tall, Rope Handle, Overlaid Royal Flemish Design	*2200.00*
Ewer with Cover, 16" Tall, Rope Handle, Royal Flemish, Coat of Arms Decoration	*5500.00*
Hatpin Holder, Mushroom-Shaped, Lusterless, Satin Finish, Fern and Flower Design	*300.00*
Lamp, 19¾" Tall, Kerosene, Milk Shade, Pink and Yellow Floral Design, Globular Glass Base, Footed (Shells and Ram's Head)	*1750.00*
Lamp, 42" Tall, Electric, Crystal Shade, Blue Aqua, Gold Lions and Shields, Red Accents, Royal Flemish Design	*7500.00*
Mustard Jar with Hinged Cover, Leaf Design on Pink and White Background	*325.00*
Paperweight, 4⅛" Diameter, Blue and White Shaded Rose, Green Stem, Serrated Green Leaves	*25,000.00*
Pitcher, Syrup, with Lid, Multicolored Floral Design Outlined in Gold	*2000.00*
Pitcher, Syrup, with Metal Lid, Barrel-Shaped, Ribbed, Metal Handle, Floral Design	*500.00*
Pitcher, Water, 9" Tall, Tan and Brown with Red Scrolls, Royal Flemish Design	*2750.00*
Pitcher, Syrup, with Lid, Multicolored Floral Design Outlined in Gold	*2000.00*
Pitcher, Syrup, with Metal Lid, Barrel-Shaped, Ribbed, Metal Handle, Floral Design	*500.00*
Pitcher, Water, 9" Tall, Tan and Brown with Red Scrolls, Royal Flemish Design	*2750.00*
Pitcher, Water, 10" Tall, Crystel, Crab Decoration	*750.00*
Plate, 10", Lusterless, Enameled Pansies	*75.00*
Plate, 12", Lusterless, Enameled Portrait of Woman	*125.00*
Salt Dip, 4-Footed, Ribbed, Pink and Yellow Pansies with Gold Highlights	*225.00*
Salt and Pepper Shakers, 2½" Tall, Egg-Shaped, Pewter Tops, Opaque White with Various Enameled Floral Designs	*450.00*
Salt Shaker, Egg-Shaped, White with Enameled Foliage, Metal Chick's Head Top	*425.00*
Salt Shaker, Rose Amber, Inverted Thumbprint Pattern	*175.00*
Sugar Shaker, Cream White with Pink and Blue Enameled Floral Design	*425.00*
Sugar Shaker, Ribbed, Purple Violet Design	*275.00*

Toothpick Holder, 2⅛" Tall, Lusterless, White with Enameled Leaves *$325.00*
Vase, 3¾" Tall, Lava with White Outlines, Multicolored Mica Chips *2000.00*
Vase, 4½" Tall, Lava, Applied Handles, Acidized *2000.00*
Vase, 4¾" Tall, Satin Finish, Enameled Forget-Me-Not Design *625.00*
Vase, 5¼" Tall, Rolled Rim, Venetian Diamond, Enameled Floral Design *600.00*
Vase, 6" Tall, Opaque White, Pink Ground, Gilded Rings, Enameled Bird on Branch .*125.00*
Vase, 6½" Tall, Lava, Multicolored Imbedded Glass Flecks *3500.00*
Vase, 7¼" Tall, Gold Tracing and Edging, Floral Design *2250.00*
Vase, 7½" Tall, 2-Handled, Royal Flemish, Tan and Brown Medallion Design *2000.00*
Vase, 8" Tall, Brown Shading, Gold Outlining, Royal Flemish Design with Winged Gargoyle
. . . .*3500.00*
Vase, 8¼" Tall, Pear-Shaped, Floral Design, Inscribed "Progressive/Fuchre/November 16,
1886" *2000.00*
Vase, 9" Tall, 7½" Diameter, Yellow Opal, Chrysanthemum Design *625.00*
Vase, 9" Tall, Globe Base, Gold Trim, Frog and Reeds Design, Signed "Napoli" . . .*1000.00*
Vase, 10" Tall, Enameled Floral Design, Signed "Napoli" *625.00*
Vase, 10½" Tall, Enameled Dragonflies and Floral Design *750.00*
Vase, 10½" Tall, Tan and Red Panels, Gold Beading at Top and Base, Red Top, Royal Flemish Design, Gold Serpent and Falcon on Front and Back *4500.00*
Vase, 11" Tall, Gourd-Shaped, Brown to Gold Satin, Seaweed Design *525.00*
Vase, 13" Tall, Royal Flemish, Camel and Rider Paneled Design *5500.00*
Vase, 15" Tall, Royal Flemish, Duck Decorations *3250.00*
Vase, 16" Tall, Boy on Front and Foliage on Back, Signed "Verona" *1000.00*

With such influences as Deming Jarves, William L. Libbey, A. H. Seabury, and others, Mount Washington became a major producer of art glass tableware and vases in the late 19th century. A huge variety of styles and designs including "Amberina," "Burmese," "Crown Milano," "Mother-of-Pearl," "Peach Blow," and countless others were all part of Mount Washington's output. Several additional listings can be found under these designs. "Royal Flemish" refers to a Mount Washington design that resembles stained windows (individual pieces of glass separated by lead line borders).

NASH, A., DOUGLAS CORPORATION EARLY 1900S-1931

Object   *Price*
Bowl with Underplate, Iridescent Gold and Platinum, Signed, Numbered *$425.00*
Bowl, 4", Red with Silver Stripes, Chintz Design *550.00*
Bowl, 10¼", Ruffled, Iridescent Green, Signed *725.00*
Box with Hinged Cover, 5" Diameter, Blue, Chintz Design, Signed *375.00*
Candlestick, 4" Tall, Ball Stem, Red and Gray, Chintz Design *325.00*
Chalice, 4½" Tall, Fluted, Gold, Pink, and Platinum, Signed, Numbered *625.00*
Cologne Bottle with Stopper, 5" Tall, Alternating Stripes of Green and Blue, Chintz Design
. . . .*625.00*
Compote, 7¼" Diameter, 4½" Tall, Green, Chintz Design, Signed *325.00*
Compote, 8" Diameter, 5" Tall, Green with Red and Gray Spiraled Rim, Chintz Design
. . . .*475.00*
Cordial, 4" Tall, Blue and Green, Chintz Design *100.00*
Goblet, 5" Tall, Pedestal Foot, Blue and Silver, Chintz Design, Signed *150.00*

Goblet, Twisted Stem, Wafer Foot, Pink Threaded Bowl, Signed "Libbey-Nash" . . .*$175.00*
Nut Dish, 1¼" × 4", Ruffled, Iridescent Gold *275.00*
Perfume Bottle with Stopper, 8" Tall, Blown-Out Bottom, Iridescent Gold *775.00*
Plate, 6½", Chartreuse and Orchid Spirals from Center, Chintz Design *175.00*
Salt Dip, 4" Diameter, Iridescent Bronze, Blue and Violet Highlights, Signed *250.00*
Vase, 4¼" Tall, Flared, Iridescent Amber, Signed "Nash-544" *550.00*
Vase, 5½" Tall, Stretched Iridescent Gold *450.00*
Vase, 5¾" Tall, Red Ground with Silver Stripes, Chintz Design, Signed *800.00*
Vase, 6¾" Tall, Square Curved Rim, Iridescent Gold, Signed "Nash-539" *475.00*
Vase, 10" Tall, Trumpet-Shaped, Green and Blue, Chintz Design, Signed *525.00*
Wineglass, 6" Tall, Green and Lavender, Chintz Design, Signed *100.00*

The Nashes, including Arthur J., A. Douglas, and Leslie, all worked for various glass companies in England and America. The A. Douglas Nash Corporation produced art glass for the most part in the style of Tiffany (Leslie Nash once managed the Tiffany Glass Furnace at Corona, New York).

"Chintz" glass is the most recognizable form of Nash design and is characterized by a spoked, rayed, or striped pattern emanating from the center of an object. A multitude of colors on iridescent backgrounds is also characteristic of Nash's products. Some pieces were decorated in gold or platinum luster or trims as well.

NEW ENGLAND GLASS COMPANY EARLY 1800S–1880S

Object	Price
Bowl, Finger, 4½", Scalloped, Agata Style	*$850.00*
Bowl, 7", Opaque Blue	*775.00*
Bowl, 8", Opaque Green	*1250.00*
Bowl, 8½", Ruffled, Amber Rim, Pomona Style	*225.00*
Creamer, Agata Style	*1250.00*
Cruet with Stopper, 5½" Tall, Opaque Green	*1500.00*
Cruet with White Stopper, 5½" Tall, Globe-Shaped, Ruffled, Pink Handle, Agata Style	*1500.00*
Paperweight, 2⅝" Diameter, Latticino Ground, 3 Red and White Flower Buds, Green Leaf Tips	*3250.00*
Paperweight, 2¾" Diameter, Pink Poinsettia with White Center and Green Stem and Leaves, White Latticino Basket	*800.00*
Paperweight, Apple with Cut Slice, 3" Diameter, Crystal Base (Francois Pierre)	*3000.00*
Pitcher, 4¼" Tall, Square Top, White Reeded Handle, Agata Style	*1500.00*
Pitcher, 6¼" Tall, Square Top, Pomona Style, Cornflower Design	*500.00*
Pitcher, 8¼" Tall, Amber Top, Pomona Style, Cornflower Design	*350.00*
Pitcher, 10" Tall, Pear-Shaped, Crystal with Vertical Cleats Below the Waist	*225.00*
Plate, 6½", Fluted Rim, Agata Style	*900.00*
Punch Bowl, 9¼", Amber Trim, Pomona Style	*1000.00*
Punch Cup, Amber Trim, Pomona Style	*100.00*
Salt Dip, 3" Long, 2⅛" Tall, 4-Footed, Floral Design, Signed	*250.00*
Salt Shaker, 3¾" Tall, Agata Style	*500.00*
Spooner, 4½" Tall, Opaque Green with Gold Band	*1000.00*
Sugar, 3" Tall, 2 Handles, Gold Band of Berries and Leaves, Pomona Style	*400.00*
Sugar, 4" Tall, Flared, Square Neck, 2 Handles, Gold Decoration, Agata Style	*1750.00*

Sugar Shaker, 4" Tall, Ribbed, Fig Form, Lime Opal with Pink Floral Design *$825.00*
Toothpick Holder, Square Top, Agata Style *650.00*
Toothpick Holder, Gold-Stained Collar, Pomona Style *350.00*
Tray, 12½" × 7½", Ruffled, Gold Rim, Stained Cornflower Design, Pomona Style ..*800.00*
Tumbler, 3¾" Tall, Agata Style *750.00*
Tumbler, 3¾" Tall, Opaque Green with Gold Band (Several Styles) *1000.00*
Tumbler, 3¾" Tall, Amber Top, Pomona Style, Cornflower Design *200.00*
Tumbler, 4" Tall, Agata Style *800.00*
Vase, 4½" Tall, 4 Pinched Sides, Ruffled, Crimped, Agata Style *2250.00*
Vase, 5¾" Tall, Agata Style *2000.00*
Vase, 6" Tall, Circular Foot, Agata Style *2500.00*
Vase, 7" Tall, Trumpet-Shaped, Footed, Amethyst Molded Ovals Design *200.00*

Another Deming Jarves–founded company, New England Glass was blessed with
many other gifted designers: Joseph Locke, Henry Whitney, and Louis Vaupel, to
name just a few. The company's output was huge and spanned all lines of glass
from early pressed practical wares to fancy art glass. New England's art examples
included "Agata," "Amberina," "Pomona," and a host of others.

ONYX GLASS   VARIOUS COMPANIES, 1889–EARLY 1900S

Object	*Price*
Bowl, 4", Red and White Floral Design	*$1250.00*
Bowl, 8", White with Silver Flowers	*1000.00*
Butter Dish with Cover, 6" Diameter, 4½" Tall, Platinum Design on Cream Background	*1750.00*
Creamer, Raised White Opalescent Design on Red Background	*1100.00*
Muffineer, 5", White	*500.00*
Paperweight, Pig, Findlay	*225.00*
Pitcher, Syrup, with Silverplated Lid, 7" Tall, Ivory with Gold Decoration	*600.00*
Pitcher, Syrup, with Silverplated Lid, 7½" Tall, Metal Handle, Silver Design on Ivory Background	*575.00*
Pitcher, Water, 8" Tall, Silver Color, Findlay	*1100.00*
Salt Shaker with Metal Cover, 2¾" Tall, Silver Flowers on Brown Background	*450.00*
Salt Shaker with Metal Cover, 2¾" Tall, Raised Silver Flowers on Cream Background	*350.00*
Spooner, Opalescent White Flowers on Red Background	*900.00*
Spooner, Silver Design on Cream Background	*525.00*
Sugar with Cover, Raised White Opalescent Design	*1200.00*
Sugar with Cover, 6" Tall, Platinum Flowers on Cream Background	*650.00*
Sugar Shaker, 5" Tall, Light Brown	*650.00*
Sugar Shaker with Metal Cover, 5¾" Tall, Silver Flowers on Cream Background	*500.00*
Toothpick Holder, Raised Silver Design on Ivory Background	*275.00*
Tumbler, 3¼" Tall, Barrel-Shaped, Silver Design on Cream Background	*400.00*
Tumbler, 3½" Tall, White with Silver Floral Design	*450.00*
Tumbler, 4" Tall, Dark Red and White Floral Design	*1250.00*
Vase, 5" Tall, Cream with Silver Floral Design	*650.00*
Vase, 6½" Tall, Raised Silver Flowers on Cream Background, Findlay	*700.00*

The first patent was obtained by George Leighton in 1889 while working for the

Dalzell, Gilmore, and Leighton Company. They referred to their design as "Findlay Onyx." They experienced difficulties in perfecting a durable formula, for their onyx products were brittle and cracked easily.

"Onyx Glass" is characterized by parallel layers of colors, at times thin enough to be translucent. Lustrous forms of platinum or silver, opal forms, concentric rings on the base, and varying degrees of relief because of the layering technique are all aspects of "Onyx glass."

PAIRPOINT MANUFACTURING COMPANY, INC.
1894–1957

Object	*Price*
Bowl, Bride's, 9", Cut Rim, Medallion Design, Footed Silverplated Frame	*$300.00*
Bowl, Bride's, Daisy and Bluebell Design, Silverplated Holder, Signed "Pairpoint"	*750.00*
Bowl, Green with Crystal Swan Handles (Small), (Gunderson-Pairpoint)	*150.00*
Bowl, Footed, Green with Crystal Swan Handles, (Large) (Gunderson-Pairpoint)	*350.00*
Bowl, 12", Footed Base, Ruby and Blue Twist Design	*300.00*
Bowl, 14", Footed Base, Ruby and Blue Twist Design	*350.00*
Bowl, 16", Footed Base, Ruby and Blue Twist Design	*400.00*
Bowl, Centerpiece, Turned-Down Rim, Amber with Silver Overlay	*300.00*
Bowl with Cover, 8", 6¹/₂" Tall, 2 Handles, Fish with Chrysanthemum Design, Signed "Pairpoint Limoges 2502/50"	*850.00*
Box with Hinged Cover, Oval, Cream with Gold Foliage, Signed "Pairpoint"	*550.00*
Box with Hinged Cover, Oval, Scalloped, Cream with Gold Foliage, Signed "Pairpoint"	*575.00*
Candlestick, 4¹/₂" Tall, Mushroom Top, Green with Crystal Bubble in Stem	*75.00*
Candlestick, 5" Tall, Ruby and Blue Twist Design	*225.00*
Candlestick, 10" Tall, Engraved Floral Holder, Air-Twist Stem, Veneti Design	*250.00*
Candlestick, 16" Tall, Emerald Green	*300.00*
Candlestick, Prism Cut, Ball Connector, Emerald Green	*200.00*
Candy Dish with Cover, Engraved Dew Drop Design, Canaria Pattern, Crystal Bubble Finial	*200.00*
Compote, 4" Tall, 6" Diameter, Aurora Pattern	*125.00*
Compote, 4¹/₄" Tall, 6" Diameter, Ruby with Crystal Bubble in Stem	*125.00*
Compote, 4⁵/₈" Tall, 8" Diameter, Ruby and Blue Twist Design	*200.00*
Compote, 5" Tall, Ruby with Crystal Bubble in Stem	*225.00*
Compote, 6¹/₂" Tall, 12" Diameter, Paperweight Base, Amber with Crystal Bubble in Stem	*175.00*
Compote, 6¹/₂" Tall, 10¹/₂" Diameter, Green with Crystal Bubble in Stem	*175.00*
Compote, 7¹/₄" Tall, 6¹/₄" Diameter, Amber with Crystal Bubble in Stem	*175.00*
Compote, 7¹/₂" Tall, Black with Silver Overlay	*375.00*
Compote, 8" Tall, 8" Diameter, Floral Design, Green with Crystal Ball Stem, Silver Overlay, Marked "Rockwell"	*275.00*
Compote, Upturned Foot, Colias Pattern, Light Green with Crystal Ball Connector	*300.00*
Compote with Cover, Green with Crystal Bubble Connector	*150.00*
Cracker Jar with Cover, Melon with Gold Tracings, Signed "Pairpoint" (Cover Signed "M.W.")	*450.00*
Goblet, Engraved Grape Design, Canaria Pattern	*125.00*
Hat, 3¹/₄" Tall, Opaque Pink to Blue Coloring	*75.00*
Lamp, Boudoir, 5" Diameter Shade, Rose Bouquet Design, Tree Trunk Base, Signed "Pairpoint"	*2250.00*

Lamp, Table, 8" Diameter Shade, Brass Base, Dogwood Border, Signed "Pairpoint" ..$2500.00

Lamp, 9¼" Tall, Miniature, Kerosene, Blue and White Windmill Design, Signed "Delft"
. . . . .500.00

Lamp, 13¾" Tall, 4-Sectioned Shade, Metal Base (Tree), Enameled Apples and Apple
Blossoms 5500.00

Lamp, 15¾" Tall, Frosted Domed Shade, Enameled Desert Scene (Sunset) 2750.00

Lamp, 21" Tall, Metal Base, Multicolored Leaf Design, Grape Pattern, Shade Stamped "The
Pairpoint Corp." 3500.00

Lamp, 21" Tall, 14" Diameter Shade, Brass Base, Floral and Butterfly Design, Papillon
Pattern 4500.00

Lamp, 24¼" Tall, Red Domed Shade, Green and Black Flower Blossoms in Relief .1750.00

Lamp, Floor, Metal Base, Signed Shade "Garden of Allah" (on Reverse) 4750.00

Paperweight, Crystal Cut Base, Yellow Rose Design (Bryden-Pairpoint) 200.00

Paperweight, 7" Tall, Crystal Fish with Bubbles Design 75.00

Pitcher, Miniature, 3" Tall, Violet with White Design, Paper Label "Pairpoint-Bryden" .100.00

Plate, 8", Enameled Floral, Spanish Galleon, or Whale Decoration 100.00

Plate, 12", Enameled Floral, Spanish Galleon, or Whale Decoration 150.00

Powder Jar with Hinged Cover, 6" Diameter, Crystal, Viscaria Pattern 250.00

Swan, 12" Tall, Crystal Head and Neck, Ruby Red Body .550.00

Tumbler, 8" Tall, Enameled Floral, Spanish Galleon, or Whale Decoration 150.00

Urn with Cover, 6" Tall, Osiris Design (Amethyst, Blue, Green, or Yellow) 250.00

Urn with Cover, 6½" Tall, Osiris Design (Amethyst, Blue, Green, or Yellow) 250.00

Vase, 5" Tall, Ruffled, Cobalt with Crystal Bubble in Stem 200.00

Vase, 8" Tall, Enameled Floral, Spanish Galleon, or Whale Decoration 350.00

Vase, 8" Tall, Rolled Rim, Ruby with Crystal Bubble in Stem 200.00

Vase, 8" Tall, Osiris Design, Various Styles and Colors (Amethyst, Blue, Green, or Yellow)
. . . . .200.00

Vase, 9" Tall, Osiris Design, Various Styles and Colors (Amethyst, Blue, Green, or Yellow)
. . . . .250.00

Vase, 10" Tall, Osiris Design, Various Styles and Colors (Amethyst, Blue, Green, or Yellow)
. . . . .300.00

Vase, 9" Tall, Ruby Cornucopia Design with Crystal Bubble in Stem 200.00

Vase, 9" Tall, Village Scene, Signed "Ambero" 1000.00

Vase, 9¾" Tall, Cut Green to Crystal Design, Colias Pattern 275.00

Vase, 10" Tall, Ruby with Crystal Bubble in Stem 250.00

Vase, 12" Tall, Flared, Ruby with Crystal Ball Connector 325.00

Vase, 14½" Tall, Cameo Vintage Design, Signed 1250.00

Vase, 15" Tall, Amethyst with Cover 275.00

Wineglass, Black Foot and Stem, Red Bowl, with or without Silver Overlay 100.00

Pairpoint merged with and eventually resumed all glass manufacturing operations
from Mount Washington by 1894. Pairpoint produced a wide variety of items, from
functional tableware and lamps to fancy art glass and cut designs. Robert Gunderson and Robert Bryden were also active with the firm in the mid-20th century.

PEACH BLOW VARIOUS COMPANIES, 1880S–1950S

Object   *Price*
Bottle, Banjo, 6¼" Tall (Gunderson) $200.00
Bottle, Water, 7" Tall, Pyramid Shape (Wheeling) 1250.00

Bowl, Finger, 2½", Crimped, Acid Finish (New England) $750.00
Bowl, 3½", Applied Leaf Design (Gunderson) *100.00*
Bowl, 4", Pinched Edge (Mt. Washington) *2500.00*
Bowl, 4", Scalloped, Diamond Quilted Pattern (Mt. Washington) *2250.00*
Bowl, 4½" Diameter, 2½" Tall, White Interior (Hobbs Brocunier) *300.00*
Bowl, 4½" Diameter, 3" Tall, Ruffled, 3-Footed (Mt. Washington) *1500.00*
Bowl, 5½" Diameter, 2½" Tall, 10 Pleated Sides, Wild Rose Pattern (New England) *.400.00*
Bowl, 8" Diameter, Ruffled (New Martinsville) *150.00*
Bowl, 10", Ruffled, Ribbed, Yellow Interior, Gilded (Mt. Washington) *600.00*
Bowl, Bride's, 10¾" Diameter, Fluted (New Martinsville) *225.00*
Bowl, Ruffled, Sharp Vibrant Color (Boston & Sandwich) *400.00*
Bowl, Rose, 5", Floral Decoration (New England) *575.00*
Bowl, Rose, Gold Design, Marked "World's Fair 1893," Libbey *525.00*
Celery Dish, 4¾" Tall, Square Top, Scalloped (New England) *625.00*
Creamer, Handled (Mt. Washington) *3000.00*
Creamer, Cased White Interior (Wheeling) *600.00*
Cruet with Cut Stopper, Tri-Cornered Spout, Crystal Handle (Wheeling) *1750.00*
Cruet with Stopper, 7" Tall, Acid Finish (Wheeling) *1250.00*
Cup, Satin Finish (Gunderson) *150.00*
Darner, Stocking (New England) *150.00*
Decanter with Amber Stopper, 9" Tall, Amber Handle Acid Finish (Wheeling) ...*1500.00*
Ewer, 6" Tall, (Gunderson) *200.00*
Ewer, 8" Tall, Rigaree Decoration (Wheeling) *1500.00*
Hat, 2⅞", Diamond Quilted Pattern (Gunderson) *125.00*
Lamp, Hall, Brass Frame *1500.00*
Muffineer, 5½" (Hobbs Brocunier) *625.00*
Pear, 4½" Tall, Blown, Curved Stem (New England) *400.00*
Perfume Bottle with Stopper, Enameled Apple Blossoms (Mt. Washington) *2500.00*
Pitcher, Acidized, Yellow Handle (Mt. Washington) *3000.00*
Pitcher, 5" Tall, Square Top, Amber Handle (Wheeling) *1000.00*
Pitcher, Syrup, with Pewter Lid, 7" Tall (Wheeling) *1250.00*
Pitcher, Water, 7", Amber Handle (Hobbs Brocunier) *1500.00*
Pitcher, Water, 8½" Tall, Acid Finish (Wheeling) *1250.00*
Pitcher, Water, 10" Tall, Amber Ring Handle (Wheeling) *1750.00*
Powder Jar with Silverplated Lid, 4" Tall, Floral and Leaf Design *250.00*
Punch Cup, 2" Tall, Dull Acid Finish (New England) *450.00*

"Peachblow" art glass. Courtesy of the Corning Museum of Glass.

Punch Cup, Gloss Finish (New England) $450.00
Punch Cup, Amber Handle, Opaque White Handle (Wheeling) 500.00
Salt Shaker, 3" Tall 500.00
Saucer, Satin Finish (Gunderson) 100.00
Spooner, 5" Tall, Ruffled (New England) 325.00
Sugar, 2½" Tall, Handled, Label (Mt. Washington) 2400.00
Sugar, Enameled "World's Fair 1893" (Libbey) 600.00
Sugar Shaker, 5½" Tall (New England) 1000.00
Sugar Shaker, 5½" Tall, Ringed Neck (Wheeling) 625.00
Sugar Shaker with Silverplated Top, 5" Tall, Dull Acid Finish (Wheeling) 550.00
Toothpick Holder, 2¼" Tall, Tri-Cornered Top, Satin Finish (New England) 650.00
Toothpick Holder, 2½" Tall, Square Rim, Silverplated Holder 5½" Tall (New England)
.... .800.00
Toothpick Holder, 2¾" Tall, Enameled Floral Design (Mt. Washington) 3600.00
Tumbler, 3¾" Tall (New England) 650.00
Tumbler, 4" Tall, Acid Finish, Daisy Decoration (Mt. Washington) 2250.00
Tumbler, Dark Gloss Cobalt Finish (Hobbs Brocunier) 400.00
Vase, 2¼" Tall, Miniature, Acid Finish, Gold Decoration (Wheeling) 750.00
Vase, 3" Tall, Applied Prunts (Mt. Washington) 275.00
Vase, 4¼" Tall, Crimped (New England) 375.00
Vase, 4½" Tall, Ruffled, Fold-Over Rim, 5 Frosted Feet (Boston & Sandwich) 300.00
Vase, 4½" Tall, Scalloped, Flared, Ribbed (Mt. Washington) 2500.00
Vase, 6¼" Tall, Trumpet-Shaped (Mt. Washington) 1600.00
Vase, 8" Tall, Gourd Shape (Wheeling) 800.00
Vase, 9", Barrel-Shaped, Ruffled, Enameled Birds and Leaves and Insects (Boston &
Sandwich) 300.00
Vase, 9¼" Tall, Trefoil-Shaped (Gunderson) 375.00
Vase, 10¼" Tall, Oval, Narrow Neck, Amber Holder with 5 Griffins Design (Hobbs
Brocunier) 1750.00
Vase, 10½" Tall, Ruffled, Footed (Mt. Washington) 4200.00
Vase, 10½" Tall, Crimped, Jack-in-the-Pulpit Design (Mt. Washington) 7500.00
Vase, 11" Tall, Bulbous, Dull Finish 1000.00

"Peachblow" art glass. Photo by Mark Pickvet.

Vase, 12" Tall, Trumpet-Shaped, Rose to White Shading (New England) *$1250.00*
Vase, 18" Tall, Trumpet Shape (New England) *1750.00*
Vase, 3 Turned-Down Sides, Ruffled (Mt. Washington) *4500.00*
Whiskey Tumbler, 2" Tall, Acid Finish (New England) *350.00*

"Peach Blow" is similar to "Burmese" except that the uranium oxide was replaced with cobalt or copper oxide in the general formula. The shading of "Peach Blow" varies from light grayish-blue at the base to rose pink or peach at the top. Cobalt generally produces a slightly darker shade at the base than copper does.

Also like "Burmese," "Peach Blow" is found in numerous finishes, patterns, and enamels, tends to be thin and fragile, and is rather desirable and valuable. Unlike "Burmese," "Peach Blow" was produced by several companies such as Mt. Washington/Pairpoint/Gunderson; Hobbs, Brocunier; New Martinsville; New England/Libbey; etc. See the "Foreign Glass" chapter for "Peach Blow" items produced by Thomas Webb & Sons of England.

PHOENIX GLASS COMPANY EARLY 1900S–1940S

Object	*Price*
Ashtray, 5¹/₂" Long, Pearl Floral Design on Coral Background	*$75.00*
Banana Dish, Pearl Opalescent	*175.00*
Bowl, Ruffled, Divided, Gilded Floral Pattern on Satin Background, Opaque Pink	*400.00*
Bowl, Flower, Floral Design on Pink Background	*175.00*
Bowl, Powder, Blue Hummingbird Design	*125.00*
Bowl, Berry with Cover, Pearl Opalescent	*150.00*
Candleholder, Strawberry Shape, 4¹/₄" Tall, Tan	*75.00*
Candleholder, Water Lily Shape, 4³/₄" Tall, Green on Crystal	*110.00*
Candlestick, 6³/₄" Tall, Green, Bird of Paradise Design	*125.00*
Candy Box, 6¹/₂" Diameter, Crystal with White Violets on a Light Blue Background	*175.00*
Centerpiece Bowl, Footed, Diving Nudes, Crystal	*200.00*
Compote, Fish Design, Amber	*100.00*
Compote, 6", Pedestal Base, Amethyst Pastel, Dolphin Design	*225.00*
Compote with Cover, Pearl Opalescent	*175.00*
Creamer, Pearl Opalescent	*125.00*
Lamp, 14" Tall, Foxglove Pattern, Aqua, Orange, and White, Marble Base	*200.00*
Pitcher, Water, Pearl Opalescent	*600.00*
Sugar, Pearl Opalescent	*125.00*
Sugar with Cover, Lacy Dewdrop Pattern, Blue Design	*75.00*
Tumbler, Pearl Opalescent	*275.00*
Vase, 5" Tall, Pearl Floral Design on Light Blue Background	*75.00*
Vase, 6¹/₂" Tall, Rectangular, Frosted, Pair of Lovebirds Design	*100.00*
Vase, 7" Tall, Fern Design, Blue	*110.00*
Vase, 8" Tall, Preying Mantis Pattern, Pink	*125.00*
Vase, 8" Tall, Freesia, Flared, Crystal Satin, Sea Green Background	*100.00*
Vase, 8¹/₄" Tall, Fan-Shaped, Bronze-Colored Grasshopper	*225.00*
Vase, 8³/₄" Tall, Milk Glass on Tan Background, Primrose Design	*175.00*
Vase, 9¹/₄" Tall, Fish Design, Blue	*200.00*
Vase, 9¹/₄" Tall, Milk Glass, Wild Geese Design on Blue Background	*150.00*
Vase, 9¹/₄" Tall, Opalescent Satin, Wild Geese Design	*200.00*

Vase, 9½" Tall, Two-Toned Apricot *$125.00*
Vase, 9½" Tall, 12" Diameter, Frosted, Flying Geese Design *175.00*
Vase, 10" Tall, Frosted Madonna Pattern, Dark Blue *300.00*
Vase, 11" Tall, Brown and Green Dogwood Design *200.00*
Vase, 11" Tall, Bulbous, Red Ground with Iridescent Flowers *200.00*
Vase, 12" Tall, White, Dancing Females in Relief *175.00*
Vase, 12¼" Tall, Pink Peonies with Turquoise Leaves' Design *150.00*
Vase, 14½" Tall, Nudes, Blue and White *550.00*
Vase, 17" Tall, Blue Ground, Thistle Design *450.00*

Much of the art glass of Phoenix is similar to that of Lalique. Figures have a smooth, satiny, acidized finish and are sometimes colored. Cameo engraving, pearlized finishes, and heavy etching are also part of Phoenix's designs.

Glass made by Phoenix is also very similar to certain styles produced by Consolidated, though the colors of Phoenix are limited and more common.

PIGEON BLOOD   VARIOUS COMPANIES, LATE
1880S–EARLY 1900S

Object	Price
Bowl, 6" Diameter, Gold Floral Design	*$75.00*
Bowl, 8½" Tall, 3-Footed, Crystal Feet and Handles	*175.00*
Butter Dish with Cover, Enameled White Floral Design	*500.00*
Cookie Jar with Cover, Silverplated Cover, Handle, and Rim, Florette Pattern (Consolidated)	*250.00*
Creamer, 3½" Tall, Enameled Floral Design	*175.00*
Cruet with Stopper, 5¾" Tall, Enameled Scrolls	*150.00*
Lamp, 10½" Tall	*650.00*
Pitcher, Syrup, with Lid, 4¾" Tall	*325.00*
Pitcher, 7" Tall, Clear Handle	*225.00*
Pitcher, 7¼" Tall, Gilded, Ribbed Handle, Ruffled Top (Consolidated)	*300.00*
Pitcher, Milk, 7¼" Tall	*175.00*
Pitcher, Tankard-Style, 10" Tall, Diamond Quilted Pattern	*225.00*
Pitcher, Water, 11" Tall	*450.00*
Salt and Pepper Shakers (Consolidated)	*175.00*
Salt and Pepper Shakers, Several Styles	*175.00*
Sugar Dish, 3½" Tall Enameled Floral Design	*175.00*
Sugar Shaker, Several Styles	*325.00*
Spooner, Several Styles	*90.00*
Toothpick Holder, Ribbed	*75.00*
Toothpick Holder, Loop Pattern	*150.00*
Tumbler, Enameled Design, Several Styles	*75.00*
Vase, 8¼" Tall, Enameled Floral Design	*175.00*
Vase, 10½" Tall, Enameled Floral Design	*200.00*
Wineglass, 6" Tall	*50.00*

"Pigeon Blood" is characterized by a somewhat transparent deep scarlet red (or blood red). Pieces produced in "Pigeon Blood" tend to have a glossy or shiny finish, which was applied to many cut glass patterns.

PINK SLAG   INDIANA TUMBLER AND GOBLET COMPANY, 1880S–EARLY 1900S

Object	Price
Bowl, 6½" Inverted Fan and Feather Pattern	*$850.00*
Butter Dish with Cover, 6" Diameter, Inverted Fan and Feather Pattern	*1250.00*
Compote, 5", Inverted Fan and Feather Pattern	*725.00*
Creamer, 3½" Tall, Handled, Inverted Fan and Feather Pattern	*700.00*
Creamer, 4½" Tall, Pitcher-Style, Inverted Fan and Feather Pattern	*750.00*
Creamer, 4¾" Tall, 4-Footed, Beaded Handle, Inverted Fan and Feather Pattern	*750.00*
Cruet with Stopper, 6" Tall, Inverted Fan and Feather Pattern	*1750.00*
Lamp, 3¼" Tall	*775.00*
Pitcher, 8" Tall, Inverted Fan and Feather Pattern	*2250.00*
Punch Cup, 8" Tall, Inverted Fan and Feather Pattern	*400.00*
Salt Shaker with Metal Top, Inverted Fan and Feather Pattern	*325.00*
Sauce Dish, 2½" Tall, Ball-Shaped Feet, Inverted Fan and Feather Pattern	*375.00*
Spooner, Inverted Fan and Feather Pattern	*375.00*
Sugar with Cover, 4" Tall, Inverted Fan and Feather Pattern	*825.00*
Sugar with Cover, 5½" Tall, Inverted Fan and Feather Pattern	*875.00*
Toothpick Holder, Inverted Fan and Feather Pattern	*525.00*
Tumbler, 3½" Tall	*350.00*
Tumbler, 4" Tall, Inverted Fan and Feather Pattern	*500.00*
Tumbler, Grape and Vine Design	*175.00*

"Pink Slag" was an opaque pressed glass with swirled or marbleized shading from white to pink. It was primarily made in tableware. The rarest and most valuable (some argue the finest!) pattern was Indiana's "Inverted Fan and Feather."

"Pink Slag" is also referred to as "Agate" or "Marble." Offshoots of this marbleized design were produced by others in various colors; however, the style is not that common. Swirling is not an easy effect to achieve since colors tend to blend into one rather than remaining separate or partially mixing.

QUEZAL ART GLASS AND DECORATING COMPANY   1901–1920S

Object	Price
Bowl, 7", Fluted, Iridescent Gold	*$500.00*
Compote, 6", Pedestal Base, Iridescent Gold, Signed	*375.00*
Compote, 7", Thin Stem, Iridescent Gold, Signed	*400.00*
Cup, Scroll Handle, Iridescent Gold, Signed	*350.00*
Lamp, 6" Tall, Bronze Feet, Iridescent Gold, Signed	*1250.00*
Lamp, Double, Claw Feet, Pearlized Base, Calcite with Gold Interior	*750.00*
Perfume Bottle with Stopper, 8" Tall, 4-Sided Cone Shape, Iridescent Gold	*275.00*
Salt Dip, 2¾", Gold, Signed "Quezal"	*250.00*
Saucer, 7", Stretched, Iridescent Gold	*325.00*
Sconce, Double Branched, Gilded, 5" Shades	*500.00*
Shade, 4½" Diameter, Yellow with Gold Lining	*325.00*
Shade, 4¾" Diameter, Ribbed, Iridescent Gold with Colored Highlights	*150.00*

Shade, 6" Tall, Iridescent Gold with Blue and Violet Highlights *$200.00*

Shade, 6¾" Tall, Iridescent Green with Gold Lining, King Tut Pattern *1000.00*

Shade, 7¾" Tall, Bullet-Shaped, Opal with Green Feathers and Gold Edging *600.00*

Shade, 7" Tall, Flared, Ribbed Sides, Yellow, Signed "Quezal" *275.00*

Shade, 7" Tall, Opal with Gold Lining *900.00*

Shade, 8⅓" Tall, Opal with Yellow Feathers *700.00*

Spittoon, 3½" Tall, Bulbous, Latticed Green and White with Gold Feathers, Marked "Quezal S 813" *500.00*

Vase, 4" Tall, Ivory with Gold and Green Feather Design *1250.00*

Vase, 5" Tall, Iridescent Dark Blue, Gold Leaves *1400.00*

Vase, 6" Tall, Iridescent Reddish Gold, Lightning Design *1500.00*

Vase, 7" Tall, Footed, Fluted and Crackled Rim, Amber with White Leaves and Green Edge, Marked "Quezal 167" *1100.00*

Vase, 7¾" Tall, Gold Rim, Green with Silver Feathers, Signed "Quezal 12" *1250.00*

Vase, 8½" Tall, Jack-in-the-Pulpit Style, Overhanging Rim, Footed, Iridescent Gold with Yellow Leaves, Inscribed "Quezal" *1200.00*

Vase, 8¾" Tall, Ruffled, Iridescent Green with Gold Lining and Gold Feathers, Signed *1250.00*

Vase, 10" Tall, Iridescent Gold with Silver Overlay *1000.00*

Vase, 11" Tall, Trumpet, Ribbed, White with Gold Lattice and Gold Interior, Marked "Quezal 6" *900.00*

Vase, 12" Tall, 9" Diameter, Banded Floral and Feather Design, Gold Interior, Marked "Quezal #437" *6000.00*

Vase, 15" Tall, Jack-in-the-Pulpit Style, White with Gold and Green Feather Design *5000.00*

Wineglass, 6" Tall, Iridescent Gold, Signed *450.00*

Since Quezal was founded by two men who had worked for Tiffany (Martin Bach and Thomas Johnson), Quezal's products are very similar in nature. Brilliant iridescent forms of blue, gold, white, green, and so on were much like "Favrile." The formulas were nearly idential to Tiffany's since that is where the two men learned them. "Quezal" was patented in 1902, and the name was often engraved in silver block letters on the underside; pieces not signed are confused with both Tiffany and Steuben.

READING ARTISTIC GLASS WORKS   1884–1886

Object	*Price*
Bowl, 6", Ruffled, Opalescent Blue	*$175.00*
Carafe, 10½" Tall, Red with Crystal Spout	*250.00*
Ewer, 13" Tall, Red with Clear Spout	*225.00*
Pitcher, Water, 10½" Tall Pink, Thumbprint Pattern	*350.00*
Pitcher, 11" Tall, Pink and White Frosted Coin Dot Pattern	*350.00*
Vase, 7¾" Tall, Overshot, Blue Opal	*350.00*
Vase, 9½" Tall, Pink with Dark Red Opalescent Neck	*750.00*

Although the company went bankrupt after two short years, they did manage to produce some fine art glass, as good as that of anyone in the business. Amberina, opalescent, decorated cut patterns, and so on were all made in that short time period. The opalescent colors are particularly noteworthy and exist in beautiful blues, greens, pinks, purples, whites, etc.

RUBENA OR RUBINA CRYSTAL VARIOUS COMPANIES, 1880S–1890S

Object	Price
Basket, 6" Tall, 4" Diameter	$125.00
Bowl, 5½", Inverted Thumbprint Pattern	100.00
Bowl, 6½", Frosted	100.00
Bowl, 8", Royal Ivy Pattern	125.00
Bowl, 9", Frosted, Royal Ivy Pattern	150.00
Bowl, Oval, 9½", Overshot	200.00
Bowl, Rose, 5½", 4¾" Tall, Gold Floral Design	150.00
Butter Dish with Cover, 7" Tall, Gilded, Signed "Northwood"	250.00
Butter Dish with Cover, Frosted, Royal Ivy Pattern	200.00
Butter Dish with Cover, Royal Oak Pattern	325.00
Candlestick, 9" Tall, Cranberry to Clear Coloring	100.00
Carafe, Water, 8" Tall, Cranberry to Clear Coloring	175.00
Castor Set, Pickle Dish with Silverplated Holder and Tongs (Northwood)	300.00
Castor Set, Pickle Dish, Silverplated Frame and Cover, Frosted Insert	325.00
Cheese Dish with Cover, 6½" Tall, 10" Diameter	250.00
Compote, 8½" Tall, Footed, Honeycomb Pattern	200.00
Condiment Set, 4-Piece, 2 Square Bottles, Rectangular Salt Dip, Silverplated Holder	300.00
Cookie Jar with Cover, 9½" Tall, Ribbed	325.00
Creamer, Frosted, Royal Ivy Pattern	225.00
Creamer, Royal Oak Pattern	150.00
Creamer, Frosted, Royal Oak Pattern	325.00
Cruet with Stopper, 5¼" Tall, Frosted, Royal Ivy Pattern	400.00
Cruet with Stopper, 5½" Tall, Royal Oak Pattern	550.00
Cruet with Cut Crystal Stopper, 6" Tall, Overshot	450.00
Decanter with Stopper, 8" Tall, Signed "Northwood"	300.00
Ice Bucket, Silver Handle, Enameled	125.00
Jam Jar with Cover, Swirl Pattern	175.00
Jelly Dish, Triangular, Crimped, Silverplated Holder	225.00
Mug, 3¾" Tall, Octagonal, Gold and Silver Trim	75.00
Mustard Jar with Silverplated Color, Enameled Floral Design, Thumbprint Pattern	175.00
Perfume Bottle with Faceted Stopper, 5¾" Tall	150.00
Perfume Bottle with Silverplated Stopper, Diamond Quilted and Drape Pattern	125.00
Pitcher, Syrup with Metal Lid, 4¾" Tall	400.00
Pitcher, Syrup with Metal Lid, 5¼" Tall, Inverted Thumbprint Pattern	250.00
Pitcher, Syrup, with Metal Lid, 5¼", Tall, Royal Ivy Pattern	350.00
Pitcher, Water, 8½" Tall, Royal Ivy Pattern	525.00
Pitcher, Water, 8½" Tall, Royal Oak Pattern	425.00
Punch Cup, 4¼" Tall	50.00
Salt Dip, 2" Tall, Hexagonal, Silverplated Stand	150.00
Salt and Pepper Shakers, Frosted, Royal Ivy Pattern	150.00
Salt and Pepper Shakers, Frosted, Royal Oak Pattern	200.00
Salt Shaker, Threaded (Northwood)	125.00
Sauce Dish, Several Styles	50.00
Spooner, Frosted, Royal Ivy Pattern	100.00
Spooner, Frosted, Royal Oak Pattern	125.00
Sugar, Frosted, Royal Ivy Pattern	125.00

Sugar with Cover, Royal Oak Pattern $200.00
Sugar with Cover, Frosted, Royal Oak Pattern 375.00
Sugar Shaker, Frosted, 5¼" Tall, Royal Ivy Pattern 225.00
Sugar Shaker, Frosted, 5¼" Tall, Royal Oak Pattern 225.00
Toothpick Holder, Several Styles 150.00
Tumbler, Enameled Floral Design, 5½" Tall, Diamond Quilted Pattern 80.00
Tumbler, Enameled Design, 6" Tall, Inverted Thumbprint Pattern 100.00
Tumbler, 6" Tall, Royal Ivy Pattern 125.00
Tumbler, Frosted, 6" Tall, Royal Oak Pattern 125.00
Vase, 8" Tall, Pedestal Foot, Ribbed, Flared 100.00
Vase, 8" Tall, Enameled Floral Decoration 150.00
Vase, 8¾" Tall, Trumpet-Shaped, Ruffled, Gold Floral Decoration 250.00
Vase, 10" Tall, Footed, Applied Crystal Decoration 175.00
Vase, 13" Tall, Trumpet-Shaped, Crystal Pedestal Foot, Crystal Applied Threading ..225.00

"Rubena" is characterized by a gradual shading from crystal at the bottom to ruby red at the top. Some pieces have shading that is not gradual but contain a distinct line of color separation. Pieces are also at times accented with clear crystal (handles, lids, stoppers, feet, etc.). Many cut patterns were decorated with "Rubena" shading.

George Duncan and Sons is credited with the original introduction of this design as others soon followed.

RUBENA VERDE OR RUBINA VERDE VARIOUS
COMPANIES, 1880S–1890S

Object	*Price*
Basket, Bride's, 8" Diameter, Silverplated Holder	$275.00
Basket, Bride's, 8" Diameter, Hobnail Pattern	525.00
Bowl, 4", Threaded Design	100.00
Bowl, 4¼", Ruffled, Hobnail Pattern	110.00
Bowl, 7", Scalloped, Enameled Gold Decorations	200.00
Bowl, Rose, 5", Crimped, Hobnail Pattern	125.00
Creamer, 5" Tall, Reeded Handle, Inverted Thumbprint Pattern	450.00
Cruet with Stopper, Frosted, Hobnail Pattern (Hobbs, Brocunier)	425.00
Cruet with Stopper, 6¾" Tall, Triple-Lipped Top, Inverted Thumbprint Pattern	450.00
Epergne, 22" Tall, Trumpet in Center of Bowl, Hanging Baskets	450.00
Pitcher, Syrup, with Silverplated Lid, 5" Tall, Inverted Thumbprint Pattern	150.00
Pitcher, Syrup, with Lid, Hobnail Pattern	125.00
Pitcher, Water, 8" Tall, Square Top, Greenish-Yellow Handle, Hobnail Pattern	350.00
Pitcher, Water, 8" Tall, Clear Handle, Tri-Cornered Lip, Enameled Daisy Design	400.00
Pitcher, Water, 9" Tall, Inverted Thumbprint Pattern	350.00
Salt and Pepper Shakers, 4½" Tall, Pewter Tops, Enameled Floral Design	275.00
Sweetmeat Dish, 5¾" Tall, Octagonal, Notched Edge, Greenish-Yellow Trim, Silverplated Holder	175.00
Tumbler, 4" Tall, Diamond Quilted Pattern	150.00
Tumbler, 4" Tall, Hobnail Pattern	275.00
Vase, 6" Tall, Ruffled	175.00
Vase, 6½" Tall, Scalloped, Reverse Color Pattern	200.00
Vase, 6¾" Tall, Crimped, Footed	125.00

Vase, 8" Tall, Jack-in-the-Pulpit Style, Applied Greenish-Yellow Feet *$175.00*
Vase, 9¼" Tall, Pedestal Feet, Drape Pattern *200.00*
Vase, 11" Tall, Ruffled, Green Rim, Drape Pattern *350.00*
Wineglass, 4¼" Tall, Inverted Thumbprint Pattern *150.00*

"Rubena Verde" is similar to many of the other shaded designs as in Amberina, Peach Blow, and Rubena Crystal. The colors in "Rubena Verde" vary from aqua green or greenish-yellow at the base to ruby red at the top. Hobbs, Brocunier, and Company is usually noted as the original maker; however, others followed soon afterward.

SATIN GLASS VARIOUS COMPANIES, 1880S–EARLY 1990S

Object	*Price*
Bell, 6" Tall, Blue	*$50.00*
Biscuit Jar with Silverplated Cover and Handle, 7" Tall, Pink Florette Pattern	*350.00*
Bowl, Finger, 4½", Diamond Quilted Pattern	*50.00*
Bowl, 6½", 3-Lobed Rim, Olive Green with White Interior, Gold Floral Design	*225.00*
Bowl, 8", Ruffled, Rainbow Colors	*275.00*
Bowl, Rose, 3½", 3¼" Tall, 8-Crimped, Blue Overlay with Embossed Floral Design	*150.00*
Creamer, Blue, Marked "World's Fair—1893" (New England)	*350.00*
Cruet with Stopper, 7" Tall, Multicolored	*400.00*
Epergne, 18" Tall, Enameled Bird and Floral Design	*325.00*
Ewer, 9¾" Tall, Blue with Frosted Handle, Enameled Flower Design	*150.00*
Ewer, 12¾" Tall, Pedestal Foot, Frosted Handle, Enameled Floral Design	*200.00*
Lamp, Miniature, 8½" Tall, Globe Shade, Square Base, Red with Crystal Chimney, Drape Pattern	*400.00*
Lamp, 8½" Tall, "Gone with the Wind" Style, Brass Foot, Red with 2 Winged Griffins on Each Globe	*700.00*
Pitcher, Milk, 6½" Tall, Blue, Diamond Quilted Pattern	*750.00*
Pitcher, Water, Square Top, Reeded Handle, White Liner	*325.00*
Spittoon, White Casing on Light Blue Background	*125.00*
Sugar, Blue, Marked "World's Fair—1893" (New England)	*350.00*
Toothpick Holder, 3¼" Tall, Blue and White Enameled Design	*125.00*
Vase, 6" Tall, Conical, Ribbed, Ruffled, Blue	*150.00*
Vase, 6½" Tall, Footed, Ribbed, Pink Overlay with Enameled Floral Design	*100.00*
Vase, 7" Tall, Gourd-Shaped, Light Blue to Turquoise Coloring	*250.00*
Vase, 7½" Tall, Acid Cutback Squares, Pink Overlay with Enameled Floral Design . .	*250.00*
Vase, 8" Tall, Gourd-Shaped, Blue	*125.00*
Vase, 8" Tall, Ribbed, White with Green Lining	*150.00*
Vase, 9" Tall, Blue Overlay with Gold Scrolls and Enameled Floral Design	*125.00*
Vase, 10½" Tall, Peach Overlay with Enameled Floral Design	*125.00*
Vase, 11" Tall, Ribbed, Blue Overlay with Enameled Floral and Jewel Design	*150.00*
Vase, 18" Tall, Blue, Iris Decoration	*325.00*
Vase, Ruffled, Pink and White Swirls, White Lining, (Mount Washington)	*500.00*

"Satin" glass is characterized by opaque milk, opal, or colored glass with a distinctive white lining. The satin texture or finish was created by a thin coating or washing with hydrofluoric acid.

SINCLAIRE, H. P., COMPANY   1904–1930S

Object	Price
Bowl, 10", Pedestal Foot, Black with White Edge, Signed	.$325.00
Bowl, 11", Ruffled, Blue with Etched Floral Design	.175.00
Bowl, 11½", Pink with Etched Floral Design	.200.00
Candlestick, 7½" Tall, Blue with Etched Scrolls	.60.00
Candlestick, 8" Tall, Dark Amber Etched Design, Signed	.75.00
Candlestick, 9½" Tall, Yellow with Etched Floral Design	.100.00
Candlestick, 10" Tall, Crystal, Engraved Vintage Design, Signed	.100.00
Candlestick, 10¼" Tall, Swirl Ribbed, Light Green, Signed	.75.00
Cologne Bottle with Stopper, 5¼" Tall, Etched Floral Design, Signed	.300.00
Compote, Dark Amber, Etched Design, Signed	.175.00
Compote, Rolled Rim, Pedestal Foot, Light Green	.125.00
Pitcher, Green with Amber Handle, Etched Vintage Pattern	.250.00
Plate, 8½", Amber, Leaf Design	.50.00
Tumbler, Green with Amber Base, Etched Vintage Pattern	.75.00
Vase, 5½" Tall, 4" Diameter, Interior Ribbing, Amethyst	.75.00
Vase, 6" Tall, Amethyst to Crystal Coloring, Lily Pattern	.250.00
Vase, 12" Tall, Crystal, Etched Flower and Foliage Design	.175.00
Vase, 13½" Tall, Crystal, Etched Tulip Design	.175.00
Wineglass, Green to Crystal Coloring, Duchess Pattern	.75.00

Sinclaire was primarily a producer of cut, engraved, or etched glassware. They obtained their blanks early on from some of the best lead crystal makers (Corning, Dorflinger, Baccarat, etc.), but after 1920, they produced their own blanks. In the 1920s, Sinclaire created many art objects in various colors, similar to those of Steuben.

SMITH BROTHERS   1870S–EARLY 1900S

Object	Price
Bowl, 4", Purple Rim, Floral Design	.$225.00
Bowl, 5½", Beaded Edge, Blue and Purple Floral Design	.375.00
Bowl, 7½", Blue and White Floral Design, Gold Rim	.450.00
Bowl, 8", Green and White Floral Design Gilding	.650.00
Box with Cover, Square, 3¼" × 3¼", Pink and White Floral Design	.325.00
Cookie Jar with Cover, 7¼" Tall, Pink and White Floral Design	.800.00
Cookie Jar with Cover, 8½" Tall, Multicolored Floral Design on Cream Background, Signed	.1200.00
Cracker Jar, Cube-Shaped, Silverplated Cover and Handle, Enameled Crab Design	.750.00
Cracker Jar with Cover, 7" Tall, Silverplated Top, Ridge and Handle, Various Enameled Floral and Foliage Designs	.600.00
Creamer, Cream with Enameled Gold Flowers	.300.00
Creamer, Cream with Enameled Lady's or Soldier's Head, Silverplated Handle and Rim	.325.00
Humidor with Cover, 6" Tall, 5" Diameter, Pansy Design on Body and Cover	.225.00
Humidor with Silverplated Cover, 7" Tall, Cream, Floral Design, Signed	.625.00
Lamp Shade, Various Enameled Floral and Foliage Designs	.125.00

Mustard Dish, Handled, Pansy Design, Signed *$250.00*

Mustard Jar with Silverplated Hinged Cover, Silverplated Handle, Various Enameled Floral Designs *175.00*

Plate, 6⅛", Tall, Ship Design (Santa Maria) *550.00*

Plate, 7", Ship Design *600.00*

Salt Bowl, Various Enameled Floral Designs *75.00*

Salt Shaker, Various Enameled Floral Designs *100.00*

Salt Shaker, Egg-Shaped, Various Enameled Floral Designs *125.00*

Sugar Shaker, 3" Tall, Ribbed, Silverplated Top, White with Purple Columbines *625.00*

Sugar with Silverplated Cover, Cream with Gold Enameled Flowers, Silverplated Handle *350.00*

Sugar with Silverplated Cover, Cream with Gold Enameled Lady's or Soldier's Head, Silverplated Handle *350.00*

Sweetmeat Dish, Raised Gold, Enameled Pansies, Rampant Lion Mark *450.00*

Toothpick Holder, Vertical Ribbed (Columns), White with Enameled Flowers *150.00*

Vase, 2½" Tall, Ribbed, Daisy Design, Signed *350.00*

Vase, 2½" Tall, Ribbed, Gold Lettering "Season's Greetings," Signed *350.00*

Vase, 4½" Tall, Pinched Sides, Carnation Design *450.00*

Vase, 5" Tall, Cream with Enameled Flowers, Signed *300.00*

Vase, 8½" Tall, Flask Style, Enameled Ship (Santa Maria), Signed *1250.00*

Vase, 8½" Tall, Floral Mum Design, Signed *750.00*

Vase, 9" Tall, Cylindrical, Enameled Bird Design, Signed *275.00*

Vase, 10" Tall, Banded Glass at Top and Bottom, Pink, Enameled Bird and Reed Design *200.00*

The Smith Brothers (Harry and Alfred) were originally part of a decorating department at Mount Washington. They formed their own decorating company but still used many blanks provided by their previous employer. Smith Brothers were noted for many cut, engraved, and enameled floral patterns. They also decorated glass in the majority of the popular art designs of the day ("Burmese," "Peach Blow," gilding, silver or silverplating, and numerous other color and color effects).

SPATTER GLASS VARIOUS COMPANIES, 1880S–EARLY 1900S

Object	Price
Basket, 8¼" Tall, Green Spatter, White Lining	*$225.00*
Basket, Bride's, 10" Tall, Crimped, Rainbow Spatter	*150.00*
Bowl, 6½", Blue Spatter, White Interior	*125.00*
Bowl, 8", Pink Spatter	*150.00*
Bowl, 10", Pleated Top, Blue Spatter	*125.00*
Bowl, Rose, 4½" Tall, Blue Spatter	*75.00*
Candlestick, 8" Tall, Rainbow Spatter on Blue Background	*75.00*
Candlestick, 8½" Tall, Pink Spatter on White Background	*100.00*
Candy Jar with Cover, 6¼" Tall, 3½" Diameter, Yellow with Blue Spatter, Enameled Floral Design	*125.00*
Cruet with Stopper, 7½" Tall, Blue and Yellow Spatter	*225.00*
Cruet with Stopper, 8" Tall, Crystal Handle, Blue and White Spatter (Mt. Washington)	*250.00*

Decanter with Crystal Faceted Stopper, 10" Tall, Pinched Sides, Red and White Spatter
. . . .*$150.00*
Pitcher, Milk, 5¹/₂" Tall, Cranberry and Frosted Coloring with Rainbow Swirled Spatter *.225.00*
Pitcher, Water, 8" Tall, Rainbow Spatter on Blue Background *175.00*
Pitcher, Water, 8¹/₄" Tall, Blue and White Spatter *200.00*
Rolling Pin, 15" Long, 2" Diameter, White with Maroon and Cobalt Blue Spatter . . .*175.00*
Salt Dip, 1³/₄" Tall, Crystal Footed, Blue and White Spatter *100.00*
Toothpick Holder, 2¹/₂" Tall, Rainbow Spatter on Red Background *100.00*
Tumbler, 5³/₄" Tall, Green and White Spatter *75.00*
Vase, 5¹/₄" Tall, Blue and White Spatter *125.00*
Vase, 6" Tall, Yellow Casing with Gold Spatter *100.00*
Vase, 6" Tall, Speckled Pink and White Spatter *75.00*
Vase, 8" Tall, White Lining, Rainbow Spatter *100.00*
Vase, 8³/₄" Tall, Flared, Pink, White, and Yellow Spatter *100.00*
Vase, 9" Tall, Crystal Thorn Handles, Rainbow Spatter *150.00*
Vase, 10¹/₂" Tall, Pink, White and Red Spatter *150.00*
Vase, 12" Tall, 3-Petal Top, Yellow and White with Enameled Floral Design *150.00*

"Spatter" refers to spotted or multicolored glass that has a white inner casing and
crystal outer casing. At times, leftover colored glass was combined and blown into
a mold to create a splotching or spattering effect. Many objects of a whimsical nature were produced in this fashion.

STEUBEN GLASS WORKS   1904–1933

Object	*Price*
Ashtray, Topaz with Blue Leaf Handle, Signed	*$150.00*
Bowl, 4", Blue to Alabaster Shading, Acid Cut Back	*1750.00*
Bowl, 4³/₄" Diameter, 11" Tall, Air-Trapped Mica Flecks, Silverina Design	*900.00*
Bowl, 6" Tall, Pedestal-Base, Bubbled Crystal	*225.00*
Bowl, 8" Tall, Acid Cutback, Plum Jade	*2250.00*
Bowl, 6¹/₂" Diameter, 12" Tall, Cranberry to Clear Shading	*350.00*
Bowl, 6¹/₂" Diameter, 12" Tall, Folded Rim, Ivory	*300.00*
Bowl, Centerpiece, 13" Diameter, Selenium Red, Signed "Steuben"	*600.00*
Bowl, Centerpiece, Acid Cutback, Jade, Etched York Pattern	*2500.00*
Bowl, Centerpiece, Footed, Bristol Yellow, Signed	*750.00*
Bowl, Centerpiece, Topaz with Floral Design, Signed	*500.00*
Bowl, Footed, Green Pomona Foot, Oriental Poppy Design, Signed "Steuben"	*1000.00*
Bowl, 4-Lobed, Wavy Rim, Vertical Ribbed, Green to Clear Shading, Stamped "Steuben"	*325.00*
Candelabra, 14¹/₂" Tall, Silverina Design	*500.00*
Candelabra, Lamp-Style, Double, Rib Swirled Flame Center, Flemish Blue Design	*.400.00*
Candlestick, 6" Tall, Acid Cutback, Jade Green on Alabaster Background, Rose Pattern	*250.00*
Candlestick, 12" Tall, Ribbed, Dome Foot, Double Ball Stem, Amber	*175.00*
Candlestick, 14" Tall, Swan Stem, Venetian Style, Green	*150.00*
Candlestick, Alabaster Foot, Rosaline Designed Cup, Signed	*150.00*
Candlestick, Airtraps, Amethyst, Silverina Design, Signed	*225.00*
Candy Dish with Cover, 6" Tall, Pedestal Base, Blue and Topaz	*225.00*

Chalice, 12" Tall, Griffin Handles, Snake Stem, Cobalt with Gold Foil and White Streaks
....$300.00
Champagne Glass, 5³/₄" Tall, Crystal Twist Stem, Black Rim, Cerise Design *200.00*
Champagne Glass, 6¹/₄" Tall, Oriental Poppy Design, Signed *450.00*
Compote, Iridescent with Stripes, Rose Cintra Design, Venetian Style, Applied Prunts, Green Rim *225.00*
Compote with Cover, 12" Tall, Venetian Style, Topaz, Paperweight Pear Finial, Signed "F. Carder—Steuben" *350.00*
Cordial, 4³/₄" Tall, Knobbed Baluster Stem, Selenium Red *200.00*
Goblet, 6" Tall, Pomona Green, Signed *75.00*
Goblet, 6" Tall, Verre de Soie Design *100.00*
Goblet, 7" Tall, Green, Threaded Design, Signed *150.00*
Goblet, 7¹/₈" Tall, Cintra Design Stem and Border, Opalescent, Signed *350.00*
Goblet, 9" Tall, Twisted Amethyst Stem, Crystal Bowl *150.00*
Lamp, Marble Base with 2 Bronze Nudes (Kneeling), Moss Agate Design *3250.00*
Lamp, 17" Tall, Calcite with Gold and Green Feathers *2500.00*
Lamp Base, 14" Tall, Acid Cutback, Plum Jade, Oriental Design *1500.00*
Mug, 6" Tall, Footed, Crystal with Green Handle and Decoration, Matsu-no-ke Design *325.00*
Nude, Figural, Black Jade with Knees in Crystal Circle *1250.00*
Parfait, 6¹/₂" Tall, Stemmed, Rosaline and Alabaster Design *175.00*
Pear, 5¹/₄" Tall, Blown, Jet Black, Marked "F. Carder-Steuben" *550.00*
Perfume Bottle with Green Stopper, 4" Tall, Bulbous, Verre de Soie Design *425.00*
Perfume Bottle with Stopper, 12" Tall, Celeste Blue *550.00*
Perfume Bottle with Stopper, Bristol Yellow with Black Threading, Signed *250.00*
Plaque, 8" × 6¹/₂", Thomas Edison *850.00*
Plaque, 5¹/₂" Square, Mottled Green and White with Flesh-Toned Bare-Breasted Woman, Pate-de-Verre Design, Signed "F. Carder 1915" *1500.00*
Plate, 8", Intaglio Border, Crystal to Amethyst Coloring *125.00*
Plate, 8", Crystal with Black Threading *75.00*
Plate, 8¹/₄", Copper Wheel Engraved Rim, Marina Blue Design *150.00*
Plate, 8¹/₂", Crystal with Amethyst Rim, Signed *150.00*
Plate, 8¹/₂", Jade Green *100.00*

Left: Steuben art glass. Photo by Mark Pickvet. Right: Steuben art glass. Photo by Robin Rainwater.

Powder Jar with Cover, Rosa Design, Signed *$150.00*
Salt Dip, Verre de Soie Design *125.00*
Shade, Bell-Shaped, Verre de Soie Design *125.00*
Shade, Calcite with Acid Etched Gold Design *175.00*
Shade, Opal, Yellow Feathering Outlined in Green, Gold Lining *175.00*
Sherbet with Matching Underplate, Jade Green Design *150.00*
Sugar Shaker, 8" Tall, Verre de Soie Design *475.00*
Tumbler, 5" Tall, Amber with Flemish Blue Rim *100.00*
Tumbler, 5" Tall, Rainbow Iridescence, Verre de Soie Design *100.00*
Urn, 13" Tall, Banjo-Shaped, Footed, Venetian Style, Topaz *100.00*
Vase, 5" Tall, Yellow to White Cluthra Design *750.00*
Vase, 5" Tall, Selenium Red Design *225.00*
Vase, 6" Tall, Acid Cutback, Black Jade on Alabaster, Pussy Willow Design, Signed ..*2000.00*
Vase, 6" Tall, Pedestal Foot, Ruffled, Ribbed, Iridescent, Ivrene Design *350.00*
Vase, 6" Tall, Trumpet-Shaped, Footed, Ivrene Design, Signed *400.00*
Vase, 6" Tall, Trumpet-Shaped, Alabaster Pedestal Foot, Rosaline Design, Signed ...*250.00*
Vase, 6½" Tall, Jack-in-the-Pulpit, Iridescent Ivrene Design, Signed *500.00*
Vase, 6½" Tall, Footed, Opaque White Swirls, Oriental Jade Design *300.00*
Vase, 7" Tall, Thorned, 3-Pronged, Emerald Green Design *350.00*
Vase, 7½" Tall, Crystal, Acid Finish, Diatreta Geometric Design *15,500.00*
Vase, 8" Tall, Acid Cutback, Alabaster to Jade Shading *750.00*
Vase, 8" Tall, Acid Cutback, Alabaster, Jade Green Rim *800.00*
Vase, 8" Tall, White Cluthra Design, Signed *1250.00*
Vase, 8¼" Tall, Trumpet-Shaped, Domed Pedestal Foot, Ribbed, Celeste Blue Design ..*250.00*
Vase, 9¼" Tall, Pedestal Foot, Engraved Floral Rosaline Design *800.00*
Vase, 9¼" Tall, Alabaster Foot, Engraved Floral Rosaline Design *900.00*
Vase, 10" Tall, Flat Oval Shape, Large Bubbles, Dark Red to White Shading, Cluthra Design
....*1000.00*
Vase, 10¼" Tall, Inverted Lip, Ribbed, Ivory Design, Signed *300.00*
Vase, 10¾" Tall, Footed, Amber with Variegated Greens and Blues, Signed *1000.00*
Vase, 11½" Tall, Green to Yellow Jade Shading, Acid Cutback *1600.00*
Vase, 12" Tall, Floriform, Ivory with Black Trim *1000.00*
Vase, 13" Tall, Trumpet-Shaped, Fluted, Green Florentia Design, Signed *1750.00*
Vase, 13½" Tall, Tyrian Design, Signed *10,000.00*
Vase, 14" Tall, Blue Jade, Alabaster and Black Swirls, Acid Cutback, Signed "F. Carder"
....*5500.00*
Vase, 16" Tall, Folded Rim, Optic Ribs, Marina Blue Design *450.00*
Vase, Fish Attached to Pedestal, Red, Signed Steuben *200.00*
Wineglass, Green Swirled, Signed *150.00*
Wineglass, 4¾" Tall, Ribbed, Inverted Baluster Stem, Topaz *125.00*
Wineglass, 7¼" Tall, Twisted Stem, Jade and Alabaster, Signed *150.00*
Wineglass, 8½" Tall, 2 Knobs, Circular Foot, Oval Bowl with Molded Bubbles and Threading, Transparent Green, Marked "Steuben" *75.00*

In the pre-crystal era, few names command attention in the art glass world as do Frederick Carder and Thomas J. Hawkes, who formed Steuben. Hawkes was a maker of superb-quality crystal, while Carder, like Tiffany, studied the art movement in Europe as well as various art styles from around the world. Carder became a world-class designer, and the majority of Steuben's colored art creations are attributed to him or at the very least to his direction. The majority of the objects created were signed "Steuben" or with Carder's signature.

See "Aurene" for additional Steuben Listings. Also, see Chapter 7 for Crystal Steuben listings since 1933.

TIFFANY, LOUIS COMFORT   1880S–1920S

Object	*Price*
Bonbon Dish, 4" Diameter, Iridescent Yellow-Orange with Opalescent Foot and Stem, Signed	*$350.00*
Bowl, Finger, Matching Underplate, Ruffled, Ribbed, Iridescent Gold, Signed	*100.00*
Bowl, 5", Ruffled, Blue	*600.00*
Bowl, 7", Ruffled Iridescent Gold, Intaglio Cut	*800.00*
Bowl, 10", Iridescent Gold with Green Ivy, 2 Flower Frogs	*750.00*
Bowl, 12", Footed, Opal and Yellow, Signed	*975.00*
Bowl, 12", Centerpiece, Opalescent Pastel Blue	*1100.00*
Candlestick, 8" Tall, Iridescent Gold, Signed	*275.00*
Chalice, 11" Tall, Iridescent Gold with Green Leaves	*1250.00*
Cologne Bottle with Double-Lobed Stopper, 10" Tall, Signed	*1000.00*
Compote, 12" Diameter, Stemmed, Blue, Signed	*1200.00*
Cordial, 1½" Tall, Iridescent Gold, Signed	*275.00*
Decanter with Stopper, 8¾" Tall, Gold, Merovingian Pattern	*1450.00*
Decanter with Stopper, 9" Tall, Brown Agate Design with Vertical White Lines, Signed	*1250.00*
Inkwell, Square (4" × 4"), Hinged Lid, Insert, Bronze with Green Slag, Pine Needle Design, Signed	*400.00*
Inkwell, Square, Embossed Brass Frame, Paneled, Marked "Tiffany Studios, N.Y. 844"	*525.00*
Parfait, 5" Tall, Footed, Pastel Lavender and Opalescent, Signed	*450.00*
Plate, 6", Pastel Blue, Signed "LCT"	*350.00*
Plate, 11", Light Bluish-Green, Opalescent Starburst Design	*325.00*
Punch Goblet, 3½" Tall, Hollow Stem, Gold, Signed	*225.00*
Salt Dip, Ruffled, Iridescent Blue and Gold, Signed "Tiffany"	*225.00*
Shade, Iridescent Orange with Opal Lining, King Tut Pattern	*425.00*
Shade, 5" Tall, Opal, Green King Tut Pattern	*725.00*
Shade, 6¼" Tall, Banded at Base and Rim, Acid-Etched Leaves and Berries	*300.00*
Shade, 10" Diameter, Domed, Gray, Green, and Iridescent Amber	*1200.00*
Sherbet, 4¼" Diameter, Yellow-Orange with Opalescent Edge	*325.00*
Sherbet, 5" Tall, Blue, Signed "L.C.T. T511"	*1000.00*
Shot Glass, Iridescent Gold with Applied Lily Pads, Signed	*300.00*
Stamp Box, 3 Glass Inserts, Signed "Tiffany Studios"	*175.00*
Stamp Box, Rectangular (4" × 2¼"), Bronze with Green Slag, 3 Compartments, Pine Needle Design	*250.00*
Toothpick Holder, Iridescent Gold, Inverted Dimple Design, Signed "L.C.T.—#R8844"	*400.00*
Tumbler, 4" Tall, Pinched Sides, Iridescent Gold, Signed	*325.00*
Vase, 4" Tall, Paperweight Style, Cameo Floral and Intaglio Design, Signed	*6500.00*
Vase, 4¼" Tall, Urn-Shaped, Iridescent Gold with Opalescent White Flowers and Green Leaves, Marked "L.C.T. US099"	*5000.00*
Vase, 4¼" Tall, Paperweight Style, Crystal with Cream, Mauve, and Olive Morning Glories, Signed "L.C.T. Y6889"	*1750.00*
Vase, 4½" Tall, Lava with Cobalt Overlay, Gold Trailings, Signed	*20,000.00*
Vase, 4½" Tall, Tall Collar, Iridescent Red, Signed	*3500.00*

Left: Tiffany art glass. Photo by Mark Pickvet. Right: Tiffany art glass. Photo by Robin Rainwater.

Vase, 5¼" Tall, Cylindrical, Cream Neck, Silver Band beneath Neck, Translucent Green Glass Edge, Marked "L.C.T. Q4511" $800.00

Vase, 5¼" Tall, Ribbed, Dimpled, Iridescent Blue *800.00*

Vase, 5½" Tall, Millefiori, Iridescent Gold with White Flowers and Green Leaves ..*2000.00*

Vase, Bud, 6" Tall, Iridescent Gold, Signed, Numbered *650.00*

Vase, 6" Tall, Crystal Base, Pastel Yellow, Signed *525.00*

Vase, 6½" Tall, Iridescent Red and Black Paneled Design, Signed *4250.00*

Vase, 6½" Tall, Iridescent Lava, Banded or Beaded Decoration, Signed *6750.00*

Vase, 7" Tall, Paperweight Style, Peacock Feather Design, Signed *5500.00*

Vase, 7½" Tall, Iridescent Shades of Green, Millefiore and Gold Leaves Design, Signed
....*2250.00*

Vase, Bud, 8¼" Tall, Iridescent Gold, Green Triangle Design, Signed *600.00*

Vase, 8½" Tall, Iridescent Brown with Double Threading, Signed *1000.00*

Vase, 9½" Tall, Iridescent Brown, Cypriote Design *3250.00*

Vase, 10" Tall, Laminated Tan and Brown Agate Striped Design, Signed *3500.00*

Vase, 11" Tall, Iridescent Red with Gold Overlay, Signed *1200.00*

Vase, 12" Tall, Paperweight Style, Gladiolus Design, Signed *5500.00*

Vase, 13" Tall, Pedestal Base, Ribbed, Iridescent Gold with Blue Highlights, Signed *1750.00*

Vase, 13¼" Tall, Jack-in-the-Pulpit Style, Gold, Signed "L.C.T. W8426" *2000.00*

Vase, 14½" Tall, Trumpet-Shaped, Pedestal Base with Ball, Iridescent Gold Foliage *2500.00*

Vase, 16" Tall, Floriform, Iridescent Gold, Signed "L.C.T. 9708A" *2250.00*

Vase, 16½" Tall, Paperweight Style, Bronze Base, Blue Floral Design *8000.00*

Vase, 17¼" Tall, Curved Gooseneck Style, Amber with Gold Feathers, Signed "L.C.T. M4386" *3500.00*

Vase, 18" Tall, Flower-Form, Bronze Base, Floriform, Pink Cameo Decoration *3500.00*

Vase, 19" Tall, Stick-Shaped, Bronze Support, Iridescent Blue, Signed *1000.00*

Vase, 19" Tall, Jack-in-the-Pulpit Style, Iridescent Gold, Floriform, Signed *1250.00*

Water Goblet, 7" Tall, Iridescent Gold, Vintage Pattern, Signed *550.00*

Wineglass, 4" Tall, Gold Foot and Bowl with Amber Stem, Signed *225.00*

Wineglass, 8½" Tall, Gold with Crystal Stem, Signed "L.C.T." *1250.00*

The outright leader of the Art Nouveau period in America, Louis Comfort Tiffany, along with members of the Nash family, sparked the entire art glass movement.

Color effects, experimentation, iridescent forms, expensive metallic designs (bronze, gold, silver, platinum, etc.), and a host of original art styles from around the world are all characteristic of Tiffany's work.

Note: See "Favrile" and "Tiffany Lamps" for additional entries on Louis Comfort Tiffany.

TIFFANY LAMPS 1870S–1920S

Object	Price
Candelabrum, 15", 6-Branched, Green Glass Cabochons, Snuffer in Central Handle, Circular Mark	$3750.00
Ceiling Fixture, 17", Iridescent Gold Shades Inscribed "L.C.T."	3250.00
Chandelier, 22" Diameter, Multicolored Hanging Head Dragonfly Design, Impressed "Tiffany Studios New York"	30,000.00
Chandelier, 24" Diameter, Pink and Blue Iris Blossom Design, Impressed "Tiffany Studios New York"	25,000.00
Chandelier, 25" Diameter, Multicolored Rose Bush Design, Impressed "Tiffany Studios New York"	27,500.00
Chandelier, Wisteria, 25" Diameter, Multicolored, Impressed "Tiffany Studios New York"	35,000.00
Chandelier, 27" Diameter, Multicolored Fish Design, Impressed "Tiffany Studios New York"	31,000.00
Chandelier, 30" Diameter, Multicolored Grape Trellis, Design, Impressed "Tiffany Studios New York"	45,000.00
Lamp, Candle, 5" Tall, Turtle-Back Tile Design, Impressed "Tiffany Studios New York"	6000.00
Lamp, Bronze Desk, 11¼" Tall, Turtle-Back Tile Design, Top Hook-Loop for Hanging, Impressed "Tiffany Studios New York"	10,000.00

Tiffany art glass lamp. Photo by Robin Rainwater.

Lamp, Candle, 13" Tall, Gold Shade, Ruffled, Gold Candlestick, Opal Insert, Green Feather Design, Signed *$1500.00*

Lamp, Candle, 13" Tall, Turtle-Back Tile Design, Impressed "Tiffany Studios" *7500.00*

Lamp, Table, 13" Tall, Globular Shade, Iridescent Blue Portrait Style *2250.00*

Lamp, Bronze Desk, 14½", Adjustable Oval Shade, Circular Cast Foot, Green Glass, Cabochons, Green Floral Design, Impressed "408 Tiffany Studios New York" *2500.00*

Lamp, Electric Candle, 15" Tall, Gold Shade, Opal and Green Riser, Signed on Base and Shade *1750.00*

Lamp, "Gone with the Wind" 15", Signed Shade, Signed Bronze Base, Off-White Satin Background, Orange Feathers (Signed "Tiffany Studios") *3750.00*

Lamp, 16", Leaded Acorn, Green and White Shade, Signed *4000.00*

Lamp, 16", Red, Amber, and Green Shaded Canterbury Bells, Signed *12,000.00*

Lamp, 16¾", Pony White Wisteria with Pink and Green Florals *24,000.00*

Lamp, 16½", Leaded Amethyst and Green Shade, White and Yellow Roses and Butterflies *82,000.00*

Lamp, 18", Deep Violet 16" Dragonfly Shade, Glass Base Enclosing Fuel Canister, 5 Dragonflies and Floral Design in Relief on Base, Impressed "Tiffany Studios New York" *90,000.00*

Lamp, 20", Blue and Green Dragonfly-Design 14" Shade, Impressed "Tiffany Studios New York *55,000.00*

Lamp, Table, 20¼", Feathered Green and White Shade, Lily Pad Vase, Marked "Tiffany Studios New York 381" *8000.00*

Lamp, Bronze Table, 20½", 16" Multicolored Bamboo-Design Shade, Impressed "Tiffany Studios New York" *35,000.00*

Lamp, Bronze Table, 21¼", Leaded Shade, 4 Raised Feet, Orange Acorns, Green Panels, Marked "Tiffany Studios New York" *2500.00*

Lamp, Bronze Table, 21¼", Seven Lily-Shaped Gold Globes, Base Marked "Tiffany Studios New York" *10,500.00*

Lamp, Table, 22", Leaded Yellow Daffodil Shade, Urn-Shaped Base, Blue to Green Shading, Green Base, Signed "Grueby" on Base *16,000.00*

Lamp, Table, 22", Spider Web, Apple Blossom Design, Signed *12,500.00*

Lamp, Bronze Table, 22", Multicolored 16" Fish-Design Shade *25,000.00*

Lamp, Bronze Table, 23¼", Leaded Shade, 5 Ball Feet, Multicolored Dragonflies, Stamped "Tiffany Studios New York" *10,000.00*

Lamp, Bronze Table, 26", Leaded Hemispherical Shade "558", Bronze Base "366", Multicolored Floral and Leaf Design, Impressed "Tiffany Studios" *11,500.00*

Lamp, Bronze Table, 26½", Leaded Domical Shade, 4-Footed Bronze Base, Pink and Blue Flowers, Yellow Centers, Impressed "Tiffany Studios New York 1475–13" *25,000.00*

Lamp, Bronze Table, 27½", Leaded Domical Shade, Bronze Treeform Base, Blue Flowers with Bright Green and Yellow Leaves, Signed "Tiffany Studios New York" *52,000.00*

Lamp, Bronze Desk, 29½", Twin Green Hemispherical Shades, Bronze Base, Gravity Feed Fuel Canister *3200.00*

Lamp, 31½", 10" Diameter Globe Shade, Multicolored Autumn Leaf Design *45,000.00*

Lamp, Bronze Floor, 63", Leaded Glass Turtle-Back Tile Design 20" Shade, Impressed "Tiffany Studios New York" *15,000.00*

Lamp, Bronze Floor, 64½", Leaded Domical Shade, 4-Footed Base, Impressed "Tiffany Studios New York 387" *10,000.00*

Lamp, Bronze Floor, 68", Red and Yellow Salamander 27" Shade, Impressed "Tiffany Studios New York" *45,000.00*

Lamp, Bronze Floor, 79", Gold Patina Base, 24" Shade with Molted Yellow Flower Clusters and Green Leaves on a Blue Ground, Impressed "Tiffany Studios New York" *75,000.00*

If there was one major object or design that could be attributed to Louis Comfort

Tiffany, it would be a toss-up between "Favrile" and lamps. The world-renowned Tiffany lamps are now commanding auction prices in excess of $100,000 for many of the larger works. Reproductions pose some problems; fraudulent copies should be carefully looked out for.

A vast majority of the original lamps are signed "L.C.T.," "Louis C. Tiffany," "Tiffany Studios," or other titles containing the word "Tiffany."

See the "Favrile" section for a few additional lamp entries.

VASA MURRHINA   VARIOUS COMPANIES, 1870S–1890S

Object	Price
Basket, 6" Tall, Crystal Twisted Handle, Pink with Silver Mica	$250.00
Basket, 7" Tall, Red to Pink Coloring	325.00
Bowl, Finger, 4" Cranberry with Silver Mica	150.00
Bowl, 4³/₄", Ruffled, Pink and Red with Gold Mica	250.00
Bowl, Rose, 5", Blue with Yellow and Silver Mica	125.00
Creamer, Ribbed, Cobalt with Gold Mica	150.00
Creamer, 4¹/₂" Tall, Crystal Handle, Pink and Red with White Lining and Silver Mica	125.00
Cruet with Crystal Stopper, 6" Tall, Crystal Handle, Pink with Silver Mica	250.00
Cruet with Stopper, 6¹/₄" Tall, Blue with Silver Mica	225.00
Ewer, 9¹/₂" Tall, Ruffled, Pink, Blue, and Yellow with White Lining and Silver Mica	200.00
Mug, 4¹/₂" Tall, White with Gold Mica	125.00
Pitcher, 7³/₄" Tall, Blue with Silver Mica	175.00
Pitcher, Syrup, with Metal Lid, 5³/₄" Tall, Blue with Gold Mica	200.00
Pitcher, Water, 8¹/₂" Tall, Bulbous, Brown and Red with Gold Mica	375.00
Sugar, Ribbed, Cobalt Blue with Gold Mica	150.00
Toothpick Holder, 2" Tall, Yellow with Red and Silver Mica	125.00
Tumbler, Various Designs with Gold or Silver Mica	225.00
Vase, 6" Tall, Bulbous, White with Amber and Gold Mica	150.00
Vase, 7¹/₄" Tall, Slender, Cranberry with Gold Mica	200.00
Vase, 8" Tall, Trumpet-Shaped, Dark Red with White and Silver Mica	175.00

Vasa Murrhina art glass.
Photo by Mark Pickvet.

Vase, 8½" Tall, Yellow Design on White Background, Silver Mica, White Lining . .*$200.00*
Vase, 9¼" Tall, Blue with White and Lighter Blue Splotches, Gold Mica *200.00*
Vase, 10" Tall, Fluted Top, Multicolored Mica Flecks *175.00*
Vase, 12¼" Tall, Pink with Silver Mica *275.00*

The name "Vasa Murrhina" originated from the Vasa Murrhina Art Glass Company in 1882–83. The glass they produced was ornamented by rolling it with flakes or flecks of mica. Color glass particles or tiny metallic sprinkles produced much the same effect. The company went out of business because of flaws in their basic formulas. These flaws were responsible for causing over two-thirds of their final glass products to crack. Many other companies adopted this decorating technique and produced some glassware in this fashion.

CHAPTER 5

CARNIVAL GLASS

The problem with art glass was the same as that for fine, brilliantly cut crystal. It was too expensive for the average citizen and catered to a very exclusive, limited market. Then an inexpensive pressed substitute for Tiffany, Steuben, and English Victorian glass arrived, and that was Carnival glass. Nearly all of the Carnival glass made in the United States was produced from about 1905 to the late 1920s. In the beginning the new pressed glass was not called "Carnival"; it borrowed its name from Tiffany's Favrile and Steuben's Aurene. It soon added other exotic names, such as New Venetian Art, Parisian Art, Aurora, and Art Iridescent.

The techniques of making this glass were also borrowed from the Art Nouveau movement. Color is natural in glass, based on various oxides that are present in sand. Ordinarily, iron and common metals produce light green to brown glass. With the addition of various metallic oxides, variations in heat and length of time in the furnace, and minor formula changes, astounding color effects were produced. Carnival glass contains a base color, which is the color of the glass before any iridescence is fired upon it. The base color is usually present on the bottom underside of an iridized glass object.

There were two major groups of colored Carnival glass. The bright Carnival colors consisted of red, blue, green, purple, amethyst, amber, and marigold. The pastel colors were a bit rarer and were made up of clear, white, ice green, ice blue, clambroth, lavender, aqua opalescent, peach opalescent, and smoke. Red was the rarest and one of the most expensive to make since fair amounts of gold oxides were required to produce it. Naturally, red is the most valuable color today and commands very high prices. The pastel colors are also not as common and are quite valuable too.

Marigold was the most popular Carnival color and is the one usually envisioned when one thinks of Carnival glass. For marigold, an orange-brown flashing was applied to clear glass and then sprayed with iridescence. Pastels usually had clear bases with a very light coating of iridescence. Lavender naturally had a purple tint; aqua, a blue-green tint; peach, a yellow-orange tint; smoke, a light gray; and clambroth, a pearly white or light yellow sheen. Other opaque and opalescent shadings were made too. Of all the colors, marigold remains the most abundant and cheapest to acquire.

The glass itself was first manufactured into simple bowls and vases. As its popularity increased, water sets, table sets, punch bowls, berry and ice cream sets, dresser sets with matching cologne bottles, other bottles (wines, whiskey, soda), powder jars, trays, hatpin holders, lamps, paperweights, mugs, beads, advertising items, and souvenir pieces all followed as its popularity exploded.

Unlike fancy art glass, Carnival glass was sold in china shops, general stores, and by mail order and was used for containers for food products like pickles and mustard. It was the first to be used for prizes and promotional items for tea companies, candy companies, and furniture stores (as Depression glass would be soon afterward).

Carnival glass was exported to England and other parts of Europe. It even reached as far as Australia, and several foreign countries began producing it too, including England, Australia, Sweden, and others; however, the fad would be a short-lived one.

By the late teens, the demand lessened; and by the early 1920s, the fad had pretty much ended. The new modern decor trends of the 1920s had no place for this odd oily glassware. Manufacturers were left with huge inventories, and this remaining stock was sold to fairs, bazaars, and carnivals (hence the name Carnival glass) at below wholesale prices to rid themselves of it. Those who were stuck with it packed it away until the 1950s.

There were five major companies that produced the majority of Carnival glass in America: the Fenton Art Glass Company of Williamstown, West Virginia; the Imperial Glass Company of Bellaire, Ohio; the Millersburg Glass Company of Millersburg, Ohio; the Northwood Glass Company of Wheeling, West Virginia; and the Dugan Glass Company of Indiana, Pennsylvania.

Noted individuals were Frank and John Fenton, who founded Fenton Art Glass. With another brother, named Robert, John also went on to establish Millersburg Glass Company. Jacob Rosenthal was also employed by the Fentons and developed many Carnival glass formulas. Edward Muhleman founded the Imperial Glass Company, and Harry Northwood (son of English glass artisan John Northwood) established Northwood. Harry Northwood's managers, Thomas E. Dugan and W. G. Minnemeyer, went on to form the Dugan Glass Company.

Fenton and Imperial both made iridescent products in the modern era. Nearly all of Fenton's recent works are easily distinguished from the older versions, and Fenton continues in operation today. Imperial began reproducing Carnival glass in the early 1960s, using some of the original molds; the new glass is marked "IG" on the base or bottom. Imperial survived several rough periods in the past but finally shut down for good in 1982.

A few other companies that produced limited amounts of Carnival glass included Cambridge, Jenkins, Heisey, Indiana, Federal, Fostoria, McKee-Jeannette, Westmoreland, and U.S. Glass.

ACORN BURRS   NORTHWOOD GLASS COMPANY

Object	Marigold	Blue	Green	Amethyst	Purple
Bowl, Berry, 5"	$25.00	$35.00	$35.00	$35.00	$40.00
Bowl, Berry, 10"	75.00	125.00	125.00	125.00	150.00
Butter Dish with Cover	175.00	225.00	225.00	225.00	250.00
Creamer	55.00	80.00	80.00	80.00	80.00
Pitcher, Water	425.00	650.00	550.00	550.00	575.00
Punch Bowl with Base	500.00	750.00	750.00	750.00	800.00
Punch Cup	25.00	50.00	50.00	60.00	55.00
Spooner	100.00	160.00	160.00	160.00	125.00
Sugar Dish with Cover	65.00	90.00	90.00	90.00	90.00
Tumbler	60.00	100.00	75.00	65.00	65.00
Vase, Whimsy	2000.00			2250.00	2250.00

Object	White	Ice Blue	Ice Green	Aqua Opalescent
Bowl, Berry, 5"		$60.00	$60.00	
Bowl, Berry, 10"		350.00	350.00	

*Left: Carnival glass,
"Acorn Burrs"
pattern. Drawing
by Mark Pickvet.
Right: Carnival
glass, "Aztec"
pattern. Photo by
Robin Rainwater.*

Object	White	Ice Blue	Ice Green	Aqua Opalescent
Butter Dish with Cover	$325.00	$300.00	$300.00	
Creamer	125.00	125.00	125.00	
Pitcher, Water		1250.00	1250.00	
Punch Bowl with Base	3250.00	3000.00	3750.00	17500.00
Punch Cup	85.00	80.00	100.00	350.00
Spooner	225.00	210.00	210.00	
Sugar Dish with Cover	150.00	150.00	150.00	
Tumbler		175.00	175.00	

This pattern is characterized by raised acorns and oak leaves around each object. The opalescent varieties—white, blue, green, and aqua—are quite rare, particularly in the punch sets.

AZTEC MCKEE BROTHERS

Object	Marigold	Clambroth
Bowl, Rose		$300.00
Creamer	65.00	100.00
Pitcher, Water	1750.00	
Sugar	65.00	100.00
Tumbler	75.00	

This is the same "Whirling Star" or "Aztec" pattern pressed by McKee in clear glass. Carnival colors were added later to a few of the surviving original molds. McKee was a very small producer of Carnival glass.

BEADED SHELL DUGAN GLASS COMPANY

Object	Marigold	Blue	Amethyst	Purple	White
Bowl, Berry, 5", Footed	$25.00		$45.00	$45.00	
Bowl, Berry, 6½", Footed	30.00		50.00	50.00	
Bowl, Berry, 9", Footed	60.00		85.00	85.00	
Butter Dish with Cover	150.00		275.00	275.00	

Object	Marigold	Blue	Amethyst	Purple	White
Creamer with Cover	$75.00		$125.00	$100.00	
Mug	175.00	100.00	90.00	110.00	400.00
Mug, Whimsy (Irregular)			400.00	400.00	
Pitcher, Water	350.00	475.00	475.00	475.00	
Spooner	75.00		125.00	125.00	
Sugar with Cover	75.00		125.00	125.00	
Tumbler	60.00	85.00	85.00	85.00	

The scalloped shell of this pattern is large, and usually three or four shells together circle around each item. The beading circles out in a radius from the bottom of each shell. The rims of many pieces are simply the top of the shell, while the bases are ridged shells pointing downward.

BELLS AND BEADS   DUGAN GLASS COMPANY

Object	Marigold	Amethyst	Purple	Opalescent Peach
Bowl, 6³/₄" (Blue or Green $75.00)	$40.00		$65.00	$100.00
Bowl, 7¹/₂" (Blue or Green $80.00)	45.00		70.00	
Compote	25.00	35.00	35.00	
Gravy Boat, Handled	75.00		100.00	150.00
Hat	50.00		60.00	
Nappy	50.00		75.00	110.00
Plate, 6³/₄"		60.00	60.00	

This pattern is characterized by swirled bell-shaped flowers with beaded stems.

BIRDS AND CHERRIES   FENTON ART GLASS COMPANY

Object	Marigold	Blue	Green	Amethyst
Bonbon Dish		$75.00	$65.00	$50.00
Bowl, 5"	475.00	450.00		275.00
Bowl, 9"	800.00	775.00		650.00
Compote	100.00	90.00	65.00	75.00
Plate, 10"		1250.00	1500.00	

This pattern is characterized by five birds perched on cherry branches; the entire design is in relief. Plates and bowls are quite scarce.

Carnival glass, "Bells and Beads" pattern.
Drawing by Mark Pickvet.

BLACKBERRY WREATH   MILLERSBURG GLASS COMPANY

Object	Marigold	Blue	Green	Purple
Bowl, 5"	$40.00		$60.00	$55.00
Bowl, 7"	60.00	250.00	75.00	65.00
Bowl, 9"	70.00	125.00	110.00	85.00
Bowl, 10", Ice Cream	150.00	175.00		150.00
Plate, 6"	1250.00		1750.00	1500.00
Plate, 8"			3000.00	
Plate, 10"	3500.00			4000.00
Spittoon (Whimsy)			3000.00	

This pattern is characterized by blackberry branches curved together to form a wreath; within the wreath is fruit and foliage.

BUTTERFLY AND BERRY   FENTON ART GLASS COMPANY

Object	Marigold	Blue	Red	Green
Bowl, Berry, 5"	$35.00	$45.00	$1000.00	$55.00
Bowl, Berry, 10", Footed	75.00	100.00		100.00
Bowl, Fernery	750.00	1250.00		
Butter Dish with Cover	125.00	300.00		300.00
Creamer with Cover	100.00	150.00		200.00
Cuspidor		900.00		
Hatpin Holder	750.00	700.00		
Nut Dish		750.00		
Pitcher, Water	225.00	450.00		550.00
Plate, Footed		1500.00		
Spittoon, 2 Styles		2500.00		
Spooner	100.00	150.00		175.00
Sugar Dish with Cover	100.00	150.00		200.00
Tumbler	45.00	55.00		85.00
Vase	75.00	65.00	600.00	

Object	Amethyst	Purple	White
Bowl, Berry, 5"		$45.00	$100.00
Bowl, Berry, 10", Footed	100.00	90.00	200.00
Bowl, Fernery	1000.00	1000.00	
Butter Dish with Cover	300.00	300.00	
Creamer	175.00	175.00	
Cuspidor	900.00	900.00	
Nut Dish	750.00	750.00	
Pitcher, Water	450.00	450.00	
Spittoon, 2 Styles	2500.00	2500.00	
Spooner	150.00	150.00	
Sugar Dish with Cover	175.00	175.00	

Object	Amethyst	Purple	White
Tumbler	$75.00	$150.00	
Vase			500.00

This pattern is characterized by alternating panels of Monarch butterflies and triangular berries, along with a notched rim. Red pieces (as with most Carnival glass) are quite rare.

CAPTIVE ROSE FENTON ART GLASS COMPANY

Object	Marigold	Blue	Green
Bonbon Dish	$50.00	$60.00	$70.00
Bowl, 8½"	35.00	50.00	55.00
Bowl, 10"	40.00	55.00	60.00
Compote	35.00	50.00	75.00
Plate, 7"	40.00	55.00	60.00
Plate, 9"	75.00	110.00	125.00

Object	Amethyst	Purple	White
Bowl, 8½"	$50.00	$50.00	
Bowl, 10"	55.00	55.00	
Compote	50.00	50.00	75.00
Plate, 7"	55.00	55.00	
Plate, 9"	110.00	110.00	

This pattern is characterized by roses surrounded by diamonds, circles, and scales.

CATTAILS AND WATER LILIES FENTON ART GLASS
COMPANY, NORTHWOOD GLASS COMPANY

Object	Marigold	Blue	Amethyst	Purple
Bonbon Dish (Red $400.00)	$75.00	$85.00		$80.00
Bowl, Berry, 9"	35.00			
Bowl, Oblong, Banana, 4-Footed (Green $150.00) ...	90.00	125.00	125.00	125.00
Creamer	50.00			
Jelly Dish (Resembles Toothpick Holder)	50.00			
Pitcher, Water	100.00			
Spooner	45.00			
Tumbler	25.00			

Along with the cattails and water lilies, there is some molding at the bottom of the design (soil and grass).

CHECKERBOARD WESTMORELAND GLASS COMPANY

Object	Marigold	Purple	Clambroth
Cruet with Stopper			$600.00
Goblet	300.00	350.00	

Carnival glass, "Checkerboard" pattern. Drawing by Mark Pickvet.

Object	Marigold	Purple	Clambroth
Pitcher, Water		$3250.00	
Punch Cup	100.00	125.00	
Tumbler	650.00	500.00	
Vase		1750.00	
Wineglass	300.00		

"Checkerboard" is a diagonal cross-cut pattern, and all pieces (with the possible exception of punch cups) are quite rare.

CHERRY   MILLERSBURG GLASS COMPANY, DUGAN GLASS COMPANY

Object	Marigold	Blue	Green	Amethyst	Purple
Banana Dish	$2500.00			$2000.00	$2000.00
Bowl, 4"	25.00	450.00	55.00	55.00	55.00
Bowl, 5", Ruffled (Dugan)	30.00	50.00	50.00	50.00	50.00
Bowl, 5½"	30.00	75.00	60.00	60.00	60.00
Bowl, 6", Ruffled, Footed (Dugan)	35.00	50.00	50.00	50.00	50.00
Bowl, 7"	75.00		125.00	85.00	85.00
Bowl, 8", Ruffled (Dugan)	30.00	50.00	50.00	50.00	50.00
Bowl, 8½", Ruffled, Footed (Dugan)	150.00	200.00	200.00	175.00	175.00
Bowl, 9"	75.00	175.00	100.00	100.00	100.00
Bowl, 10", Ice Cream	100.00	500.00	175.00	150.00	150.00
Compote	550.00	1250.00	600.00	600.00	600.00
Creamer	75.00		125.00	125.00	125.00
Cruet with Stopper (Dugan) (Pastel $550.00)				150.00	150.00
Pitcher, Milk	250.00		475.00	475.00	475.00
Pitcher, Water	500.00		725.00	725.00	725.00
Plate, 6" (Dugan Peach Opalescent $400.00)	800.00				
Plate, 7½"			850.00	750.00	750.00
Plate, 10"	4000.00		4250.00		
Powder Jar with Cover			1000.00		
Spooner	60.00		125.00	125.00	125.00
Sugar Dish with Cover	125.00		175.00	175.00	175.00
Tumbler, 2 Styles	500.00		700.00	700.00	700.00

The four Dugan bowls, the Dugan plate, and the Dugan cruet are a separate pattern from the remaining Millersburg pieces. Dugan's "Cherry" is characterized by cherry branches with the fruit in medallion form within the interior of the bowls. Millersburg's "Cherry" pattern is in exterior panels of cherry foliage raised in relief.

CHERRY AND CABLE   NORTHWOOD GLASS COMPANY

Object	Marigold
Bowl, Berry, 5"	$50.00
Bowl, Berry, 9"	90.00
Butter Dish with Cover	300.00
Creamer	125.00
Pitcher, Water	1250.00
Spooner	100.00
Sugar with Cover	150.00
Tumbler	300.00

"Cherry and Cable" contains a line or cable that runs around each item; four leaves run through the cable and branch down into two groupings of three cherries. Also, around the bottom are circular thumbprints (eight total). This pattern has been reproduced in miniature.

CHERRY CIRCLES   FENTON ART GLASS COMPANY

Object	Marigold	Blue	Green	Amethyst
Bonbon Dish (Red $300.00)	$50.00	$40.00		$40.00
Bowl, 8"	55.00	60.00	60.00	60.00
Compote	90.00	100.00	100.00	100.00
Plate, 9" (White $200.00)	250.00	125.00		
Plate, 10", Chop (Clambroth Only, $225.00)				

"Cherry Circles" includes groups of three cherries in a wide band around the center of each object, surrounded by foliage wreaths.

CHERRY WREATH   DUGAN GLASS COMPANY

Object	Marigold	Blue	Green
Butter Dish with Cover	$100.00	$200.00	$185.00
Creamer	70.00	125.00	125.00
Cuspidor	1000.00		
Pitcher, Water	175.00	300.00	300.00
Sugar	70.00	125.00	125.00
Spooner	65.00	115.00	115.00
Tumbler	45.00	60.00	60.00

Object	Amethyst	Purple	White
Butter Dish with Cover	$200.00	$200.00	$300.00
Lamp, Cherub			500.00

Left: Carnival glass, "Cherry and Cable" pattern. Drawing by Mark Pickvet. "Right: Carnival glass, "Circle Scroll" pattern. Drawing by Mark Pickvet.

Object	Amethyst	Purple	White
Creamer	$125.00	$125.00	$200.00
Pitcher, Water	300.00	300.00	500.00
Sugar	125.00	125.00	200.00
Spooner	115.00	115.00	175.00
Tumbler	60.00	60.00	110.00

The cherries in this wreath design are either the color of the basic flashing or are flashed in red. For those in red, increase the above-listed prices by 25%.

CIRCLE SCROLL   DUGAN GLASS COMPANY

Object	Marigold	Amethyst	Purple
Bowl, 5"	$30.00	$40.00	$40.00
Bowl, 10"	40.00	50.00	50.00
Butter Dish with Cover	200.00	250.00	250.00
Creamer	125.00	150.00	150.00
Pitcher, Water	1250.00	2000.00	2000.00
Spooner	100.00	125.00	125.00
Sugar Dish with Cover	150.00	175.00	175.00
Tumbler	300.00	500.00	500.00
Vase	125.00	150.00	150.00

The scroll design of this pattern is inscribed in circles that band around each object. Above and below the circles are vertical panels with circular ends.

COIN DOT   FENTON ART GLASS COMPANY, WESTMORELAND GLASS COMPANY

Object	Marigold	Blue	Green	Amethyst
Basket (Westmoreland Pattern Variant)	$60.00	$75.00		
Bowl, 6" (Red $900.00)	35.00	45.00	45.00	45.00
Bowl, 9"	40.00	50.00	50.00	50.00
Bowl, 10" (Red $1000.00)	45.00	55.00	55.00	55.00
Bowl, Rose	40.00	50.00	50.00	50.00
Bowl, Rose (Westmoreland Pattern Variant)	85.00			100.00

Object	Marigold	Blue	Green	Amethyst
Bowl (Westmoreland Pattern Variant) $55.00		$90.00		$75.00
Compote (Westmoreland Pattern Variant) 75.00				
Pitcher, Water 300.00		425.00	450.00	425.00
Tumbler 60.00		100.00	110.00	100.00

Object	Purple	Aqua Opalescent	Peach Opalescent
Bowl, 6" $45.00		$225.00	
Bowl, 9" 50.00		275.00	
Bowl, 10" 55.00		300.00	
Bowl, Rose............................50.00			
Bowl (Westmoreland Pattern Variant)			150.00
Compote (Westmoreland Pattern Variant).........			175.00
Pitcher, Water........................425.00			
Tumbler 100.00			

The original "Coin Dot" was produced by Fenton and is characterized by various sizes of pressed coins around each item. Westmoreland produced a slight variant, as noted by the pieces listed above.

COLONIAL   IMPERIAL GLASS COMPANY

Object	Marigold	Red	Green
Candlestick $100.00			
Creamer 45.00		125.00	55.00
Pitcher, Water		3250.00	
Sugar 45.00		125.00	55.00
Tumbler		225.00	
Vase 55.00			65.00

This is a typical "Colonial" pattern, featuring wide, arched panels around each object.

COSMOS AND CANE   IMPERIAL GLASS COMPANY

Object	Marigold	White
Bowl, Berry, 5" $35.00		$75.00
Bowl, Berry, 8" 45.00		90.00
Bowl, Berry, 10" 50.00		100.00
Bowl, Rose (Amethyst 175.00, Amber $200.00) 125.00		650.00
Butter Dish with Cover 150.00		225.00
Compote 85.00		125.00
Creamer 75.00		110.00
Pitcher, Water 600.00		900.00
Plate, Chop 400.00		525.00
Sherbet		150.00
Spittoon 3250.00		3500.00
Spooner 65.00		100.00
Sugar 75.00		110.00
Tray		125.00

Object	Marigold	White
Tumbler	.$85.00	$125.00
Tumbler with Advertising	.250.00	

This pattern is characterized by ferns and flowers that are placed from the bottom to just below the rim; between the foliage is a diamond trellis design.

COUNTRY KITCHEN MILLERSBURG GLASS COMPANY

Object	Marigold	Green	Amethyst	Purple
Bowl, Berry, 5"	.$50.00			
Bowl, Berry, 9"	.75.00			
Butter Dish with Cover	.350.00		375.00	375.00
Creamer	.175.00	200.00	200.00	200.00
Cuspidor			3000.00	3000.00
Spittoon			3000.00	3000.00
Spooner	.150.00		175.00	175.00
Sugar	.175.00	200.00	200.00	200.00
Vase, Whimsy	.350.00		450.00	450.00

"Country Kitchen" includes flowers, triangular ridges, and wavy bands around each object. Cuspidors and spittoons are very rare and valuable.

CRACKLE VARIOUS COMPANIES

Object	Marigold	Green	Purple
Bowl, Berry, 5"	.$15.00	$20.00	$20.00
Bowl, Berry, 9"	.20.00	25.00	25.00
Candlestick, 3½" Tall	.20.00		
Candlestick, 7" Tall	.25.00		
Candy Jar with Cover	.35.00		
Creamer	.20.00	25.00	25.00
Pitcher, Water, Dome Base	.65.00	75.00	75.00
Planter, Window	.100.00		
Plate, 7"	.25.00		
Punch Bowl with Base	.100.00	125.00	125.00

 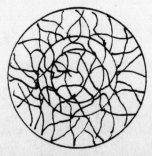

Left: Carnival glass, "Colonial" pattern. Drawing by Mark Pickvet. Right: Carnival glass, "Crackle" pattern. Drawing by Mark Pickvet.

Object	Marigold	Green	Purple
Punch Cup	.$20.00	$25.00	$25.00
Spittoon	.35.00		
Sugar	.20.00	25.00	25.00
Tumbler	.12.00	15.00	15.00
Vase, Auto	.20.00	25.00	25.00
Vase, Wall	.35.00		

If common can be attributed to any Carnival glass, then "Crackle" is a prime candidate. It is true to the name "Carnival" in that large amounts were given away as prizes at fairs, exhibitions, etc. Imperial was probably the largest maker of "Crackle" Carnival.

DAHLIA   DUGAN GLASS COMPANY

Object	Marigold	Amethyst	Purple	White
Bowl, 5", Footed	.$35.00	$45.00	$45.00	$100.00
Bowl, 10", Footed	.75.00	125.00	125.00	250.00
Butter Dish	.125.00	200.00	200.00	300.00
Creamer	.60.00	125.00	125.00	200.00
Pitcher, Water	.550.00	750.00	750.00	850.00
Spooner	.50.00	110.00	110.00	125.00
Sugar	.60.00	125.00	125.00	150.00
Tumbler	.75.00	110.00	110.00	135.00

The large dahlias in this pattern are in relief and are spaced a little farther apart than in typical pressed patterns.

DIAMOND LACE   IMPERIAL GLASS COMPANY

Object	Marigold	Purple	White
Bowl, Berry, 5½"	.$25.00	$35.00	
Bowl, Berry, 9"	.50.00	80.00	

Left: Carnival glass,
"Dahlia" pattern.
Drawing by Mark Pickvet.
Right: Carnival glass,
"Double Dolphin" pattern.
Drawing by Mark Pickvet.

Object	Marigold	Purple	White
Bowl, Fruit, 10½"	$80.00	$100.00	
Pitcher, Water	200.00	300.00	
Tumbler	45.00	75.00	85.00

This pattern is characterized by long diagonal frames with central starbursts, beading, and stippling.

DIAMOND POINT COLUMNS   IMPERIAL GLASS COMPANY, FENTON ART GLASS COMPANY

Object	Marigold	Green	Purple	White
Bowl, 4½"	$20.00			
Butter Dish	80.00			
Compote	25.00			
Creamer	35.00			
Plate, 7"	35.00			
Powder Jar with Cover	50.00			
Spooner	30.00			
Sugar	35.00			
Vase	30.00	50.00	45.00	60.00

This pattern is characterized by alternating rows of panels with checkered diamonds.

DOUBLE DOLPHIN   FENTON ART GLASS COMPANY

Object	Ice Blue	Ice Green	White
Bowl, 8"	$75.00	$75.00	
Bowl, 9", Footed	100.00	100.00	
Bowl, 10"	80.00	80.00	
Bowl, 11", Footed	110.00	110.00	
Cake Plate with Center Handle	75.00	75.00	
Candlestick	40.00	40.00	45.00
Candy Dish with Cover	100.00	100.00	
Compote	90.00	90.00	
Vase, Fan Style	90.00	90.00	100.00

Object	Pink	Topaz	Tangerine
Bowl, 8"	$75.00		
Cake Plate	45.00		
Candlestick	35.00		
Compote		100.00	100.00
Vase, Fan Style	90.00	100.00	100.00

Each object usually contains a pair of scaled dolphins with flipped tails in raised relief. The colors are light iridescent pastels.

ELKS   FENTON ART GLASS COMPANY, MILLERSBURG GLASS COMPANY, DUGAN GLASS COMPANY

Object	Blue	Green	Amethyst	Purple
Bell, 1911 Atlantic City $900.00				
Bell, 1914 Parkersburg .900.00				
Bowl, 8" (Millersburg) .500.00			500.00	500.00
Bowl, Detroit (Marigold $750.00) 300.00	400.00			
Nappy (Dugan)			3000.00	3000.00
Paperweight (Millersburg)	1250.00	1000.00	1000.00
Plate, Atlantic City 900.00	1250.00			
Plate, Parkersburg 750.00	1000.00			

This pattern is characterized by an elk head with a clock upon the antlers (pointing to 12 noon). Around the head are floral and foliage designs. Dugan made only a nappy, and Millersburg produced a bowl and paperweight; the remaining advertising pieces are Fenton.

ESTATE   WESTMORELAND GLASS COMPANY

Object	Marigold	Ice Blue	Ice Green	Aqua Opalescent	Peach Opalescent
Creamer $60.00	$100.00	$125.00	$150.00	$100. 00
Mug 100.00	125.00	150.00		
Perfume Bottle with Stopper			150.00	
Sugar 60.00	100.00	125.00	150.00	100.00
Vase, 3" Tall, Stippled 65.00	100.00	115.00		
Vase, Bud, 6" Tall, ...75.00	110.00	125.00		

FASHION   IMPERIAL GLASS COMPANY

Object	Marigold	Green	Amethyst	Purple	Smoke
Basket, Bride's $100.00				$125.00
Bowl, 9" 45.00	75.00			90.00
Bowl, Fruit, with Base 60.00	85.00			100.00
Bowl, Rose 325.00	750.00	1000.00		
Butter Dish 75.00		175.00	175.00	

Carnival glass, "Estate" pattern. Drawing by Mark Pickvet.

Object	Marigold	Green	Amethyst	Purple	Smoke
Compote					$200.00
Creamer 45.00		125.00	125.00	125.00	150.00
Pitcher, Water 175.00		1000.00	900.00	750.00	
Punch Bowl with Base (Red $10,000.00) .225.00			750.00	750.00	
Punch Cup (Red $750.00) 35.00			65.00	65.00	
Sugar 45.00		125.00	125.00	125.00	150.00
Tumbler 35.00		150.00	150.00	150.00	175.00

This pattern consists of diamonds, jewels, sunbursts, and beading over the entire surface.

FENTONIA   FENTON ART GLASS COMPANY

Object	Marigold	Blue	Green	Amethyst	Purple
Bowl, 5", Footed $35.00		$40.00	$45.00		$40.00
Bowl, 7½", Footed 40.00		75.00	85.00	75.00	75.00
Bowl, Berry, 9" 45.00		80.00	90.00	80.00	80.00
Bowl, 9½", Footed 60.00		90.00	100.00	90.00	90.00
Bowl, Fruit, 10" 70.00		95.00			
Butter Dish with Cover 150.00		200.00			
Creamer 100.00		125.00		125.00	
Pitcher, Water 425.00		600.00			
Spooner 60.00		110.00	125.00	110.00	110.00
Sugar 100.00		125.00		125.00	
Tumbler 125.00		175.00			

"Fentonia" consists of scales and stitches within beaded frames. The pattern is set diagonally on each object.

FERN   NORTHWOOD GLASS COMPANY, FENTON ART GLASS COMPANY

Object	Marigold	Blue	Green	Amethyst
Bowl, 7" $35.00		$50.00	$55.00	$50.00
Bowl, 7" (Fenton)		750.00		
Bowl, 8" (Fenton)		800.00		
Bowl, 8¼" 30.00		40.00	45.00	40.00
Bowl, 9" (Fenton)		850.00		
Compote 22.00		30.00	35.00	30.00
Hat 18.00		24.00	25.00	24.00

Object	Purple	White	Ice Blue	Ice Green
Bowl, 7" $50.00				
Bowl, 8¼" 40.00		75.00	75.00	75.00
Compote 30.00				
Hat 24.00		40.00	40.00	40.00

"Fern" is simply a series of ferns that alternate with branches emanating from the center. It is an interior pattern, but some ferns and foliage are also found on the exterior. The three Fenton bowls were made in blue; all other listed pieces are Northwood.

FIELD THISTLE   U.S. GLASS COMPANY

Object	Marigold	Green
Bowl, 6"	$40.00	
Bowl, 10"	50.00	
Butter Dish with Cover	100.00	125.00
Compote, Large	90.00	
Creamer	40.00	50.00
Plate, 6"	150.00	200.00
Plate, 9"	200.00	250.00
Pitcher, Water	250.00	350.00
Spooner	60.00	75.00
Sugar	40.00	50.00
Tumbler	55.00	70.00
Vase	60.00	75.00

This pattern consists of swirled foliage with daisies as well as a central medallion with a clear glass daisy. The pattern covers the entire exterior of each object.

FILE   IMPERIAL GLASS COMPANY

Object	Marigold	Amethyst	Purple
Bowl, 5"	$25.00	$40.00	$40.00
Bowl, 7"	30.00	45.00	45.00
Bowl, 9"	35.00	50.00	50.00
Bowl, 10"	35.00	50.00	50.00
Butter Dish with Cover	225.00		
Compote	30.00	45.00	45.00
Creamer	110.00		
Pitcher, Water	325.00		
Spooner	100.00		
Sugar Dish with Cover	150.00		
Tumbler	200.00		
Vase	90.00		

"File" is characterized by a series of rounded panels with ridges (or files). A central band divides two rows of these file designs into pyramidlike shapes. Aside from Imperial, it was also made in England.

FINE RIB   NORTHWOOD GLASS COMPANY, FENTON ART GLASS COMPANY, DUGAN GLASS COMPANY

Object	Marigold	Blue	Green	Amethyst	Purple
Bowl, 5"	$25.00	$35.00	$35.00	$35.00	$35.00

Object	Marigold	Blue	Green	Amethyst	Purple
Bowl, 9"	$55.00	$70.00	$70.00	$70.00	$70.00
Bowl, 10"	60.00	75.00	75.00	75.00	75.00
Plate, 8"	20.00			35.00	35.00
Plate, 9"	75.00			100.00	100.00
Vase, 2 Styles (Red $250.00)	25.00	40.00	50.00	40.00	40.00

Object	White	Ice Blue	Ice Green	Aqua Opalescent	Peach Opalescent
Banana Dish					$100.00
Compote					125.00
Vase, 2 Styles	55.00	55.00	55.00	65.00	65.00

This is a simple pattern of vertical ribbing. The only Fenton piece made is the red vase, and the pattern is a slight variation from the Northwood design.

FLUTE   IMPERIAL GLASS COMPANY, MILLERSBURG GLASS COMPANY, NORTHWOOD GLASS COMPANY

Object	Marigold	Blue	Green	Amethyst	Purple
Bowl, 4"		$45.00	$45.00		$45.00
Bowl, 5"	45.00	75.00	75.00	65.00	65.00
Bowl, 10"	150.00			250.00	250.00
Bowl, 10" (Northwood Only)	65.00		75.00	75.00	75.00
Bowl, Custard, 11" (Imperial Only)			300.00	275.00	275.00
Butter Dish	125.00		175.00		
Butter Dish with Cover	225.00		300.00	275.00	275.00
Celery Dish				250.00	250.00
Compote, 6", Clover-Shaped Base, Marked Crystal	400.00			450.00	450.00
Creamer	100.00	140.00	140.00	110.00	110.00
Cruet (Imperial)	100.00				
Pitcher, Water	300.00		600.00	550.00	550.00
Punch Bowl	225.00		450.00	400.00	400.00
Punch Bowl with Base	325.00		650.00	600.00	600.00
Punch Cup	35.00	45.00	45.00	40.00	40.00
Ringtree (Northwood)	200.00				

Carnival glass, "Flute" pattern. Photo by Robin Rainwater.

Object	Marigold	Blue	Green	Amethyst	Purple
Salt Dip, Footed (Northwood) (Vaseline $100.00) $50.00					
Sauce Dish, 5" Diameter 35.00					
Sherbet (Northwood) 45.00					
Spooner 65.00		100.00	100.00	100.00	
Sugar 90.00	125.00	125.00	100.00	100.00	
Sugar Dish with Cover 125.00	150.00	150.00	125.00	125.00	
Toothpick Holder (Aqua $125.00) 65.00	75.00	75.00	70.00	70.00	
Toothpick Holder, Handled (Smoke $100.00) 75.00					
Tumbler, Several Styles 65.00	110.00	110.00	125.00	125.00	
Vase 250.00		350.00	300.00	300.00	

There are quite a few "Flute" designs, but most are similar in design and price. Imperial's has wide paneled flutes, thick glass, and circular bases; some Millersburg products have 16 thin flutes, while others were made with much wider flutes; Northwood's wide flutes are more arched or ridged compared to the others.

FOUR SEVENTY-FOUR   IMPERIAL GLASS COMPANY

Object	Marigold	Green	Amethyst	Purple
Bowl, 8" $55.00		$70.00		
Bowl, 9" 60.00		75.00		
Butter Dish with Cover 125.00		225.00	225.00	225.00
Cordial 90.00			125.00	125.00
Creamer 65.00		85.00	100.00	100.00
Goblet 55.00		70.00	80.00	80.00
Pitcher, Milk 150.00		450.00	450.00	450.00
Pitcher, Water, 2 Styles 200.00		550.00	550.00	550.00
Punch Bowl with Base 225.00		575.00	575.00	575.00
Punch Cup 25.00		35.00	35.00	35.00
Sugar 65.00		85.00	100.00	100.00
Tumbler 50.00		100.00	100.00	100.00
Vase, 7" Tall 750.00		1000.00		
Vase, 14" Tall 1000.00		1250.00		
Wineglass 70.00				

Four Seventy-four consists of a large, central four-petaled flower on a large stalk with thin leaves. These flowers are framed by interlocking broken arches of sunbursts. The ridges are usually notched also.

FROSTED BLOCK   IMPERIAL GLASS COMPANY

Object	Marigold	Clambroth
Bowl, 6½" $20.00		$35.00
Bowl, 7½" 25.00		40.00
Bowl, 8" 28.00		45.00
Bowl, 9" 30.00		50.00

Object	Marigold	Clambroth
Bowl, Rose	$50.00	$75.00
Bowl, Square	40.00	70.00
Butter Dish with Cover	125.00	175.00
Compote	80.00	125.00
Creamer	35.00	65.00
Pickle Dish, Handled	40.00	70.00
Pitcher, Milk	100.00	
Plate, 7½"		60.00
Plate, 9"	35.00	65.00
Spooner	30.00	
Sugar	35.00	65.00
Tray, Celery	40.00	

This pattern is characterized by stippled glass in panels separated by beading. Some pieces may be marked: "Made in USA."

FRUIT AND FLOWERS   NORTHWOOD GLASS COMPANY

Object	Marigold	Blue	Green	Amethyst
Banana Dish, 7"			$200.00	$225.00
Bonbon Dish, Stemmed	40.00	50.00	50.00	50.00
Bowl, Berry, 5"	40.00	50.00	50.00	50.00
Bowl, Berry, 9"	55.00	65.00	65.00	65.00
Bowl, 10", Footed (Aqua Opalescent $150.00)	35.00			45.00
Plate, 7"	45.00	75.00	75.00	75.00
Plate, 8"	60.00	100.00	100.00	100.00
Plate, 9½"	175.00		225.00	225.00

Object	Purple	White	Ice Blue	Ice Green
Banana Plate, 7"	$225.00			
Bonbon Dish, Stemmed (Aqua Opalescent $500.00)	50.00	65.00	65.00	65.00
Bowl, Berry, 5"	50.00	65.00	65.00	65.00
Bowl, Berry, 9"	65.00	75.00	75.00	75.00
Bowl, 10", Footed	45.00			
Plate, 7"	75.00	125.00		
Plate, 8"	100.00	150.00	150.00	150.00
Plate, 9½"	225.00	325.00	325.00	325.00

"Fruit and Flowers" contains slight variations of apples, pears, and cherries, all with leaves, vines, and foliage.

GOLDEN HONEYCOMB   IMPERIAL GLASS COMPANY

Object	Marigold
Bonbon Dish, 5" Diameter	$65.00
Bowl, 5"	25.00
Bowl, 7"	40.00

Object	Marigold
Compote	.$30.00
Creamer	.40.00
Plate, 7"	.35.00
Sugar	.40.00

This pattern contains a large central medallion of a sunburst at the base, while the exterior surface contains rows of thumbprints inscribed within squares (or honeycombs).

GRAPE   IMPERIAL GLASS COMPANY

Object	Marigold	Green	Amethyst	Purple	Amber	Smoke
Basket $75.00		$100.00				$175.00
Bottle, Water						
(Clambroth $250.00) 125.00		200.00		175.00		
Bowl, Berry, 5" 25.00		35.00		35.00		45.00
Bowl, Fruit, 8¾" (Red $275.00) .30.00		40.00		40.00		50.00
Bowl, Berry, 10" 35.00		45.00		45.00		55.00
Bowl, Rose 175.00		200.00	200.00	200.00		225.00
Compote 30.00		40.00	40.00	40.00		
Cup 35.00		45.00				50.00
Cuspidor 800.00		900.00				
Decanter, with Stopper, Wine ..65.00		100.00	100.00	100.00		
Goblet 40.00		75.00	75.00	75.00	85.00	90.00
Lamp Shade 50.00						
Nappy 25.00		35.00				40.00
Pitcher, Milk 225.00		325.00	350.00	350.00		500.00
Pitcher, Water 150.00		300.00	300.00	300.00		450.00
Plate, 7" $150.00) 60.00		150.00	250.00	250.00		275.00
Plate, 8½" 65.00		150.00				
Ruffled 70.00		80.00	80.00	80.00		90.00
Plate, 12" (Blue $175.00) 70.00		175.00	275.00	275.00		300.00
Punch Bowl with Base 175.00		325.00	325.00	325.00	425.00	450.00
Punch Cup 25.00		30.00	30.00	30.00	35.00	40.00
Saucer 25.00		30.00				35.00
Spittoon 1000.00		2000.00				
Tray, Center Handle 40.00						
Tumbler 30.00		55.00	55.00	55.00	70.00	75.00
Wine Glass 30.00		35.00	35.00	35.00		

Imperial's "Grape" is a fairly common pattern except for the larger items (cuspidors, pitchers, and punch bowls).

GRAPE AND CABLE   NORTHWOOD GLASS COMPANY,
FENTON ART GLASS COMPANY

Object	Marigold	Blue	Red	Green	Amethyst
Banana Boat, 12", Footed $175.00		$300.00		$300.00	$275.00
Bonbon Dish..........................35.00					40.00

Object	Marigold	Blue	Red	Green	Amethyst
Bowl, 4", Ice Cream	$35.00	$40.00		$40.00	$40.00
Bowl, Berry, 5"	25.00	35.00		35.00	35.00
Bowl, 5½"	25.00	35.00		35.00	35.00
Bowl, 5½", Scalloped	35.00	45.00		45.00	45.00
Bowl, 7" (Fenton)	65.00	55.00	450.00	55.00	55.00
Bowl, 7", Scalloped	50.00	85.00		85.00	85.00
Bowl, 7", Footed	55.00	90.00		90.00	90.00
Bowl, 8¼", Footed	75.00	60.00		60.00	60.00
Bowl, Berry, 9"	90.00	70.00		70.00	70.00
Bowl, 9", Footed	65.00	100.00		100.00	100.00
Bowl, Berry, 10"	100.00	80.00		80.00	80.00
Bowl, 11", Ice Cream	125.00	225.00		225.00	225.00
Bowl, 11½", Scalloped	45.00	55.00		55.00	55.00
Bowl, Orange (Fenton)	125.00	175.00		175.00	175.00
Bowl, Orange, Footed	150.00	200.00		200.00	200.00
Bowl, Footed (Fenton)	175.00	225.00	550.00	225.00	225.00
Butter Dish	200.00	225.00		225.00	225.00
Candlestick	100.00	150.00		150.00	150.00
Centerpiece, Footed	350.00	450.00		450.00	450.00
Cologne Bottle with Stopper	200.00			225.00	225.00
Compote	525.00	400.00		400.00	400.00
Compote with Cover	2500.00				600.00
Cookie Jar with Cover	250.00	300.00		300.00	300.00
Creamer	65.00	100.00		100.00	100.00
Cup	100.00				125.00
Cuspidor	3000.00	3000.00		3000.00	3000.00
Decanter with Stopper	1000.00	1250.00		1250.00	1250.00
Dresser Tray	175.00	225.00		225.00	225.00
Fernery	1750.00	1000.00		1000.00	950.00
Hat	35.00			50.00	50.00
Hatpin Holder	150.00	225.00		225.00	225.00
Lamp, Candle	125.00	175.00		175.00	175.00
Lamp Shade	225.00	200.00		200.00	200.00
Nappy	85.00	100.00		100.00	100.00
Pin Tray	150.00	200.00		200.00	200.00
Pitcher, Tankard	1000.00	900.00		900.00	900.00
Pitcher, Water	350.00	500.00		475.00	475.00
Plate, 6"	100.00	400.00		375.00	200.00
Plate, 7½"	90.00	100.00		100.00	100.00
Plate, 9½"	110.00	425.00		400.00	225.00
Plate, Footed	100.00	125.00		125.00	125.00
Plate, Footed (Fenton)	75.00	100.00	450.00	100.00	100.00
Plate with Advertising				350.00	
Powder Jar with Cover	90.00	100.00		100.00	100.00
Punch Bowl with Base, 12"	400.00	500.00		500.00	500.00
Punch Bowl, 16"	450.00	600.00		600.00	600.00
Punch Bowl, with Base, 24"	2000.00	3500.00		2500.00	2500.00
Punch Cup	25.00	35.00		35.00	35.00
Saucer	75.00				90.00
Sherbet	35.00			50.00	50.00

Carnival glass, "Grape and Cable" pattern. Photo by Robin Rainwater.

Object	Marigold	Blue	Red	Green	Amethyst
Shot Glass...................	$200.00				$225.00
Spittoon....................	4250.00			6500.00	6000.00
Spooner....................	75.00	175.00		175.00	175.00
Sugar......................	75.00	100.00		100.00	100.00
Sugar with Cover...........	100.00	225.00		150.00	200.00
Sweetmeat Dish.............	500.00	300.00		300.00	300.00
Sweetmeat Compote..........	750.00				225.00
Tobacco Jar with Cover.....	425.00	450.00		450.00	450.00
Tray, Dresser	125.00			175.00	175.00
Tumbler, 6 oz.	75.00	85.00		65.00	55.00
Tumbler, 12 oz.	65.00	100.00		85.00	85.00

Object	Purple	White	Ice Blue	Ice Green	Aqua Opalescent
Banana Boat, 12", Footed	$300.00	$425.00	$425.00	$425.00	
Bonbon Dish.................	40.00	550.00	550.00	550.00	750.00
Bowl, 4", Ice Cream	40.00	100.00	100.00	100.00	
Bowl, Berry, 5"	35.00	60.00	60.00	60.00	
Bowl, 5½"	35.00	60.00	60.00	60.00	
Bowl, 5½", Scalloped	45.00	70.00	70.00	70.00	700.00
Bowl, 7" (Fenton)	55.00				
Bowl, 7", Scalloped...........	85.00	110.00	110.00	110.00	
Bowl, 7", Footed	90.00	125.00	125.00	125.00	
Bowl, 8¼", Footed	60.00				
Bowl, Berry, 9"	70.00	110.00	110.00	110.00	
Bowl, 9", Footed	100.00	135.00	135.00	135.00	
Bowl, Berry, 10"	80.00	125.00	125.00	125.00	
Bowl, 11", Ice Cream	225.00	300.00	300.00	300.00	
Bowl, 11½", Scalloped	55.00	85.00	85.00	85.00	750.00
Bowl, Orange (Fenton)	125.00				
Bowl, Orange, Footed	200.00			1750.00	3000.00
Bowl, Footed (Fenton)	225.00				900.00
Butter Dish.................	150.00	300.00	300.00	300.00	
Candlestick.................	150.00				

Object	Purple	White	Ice Blue	Ice Green	Aqua Opalescent
Centerpiece, Footed	$450.00	$600.00	$600.00	$600.00	
Cologne Bottle with Stopper. . .	225.00				
Compote	400.00	750.00	750.00	750.00	
Compote with Cover	450.00				
Cookie Jar With Cover	300.00	750.00	750.00	750.00	3250.00
Creamer	100.00	175.00	175.00	175.00	
Cup	125.00		175.00	175.00	
Cuspidor	3000.00				
Decanter with Stopper	1250.00				
Dresser Tray	225.00	350.00	350.00	350.00	
Fernery, Footed	950.00	1250.00	3000.00	1500.00	
Hat.	50.00	75.00	75.00	75.00	
Hatpin Holder	225.00	375.00	375.00	375.00	2500.00
Lamp, Candle	175.00				
Lamp Shade	200.00				
Nappy	100.00	175.00	125.00	125.00	
Pin Tray	200.00	300.00	300.00	300.00	
Pitcher, Tankard	900.00		3500.00	3000.00	
Pitcher, Water.	475.00				
Plate, 6".	200.00	450.00	450.00	450.00	2500.00
Plate, 7½".	100.00	200.00	200.00	200.00	500.00
Plate, 9½".	225.00	475.00	475.00	475.00	2750.00
Plate, Footed	125.00	225.00	225.00	225.00	
Plate, Footed (Fenton)	100.00				
Powder Jar with Cover	100.00	200.00	200.00	200.00	350.00
Punch Bowl with Base, 12"	500.00				
Punch Bowl, 16".	600.00	1250.00	1750.00	1750.00	
Punch Bowl, with Base, 24". . .	2500.00	5000.00	5000.00	5000.00	10000.00
Punch Cup	35.00	55.00	55.00	55.00	250.00
Saucer	90.00		100.00	100.00	
Sherbet	50.00	75.00	75.00	75.00	
Shot Glass	225.00				
Spittoon.	6000.00				
Spooner.	175.00		250.00	250.00	
Sugar.	100.00	175.00	175.00	175.00	
Sugar with Cover	200.00		300.00	300.00	
Sweetmeat Dish	300.00				
Sweetmeat Compote	225.00				
Tobacco Jar with Cover	450.00				
Tray, Dresser	175.00		750.00	750.00	
Tumbler, 6 oz.	55.00		100.00	100.00	
Tumbler, 10 oz.	85.00		125.00	125.00	

Fenton produced only those pieces noted above. The Fenton pattern contains grape bunches alternating with large-veined leaves, all attached to a vine; the cable is a diagonal series of ridges curving up and down directly below the rim. Northwood pattern contains large bunches of grapes that are raised in relief from the center, and they too alternate with leaves; the cable is formed at the base with teardrops.

This is one of the most prolific patterns of Carnival glass in terms of variety of pieces produced; however, assembling all of them would be a monumental task.

*Left: Carnival glass, "Grape and Gothic Arches" pattern. Drawing by Mark Pickvet.
Right: Carnival glass, "Hobnail" pattern. Photo by Mark Pickvet. Courtesy of the
Fenton Art Glass Museum.*

GRAPE AND GOTHIC ARCHES NORTHWOOD
GLASS COMPANY

Object	Marigold	Blue	Green	Amethyst	Purple	Pearl
Bowl, 5"	$30.00	$50.00	$50.00	$50.00	$50.00	
Bowl, Berry, 10"	45.00	75.00	75.00	75.00	75.00	
Butter Dish with Cover	100.00	125.00	125.00	125.00	125.00	300.00
Creamer	50.00	75.00	75.00	75.00	75.00	175.00
Pitcher, Water	225.00	350.00	350.00	350.00	350.00	600.00
Spooner	45.00	65.00	65.00	65.00	65.00	150.00
Sugar Dish with Cover	65.00	90.00	90.00	90.00	90.00	200.00
Tumbler	35.00	50.00	50.00	50.00	50.00	175.00

This typical grape pattern includes leaves and large grape bunches connected by a
vine around each piece. In the background are pointed arches that resemble a picket
fence.

GREEK KEY NORTHWOOD GLASS COMPANY

Object	Marigold	Blue	Green	Purple
Bowl, 7"	$55.00		$70.00	$70.00
Bowl, 8½"	60.00		75.00	75.00
Bowl, 8½", Dome Footed	65.00		80.00	80.00
Hatpin (Pattern Variant)				45.00
Pitcher, Water	550.00		300.00	300.00
Plate, 9" (Aqua Opalescent $800.00)	500.00	700.00	375.00	600.00
Plate, 11" (Aqua Opalescent $850.00)	550.00	750.00	425.00	650.00
Tumbler	65.00		100.00	100.00

"Greek Key" is a common pattern, found in other mediums, and consists of interlocking "e" designs. At the top are semicircles with tiny flower circles surrounded
by seven petals, in the middle is the maze design, and at the bottom are stretched diamonds with circles at the top.

HEISEY CARNIVAL GLASS   A.H. HEISEY COMPANY

Object	Marigold	Ice Blue	Clambroth	Pastel
Bottle, Water (Line #357)	*$125.00*			
Breakfast Set				200.00
Candy Jar with Cover, 11" Tall, Stemmed, Floral Spray Design		125.00		
Compote, Cartwheel Style	*100.00*		125.00	
Creamer	*100.00*	200.00	200.00	
Frog Dish with Cover (White or Ice Green $500.00)	*400.00*	500.00		
Punch Cup (Flute Design)	*35.00*			
Sugar	*100.00*	200.00	200.00	
Toothpick Holder	*100.00*		150.00	
Tray	*90.00*	175.00	175.00	
Tumbler (Line #357)	*50.00*			
Turtle Dish with Cover (Green or Pink $400.00)				

Although not a huge producer of Carnival glass, Heisey did make some iridized glass during this time period.

HOBNAIL   MILLERSBURG GLASS COMPANY

Object	Marigold	Blue	Green	Amethyst	Purple
Bowl (Marigold has Cherries in Pattern) .	*$700.00*	*$1100.00*	*$600.00*	*$600.00*	*$600.00*
Bowl, Rose	125.00	300.00	150.00	150.00	150.00
Bowl, Rose (Pattern Variant)	950.00				
Butter Dish	500.00	600.00	300.00	300.00	300.00
Creamer	225.00	325.00	175.00	175.00	175.00
Jardiniere (Pattern Variant)	1250.00			1000.00	
Pitcher, 6" Tall, Miniature	225.00				
Pitcher, Water	1750.00	5500.00	2500.00	2500.00	2500.00
Spittoon	300.00	650.00	350.00	350.00	350.00
Spooner		325.00	175.00	175.00	175.00
Sugar Dish with Cover	300.00	400.00	250.00	250.00	250.00
Tumbler, 2½" Tall, Miniature	55.00				
Tumbler	350.00	900.00	425.00	425.00	425.00
Vase			175.00	175.00	
Vase (Pattern Variant)	1000.00		1000.00	1000.00	

In general, hobnail patterns are quite common, especially with Westmoreland; however, in Carnival glass it is quite rare. The knobs of the Millersburg pieces are very glossy and refract well.

HOBSTAR   IMPERIAL GLASS COMPANY

Object	Marigold	Green	Amethyst	Purple	Smoke
Basket, Bride's	*$75.00*				

Object	Marigold	Green	Amethyst	Purple	Smoke
Bowl, 5"	$25.00				$35.00
Bowl, 6", Ruffled	30.00				40.00
Bowl, 8", Ruffled	35.00				45.00
Bowl, 9" (Pattern Variant)	40.00	50.00	50.00		75.00
Bowl, 10"	45.00				60.00
Bowl, 12", Ruffled	60.00				75.00
Bowl, Fruit, with Base	60.00	75.00	75.00	75.00	
Bowl, Fruit, with Base (Pattern Variant) ..	100.00	125.00	125.00		150.00
Butter Dish with Cover	100.00	225.00	225.00	225.00	
Cookie Jar with Cover	125.00				
Creamer	35.00	125.00	125.00	125.00	
Pickle Castor	400.00				
Spooner	30.00	110.00	110.00	110.00	
Sugar Dish with Cover	45.00	150.00	150.00	150.00	

This hobstar design is the same pattern as those typically found on cut glass. The molding contains some fine faceting and is often confused with cut glass. The pattern variant contains hobstars surrounded by beaded broken arches.

HOBSTAR AND FEATHER MILLERSBURG GLASS COMPANY

Object	Marigold	Blue	Green	Amethyst	Purple
Bowl, 5"				$450.00	$450.00
Bowl, 5", Diamond-Shaped.............	400.00				
Bowl, 5", Heart-Shaped................	350.00				
Bowl, 10", Square........................					1750.00
Bowl, Rose	2000.00		2250.00		2250.00
Butter Dish with Cover..............	1250.00		1750.00		1750.00
Compote...........................	1750.00			5000.00	5000.00
Creamer..........................	750.00		850.00		850.00
Punch Bowl with Base..............	2250.00	3750.00	3250.00	3250.00	3250.00
Punch Cup	225.00	300.00	275.00	275.00	275.00
Sherbet	600.00				
Spooner...........................	700.00		800.00		800.00
Sugar Dish with Cover	800.00		900.00		900.00
Vase..............................	1750.00		2000.00	2000.00	2000.00

The feathers surround a finely molded hobstar in this pattern. Rims are usually scalloped, and the bottom contains a horizontal band. A punch set with bowl and 12 matching cups is a very impressive showing indeed in this pattern.

HOBSTAR BAND IMPERIAL GLASS COMPANY

Object	Marigold
Bowl	$65.00
Celery Dish	65.00
Compote	90.00

Pitcher, 2 Styles $225.00
Tumbler, 2 Styles 55.00

Small hobstars are contained within pointed ovals at the top of each object. The lower part contains vertical beading.

HOLLY   FENTON ART GLASS COMPANY

Object	Marigold	Blue	Red	Green	Amethyst	White
Bowl, 7¼"	$25.00	$45.00	$650.00	$45.00	$45.00	$75.00
Bowl, 8"	.25.00	45.00	650.00	45.00	45.00	75.00
Bowl, 10"	.30.00	50.00	675.00	50.00	50.00	85.00
Compote, 5" (Small)	.20.00	40.00	250.00	40.00	40.00	55.00
Goblet	.20.00	35.00	200.00	35.00	35.00	50.00
Hat Vase	.18.00	30.00	375.00	30.00	30.00	45.00
Plate	.60.00	75.00	75.00	75.00	75.00	150.00

Object	Ice Blue	Ice Green	Vaseline	Peach Opalescent
Bowl, 7¼"	$75.00	$75.00	$75.00	$750.00
Bowl, 8"	.75.00	75.00	75.00	750.00
Bowl, 10"	.85.00	75.00	85.00	
Compote (Small)	.55.00	55.00	55.00	
Goblet	.50.00	50.00	50.00	
Hat Vase	.45.00	45.00	45.00	
Plate	.125.00	125.00	125.00	

"Holly" is characterized by holly leaves and vines emanating from the center. The foliage also creates a raised circular pattern in relief.

INVERTED FEATHER   CAMBRIDGE GLASS COMPANY

Object	Marigold	Green	Amethyst
Butter Dish with Cover	$250.00		$275.00
Compote	.50.00		
Cracker Jar with Cover		300.00	
Creamer	.200.00		225.00
Parfait Dish	.65.00		
Pitcher, Milk	.225.00		
Pitcher, Water	.3750.00	3750.00	
Punch Bowl with Base	.2250.00		
Punch Cup	.60.00	75.00	
Spooner	.175.00		
Sugar	.200.00		225.00
Tumbler	.550.00	650.00	
Wineglass	.100.00		

Cambridge was not a major producer of iridized or Carnival glass; however, they did manufacture a few inverted patterns. "Inverted Feather" covers the entire pieces with scrolls, hobstars, ridged frames, florals, and draped beading.

INVERTED STRAWBERRY   CAMBRIDGE GLASS
COMPANY

Object	Marigold	Blue	Green	Amethyst	Purple
Bowl, Berry, 5"	$45.00	$75.00	$65.00	$70.00	
Bowl, Berry, 9"	75.00		100.00	110.00	
Bowl, 10½"	80.00		110.00	125.00	
Butter Dish with Cover	250.00		325.00	350.00	
Candlestick	125.00		150.00	175.00	
Celery Dish		375.00		300.00	
Compote (Small)	350.00	400.00			
Compote (Large)	275.00		375.00	425.00	
Creamer	100.00		125.00	150.00	300.00
Cuspidor	1000.00	1250.00	1100.00	1150.00	
Honey Dish	85.00				
Pitcher, Milk	1000.00		1250.00	1500.00	
Pitcher, Water	2000.00		2750.00	3000.00	
Powder Jar	100.00		125.00		
Spittoon	600.00		650.00	700.00	
Spooner	90.00		100.00		150.00
Sugar	100.00		125.00	150.00	
Sugar, Stemmed					300.00
Tumbler	350.00	400.00	400.00	300.00	

The second of Cambridge's inverted patterns, this one is characterized by diamond-molded strawberries with branches and leaves around each item.

INVERTED THISTLE   CAMBRIDGE GLASS COMPANY

Object	Marigold	Green	Amethyst
Bowl, 5"		$200.00	$200.00
Bowl, 9"		300.00	300.00
Box with Cover (Peach Opalescent $500.00)			
Butter Dish with Cover	.350.00	500.00	500.00
Creamer	.375.00	425.00	425.00
Pitcher, Milk			2750.00
Pitcher, Water	.3250.00		3500.00

Left: Carnival glass, "Inverted Thistle" pattern. Drawing by Mark Pickvet. Right: Carnival glass, "Lustre and Clear" pattern. Drawing by Mark Pickvet.

Object	Marigold	Green	Amethyst
Plate, Chop			$2250.00
Spittoon			3500.00
Spooner	.350.00	400.00	400.00
Sugar	.375.00	425.00	425.00
Tumbler	.425.00		450.00

This pattern is similar to "Inverted Strawberry" except that the strawberries are replaced with thistle. The thistle branches and leaves are also formed into scrolls.

KITTENS   FENTON ART GLASS COMPANY

Object	Marigold	Cobalt Blue	Purple	Vaseline
Bowl, 4"	.$125.00	$225.00	$275.00	$275.00
Bowl, Flared Straight Sides	.125.00	225.00	150.00	
Bowl, 6"	.150.00	250.00		
Cup	.150.00	375.00		
Plate, 4¹/₂"	.150.00	225.00		
Saucer	.100.00	325.00		
Spittoon	.3250.00	3750.00		
Spooner	.100.00	300.00		250.00
Vase, 3–3¹/₄" Tall	.175.00	225.00		250.00

This is a cute pattern, consisting of kittens scrambling over each other to drink from a long oval bowl.

LEAF TIERS   FENTON ART GLASS COMPANY

Object	Marigold	Blue	Green	Purple
Banana Dish, Footed	.$200.00			
Bowl, Berry, 5", Footed	.40.00	65.00	75.00	55.00
Bowl, Berry, 10", Footed	.65.00	100.00	110.00	90.00
Butter Dish, Footed	.175.00	250.00	275.00	225.00
Creamer, Footed	.90.00	125.00	150.00	110.00
Pitcher, Water, Footed	.500.00	750.00	850.00	650.00
Spooner, Footed	.80.00	110.00	125.00	100.00
Sugar Dish, Footed	.90.00	125.00	150.00	110.00
Tumbler, Footed	.90.00	125.00	150.00	110.00

"Leaf Tiers" contains rows of overlapping leaves around each object. Purple is a little more common than blue or green, and all of the pieces are footed.

LUSTRE AND CLEAR   IMPERIAL GLASS COMPANY

Object	Marigold
Bowl, 5"	.$25.00
Bowl, 10"	.35.00
Bowl, Rose	.65.00

Butter Dish *$75.00*
Compote . . . .*.45.00*
Creamer . . . .*.50.00*
Nappy . . . .*.45.00*
Pitcher, Water . . . .*.225.00*
Salt and Pepper Shakers . . . .*.75.00*
Sugar . . . .*.50.00*
Tray, Celery, 8" . . . .*.35.00*
Tumbler . . . .*.55.00*
Vase, 8", Footed . . . .*.85.00*
Vase, Wall . . . .*.35.00*

This is a somewhat transparent marigold color with pillars that end at the rim and matching flutes.

LUSTRE FLUTE   NORTHWOOD GLASS COMPANY

Object	Marigold	Green	Amethyst	Purple
Bonbon Dish		*$60.00*	*$55.00*	*$55.00*
Bowl, 5½"	*.35.00*			
Bowl, 8"	*.45.00*	*65.00*	*65.00*	*65.00*
Compote	*.40.00*	*55.00*	*55.00*	*55.00*
Creamer	*.45.00*	*65.00*	*65.00*	*65.00*
Hat	*.30.00*	*35.00*	*40.00*	*40.00*
Nappy	*.35.00*	*50.00*	*50.00*	*50.00*
Punch Bowl with Base	*.250.00*	*325.00*	*425.00*	*425.00*
Punch Cup	*.65.00*	*75.00*	*90.00*	*90.00*
Sherbet	*.30.00*			
Sugar	*.45.00*	*65.00*	*65.00*	*65.00*

This pattern is characterized by vertical flutes or columns topped off by a band of lattice work.

LUSTRE ROSE   IMPERIAL GLASS COMPANY

Object	Marigold	Green	Purple	Amber	Smoke	Clambroth
Bowl, Berry, 5"	*$35.00*	*$45.00*	*$45.00*	*$65.00*	*$65.00*	*$65.00*

Carnival glass, "Lustre Flute" pattern.
Drawing by Mark Pickvet.

Object	Marigold	Green	Purple	Amber	Smoke	Clambroth
Bowl, 7"	$40.00	$50.00	$50.00	$70.00	$70.00	$70.00
Bowl, 8"	45.00	55.00	55.00	75.00	75.00	75.00
Bowl, 9"	50.00	60.00	60.00	80.00	80.00	80.00
Bowl, Berry, 9", Footed (Red $2000.00)	55.00	65.00	65.00	85.00	85.00	85.00
Bowl, 11"	50.00	60.00	60.00	80.00	80.00	80.00
Bowl, 12", Footed (Red $2500.00)	50.00	65.00	65.00	85.00	85.00	85.00
Bowl, Rose	60.00	80.00	75.00			100.00
Butter Dish	60.00	75.00	75.00			
Creamer	40.00	55.00	55.00	75.00		
Fernery	50.00	75.00	65.00	110.00	110.00	125.00
Pitcher, Milk	75.00	100.00		125.00		
Pitcher, Water	125.00	150.00	150.00	200.00	200.00	225.00
Plate, 6"	55.00	70.00	65.00	85.00	85.00	85.00
Plate, 9"	60.00	75.00	70.00	90.00	90.00	90.00
Plate, Footed	55.00	65.00				
Spooner	35.00	50.00	50.00	70.00		
Sugar	40.00	55.00	55.00	75.00		
Tumbler	45.00	50.00	50.00	65.00	65.00	75.00

This early Imperial pattern consists of a band of roses within thorns and other foliage.

MAPLE LEAF   DUGAN GLASS COMPANY

Object	Marigold	Blue	Amethyst	Purple
Bowl, 4¹/₂", Ice Cream, Stemmed (Small)	$65.00	$85.00	$100.00	$85.00
Bowl, 9", Ice Cream, Stemmed (Large)	80.00	100.00	125.00	100.00
Butter Dish with Cover	125.00	150.00	175.00	150.00
Creamer	65.00	75.00	85.00	75.00
Pitcher, Water	175.00	350.00	375.00	300.00
Spooner	60.00	70.00	75.00	70.00
Sugar Dish with Cover	85.00	100.00	115.00	100.00
Tumbler	45.00	50.00	60.00	50.00

The maple leaves in this pattern are intertwined within ridging that gives a raised appearance. Above the design is a horizontal line of semicircles around each piece.

OCTAGON   IMPERIAL GLASS COMPANY

Object	Marigold	Green	Amethyst	Purple	White	Aqua
Bowl, 4¹/₂"		$30.00	$30.00	$30.00		
Bowl, 8¹/₂"	40.00					
Butter Dish with Cover	100.00	150.00		150.00		
Cordial	110.00				175.00	
Creamer	55.00	75.00		65.00		
Decanter	125.00			300.00	125.00	110.00

Object	Marigold	Green	Amethyst	Purple	White	Aqua
Goblet	$75.00			$85.00		
Pitcher, Milk	125.00	175.00	225.00			
Pitcher, Water	150.00	350.00	300.00			
Salt and Pepper Shakers			150.00			
Spooner	55.00	75.00		65.00		
Sugar Dish with Cover	65.00	85.00		75.00		
Toothpick Holder	125.00					
Tumbler (Smoke $125.00)	35.00	100.00	65.00			110.00
Vase	85.00	125.00	125.00	125.00		
Wineglass	40.00			65.00		

"Octagon," as the name would imply, consists of eight heavy mold-designed panels; the panels contain a variety of stars, diamonds, beading, arches, and other geometrical designs.

OPTIC AND BUTTONS   IMPERIAL GLASS COMPANY

Object	Marigold
Bowl, 5"	$25.00
Bowl, 6"	30.00
Bowl, 8"	35.00
Bowl, 10"	40.00
Bowl, 12", Handled	50.00
Cup	30.00
Goblet	65.00
Plate, 7"	40.00
Plate, 10½"	65.00
Saucer	20.00
Tumbler, 2 Styles	75.00

Vertical panels with a band of beads at the top make up this simple pattern by Imperial.

ORANGE TREE   FENTON ART GLASS COMPANY

Object	Marigold	Blue	Green	Red	Amethyst	Purple
Bowl, Berry, 5½", Footed	$35.00	$40.00	$40.00			
Bowl, 8"	30.00	40.00	40.00	650.00	45.00	45.00
Bowl, Berry, 9", Footed	40.00	50.00	50.00			
Bowl, 10"	35.00	45.00	45.00	700.00	50.00	50.00
Bowl, 11", Footed	90.00	150.00	150.00		125.00	100.00
Bowl, Orange, Footed	90.00	150.00	150.00		125.00	100.00
Bowl, Rose	50.00	55.00	60.00	750.00	60.00	60.00
Butter Dish with Cover	150.00	175.00				
Centerpiece, 12", Footed	750.00	2750.00	1250.00			
Compote	35.00	45.00	50.00		40.00	40.00
Creamer	55.00	75.00				
Cruet		1250.00				

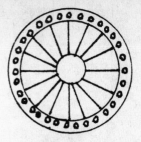 

Left: Carnival glass, "Optic and Buttons" pattern. Drawing by Mark Pickvet. Right: Carnival glass, "Orange Tree" pattern. Photo by Mark Pickvet. Courtesy of the Fenton Art Glass Museum.

Object	Marigold	Blue	Green	Red	Amethyst	Purple
Goblet	$80.00					
Hatpin Holder	125.00	200.00	225.00			
Mug (Vaseline $200.00)	45.00	55.00	75.00	500.00	55.00	50.00
Mug, Shaving	60.00	80.00	80.00		80.00	75.00
Pitcher, Water, Footed	250.00	325.00				
Pitcher, Water, Pattern Contains Scrolls	325.00		500.00		500.00	
Plate, 8"	90.00	125.00	125.00		125.00	115.00
Plate, 9½"	100.00	135.00	135.00		135.00	125.00
Powder Jar with Cover	100.00	125.00			110.00	110.00
Punch Bowl with Base	225.00	325.00			275.00	275.00
Punch Cup	35.00	45.00			45.00	40.00
Sherbet	25.00	30.00				
Spooner	70.00	100.00				
Sugar	80.00	125.00				
Tumbler, Footed	45.00	55.00				
Tumbler, Pattern Contains Scrolls	55.00	75.00			75.00	
Wineglass	35.00					

Object	White	Ice Blue	Ice Green	Aqua Opalescent	Peach Opalescent
Bowl, Berry, 5½", Footed	$75.00				
Bowl, 8"	50.00				
Bowl, Berry, 9", Footed	90.00				
Bowl, 10" (Milk Glass $200.00)	55.00				
Bowl, 11", Footed	175.00				
Bowl, Orange, Footed	175.00				
Bowl, Rose	225.00				
Butter Dish with Cover	225.00	325.00	325.00		
Compote	75.00	75.00	75.00		
Creamer	125.00		125.00		
Hatpin Holder	325.00				2500.00

Carnival glass, "Orange Tree" pattern. Photo by Mark Pickvet. Courtesy of the Fenton Art Glass Museum.

Object	White	Ice Blue	Ice Green	Aqua Opalescent	Peach Opalescent
Mug (Amber $200.00) $1250.00				$200.00	
Pitcher, Water, Footed 550.00					
Plate, 8" 175.00					1750.00
Plate, 9½" 200.00					2000.00
Powder Jar with Cover 150.00					
Punch Bowl with Base 375.00				1500.00	
Punch Cup 50.00					200.00
Spooner 175.00			175.00		
Sugar 175.00			175.00		
Tumbler, Footed 90.00				100.00	
Tumbler, Pattern Contains Scrolls . .100.00					
Wineglass				100.00	100.00

This pattern is characterized by a thick tree trunk with three branches; the branches contain orange blossoms with stippled centers.

PALM BEACH   U.S. GLASS COMPANY

Object	Marigold	Purple	White
Banana Dish $125.00		$250.00	
Bowl, 5" 35.00			55.00
Bowl, 9" 55.00			85.00
Bowl, Rose 100.00			150.00
Butter Dish 150.00			225.00
Creamer 85.00			150.00
Pitcher, Water 500.00			800.00
Plate, 9" 175.00		275.00	250.00
Spooner 75.00			110.00
Sugar Dish with Cover 110.00			175.00

Object	Marigold	Purple	White
Tumbler	.$135.00		$200.00
Vase	.100.00	150.00	175.00

Although U.S. Glass was not a huge maker of iridized glass, they did produce a few odd pieces and patterns during the Carnival glass era.

PANSY   IMPERIAL GLASS COMPANY

Object	Marigold	Blue	Green	Amethyst
Bowl, 8¾"	.$50.00	$60.00	$60.00	$55.00
Creamer	.40.00		50.00	45.00
Dresser Tray	.65.00		100.00	
Nappy	.25.00		35.00	
Pickle Dish, Oval	.30.00		45.00	50.00
Plate, Ruffled	.75.00		85.00	90.00
Relish Dish	.45.00		65.00	60.00
Sugar	.40.00		50.00	45.00

Object	Purple	Amber	Smoke	Aqua Opalescent
Creamer		$90.00	$75.00	
Dresser Tray	.90.00		125.00	
Pickle Dish			75.00	
Plate, Ruffled			100.00	
Relish Dish		100.00	90.00	350.00
Sugar		90.00	75.00	

The pansies in this pattern are cluttered with arches and other foliage on a stippled background.

PEACH   NORTHWOOD GLASS COMPANY

Object	Cobalt Blue	White
Bowl, Berry, 5"		$75.00
Bowl, Berry, 9"		225.00
Butter Dish with Cover		275.00
Creamer		150.00
Pitcher, Water	.650.00	750.00
Spooner		125.00

Carnival glass, "Peach" pattern. Drawing by Mark Pickvet.

Object	Cobalt Blue	White
Sugar		$150.00
Tumbler	100.00	125.00

Two peaches are bunched together with branches and vines and framed with horizontal beading in this pattern. The design is set in relief and also contains two outer horizontal bands (one near the top and one at the bottom).

PEACOCK MILLERSBURG GLASS COMPANY

Object	Marigold	Green	Amethyst	Purple	Vaseline
Banana Dish			$2500.00	$2500.00	
Bowl, 5"	.50.00	65.00	65.00	60.00	
Bowl, 6"			125.00	125.00	
Bowl, 7½"	.450.00	400.00	400.00	400.00	
Bowl, 9"	175.00	325.00	300.00	275.00	2750.00
Bowl, 10", Ice Cream	.400.00	500.00		600.00	
Bowl, Rose				2250.00	3500.00
Plate, 6"	.550.00		425.00	600.00	
Plate, Chop	.1250.00				
Spittoon	.4000.00		6000.00	6000.00	

The feathers of the peacock in this pattern are set in relief, while the peacock itself is framed by a wreath of foliage. In the background are Greek columns and ferns at the bird's feet. Vaseline items are extremely rare and valuable.

PEACOCK AND URN FENTON ART GLASS COMPANY,
MILLERSBURG GLASS COMPANY, NORTHWOOD GLASS COMPANY

Object	Marigold	Blue	Red	Green	Amethyst
Bowl (Fenton Only) (Peach Opalescent $1250.00)	$65.00	$85.00	$2000.00	$85.00	$80.00
Bowl, 5"		55.00		55.00	55.00
Bowl, 6", Ice Cream (White $275.00)......	65.00	90.00		85.00	65.00
Bowl, 6" (Pattern Variant, Millersburg)	55.00	500.00		175.00	75.00
Bowl, 8½" (Pattern Variant, Millersburg)..	350.00				425.00
Bowl, 9"...........................	100.00			300.00	175.00
Bowl, 9½" (Pattern Variant, Millersburg ..	125.00			200.00	175.00
Bowl, 10", Ice Cream (White $850.00)....	200.00	300.00		275.00	
Bowl, 10" (Pattern Variant, Millersburg) ..	300.00	2000.00		500.00	400.00
Compote	45.00	55.00	1000.00	65.00	55.00
Compote, Small (Pattern Variant, Millersburg).............	40.00	50.00		50.00	50.00
Compote, Large (Pattern Variant, Millersburg)..........	1250.00		1100.00		1000.00
Goblet	75.00	90.00			100.00
Plate, 6" (White $225.00)	125.00	200.00		225.00	175.00
Plate, 10½" (Pattern Variant Millersburg) .	2000.00				5000.00
Plate, 11"............................	1000.00				1250.00

Carnival glass, "Peacock and Urn" pattern. Photo by Robin Rainwater.

Object	Marigold	Blue	Red	Green	Amethyst
Plate, Chop	$1500.00				$750.00
Spittoon	2250.00				2500.00

Object	Purple	Ice Blue	Ice Green	Vaseline	Aqua Opalescent
Bowl, 5"	$55.00	$75.00	$75.00		$2000.00
Bowl, 6", Ice Cream	85.00	350.00	550.00		1750.00
Bowl, 9"	175.00				
Bowl, 10", Ice Cream (Plain Aqua $3250.00)	250.00	1250.00	1750.00		4000.00
Compote	60.00			150.00	
Goblet				125.00	
Plate, 11"	1250.00				
Plate, Chop			1750.00		
Spittoon	2500.00				

The patterns are similar for the three companies who produced it. The ridgework on the urn is more rigid in Millersburg as opposed to Fenton; Millersburg also contains a stylized bee within the bird's beak. The circle of leaves within the foliage wreath contains less detail and more plain glossy space on the Northwood design.

One of the Millersburg variants includes wreaths that are sprays of foliage rather than a complete, all-encompassing design. Some of the scrolling has no beading, as in the original pattern.

PEACOCK AT THE FOUNTAIN NORTHWOOD GLASS COMPANY, DUGAN GLASS COMPANY

Object	Marigold	Blue	Green	Amethyst	Purple
Bowl, Berry, 5"	$40.00	$55.00	$50.00	$50.00	$55.00
Bowl, Berry, 9"	50.00	65.00	60.00	60.00	65.00
Bowl, Orange, Footed	175.00	325.00	225.00	325.00	225.00
Butter Dish with Cover	150.00	250.00	225.00	225.00	200.00
Compote	225.00	300.00	300.00	300.00	300.00
Creamer	75.00	100.00	100.00	90.00	90.00
Pitcher, Water	300.00	800.00	650.00		500.00
Pitcher, Water (Dugan)	275.00	375.00			375.00
Punch Bowl with Base	325.00	750.00	600.00	550.00	550.00

Object	Marigold	Blue	Green	Amethyst	Purple
Punch Cup	$25.00	$45.00	$40.00	$35.00	$35.00
Spittoon			3000.00		
Spooner	65.00	90.00	85.00		80.00
Sugar	75.00	100.00	100.00	90.00	90.00
Tumbler	45.00	55.00	500.00		55.00
Tumbler (Dugan)	45.00	60.00			55.00

Object	White	Ice Blue	Ice Green	Aqua Opalescent
Bowl, Berry, 5"	$75.00	$75.00	$100.00	
Bowl, Berry, 9"	85.00	85.00	110.00	
Bowl, Orange	650.00	650.00	750.00	3500.00
Butter Dish with Cover	300.00	300.00	400.00	
Compote	350.00	350.00	450.00	375.00
Creamer	150.00	175.00	225.00	
Pitcher, Water	1000.00	1000.00	1750.00	
Punch Bowl with Base	850.00	850.00	2250.00	10,000.00
Punch Cup	50.00	50.00	75.00	200.00
Spooner	125.00	135.00	175.00	
Sugar	150.00	175.00	225.00	
Tumbler	175.00	275.00	375.00	

There are only two Dugan pieces, a pitcher and tumbler noted above. The peacock in this pattern is quite large, standing upright on a block pedestal that contains a daisy growing from between the bricks. The fountain contains lined ridges where the water sprays from it. This is a very popular, elegant design, and the aqua opalescent punch set is quite impressive (in value and beauty).

PERSIAN GARDEN DUGAN GLASS COMPANY

Object	Marigold	Blue	Green
Bowl, Berry, 5"	$50.00		
Bowl, Ice Cream, 6"	75.00	100.00	90.00
Bowl, Berry, 10"	150.00		
Bowl, Ice Cream, 11"	200.00	325.00	300.00
Bowl, Fruit with Base	125.00		
Plate, 6"	65.00	110.00	100.00

Object	Purple	White	Peach Opalescent
Bowl, Berry, 5"	$65.00	$75.00	
Bowl, Ice Cream, 6"	75.00	110.00	
Bowl, Berry, 10"	175.00	225.00	
Bowl, Ice Cream, 11"	200.00	250.00	300.00
Bowl, Fruit with Base	225.00	300.00	450.00
Plate, 6"	85.00	125.00	225.00
Plate, Chop, 13"	2750.00	2000.00	5000.00

"Persian Garden" is a geometric pattern with a center medallion; rows of arches with flowers and checkerboards flow outward, ending in a band of fountains with teardrops near the rim of each piece.

PERSIAN MEDALLION   FENTON ART GLASS COMPANY

Object	Marigold	Red	Blue	Green	Amethyst
Bonbon Dish	$45.00	$750.00	$65.00	$65.00	$60.00
Bowl, 5"	35.00		45.00	50.00	
Bowl, 8¾"	45.00	900.00	55.00	60.00	
Bowl, 10", Collar Base	55.00		65.00	75.00	
Bowl, Orange	90.00		150.00	175.00	150.00
Bowl, Rose	75.00		75.00	80.00	
Compote	50.00	500.00	75.00	65.00	
Hair Receiver	60.00		65.00		65.00
Plate, 7"	80.00		100.00	90.00	
Plate, 9"	150.00		275.00	300.00	
Plate, Chop			325.00		
Punch Bowl with Base	250.00		325.00	400.00	350.00
Punch Cup	25.00		30.00	40.00	35.00

Object	Purple	White	Amber	Ice Blue	Vaseline
Bonbon Dish		$100.00	$100.00	$500.00	$100.00
Bowl, 5"	50.00				
Bowl, 8¾"	60.00				
Bowl, 10", Collar Base	75.00				
Bowl, Orange	150.00				
Bowl, Rose	90.00	125.00	100.00		
Hair Receiver	65.00				
Plate, 7"	100.00	125.00			125.00
Plate, 9"	200.00	550.00			
Plate, Chop	70.00	325.00			
Punch Bowl with Base	350.00				
Punch Cup	35.00				

This pattern is characterized by varying shapes of floral medallions with bands of petaled circles and teardrops inscribed within the circles.

Left: Carnival glass, "Persian Medallion" pattern. Photo by Mark Pickvet. Courtesy of the Fenton Art Glass Museum. Right: Carnival glass, "Persian Medallion" pattern. Photo by Mark Pickvet. Courtesy of the Fenton Art Glass Museum.

RASPBERRY NORTHWOOD GLASS COMPANY

Object	Marigold	Blue	Green	Purple
Bowl, Berry, 5"	$35.00		$45.00	$45.00
Bowl, Berry, 9"	55.00		75.00	70.00
Bowl, Serving, Footed	55.00	175.00	75.00	70.00
Compote	50.00		65.00	60.00
Pitcher, Milk	150.00		200.00	175.00
Pitcher, Water	175.00	450.00	250.00	250.00
Sauce Boat, Footed	80.00	175.00		125.00
Tumbler	45.00	100.00	50.00	50.00

Object	White	Ice Blue	Ice Green
Pitcher, Milk	$1250.00	$1500.00	$1750.00
Pitcher, Water	1750.00	2000.00	2250.00
Tumbler	300.00	325.00	350.00

The raspberries of this pattern are shaped by beaded circles in low relief. Below the raspberries is a wide basketweave panel.

SEAWEED MILLERSBURG GLASS COMPANY

Object	Marigold	Green	Purple
Bowl, 5"	$425.00	$500.00	
Bowl, 9"	275.00	375.00	
Bowl, 10"	825.00	1000.00	1000.00
Bowl, 10½", Ice Cream	425.00	500.00	500.00
Bowl, 10½", Ruffled	200.00	225.00	250.00
Lamp	225.00		
Plate, 10"	825.00	950.00	

This design consists of beads in bubble form, spiraling scrolls that twirl outward from the center, and a wavy background.

SINGING BIRDS NORTHWOOD GLASS COMPANY

Object	Marigold	Blue	Green	Amethyst	Purple
Bowl, Berry, 5"			$50.00	$45.00	$40.00
Bowl, Berry, 10"			90.00	80.00	75.00
Butter Dish with Cover	225.00		350.00	325.00	325.00
Creamer	90.00		150.00	125.00	125.00
Mug (Ice Blue or Ice Green $800.00; Aqua Opalescent $1250.00)	225.00	325.00	400.00	175.00	
Pitcher, Water	275.00		450.00	300.00	300.00
Sherbet				100.00	100.00

Object	Marigold	Blue	Green	Amethyst	Purple
Spooner	$80.00		$125.00	$110.00	$110.00
Sugar	125.00		175.00	150.00	150.00
Tumbler	55.00		75.00	65.00	65.00

As the pattern name implies, the birds sitting on the branches have their beaks open as if they are singing.

SPRINGTIME   NORTHWOOD GLASS COMPANY

Object	Marigold	Green	Amethyst
Bowl, Berry, 5"		$70.00	$60.00
Bowl, Berry, 9"		150.00	125.00
Butter Dish with Cover	200.00	300.00	275.00
Creamer	150.00	250.00	225.00
Pitcher, Water	550.00	1000.00	925.00
Spooner	125.00	225.00	200.00
Sugar	150.00	250.00	225.00
Tumbler	75.00	150.00	135.00

"Springtime" contains chained daisies within panels set in relief; along the top and bottom are basketweave borders.

STAR AND FILE   IMPERIAL GLASS COMPANY

Object	Marigold
Bonbon Dish	$40.00
Bowl, 7"	35.00
Bowl, 9½"	50.00
Bowl, Rose (Pastel Green $125.00)	75.00
Celery Vase (Smoke $110.00)	50.00
Compote	45.00
Creamer	35.00
Cup, Custard	30.00
Decanter with Stopper	125.00
Pickle Dish	45.00
Pitcher, Water	250.00
Plate, 6"	55.00
Sherbet	35.00
Spooner	30.00
Sugar	35.00
Tumbler	75.00
Wineglass	40.00

This is a simple geometric pattern consisting of a wide chain of hobstars separated by filed spears.

STAR MEDALLION   IMPERIAL GLASS COMPANY

Object	Marigold	Smoke	Clambroth
Bonbon Dish	$45.00		
Bowl, 7"	35.00	45.00	
Bowl, 7", Square	40.00	50.00	
Bowl, 9", Square	45.00	55.00	
Butter Dish with Cover	100.00		
Celery Dish, Handled	80.00		
Compote	45.00		
Creamer	55.00		
Cup, Custard	25.00		
Goblet	55.00		
Pickle Dish	40.00		
Pitcher, Milk	65.00	75.00	75.00
Pitcher, Water	100.00		
Plate, 5"	60.00		
Plate, 10"		75.00	
Punch Bowl	125.00		
Punch Cup	35.00		
Sherbet	35.00		
Spooner	50.00		
Sugar	55.00		
Tray, Celery	65.00		
Tumbler	45.00	60.00	
Vase, 6" Tall	40.00		

A wide band encompasses about three quarters of each piece; in the center are sharp-edged patterned stars. Surrounding the stars are hobstars extending out from small diamond patterning.

STIPPLED RAYS   FENTON ART GLASS COMPANY, IMPERIAL GLASS COMPANY, NORTHWOOD GLASS COMPANY

Object	Marigold	Blue	Red	Green
Bonbon Dish	$35.00	$50.00	$500.00	$50.00
Bowl, 5"	35.00	50.00	400.00	50.00
Bowl, 8" (Northwood)	45.00			60.00
Bowl, 9"	45.00	60.00	500.00	60.00
Bowl, 10"	50.00			65.00
Compote	45.00	50.00		50.00
Creamer	35.00	40.00	375.00	40.00
Creamer, Footed (Imperial)	55.00			55.00
Plate, 7"	40.00	60.00	450.00	60.00
Sugar	35.00	40.00	375.00	40.00
Sugar, Footed (Imperial)	55.00			55.00

Object	Amethyst	White	Smoke
Bonbon Dish	$50.00		

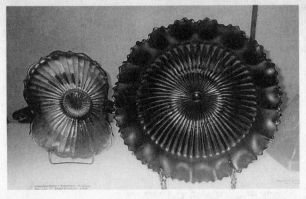

Carnival glass, "Stippled Rays" pattern. Photo by Mark Pickvet. Courtesy of the Fenton Art Glass Museum.

Object	Amethyst	White	Smoke
Bowl, 5"	$50.00	$75.00	
Bowl, 8"	.60.00		
Bowl, 9"	.60.00	90.00	
Bowl, 10"	.65.00		
Compote	.50.00		
Creamer	.40.00		
Creamer, Footed (Imperial)			65.00
Plate	.60.00		
Sugar	.50.00		
Sugar, Footed (Imperial)			65.00

The Fenton version contains the most variety of pieces, all except the footed creamer and sugar. This interior pattern is characterized by alternating stippled spears with clear portions that emanate from the center into a large star.

The Imperial pattern is in low relief and has scalloped edges. The only two pieces that are known to be made by Imperial are the footed creamer and sugar.

Northwood produced a compote along with the 8" and 10" bowls.

STORK AND RUSHES   DUGAN GLASS COMPANY

Object	Marigold	Blue	Amethyst	Purple	Aqua Opalescent
Bowl, Berry, 4½"	$35.00		$40.00	$40.00	
Bowl, Berry, 10"	.55.00		65.00	65.00	
Hat Vase	.55.00		65.00	65.00	
Mug	.50.00	425.00		375.00	500.00
Pitcher, Water	.250.00	375.00	325.00	325.00	
Punch Bowl	.225.00	300.00	275.00	275.00	
Punch Cup	.25.00	40.00	35.00	35.00	
Tumbler	.40.00	50.00	45.00	45.00	

The stork is common bird found in many Carnival examples. Imperial also made several items, such as vases and ABC plates, with a stork pattern motif (see the section at the end of the chapter on Imperial).

Carnival glass, "Tree Bark" pattern. Drawing by Mark Pickvet.

TREE BARK IMPERIAL GLASS COMPANY

Object	Marigold
Bowl, 7½"	.$25.00
Candle Holder with Stand, Pattern Variant	.80.00
Candlestick, 4½"	.25.00
Candlestick, 7"	.20.00
Candy Jar with Cover	.30.00
Pickle Jar, 7½"	.45.00
Pitcher	.75.00
Pitcher with Lid	.90.00
Sauce Dish, 4"	.15.00
Tumbler, 2 Styles	.25.00

"Tree Bark" is a very simple rough pattern. The exterior contains haphazard vertical ridges that resemble the bark of trees.

TWINS IMPERIAL GLASS COMPANY

Object	Marigold	Blue	Green	Purple	Smoke
Basket, Bride's	.$75.00				
Bowl, Berry, 5"	.35.00		45.00		
Bowl, 7", Footed	.40.00			50.00	
Bowl, 8"	.40.00				60.00
Bowl, Berry, 9"	.45.00		55.00		
Bowl, 10", Footed	.50.00			60.00	
Bowl, Fruit with Base	.65.00				
Plate, 9½"	.225.00				
Plate, 13"	.375.00	425.00	425.00		
Punch Bowl with Base	.75.00				
Punch Cup	.25.00				

This pattern contains a sunburst in the center surrounded by a wreath of teardrop rosettes. The remaining portion consists of rounded arches and ridges in relief. It is an allover pattern resembling that of cut glass.

VINTAGE   FENTON ART GLASS COMPANY

Object	Marigold	Blue	Red	Green	Amethyst
Bowl, Berry, 4½"	$35.00	$45.00		$45.00	$45.00
Bowl, 6½"	30.00	40.00		40.00	40.00
Bowl, Berry, 8"	45.00	55.00		55.00	55.00
Bowl, 8", Flat	25.00	35.00	1500.00	35.00	35.00
Bowl, 10", Flat	30.00	40.00	1750.00	40.00	40.00
Bowl, Fernery, Footed	50.00	60.00	750.00	60.00	60.00
Bowl, Orange, Footed	80.00	110.00		115.00	100.00
Bowl, Rose	70.00	90.00		100.00	90.00
Compote	45.00	55.00		60.00	55.00
Cup	25.00	40.00		35.00	30.00
Epergne, 2 Styles	125.00	150.00		175.00	150.00
Fernery, 2 Styles	50.00	65.00	750.00	65.00	60.00
Fernery, Whimsy					175.00
Nut Dish, Tri-Footed	40.00	55.00		60.00	55.00
Nut Dish, 6-Footed	55.00	85.00		90.00	85.00
Plate, 7"		75.00		80.00	75.00
Plate, 7¾"		80.00		85.00	80.00
Plate, 9"	250.00	750.00			
Plate, 11", Ruffled	175.00	250.00		225.00	
Punch Bowl with Base	225.00	400.00		400.00	375.00
Punch Cup	35.00	50.00		50.00	45.00
Sandwich Server	75.00				
Tray, Card	45.00				
Wine Glass	25.00				40.00

Object	Purple	Amber	Amberina	Aqua Opalescent
Bowl, Berry, 4½"	$45.00	$65.00		
Bowl, 6½"	40.00	60.00		
Bowl, Berry, 8"	55.00	75.00		
Bowl, 8", Flat	35.00	40.00		1000.00
Bowl, 10", Flat	40.00	50.00		1250.00
Bowl, Fernery, Footed	60.00	90.00		
Bowl, Orange, Footed	110.00	125.00		

Carnival glass, "Vintage" pattern. Photo by Mark Pickvet. Courtesy of the Fenton Art Glass Museum.

Object	Purple	Amber	Amberina	Aqua Opalescent
Bowl, Rose	$90.00	$100.00	$125.00	
Compote	.50.00			
Cup	.30.00			
Epergne, 2 Styles	.150.00			
Fernery, 2 Styles	.60.00	75.00		
Fernery, Whimsy	.175.00			
Nut Dish, Tri-Footed	.55.00	65.00		
Nut Dish, 6-Footed	.85.00	100.00		
Plate, 7"	.75.00			
Plate, 7¾"	.80.00			
Punch Bowl with Base	.375.00	425.00		
Punch Cup	.45.00	55.00		
Sandwich Dish			100.00	
Wineglass	.40.00			

"Vintage" is another common grape and leaf pattern that is somewhat sparse and in low relief on each piece.

WAFFLE BLOCK   IMPERIAL GLASS COMPANY

Object	Marigold	Purple	Clambroth	Teal
Basket, 10"	$65.00		$90.00	
Bowl, 7"	.35.00			
Bowl, 9"	.40.00			
Bowl, Fruit with Base			200.00	
Bowl, Rose	100.00		300.00	
Creamer	.60.00			
Nappy	.40.00			
Parfait	.45.00		75.00	
Pitcher, Water	.150.00		200.00	
Plate, 10"	.75.00			125.00
Plate, 12"	.85.00			150.00
Punch Bowl	.200.00	250.00	350.00	250.00
Punch Cup	.20.00	40.00	50.00	40.00
Salt and Pepper Shakers	.75.00			
Sherbet			50.00	
Sugar	.60.00			
Tumbler	.225.00			

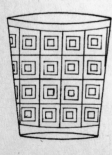

Carnival glass, "Waffle Block" pattern. Drawing by Mark Pickvet.

Object	Marigold	Purple	Clambroth	Teal
Vase, 8" Tall $45.00			$80.00	
Vase, 11" Tall 55.00			90.00	

A simple allover square pattern resembling waffles, as the name implies.

WIDE PANEL IMPERIAL GLASS COMPANY, FENTON ART GLASS COMPANY, NORTHWOOD GLASS COMPANY, WESTMORE-LAND GLASS COMPANY

Object	Marigold	Purple	Red	Ice Blue	Ice Green
Bowl, 7¹/₂" (Teal $65.00) (Westmoreland)					
Bowl, 8¹/₄" (Amber $70.00) (Westmoreland)					
Bowl, 9" $40.00		$85.00			
Cake Plate, 12" 60.00		90.00	350.00		
Cake Plate, 15" 70.00		100.00	400.00		
Candy Dish with Cover 55.00		65.00	500.00	75.00	75.00
Compote 45.00					
Compote, Miniature 40.00					
Console Set 100.00				125.00	125.00
Epergne (Blue $800.00) 500.00		650.00	900.00		
Goblet (Small) 45.00					
Goblet (Large) 50.00			250.00		
Pitcher, Water or Lemonade 125.00					
Plate, 10" 35.00					
Punch Bowl 150.00			2250.00		
Punch Cup 35.00			150.00		
Spittoon 350.00					
Vase (Blue or Green $45.00, Peach Opalescent $75.00) 35.00		45.00	750.00		

*Carnival glass, "Wide Panel" pattern.
Reproduced from a 1912 advertisement. From the
Baltimore Bargain Book Catalog.*

Object	White	Smoke	Clambroth	Vaseline	Pink
Bowl, 9"		$100.00			
Cake Plate, 12"	.125.00		125.00	125.00	125.00
Cake Plate, 15"	.150.00		150.00	150.00	150.00
Candy Dish with Cover	.75.00				75.00
Console Set				125.00	125.00
Epergne (Aqua Opalescent $5500.00)	.900.00				
Plate, 10"		75.00	75.00		
Punch Bowl	.250.00				250.00
Punch Cup	.50.00				50.00

The panels extend about three quarters of the way up the glass and end in three horizontal bands at the top for the most common items in this pattern. With so many companies producing this simple design, there are a number of variations, including varying degrees of width in the panels, pieces with only one or no top bands, and so on.

WINDMILL   IMPERIAL GLASS COMPANY

Object	Marigold	Green	Purple	Smoke
Bowl, Berry, 5"	.$25.00	$40.00	$35.00	
Bowl, Berry, 9"	.35.00	50.00	45.00	
Bowl, Fruit, 10½"	.40.00	55.00	50.00	
Pickle Dish	.25.00	55.00	45.00	
Pitcher, Milk	.65.00	150.00	125.00	
Pitcher, Water	.85.00	200.00	175.00	450.00
Tray	.50.00	85.00	75.00	100.00
Tumbler	.20.00	35.00	65.00	80.00

The windmill in this pattern is raised in the center and is surrounded by trees within a ridged oval. Outside the oval frame are floral designs and paneled sides.

WISHBONE   NORTHWOOD GLASS COMPANY

Object	Marigold	Blue	Green	Purple
Bowl, 8"	.$45.00	$100.00	$75.00	$75.00
Bowl, 9", Footed	.50.00	85.00	85.00	85.00
Bowl, 10"	.65.00	175.00	100.00	100.00
Epergne	.$200.00	$225.00	$325.00	$300.00
Pitcher, Water	.950.00		1100.00	1250.00
Plate, 9", Footed	.100.00		150.00	175.00
Plate, 10"	.425.00		450.00	400.00
Tumbler	.100.00		150.00	175.00

Object	White	Ice Blue	Ice Green	Aqua Opalescent
Bowl, 8"	.$600.00	$150.00	$150.00	
Bowl, 9", Footed	.175.00	175.00	175.00	2000.00
Bowl, 10"	.650.00	175.00	175.00	

Object	White	Ice Blue	Ice Green	Aqua Opalescent
Epergne	.$500.00	$500.00	$750.00	
Tumbler	.325.00			

"Wishbone" contains a small, central, circular medallion surrounded by curving tweezerlike spears shaped like wishbones. Overlapping these wishbone designs are winged mothlike critters, and finally, beyond them is a continuous line of scrolling.

WREATH OF ROSES FENTON ART GLASS COMPANY, DUGAN GLASS COMPANY

Object	Marigold	Blue	Green	Amethyst	White
Bonbon Dish	.$25.00	$40.00	$40.00	$40.00	$65.00
Bonbon Dish, Stemmed	.45.00	65.00	65.00	65.00	100.00
Bowl, Rose	.50.00			75.00	
Compote	.30.00	50.00	50.00	50.00	
Compote (Dugan Pattern Variant)	.50.00	60.00	60.00	60.00	
Punch Bowl with Base	.275.00	350.00	350.00	350.00	
Punch Cup	.25.00	35.00	35.00	35.00	
Spittoon	.75.00				

Wreaths of vines and foliage surround this simple rose design. The only Dugan pieces are the rose bowl, the spittoon, and the compote pattern variant.

WREATHED CHERRY DUGAN GLASS COMPANY

Object	Marigold	Amethyst	Purple	White
Bowl, Berry, 5", Oval	.$25.00	$35.00	$35.00	$50.00
Bowl, Berry, 10½", Oval	.85.00	150.00	150.00	350.00
Butter Dish with Cover	.125.00	200.00	200.00	250.00
Creamer	.75.00	125.00	125.00	150.00
Pitcher, Water	.250.00	500.00	500.00	900.00
Spooner	.65.00	110.00	110.00	125.00
Sugar	.75.00	125.00	125.00	150.00
Toothpick Holder		200.00		
Tumbler	.40.00	75.00	75.00	200.00

The cherries in this pattern are of a slightly darker color and are raised in relief. Surrounding the cherries is a wreath of draped scalloped ridges that form a continuous band. Each wreath frames a bunch of three cherries.

The remaining pages in this chapter include miscellaneous patterns by the five major American Carnival glass producers (Dugan, Fenton, Imperial, Millersburg, and Northwood). Very little variety of pieces (fewer than five in each pattern) exist in the following listings:

DUGAN GLASS COMPANY MISCELLANEOUS
PATTERNED CARNIVAL GLASS

Object	Price
Ashtray, Polo Pony Pattern (Marigold $50.00, Pastels $125.00)	*$65.00*
Banana Bowl, Dogwood Sprays Pattern (Peach Opalescent $100.00)	*110.00*
Banana Bowl, Petals Pattern (Marigold $75.00, Pastels $150.00)	*110.00*
Banana Bowl, Single Flower Pattern, Peach Opalescent Only	*175.00*
Basket, Beaded Basket Pattern (Marigold $60.00, Smoke $125.00)	*90.00*
Basket, Big Basketweave Pattern	*50.00*
Basket, Ski Star Pattern	*550.00*
Bonbon Dish, 2-Handled, Puzzle Pattern (Marigold $50.00, Pastels $90.00)	*65.00*
Bonbon Dish, Question Marks Pattern (Marigold $50.00, Pastels $100.00)	*65.00*
Bowl, 9", Apple Blossoms Pattern	*65.00*
Bowl, with or without Foot, Border Plants Pattern (Pastels $100.00)	*75.00*
Bowl, Round or Square, Butterfly and Tulip Pattern (Marigold $450.00)	*1000.00*
Bowl, 5", Cobblestones Pattern	*50.00*
Bowl, 8", Corinth Pattern (Marigold $35.00, Pastels $125.00)	*45.00*
Bowl, 9", Footed, Dogwood Sprays Pattern (Pastels $150.00)	*55.00*
Bowl, Double Stem Rose Pattern (Marigold $40.00, Peach Opalescent $125.00)	*65.00*
Bowl, Fish on Lily Pad Pattern (Pastels $75.00)	*30.00*
Bowl, Footed, Five Hearts Pattern (Marigold $50.00)	*70.00*
Bowl, Flowers and Frames Pattern (Marigold $35.00, Pastels $100.00)	*60.00*
Bowl, 5", Flowers and Spades Pattern (Marigold $40.00, Pastels $100.00)	*65.00*
Bowl, 10", Flowers and Spades Pattern (Marigold $55.00, Pastels $125.00)	*80.00*
Bowl, 6¼", Four Flowers Pattern (Blue or Peach Opalescent $75.00)	*55.00*
Bowl, 10", Four Flowers Pattern (Blue or Peach Opalescent)	*80.00*
Bowl, 7", Golden Grape Pattern (Marigold $35.00)	*40.00*
Bowl, 7½", Grape Vine Lattice Pattern (Marigold $30.00, White $75.00)	*50.00*
Bowl, 5", Heavy Grape Pattern (Marigold $50.00)	*75.00*
Bowl, 10", Heavy Grape Pattern (Marigold $100.00, Peach Opalescent $750.00)	*75.00*
Bowl, Holly and Berry Pattern (Marigold $45.00, Peach Opalescent $80.00)	*60.00*
Bowl, 5", Jewled Heart Pattern (Peach Opalescent $100.00)	*55.00*
Bowl, 10", Jewled Heart Pattern (Peach Opalescent $175.00)	*110.00*
Bowl, Lattice Pattern (Marigold $65.00)	*75.00*
Bowl, 9", Lattice and Daisy Pattern, Marigold Only	*75.00*
Bowl, Long Leaf Pattern, Peach Opalescent Only	*75.00*
Bowl, Long Thumbprint Pattern (Marigold $40.00)	*50.00*
Bowl, 9", Malaga Pattern (Marigold $80.00)	*110.00*
Bowl, 5", Petal and Fan Pattern (Marigold $45.00, Pastels $90.00)	*60.00*
Bowl, 10", Petal and Fan Pattern (Marigold $55.00, Pastels $125.00)	*85.00*
Bowl, 8½", Petals Pattern (Marigold $55.00, Pastels $85.00)	*65.00*
Bowl, Pony Polo Pattern (Marigold, $80.00, Pastels $550.00)	*175.00*
Bowl, 9", Raindrops Pattern (Pastels $75.00)	*125.00*
Bowl, Round-Up Pattern (Marigold $75.00)	*100.00*
Bowl, Single Flower Pattern (Marigold $35.00, Pastels $75.00)	*45.00*
Bowl, 9", Single Flower Framed Pattern (Marigold $55.00, Pastels $200.00)	*100.00*
Bowl, Six Petals Pattern (Marigold $45.00, Pastels $200.00)	*55.00*
Bowl, 5", Ski Star Pattern	*65.00*
Bowl, 10", Ski Star Pattern	*85.00*

Bowl, 4¹/₂", Soda Gold Spears Pattern, Marigold Only *$35.00*

Bowl, 8¹/₂", Soda Gold Spears Pattern, Marigold Only . . . . *.45.00*

Bowl, Stippled Flower Pattern, Peach Opalescent Only . . . . *.75.00*

Bowl, Stippled Petals Pattern . . . . *.100.00*

Bowl, Victorian Pattern (Peach Opalescent $1500.00) . . . . *.300.00*

Bowl, Vining Twigs Pattern (Marigold $35.00, White $60.00) . . . . *.45.00*

Bowl, with or without Dome Base, Weeping Cherry Pattern (Marigold $60.00, Pastels $125.00, Peach Opalescent $300.00) . . . . *.90.00*

Bowl, Wind Flower Pattern (Marigold $50.00) . . . . *.60.00*

Bowl, Rose, Fluted Scroll Pattern, Amethyst Only *1250.00*

Bowl, Rose, Golden Grape Pattern (Marigold $55.00) . . . . *.65.00*

Bowl, Rose, Grape Delight Pattern (Marigold $60.00, White $100.00) . . . . *.80.00*

Bowl, Rose, Honeycomb Pattern (Peach Opalescent $200.00) *125.00*

Coaster, Concave Diamond Pattern . . . . *.30.00*

Compote, Coin Spot Pattern (Marigold $30.00, Pastels $75.00) . . . . *.50.00*

Compote, Constellation Pattern (Marigold $30.00, Pastels $100.00) . . . . *.50.00*

Compote, Dogwood Sprays Pattern (Marigold $30.00) . . . . *.75.00*

Compote, Floral and Wheat Pattern (Marigold $25.00, Pastels $50.00, Peach Opalescent $100.00) . . . . *.40.00*

Compote, Georgia Belle Pattern (Marigold $50.00, Peach Opalescent $100.00) . . . . . *.60.00*

Compote, Long Thumbprint Pattern (Marigold $45.00) . . . . *.55.00*

Compote, Petals Pattern (Marigold $60.00, Pastels $100.00) . . . . *.75.00*

Compote, Puzzle Pattern (Marigold $50.00, Pastels $90.00) . . . . *.65.00*

Compote, Question Marks Pattern (Marigold $50.00, Pastels $90.00) . . . . *.60.00*

Compote, Starfish Pattern (Marigold $50.00, Peach Opalescent $100.00) . . . . *.65.00*

Creamer, Long Thumbprint Pattern (Marigold $50.00) . . . . *.60.00*

Creamer, S-Repeat Pattern . . . . *.75.00*

Hat Vase, Daisy Web Pattern (Marigold $50.00, Peach Opalescent $100.00) . . . . *.75.00*

Hatpin Holder, Formal Pattern *200.00*

Mug, Fish on Lily Pad Pattern (Pastels $1000.00) *150.00*

Mug, Heron Pattern (Marigold $100.00) *150.00*

Left: Carnival glass, "Question Marks" pattern, by Dugan. Photo by Mark Pickvet. Courtesy of the Fenton Art Glass Museum. Right: Carnival glass, "Fanciful" pattern, by Dugan. Photo by Mark Pickvet. Courtesy of the Fenton Art Glass Museum.

Mug, Vintage Banded Pattern (Marigold $50.00), Smoke *$65.00*

Nappy, Handled, Holly and Berry Pattern (Marigold $55.00, Peach Opalescent $100.00) *80.00*

Nappy, Leaf Rays Pattern (Marigold $35.00, Pastels $55.00) *45.00*

Nappy, Wind Flower Pattern (Marigold $65.00) *75.00*

Nut Dish, Grape Delight Pattern (Marigold $60.00, White $100.00) *80.00*

Pitcher, Water, Concave Diamond Pattern (Green $650.00) *425.00*

Pitcher, Water, Floral and Grape Pattern (Marigold $125.00, White $500.00) *275.00*

Pitcher, Water, God and Home Pattern, Blue Only *1500.00*

Pitcher, Water, Heavy Iris Pattern (Marigold $600.00, Peach Opalescent $1500.00) . .*900.00*

Pitcher, Water, Jewled Heart Pattern, Marigold Only *850.00*

Pitcher, Water, Tankard-Style, Lattice and Daisy (Marigold $150.00) *225.00*

Pitcher, Water, Quill Pattern (Marigold $1750.00) *3000.00*

Pitcher, Water, Rambler Rose Pattern (Marigold $150.00) *225.00*

Pitcher, Water, Vineyard Pattern (Marigold $100.00) *350.00*

Pitcher, Water, Vintage Banded Pattern, Marigold Only *275.00*

Plate, 8¹/₂", Apple Blossoms Pattern *125.00*

Plate, Dome Foot, Double Stem Rose Pattern, Peach Opalescent Only *175.00*

Plate, 7", Fish on Lily Pad Pattern (Marigold $35.00, Pastels $100.00) *60.00*

Plate, 6¹/₂", Four Flowers Pattern (Peach Opalescent $125.00) *100.00*

Plate, 10¹/₂", Four Flowers Pattern, Green Only *750.00*

Plate, Grill, Four Flowers Pattern (Purple $800.00, Peach Opalescent $600.00) *350.00*

Plate, 7¹/₂", Grape Vine Lattice Pattern (Marigold $50.00, White $100.00) *75.00*

Plate, 6", Ruffled, Petal and Fan Pattern (Marigold $75.00, Pastels $200.00) *125.00*

Plate, Polo Pony Pattern (Marigold $225.00) *300.00*

Plate, Round-Up Pattern (White, $250.00, Peach Opalescent $400.00) *175.00*

Plate, Soda Gold Spears Pattern, Marigold Only *60.00*

Plate, 9¹/₂", 1" Dome Footed, Vintage Pattern (Marigold $400.00) *600.00*

Plate, Wind Flower Pattern (Marigold $150.00) *200.00*

Powder Jar with Cover, Vintage Pattern (Marigold $75.00, White $350.00) *200.00*

Punch Bowl with Base, Many Fruits Pattern (Marigold $250.00, White $1250.00) . . .*500.00*

Punch Bowl, S-Repeat Pattern *2000.00*

Punch Cup, Many Fruits Pattern (Marigold $30.00, White $50.00) *40.00*

Punch Cup, S-Repeat Pattern *50.00*

Sauce Dish, Fan Pattern (Marigold $25.00) *40.00*

Sugar, Long Thumbprint Pattern (Marigold $50.00) *60.00*

Swan Figurine (Marigold $75.00, Pastels $65.00, Peach Opalescent $175.00) *110.00*

Toothpick Holder, S-Repeat Pattern *250.00*

Tray, Dresser, Vintage Pattern, Marigold Only *100.00*

Tumbler, Concave Diamond Pattern (Green $425.00) *45.00*

Tumbler, Floral and Grape Pattern (Marigold $30.00, White $75.00) *50.00*

Tumbler, Heavy Iris Pattern (Marigold $55.00, White $100.00) *75.00*

Tumbler, Jeweled Heart Pattern (White $625.00) *110.00*

Tumbler, Quill Pattern (Marigold $425.00) *525.00*

Tumbler, Rambler Rose Pattern (Marigold $35.00) *55.00*

Tumbler, Vineyard Pattern (Marigold $35.00) *55.00*

Tumbler, Vintage Banded Pattern, Marigold Only *425.00*

Vase, Beauty Bud Pattern (with Feet $175.00) *75.00*

Vase, Big Basketweave Pattern (Marigold $30.00, Pastels $100.00) *60.00*

Vase, 7" Tall, Corinth Pattern (Marigold $25.00, Pastels $55.00) *40.00*

Vase, Jack-in-the-Pulpit Style, Formal Pattern (White $200.00) *75.00*

Vase, Lattice and Points Pattern (Marigold $45.00, White $75.00) *$55.00*

Vase, Lined Lattice Pattern (Marigold $45.00, Pastels $75.00) *60.00*

Vase, 3-Handled, Mary Ann Pattern, Marigold Only *300.00*

Vase, Paneled Hobnail Pattern (Marigold $55.00, Pastels $125.00) *85.00*

Vase, 7" Tall, Paneled Tree Trunk Pattern (Marigold $85.00, Pastels $200.00) *125.00*

Vase, Pulled Loop Pattern (Marigold $35.00, Peach Opalescent $75.00) *50.00*

Vase, Spider Web and Tree Bark Pattern, White Only *75.00*

Vase, Summer Days Pattern (Marigold $55.00) *75.00*

Vase, 6" Tall, Three Diamonds Pattern (Marigold $40.00, White $75.00, Peach Opalescent $100.00) *60.00*

Vase, Wide Rib Pattern (Marigold $50.00, Pastels $125.00) *60.00*

In the past, much of Dugan's work was attributed to Northwood since they leased a factory from Harry Northwood; however, they have now been recognized as a distinct maker of Carnival glass with many of their own unique patterns. Copying was still taking place between the different firms but to a lesser degree than in the pressed glass era; most copying would be finished by the Depression as companies became much more careful at applying for and obtaining patents.

FENTON ART GLASS COMPANY MISCELLANEOUS
PATTERNED CARNIVAL GLASS

Object	*Price*
Banana Boat, Cherry and Daisies Pattern (Marigold $800.00)	*$1000.00*
Basket, Pearl and Jewels Pattern, White Only	*110.00*
Bonbon Dish, Butterflies Pattern (Marigold $50.00)	*75.00*
Bonbon Dish, Daisy Pattern (Marigold $40.00)	*60.00*
Bonbon Dish, Honeycomb and Clover Pattern (Marigold $45.00, Amber $80.00)	*65.00*

Left: Carnival glass, "Panelled Dandelion" pattern, by Fenton. Photo by Robin Rainwater. Right: Carnival glass, "Butterfly and Fern" pattern, by Fenton. Photo by Mark Pickvet. Courtesy of the Fenton Art Glass Museum.

Bonbon Dish, Illusion Pattern (Marigold $55.00) $85.00

Bonbon Dish, Leaf Chain Pattern (Marigold $45.00) 60.00

Bonbon Dish, Lotus and Grape Pattern (Marigold $45.00, Vaseline $125.00, Red $750.00) 55.00

Bonbon Dish, Handled, Peacock Tail Pattern (Marigold $25.00) 35.00

Bonbon Dish, Pond Lily Pattern (Marigold $45.00, White $80.00) 55.00

Bonbon Dish, Prayer Rug Pattern, Milk White or Peach Opalescent Only 525.00

Bowl, 7", Acorn Pattern (Marigold $40.00, Red $500.00) 65.00

Bowl, Age Herald Pattern, Amethyst Only 1250.00

Bowl, Autumn Acorns Pattern 65.00

Bowl, Blackberry Pattern 45.00

Bowl, 10", Chrysanthemum Pattern (Pastels $75.00, Red $750.00) 65.00

Bowl, 10", Footed, Chrysanthemum Pattern (Pastels $150.00, Red $800.00) 75.00

Bowl, 8", Concord Pattern (Marigold $75.00) 110.00

Bowl, 8³/₄", Coral Pattern (Marigold $60.00) 110.00

Bowl, Cut Arcs Pattern 40.00

Bowl, 9", with or without Feet, Dragon and Strawberry Pattern (Marigold $200.00) ..325.00

Bowl, 11", Footed, Dragon's Tongue Pattern, Marigold Only 325.00

Bowl, with or without Foot, Dragon and Lotus Pattern (Marigold $50.00, Peach Opalescent $325.00, Red $1000.00) 75.00

Bowl, 5", Fan-Tails Pattern (Marigold $30.00) 40.00

Bowl, 9" or 10¹/₂", Feathered Serpent Pattern (Marigold $50.00) 75.00

Bowl, 5", Footed, Feathered Serpent Pattern (Marigold $50.00) 75.00

Bowl, 8¹/₂", Feather Stitch Pattern (Marigold $60.00) 85.00

Bowl, Goddess of Harvest Pattern 3500.00

Bowl, 9", Heart and Horseshoe Pattern (Marigold $50.00) 65.00

Bowl, 9", Heart and Vine Pattern (Marigold $100.00) 55.00

Bowl, 8", Hearts and Trees Pattern 175.00

Bowl, Heavy Pineappple Pattern 600.00

Bowl, 7", with or without Foot, Horse's Head Pattern, (Marigold $70.00, Vaseline $200.00) 65.00

Left: Carnival glass, "Goddess of Harvest" pattern, by Fenton. Photo by Mark Pickvet. Courtesy of the Fenton Art Glass Museum. Right:Carnival glass, "Ribbon Tie" pattern, by Fenton. Photo by Mark Pickvet. Courtesy of the Fenton Art Glass Museum.

Bowl, Illusion Pattern (Marigold $85.00) *$110.00*

Bowl, Leaf Chain Pattern (Marigold $50.00) *65.00*

Bowl, 7", Lion Pattern (Marigold $100.00) *175.00*

Bowl, 7½", Lion Pattern (Marigold $350.00) *500.00*

Bowl, 8" or 9", Little Daisies Pattern, Marigold Only *200.00*

Bowl, 5½", Little Fishes Pattern (Marigold $50.00, Purple or Amethyst $125.00) *75.00*

Bowl, 10", Little Fishes Pattern (Marigold $90.00, White $950.00) *125.00*

Bowl, 5" Little Flowers Pattern (Marigold $35.00, Vaseline $65.00, Amber $125.00) .. *55.00*

Bowl, 9", Little Flowers Pattern (Marigold $55.00, Red $1750.00) *100.00*

Bowl, Lotus and Grape Pattern (Marigold $50.00) *60.00*

Bowl, Northern Star Pattern, Marigold Only *40.00*

Bowl, 11", Panels and Ball Pattern (Marigold $60.00) *100.00*

Bowl, 5", Footed, Panther Pattern (Marigold $70.00, White $300.00, Red $750.00) ..*110.00*

Bowl, 9", Footed, Panther Pattern (Marigold $110.00, White $1000.00) *200.00*

Bowl, 9", Peacock and Dahlia Pattern (Marigold $65.00, Blue $110.00, Pastels $100.00) *75.00*

Bowl, Peacock and Grapes Pattern (Marigold $45.00, Peach Opalescent $325.00, Red $650.00) *55.00*

Bowl, 9", Peacock Tail Pattern (Marigold $35.00) *45.00*

Bowl, Peter Rabbit Pattern (Marigold $800.00) *1000.00*

Bowl, Pine Cone Pattern (Marigold $40.00) *50.00*

Bowl, Plaid Pattern (Marigold $55.00, Pastels $750.00, Red $2,000.00) *65.00*

Bowl, Ragged Robin Pattern (Marigold $65.00, White $100.00) *75.00*

Bowl, Ribbon Tie Pattern (Marigold $55.00, Red $1750.00) *70.00*

Bowl, 10", Rose Tree Pattern (Marigold $250.00) *325.00*

Bowl, 6", Sailboats Pattern (Marigold $40.00, Red $375.00) *80.00*

Bowl, Scale Band Pattern (Marigold $40.00) *55.00*

Bowl, Footed, Stag and Holly Pattern (Marigold $100.00, Red $1500.00) *200.00*

Bowl, 9½", Stream of Hearts Pattern (Marigold $85.00) *110.00*

Bowl, Ten Mums Pattern (Marigold $90.00, White $150.00) *115.00*

Bowl, Two Flowers Pattern (White $425.00, Red $1,500.00) *60.00*

Bowl, Footed, Two Flowers Pattern (White $500.00, Red $1,750.00) *75.00*

Bowl, Two Fruits Pattern (Marigold $75.00, White $150.00) *125.00*

Bowl, Wild Blackberry Pattern (Marigold $60.00) *75.00*

Bowl, Rose, Garland Pattern (Marigold $50.00) *70.00*

Bowl, Rose, Horse's Head Pattern (Marigold $100.00, Vaseline $250.00) *125.00*

Bowl, Rose, Small Rib Pattern (Marigold Only $50.00) *60.00*

Bowl, Rose, Stag and Holly Pattern (Marigold $225.00) *400.00*

Bowl, Rose, Two Flowers Pattern (Marigold $50.00, Vaseline $80.00) *65.00*

Candlestick, Cut Ovals Pattern (Marigold $20.00, ... *30.00*

Candlestick, Florentine Pattern (Marigold $50.00, Red $300.00) *150.00*

Candy Dish, Basketweave Pattern (Pastels $75.00) *50.00*

Compote, Blackberry Bramble Pattern *75.00*

Compote, Coral Pattern (Marigold $50.00, Pastels $150.00) *75.00*

Compote, Cut Arcs Pattern *55.00*

Compote, Fan-Tails Pattern (Marigold $40.00) *55.00*

Compote, Iris Pattern (Marigold $60.00, White $400.00) *80.00*

Compote, Mikado Pattern (Marigold $125.00, White or Green $600.00) *325.00*

Compote, Peacock Tail Pattern (Marigold $45.00) *60.00*

Compote, Scotch Thistle Pattern *60.00*

Compote, Small Rib Pattern (Marigold $45.00) *55.00*

Left: Carnival glass, "Plaid" pattern, by Fenton. Photo by Mark Pickvet. Courtesy of the Fenton Art Glass Museum. Right: Carnival glass, "Milady" pattern, by Fenton. Photo by Mark Pickvet. Courtesy of the Fenton Art Glass Museum.

Compote, Stream of Hearts Pattern (Marigold $65.00) *$85.00*
Compote, Sunray Pattern, Marigold Only *75.00*
Epergne, Dahlia Twist Pattern (Marigold $300.00) *400.00*
Goblet, Iris Pattern (Marigold $60.00) *80.00*
Goblet, Sailboats Pattern (Marigold $45.00) *350.00*
Hat Vase, Basketweave Pattern (Red $325.00) *50.00*
Hat Vase, Blackberry Pattern (Pastels $75.00, Red $250.00) *50.00*
Hat Vase, Blackberry Banded Pattern *35.00*
Hat Vase, Fern Panels Pattern (Marigold $30.00, Red $175.00) *40.00*
Hat Vase, Peacock Tail Pattern (Marigold $40.00) *55.00*
Jardiniere, Diamond and Rib Pattern (Marigold $425.00) *750.00*
Pitcher, Water, Apple Tree Pattern (Marigold $175.00, White $750.00) *325.00*
Pitcher, Water, Banded Drape Pattern (Marigold $100.00, White $500.00) *350.00*
Pitcher, Water, Blackberry Block Pattern (Pastels $1250.00) *450.00*
Pitcher, Water, Blueberry Pattern *500.00*
Pitcher, Water, Bouquet Pattern (Marigold $275.00) *450.00*
Pitcher, Water, Butterfly and Fern Pattern (Marigold $250.00) *550.00*
Pitcher, Water, Cherry Blossoms Pattern, Blue Only *150.00*
Pitcher, Water, Fluffy Peacock Pattern (Marigold $500.00, Blue $1250.00) *600.00*
Pitcher, Water, Inverted Coin Dot Pattern (Marigold $250.00) *500.00*
Pitcher, Water, Tankard-Style, Lattice and Grape Pattern (Marigold $175.00, White $725.00) *350.00*
Pitcher, Water, Lily of the Valley Pattern (Marigold $2000.00), Marigold and Cobalt Blue Only *5000.00*
Pitcher, Water, Milady Pattern (Marigold $525.00) *675.00*
Pitcher, Water, Orange Tree Orchards Pattern (Marigold $225.00, White $500.00) ..*275.00*
Pitcher, Water, Paneled Dandelion Pattern (Marigold $425.00) *550.00*
Pitcher, Water, Applied Decoration, Prism Band Pattern (Marigold $200.00) *425.00*
Pitcher, Water, Scale Band Pattern (Marigold $150.00) *225.00*
Pitcher, Water, Silver Queen Pattern, Marigold Only *225.00*

Pitcher, Water, Strawberry Scroll Pattern (Marigold $2250.00) *$2000.00*
Pitcher, Water, Ten Mums Pattern (Marigold $450.00, White $1300.00) *1000.00*
Pitcher, Cider, Wine and Roses Pattern, Marigold Only *500.00*
Pitcher, Water, Zig Zag Pattern (Marigold $225.00, Green $425.00) *325.00*
Plate, 9", Acorn Pattern *375.00*
Plate, Age Herald Pattern, Amethyst Only *1250.00*
Plate, 7½", Autumn Acorns Pattern *90.00*
Plate, 9", Concord Pattern (Marigold $300.00) *425.00*
Plate, 8¼", Coral Pattern (Marigold $225.00) *375.00*
Plate, Dragon and Lotus Pattern (Marigold $250.00) *400.00*
Plate, 9", Heart and Horseshoe Pattern (Marigold $100.00) *150.00*
Plate, 8", Heart and Vine Pattern (Marigold $100.00) *150.00*
Plate, 6½", Horse's Head Pattern (Marigold ($100.00) *150.00*
Plate, 7", Leaf Chain Pattern (Marigold $325.00) *125.00*
Plate, 9", Leaf Chain Pattern (Marigold $75.00, Red $550.00, Aqua Opalescent $2500.00)
....*125.00*
Plate, 7", Little Flowers Pattern, Marigold Only *100.00*
Plate, 10", Little Flowers Pattern, Marigold Only *225.00*
Plate, Lotus and Grape Pattern (Marigold $100.00) *600.00*
Plate, Northern Star Pattern, Marigold Only *80.00*
Plate, 8½", Peacock and Dahlia Pattern (Marigold $225.00) *300.00*
Plate, Peacock and Grapes Pattern (Marigold $150.00) *300.00*
Plate, Peter Rabbit Pattern (Marigold $2000.00) *2500.00*
Plate, 6", Pine Cone Pattern (Marigold $65.00) *75.00*
Plate, 8", Pine Cone Pattern *125.00*
Plate, Plaid Pattern (Marigold $150.00) *200.00*
Plate, Ribbon Tie Pattern (Marigold $250.00) *100.00*
Plate, Sailboats Pattern (Marigold $225.00) *300.00*
Plate, Footed, Scale Band Pattern (Marigold $55.00) *75.00*
Plate, Soldiers and Sailors Pattern (Marigold $650.00) *1000.00*
Plate, 9", Footed, Stag and Holly Pattern, Marigold Only *450.00*
Plate, 13", Footed, Stag and Holly Pattern (Marigold $225.00) *400.00*

Left: Carnival glass, "Peacock and Grapes" pattern, by Fenton. Photo by Mark Pickvet. Courtesy of the Fenton Art Glass Museum. Right: Carnival glass, "Dragon and Lotus" pattern, by Fenton. Photo by Mark Pickvet. Courtesy of the Fenton Art Glass Museum.

Carnival glass, "Butterfly and Berry" pattern, by Fenton. Photo by Mark Pickvet. Courtesy of the Fenton Art Glass Museum.

Shot Glass, Arched Flute Pattern (Marigold $75.00) $100.00
Spittoon, Blackberry Pattern 3250.00
Spittoon, Rib and Panel Pattern, Marigold Only 150.00
Tumbler, Apple Tree Pattern (Marigold $50.00, White $100.00) 70.00
Tumbler, Banded Drape Pattern (Marigold $35.00, White $55.00) 45.00
Tumbler, Blackberry Block Pattern (Pastels $125.00) 100.00
Tumbler, Blueberry Pattern 85.00
Tumbler, Bouquet Pattern 100.00
Tumbler, Butterfly and Fern Pattern (Marigold $50.00) 65.00
Tumbler, Cherry Blossoms Pattern, Blue Only 35.00
Tumbler, Fluffy Peacock Pattern (Marigold $40.00, Blue $100.00) 50.00
Tumbler, Inverted Coin Dot Pattern (Marigold $90.00) 125.00
Tumbler, Lattice and Grape Pattern (Marigold $45.00, White $225.00) 55.00
Tumbler, Lily of the Valley Pattern (Marigold $500.00), Marigold and Cobalt Blue Only
.... 750.00
Tumbler, Milady Pattern (Marigold $110.00) 175.00
Tumbler, Orange Tree Orchards Pattern (Marigold $50.00, White $100.00) 65.00
Tumbler, Paneled Dandelion Pattern (Marigold $60.00) 75.00
Tumbler, Applied Decoration, Prism Band Pattern, (Marigold $40.00) 85.00
Tumbler, Scale Band Pattern (Marigold $35.00, Green $250.00) 45.00
Tumbler, Silver Queen Pattern, Marigold Only 60.00
Tumbler, Strawberry Scroll Pattern (Marigold $400.00) 350.00
Tumbler, Ten Mums Pattern (Marigold $65.00, White $350.00) 110.00
Tumbler, Zig Zag Pattern (Marigold $45.00, Blue $75.00) 60.00
Vase, April Showers Pattern 55.00
Vase, Cut Arcs Pattern 60.00
Vase, Diamond and Rib Pattern (Marigold $30.00, Smoke $50.00) 40.00
Vase, Heavy Hobnail Pattern 600.00
Vase, Knotted Beads Pattern (Marigold $40.00, Amber or Vaseline $125.00) 50.00
Vase, Leaf Swirl and Flower Pattern (Marigold $55.00) 75.00
Vase, Paneled Diamond and Bows Pattern (Marigold $40.00, Pastels $80.00) 55.00

Vase, Plume Panels Pattern (Marigold $50.00, Pastels $150.00, Red $500.00) *$65.00*

Vase, Pulled Loop Pattern (Marigold $40.00, Pastels $125.00, Red $500.00) . . . . *.50.00*

Vase, Rib and Panel Pattern, Marigold Only . . . . *.75.00*

Vase, Rustic Pattern (Marigold $40.00, Pastels $75.00, Red $750.00) . . . . *.55.00*

Vase, Swirled Flute Pattern (Marigold $40.00, White $60.00, Red $525.00) . . . . *.55.00*

Vase, 7" Diameter, Target Pattern (Marigold $40.00, Peach Opalescent $110.00) . . . . *.55.00*

Wineglass, Wine and Roses Pattern (Marigold $60.00, Pastels $150.00) . . . . *.100.00*

Many of the basic Carnival glass companies responsible for the majority of its production were interrelated. Fenton, like Dugan, was no exception, as Frank L. Fenton had previously worked as apprentice and then foreman at one of the Northwood
factories.

Fenton produced a huge amount of Carnival glass from their inception in 1907 to
about 1920. There are more red Carnival examples by Fenton as well as different
water sets (pitchers and tumblers) than by any other maker. The most noteworthy of
Fenton's colors was a bright iridescent blue or cobalt blue. Fenton is the only original Carnival glassmaker in operation today, and they have revived many iridescent
forms in the recent past.

IMPERIAL GLASS COMPANY MISCELLANEOUS PAT-
TERNED CARNIVAL GLASS

Object	*Price*
Basket, Plain Jane Pattern, Marigold Only	*$75.00*
Basket, Spring Basket Pattern (Marigold $50.00)	*.60.00*
Bonbon Dish, Honeycomb Pattern	*.50.00*
Bonbon Dish, Cobblestone Pattern (Marigold $45.00)	*.60.00*
Bowl, 8" Acanthus Pattern	*.85.00*
Bowl, 9½", Acanthus Pattern	*.65.00*
Bowl, 10", A Dozen Roses Pattern	*.175.00*
Bowl, Arcs Pattern (Marigold $25.00, Smoke $55.00)	*.40.00*
Bowl, Blossoms and Band Pattern, Marigold Only	*.30.00*
Bowl, 8", Broken Arches Pattern	*.65.00*
Bowl, 7½" or 10" Oval, Cane Pattern	*.45.00*
Bowl, 6", Handled, Honeycomb Pattern, Marigold Only	*.40.00*
Bowl, 5" or 9", Cobblestone Pattern (Marigold $45.00)	*.60.00*
Bowl, Diamond and Sunburst Pattern (Marigold $40.00)	*.65.00*
Bowl, Diamond Ring Pattern (Marigold $35.00)	*.55.00*
Bowl, 9", Footed, Double Dutch Pattern (Marigold $35.00)	*.55.00*
Bowl, Dome Foot or Oval, Double Scroll Pattern (Marigold $30.00, Red $275.00)	*.50.00*
Bowl, 9", Hat-Tie Pattern (Marigold $55.00, Smoke $75.00)	*.65.00*
Bowl, Heavy Diamond Pattern, Marigold Only	*.25.00*
Bowl, 5", Heavy Grape Pattern (Marigold $30.00, Amber $75.00)	*.40.00*
Bowl, 9", Heavy Grape Pattern (Marigold $65.00, Amber $125.00)	*.85.00*
Bowl, 8", Long Hobstar Pattern, Marigold Only	*.55.00*
Bowl, 10", Long Hobstar Pattern, Marigold Only	*.65.00*
Bowl, Mayflower Pattern (Marigold $35.00, Peach Opalescent $75.00)	*.55.00*
Bowl, 5", Optic Flute Pattern (Smoke $45.00)	*.35.00*
Bowl, 10", Optic Flute Pattern (Smoke $60.00)	*.50.00*
Bowl, Premium Pattern (Marigold $55.00)	*.125.00*

Bowl, Rococo Pattern (Marigold $35.00) *$50.00*

Bowl, Fruit, with Base, Royalty Pattern (Marigold $30.00) *35.00*

Bowl, Scroll Embossed Pattern (Marigold $45.00) *55.00*

Bowl, Shell Pattern (Marigold $40.00, Smoke $125.00) *50.00*

Bowl, Soda Gold Pattern (Marigold $55.00) *75.00*

Bowl, Star Center Pattern (Marigold $40.00, Smoke $60.00) *50.00*

Bowl, Star of David Pattern (Marigold $75.00, Smoke $125.00) *95.00*

Bowl, 7", Star Spray Pattern (Marigold $35.00) *50.00*

Bowl, 9", Wheels Pattern, Marigold Only *60.00*

Bowl, Whirling Star Pattern (Marigold $50.00) *75.00*

Bowl, Rose, Hat-Tie Pattern, Marigold Only *75.00*

Cake Plate with Center Handle, Balloons Pattern *125.00*

Candlestick, Double Scroll Pattern (Marigold $25.00, Red $250.00) *45.00*

Candlestick, Premium Pattern (Marigold $40.00) *75.00*

Candlestick, Soda Gold Pattern (Marigold $40.00) *45.00*

Candy Dish, Propeller Pattern (Marigold $40.00) *45.00*

Candy Jar, Melon Rib Pattern, Marigold Only *40.00*

Compote, Arcs Pattern (Marigold $25.00, Smoke $55.00) *40.00*

Compote, Balloons Pattern *115.00*

Compote, Columbia Pattern *25.00*

Compote, Honeycomb and Clover Pattern (Marigold $45.00) *100.00*

Compote, Long Hobstar Pattern, Marigold Only *75.00*

Compote, Mayflower Pattern (Marigold $45.00, Smoke $75.00) *60.00*

Compote, Optic Flute Pattern, Marigold Only *40.00*

Compote, Propeller Pattern (Marigold $45.00) *50.00*

Compote, Whirling Star Pattern (Marigold $75.00) *100.00*

Creamer, Heavy Diamond Pattern, Marigold Only *20.00*

Creamer, Ranger Pattern, Marigold Only *55.00*

Decanter with Stopper, Diamond and Sunburst Pattern (Marigold $150.00) *225.00*

Decanter with Stopper, Forty-Niner Pattern, Marigold Only *150.00*

Goblet, Flute and Cane Pattern, Marigold Only *50.00*

Goblet, Tulip and Cane Pattern (Marigold $75.00) *90.00*

Hat Vase, Florentine Pattern, Pastels Only *100.00*

Hat Vase, Mayflower Pattern (Marigold $40.00, Smoke $70.00) *55.00*

Lamp, Zipper Loop Pattern (Marigold $500.00), Marigold and Smoke Only *600.00*

Lamp Shade, Mayflower Pattern (Marigold $45.00, Smoke $60.00) *50.00*

Mug, Robin Pattern, Marigold Only *75.00*

Paperweight, Plain Jane Pattern, Marigold Only *100.00*

Pitcher, Milk, Beaded Acanthus Pattern (Green $175.00) *85.00*

Pitcher, Water, Chatelaine Pattern, Purple Only *1750.00*

Pitcher, Milk, Field Flower Pattern (Marigold $100.00) *175.00*

Pitcher, Water, Field Flower Pattern (Marigold $200.00) *250.00*

Pitcher, Milk, Flute and Cane Pattern, Marigold Only *150.00*

Pitcher, Water, Forty-Niner Pattern, Marigold Only *300.00*

Pitcher, Water, Oklahoma Pattern, Marigold Only *525.00*

Pitcher, Milk, Poinsettia Pattern (Marigold $100.00, Smoke $150.00) *275.00*

Pitcher, Milk, Ranger Pattern. Marigold Pattern *200.00*

Pitcher, Water, Robin Pattern, Marigold Only *400.00*

Pitcher, Water, Soda Gold Pattern (Marigold $250.00) *350.00*

Pitcher, Water, Studs Pattern, Marigold Only *85.00*

Pitcher, Water, Tiger Lily Pattern (Marigold $200.00) *350.00*

Plate, 9½", Acanthus Pattern $165.00

Plate, 7", Honeycomb Pattern, Purple Only 100.00

Plate, 9", Hat-Tie Pattern (Marigold $100.00, Smoke $175.00, Amber $1,500.00) ...140.00

Plate, 7", Heavy Grape Pattern (Marigold $65.00, Amber $125.00) 85.00

Plate, Grill, 12", Heavy Grape Pattern (Marigold $225.00, Amber $450.00) 350.00

Plate, Laurel Leaves Pattern (Mrigold $60.00) 75.00

Plate, Scroll Embossed Pattern (Marigold $65.00, Purple $110.00) 90.00

Plate, Shell Pattern (Marigold $90.00, Smoke $350.00) 150.00

Plate, Star Center Pattern (Marigold $65.00, Smoke $100.00) 75.00

Plate, 7½", Star Spray Pattern (Marigold $60.00) 85.00

Plate, 7", Stork ABC Pattern, Marigold Only 100.00

Puff Box, Melon Rib Pattern, Marigold Only 50.00

Punch Bowl with Base, Broken Arches Pattern 450.00

Punch Bowl with Base, Whirling Star Pattern (Marigold $250.00) 1250.00

Punch Cup, Broken Arches Pattern 35.00

Punch Cup, Royalty Pattern (Marigold $30.00) 35.00

Punch Cup, Whirling Star Pattern (Marigold $30.00) 75.00

Salt and Pepper Shakers, Melon Rib Pattern, Marigold Only 75.00

Spooner, Honeycomb and Clover Pattern, Marigold Only 100.00

Sugar, Heavy Diamond Pattern, Marigold Only 20.00

Sugar Dish with Cover, Hexagon and Cane Pattern, Marigold Only 75.00

Toothpick Holder, Ranger Pattern, Marigold Only 100.00

Toothpick Holder, Square Daisy and Button Pattern, Smoke Only 150.00

Tray, Studs Pattern, Marigold Only 75.00

Tray, Center Handle, Three Flowers Pattern (Marigold $55.00) 65.00

Tumble-Up, Oklahoma Pattern, Marigold Only 200.00

Tumbler, Chatelaine Pattern, Purple Only 325.00

Tumbler, Field Flower Pattern (Marigold $35.00) 60.00

Tumbler, Forty-Niner Pattern, Marigold Only 85.00

Tumbler, Ranger Pattern, Marigold Only 300.00

Tumbler, Soda Gold Pattern (Marigold $55.00) 85.00

Tumbler, Studs Pattern, Marigold Only 40.00

Tumbler, Tiger Lily Pattern (Marigold $50.00) 75.00

Vase, Beaded Bull's Eye Pattern 50.00

Vase, Colonial Lady Pattern 75.00

Vase, 4" Tall, Columbia Pattern 25.00

Vase, Loganberry Pattern (Marigold $125.00, Amber or Smoke $250.00) 200.00

Vase, Mitered Ovals Pattern (Marigold $2250.00) 2000.00

Vase, Parlor Panels Pattern (Marigold $55.00) 100.00

Vase, Poppy and Fish Net Pattern, Red Only 750.00

Vase, Poppy Show Pattern (Marigold $325.00, Pastels $1000.00) 550.00

Vase, 14" Tall, Ripple Pattern (Marigold $35.00, Pastels $55.00, Red $375.00) 45.00

Vase, Rococo Pattern (Marigold $45.00) 75.00

Vase, Scroll and Flowers Panels Pattern (Marigold $110.00) 250.00

Vase, Star and Fan Pattern 275.00

Vase, Stork Pattern, Marigold Only 60.00

Vase, Thumbprint and Oval Pattern (Marigold $200.00) 225.00

Wineglass, Cane Pattern 35.00

Wineglass, Diamond and Sunburst Pattern (Marigold $25.00) 60.00

Wineglass, Flute and Cane Pattern, Marigold Only 40.00

Wineglass, Forty-Niner Pattern, Marigold Only 65.00

Imperial's founder, Edward Muhleman, was related to the Fentons but established his own company four years before the Fenton Brothers.

Imperial stopped making Carnival glass when the market turned sour; however, they reproduced a good deal of iridescent glass, using many of the original molds, in the 1960s and 1970s. All reissues are marked "IG" (overlapping letters) for easy identification.

MILLERSBURG GLASS COMPANY MISCELLANEOUS PATTERNED CARNIVAL GLASS

Object	Price
Bonbon Dish, Night Stars Pattern (Amethyst $525.00)	.$275.00
Bonbon Dish, Strawberry Pattern (Marigold $40.00, Vaseline $125.00, Amberina $250.00, Red $500.00, Vaseline Opalescent $750.00)	.75.00
Bonbon Dish, Tracery Pattern	.750.00
Bowl, Advertising (Bernheimer), Blue Only	.675.00
Bowl, 8¼" or 9½", Cactus Pattern (Marigold $35.00)	.50.00
Bowl, 9" or 9¾", Big Fish Pattern (Marigold $35.00)	.250.00
Bowl, Fleur De Lis Pattern (Marigold $65.00)	.85.00
Bowl, Footed, Fleur De Lis Pattern (Marigold $75.00, Amethyst $325.00)	.125.00
Bowl, Grape Leaves Pattern (Marigold $75.00, Vaseline $1000.00)	.125.00
Bowl, Grape Wreath Pattern (Marigold $55.00)	.75.00
Bowl, Greengard Furniture Pattern, Amethyst Only	.350.00
Bowl, Holly Sprig Pattern (Marigold $50.00)	.75.00
Bowl, 9", Fluted Edge, Many Stars Pattern (Blue $850.00)	.350.00
Bowl, Round, Many Stars Pattern	.350.00
Bowl, Mayan Pattern	.55.00
Bowl, 10", Nesting Swan Pattern (Marigold $175.00, Blue or Vaseline $3,250.00)	. ..275.00
Bowl, Primrose Pattern (Marigold $150.00, Blue $2750.00)	.125.00
Bowl, Rays and Ribbons Pattern (Marigold $60.00)	.80.00
Bowl, Strawberry Pattern (Marigold $150.00)	.250.00
Bowl, Trout and Fly Pattern (Marigold $450.00, Lavender $1000.00)	.500.00
Bowl, 5", Vintage Pattern	.750.00
Bowl, 9", Vintage Pattern (Blue $3500.00)	.800.00
Bowl, 9", Whirling Leaves Pattern (Marigold $85.00, Vaseline $500.00)	.110.00
Bowl, 11", Whirling Leaves Pattern (Marigold $100.00, Vaseline $600.00)	.125.00
Bowl, Zig Zag Pattern (Marigold $300.00)	.425.00
Bowl, Rose, Big Fish Pattern, Vaseline Only	.7500.00
Bowl, Rose, Daisy Squares Pattern (Gold $400.00)	.300.00
Bowl, Rose, Nesting Swan Pattern, Marigold Only	.2250.00
Bowl, Rose, Swirl Hobnail Pattern (Marigold $300.00, Green $550.00)	.350.00
Card Tray, Night Stars Pattern (Amethyst $625.00)	.425.00
Card Tray, Zig Zag Pattern, Green Only	.1000.00
Compote, Acorn Pattern (Vaseline $3500.00)	.425.00
Compote, Boutonniere Pattern	.60.00
Compote, Deep Grape (Relief) Pattern (Marigold $900.00, Vaseline $3500.00)	....1250.00
Compote, Dolphins Design, Pedestal Feet, Scalloped (Blue $1250.00)	.750.00
Compote, Flowering Vine Pattern	.400.00
Compote, 1 Handle, Fruit Basket Pattern, Amethyst Only	.1250.00

Compote, Miniature, Leaf and Little Flowers Pattern (Marigold $350.00) *$475.00*

Compote, Olympic Pattern (Purple $550.00) *1250.00*

Compote, Peacock Tail Pattern (Marigold $35.00) *45.00*

Compote, Poppy Pattern *675.00*

Compote, Strawberry Pattern (Marigold $175.00) *300.00*

Compote, 9", Tulip Pattern (Marigold $625.00) *1000.00*

Compote, Wild Flower Pattern (Marigold $1250.00, Green $2000.00) *200.00*

Nappy, Holly Sprig Pattern (Marigold $50.00) *75.00*

Pin Tray, Sea Coast Pattern *325.00*

Pin Tray, Sunflower Pattern *450.00*

Pitcher, Water, Diamonds Pattern (Marigold $250.00) *750.00*

Pitcher, Water, Feather and Heart Pattern (Marigold $600.00) *900.00*

Pitcher, Water, Fruits and Flowers Pattern (Marigold $7500.00) *8500.00*

Pitcher, Water, Gay '90s Pattern *7500.00*

Pitcher, Water, Marilyn Pattern (Marigold $550.00, Green, $1500.00) *900.00*

Pitcher, Water, Morning Glory Pattern (Marigold $7500.00) *10,000.00*

Pitcher, Water, Perfection Pattern *4000.00*

Pitcher, Milk, Potpourri Pattern, Marigold Only *1250.00*

Plate, 9", Cosmos Pattern, Green Only *125.00*

Plate, Mayan Pattern *450.00*

Plate, Rays and Ribbons Pattern (Marigold $125.00) *200.00*

Plate, Spring Opening Pattern, Amethyst Only *300.00*

Plate, Trout and Fly Pattern, Purple Only *7500.00*

Punch Bowl with Base, Big Thistle Pattern *7500.00*

Punch Bowl with Base, Diamonds Pattern *2500.00*

Punch Bowl, Fruits and Flowers Pattern (Marigold $1250.00, Blue $3500.00) *1500.00*

Punch Cup, Fruits and Flowers Pattern (Marigold $50.00, Blue $100.00) *65.00*

Sauce Dish, Holly Sprig Pattern, Marigold Only *175.00*

Sherbet, Fruits and Flowers Pattern *800.00*

Spittoon, Grape Wreath Pattern, Marigold Only *750.00*

Spittoon, Nesting Swan Pattern, Green Only *4500.00*

Spittoon, Swirl Hobnail Pattern (Marigold $500.00) *600.00*

Tumbler, Diamonds Pattern *50.00*

Tumbler, Feather and Heart Pattern (Marigold $150.00) *200.00*

Tumbler, Gay '90s Pattern *750.00*

Carnival glass, "Acorn" pattern, by Millersburg. Photo by Mark Pickvet. Courtesy of the Fenton Art Glass Museum.

Tumbler, Marilyn Pattern (Marigold $150.00, Green $425.00) *$175.00*
Tumbler, Morning Glory Pattern, (Marigold $650.00) *1000.00*
Tumbler, Perfection Pattern *700.00*
Vase, Bull's Eye and Loop Pattern, Amethyst Only *225.00*
Vase, Honeycomb and Hobstar Pattern *1500.00*
Vase, People's Vase Pattern, Elaborate Design of an Adult Watching Children Inscribed within a Circle *9000.00*
Vase, Rose Columns Pattern (Blue $10,000.00) *1750.00*
Vase, Tulip Scroll Pattern (Marigold $200.00) *250.00*

Established by a member of the Fenton family, Millersburg has the distinction of being the scarcest of the big five in the Carnival glass world. The company operated only a few short years, and an archaeological dig where the original factory was destroyed was necessary for some pattern identification. As many of the prices indicate, there are several rare and valuable Millersburg items.

NORTHWOOD GLASS COMPANY MISCELLA-
NEOUS PATTERNED CARNIVAL GLASS

Object	*Price*
Basket, Basket Pattern (Pastels $400.00)	*$200.00*
Basket, Bride's, Grape Leaves Pattern	*250.00*
Bonbon Dish, Butterfly Pattern	*40.00*
Bonbon Dish, Rose Wreath Pattern, Amethyst Only	*300.00*
Bonbon Dish, Three Fruits Pattern (Marigold $55.00, Pastels $95.00, Aqua Opalescent $500.00)	*75.00*
Bowl, 10", Apple and Pear Pattern, Marigold Only	*100.00*
Bowl, 8" or 9", Beaded Pattern	*50.00*
Bowl, Beaded Hearts Pattern	*75.00*
Bowl, 3-Footed, Blackberry Pattern	*75.00*
Bowl, 8½", Bull's Eye and Leaves Pattern	*65.00*
Bowl, 9", Embroidered Mums Pattern (Pastels $100.00, Aqua Opalescent $300.00) ...	*60.00*
Bowl, 9", Good Luck Pattern (Marigold $85.00, Pastels $750.00)	*150.00*
Bowl, 7½", Grape Leaves Pattern (Marigold $60.00, Ice Blue $150.00)	*90.00*
Bowl, 9", Hearts and Flowers Pattern (Marigold $50.00, Pastels $100.00)	*80.00*
Bowl, Lovely Pattern (Marigold $75.00)	*175.00*
Bowl, Berry, Memphis Pattern (Marigold $75.00)	*110.00*
Bowl, Fruit with Base, Memphis Pattern (Marigold $150.00, Pastels or Blue $1500.00) .	*300.00*
Bowl, 9", Nippon Pattern (Marigold $60.00, Pastels $175.00, Aqua Opalescent $550.00) .	*75.00*
Bowl, 9", Octet Pattern (Marigold $45.00, White $80.00)	*65.00*
Bowl, Paneled Holly Pattern	*65.00*
Bowl, Poinsettia Pattern (Marigold $110.00, Pastels $500.00)	*175.00*
Bowl, Poppy Pattern (Marigold $35.00)	*45.00*
Bowl, Poppy Show Pattern (Marigold $175.00)	*250.00*
Bowl, 8", Rose Show Pattern (Marigold $175.00, Aqua Opalescent $500.00)	*225.00*
Bowl, Rosette Pattern (Marigold $55.00)	*100.00*
Bowl, Footed, Rosette Pattern (Marigold $65.00)	*110.00*
Bowl, Ruffled, Rib Pattern (Marigold $55.00)	*70.00*
Bowl, Ruffled, Rings and Daisy Band Pattern, Amethyst Only	*110.00*
Bowl, 6", Smooth Rays Patter (Marigold $55.00, Pastels $75.00)	*65.00*

Bowl, Soutache Pattern, Marigold Only $75.00

Bowl, Star of David and Bows Pattern (Marigold $60.00) *80.00*

Bowl, 5", Strawberry Pattern (Marigold $35.00) *40.00*

Bowl, 8¹/₂", Strawberry Pattern (Marigold $60.00, Pastels $500.00, Aqua Opalescent $3000.00)...*75.00*

Bowl, 5", Strawberry Intaglio Pattern, Marigold Only *40.00*

Bowl, 9", Strawberry Intaglio Pattern, Marigold Only *65.00*

Bowl, 8¹/₂", Sunflower Pattern (Marigold $65.00, Pastels $125.00, Blue $350.00) *80.00*

Bowl, 5", Three Fruits Pattern (Marigold $35.00, Pastels $50.00, Aqua Opalescent $150.00) *40.00*

Bowl, 10", Three Fruits Pattern (Marigold $45.00, Pastels $85.00, Aqua Opalescent $450.00) *65.00*

Bowl, 5", Valentine Pattern (Marigold $100.00) *150.00*

Bowl, 10", Valentine Pattern (Marigold $175.00) *225.00*

Bowl with Cover, Wheat Pattern, Amethyst Only *2500.00*

Bowl, 6", Fluted, Wild Rose Pattern (Marigold $50.00).........................*60.00*

Bowl, 8", Wild Rose Pattern (Marigold $45.00, Ice Blue $500.00) *55.00*

Bowl, 8¹/₂", Wild Strawberry Pattern, Purple and Green Only *80.00*

Bowl, Rose, Beaded Cable Pattern (Pastels $750.00) *100.00*

Bowl, Rose, Daisy and Plume Pattern (Marigold $40.00, Pastels $100.00, Aqua Opalescent $2000.00)..*75.00*

Bowl, Rose. Drapery Pattern (Marigold $50.00, Pastels $100.00, Squa Opalescent $275.00) *65.00*

Bowl, Rose, Fine Cut and Roses Pattern (Marigold $70.00, Pastels $125.00, Aqua Opalescent $750.00)..*90.00*

Bowl, Rose, Footed, Leaf and Beads Pattern (Marigold $55.00, Pastels $150.00, Aqua or Peach Opalescent $350.00) *80.00*

Bowl, Rose, Smooth Rays Pattern (Marigold $50.00) *65.00*

Candy Dish, Beaded Cable Pattern *60.00*

Candy Dish, Daisy and Plume Pattern (Marigold $25.00, Pastels $100.00) *45.00*

Candy Dish, Drapery Pattern (Marigold $35.00, Pastels $70.00, Aqua Opalescent $250.00) *50.00*

Candy Dish, Footed, Fine Cut and Roses Pattern (Marigold $40.00, Pastels $110.00) ..*90.00*

Candy Dish, Leaf and Beads Pattern (Marigold $50.00, Pastels $150.00, Aqua Opalescent $225.00)...*75.00*

Compote, Amaryllis Pattern (Marigold $65.00) *90.00*

Compote, Blackberry Pattern *55.00*

Compote, Blossomtime Pattern (Pastels $100.00) *65.00*

Compote, Daisy and Plume Pattern (Marigold $60.00, Pastels $125.00) *85.00*

Compote, Hearts and Flowers Pattern (Marigold $60.00, Pastels $250.00) *100.00*

Compote, Hobstar Flower Pattern (Marigold $75.00) *100.00*

Compote, Small Blackberry Pattern (Marigold $55.00) *65.00*

Compote, Smooth Rays Pattern, Marigold Only *45.00*

Creamer, Double Loop Pattern (Marigold $40.00, Aqua Opalescent $225.00) *60.00*

Jardiniere, Tree Trunk Pattern (Marigold $350.00) *500.00*

Lamp Shade, Leaf Column Pattern, White Only *125.00*

Lamp Shade, Pearl Lady Pattern, White Only *75.00*

Mug, Dandelion Pattern (Marigold $85.00, Aqua Opalescent $350.00) *125.00*

Pitcher, Water, Tankard Style, Dandelion Pattern (Marigold $200.00, Pastels $750.00) *425.00*

Pitcher, Water, Tankard Style, Grape Arbor Pattern (Marigold $250.00, White $1000.00, Ice Blue or Green $3000.00) *600.00*

Pitcher, Water, Tankard Style, Oriental Poppy Pattern (Marigold $450.00, Blue $2750.00, Pastels $1100.00, Ice Green $2250.00) *$600.00*

Pitcher, Water, Paneled Holly Pattern, Amethyst Only *2250.00*

Pitcher, Water, Pretty Panels Pattern (Marigold $150.00) *550.00*

Pitcher, Water, Swirl Rib Pattern, Marigold Only *200.00*

Plate, Embroidered Mums Pattern (Marigold $75.00, Pastels $100.00) *125.00*

Plate, 9", Good Luck Pattern (Marigold $150.00, Pastels $350.00) *250.00*

Plate, 9½", Hearts and Flowers Pattern (Marigold $150.00, Pastels $400.00, Aqua Opalescent $1000.00) *300.00*

Plate, 9", Nippon Pattern (Marigold $350.00, White $750.00) *450.00*

Plate, Poppy Show Pattern (Marigold $250.00, Green $1000, Aqua Opalescent $5000.00) *425.00*

Plate, Rose Show Pattern (Marigold $275.00, Milk $1250.00, Lime Green Opalescent $3000.00) *400.00*

Plate, 7", Smooth Rays Pattern, Marigold Only *70.00*

Plate, Soutache Pattern, Peach Opalescent Only *425.00*

Plate, 7", Strawberry Pattern (Marigold $90.00) *125.00*

Plate, 9", Strawberry Pattern (Marigold $100.00, White $225.00) *150.00*

Plate, Footed, Sunflower Pattern (Marigold $200.00) *400.00*

Plate, Three Fruits Pattern (Marigold $85.00, Pastels $750.00, Aqua Opalescent $850.00) *150.00*

Plate, 7", Wild Strawberry Pattern, Purple and Green Only *90.00*

Plate, 8", Wild Strawberry Pattern, Purple and Green Only *150.00*

Punch Bowl with Base, Memphis Pattern (Marigold $250.00, Pastels $2,500.00) *375.00*

Punch Cup, Memphis Pattern (Marigold $40.00, Pastels $55.00) *45.00*

Relish Dish, Poppy Pattern (Marigold $60.00, Pastels $100.00) *75.00*

Spooner, Two Fruits Pattern, Blue Only *550.00*

Sugar, Double Loop Pattern (Marigold $40.00, Aqua Opalescent $225.00) *60.00*

Sugar, Two Fruits Pattern, Blue Only *550.00*

Tray, 11" Round, Holiday Pattern, Marigold Only *225.00*

Tumbler, Dandelion Pattern (Marigold $55.00, Pastels $125.00) *85.00*

Tumbler, Grape Arbor Pattern (Marigold $50.00, Pastels $200.00) *75.00*

Tumbler, Interior Poinsettia Pattern, Marigold Only *525.00*

Tumbler, Oriental Poppy Pattern (Marigold $50.00, Pastels $125.00, Ice Green $250.00, Blue $300.00) *75.00*

Tumbler, Poinsettia Pattern, Marigold Only *350.00*

Tumbler, Pretty Panels Pattern *75.00*

Tumbler, Swirled Rib Pattern, Marigold Only *75.00*

Vase, Ear of Corn Style (Pastels $650.00) *325.00*

Vase with Husk Base, Ear of Corn Style *3000.00*

Vase, Daisy and Drape Pattern (Marigold $125.00, Pastels $1,000.00) *225.00*

Vase, 11" Tall, Diamond Point Pattern (Pastels $350.00) *50.00*

Vase, Drapery Pattern (Marigold $30.00, Pastels $55.00) *45.00*

Vase, 7" Tall, Feathers Pattern (Marigold $25.00, Pastels $50.00) *40.00*

Vase, Graceful Pattern (Marigold $65.00) *110.00*

Vase, Leaf Column Pattern (Marigold $40.00, White $65.00) *50.00*

Vase, Pulled Corn Husk Pattern, Purple or Green Only *2750.00*

Vase, Superb Drape Pattern, Aqua Opalescent Only *1250.00*

Vase, Tornado Pattern (Marigold $300.00, White $750.00, Blue $1000.00) *350.00*

Vase, Ribbed, Tornado Pattern (Marigold $325.00, Blue or Ice Blue $1250.00) *375.00*

Vase, Tree Trunk Pattern (Marigold $125.00, Pastels $225.00, Aqua or Peach Opalescent $1000.00) *175.00*

Northwood and Fenton were the two largest producers of Carnival glass. Harry North-wood obtained a good deal of experience in glassmaking by working for several firms during much of the late 19th century.

Northwood experimented with and produced more original colors than the other firms, particularly the pastel examples. Only red seems to be lacking in North-wood's Carnival glass. When Harry Northwood passed away in 1923, Northwood's output died with him, though Carnival items had already severely declined by the late teens.

CHAPTER 6

DEPRESSION GLASS

It had been nearly 40 years since the American nation had experienced a serious economic downswing. Many, including a new generation, had either forgotten or had not lived through the hard times of the 1890s. A major shock was on its way, for looming over the horizon was the nation's greatest and worst recession: the Great Depression of the late 1920s and the 1930s.

Several factors were responsible for this decline. The Agricultural Marketing Act of 1929 and the Hawley-Smoot tariff, enacted in 1930, increased rates on both farm and manufacturing goods. President Herbert Hoover signed the bill despite widespread opposition by most leading economists. The tariff alone raised the cost of living, encouraged inefficient production, and hampered exports. Foreign retaliation against expensive exports followed.

Through September of 1929, the stock market continued an upward trend, but the increase was due to speculation and manipulation of existing securities. Banks gambled heavily on this speculation, business overstocked inventories, consumer spending was suddenly reduced by a factor of 4, commodity prices rapidly declined, and interest rates soared. Despite these poor economic indicators, the stock market boomed, but it all came to a grinding halt on October 23, 1929. Security prices unexpectedly fell drastically from panic selling. The following day nearly 13 million shares were dumped on the market, a new record. Five short days later, the record was broken again as the volume reached 16 million shares.

The dumping of so many shares crashed the market and spawned the Great Depression. Thousands of banks closed, robbing nearly $3 billion from depositors; over 100,000 businesses went bankrupt; the Gross National Product was nearly cut in half; and millions of Americans were out of work. Even agricultural output suffered from poor weather conditions and incredible low prices. As a result, massive foreclosures followed.

Despite the nation's severe problems, more glass was manufactured during these years than at any other period in American history—an amazing feat considering the state of the nation's economy. A great battle ensued in the glass industry between houses producing handmade glass and those that made machineware. Handcut crystal was far superior in quality, but it was very expensive and lost out to mass-produced machine-made glass on price alone.

The new manufactured glass was flawed and cheaply made, but the price was several times lower than that of handmade glass. Flaws included noticeable air bubbles, slightly inconsistent coloring, tiny trails of excess glass, and so on. These minor flaws do not detract from the value, but chips and cracks render glass virtually worthless. The glass companies that folded during the Depression were those that did not convert to automation. Competing with "2 for a Nickel" tumblers and complete sets of tableware that sold for as little as $2 was impossible, especially considering the depressed state of the nation.

Machine-made glassware first appeared on the market in significant quantities after World War I. It sold well, but intense competition and price cutting followed. The profit margin on such products was very low, and a higher sales volume was required to sustain such profits—not an easy objective to achieve with a depression ahead. Cheap handmade imported glass also nearly tripled in the 1920s, providing even more competition for American glass manufacturers.

Despite these difficulties, the Depression era was a banner time for glass production in the United States. More patterns, shapes, and colors were produced in this period than at any other time, past or present, in American glass history. Depression glass includes nearly all glass made in America from the 1920s and 1930s. It was marketed to middle- and working-class Americans since it sold very inexpensively. The affordable glass could be purchased by the piece or in complete sets. It was available from general or department stores, factory outlets, mail order, and wherever house furnishings and kitchenware were sold. Table sets usually included soup and serving bowls, tumblers, plates, and saucers. Added to this could be creamers and sugars, punch sets, vases, candy and cracker jars, water pitchers, butter dishes, dessert dishes, serving platters, salt and pepper shakers, measuring cups, and nearly everything imaginable for the table. Some sets number over 100 distinct pieces in the same pattern!

The gaudy art and oily Carnival glass colors went out of style quickly and were replaced by the simple, singular, non-opaque colors of the new Depression glass. Color was added to much of America's gadgets in the Roaring Twenties, including such things as automobiles and appliances. Colored glass was used as cheap prizes at fairs and exhibitions; complete sets were given away as promotional items with furniture and appliance purchases; and smaller pieces served as bonuses in oatmeal cans, cereal boxes, and household supply containers. With the coming of Depression glass, glass was so inexpensive that it was no longer a luxury for the well-to-do only. Middle- and working-class Americans purchased it in large quantities.

Colored glass had been in existence for centuries, but the Depression was a time when it reached its peak in popularity. It was also a time when nearly every company producing glass in America perfected color and further experimented with new combinations. Pink was by far the most common, which is evidenced by the slightly lower value for pink Depression glass. In terms of quantity, green was a close second to pink, followed by amber. Other colors, though somewhat rarer, can also be found in glass of this period. To produce color, metallic as well as nonmetallic elements are necessary. Metals produce the most vibrant and distinct colors, while the nonmetallic agents of phosphorus, selenium, sulfur, and tellurium serve to heighten or intensify specific colors.

The metal manganese produces an amethyst color and is the oldest known, dating back to Egyptian times, around 1400 B.C. Copper imparts a light blue and was also utilized by the ancient Egyptians. Cobalt is responsible for the richest, deepest, and most powerful blue coloring. Cobalt blue has long been a staple throughout history. Examples of this beautiful blue glass were found in King Tut's tomb and in stained glass windows of 12th-century Europe. It was also used extensively as a pottery glaze for both the Tang and Ming dynasties of China.

Lead naturally produces the most outstanding clear crystal. Generally, the higher concentration of lead, the better clarity and quality of the crystal. Silver also produces crystal, though not as fine nor as cheaply as lead. Chromium is responsible for a dark green color that can be heightened by other elements. Iron can be mixed with chromium for a darker green or with sulfur and carbon to produce amber-colored glass. Manufacturers usually avoid sand containing high concentrations of iron, since it tends to make glass a murky green or dull brown. Gold, one of the more expensive coloring agents, imparts a brilliant ruby red color. Andread Cassius is usually credited with this discovery in 1685. Luxurious ruby red glass generally has a higher value than most other colors because of the addition of gold. Rarer colors exist too, such as a prominent bright yellow produced from uranium and a smoky gray glass from nickel.

Aside from coloring, decorating techniques flourished during the Depression years. Some hand etching and copper wheel engraving survived, but technological advances made it possible for machines to do the work more quickly and efficiently. The quality did suffer to some extent, but the labor savings alone more than made up for it. Crackle glass was made by dipping hot glass fresh from a machine mold into cold water to induce numerous cracks over the entire surface of the glass. It was then necessary to reheat the cracked glass and reform it within the mold. Frosted glass gained some popularity; it involved a complete light acid etching over the entire exterior surface of the glass object. The result was a murky light gray coloring.

Machines applied enameling in exactly the right position, which was much quicker than application by hand. Enameled glass was then refired to fuse the paint-like substance permanently. Silk screens were also used to apply patterns, monograms, crests, and so forth. Even decals were fired on some cheaper glassware. Aside from these numerous innovations, the most permanent trademark decorating technique applied to Depression glass was simple patented patterns pressed into molds by machine.

The popularity of Depression glass faltered in the late 1930s as Americans tired of the colored glass. A return to crystal, as well as new technological advances in ceramics and plastics, ended one of the most notable and prolific periods in American glass history. Depression glass was packed away for years until collectors of the 1960s began reassembling sets. Depression glass popularity ever since has produced a multitude of collectors; skyrocketing prices; numerous clubs, books, and newsletters; and simply the most popular glass collecting medium in America.

ADAM JEANNETTE GLASS COMPANY, 1932–1934

Object	Price
Ashtray	$20.00
Bowl, 4¾"	10.00
Bowl, 5¾"	12.00
Bowl, 7¾"	16.00
Bowl, 9", with Cover	50.00
Bowl, 10" Oval	20.00
Butter Dish with Cover (Green Is Rare—$500)	75.00
Butter Dish with Cover (Sierra Pattern)	600.00
Cake Plate	20.00
Candlestick	35.00
Candy Jar with Cover	75.00
Coaster	15.00
Creamer	15.00
Cup	20.00
Lamp	250.00
Pitcher, Milk, 1 qt.	40.00
Plate, 6"	5.00

Plate, 7³/₄" Square $10.00
Plate, 7³/₄" Round 50.00
Plate, 9" Square 20.00
Plate, 9" Grill, 3 Divisions 20.00
Platter, 11³/₄" 25.00
Relish Dish 15.00
Salt and Pepper Shakers 75.00
Saucer, 6" Square 5.00
Saucer, 6" Round 50.00
Sherbet 25.00
Sugar with Cover 35.00
Tumbler, Several Styles 30.00
Vase, 7¹/₂" (Pink Is Rare—$200) ....

A few odd pieces were made in yellow and opaque blue (or delphite); triple the above prices. With most patterns, green is slightly more valuable than pink, but the "Adam" pattern is an exception. A good deal of green is available along with the pink. The pattern contains a large central flower with vertical ribbing.

There are a few rare pieces including two versions of the original butter dish. Be careful that the "Adam Sierra" butter dish bottom or top is not mixed up with the plain "Adam" or plain "Sierra" pattern (see the "Sierra" listings).

Also note that the butter dish has been reproduced, but the new color is shaded more lightly than the original.

One final comment is that the candy lid and sugar lid are identical, a common occurrence in Jeannette's glassware.

AMERICAN PIONEER   LIBERTY WORKS, 1931–1934

Object	Price
Bowl, 5", 2-Handled	.$15.00
Bowl with Cover, 8³/₄"	.85.00
Bowl, 9", 2-Handled	.20.00
Bowl with Cover, 9³/₄"	.100.00
Bowl, 10³/₄"	.50.00
Candlestick	.40.00
Candy Jar with Cover, 2 Varieties (Narrow and Wide)	.100.00
Cheese and Cracker Set, 2-Piece, Plate with Indentation and Matching Compote	.50.00
Coaster	.20.00
Creamer	.20.00
Cup	.12.00
Dresser Set, 2 Cologne Bottles with Stoppers, Powder Jar, and Matching Tray	.350.00
Goblet	.40.00
Ice Bucket or Pail	.50.00
Lamp	.100.00
Mayonnaise Dish	.75.00
Pitcher with Cover, 5" Tall	.150.00
Pitcher with Cover, 7" Tall	.200.00
Plate, 6"	.12.00
Plate, 6", 2-Handled	.15.00
Plate, 8"	.10.00

Plate, 11½", 2-Handled *$15.00*
Saucer *5.00*
Sherbet *20.00*
Sugar, 2-Handled *20.00*
Tumbler, Several Styles *30.00*
Vase, 7" Tall, Several Styles *75.00*
Vase, 9" Tall *225.00*
Whiskey Tumbler, 2¼" Tall, 2 oz. *50.00*
Wine Goblet *35.00*

Color and size variances are often found in nearly if not all Depression patterns. Differing shades of green are quite common in the "American Pioneer" pattern. Piece sizes often vary because of mold or manufacturing changes.

Primary colors include pink, green, and crystal. For crystal, reduce the above prices somewhat—25%. A few pieces have also been discovered in amber; double the above-listed prices. "American Pioneer" is a round hobnail pattern.

AMERICAN SWEETHEART   MACBETH-EVANS GLASS
COMPANY, 1930–1936

Object	Pink
Bowl, 3¾" or 4½"	*$35.00*
Bowl, 6"	*10.00*
Bowl, 9" or 9½"	*35.00*
Bowl, 10", Oval	*40.00*
Bowl, 18" Console	*300.00*
Creamer	*7.50*
Cup	*10.00*
Pitcher, 2 qt.	*400.00*
Pitcher, 2½ qt.	*450.00*
Plate, 6" or 6½"	*3.00*
Plate, 8"	*8.00*
Plate, 9"	*10.00*
Plate, 9¾", 10¼", or 11"	*15.00*
Plate, 12"	*17.50*
Platter, 13" Oval	*35.00*
Platter, 15½" Round	*175.00*
Salt and Pepper Shakers	*300.00*
Saucer	*3.00*
Sherbet	*15.00*
Sugar Dish	*7.50*
Tid-bit, 2-Tier	*75.00*
Tumbler, Various Styles	*60.00*

"American Sweetheart" comes in a wide variety of opaque or nearly opaque colors. A light, nearly transparent milk white, a deep cobalt blue, ruby red, beige, and some pieces trimmed in gold can all be found. Blue and red are beautiful but rare (double the above-listed prices).

The pattern contains a slightly irregular edge caused by sets of three vertical ribs. The ribbing is only on the edges for the flatter pieces.

AUNT POLLY   U.S. GLASS COMPANY, LATE 1920S

Object	Blue
Bowl, 4³/₄"	$20.00
Bowl, 5¹/₂", 1 Handle Tab	.25.00
Bowl, 7¹/₄" Oval, 2-Handled	.30.00
Bowl, 8"	.30.00
Bowl, 8¹/₂" Oval	.55.00
Butter Dish with Cover	.250.00
Candy Jar with Cover, 2-Handled	.500.00
Compote, 5¹/₄", Footed, 2-Handled	.75.00
Creamer	.37.50
Pitcher, 1¹/₂ qt.	.200.00
Plate, 6"	.12.00
Plate, 8"	.15.00
Salt and Pepper Shakers	.225.00
Sherbet	.15.00
Sugar Dish with Cover	.150.00
Tumbler, 3¹/₂" Tall, 8 oz.	.35.00
Tumbler, 6¹/₂" Tall, Footed	.50.00

"Aunt Polly" patterned glass is difficult to find in perfect condition. Minor flaws are evident in much Depression glass, but the seams and mold lines are rather heavy and uneven with this pattern. The pattern is diamond on the bottom half and paneled on the top half (plates are just the opposite).

The blue is a light color and is the most popular, while there are varying shades of green and a few iridescent pieces (cut the price in half for colors other than blue).

AURORA   HAZEL ATLAS GLASS COMPANY, LATE 1930S

Object	Price
Bowl, 4¹/₂"	$25.00
Bowl, 5¹/₂"	.15.00
Cup	.10.00
Pitcher, Milk, 4¹/₂" Tall	.20.00
Plate, 6¹/₂"	.10.00

Depression glass, "Aurora" pattern. Drawing by Mark Pickvet.

Saucer *$5.00*
Tumbler, 4³/₄" Tall . . . . *.20.00*

The prices are primarily for cobalt blue, which is the desirable color. Pieces were also made in pink and green.

AVOCADO (NO. 601)   INDIANA GLASS COMPANY, 1923–1933

Object	*Price*
Bowl, 5¹/₄", 2-Handled	*$30.00*
Bowl, 7", 1 Handle	*.25.00*
Bowl, 7¹/₂"	*.40.00*
Bowl, 8" Oval, 2-Handled	*.45.00*
Bowl, 9¹/₂"	*.100.00*
Creamer	*.35.00*
Cup	*.35.00*
Pitcher, 1 qt.	*.750.00*
Plate, 6¹/₂"	*.15.00*
Plate, 8¹/₄"	*.20.00*
Plate, 10¹/₄" Cake, 2-Handled	*.50.00*
Relish	*.25.00*
Saucer	*.25.00*
Sherbet	*.50.00*
Sugar	*.35.00*
Tumbler	*.150.00*

The primary colors in this pattern are pink and green, with a bit of crystal. Reproductions abound in this pattern as is typical with the Indiana Glass Company. The "Avocado" pattern was remade in the 1970s under the Tiara product line in pink, frosted pink, yellow, blue, red, amber, amethyst, and dark green.

BEADED BLOCK   IMPERIAL GLASS COMPANY, 1927–1930S

Object	*Price*
Bowl, 4¹/₂", 5¹/₂", 6", or 6¹/₂"; with or without Handles	*$10.00*
Bowl, 7¹/₂" or 8¹/₄"	*.15.00*
Celery Dish	*.15.00*
Compote	*.16.00*
Creamer	*.17.50*
Marmalade Dish	*.12.00*
Pitcher, 1 pt.	*.100.00*
Plate, 7³/₄" Square	*.5.00*
Plate, 8³/₄"	*.12.00*
Sugar	*.17.50*
Vase, 6", Footed	*.15.00*

"Beaded Block" comes in a wide variety of colors, primarily green, pink, and amber. For crystal, cut the above prices by half to a quarter. Other colors include blue, vaseline, iridescent, red, opalescent, and milk white (double the above prices).

The pattern contains squares separated by vertical and horizontal beaded rows. Imperial reproduced a few of these but all of Imperial's reproductions are marked "IG" on the bottom.

BLOCK OR BLOCK OPTIC HOCKING GLASS
COMPANY, 1929–1933

Object	Price
Bowl, 4¼" or 5¼"	*$7.50*
Bowl, 7"	*15.00*
Bowl, 8½"	*20.00*
Butter Dish with Cover	*50.00*
Candlestick	*40.00*
Candy Jar with Cover	*50.00*
Cocktail Glass, 4¼" Tall	*30.00*
Compote	*35.00*
Creamer, Several Styles	*12.50*
Cup, Several Styles	*6.00*
Goblet, Several Styles	*30.00*
Ice Bucket	*35.00*
Mug	*30.00*
Pitcher, Water, Several Styles	*75.00*
Plate, 6"	*3.00*
Plate, 8"	*4.00*
Plate, 9"	*10.00*
Plate, 9" Grill (Divided)	*15.00*
Plate, 10¼"	*20.00*
Reamer	*10.00*
Salt and Pepper Shakers	*75.00*
Sandwich Server with Handle	*50.00*
Saucer	*8.00*
Sherbet, Several Styles	*10.00*
Sugar, Several Styles	*12.50*
Tumbler, 3" Tall	*15.00*
Tumbler, Several Styles	*17.50*
Tumble-Up, Bottle with Matching Tumbler	*50.00*
Vase, 5¾" Tall	*200.00*

Left: Depression glass, "Avocado" pattern. Drawing by Mark Pickvet. Right: Depression glass, "Block" pattern. Drawing by Mark Pickvet.

Whiskey Tumbler *$25.00*
Wine Glass .... *.35.00*

The basic colors are green, pink, and yellow. A few frosted pieces exist but are not highly desired (reduce the above prices by half). The covered butter dish comes in a few rare colors such as cobalt blue ($400) and opalescent green ($200).

The pattern consists of ridged horizontal ribbing intersecting with vertical ribbing to create the block effect.

BOW KNOT   UNKNOWN MANUFACTURER, DEPRESSION YEARS

Object	*Green*
Bowl, 4½"	*$10.00*
Bowl, 5½"	*.14.00*
Cup	*.6.00*
Plate, 7"	*.8.00*
Sherbet	*.10.00*
Tumbler, 5" Tall, with or without Foot	*.15.00*

In her classic books on Depression glass, Hazel Marie Weatherman listed this pattern as unknown, and no one has identified it yet!

The only color is green, and the center consists of a hexagonal flower surrounded by scrolling bowlike designs.

CAMEO OR BALLERINA OR DANCING GIRL
HOCKING GLASS COMPANY, 1930–1934

Object	*Price*
Bowl, 4¾"	*.50.00*
Bowl, 5½"	*.25.00*
Bowl, 7¼", 8¼", or 9"	*.35.00*
Bowl, 10" Oval	*.20.00*
Bowl, 11", 3 Legs	*.50.00*
Butter Dish with Cover	*.175.00*
Cake Plate, 10", 3 Legs	*.15.00*
Cake Plate, 10½"	*.50.00*
Candlestick	*.35.00*
Candy Jar with Cover, 4" Tall	*.50.00*
Candy Jar with Cover, 6½" Tall	*.75.00*
Compote	*.25.00*
Cookie Jar with Cover	*.50.00*
Creamer	*.20.00*
Cup	*.10.00*
Decanter with Stopper, 10" Tall	*.125.00*
Domino Tray	*.100.00*
Goblet, 6" Tall	*.50.00*

Depression glass, "Cameo" pattern. Photo by Robin Rainwater.

Ice Bucket, 2 Tab Handles *$200.00*
Jam Jar with Cover, 2" Tall *150.00*
Pitcher, Milk, 1 pt. *200.00*
Pitcher, 1 qt. *50.00*
Pitcher, Water, 2 qt. *50.00*
Plate, 6", 7", or 8" *5.00*
Plate, 8¹/₂" Square *25.00*
Plate, 9¹/₂", 10", or 10¹/₂" *10.00*
Plate, 10¹/₂", 2 Tab Handles *12.00*
Platter, 12", 2 Tab Handles *25.00*
Relish, Footed, 3 Divisions *25.00*
Salt and Pepper Shakers *75.00*
Sandwich Server with Center Handle (Rare) *3000.00*
Saucer, 6" *4.00*
Saucer with Ring *125.00*
Sherbet, 3" Tall *10.00*
Sherbet, 5" Tall *25.00*
Sugar *20.00*
Tumbler, Various Styles *25.00*
Vase, 5³/₄" *125.00*
Vase, 8" Tall *20.00*
Water Bottle *20.00*
Wineglass, 4" Tall *50.00*

"Cameo" is the queen of Depression glass patterns. It is very beautiful, highly collectible, and easily recognizable with the cameo dancing girl design. Pink, green, and yellow are the primary colors. A few pieces were made in crystal with a platinum rim (reduce the above prices by 25%); a few others appear in frosted green (reduce the above prices by 50%).

Reproductions of the salt and pepper shakers in pink, green, and cobalt blue (1970s) exist, but the colors are weaker and easily distinguished from the originals.

Miniature sets that contain about 40 pieces have been reproduced in pink, green, and yellow and are easily distinguished because of their tiny size (see the chapter on modern collectible glass for pricing information).

CHERRY BLOSSOM JEANNETTE GLASS COMPANY,
1930–1939

Object	Price
Bowl, 4³/₄"	$12.00
Bowl, 5³/₄"	.25.00
Bowl, 7³/₄" or 8¹/₂"	.35.00
Bowl, 9" Oval	.25.00
Bowl, 9", 2-Handled	.20.00
Bowl, 10¹/₂", 3 Legs	.45.00
Butter Dish with Cover	.75.00
Cake Plate, 10¹/₄", 3 Legs	.20.00
Coaster	.10.00
Creamer	.12.50
Cup	.15.00
Mug	.150.00
Pitcher, Milk, 1 qt.	.40.00
Pitcher, 1¹/₂ qt.	.45.00
Plate, 6"	.5.00
Plate, 7"	.12.00
Plate, 9"	.14.00
Plate, Grill, 3 Divisions	.20.00
Platter, 11" Oval	.25.00
Platter, 13" Oval	.40.00
Platter, 13" Oval, 3 Divisions	.50.00
Salt and Pepper Shakers	.1000.00
Saucer	.3.00
Sherbet	.12.00
Sugar with Cover	.25.00
Tray, 10¹/₂"	.15.00
Tumbler, Various Styles	.20.00

*Depression glass, "Cherry Blossom"
pattern. Reproduced from a 1935
advertisement.*

*Creamer *$35.00*
*Sugar .... *.35.00*
*Plate, 6" .... *.10.00*
*Cup .... *.30.00*
*Saucer .... *.6.00*
*14 Piece Set .... *.250.00*

The primary colors are pink and green. A few were made in a light opaque blue sometimes referred to as delphite blue (same prices as above). A few others were made in yellow, amber, and opaque green; quadruple the above prices.

A few reproductions have been made in "Cherry Blossom," including water sets (pitchers and tumblers), bowls, cups and saucers, butter dishes, salt and pepper shakers, the 2-handled tray, and the cake plate (cut the above prices in half). The colors differ in the reproductions and include brighter versions of pink and green, yellow, cobalt blue, ruby red, and transparent blue.

*The pieces above marked with an asterisk (*) were part of a children's miniature set.

CHERRYBERRY   U.S. GLASS COMPANY, EARLY 1930S

Object	*Price*
Bowl, 4"	*$8.00*
Bowl, 6¼"	*.40.00*
Bowl, 6½" or 7½"	*.15.00*
Butter Dish with Cover	*.150.00*
Compote	*.15.00*
Creamer, Small	*.15.00*
Creamer, Large, 4½" Tall	*.20.00*
Olive Dish, 5", 1 Tab Handle	*.15.00*
Pickle Dish, 8¼" Oval	*.15.00*
Pitcher	*.150.00*
Plate, 6"	*.6.00*
Plate, 7½"	*.8.00*
Sherbet	*.6.00*
Sugar, Small (Open)	*.15.00*
Sugar, Large, with Cover	*.35.00*
Tumbler	*.20.00*

The basic colors are pink and green; however, most pieces can be found in crystal and a light iridized marigold color (reduce the above prices by 25% for crystal or marigold).

The iridized pieces are often confused with earlier Carnival glass because of the similar marigold color. "Cherryberry" is very similar to "Strawberry" except for the difference in the berry pattern.

CIRCLE   HOCKING GLASS COMPANY, 1930S

Object	*Price*
Bowl, 4½" or 5½"	*$6.00*
Bowl, 8"	*.12.00*

Left: Depression glass, "Circle" pattern. Photo by Robin Rainwater. Right: Depression glass, "Cloverleaf" pattern. Drawing by Mark Pickvet.

Bowl, 9½"	*$14.00*
Creamer	*.7.50*
Cup	*.5.00*
Decanter	*.30.00*
Goblet	*.10.00*
Pitcher, 2 or 2½ qt.	*.30.00*
Plate, 6"	*.3.00*
Plate, 8¼"	*.5.00*
Reamer (Fits the 2½ qt. Pitcher)	*.10.00*
Saucer	*.3.00*
Sherbet	*.5.00*
Sugar	*.7.50*
Tumbler, Various Styles	*.10.00*

Pink and green are the two primary colors. Many goblets have green stems with crystal bowls (same price). As with a good deal of Depression glass, color variations from one batch to the next often vary, and many pieces of "Circle" have a yellowish green tone.

Many pieces have a star on the bottom, but all contain horizontal circular ribbing.

CLOVERLEAF   HAZEL ATLAS GLASS COMPANY, 1930–1936

Object	*Price*
Ashtray	*$15.00*
Bowl, 4" or 5"	*.20.00*
Bowl, 7" or 8"	*.40.00*
Candy Dish with Cover	*.50.00*
Creamer	*.15.00*
Cup	*.5.00*
Plate, 6"	*.5.00*
Plate, 8"	*.7.50*
Plate, 10¼" Grill, 3 Divisions	*.20.00*
Salt and Pepper Shakers	*.35.00*
Saucer	*.3.00*
Sherbet	*.5.00*
Sugar, 2-Handled	*.15.00*
Tumbler, Various Styles	*.25.00*

The primary colors are pink, green, and yellow. The pattern was also produced in black (double the above prices).

The clover leaves are placed between two circular bands near the tops or outer rims of each piece.

COLONIAL BLOCK   HAZEL ATLAS GLASS COMPANY, EARLY 1930S

Object	Price
Bowl, 4"	$6.00
Bowl, 7"	15.00
Butter Dish with Cover	50.00
Butter Tub with Cover	40.00
Candy Jar with Cover	40.00
Creamer	10.00
Goblet	10.00
Pitcher	35.00
Sugar Dish with Cover, 2-Handled	20.00

The prices above are for green and pink. For crystal and reproduction milk glass, reduce the above prices by 50%.

Most pieces in this pattern are marked with the Hazel-Atlas "H" and "A" overlapping symbol. This symbol is sometimes confused with both Atlas-Mason (overlapping "A" and "M") and Anchor-Hocking because of the "A" and "H" beginning letters. See the history section on Hazel Atlas and the collection of symbols for the true Hazel-Atlas symbol.

The block pattern is similar to "Block Optic" except that "Colonial Block" contains a star in the bottom or center of each piece.

COLONIAL FLUTED OR ROPE   FEDERAL GLASS COMPANY, 1928–1933

Object	Price
Bowl, 4"	$5.00
Bowl, 6"	8.00
Bowl, 6½" or 7½"	15.00
Creamer	6.00

Left: Depression glass, "Colonial Block" pattern. Drawing by Mark Pickvet. Right: Depression glass, "Colonial Rope" pattern. Drawing by Mark Pickvet.

Cup *$4.00*
Plate, 6" .... *.3.00*
Plate, 8" .... *.4.00*
Saucer .... *.2.00*
Sherbet .... *.5.00*
Sugar with Cover, 2-Handled .... *.15.00*

The basic colors are green and pink. Some pieces are marked with the Federal trademark ("F" inscribed in a shield).

The pattern is vertically ribbed with a roping on the outer or top edge.

COLONIAL KNIFE AND FORK   HOCKING GLASS
COMPANY, 1934–1938

Object	*Price*
Bowl, 4½", 5½", or 7"	*$40.00*
Bowl, 9"	*.25.00*
Bowl, 10" Oval	*.30.00*
Butter Dish with Cover	*.50.00*
Celery Dish	*.100.00*
Cheese Dish with Cover	*.100.00*
Claret Glass, 5¼" Tall	*.20.00*
Cocktail Glass, 4" Tall	*.20.00*
Cordial Glass	*.25.00*
Creamer	*.20.00*
Cup	*.10.00*
Goblet, 5¾" Tall	*.25.00*
Mug, 4½" Tall	*.125.00*
Pitcher, 7" or 8" Tall, with or without Ice Lip	*.50.00*
Plate, 6"	*.4.00*
Plate, 8½"	*.6.00*
Plate, 10"	*.35.00*
Plate, 10" Grill, 3 Divisions	*.25.00*

 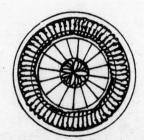 

Left: Depression glass, "Colonial Knife and Fork" pattern. Photo by Robert Darnold. Center: Depression glass, "Coronation" pattern. Drawing by Mark Pickvet. Right: Depression glass, "Crackle" pattern. Photo by Robin Rainwater.

Platter, 10" Oval *$25.00*
Salt and Pepper Shakers *125.00*
Saucer *4.00*
Sherbet *12.00*
Sugar with Cover, 2-Handled *35.00*
Tumbler, 3", 3¹/₄", or 4" Tall, with or without Feet *25.00*
Tumbler, 5" or Taller, with or without Feet *40.00*
Whiskey Tumbler, 2¹/₂" Tall, 1¹/₂ oz. *10.00*
Wineglass, 4¹/₂" Tall *20.00*

The basic colors are pink, green, and crystal. For crystal, reduce the above prices by 50%. A few pieces were produced in milk white too (same price as listed above) as well as the darker royal ruby (quadruple the above prices). The pattern consists of wide arched flutes with extra vertical ribbing between the flutes.

CORONATION OR BANDED RIB OR SAXON
HOCKING GLASS COMPANY, 1936–1940

Object	*Price*
Bowl, 4¹/₄"	*$10.00*
Bowl, 4¹/₄", 2 Tab Handles	*5.00*
Bowl, 6¹/₂"	*5.00*
Bowl, 8"	*25.00*
Bowl, 8", 2 Tab Handles	*10.00*
Cup	*5.00*
Pitcher	*150.00*
Plate, 6"	*2.00*
Plate, 8¹/₂"	*5.00*
Saucer	*2.00*
Sherbet	*4.00*
Tumbler, 5" Tall, Footed	*20.00*

The above-listed prices are for pink and green. Saucers were made in crystal ($1.00), and several pieces were also made in the darker royal ruby (double the above prices).

The wide vertical ribbing ends about halfway up, with very thin banded rims spaced closely together.

CRACKLE GLASS   VARIOUS COMPANIES, 1920S–1930S

Object	*Price*
Candlestick, "By Cracky" Pattern (L.E. Smith)	*$12.00*
Candy Jar, "By Cracky" Pattern (L.E. Smith)	*35.00*
Frog, "By Cracky" Pattern (L.E. Smith)	*20.00*
Pitcher, Iced Tea, with Cover, "Craquel" Pattern (U.S. Glass)	*100.00*
Pitcher, Iced Tea, with Cover, Jack Frost Design (Federal)	*90.00*
Pitcher, Lemonade, Jack Frost Design (Federal)	*75.00*
Pitcher, Water, Jack Frost Design, Depression Colors (Federal)	*75.00*
Plate, 8" Octagonal, "By Cracky" Pattern (L.E. Smith)	*18.00*

L. E. SMITH GLASS CO.
MOUNT PLEASANT, PA.

1.   No. 33 Candle Holder
2.   3 inch Flower Block
3.   8 inch Octagon Plate
4.   Luncheon Set with Sherbet

MADE IN CRYSTAL, CANARY AND AMBER

Depression glass, "Crackle" pattern. Reproduced from a 1928 advertisement.

Depression glass, "Cube" pattern. Reproduced from a 1930 advertisement.

Left: Depression glass, "Cube" pattern. Photo by Robin Rainwater. Right: Depression glass, "Cube" pattern. Photo by Robin Rainwater.

Sherbet, "By Cracky" Pattern (L.E. Smith) *$10.00*
Tumbler, Iced Tea, Jack Frost Design (Federal) .... *.15.00*
Tumbler, Lemonade, Jack Frost Design (Federal) .... *.14.00*
Tumbler, Water, Jack Frost Design (Federal) .... *.14.00*

"Crackle" glass was made by plunging hot objects into lukewarm or cold water to induce cracks; the object was then refired. It was produced by many but not in huge quantities. There are still good buys out there in Depression-style "Crackle" glass.

The colors are usually amber, green, and pink. For crystal, reduce the above-listed prices by half.

CUBE OR CUBIST   JEANNETTE GLASS COMPANY, 1929–1933

Object	*Price*
Bowl, 4½"	*$6.00*
Bowl, 6½"	*.10.00*
Butter Dish with Cover	*.75.00*
Candy Jar with Cover	*.35.00*
Coaster	*.5.00*
Creamer	*.6.00*
Cup	*.6.00*
Pitcher	*.200.00*
Plate, 6"	*.4.00*
Plate, 8"	*.6.00*
Powder Jar with Cover, 3 Legs	*.20.00*
Salt and Pepper Shakers	*.35.00*
Saucer	*.3.00*
Sherbet	*.6.00*
Sugar with Cover	*.14.00*
Tumbler, 4" Tall	*.40.00*

The basic colors are pink and green, but quite a few other colors exist. For crystal, amber, or milk white, reduce the above prices by half.

"Cube" is often mixed up with many similar pressed crystal patterns, such as Fostoria's "American" pattern.

CUPID   PADEN CITY GLASS COMPANY, 1930S

Object	*Price*
Bowl, 8½" Footed	*$100.00*
Bowl, 9¼" Footed	*.90.00*
Bowl with Center Handle, 9¼"	*.100.00*
Bowl, 10½" or 11"	*.90.00*
Cake Plate, 11¾"	*.95.00*
Cake Stand, Footed	*.85.00*
Candlestick	*.55.00*
Candy Jar with Lid, with or without Foot	*.125.00*
Compote	*.75.00*

Depression glass. "Cupid" pattern. Reproduced from a 1929 Paden City patent submission.

Creamer	*$75.00*
Ice Bucket or Tub	*150.00*
Lamp with Silver Trimming	*350.00*
Mayonnaise Dish	*125.00*
Plate, 10½"	*75.00*
Samovar	*800.00*
Sugar, 2-Handled	*75.00*
Tray with Center Handle, 10¾"	*80.00*
Tray, 11", Footed	*125.00*
Vase, 8¼"	*250.00*
Vase, Fan-Shaped	*175.00*

The primary colors are pink and light blue, but pieces have been found in Cobalt blue, black, and yellow (increase the above prices by 50%). A samovar is an urn with a spigot at its base. Samovars originated in Russia decades ago. Two winged Cupid figures face each other between a cameolike bell in this pattern.

DIAMOND QUILTED OR FLAT DIAMOND
IMPERIAL GLASS COMPANY, LATE 1920S–EARLY 1930S

Object	*Price*
Bowl, 4¾", 5", or 7"	*$8.00*
Bowl, 5½", One Tab Handle	*.8.00*
Bowl, 10½"	*15.00*
Cake Salver, 10"	*50.00*
Candlestick	*12.50*
Candy Jar with Cover, Footed	*75.00*
Compote with Cover, 11½"	*75.00*
Cordial	*10.00*
Creamer	*7.50*
Cup	*10.00*
Goblet, 6" Tall	*10.00*
Ice Bucket	*50.00*
Mayonnaise Set with Ladle, Plate, and Compote	*50.00*
Pitcher, 2 qt.	*50.00*
Plate, 6"	*4.00*
Plate, 7" or 8"	*5.00*
Platter, 14"	*10.00*
Punch Bowl with Stand	*400.00*
Sandwich Server with Center Handle	*35.00*

Saucer *$4.00*
Sherbet ....*.5.00*
Sugar, 2-Handled ....*.7.50*
Tumbler, Several Styles ....*.8.00*
Whiskey, 1½ oz. ....*.10.00*
Wineglass, 2 or 3 oz. ....*.10.00*

The prices listed above are for pink and green. For the rarer colors, such as light blue, black, red, and amber, double the above prices; for crystal, reduce them by 50%. Be careful not to confuse this pattern with a similar diamond pattern by Hazel Atlas. The quilting on Hazel Atlas pieces ends in a straight line at the top of each piece, while that of Imperial ends unevenly in points at the top.

DIANA   FEDERAL GLASS COMPANY, 1937–1941

Object	*Price*
Ashtray, 3½"	*$3.00*
Bowl, 5", 5½", or 9"	*.8.00*
Bowl, 11" or 12"	*.10.00*
Candy Jar with Cover	*.25.00*
Coaster	*.5.00*
Creamer	*.7.50*
Cup	*.5.00*
Cup, 2 oz. Demitasse	*.10.00*
Plate, 6"	*..2.00*
Plate, 9½" or 11¾"	*.8.00*
Platter, 11¾"	*.10.00*
Platter, 12" Oval	*.12.00*
Salt and Pepper Shakers	*.75.00*
Saucer	*.2.00*
Saucer, Demitasse (4½")	*.5.00*
Sherbet	*.5.00*
Sugar, 2-Handled	*.7.50*
Tumbler	*.15.00*

Basic colors consist of pink and amber. For crystal, crystal trimmed in colors, or frosted pieces, reduce the above prices by 50%.

"Diana" is sometimes confused with spirals, swirls, and twisted patterns; however, the centers of "Diana" pieces are swirled where the others are plain. The shading also seems to be a little duller on the "Diana" pieces.

Depression glass, "Diana" pattern. Drawing by Mark Pickvet.

DOGWOOD OR APPLE BLOSSOM OR WILD ROSE   MACBETH-EVANS GLASS COMPANY, 1928–1932

Object	Price
Bowl, 5½"	.$20.00
Bowl, 8½"	.50.00
Bowl, 10¼"	.150.00
Cake Plate, 11" Footed	.200.00
Cake Plate, 13" Footed	.100.00
Creamer	.15.00
Cup	.10.00
Pitcher	.325.00
Plate, 6" or 8"	.7.50
Plate, 9¼"	.15.00
Plate, 10½" Grill, 3 Divisions	.15.00
Platter, 12" Salver	.20.00
Platter, 12" Oval	.300.00
Saucer	.5.00
Sherbet, Footed	.25.00
Sugar, 2-Handled	.10.00
Tid-Bit Set, 2-Tiered (8" and 12" Plates with Metal Handle)	.100.00
Tumbler, Several Styles	.35.00

The primary pieces include pink and green. For yellow, double the above prices; for the opaque cremax, monax, and crystal pieces, reduce the above prices by 50%.

Beware of undecorated glass made by MacBeth-Evans in the same shape as "Dogwood" patterned glass; sometimes it is passed off as this pattern but is worth much less.

DORIC   JEANNETTE GLASS COMPANY, 1935–1938

Object	Price
Bowl, 4½"	.$6.00
Bowl, 5½"	.30.00
Bowl, 8¼"	.10.00
Bowl, 9", 2-Handled	.10.00
Bowl, 9", Oval	.15.00

Depression glass, "Doric" pattern. Drawing by Mark Pickvet.

Butter Dish with Cover *$75.00*
Cake Plate, 10", 3 Legs *15.00*
Candy Dish, 3-Part *6.00*
Candy Dish, 3 Part in Metal Holder *40.00*
Candy Dish with Cover *35.00*
Coaster *10.00*
Creamer *7.50*
Cup *6.00*
Pitcher, 1 qt. *35.00*
Pitcher, 1½ qt. *400.00*
Plate, 6" *3.00*
Plate, 7" or 9" *12.00*
Plate, 9" Grill, 3 Divisions *14.00*
Platter, 12", Oval *15.00*
Relish *10.00*
Salt and Pepper Shakers *40.00*
Saucer *3.00*
Sherbet *10.00*
Sugar with Cover, 2-Handled *30.00*
Tray, 8" Square *15.00*
Tray, 10", 2-Handled *17.50*
Tumbler, Several Styles *50.00*

The primary colors are pink and green. For the rare opaque delphite blue, quadruple the above prices. A reproduction iridescent three-part candy dish was produced in the 1970s in the "Doric" pattern with the original molds and is priced at about $10.00. The candy and sugar lids are not interchangeable as in most Jeannette patterns since the candy lid is a little wider and much taller than the sugar lid. The complete relish set in "Doric" consists of the 8" × 8" bottom tray, two 4" × 4" top trays, and one 4" × 8" top tray.

DORIC AND PANSY   JEANNETTE GLASS COMPANY,
1937–1938

Object	*Price*
Bowl, 4½"	*$10.00*
Bowl, 8"	*50.00*
Bowl, 9", 2-Handled	*25.00*
Butter Dish with Cover	*450.00*
Cup	*15.00*
Creamer	*75.00*
Plate, 6"	*8.00*
Plate, 7" or 9"	*25.00*
Salt and Pepper Shakers	*325.00*
Saucer	*4.00*
Sugar, 2-Handled	*75.00*
Tray, 10", 2-Handled	*25.00*
Tumbler	*50.00*

DORIC AND PANSY   "PRETTY POLLY PARTY DISHES"
(CHILDREN'S SET)

Object	*Price*
Cup	.$30.00
Saucer	.4.00
Plate	.8.00
Creamer	.30.00
Sugar	.30.00
14-Piece Tea Set	.225.00

Colors consist of pink, green, and ultramarine. For crystal, reduce the above-listed prices by 50%. Color variations exist in the ultramarine, from a bluelike tint to almost green.

This pattern is a derivative of the plain "Doric" in that it has flowers (pansies) inserted where the original "Doric" has blank or clear glass.

EARLY AMERICAN SANDWICH   DUNCAN AND
MILLER GLASS COMPANY 1925–1930S

Object	*Price*
Ash Tray, 2³/₄" Square	.$5.00
Basket, 6" Tall	.65.00
Basket, 10" Tall	.50.00
Basket, 10" Tall, Ruffled	.65.00
Bonbon Dish with Handle	.14.00
Bonbon with Cover, 7¹/₂" Tall	.55.00
Bowl, 4"	.4.00
Bowl, 4" (Fits 6¹/₂" Plate)	.5.00
Bowl, 5"	.6.00
Bowl, 5", Footed	.8.00
Bowl, 6", 3 Styles	.7.00
Bowl, 6", Footed	.8.00
Bowl, 10", 3 Divisions	.20.00
Bowl, 11", 2" Tall, Serrated	.30.00
Bowl, 11¹/₂", Shallow (1¹/₂" Tall)	.10.00
Bowl, 11¹/₂", Crimped	.12.00
Bowl, 12", Oblong, 3³/₄" Tall	.22.00
Bowl, 12", Flared	.18.00
Butter Dish with Cover	.175.00
Candelabrum, 1-Light	.40.00
Candelabrum, 3-Light, 10"	.80.00
Candelabrum, 3-Light, 16"	.90.00
Candlestick, 4"	.6.00
Candlestick, 2-Branch, 5"	.16.00
Candlestick, 3-Branch, 5"	.18.00
Candy Jar with Cover, 5" Tall	.65.00
Candy Jar with Cover, 8¹/₂" Tall	.90.00
Cigarette Box with Cover	.35.00

Cigarette Holder, 3", Footed *$30.00*
Compote, 5¹/₂", Inner Liner *25.00*
Compote, 6" (2 Styles) *30.00*
Compote, 7¹/₂", Flared *40.00*
Cheese and Cracker Set, 2-Piece (13" Plate, 5¹/₂" Cheese Stand) *45.00*
Creamer, 3" Tall *14.00*
Creamer, 4" Tall *16.00*
Cruet with Stopper 5³/₄" Tall, 3 oz. *20.00*
Cup, 6 oz. *3.00*
Deviled Egg Platter, 12" (Holds 1 Dozen Eggs) *125.00*
Fruit Cup, 2¹/₂", 6 oz. *7.00*
Jelly Dish, 3" Diameter *5.00*
Ladle *20.00*
Lamp, Hurricane, 15" *100.00*
Mayonnaise, 2³/₄" Tall, 5" Diameter *6.00*
Parfait, 5¹/₄", 4 oz. *12.00*
Pickle Dish, Oval (7" × 3³/₄") *10.00*
Pitcher, Syrup, 1 pt. *70.00*
Pitcher, 1 qt. *100.00*
Plate, 5" *4.00*
Plate, 6" *5.00*
Plate, 6¹/₂" Indentation for 4" Finger Bowl *6.00*
Plate, 7" *6.00*
Plate, 8" *8.00*
Plate, 9¹/₂" *10.00*
Plate, 12" *12.00*
Plate, 12" Grill, 3 Divisions *16.00*
Plate, 13" *14.00*
Relish, Oval (7" × 3³/₄"), 3 Divisions *10.00*
Relish, Oval (10" × 4¹/₂"), 3 Divisions *10.00*
Relish, Rectangular (10¹/₂" × 6³/₄"), 3 Divisions *12.00*
Salt and Pepper Shakers with Glass Tops *50.00*
Salver, Cake, 12" *25.00*
Salver, Cake, 13" *30.00*
Saucer *3.00*
Sherbet, 4¹/₄", 5 oz. *8.00*
Stemware, 2³/₄", 5 oz., Low Foot *6.00*
Stemware, 4¹/₄" or 4¹/₂", 3 oz. *8.00*
Stemware, 5¹/₄", 5 oz. *10.00*
Stemware, 6", 9 oz. *12.00*
Sugar, 2³/₄" Tall, Low Footed, 2-Handled *14.00*
Sugar, 3¹/₄" Tall, Low Footed, 2-Handled *20.00*
Sugar Shaker, 13 oz. *18.00*
Sundae, 3¹/₂", 5 oz., Flared *14.00*
Tray, 6" Round, 1 Handle *6.00*
Tray, 8" Oval, 2 Handles *12.00*
Tray, 10" Oval *14.00*
Tray, Rectangular (10¹/₂" × 6³/₄") *12.00*
Tumbler, 3¹/₄" Tall, 5 oz., Footed *12.00*
Tumbler, 4³/₄" Tall, 9 oz., Footed *14.00*
Tumbler, 5¹/₄" or 5¹/₂" Tall *18.00*

Urn with Cover, 12" *$100.00*
Vase, 3" Tall, Footed *12.00*
Vase, 4½" Tall *12.00*
Vase, 5" Tall, Footed *20.00*
Vase, 10" Tall, Footed *40.00*

The primary colors are pink, green, and amber. For crystal, reduce the above prices by 50%. Duncan and Miller were the first to re-create the old "Sandwich" designs in the new automatic machine-pressed process of the Depression. Ruby red and a yellow-green color were added in the 1940s (same price as above).

Indiana later acquired a few of the molds and reproduced some items, but the colors are different. Indiana also developed their own "Sandwich" pattern that does not contain as many spirals as the original Duncan and Miller products. The prices actually tend to stay down because of the amount and different varieties of "Sandwich" out there.

ENGLISH HOBNAIL   WESTMORELAND GLASS COMPANY, 1920S–1970S

Object	*Price*
Ashtray, (Many Styles)	*$15.00*
Bowl, 4½", 5", or 6", Round or Square Styles	*18.00*
Bowl, 8"	*20.00*
Bowl, 8", Footed, 2-Handled	*50.00*
Bowl, 8" or 9", Oval	*20.00*
Bowl, 11" or 12"	*35.00*
Bowl, 12", Oval	*25.00*
Candlestick, 3½" Tall	*15.00*
Candlestick, 8½" Tall	*25.00*
Candy Jar with Cover, Small	*50.00*
Candy Jar with Cover, Large, 15" Tall	*200.00*
Celery Dish, 9" Tall	*18.00*
Celery Dish, 12" Tall	*20.00*
Cigarette Box	*25.00*
Claret Glass, 5 oz.	*20.00*
Cocktail Glass, 3 oz.	*15.00*
Cologne Bottle with Stopper	*30.00*
Cordial	*25.00*
Creamer	*20.00*
Cup	*15.00*
Decanter with Stopper	*100.00*
Demitasse Cup and Saucer	*25.00*
Egg Cup	*40.00*
Goblet, 6¼ oz.	*25.00*
Jam Jar with Cover	*35.00*
Lamp, 6¼" Tall	*50.00*
Lamp, 9¼" Tall	*100.00*
Pitcher, 1½ pt.	*150.00*
Pitcher, 1 qt.	*175.00*
Pitcher, 2 qt.	*200.00*

555/5oz. Toilet Bottle   555 Cig. Jar and Cover   555 Marmalade and Cover
(Notched)

Depression glass, "English Hobnail" pattern. Reproduced from a 1926 Westmoreland catalog.

555 Ftd. Sugar and Cream Set

Plate, 5½", 6½", or 7½" *$6.00*
Plate, 8", Round or Square .... *.8.00*
Plate, 10" .... *.20.00*
Salt Dip, 2", Footed .... *.20.00*
Salt and Pepper Shakers .... *.100.00*
Saucer .... *.4.00*
Sherbet .... *.15.00*
Sugar, 2-Handled .... *.20.00*
Tumbler, Several Styles .... *.15.00*
Vase .... *.155.00*
Whiskey, 1½ oz. .... *.20.00*
Wineglass, 2 oz. .... *.20.00*

The colors covered in the pricing include pink, green, amber, and a light copper blue. For cobalt blue, double the above prices; for crystal, reduce them by 50%. In the earliest of Westmoreland's advertisements, "English Hobnail" was referred to as a "Sandwich Reproduction." It is also Westmoreland's #555 pattern.

FIRE-KING DINNERWARE (PHILBE FIRE-KING)
HOCKING GLASS COMPANY, 1937–1938

Object   *Price*
Bowl, 5½" or 7¼" *$30.00*

Depression glass, Philbe Fire-King dinnerware. Reproduced from a 1937 patent design.

Bowl, 10" Oval . . . . *.$50.00*
Candy Jar with Cover . . . . *.400.00*
Cookie Jar with Cover . . . . *.600.00*
Creamer . . . . *.75.00*
Cup . . . . *.75.00*
Goblet . . . . *.125.00*
Pitcher, 1 qt. . . . . *.750.00*
Pitcher, 2 qt. . . . . *.1000.00*
Plate, 6" or 8" . . . . *.35.00*
Plate, 10" or 10½" . . . . *.50.00*
Plate, 10½" Grill, 3 Divisions . . . . *.50.00*
Platter, 11½" . . . . *.40.00*
Platter, 12", 2 Tab Handled . . . . *.60.00*
Saucer, 6" . . . . *.25.00*
Sugar, 2-Handled . . . . *.75.00*
Tumbler, Several Styles . . . . *.75.00*

The primary colors include pink, green, and a light copper blue. For crystal, reduce the above prices by 50%. The original "Fire-King Dinnerware" was introduced by Hocking near the end of the Depression glass era. Many pieces are trimmed in platinum. After the Depression and the merger with Anchor, an incredible amount of Fire-King products can be found in a wide variety of styles (see Chapter 7).

FLORAL AND DIAMOND BAND U.S. GLASS
COMPANY, 1920S

Object	*Price*
Bowl, 4½"	*.$6.00*
Bowl, 5¾", 2 Handles	*.8.00*
Bowl, 8"	*.12.00*
Butter Dish with Cover	*.125.00*
Compote	*.12.00*
Creamer	*.12.50*
Pitcher	*.100.00*
Plate, 8"	*.25.00*
Sherbet	*.6.00*

Sugar with Cover, 2 Handles $75.00
Tumbler, 4" or 5" Tall *20.00*

Colors include pink and many varying shades of green, ranging from light green to bluish or aqua-greens. For marigold or black pieces, double the above prices; for crystal, reduce them by 50%.

Some green is nearly opaque and appears frosted or satinized. The mold lines also tend to be a little rough with "Floral and Diamond Band" articles.

The pattern contains a large six-petal flower with diamond bands near the top or outer rim. The diamond banding is not complete for it is cut off by smaller six-petal flowers.

FLORAL POINSETTIA   JEANNETTE GLASS COMPANY, 1931–1935

Object	Price
Bowl, 4" or 7½"	$15.00
Bowl with Cover, 8"	*35.00*
Bowl, 9" Oval	*15.00*
Butter Dish with Cover	*100.00*
Candy Jar with Cover	*40.00*
Creamer	*12.50*
Coaster	*10.00*
Compote, 9"	*750.00*
Cup	*10.00*
Ice Tub, 3½" Oval, 2 Tab Handles	*750.00*
Lamp	*250.00*
Pitcher, Milk, 1½ pt.	*500.00*
Pitcher, 1 qt.	*35.00*
Pitcher, 1½ qt.	*200.00*
Plate, 6"	*6.00*
Plate, 8" or 9"	*10.00*
Plate, 9" Grill, 3 Divisions	*175.00*
Platter, 10¾" Oval	*25.00*
Platter, 12"	*75.00*
Refrigerator Dish with Cover, Square	*60.00*
Relish Dish, Oval, 2-Part, 2 Tab Handles	*15.00*
Salt and Pepper Shakers	*60.00*
Saucer	*8.00*
Sherbet	*15.00*
Sugar with Cover, 2-Handled	*27.50*
Tray, 6" Square, 2-Handled	*15.00*
Tumbler, Several Styles	*20.00*
Vase, Various Styles	*400.00*

The primary colors are pink and green, but there are other variations. For opaque blue or delphite, yellow or red, triple the above prices; for crystal, reduce them by 50%.

The salt and pepper shakers have been reproduced in pink, dark green, and cobalt blue.

"Floral Poinsettia" is an allover pattern of large poinsettia blossoms along with vertical ribbing.

FLORENTINE NO. 1 OR OLD FLORENTINE OR POPPY NO. 1   HAZEL ATLAS GLASS COMPANY, 1932–1935

Object	Price
Ashtray	$20.00
Bowl, 5"	12.00
Bowl, 6" or 8½"	20.00
Bowl with Cover, 9½", Oval	50.00
Butter Dish with Cover	150.00
Coaster	20.00
Compote	20.00
Creamer	12.50
Cup	8.00
Pitcher, 1 qt.	50.00
Pitcher, 1½ qt.	100.00
Plate, 6"	5.00
Plate, 8½"	10.00
Plate, 10"	15.00
Plate, 10" Grill, 3 Divisions	15.00
Platter, 11½" Oval	20.00
Salt and Pepper Shakers	75.00
Saucer	4.00
Sherbet	7.50
Sugar with Cover	27.50
Tumbler, Several Styles	15.00

The colors included in the pricing above consist of pink, green, and yellow. For cobalt blue, double the above prices; for crystal, reduce them by 50%.

"Florentine No. 1" is not difficult to distinguish from "Florentine No. 2," following. The main difference is that the majority of pieces in No. 1 are hexagonal while all in No. 2 are round.

Note that in both "Florentine" designs, the butter and oval bowl covers are interchangeable. Also, the salt and pepper shakers have been reproduced in pink and cobalt blue.

FLORENTINE NO. 2 OR POPPY NO. 2   HAZEL ATLAS GLASS COMPANY, MID- TO LATE 1930S

Object	Price
Bowl, 4½" or 4¾"	$15.00
Bowl, 5½", 6", 7½", 8", or 9"	20.00
Bowl with Cover, 9", Oval	50.00
Butter Dish with Cover	150.00
Candlestick	30.00
Candy Dish with Cover	125.00
Coaster	15.00

Compote *$20.00*
Creamer .... *.10.00*
Cup .... *.6.00*
Custard Cup .... *.50.00*
Gravy Boat .... *.75.00*
Parfait, 6" Tall .... *.30.00*
Pickle Dish, 10" Oval .... *.20.00*
Pitcher, Milk .... *.50.00*
Pitcher, Water .... *.100.00*
Plate, 6" .... *.3.00*
Plate, 8½" .... *.8.00*
Plate, 10" .... *.10.00*
Plate, 10¼" Grill, 3 Divisions or with Ring for 4¾" Bowl ...... *.15.00*
Platter, 11" Oval .... *.15.00*
Platter, 11½", Matches Gravy Boat .... *.50.00*
Relish Dish, 10", 3 Divisions .... *.25.00*
Salt and Pepper Shakers .... *.60.00*
Saucer .... *.3.00*
Sherbet .... *.7.50*
Sugar with Cover, 2-Handled .... *.20.00*
Tumbler, Various Styles .... *.15.00*

As with Florentine No. 1, the prices include pink, green, and yellow. For odd colors such as amber, cobalt blue, light blue, and fired-on versions, double the above prices; for crystal, reduce them by 50%.

FLOWER GARDEN WITH BUTTERFLIES OR BUTTERFLIES AND ROSES U.S. GLASS COMPANY, LATE 1920S

Object	*Price*
Ashtray	*$100.00*
Bowl, 8½" or 9"	*.55.00*
Bowl, 11" or 12"	*.65.00*
Candlestick, 4"	*.30.00*
Candlestick, 8"	*.50.00*
Candy Jar with Cover	*.150.00*
Cologne Bottle with Stopper	*.150.00*
Compote, Various Styles, 5" Tall and Under	*.35.00*
Compote, Various Styles, 6" Tall and Over	*.75.00*
Creamer	*.50.00*
Cup	*.40.00*
Heart-Shaped Jar with Cover	*.500.00*
Mayonnaise Set, Dish, Plate, and Ladle	*.75.00*
Plate, 7" or 8"	*.20.00*
Plate, 10" with or without Indentation	*.35.00*
Powder Jar with Cover	*.75.00*
Sandwich Server with Center Handle	*.75.00*
Saucer	*.12.00*
Sugar, 2-Handled	*.50.00*

Tray, Various Styles *$55.00*
Tumbler, Various Styles *100.00*
Vase, 6¹/₄" or 8" Tall *75.00*
Vase, 10" or 10¹/₂" Tall *100.00*

The colors included in the pricing are pink, green, and amber. For light blue or yellow, increase the above prices by 50%; for crystal, decrease them by 50%; and for black, quadruple the above prices. The black pieces are rare and particularly valuable, as is most black Depression glass. Note that some of the pieces have gold banding or rings near the top or around the edging, but the prices do not vary for these.

This is a very dense allover pattern of leaves, butterflies, and five-petal flowers.

FORTUNE HOCKING GLASS COMPANY, 1936–1938

Object *Price*
Bowl, 4", 4¹/₂", or 5¹/₄" *$5.00*
Bowl, 4¹/₂" with 2 Tab Handles *6.00*
Bowl, 7³/₄" *8.00*
Candy Dish with Cover *20.00*
Cup *4.00*
Plate, 6" *3.00*
Plate, 8" *6.00*
Saucer *2.00*
Tumbler, 3¹/₂" Tall *4.00*
Tumbler, 4" Tall *6.00*

The only colored glass in this pattern is pink. For crystal, reduce the price by 50%. The pattern contains angled vertical flutes for somewhat of an optic effect. This angling also produces a notched edge except for the drinking vessels, which are cut off by a horizontal line and therefore have a smooth outer edge.

FRUITS HAZEL ATLAS GLASS COMPANY, 1931–1933

Object *Price*
Bowl, 5" *$15.00*
Bowl, 8" *30.00*
Cup *5.00*
Pitcher *50.00*
Plate, 8" *5.00*
Saucer *3.00*
Sherbet *6.00*
Tumbler, Various Styles *10.00*

The primary colors in this pattern are pink and green. For crystal, reduce the price by 50%; for iridized pieces, use the same prices as for pink and green. A pair of fruits appear together with leaves at the top or outer edge of this vertically paneled pattern.

Left: Depression glass, "Fortune" pattern. Drawing by Mark Pickvet. Right: Depression glass, "Georgian Lovebirds" pattern. Photo by Robin Rainwater.

GEORGIAN LOVEBIRDS FEDERAL GLASS COMPANY, 1931–1936

Object	Price
Bowl, 4½"	$8.00
Bowl, 5¾"	15.00
Bowl, 6½" or 7½"	50.00
Bowl, 9" Oval	55.00
Butter Dish with Cover	100.00
Coaster	10.00
Creamer	10.00
Cup	8.00
Hotplate	35.00
Pitcher	300.00
Plate, 6" or 8"	4.00
Plate, 9¼"	15.00
Platter, 11½", 2 Tab Handles	50.00
Saucer	2.00
Sherbet	8.00
Sugar with Cover, 2-Handled	35.00
Tumbler, 4" Tall	40.00
Tumbler, 5¼" Tall	75.00

The only color made in this pattern was green. For crystal, reduce the above prices by 50%. This is a pretty pattern, with lovebirds sitting side by side on most pieces except tumblers, hotplates, and some plates. Also, on some pieces, the design is in the center only, while others include it on the edges too.

HERITAGE FEDERAL GLASS COMPANY, 1930S–1970S

Object	Price
Bowl, 5"	$30.00
Bowl, 8½"	75.00
Bowl, 10½"	20.00
Creamer	35.00
Cup	5.00

Plate, 8" or 9¼" *$7.50*
Plate, 12" *10.00*
Saucer *2.00*
Sugar, 2-Handled *35.00*

The basic colors priced above are pink and green. For light blue, increase them by 50%; for crystal, decrease them by 50%.

This pattern was reproduced in the 1960s and 1970s in green, amber, and crystal. Most are marked "MC" (for McCrory's), and the patterns are weaker for the new pieces. The new green is also darker than the original, and some of the crystal was trimmed in gold. "Heritage" is similar to "Sandwich" patterns in that it includes an allover pressed pattern.

HEX OPTIC OR HONEYCOMB   JEANNETTE GLASS
COMPANY, 1928–1932

Object	Price
Bowl, 4¼"	*$5.00*
Bowl, 7¼", 7½", or 8¼"	*10.00*
Bowl, 9" or 10"	*15.00*
Butter Dish with Cover	*75.00*
Creamer	*5.00*

Depression glass, "Hex Optic" or "Honeycomb" pattern. Reproduced from a 1930 advertisement.

Cup	*$4.00*
Ice Bucket with Metal Handle	*25.00*
Pitcher, Milk, 1 qt.	*20.00*
Pitcher, Water 1½ qt.	*35.00*
Plate, 6"	*3.00*
Plate, 8"	*5.00*
Platter, 11"	*10.00*
Reamer (Fits Ice Bucket)	*20.00*
Refrigerator Dish with Cover	*15.00*
Salt and Pepper Shakers	*25.00*
Saucer	*3.00*
Sherbet	*4.00*
Sugar, 2-Handled	*5.00*
Sugar Shaker	*150.00*
Tumbler, Various Styles	*6.00*
Whiskey, 2" Tall, 1 oz.	*7.50*

The primary Depression colors include pink and green. Iridescent or light marigold pieces were reproduced in the 1950s (reduce the above prices by 25%). This is a rather simple pressed hexagonal pattern.

HORSESHOE OR NO. 612   INDIANA GLASS COMPANY, 1930–1933

Object	*Price*
Bowl, 4½", 6½", or 7½"	*$15.00*
Bowl, 8½" or 9½"	*25.00*
Bowl, 10½", Oval	*25.00*
Butter Dish with Cover	*500.00*
Candy Dish with Cover, Metal Holder	*100.00*
Creamer	*12.50*
Cup	*10.00*
Pitcher	*250.00*
Plate, 6"	*6.00*
Plate, 8½" or 9½"	*8.00*
Plate, 10½"	*15.00*

Depression glass, "Horseshoe" or "No. 612" pattern. Photo by Robin Rainwater.

Plate, 10½" Grill, 3 Divisions	.$50.00
Platter, 10¾" Oval	.20.00
Platter, 11½"	.20.00
Relish, 3-Part	.20.00
Saucer	.4.00
Sherbet	.14.00
Sugar, 2-Handled	.12.50
Tumbler, 4¼" or 4¾" Tall	.75.00
Tumbler, 5½" Tall, Footed	.20.00
Tumbler, 6¼" Tall, Footed	.100.00

Basic colors include green and yellow. Pink pieces are rare—quadruple the above prices; for crystal, reduce them by 50%. This is a pattern that Indiana did not patent a name for except the designation, "No. 612." "Horsehoe" is simply a nickname that stuck because of the large ovals on the pattern that curl in like horseshoes at the end. "Horsehoe" pieces also vary in thickness; some are thin and some are thick.

IRIS OR IRIS AND HERRINGBONE JEANNETTE
GLASS COMPANY, 1928–1932, 1950S–1970S

Object	*Price*
Bowl, 4½" or 5"	.$10.00
Bowl, 7½" or 8"	.25.00
Bowl, 9½"	.15.00
Bowl, 11" or 11½"	.20.00
Butter Dish with Cover	.50.00
Candlestick	.14.00
Candy Jar with Cover	.100.00
Claret Glass	.15.00
Coaster	.25.00
Creamer	.10.00
Cup	.8.00
Demitasse Cup and Saucer	.100.00
Goblet, Various Styles	.15.00
Lamp Shade, 11½"	.40.00
Nut Set (Metal Base and Holder for Nut Crackers and Picks)	.55.00
Pitcher	.35.00
Plate, 5½"	.8.00
Plate, 8" or 9"	.40.00
Platter, 11¾"	.25.00
Saucer	.5.00
Sherbet	.15.00
Sugar with Cover, 2-Handled	.20.00
Tumbler, Various Styles	.15.00
Vase, 9"	.20.00
Wineglass	.15.00

The items priced above are for crystal and the reproduction marigold (1950s–1970s). For the rarer green and pink, quadruple the above prices.

The pattern consists of irises along with vertical ribbing.

Left: Depression glass, "Iris" pattern. Photo by Robin Rainwater. Right: Depression glass, "Jubilee" pattern. Drawing by Mark Pickvet.

JUBILEE   LANCASTER GLASS COMPANY, EARLY 1930S

Object	Price
Bowl, 8", 3-Footed	$175.00
Bowl, 9", 2-Handled	75.00
Bowl, 11", 3-Footed	175.00
Candlestick	75.00
Cheese and Cracker Set	125.00
Cordial	125.00
Creamer	25.00
Cup	17.50
Goblet	60.00
Mayonnaise Set (Plate, Bowl, and Ladle)	200.00
Plate, 7" or 8³/₄"	12.00
Platter, 13¹/₂"	50.00
Saucer	10.00
Sherbet	35.00
Sugar, 2-Handled	17.50
Tray, 11", 2-Handled	40.00
Tray, 11", with Center Handle	80.00
Wineglass	50.00

The only two colors are pink and yellow. "Jubilee" is a difficult pattern to obtain for there are few common pieces. Be very careful of other less valuable Lancaster patterns. "Jubilee" has an open-centered flower in the pattern with 12-petal flowers surrounding it. Other patterns have 16 petals or 12 petals with a smaller petal between two large ones.

KITCHENWARE   VARIOUS COMPANIES, 1920S–1930S

Object	Price
Bowl, Mixing, up to 7"	$10.00
Bowl, Mixing, 7¹/₈" to 9"	14.00
Bowl, Mixing, Over 9"	16.00

KITCHEN GLASSWARE

Depression glass, kitchenware. Reproduced from a Butler Brother's catalog advertisement.

Depression glass, ladle, kitchenware. Photo by Robin Rainwater.

TABLE GLASSWARE

BUTLER BROTHERS

Depression glass, kitchenware. Reproduced from a Butler Brother's catalog advertisement.

Butter Dish with Cover, ¼ lb. $25.00

Butter Dish with Cover, 1 lb. 35.00

Cake Preserver with Cover 75.00

Cake Tub 35.00

Canister, Covered, up to 16 oz. 25.00

Canister, Covered, 17–28 oz. 30.00

Canister, Covered, 29–48 oz. 35.00

Canister, Covered, over 48 oz. 50.00

Cookie Jar with Cover 20.00

Cruet with Stopper 45.00

Egg Cup 10.00

Funnel 50.00

Juice Dispenser 100.00

Knife 25.00

Ladle 20.00

Measuring Cup, ¼ Cup *$6.00*
Measuring Cup, ⅓ Cup .... *.7.00*
Measuring Cup, ½ Cup .... *.8.00*
Measuring Cup, 1 Cup .... *.10.00*
Measuring Cup, 2 Cup .... *.12.00*
Measuring Cup, over 2 Cups .... *.15.00*
Mechanical Attachments .... *.30.00*
Pie Dish .... *.35.00*
Pitcher, Syrup, up to 16 oz. .... *.50.00*
Pitcher, 17–28 oz. .... *.60.00*
Pitcher, 29–48 oz. .... *.75.00*
Pitcher, over 48 oz. .... *.85.00*
Punch Ladle .... *.35.00*
Range Bowl, Uncovered .... *.15.00*
Range Bowl, Covered .... *.25.00*
Reamer, Lemon, Small, under 3" Tall .... *.8.00*
Reamer, Lemon, Small, over 3" Tall .... *.12.00*
Reamer, Orange, Large, under 3" Tall .... *.12.00*
Reamer, Orange, Large, over 3" Tall .... *.15.00*
Refrigerator Bowl with Cover, Round, up to 6" Diameter .... *.20.00*
Refrigerator Bowl with Cover, Round, over 8" Diameter .... *.25.00*
Refrigerator Dish with Cover, Square or Rectangular, up to 32 Square Inches ..... *.25.00*
Refrigerator Dish with Cover, Square or Rectangular, over 32 Square Inches ...... *.35.00*
Rolling Pin .... *.100.00*
Salt Box .... *.75.00*
Salt and Pepper Shakers .... *.50.00*
Tray, Oval or Rectangular (Opaque 25.00) .... *.25.00*
Tumblers, up to 8 oz. .... *.10.00*
Tumblers, over 8 oz. .... *.15.00*
Water Bottle .... *.25.00*
Water Cooler with Spout .... *.100.00*

The basic colors include pink, green, amber, yellow, and light blue. For opaque versions and crystal, reduce the above prices by 50%. For cobalt blue, ruby red, or ultramarine, double the above prices. For black, quadruple the above prices.

Some of the largest makers of kitchen products during the Depression era were Hocking/Anchor-Hocking (many canister sets, Vitrock, Fire King, and nearly every type of product made); Jeannette (Jennyware products—most made in ultramarine as well as other colors); Hazel Atlas (famous for the "Crisscross" pattern); McKee (many opaque and milk-white patterns—some with colored dots, red or black ships, etc.); and a host of others.

Kitchenware can be difficult to identify at times because of the many plain and unmarked styles. These products were also made in every color, including the opaque styles of delphite blue, jadite green, custard yellow or beige, milk whites, fired-on colors, etc. Many were decorated by embossing and enameling as well as with fired-on decals or transfers.

Cookie jars are generally larger than patterned cracker jars. Canisters come in a huge variety of shapes and markings—flour, sugar, coffee, tea, cereal, spices, salt, oatmeal, cocoa, etc. Glass "silverware," primarily knives, serving spoons, and ladles are getting more difficult to find. Cups may have up to three spouts; range bowls or sets are often marked "drips" or "drippings" and have matching canisters.

The only known cobalt blue water cooler was made by L.E. Smith. Reamers are probably the most prolific—increase price by 50% if there is a matching collecting bowl or cup. Mechanical items (such as extractors, grinders, etc.) should include a glass collector.

LACE EDGE OR OPEN LACE HOCKING GLASS
COMPANY, 1935–1938

Object	Price
Bowl, 6¹/₂", 7³/₄", 8¹/₄", or 9¹/₂"	*$15.00*
Bowl, 10¹/₂", 3 Legs	*125.00*
Butter Dish with Cover	*75.00*
Candlestick	*75.00*
Candy Jar with Cover	*45.00*
Compote with Cover	*40.00*
Cookie Jar with Cover	*65.00*
Creamer	*20.00*
Cup	*20.00*
Flower Bowl with Crystal Frog	*25.00*
Plate, 8¹/₄" or 8³/₄"	*15.00*
Plate, 10¹/₂"	*20.00*
Plate, 10¹/₂" Grill, 3 Divisions	*20.00*
Plate, 10¹/₂" Relish, 3-Part (Parallel Divisions)	*20.00*
Platter, 12³/₄", or 13", with or without Divisions	*25.00*
Relish Bowl, 7¹/₂", 3-Part	*50.00*
Saucer	*.8.00*
Sherbet	*75.00*
Sugar, 2-Handled	*20.00*
Tumbler, 3¹/₂" or 4¹/₂" Tall	*15.00*
Tumbler, 5" Tall	*25.00*
Vase, 7" Tall	*200.00*

The primary color is transparent pink. For satinized or frosted pink and crystal, reduce the above prices by 50%. "Lace" patterns are notorious for chipping and cracking because of the delicate edging. Be sure to scrutinize pieces very carefully before purchasing. Chipped, cracked, or damaged glass has little value except for historical purposes. Several companies produced "Lace" glassware, but Hocking's pink is a bit duller than others.

LACED EDGE OR KATY BLUE IMPERIAL GLASS
COMPANY, EARLY 1930S

Object	Price
Bowl, 4¹/₂", 5", 5¹/₂", or 7"	*$20.00*
Bowl, 9"	*40.00*
Bowl, 11" Oval, with or without Divisions	*50.00*
Creamer	*25.00*
Cup	*20.00*
Mayonnaise, 3-Piece (Bowl, Plate, and Ladle)	*100.00*

Depression glass, "Lace Edge" pattern. Drawing by Mark Pickvet.

Plate, 6½"	$10.00
Plate, 8"	15.00
Plate, 10"	35.00
Platter, 12"	50.00
Platter, 13"	60.00
Saucer	8.00
Sugar, 2-Handled	25.00
Tid-bit, 2-Tiered	75.00
Tumbler, Various Styles	30.00
Vase	40.00

The colors priced above are for light blue and green, with opalescent edging on all pieces. The opalescent coloring was referred to by Imperial as "Sea Foam." As with Hocking's Lace Edge, beware of damaged edges.

LINCOLN INN   FENTON GLASS COMPANY, LATE 1920S

Object	*Price*
Ashtray	$10.00
Bonbon, Square or Oval, 2-Handled	12.00
Bowl, 4", 5", or 6"	10.00
Bowl, 9" or 9¼"	15.00
Bowl, 10½", Footed	25.00
Candy Dish, Oval, Footed	15.00
Compote	15.00
Creamer	15.00
Cup	10.00
Goblet	20.00
Nut Dish, Footed	10.00
Olive Dish	12.00
Pitcher	750.00
Plate, 6"	5.00
Plate, 8" or 9½"	8.00
Platter, 12"	15.00
Salt and Pepper Shakers	125.00
Saucer	4.00
Sherbet	12.00
Sugar, 2-Handled	15.00
Tumbler, Various Styles	15.00

Vase, 12" Tall, Footed *$75.00*
Wineglass . . . .*.20.00*

This pattern contains more colors than most others. Basic prices above include pink, green, light blue, amethyst, amber, and opaque shades of green. For cobalt blue, ruby red, and black, double the above prices; for crystal, reduce them by half. This is a fairly simple pattern characterized by vertical ribbing that does not quite extend to the top of each piece.

Depression glass, "Lincoln Inn" pattern. Reproduced from a 1929 advertisement.

LORAIN BASKET   INDIANA GLASS COMPANY, 1929–1932

Object	Price
Bowl, 6" or 7¹/₄"	$35.00
Bowl, 8"	.75.00
Bowl, 9³/₄", Oval	.40.00
Creamer	.15.00
Cup	.10.00
Plate, 5¹/₂"	.6.00
Plate, 7³/₄"	.8.00
Plate, 8¹/₂"	.15.00
Plate, 10¹/₄"	.30.00
Platter, 11¹/₂"	.35.00
Relish, 4-Part	.20.00
Saucer	.4.00
Sherbet	.20.00
Sugar, 2-Handled	.15.00
Tumbler	.20.00

The primary colors are green and yellow. For crystal, reduce the prices by 50%. Edges tend to be a bit rough because of poor molding, especially the inner rims of bowls. Note that sherbets were reproduced in milk white and an opaque green in the 1950s and 1960s.

This pattern is also referred to as Indiana's "No. 615" and consists of heavy scrolling around the edges and corners with a large center design.

MADRID   FEDERAL GLASS COMPANY, 1932–1938

Object	Price
Ashtray, 6", Square	$100.00
Bowl, 4³/₄" or 5"	.8.00
Bowl, 7" or 8"	.12.00
Bowl, 9¹/₂"	.20.00
Bowl, 10", Oval	.15.00
Bowl, 11"	.15.00
Butter Dish with Cover	.75.00
Candlestick	.8.00
Coaster	.30.00
Cookie Jar with Cover	.50.00
Creamer	.7.50
Cup	.6.00
Gravy Boat with Platter	.1000.00
Marmalade	.15.00
Pitcher, Milk, 1 qt.	.35.00
Pitcher, 2 qt.	.45.00
Pitcher, 2¹/₂", with or without Ice Lip	.55.00
Plate, 6"	.3.00
Plate, 7¹/₂" or 9"	.8.00
Plate, 10¹/₂"	.20.00

Plate, 10½" Grill, 3 Divisions *$15.00*
Platter, 11¼" *15.00*
Platter, 11½", Oval *17.50*
Salt and Pepper Shakers *75.00*
Saucer *3.00*
Sherbet *8.00*
Sugar with Cover *25.00*
Tumbler, 4¼" Tall *15.00*
Tumbler, Various Styles *20.00*

The basic colors consist of pink, green, and amber. Light blue is rarer—double the above prices. For crystal, reduce them by 50%. The blue was referred to by Federal as "Madonna Blue." "Madrid" is characterized by a large center diamond shape surrounded by scrolling. Scrolling occurs on the edges as well.

Reproductions are a problem with "Madrid." In 1976, Federal reproduced "Madrid" under the name of "Recollection" for America's Bicentennial. It was issued in amber only and dated "1976." When Federal went out of business, the Indiana Glass Company purchased the molds and removed the "1976" date from them. Indiana has also reproduced many pieces in a lighter pink and brighter blue.

MANHATTAN OR HORIZONTAL RIBBED
ANCHOR HOCKING GLASS COMPANY 1938–1943

Object	Price
Ashtray	*$10.00*
Bowl, 4½", 5½", or 7½", with or without Handles	*10.00*
Bowl, 8" or 9", with or without Handles	*15.00*
Bowl, 9½", 1 Handle	*20.00*
Candlestick	*7.50*
Candy Dish, 3 Legs	*12.00*
Coaster	*10.00*
Compote	*20.00*
Creamer	*10.00*
Cup	*50.00*
Pitcher, Milk	*35.00*
Pitcher, 2½ qt.	*50.00*
Plate, 6", 8½", or 10¼"	*15.00*
Platter, 14"	*20.00*
Relish Tray,	*30.00*

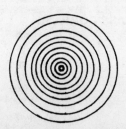

Depression glass, "Manhattan" pattern. Drawing by Mark Pickvet.

Relish Tray Insert (Ruby Red $5.00) *$4.00*
Salt and Pepper Shakers .... *.50.00*
Saucer .... *.15.00*
Sherbet .... *.7.50*
Sugar, 2-Handled .... *.10.00*
Tumbler, Various Styles .... *.15.00*
Vase .... *.14.00*
Wineglass .... *.15.00*

The basic Depression color is pink. For crystal, reduce the above prices by 50%. For ruby red, double the above prices. The pattern is a rather simple vertically ribbed design. Anchor Hocking produced a similar pattern in 1987 named "Park Avenue," but the pieces have different dimensions.

MAYFAIR   FEDERAL GLASS COMPANY, 1934

Object	Price
Bowl, 5", Shallow	*$8.00*
Bowl, 5" Deep or 6"	*.15.00*
Bowl, 10" Oval	*.25.00*
Creamer	*.15.00*
Cup	*.7.50*
Plate, 6¾"	*.6.00*
Plate, 9½"	*.10.00*
Plate, 9½" Grill, 3 Divisions	*.12.00*
Platter, 12" Oval	*.25.00*
Saucer	*.2.00*
Sugar	*.15.00*
Tumbler, 4½" Tall	*.20.00*

Prices are for green and amber; for crystal, reduce them by 50%. The green pieces actually differ in pattern somewhat from the amber and crystal. Hocking obtained a patent on the name "Mayfair" before Federal did; as a result, Federal redesigned the molds twice in order to produce the "Rosemary" pattern (listed further on in this chapter). The green pieces are part "Mayfair" and part "Rosemary" since they were a result of Federal's design before the final conversion. Most consider the green as "Mayfair."

The pieces made during the switch have arching in the bottom but no waffling or grid design between the top arches as in the original "Mayfair." The glass under the arches in "Rosemary" is plain.

MAYFAIR OPEN ROSE   HOCKING GLASS COMPANY, 1931–1937

Object	Price
Bowl, 5", 5½", or 7"	*$40.00*
Bowl, 9½", Oval	*.40.00*
Bowl with Cover, 10"	*.75.00*
Bowl, 11¾" or 12"	*.50.00*

Butter Dish with Cover *$125.00*

Cake Plate, 10" Footed . . . . *.40.00*

Cake Plate, 12", 2-Handled . . . . *.50.00*

Candy Dish with Cover . . . . *.75.00*

Celery Dish, 9" or 10", with or without Divisions . . . . *.40.00*

Claret Glass, 5¼" Tall . . . . *.125.00*

Cocktail Glass, 4" Tall . . . . *.75.00*

Cookie Jar with Cover . . . . *.50.00*

Cordial, 1 oz. . . . . *.125.00*

Creamer . . . . *.25.00*

Cup . . . . *.25.00*

Decanter with Stopper, 1 qt. . . . . *.125.00*

Goblet, 5–8" Tall . . . . *.125.00*

Pitcher, Milk, 1 qt. . . . . *.75.00*

Pitcher, 8" Tall, 2 qt. . . . . *.85.00*

Pitcher, 8½" Tall, 2½ qt. . . . . *.100.00*

Plate, 5¾" or 6½" . . . . *.12.00*

Plate, 8½" . . . . *.20.00*

Plate, 9½" . . . . *.35.00*

Plate, 9½" Grill, 3 Divisions . . . . *.40.00*

Plate, 11½" Grill, 2-Handled . . . . *.50.00*

Platter, 12" Oval, 2-Handled, with or without Divisions . . . . *.50.00*

Relish, 8½", with or without Divisions . . . . *.40.00*

Salt and Pepper Shakers . . . . *.75.00*

Sandwich Server with Center Handle . . . . *.40.00*

Saucer . . . . *.25.00*

Sherbet, 2¼" Tall . . . . *.75.00*

Sherbet, 3" Tall . . . . *.25.00*

Sherbet, 4¾" Tall . . . . *.60.00*

Sugar . . . . *.35.00*

Tumbler, Various Styles . . . . *.35.00*

Vase . . . . *.100.00*

Whiskey Tumbler, 2¼" Tall, 1½ oz. . . . . *.50.00*

Wineglass, 4½" Tall . . . . *.75.00*

Pink and ice blue are the colors priced above. Green and yellow are much rarer—double the above prices; for crystal, reduce them by 50%. "Mayfair Open Rose" is probably the most popular and most recognized pattern of all with the stemmed

Depression glass, "Mayfair Open Rose" pattern. Photo by Robert Darnold.

rose and vertical ribbing. "Cameo" is probably its only serious competition for the sheer number of different pieces made as well as rare and valuable pieces.

Since the 1970s, there have been many reproductions of this pattern. The colors as well as some dimensions are different from the new pieces. Salt and pepper shakers, cookie jars, and whiskey tumblers have all been reproduced.

MISS AMERICA OR DIAMOND HOCKING GLASS COMPANY, 1933–1937

Object	Price
Bowl, 4½" or 6½"	$10.00
Bowl, 8" or 8¾"	45.00
Bowl, 10" Oval	20.00
Butter Dish with Cover	500.00
Cake Plate, 12" Footed	35.00
Candy Jar with Cover	125.00
Celery Dish	20.00
Coaster	15.00
Compote	20.00
Creamer	15.00
Cup	15.00
Goblet	50.00
Pitcher	125.00
Plate, 5¾" or 6¾"	6.00
Plate, 8½"	15.00
Plate, 10¼"	20.00
Plate, 10¼" Grill, 3 Divisions	25.00
Platter, 12¼" Oval	25.00
Relish Dish	20.00
Salt and Pepper Shakers	75.00
Saucer	5.00
Sherbet	12.00
Sugar	15.00
Tumbler, Various Styles	35.00
Wineglass	50.00

The basic colors are pink and green. For ruby red, quadruple the above prices; for crystal or flashed-on crystal, reduce them by 50%. "Miss America" is a pressed diamond pattern with rays in the center of equal length.

Reproductions do cause problems with this pattern. Butter dishes, shakers, tumblers, and pitchers were all remade; however, with most reproductions, the colors do vary significantly from the original Depression colors.

MT. PLEASANT DOUBLE SHIELD L.E. SMITH COMPANY, 1920S–1934

Object	Price
Bonbon, 7" with Handle	$15.00
Bowl, 4"–10", with or without Handles	15.00

Candlestick, Single *$10.00*
Candlestick, Double *12.50*
Creamer *17.50*
Cup *7.50*
Leaf Dish *10.00*
Mayonnaise Dish, Footed *15.00*
Mint Dish, 6", Center Handle *15.00*
Plate, 7"–9", with or without Handles *10.00*
Plate, 9", Grill, 3 Divisions *12.00*
Plate, 10½", 2-Handled *15.00*
Platter, 12", 2-Handled *20.00*
Salt and Pepper Shakers *35.00*
Sandwich Server with Center Handle *20.00*
Saucer *3.00*
Sherbet *10.00*
Sugar, 2-Handled *17.50*
Tumbler, Footed *10.00*
Vase *20.00*

The basic colors are pink and green. For cobalt blue and dark amethyst (almost black), double the above prices. Many pieces were trimmed in platinum, and if the band is completely intact, the pieces are worth a little bit more. For crystal, reduce the above listed prices by 50%. In case the band is scattered or only partial, the remaining part can be erased lightly with a pencil eraser.

The pattern is plain and simple with elegant banding, arcs, and rounded triangles around the edges.

NEW CENTURY HAZEL ATLAS GLASS COMPANY, 1930–1935

Object	*Price*
Bowl, 4½"–8"	*$10.00*
Bowl with Cover, 9"	*50.00*
Butter Dish with Cover	*75.00*
Coaster	*20.00*

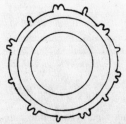  

Left: Depression glass, "Mt. Pleasant" pattern. Drawing by Mark Pickvet. Center: Depression glass, "New Century" pattern. Reproduced from a 1930 trade catalog. Right: Depression glass, "New Century" pattern. Reproduced from a 1930 trade catalog.

Cordial *$15.00*
Creamer .... *.7.50*
Cup .... *.6.00*
Decanter with Stopper .... *.55.00*
Pitcher, 7³/₄" Tall, 2 qt. .... *.35.00*
Pitcher, 8" Tall, 2¹/₂ qt. .... *.45.00*
Plate, 6" .... *.3.00*
Plate, 7" or 8¹/₂" .... *.6.00*
Plate, 10" .... *.10.00*
Plate, 10" Grill, 3 Divisions .... *.12.00*
Platter, 11" Oval .... *.15.00*
Salt and Pepper Shakers .... *.50.00*
Saucer .... *.3.00*
Sherbet .... *.6.00*
Sugar with Cover .... *.22.50*
Tumbler, Various Styles .... *.12.00*
Whiskey, 2¹/₂" Tall, 1¹/₂ oz. .... *.10.00*
Wineglass .... *.15.00*

The basic colors are pink and green. Double the prices for cobalt blue or amethyst; reduce them by 50% for crystal.

This pattern is sometimes referred to as "Lydia Ray" which was a temporary name used by Hazel Atlas but was not patented. It is characterized by vertical ribbing cut off near the top with three horizontal bands. Round pieces usually have rays that are equidistant from the center.

NEWPORT HAIRPIN   HAZEL ATLAS GLASS COMPANY, LATE 1930S

Object	*Price*
Bowl, 4¹/₄" or 4³/₄"	*$6.00*
Bowl, 5¹/₄"	*.10.00*
Bowl, 8¹/₄"	*.15.00*
Creamer	*.7.50*
Cup	*.5.00*
Plate, 6"	*.3.00*
Plate, 8¹/₂"	*.6.00*
Platter, 11¹/₂"	*.15.00*
Platter, 11³/₄", Oval	*.17.50*
Salt and Pepper Shakers	*.40.00*
Saucer	*.2.50*
Sherbet	*.7.50*
Sugar, 2-Handled	*.7.50*
Tumbler	*.10.00*

The color priced above is for pink. For cobalt blue and dark amethyst, double the above prices. Platonite colors were made in the 1940s–1950s and can be found in the following chapter.

This pattern was made near the end of the Depression and is characterized by intersecting vertical waves.

*Depression glass, "Nora Bird"
pattern. Reproduced from a 1929
Paden City patent design.*

NORA BIRD   PADEN CITY GLASS COMPANY, 1929–1930S

Object	Price
Candlestick	$25.00
Candy Dish with Cover	.75.00
Creamer	.30.00
Cup	.40.00
Ice Tub, 6"	.100.00
Mayonnaise Dish with Inner Liner	.75.00
Plate, 8"	.20.00
Saucer	.15.00
Sugar, 2-Handled	.30.00
Tumbler, Various Styles	.30.00

The primary Depression colors are pink and green. There are a few crystal pieces in
this pheasantlike etched pattern (reduce the above prices by half). The bird on each
piece is etched in two poses: one in flight and the other ready for take-off.

NORMANDIE BOUQUET AND LATTICE
FEDERAL GLASS COMPANY, 1933–1940

Object	Price
Bowl, 5"	$5.00
Bowl, 6½" or 8½"	.15.00
Bowl, 10", Oval	.20.00
Creamer	.10.00
Cup	.6.00
Pitcher	.100.00
Plate, 6"	.3.00
Plate, 7¾" or 9¼"	.10.00
Plate, 11"	.25.00
Plate, 11", Grill, 3 Divisions	.20.00
Platter, 11¾"	.25.00
Salt and Pepper Shakers	.75.00
Saucer	.2.00
Sherbet	.7.50

Sugar with Cover *$125.00*
Tumbler, Various Styles ....*.40.00*

The basic colors priced above are pink and amber. For the light iridescent marigold color, reduce the above prices by 25%. Depression iridescent as a general rule is much cheaper than true Carnival glass and does not cause too many problems for experienced collectors.

OLD CAFE   HOCKING GLASS COMPANY, 1936–1940

Object	Price
Bowl, 3³/₄"–5¹/₂", with or without Handles	*$4.00*
Bowl, 9", 2-Handled	*.10.00*
Candy Dish	*.7.50*
Cup	*.4.00*
Lamp	*.17.50*
Olive Dish	*.5.00*
Pitcher, Milk, 1 qt.	*.75.00*
Pitcher, 2¹/₂ qt.	*.100.00*
Plate, 6"	*.2.00*
Plate, 10"	*.20.00*
Saucer	*.2.00*
Sherbet	*.5.00*
Tumbler, 3" or 4" Tall	*.10.00*
Vase, 7¹/₄" Tall	*.15.00*

The primary color is pink. For crystal, reduce the above prices by 50%. The royal ruby red color was produced for one year only, 1940 (double the above prices). "Old Cafe" was produced near the end of the Depression glass era.

OLD ENGLISH THREADING   INDIANA GLASS COMPANY, 1930S

Object	Price
Bowl, 4"	*$15.00*
Bowl, 9" or 9¹/₂"	*.25.00*
Candlestick	*.12.00*
Candy Dish with Cover	*.60.00*
Candy Jar with Cover	*.75.00*
Compote	*.15.00*
Creamer	*.15.00*
Egg Cup	*.10.00*
Fruit Stand	*.50.00*
Goblet	*.30.00*
Pitcher with Cover	*.125.00*
Plate	*.20.00*
Sandwich Server with Center Handle	*.60.00*
Sherbet	*.17.50*
Sugar with Cover, 2-Handled	*.35.00*

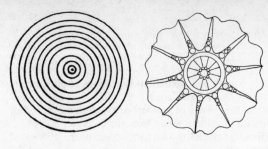

Left: Depression glass, "Old English Threading" pattern. Drawing by Mark Pickvet. Right: Depression glass, "Oyster and Pearl" pattern. Drawing by Mark Pickvet.

Tumbler, Various Styles *$20.00*
Vase, Various Styles .... *.50.00*

The basic Depression colors are pink, green, and amber. For crystal, reduce the above prices by 50%. The pattern contains many concentric ribs spaced very closely together.

ORCHID   PADEN CITY GLASS COMPANY, 1930S

Object	*Price*
Bowl, 5"	*$12.50*
Bowl, 8½" or 8¾", with or without Handles	*.25.00*
Bowl, 10"	*.35.00*
Candlestick	*.20.00*
Compote	*.17.50*
Creamer	*.25.00*
Ice Bucket	*.75.00*
Mayonnaise Set (Bowl, Plate and Ladle)	*.75.00*
Plate, 8½"	*.25.00*
Sandwich Server with Center Handle	*.35.00*
Sugar, 2-Handled	*.25.00*
Vase	*.50.00*

The colors priced above include pink, green, yellow, and amber. For the more desirable cobalt blue and ruby red, double the above prices; for the rare black, triple them.

As the name indicates, this pattern is characterized by etched orchids. Leaves and stems are also included in the design. Many of the pieces are square in shape or contain square bases.

OYSTER AND PEARL   ANCHOR HOCKING GLASS CORPORATION, 1938–1940

Object	*Price*
Bowl, 5½", 1 Handle	*$7.50*
Bowl, 6½", 2-Handled	*.10.00*
Bowl, 10½"	*.17.50*

Candleholder *$10.00*
Heart-Shaped Bowl, 1 Handle .... *.7.50*
Platter, 13½" .... *.15.00*
Relish Dish .... *.10.00*

The pieces priced above include crystal, pink, and fired-on versions of pink, green, and white. For ruby red, double the above-listed prices.

"Oyster and Pearl" was made at the tail end of the Depression, after the merger of the two companies. It represents a transition period from the colored glass of the Depression to the more ceramic- and porcelain-like solid colors of the 1940s and later. The pattern consists of a starlike outcropping from a circular center. On the arms or legs of the star are three progressively smaller circles.

PANELLED ASTER   U.S. GLASS COMPANY, EARLY 1930S

Object	Price
Bowl, 4½" or 5½"	*$10.00*
Bowl, 8" or 9"	*.15.00*
Cake Plate, 10", 3-Footed	*.20.00*
Coaster	*.8.00*
Creamer	*.10.00*
Cup	*.7.50*
Pitcher	*.150.00*
Plate, 7½"	*.7.50*
Plate, 10"	*.10.00*
Plate, 10", Grill, 3 Divisions	*.10.00*
Saucer	*.2.50*
Sherbet	*.10.00*
Sugar	*.7.50*
Tumbler, Various Styles	*.15.00*

The colors priced above include pink, green, and light amber.

As the name indicates, the pattern contains asters separated into vertical sections. Watch for rough mold seams with this pattern.

PARROT   FEDERAL GLASS COMPANY, 1931–1932

Object	Price
Bowl, 5"	*$15.00*
Bowl, 7"	*.30.00*
Bowl, 8"	*.60.00*
Bowl, 10", Oval	*.60.00*
Butter Dish with Cover	*.350.00*
Creamer	*.25.00*
Cup	*.25.00*
Marmalade Dish	*.30.00*
Pitcher, 2½ qt.	*.1250.00*
Plate, 5¾" or 7½"	*.25.00*
Plate, 9"	*.35.00*

Depression glass, "Parrot" pattern. Drawing by Mark Pickvet.

Plate, 10¹/₂", Grill, Round or Square, 3 Divisions *$35.00*
Platter, 11¹/₄", Oblong . . . .*.50.00*
Salt and Pepper Shakers *300.00*
Saucer . . . .*.10.00*
Sherbet . . . .*.20.00*
Sugar with Cover, 2-Handled *150.00*
Tumbler, Various Styles *100.00*

The basic colors are pink and amber. For light blue, double the above prices; for crystal, reduce them by 50%. "Parrot" is an easily recognized pattern and consists of two parrots sitting together on one branch and a lone parrot on the other branch. The branches contain palmlike leaves.

PATRICIAN OR SPOKE   FEDERAL GLASS COMPANY, 1933–1937

Object	Price
Bowl, 4³/₄", 5", or 6"	*$15.00*
Bowl, 8¹/₂"	*.25.00*
Bowl, 10", Oval	*.25.00*
Butter Dish with Cover	*200.00*
Cookie Jar with Cover	*100.00*
Creamer	*.10.00*
Cup	*.8.00*
Marmalade Dish	*.10.00*
Pitcher	*100.00*
Plate, 6"	*.8.00*
Plate, 7¹/₂" or 9"	*.12.00*
Plate, 10¹/₂"	*.6.00*
Plate, 10¹/₂", Grill, 3 Divisions	*.15.00*
Platter, 11¹/₂", Oval	*.20.00*
Salt and Pepper Shakers	*.75.00*
Saucer	*.6.00*
Sherbet	*.10.00*
Sugar with Cover, 2-Handled	*.50.00*
Tumbler, Various Styles	*.25.00*

The Depression colors include pink, green, and amber. For crystal, reduce the prices by 50%. The inner circle of each piece resembles a wheel with spokes, hence the nickname. The pattern also develops into a star, contains zigzag designs near the outer edges or tops of the pieces, and has an additional edging made of semicircles.

PATRICK   LANCASTER GLASS COMPANY, 1930S

Object	Price
Bowl, 5³/₄"	$25.00
Bowl, 9", 2-Handled	.40.00
Bowl, 11"	.50.00
Candlestick	.25.00
Candy Dish, 3-Footed	.50.00
Creamer	.20.00
Cup	.15.00
Goblet	.25.00
Mayonnaise Set (Bowl, Plate, and Ladle)	.100.00
Plate, 7", 7¹/₂", or 8"	.10.00
Sandwich Server with Center Handle	.50.00
Saucer	.3.00
Sherbet	.25.00
Sugar, 2-Handled	.20.00
Tray	.50.00
Tumbler, Several Styles	.35.00
Wineglass	.25.00

"Patrick" was made in two colors, pink and yellow. The pattern consists of etched floral and scrolled designs.

PEACOCK REVERSE   PADEN CITY GLASS COMPANY, 1930S

Object	Price
Bowl, 4¹/₂" or 5"	$20.00
Bowl, 8³/₄" Square	.45.00
Bowl, 8³/₄" Square, 2-Handled	.55.00
Bowl, 11³/₄"	.75.00
Candlestick	.30.00

Depression glass, "Peacock Reverse" pattern. Reproduced from a 1929 Paden City patent design.

Candy Dish, Square *$55.00*
Compote .... *.40.00*
Creamer .... *.50.00*
Cup .... *.40.00*
Plate, 6" or 7½" .... *.25.00*
Plate, 8½" .... *.35.00*
Plate, 10½", 2-Handled .... *.45.00*
Sandwich Server with Center Handle .... *.75.00*
Saucer .... *.15.00*
Sherbet .... *.40.00*
Sugar, 2-Handled .... *.50.00*
Tumbler, Several Styles .... *.50.00*
Vase, Several Styles .... *.100.00*

The above prices are for pink, green, yellow, and amber. For ruby red and cobalt blue, double the above prices; for black, triple them; for crystal, reduce them by 50%. This pattern was supposedly made in pink, green, yellow, amber, blue, red, black, and crystal. Advertisements and catalogs list all of the above colors, including crystal, but not all have been rediscovered at this point. As is common with Paden City's glassware, there is a limited variety of pieces, and what is for sale is difficult to locate.

The peacock in the pattern is referred to as "Reverse" because the head of the peacock is turned to face its tail section while the body remains straight.

PEACOCK AND WILD ROSE   PADEN CITY GLASS COMPANY, 1930S

Object	Price
Bowl, 5"	*$25.00*
Bowl, 8½" or 8¾", with or without Feet	*.30.00*
Bowl, 8½" Oval, Footed	*.45.00*
Bowl, 9½", 10", 10½", or 11", with or without Handles or Feet	*.40.00*
Bowl, 14"	*.50.00*
Candlestick	*.35.00*
Candy Dish with Cover	*.100.00*
Compote	*.25.00*
Ice Bucket or Tub	*.65.00*

Depression glass, "Peacock and Wild Rose" pattern. Reproduced from a 1928 Paden City patent design.

Depression glass, "Peacock and Wild Rose" pattern. Reproduced from a 1928 advertisement.

Pitcher, Milk, 1 qt. *$125.00*
Pitcher, Water, 2 qt. *250.00*
Plate, 7¹/₂" *50.00*
Plate, Cake, Footed *40.00*
Relish, 3 Divisions *35.00*
Tumbler, Several Styles *75.00*
Vase, Several Styles *75.00*

Once again, there is a wide variety of colors in this Paden City pattern. Those priced above include pink, green or blue-green, and yellow. For ruby red and cobalt blue, double the above prices; for black, triple them; and for crystal, reduce them by 50%.

If any of Paden City's glassware could be considered common, this "Peacock and Wild Rose" pattern would be at the top of the list; however although common for Paden City it is still rare compared to typical Depression glass patterns. Black is about the only color in all of Depression glass that outprices ruby red and cobalt blue. This holds true in this pattern. The green is a very pale bluish green, much like a light ultramarine. The pattern is similar to "Peacock Reverse," only the peacock faces forward.

PRETZEL　　INDIANA GLASS COMPANY, 1930S

Object	Price
Bowl, 4¹/₂"	*$3.00*
Bowl, 7¹/₂"	*8.00*

Pattern No. 622
MACHINE MADE
Design Patent Number D-104618—D-104619

Handled Cream
4 doz. ctn. 31 lbs.

Cup
6 doz. ctn. 31 lbs.
Saucer
6 doz. ctn. 25 lbs.

Handled Sugar
4 doz. ctn. 35 lbs.

7½" Coupe Soup
4 doz. ctn. 47 lbs.

9¾" Berry
2 doz. ctn. 42 lbs.

9¾" Berry with 11½" Plate makes 2-piece Salad Set

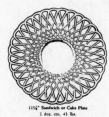

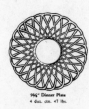

11½" Sandwich or Cake Plate
2 doz. ctn. 43 lbs.

9¾" Dinner Plate
4 doz. ctn. 47 lbs.

8¾" Salad Plate
4 doz. ctn. 37 lbs.

6" Plate
6 doz. ctn. 25 lbs.

Depression glass, "Pretzel" pattern. Reproduced from a 1935 trade catalog.

Depression glass, "Pretzel" pattern. Photo by Robin Rainwater.

Bowl, 9½"	*$12.00*
Celery Tray, 10¼"	*10.00*
Creamer	*5.00*
Cup	*4.00*
Leaf-Shaped Dish	*5.00*
Pickle Dish, 2-Handled	*5.00*
Pitcher, 1 qt.	*125.00*
Plate, 6"	*3.00*
Plate, 6", 1 Handle	*4.00*
Plate, 7¼" Square	*6.00*
Plate, 8½" or 9½"	*5.00*

Platter, 11¹/₂" *$7.00*
Saucer *10.00*
Sugar, 2-Handled *5.00*
Tumbler, Various Styles *17.50*

The pricing above includes crystal or embossed crystal pieces; for ultramarine, double the above prices. As with many of Indiana's numbered patterns, "Pretzel" is this one's adopted name because of its wavy overlapping pretzel-like design. It was patented simply as "No. 622."

As with so much of Indiana's glass, "Pretzel" did not escape reproductions. The celery dish was reissued in the 1970s in amber, avocado green, and blue and is still being made today.

PRINCESS   HOCKING GLASS COMPANY, 1931–1935

Object	*Price*
Ashtray	*$50.00*
Bowl, 4¹/₂" or 5"	*20.00*
Bowl, 9" or 9¹/₂"	*30.00*
Bowl, 10", Oval	*25.00*
Butter Dish with Cover	*100.00*
Cake Stand, 10"	*20.00*
Candy Dish with Cover	*50.00*
Coaster	*50.00*
Cookie Jar with Cover	*45.00*
Creamer	*12.50*
Cup	*10.00*
Pitcher, Milk, 1 qt.	*50.00*
Pitcher, 2 qt.	*50.00*
Plate, 5¹/₂"	*6.00*
Plate, 8" or 9"	*12.00*
Plate, 9" Grill, 3 Divisions	*12.00*
Plate, 10¹/₂" Grill, 3 Divisions, 2-Handled	*15.00*
Platter, 12", 2-Handled	*25.00*
Relish	*20.00*
Salt and Pepper Shakers	*50.00*
Sandwich Server with Center Handle	*25.00*

Depression glass, "Princess" pattern. Photo by Robin Rainwater.

Saucer *$6.00*
Sherbet *12.50*
Sugar with Cover *27.50*
Sugar Shaker *25.00*
Tumbler, 3"–6" Tall *30.00*
Tumbler, over 6" Tall *40.00*
Vase *30.00*

The basic prices above include the colors pink, green, and light amber. For bright yellow (named "Topaz" by Hocking) and light blue, double the above prices.

"Princess" is a pretty, popular pattern characterized by a somewhat paneled curtain design. Note that many pieces are octagonal in shape.

PYRAMID OR NO. 610   INDIANA GLASS COMPANY,
1926–1932

Depression glass, "Pyramid" or "No. 610" pattern. Reproduced from a 1930 trade catalog.

Object	Price
Bowl, 5" or 6"	*$15.00*
Bowl, 8½" or 9½"	*25.00*
Creamer	*17.50*
Ice Tub	*75.00*
Ice Tub with Cover	*700.00*
Pitcher, Milk, 1 qt.	*250.00*
Pitcher, Water, 2 qt.	*300.00*
Relish Tray, 4 Divisions, 2-Handled	*50.00*
Sugar	*17.50*
Tumbler, Various Styles	*30.00*

"Pyramid," priced above, includes the colors pink, green, and yellow. For crystal or milk glass, reduce the prices by 50%. Like a few of Indiana's numbered patterns, the name "Pyramid" was unpatented but nicknamed by dealers and collectors because of the pattern's shape.

Under the "Tiara" name, "Pyramid" pieces were reproduced in blue and black in the 1970s (same price as crystal).

QUEEN MARY   HOCKING GLASS COMPANY, 1936–1939

Object	Pink
Ashtray	*$3.00*
Bowl, 4"–5¾", with or without Handles	*5.00*
Bowl, 6"–9"	*10.00*
Butter Dish with Cover	*125.00*
Candlestick, Double	*12.50*
Candy Dish with Cover	*25.00*
Cigarette Jar, Oval	*7.50*
Coaster, Round	*3.00*
Coaster, Square	*5.00*
Compote	*10.00*
Creamer, Footed	*15.00*
Creamer, Oval	*7.50*
Cup	*4.00*
Pickle Dish	*15.00*
Pitcher	*125.00*
Plate, 6" or 6½"	*3.00*
Plate, 8¾"	*15.00*
Plate, 9¾"	*20.00*
Platter, 12"	*15.00*
Platter, 14"	*20.00*
Salt and Pepper Shakers	*75.00*
Saucer	*2.00*
Sherbet	*5.00*
Sugar, Footed	*15.00*
Sugar, Oval	*7.50*
Tray, 12" or 14"	*20.00*
Tumbler, 3½" or 4" Tall	*10.00*
Tumbler, 5" Tall	*25.00*

The original Depression color was pink, which was produced in the late 1930s. Reduce the above prices by 50% for crystal. For royal ruby and forest green, which were produced in the 1950s, use the same prices as for the pink.

This pattern is sometimes referred to as "Vertical Ribbed" obviously because of the up-and-down or vertical ribbing.

RAINDROPS OR OPTIC DESIGN   FEDERAL GLASS
COMPANY, 1929–1933

Object	*Price*
Bowl, 4½" or 6"	$5.00
Bowl, 7½"	10.00
Creamer	5.00
Cup	4.00
Plate, 6"	2.00
Plate, 8"	4.00
Salt and Pepper Shakers	200.00
Saucer	2.00
Sherbert	5.00
Sugar with Cover	35.00
Tumbler, 3" or 4" Tall	4.00
Tumbler, 5" Tall	7.50
Whiskey Tumbler, 1¾" or 2¼" Tall	6.00

"Raindrops" is a rather simple pattern with small pressed circles. The prices above are for green; for crystal, reduce them by 50%.

RIBBON   HOCKING GLASS COMPANY, 1927–1933

Object	*Price*
Bowl, 4" or 5"	$7.50
Bowl, 7" or 8"	15.00
Candy Jar with Cover	50.00
Creamer	10.00
Cup	5.00

Left: Depression glass, "Raindrops" or "Optic" pattern. Photo by Robin Rainwater.
Right: Depression glass, "Ribbon" pattern. Photo by Robin Rainwater.

Plate, 6¼" *$3.00*
Plate, 8" *5.00*
Salt and Pepper Shakers *50.00*
Saucer *2.00*
Sherbet *5.00*
Sugar, 2-Handled *10.00*
Tumbler, 5½" or 6" Tall *20.00*

The basic colors are pink and green. For black, double the above prices; for crystal, reduce them by 50%. This is another simple Depression pattern of vertical panels that nearly reach the top of each item.

RINGS OR BANDED RINGS   HOCKING GLASS
COMPANY, 1927–1933

Object	*Price*
Bowl, 5"	*$5.00*
Bowl, 5¼", 2 Divisions	*10.00*
Bowl, 7" or 8"	*10.00*
Cocktail Shaker	*25.00*
Creamer	*6.00*
Cup	*5.00*
Decanter with Stopper	*35.00*
Goblet	*15.00*
Ice Bucket or Tub	*20.00*
Pitcher, 2 qt.	*25.00*
Pitcher, 2½ qt.	*30.00*
Plate, 6¼"	*2.00*
Plate, 6½" with Off-Center Ring for Sherbet	*5.00*
Plate, 8"	*4.00*
Salt and Pepper Shakers	*35.00*
Sandwich Server with Center Handle	*25.00*
Saucer	*2.00*
Sherbet	*10.00*
Sugar	*6.00*
Tumbler, Various Styles	*7.50*
Vase	*17.50*
Whiskey, 2" Tall, 1½ oz.	*6.00*

Hocking produced many, many banded ring combinations. These bands include an incredible number of colors, including black, blue, green, orange, pink, red, yellow, and differing shades of these colors. They even trimmed or ringed them in metals, including gold, silver, and platinum. For plain crystal, reduce the above prices by 50%.

The biggest problem with these fired-on enameled rings is that they are difficult to find completely intact. Nicks, scratches, incomplete bands, fading, worn out, and other problems plague this type of banding. Damaged banded glass is not worth nearly as much as completely intact glass (the prices above reflect complete, undamaged banding).

ROCK CRYSTAL OR EARLY AMERICAN ROCK CRYSTAL   MCKEE GLASS COMPANY, 1920S–1930S

Object	Price
Bonbon Dish	$25.00
Bowl, 4"–6"	15.00
Bowl, 7"–9"	25.00
Bowl, 10"–12"	35.00
Bowl, 12½"–14"	75.00
Butter Dish with Cover	300.00
Candelabra, Double or Triple	75.00
Candlestick, Various Styles	35.00
Candy Jar with Cover	75.00
Cake Stand, 11", Footed	40.00
Compote, 7"	25.00
Cordial	25.00
Creamer	25.00
Cruet with Stopper	100.00
Cup	20.00
Goblet, Various Styles	25.00
Marmalade Dish	20.00
Lamp, Electric	225.00
Parfait	30.00
Pitcher, Syrup with Lid	150.00
Pitcher, Milk, 1 qt.	300.00
Pitcher, Water, 2 qt.	400.00
Pitcher with Cover, 3 qt.	500.00
Plate, 6"	7.50
Plate, 7½" or 8½"	10.00
Plate, 9", 10", or 10½"	25.00
Platter, 11½"	30.00
Punch Bowl with Stand	500.00
Salt Dip	40.00
Salt and Pepper Shakers	125.00
Sandwich Server with Center Handle	35.00
Saucer	7.50
Sherbert	20.00
Spooner	40.00
Sugar with Cover, 2-Handled	60.00
Tray, Oval	50.00
Tumbler, Various Styles	20.00
Vase, Various Styles	75.00
Wineglass	25.00

"Rock Crystal" is one of the most prolific patterns in Depression glass and comes in a wide variety of colors including varying shades of amber, amethyst, aquamarine, light blue, frosted or decorated crystal, green, milk, pink, vaseline, yellow, frosted colors, and so on. The prices only vary for ruby red and cobalt blue (double the above prices), and plain crystal (reduce them by 50%). The pattern contains a good deal of scrolling and vining around five-petal flowers.

ROSE CAMEO   BELMONT TUMBLER COMPANY, 1931

Object	Price
Bowl, 4½"	.$7.50
Bowl, 5"	.10.00
Bowl, 6"	.12.50
Plate, 7"	.7.50
Sherbet	.10.00
Tumbler, 5" Tall, Rim Design Varies	.15.00

The only color made in this pattern was green. The Belmont Tumbler Company is the only company to file on a patent on this pattern, which they did in 1931. Do not confuse this pattern with Hocking's "Ballerina." In "Rose Cameo," a rose is encircled within the cameo. In Hocking's, a dancing girl or ballerina is encircled.

ROSEMARY OR DUTCH ROSE   FEDERAL GLASS COMPANY, 1935–1936

Object	Price
Bowl, 5"	.$7.50
Bowl, 6"	.20.00
Bowl, 10", Oval	.25.00
Creamer	.10.00
Cup	.7.50
Plate, 6¾"	.7.50
Plate, 9½"	.10.00
Plate, 9½", Grill, 3 Divisions	.12.00
Platter, 12", Oval	.20.00
Saucer	.2.50
Sugar, 2-Handled	.10.00
Tumbler	.25.00

The prices are for green and amber. Pink is much rarer (increase the above prices by 50%).

 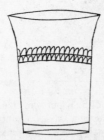 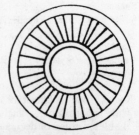

Left: Depression glass, "Rosemary" pattern. Drawing by Mark Pickvet. Center: Depression glass, "Roulette" pattern. Drawing by Mark Pickvet. Right: Depression glass, "Round Robin" pattern. Drawing by Mark Pickvet.

"Rosemary" is a derivative of Federal's "Mayfair" pattern and includes rose blossoms in the center and within the arches.

ROULETTE   HOCKING GLASS COMPANY, 1935–1938

Object	Price
Bowl, 8" or 9"	$10.00
Cup	5.00
Pitcher, 1 qt.	40.00
Plate, 6"	3.00
Plate, 8½"	6.00
Platter, 12"	15.00
Saucer	3.00
Sherbert	5.00
Tumbler, Several Styles	20.00
Whiskey Tumbler, 2½" Tall, 1½ oz.	15.00

The primary Depression colors include pink and green; for crystal, reduce the prices by 50%. "Roulette" is sometimes nicknamed "Many Windows" because of the two horizontal rows of miniature rectangles.

ROUND ROBIN   UNKNOWN MANUFACTURE, 1920S–1930S

Object	Price
Bowl, 4"	$5.00
Creamer	7.50
Cup	5.00
Domino Tray	35.00
Plate, 6"	3.00
Plate, 8"	4.00
Platter, 12"	10.00
Saucer	2.00
Sherbert	5.00
Sugar, 2-Handled	7.50
Tumbler	15.00

The colors include green and light marigold. For crystal, reduce the prices by 50%. This is another simple vertically ribbed pattern but with no sure patents. The domino tray is unique to this pattern; it consists of a center ring for a creamer and the remaining surrounding area for sugar cubes.

ROYAL LACE   HAZEL ATLAS GLASS COMPANY, 1934–EARLY 1940S

Object	Price
Bowl, 4¾" or 5"	$15.00
Bowl, 10", with or without Legs	25.00
Bowl, 11", Oval	30.00

Butter Dish with Cover *$150.00*
Candlestick, Various Styles *20.00*
Cookie Jar with Cover *50.00*
Creamer *15.00*
Cup *12.00*
Nut Bowl *150.00*
Pitcher, 1½ qt. *60.00*
Pitcher, 1 qt. *75.00*
Pitcher, 1½ qt. *85.00*
Plate, 6" *5.00*
Plate, 8½" *7.50*
Plate, 9" Grill, 3 Divisions *12.50*
Plate, 10" *15.00*
Platter, 13", Oval *20.00*
Salt and Pepper Shakers *75.00*
Saucer *4.00*
Sherbert *15.00*
Sugar with Cover, 2-Handled *50.00*
Tumbler, Several Styles *25.00*

The colors priced above include pink and green. For amethyst and cobalt blue, double the above prices; for crystal, reduce them by 50%. Production of this paneled lace pattern by Hazel Atlas continued into the 1940s, but the majority of the colored glass was made in the 1930s.

The interesting story of "Royal Lace" is that General Mills had commissioned Hazel Atlas to manufacture Shirley Temple pieces (cobalt blue glass with pictures of Shirley Temple applied as decals). When General Mills discontinued the order, Hazel Atlas was left with several tanks of molten blue glass. The "Royal Lace" molds were nearby and were promptly filled with the blue glass.

SANDWICH INDIANA GLASS COMPANY, 1920S–1930S

Object	Pink	Green	Amber	Crystal
Ashtray Set, 4-Piece Card Suits	*$15.00*	*$20.00*		*$4.00*
Basket, 10" Tall			*35.00*	*30.00*
Bowl, 4¼"	*6.00*	*8.00*	*4.00*	*3.00*
Bowl, 6"	*5.00*	*6.00*	*3.00*	*2.00*
Bowl, 6", Hexagonal	*10.00*	*12.00*	*5.00*	*4.00*

Depression glass, "Sandwich" pattern. Photo by Robin Rainwater.

INDIANA GLASS COMPANY
DUNKIRK, INDIANA

Manufacturers Of

PRESSED AND BLOWN GLASSWARE
CRYSTAL, COLORED AND DECORATED

SANDWICH PATTERN
No. 170—8¼" Salad Plate

Depression glass,
"Sandwich" pattern.
Reproduced from a
1925 advertisement.

Object	Pink	Green	Amber	Crystal
Bowl, 8½"	$12.00	$14.00	$10.00	$8.00
Bowl, 9"	16.00	20.00	14.00	12.00
Bowl, 11½"	25.00	30.00	18.00	16.00
Butter Dish Bottom	50.00	75.00	10.00	8.00
Butter Dish with Cover	180.00	230.00	32.00	25.00
Butter Dish Top	125.00	150.00	20.00	15.00
Candlestick, 3½"	15.00	20.00	10.00	8.00
Candlestick, 7"	20.00	25.00	14.00	12.00
Celery, 10½"	20.00	25.00	14.00	12.00
Creamer	15.00	20.00	10.00	8.00
Creamer and Sugar Set on Diamond-Shaped Tray	35.00	45.00	25.00	20.00
Cup	5.00	6.00	3.00	2.00
Decanter with Stopper	90.00	100.00	25.00	20.00
Goblet, 9 oz.	16.00	20.00	14.00	12.00
Mayonnaise			14.00	12.00
Pitcher, 68 oz.	125.00	150.00	40.00	30.00
Plate, 6"	5.00	6.00	3.00	2.00
Plate, 7"	6.00	7.00	4.00	3.00
Plate, 8", Oval with Indentation for the Sherbet	7.00	8.00		
Plate, 8⅜"	6.00	7.00	4.00	3.00
Plate, 10½"	15.00	20.00	10.00	8.00
Plate, 13"	20.00	25.00	14.00	10.00
Puff Box			16.00	14.00
Punch Bowl, 13"		200.00		
Punch Cup		10.00		
Salt and Pepper Shakers			18.00	16.00
Sandwich Server with Center Handle	30.00	35.00	22.00	18.00

Object	Pink	Green	Amber	Crystal
Saucer	$4.00	$5.00	$3.00	$2.00
Sherbet, 3¹/₄"	8.00	10.00	6.00	5.00
Sugar	15.00	20.00	10.00	8.00
Sugar Cover			14.00	12.00
Tumbler, 3 oz. Footed	15.00	20.00	10.00	8.00
Tumbler, 8 oz. Footed	20.00	25.00	14.00	10.00
Tumbler, 12 oz. Footed	25.00	30.00	15.00	12.00
Wine, 3", 4 oz.	20.00	25.00	8.00	6.00

Indiana's "Sandwich" causes more problems than any other pattern. All of the above colors were made during the Depression era; however, all except the pink have been reproduced since. The crystal and amber reflect prices for the new as well as the old; they're quite a bit lower than what the originals would be on their own. The problem that arises is that the majority of the original molds were put back into service to make virtually identical pieces.

The pink is the only true original color that is easily distinguished, since it is all old. The original green is a yellowish green, while the new is a paler shade of green. The original also glows under a dark or black light (a common test for older Depression glass because of the ores utilized in the ingredients); the new does not glow.

Other colors of Indiana's "Sandwich" were produced after the Depression and appear in the next chapter. These include teal blue, smokey blue, milk white, and red. A few red original pieces were made in the 1930s but are nearly impossible to tell from the reproductions.

SHARON CABBAGE ROSE FEDERAL GLASS
COMPANY, 1935–1939

Object	Price
Bowl, 5" or 6"	$10.00
Bowl, 7¹/₂", 8¹/₂", or 9¹/₂"	15.00
Bowl, 10¹/₂"	25.00
Butter Dish with Cover	75.00
Cake Plate, 11¹/₂", Footed	30.00

Left: Depression glass, "Sharon Cabbage Rose" pattern. Right: Depression glass, "Sierra Pinwheel" pattern. Photos by Robin Rainwater.

Candy Jar with Cover	*$50.00*
Creamer	*12.50*
Cup	*10.00*
Marmalade Dish	*35.00*
Pitcher, 2½ qt.	*125.00*
Plate, 6"	*5.00*
Plate, 7½" or 9½"	*12.50*
Platter, 12½", Oval	*20.00*
Salt and Pepper Shakers	*50.00*
Saucer	*5.00*
Sherbet	*12.50*
Sugar with Cover, 2-Handled	*27.50*
Tumbler, Various Styles	*30.00*
Vase	*50.00*

The Depression colors priced above include pink, green, and amber; for crystal, reduce the prices by 50%. This pattern gets its name from the roses that resemble cabbage heads.

There are several reproductions to be aware of in this pattern. Butter dishes were produced in 1976 in pink, dark pink, green, dark or forest green, and light blue. The regular pink and green are the only trouble, since they resemble the originals. Creamer and sugar sets as well as salt and pepper shakers in very light pink were reissued in the late 1970s and 1980s, but the color is much fainter than the original. Candy jars were also reproduced in both pink and green.

SIERRA PINWHEEL   JEANNETTE GLASS COMPANY, 1931–1933

Object	*Price*
Bowl, 5½"	*$10.00*
Bowl, 8½"	*15.00*
Bowl, 9¼", Oval	*35.00*
Butter Dish with Cover	*60.00*
Creamer	*15.00*
Cup	*12.00*
Pitcher, Milk, 1 qt.	*75.00*
Plate, 9"	*12.50*
Platter, 11", Oval	*35.00*
Salt and Pepper Shakers	*50.00*
Saucer	*5.00*
Sugar with Cover, 2-Handled	*35.00*
Tray, 10¼", 2-Handled	*20.00*
Tumbler	*45.00*

The primary colors are pink and green, but there were a few pieces made in ultramarine (same price). The pattern consists of vertical ribbing that extends out to an irregular edge that is prone to chipping, so examine pieces carefully.

Jeannette did make a butter dish and cover with a combination of the "Adam" (see first listing in this chapter) and the "Sierra" pattern. This dish along with the cover happens to be worth about $600.00!

SPIRAL   HOCKING GLASS COMPANY, 1928–1930

Object	Price
Bowl 4³/₄"	.$5.00
Bowl, 7"	.8.00
Bowl, 8"	.10.00
Bowl, 9"	.12.50
Creamer	.7.50
Cup	.4.00
Ice Tub	.25.00
Marmalade with Cover	.25.00
Pitcher, 1 qt.	.30.00
Plate, 6"	.2.00
Plate, 8"	.3.00
Platter, 12"	.20.00
Salt and Pepper Shakers	.50.00
Sandwich Server with Center Handle	.40.00
Saucer	.2.00
Sherbert	.5.00
Sugar, 2-Handled	.7.50
Tumbler, Various Styles	.5.00

The two Depression colors made in this pattern are pink and green. This pattern is sometimes confused with "Swirl" and "Twisted Optic." "Swirl" is easy to identify, because the arcs and curves are a bit straighter or not as sharply angled. Like "Twisted Optic," "Swirl" curves go counterclockwise; "Spiral" curves move clockwise. The important thing to remember is to look at the piece from the correct angle!

STRAWBERRY   U.S. GLASS COMPANY, EARLY 1930S

Object	Price
Bowl, 4"	.$8.00
Bowl, 6¹/₄"	.40.00
Bowl, 6¹/₂"	.15.00
Bowl, 7¹/₂"	.16.00
Butter Dish with Cover	.150.00
Compote	.15.00
Creamer, Small	.15.00
Creamer, Large, 4¹/₂" Tall	.20.00
Olive Dish, 5", 1 Tab Handle	.15.00
Pickle Dish, 8¹/₄" Oval	.15.00
Pitcher	.150.00
Plate, 6"	.6.00
Plate, 7¹/₂"	.8.00
Sherbet	.6.00
Sugar, Small (open)	.15.00
Sugar, Large with Cover	.35.00
Tumbler	.20.00

The basic colors are pink and green; however, most pieces can be found in crystal and a light iridized marigold color (reduce the above prices by 25% for crystal or marigold).

This is the sister pattern of "Cherryberry," also produced by U.S. Glass. The dimensions of the pieces are identical, but the fruits on the pattern are obviously different.

SUNFLOWER   JEANNETTE GLASS COMPANY, 1930S

Object	Price
Ashtray, 5"	*$10.00*
Cake Plate, 10" with 3 Legs	*.8.00*
Creamer	*.17.50*
Cup	*.12.50*
Plate, 9"	*.12.50*
Saucer	*.7.50*
Sugar, 2-Handled	*.17.50*
Trivet, 7" with 3 Legs	*.225.00*
Tumbler	*.25.00*

The basic colors are pink and green. For odd colors like ultramarine, delphite blue, and other opaque colors, triple the above prices. The pattern consists of sunflower blossoms connected by long stalks or vines along with one large sunflower blossom in the center. The cake plate was once given away free in flour bags and remains one of the most commonly found Depression glass items.

SWIRL OR PETAL SWIRL   JEANNETTE GLASS COMPANY, 1937–1938

Object	Price
Bowl, 6¼"	*$10.00*
Bowl, 9"	*.15.00*
Bowl, 10" or 10½", with or without Handles or Feet, Closed Handles	*.25.00*
Butter Dish with Cover	*.200.00*
Candleholders, Single or Double	*.25.00*
Candy Dish with 3 Legs	*.12.50*

Left: Depression glass, "Spiral" pattern. Photo by Robin Rainwater. Right: Depression glass, "Swirl" pattern. Drawing by Mark Pickvet.

Candy Dish with Cover	*$100.00*
Coaster	*7.50*
Creamer	*10.00*
Cup	*8.00*
Pitcher, 1½ qt.	*350.00*
Plate, 6½"	*7.50*
Plate, 7¼" or 8"	*10.00*
Plate, 9¼"	*12.00*
Plate, 10½"	*15.00*
Platter, 12", Oval	*25.00*
Platter, 12½"	*25.00*
Salt and Pepper Shakers	*75.00*
Saucer	*5.00*
Sherbet	*10.00*
Sugar, 2-Handled	*10.00*
Tray, 10½", 2-Handled	*25.00*
Tumbler, Various Styles	*25.00*
Vase, Various Styles	*25.00*

"Swirl" pieces come with two different edge designs; some are plain and others are ruffled. The values are the same for both. The colors priced above include pink, ultramarine, amber, and blue.

"Swirl" is fairly easy to keep separate from the "Spiral" and "Twisted Optic" patterns because its curves and arcs are not as wide as those of the other two.

TEA ROOM   INDIANA GLASS COMPANY, 1926–1931

Object	*Price*
Banana Boat, with or without Feet	*$75.00*
Bowl, 4" or 5"	*45.00*
Bowl, 8½" or 8¾"	*50.00*
Bowl, 9½", Oval	*60.00*
Candlestick	*25.00*
Creamer, Several Styles	*17.50*
Cup	*40.00*
Goblet	*60.00*
Ice Bucket	*50.00*
Lamp, 9", Electric	*50.00*
Marmalade with Notched Cover	*175.00*
Mustard Jar with Cover	*125.00*
Parfait	*55.00*
Pitcher, 1 qt.	*125.00*
Plate, 6½" or 8¼"	*30.00*
Plate, 10½", 2-Handled	*45.00*
Relish	*20.00*
Salt and Pepper Shakers	*75.00*
Sandwich Server with Center Handle	*150.00*
Saucer	*25.00*
Sherbet, Several Styles	*30.00*
Sugar, 2-Handled, Several Styles	*17.50*

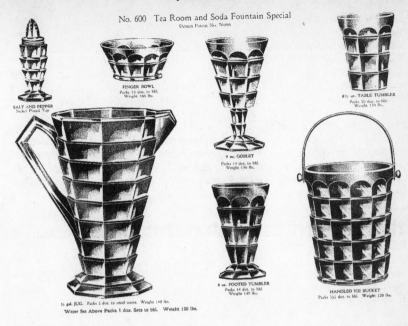

No. 600 Tea Room and Soda Fountain Special
Design Patent No. 76086

SALT AND PEPPER
Nickel Plated Top

FINGER BOWL
Packs 14 doz. to bbl.
Weight 160 lbs.

9 oz. GOBLET
Packs 10 doz. to bbl.
Weight 130 lbs.

8½ oz. TABLE TUMBLER
Packs 20 doz. to bbl.
Weight 130 lbs.

8 oz. FOOTED TUMBLER
Packs 14 doz. to bbl.
Weight 140 lbs.

HANDLED ICE BUCKET
Packs 5½ doz. to bbl. Weight 120 lbs.

½ gal. JUG. Packs 2 doz. to small tierce. Weight 140 lbs.
Water Set Above Packs 1 doz. Sets to bbl. Weight 120 lbs.

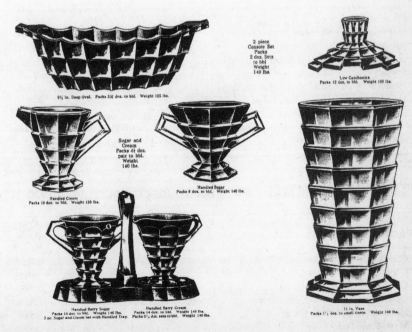

9½ in. Deep Oval. Packs 5½ doz. to bbl. Weight 125 lbs.

3 piece Console Set
Packs 2 doz. Sets to bbl. Weight 140 lbs.

Low Candlestick
Packs 12 doz. to bbl. Weight 150 lbs.

Sugar and Cream
Packs 4½ doz. pair to bbl. Weight 140 lbs.

Handled Sugar
Packs 8 doz. to bbl. Weight 140 lbs.

Handled Cream
Packs 10 doz. to bbl. Weight 120 lbs.

Handled Berry Sugar
Packs 14 doz. to bbl. Weight 140 lbs.
3 pc. Sugar and Cream Set with Handled Tray. Packs 5½ doz. sets to bbl. Weight 140 lbs.

Handled Berry Cream
Packs 14 doz. to bbl. Weight 140 lbs.

11 in. Vase
Packs 1½ doz. to small tierce. Weight 140 lbs.

Depression glass, "Tea Room" pattern. Reproduced from a 1930 trade catalog.

Sugar with Cover, Several Styles	*$125.00*
Sundae Dish	*75.00*
Tray for Rectangular Creamer and Sugar	*40.00*
Tumbler, Several Styles	*35.00*
Vase, 6½" Tall	*100.00*
Vase, 9½" Tall	*75.00*
Vase, 11" Tall	*125.00*

Colors include pink, green, and amber; for crystal, reduce the above prices by 50%. "Tea Room" is an extremely popular, expensive pattern. If you can find a piece under $10.00, buy it! There are many fountain items that were made for ice cream stores (banana boats or splits, parfait glasses, and footed tumblers, for instance); tea rooms, as its name implies (several creamer and sugars, mustards, marmalades, etc.); and restaurants.

THUMBPRINT OR PEAR OPTIC   FEDERAL GLASS COMPANY, 1929–1930

Object	*Green*
Bowl, 4¾" or 5"	*$3.00*
Bowl, 7" or 8"	*8.00*
Creamer	*12.50*
Cup	*3.00*
Plate, 6"	*2.00*
Plate, 8"	*3.00*
Plate, 9¼"	*5.00*
Salt and Pepper Shakers	*35.00*
Saucer	*2.00*
Sherbet	*5.00*
Sugar	*12.50*
Tumbler, Various Styles	*5.00*
Whiskey Tumbler, 2¼" Tall, 1¼ oz.	*7.50*

"Pear Optic" is Federal's official name for this pattern, but it is more commonly referred to as "Thumbprint." It is green and contains a common elongated pressed thumbprint design.

TWISTED OPTIC   IMPERIAL GLASS COMPANY, 1927–1930

Object	*Price*
Bowl, 4¾" or 5"	*$7.50*
Bowl, 7" or 8"	*10.00*
Candlestick	*7.50*
Candy Jar with Cover	*30.00*
Creamer	*7.50*
Cup	*5.00*
Marmalade Dish with Cover	*25.00*
Mayonnaise	*15.00*
Pitcher, 2 qt.	*30.00*

Depression glass, "Twisted Optic" pattern. Photo by Robin Rainwater.

Plate, 6" or 7" *$4.00*
Plate, 8" .... *.5.00*
Plate, 9", Oval with Indentation .... *.6.00*
Plate, 10" .... *.7.50*
Sandwich Server with Center Handle .... *.25.00*
Saucer .... *.3.00*
Sherbet .... *.7.50*
Sugar, 2-Handled .... *.7.50*
Tray, 2-Handled .... *.15.00*
Tumbler, Several Styles .... *.6.00*

The Depression colors in the pricing consist of pink, green, amber, yellow, and a light copper blue.

"Twisted Optic" is commonly confused with Hocking's "Spiral" pattern and less so with some "Swirl" patterns. The curving spirals of "Twisted Optic" go counterclockwise, while "Spiral" curves move in a clockwise direction. "Spiral" was only made in pink and green, while "Twisted Optic" includes light blue, amber, and yellow pieces.

U.S. SWIRL   U.S. GLASS COMPANY, LATE 1920S

Object	*Price*
Bowl, 4½"	*$5.00*
Bowl, 5½", 1 Handle	*.10.00*
Bowl, 8"	*.15.00*
Bowl, 8¼", Oval	*.20.00*
Bowl, 10", Octagonal, Footed	*.25.00*
Butter Dish with Cover	*.75.00*
Candy Jar with Cover, 2-Handled	*.30.00*
Creamer	*.12.50*
Pitcher, 1½ qt.	*.40.00*
Plate, 6"	*.2.00*
Plate, 8"	*.5.00*
Salt and Pepper Shakers	*.50.00*
Sherbet	*.5.00*
Sugar with Cover, 2-Handled	*.30.00*

Tumbler, Several Styles *$12.50*
Vase *15.00*

The basic colors include pink and green; for crystal, reduce the prices by 50%. Most of the "U.S. Swirl" pieces have a star in the bottom, which helps in differentiating it from the other swirls, spirals, and twisted patterns out there.

VICTORY   DIAMOND GLASS-WARE COMPANY, 1929–1932

Object	*Price*
Bonbon Dish	*$12.50*
Bowl, 6½"	*12.50*
Bowl, 8½"	*15.00*
Bowl, 9", Oval	*30.00*
Bowl, 11", 12", or 12½"	*30.00*
Candlestick	*15.00*
Cheese and Cracker Set (Indented Plate with Compote)	*50.00*
Compote	*12.50*
Creamer	*12.50*
Cup	*10.00*
Goblet	*20.00*
Gravy Boat with Matching Platter	*175.00*
Mayonnaise Set, Dish, Underplate, and Ladle	*75.00*
Pitcher, 2 qt.	*100.00*
Plate, 6", 7", or 8"	*6.00*
Plate, 9"	*12.50*
Platter, 12"	*20.00*
Sandwich Server with Center Handle	*35.00*
Saucer	*4.00*
Sherbet	*12.50*
Sugar, 2-Handled	*12.50*
Tumbler, Various Styles	*25.00*

The colors priced above include amber, pink, and green. For cobalt blue, double the above prices; for black, triple them. The cobalt blue and the opaque black glass are highly desirable and collectible. They're not cheap either! Some of the black pieces are trimmed in gold and decorated with flower patterns or other designs (the value is the same as the usual black). Gravy boats and platters are not common pieces found in Depression sets, and the one here is also quite rare.

The pattern is one of simplicity consisting of vertical panels (much like a spoke design on the flat rounded pieces).

WATERFORD OR WAFFLE   HOCKING GLASS
COMPANY, 1938–1944

Object	*Price*
Ashtray, 4", with or without Advertising	*$7.50*
Bowl, 5" or 5½"	*10.00*
Bowl, 8¼	*12.50*

Butter Dish with Cover	*$150.00*
Coaster	*.7.50*
Creamer	*.12.50*
Cup	*.10.00*
Goblet	*.12.50*
Lamp, Miniature	*.25.00*
Pitcher, Milk, 1 qt.	*.75.00*
Pitcher, Water, 2½ qt.	*.100.00*
Plate, 6"	*.6.00*
Plate, 7"	*.7.50*
Plate, 9½"	*.10.00*
Plate, 10¼", 2-Handled	*.12.50*
Platter, 13¾"	*.25.00*
Relish	*.20.00*
Salt and Pepper Shakers	*.75.00*
Saucer	*.4.00*
Sherbet	*.12.50*
Sugar with Cover	*.37.50*
Tumbler, Several Styles	*.12.50*
Wineglass	*.12.50*

The basic color is pink; for crystal, reduce prices by 50%. Pieces can also be found in milk white, yellow, and reproduction forest green; reduce the above prices by 25%.

This pattern is similar to Hocking's "Miss America" in more ways than one. First it has a similar diamond shape, but the diamonds are much larger on the "Waterford." Some pieces have the exact same mold design too, only the patterns differ. Note that "Waffle" is a nickname only, which aids in describing the pattern. This pattern was also made after "Miss America" at the tail end of the Depression era.

WINDSOR OR WINDSOR DIAMOND   JEANNETTE
GLASS COMPANY, 1936–1937

Object	*Price*
Ashtray	*$15.00*
Boat Dish, 11¾" Oval	*.50.00*
Bowl, 4¾" or 5"	*.7.50*
Bowl, 5½"	*.10.00*
Bowl, 7", 3 Legs	*.15.00*
Bowl, 8", 8¼", or 8½", with or without Handles	*.17.50*
Bowl, 9½", Oval	*.20.00*
Bowl, 10½"	*.25.00*
Bowl, 12½"	*.75.00*
Butter Dish with Cover	*.100.00*
Cake Plate, 10¾", Footed	*.20.00*
Candlestick	*.35.00*
Candy Jar with Cover	*.55.00*
Coaster	*.15.00*
Compote	*.12.50*
Creamer	*.12.50*
Cup	*.10.00*

Depression glass, "Windsor Diamond" pattern. Drawing by Mark Pickvet.

Pitcher, 1 pt. *$100.00*
Pitcher, 1½ qt. *75.00*
Plate, 6" *5.00*
Plate, 7" *10.00*
Plate, 9" *12.50*
Plate, 10¼", 2-Handled *15.00*
Platter, 11½", Oval *20.00*
Platter, 13½" *35.00*
Powder Jar *75.00*
Salt and Pepper Shakers *50.00*
Saucer *4.00*
Sherbet *15.00*
Sugar with Cover *27.50*
Tray, 4", Square *35.00*
Tray, 4", Square, 2-Handled *25.00*
Tray, 9" Oval, with or without Handles *20.00*
Tray, 9¾" Oval, with or without Handles *25.00*
Tumbler, Several Styles *25.00*

The basic colors include pink and green. For odd-colored pieces, including light blue, delphite blue, and yellow, double the above prices. For the rare red amberina, quadruple them. As with most Depression glass, colored glass production ended with this pattern by 1940; however, pieces were still made in crystal (reduce the prices by 50%).

The pressed diamond pattern is an allover one; that is, it covers most pieces from top to bottom.

CHAPTER 7

MODERN AND MISCELLANEOUS AMERICAN GLASS

At the turn of the century, America was on a wave of growth fueled by invention, technology, industrialization, and the rise of powerful corporations. The glass industry was no exception. After the Depression, smaller companies were overtaken by larger, machine-production-oriented corporations.

Colored glass production of the Depression era was drastically reduced for two primary reasons. One is that many of the elemental metals necessary for coloring were needed for World War II weapons manufacture. The other is that the Depression colors simply went out of style. Many glass manufactures qualified as industry essentials and produced glass for the war effort. These included radar, X-ray, and electronic tubes as well as heat-treated tumblers manufactured specifically for extra strength.

After the war, big corporations such as Libbey (a division of Owens-Corning) and Anchor Hocking emerged as industrial giants boasting high-speed machinery and huge-volume capacity. Handmade glass, hand-cut, hand-etched, and nearly all other hand operations that had squeaked through the Depression, folded by the late 1950s. Such names as Pairpoint, Heisey, Cambridge, and many more shut down permanently.

A few others like Fostoria and Westmoreland, survived into the 1980s, but many more were purchased and swallowed by larger firms; some continued operation as divisions (Hazel-Ware under Continental Can for instance). Finally there were a rare few, like Fenton and Steuben, who survived the economic downswings and hard times of the marketplace. They have operated continuously since the turn of the century and continued to etch their mark in glassmaking history.

Despite the difficulties of many companies, a huge variety of collectible glassware has been produced in America since the Depression era. Colors were not totally eradicated, especially in the case of Jeannette, which made several Depression lookalike patterns such as "Anniversary." Darker colors like forest green and royal ruby (Anchor Hocking) and Moroccan amethyst (Hazel-Ware) were made in large table sets.

Animal figures and covered animal dishes have been popular since the 19th century and modern examples have been made by numerous companies (Heisey, New Martinsville, Fenton, Steuben, etc). The Boyd Art Glass Company has been in existence only since 1978 and already is well established in the collector field, with miniature animals and other colorful figurines. Decorated enameled wares include not only animals but a host of other character figures too. Swanky Swigs (a product of Kraft Cheese spreads), tumblers, pitchers, and a host of other items with machine-applied enameling or transfers have flourished over the past fifty years.

As the Depression colors phased out, a good deal of crystal, milk, and porcelain-like items were produced afterward. Heisey, Cambridge, and Fostoria all made quality crystal table sets in the 1940s and 1950s. Westmoreland's "Paneled Grape" and Fenton's "Crest" patterns were the largest sets ever produced in milk glass. Chinex, Fire-King, and a host of others produced both oven and tableware that resemble porcelain in a wide variety of colors.

Modern collectible glass includes many reproduction forms such as Imperial's "New Carnival," other iridescent forms, carnival-like punch bowls and water sets, popular Depression patterns, Jeannette's miniature "Cameo Ballerina," and others that at times can be quite confusing when compared to the originals. One company that has been quite controversial in making reproductions is the Indiana Glass Company. In the past two decades the company has reproduced a wide variety of items in the Sandwich pattern that originally dates back to the early Depression years.

Naturally, the people most upset with reproductions are those who have invested or collected the original, but it is partly selfishness; after all, a company has a legal right to do what it wishes with its own patented lines and machinery. Reproductions give new collectors a chance to acquire beautiful and appealing patterns. Hundreds of years from now, it will probably matter little if a particular pattern was produced in the 1930s or 1970s.

On the side of the collector, no one really wishes to see a collection devalued or harmed because of remakes. Some companies have responded and made their new pieces with slightly different dimensions in new molds or even with different colors. Exact reproductions with original molds can be confusing to buyers and sellers alike, especially if new pieces are advertised or sold unknowingly as antiques. It is still up in the air whether or not reproductions help or hamper the collector market; some companies have had mixed results remaking certain styles and patterns of old.

A resurgence in glass and glass collecting has occurred in America in the past twenty years. A host of new art glass companies have surfaced, as well as a few older ones which has resulted in a good deal of new quality glassware available in the marketplace. Fenton continues to pour out fancy colored baskets; Steuben, the finest crystal; Pilgrim, a return to cameo engraving; and such items as spun glass Christmas ornaments are now available.

There are also companies that are not involved directly in the manufacturing or production of glass but continue to commission glass lines and new products from various makers. Avon, for example, commissioned Fostoria to make its own "Coin Glass" items; French producers, their Hummingbird tableware; and others.

Along with modern glassware, the remaining portion of this chapter also contains some miscellaneous older collectible glass items that do not fit well into the other categories, such as fruit or canning jars, marbles, some animal figurines, and so on.

AKRO AGATE   AKRO AGATE COMPANY, 1914–1951

Object	Price
Ashtray, 4", Hotel Edison or Hotel Lincoln	$40.00
Basket, 4" Tall, 2-Handled, Green and White Marbleized	30.00
Bell, 5¼" Tall, Solid Colors	30.00
Bell, 5¼" Tall, Marbleized Colors	45.00
Bowl, 5¼", 3-Footed, Solid Colors	15.00

Bowl, 5¼", 3-Footed, Marbleized Colors *$25.00*

Bowl, 7¼", 2 Tab Handles, Solid Colors *20.00*

Bowl, 7¼", 2 Tab Handles, Marbleized Colors *30.00*

Candlestick, 3¼" Tall, Solid Colors *15.00*

Candlestick, 3¼" Tall, Marbleized Colors *25.00*

Children's Play Set, 8-Piece Concentric Ring Style (Teapot and Cover, Sugar and Creamer, 4 Saucers), Solid Colors *100.00*

Children's Play Set, 8-Piece concentric Ring Style (Teapot and Cover, Sugar and Creamer, 4 Saucers), Marbleized Colors *225.00*

Children's Play Set, 16-Piece Concentric Ring Style (Teapot and Cover, Creamer and Sugar, 4 Cups and 4 Saucers, 4 Plates), Solid Colors *150.00*

Children's Play set, 16-Piece Concentric Ring Style (Teapot and Cover, Creamer and Sugar, 4 Cups and 4 Saucers, 4 Plates), Marbleized Colors *325.00*

Children's Play Set, 21-Piece Concentric Ring Style (Teapot and Cover, Creamer and Covered Sugar, 4 Cups and 4 Saucers, 4 Cereal Bowls, 4 Plates), Solid Colors *200.00*

Children's Play Set, 21-Piece Concentric Ring Style (Teapot and Cover, Creamer and Covered Sugar, 4 Cups and 4 Saucers, 4 Cereal Bowls, 4 Plates), Marbleized Colors *450.00*

Children's Play Set, 21-Piece Octagonal Style; Dark Green, Blue, or White (4 Plates, 4 cups, 4 Saucers, Pitcher, 4 Tumblers, Teapot with Cover, Creamer, and Sugar) *150.00*

Children's Play Set, 21-Piece Octagonal Style; Lemonade or Ox Blood (4 Plates, 4 Cups, 4 Saucers, Pitcher, 4 Tumblers, Teapot with Cover, Creamer, and Sugar) *400.00*

Children's Play Set, 8-Piece Stacked Disk Style (Pitcher with Cover, 2 Cups, 2 Saucers, and 2 Plates), Solid Green or White *45.00*

Children's Play Set, 8-Piece Stacked Disk Style (Teapot with Cover, 2 Cups, 2 Saucers, and 2 Plates), Solid Colors Other than Green or White *75.00*

Children's Play Set, 21-Piece Stacked Disk Style (Teapot with Cover, Creamer and Sugar, 4 Cups and 4 Saucers, 4 Plates, Pitcher and 4 Tumblers), Solid Green or White *100.00*

Children's Play Set, 21-Piece Stacked Disk Style (Teapot with Cover, Creamer and Sugar, 4 Cups and 4 Saucers, 4 Plates, Pitcher and 4 Tumblers), Solid Colors Other than Green or White *175.00*

Children's Play Set, 8-Piece Stacked Disk and Interior Panel Design (Teapot with Cover, 2 Cups, 2 Saucers, and 2 Plates), Solid Opaque Colors *75.00*

Children's Play Set, 8-Piece Stacked Disk and Interior Panel Design (Teapot with Cover, 2 Cups, 2 Saucers, and 2 Plates), Transparent Cobalt Blue *125.00*

Children's Play Set, 21-Piece Stacked Disk and Interior Panel Design (Teapot with Cover, Creamer and Sugar, 4 Cups and 4 Saucers, 4 Plates, Pitcher and 4 Tumblers), Solid Opaque Colors *325.00*

Children's Play Set, 21-Piece Stacked Disk and Interior Panel Design (Teapot with Cover, Creamer and Sugar, 4 Cups and 4 Saucers, 4 Plates, Pitcher and 4 Tumblers), Transparent Cobalt Blue *450.00*

Cup and Saucer, Demitasse, 2⅛" Tall, 4¼" Diameter, Solid Colors *10.00*

Cup and Saucer, Demitasse, 2⅛" Tall, 4¼" Diameter, Marbleized Colors *15.00*

Flowerpot, 3" Tall, Smooth or Scalloped Top, Solid Colors *15.00*

Flowerpot, 3" Tall, Smooth or Scalloped Top, Marbleized Colors *25.00*

Jardiniere, 5" Tall, Scalloped or Rectangular Top, with or without Tab Handles, Solid Colors *20.00*

Jardiniere, 5" Tall, Scalloped or Rectangular Top, with or without Tab Handles, Marbleized Colors *30.00*

Marbles, Glass, 5-Piece Set with Original Box *10.00*

Marbles, Glass, 10-Piece Set with Original Box *18.00*

Marbles, Glass, 25-Piece Set with Original Box *35.00*

Marbles, Glass 50-Piece Set with Original Box *60.00*

Marbles, Glass, 100-Piece Set with Original Box *100.00*

Marbles, Glass, Solitary Checker Set, 25-Piece *50.00*

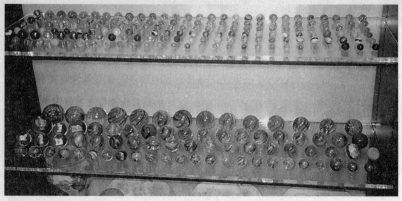

Akro Agate Marbles. Photo by Mark Pickvet.

Marbles, Glass, Chinese Checker Set, 36-Piece $70.00
Puff Box with Colonial Lady Cover, Solid Colors *75.00*
Puff Box with Scottish Terrier Cover, Solid Colors *75.00*
Puff Box with Scottish Terrier Cover, Transparent *100.00*
Urn, 3¹/₄" Tall, Square Foot, Marbleized Colors *20.00*
Vase, 3¹/₄" Tall, Cornucopia, Marbleized Colors *20.00*
Vase, 6¹/₄" Tall, Scalloped or Smooth Top, with or without Tab Handles, Solid Colors *.25.00*
Vase, 6¹/₄" Tall, Scalloped or Smooth Top, with or without Tab Handles, Marbleized Colors
. . . .*35.00*

Akro Agate began as a marble manufacturer and quickly became America's leading
maker of marbles. They expanded into novelties, children's miniature dishes, and
other generally small items. They made glass in solid, opaque, and transparent colors, but their most famous designs were the swirled or spiraled marblelike colors
such as red onyx, blue onyx, etc. The most common trademark used was a crow in
flight clutching marbles within its claws.

ANNIVERSARY　JEANNETTE GLASS COMPANY, 1947–1949, 1970S

Object	Pink	Crystal
Bowl, 4³/₄" Berry	$6.00	$2.00
Bowl, 7¹/₂"	14.00	6.00
Bowl, 9"	18.00	10.00
Butter Dish with Cover	50.00	20.00
Cake Plate, 12¹/₂"	12.00	6.00
Cake Plate with Metal Cover	15.00	8.00
Candlestick	10.00	5.00
Candy Jar and Cover	30.00	15.00
Compote, 3-Legged	10.00	3.00
Creamer	10.00	3.00
Cup	8.00	2.00

Object	Pink	Crystal
Pickle Dish	*$8.00*	*$3.00*
Plate, 6¼"	*.3.00*	*1.00*
Plate, 9"	*.8.00*	*2.00*
Platter, 12½"	*.10.00*	*3.00*
Relish Dish	*.10.00*	*3.00*
Saucer	*.4.00*	*2.00*
Sherbet	*.8.00*	*3.00*
Sugar with Cover	*.20.00*	*7.00*
Sugar Lid	*.8.00*	*3.00*
Vase	*.25.00*	*10.00*
Wineglass, 2½ oz.	*.15.00*	*6.00*

Pink and crystal "Anniversary" pattern glass is easily confused with Depression glass, while the newer iridized pieces are confused with Carnival glass; however, both were produced years later than the older periods. Iridized pieces sell for slightly less than pink or about double the crystal prices.

AVON GLASS COLLECTIBLES 1920S–PRESENT

Object	Price
Basket, Candle, Crystal with Gold Handle, Diamond Pattern, Fostoria	*$15.00*
Bell, 4¾" Tall, Crystal with Red Heart Handle	*.15.00*
Bell, 5" Tall, Crystal Heart Handle and Heart Pattern, Fostoria	*.15.00*
Bell, 5¾" Tall, Etched Frosted Hummingbird Pattern	*.15.00*
Bell, 6½" Tall, Red, Cape Cod Pattern	*.15.00*
Bowl, Finger, Small (Held Bath Cubes), Red, Cape Cod Pattern	*.10.00*
Bowl, 5¼", Etched Frosted Hummingbird Pattern	*.12.00*
Butter Dish with Cover, 7" Long, ¼ lb. Size, Red, Cape Cod Pattern	*.20.00*
Cake Plate, 12" Diameter, Footed, Etched Frosted Hummingbird Pattern	*.35.00*
Candle Holder, 2⅝" Tall, Etched Frosted Hummingbird Pattern	*.12.00*
Candle Holder, Hurricane, Red, Cape Cod Pattern	*.15.00*
Candle Holder, 3¾" Diameter, Red, Cape Cod Pattern	*.10.00*
Candlestick, 3" Tall, Crystal with Holly Decoration	*.6.00*
Candlestick, 7" Tall, Crystal Heart Pattern, Fostoria	*.16.00*
Candlestick Cologne Bottle with Stopper, 5 oz., Red, Cape Cod Pattern	*.12.00*
Candlette, Turtle Figure (Shell Holds Candle), 4½" Long, Crystal Diamond Pattern ..	*.12.00*
Candy Dish, 3½" Tall, 6" Diameter, Red, Cape Cod Pattern	*.15.00*
Candy Dish with Cover, 6" Tall, Etched Frosted Hummingbird Pattern	*.35.00*
Canning Jar Replica, Blue Glass with Glass Lid and Wire Bail, Pressed Sunburst (Aztec) Pattern	*.8.00*
Champagne Glass, 9" Tall, Etched Frosted Hummingbird Pattern	*.15.00*
Chess Set, 3 oz. Amber Bottles, 6-Piece Set (King, Queen, Rook, Bishop, Knight, and Pawn)	*.80.00*
Chess Set, 16 Dark Amber and 16 Light Amber 3 oz. Bottles with Silverplated Chess Piece Tops (Complete 32-Piece Set)	*.400.00*
Christmas Ornament, 3¼" Across, Hexagon, Red with Plaid Cloth Bow, Cape Cod Pattern	*.10.00*
Christmas Ornament, 3½" Tall, Etched Frosted Hummingbird Pattern	*.10.00*
Cold Cream Box with Silver Color, Rose Brand, Milk White, Early 1930s	*.50.00*

Avon, Fostoria Coin glass. Photo by Robin Rainwater.

Compote, 4" Tall, Crystal with Holly Decoration *$15.00*
Condiment Tray, Small, Red, Cape Cod Pattern *15.00*
Creamer, 3¹/₂" Tall, Red, Cape Cod Pattern *12.00*
Cruet with Stopper, 5 oz., Red, Cape Cod Pattern *12.00*
Cup, 3¹/₂" Tall, Red, Cape Cod Pattern *10.00*
Cup, Loving, No Handle, 6⁷/₈" Tall, Crystal Heart Pattern, Fostoria *18.00*
Decanter, Miniature with Stopper, 5 oz. Bath Oil, Milk White, Hobnail Design, 1972 ..*7.00*
Decanter, Wine, with Stopper, 16 oz. (Held Bubble Bath), Red, Cap Cod Pattern *20.00*
Goblet, 8¹/₈" Tall, Blue with Frosted George Washington Medallion, Fostoria Coin Glass *.22.00*
Goblet, 8¹/₈" Tall, Blue with Frosted Martha Washington Medallion, Fostoria Coin Glass
....*22.00*
Goblet, 8¹/₄" Tall, Etched Frosted Hummingbird Pattern *15.00*
Goblet, Water, with Candle, Red, Cape Cod Pattern *12.00*
Harvester, Amber, 1973 ....*6.00*
Heart Box with Cover, 4" Across, Red, Cape Cod Pattern *18.00*
Mug, 5" Tall, Footed, Red, Cape Cod Pattern *6.00*
Napkin Ring, 1¹/₂" Long, Red, Cape Cod Pattern *6.00*
Pitcher, Miniature Grecian, 5 oz. Bath Oil, Mild White, 1972 ....*6.00*
Pitcher, Sauce, 5¹/₂" Tall, Blue with Frosted Mount Vernon Medallion, Fostoria Coin Glass
....*25.00*
Pitcher, Milk, 8" Tall, Etched Frosted Hummingbird Pattern *30.00*
Pitcher, Water, 8¹/₄" Tall, Red, Cape Cod Pattern *25.00*
Plate, 7¹/₂", Etched Frosted Hummingbird Pattern *12.00*
Plate, Dessert, Red, Cape Cod Pattern *15.00*
Plate, Dinner, Red, Cape Cod Pattern *18.00*
Platter, Round 11", Crystal with Holly and Berry Design *16.00*
Platter, Round 12¹/₂", Etched Frosted Hummingbird Pattern *40.00*
Powder Box, 3 oz. "Nearness Body," Satin with Blue Speckled Lid, 1956 ....*16.00*
Powder Sachet, 1¹/₂ oz., Cranberry with Silver Cover, 1969 ....*12.00*
Salt Cellar, 4 Feet, Crystal with Matching Silver Spoon, Fostoria *12.00*
Salt Shaker, Red, Cape Cod Pattern *8.00*
Salt and Pepper Shakers with Stainless Steel Tops, 3" Tall, Etched Frosted Hummingbird
Pattern *20.00*
Sauce Boat, 8" Long, 1 Handle, Pouring Lip, Red, Cape Cod Pattern *30.00*
Saucer, 5³/₄", Red, Cape Cod Pattern *10.00*
Sugar, 3¹/₂" Tall, Red, Cape Cod Pattern *12.00*

Tumbler, 3¼" Tall, Footed, Red, Cape Cod Pattern *$10.00*
Tumbler, 5½" Tall, Red, Cape Cod Pattern *10.00*
Vase, Grape Bud, 6 oz. Bath Oil, Amethyst, 1973 .... *7.00*
Vase, 5" Tall, Crystal, Heart-Shaped, Fostoria *12.00*
Vase, 7½" Tall, Thick, Etched Frosted Hummingbird Pattern *35.00*
Vase, 8" Tall, Red, Cape Cod Pattern *20.00*
Vase, Bud, 9½" Tall, Etched Frosted Hummingbird Pattern *25.00*
Wineglass, 6¾" Tall, Etched Frosted Hummingbird Pattern *15.00*
Wineglass with Candle, Red, Cape Cod Pattern *12.00*

Though not a maker of glass products, Avon has commissioned hundreds of products since the late 1920s. Popular modern sets that are issued a piece at a time (two or three annually) include the ruby red "Cape Cod" pattern, the "Hummingbird" crystal pattern (made in France), and even some coin glass and other glass products made by Fostoria.

BEADED EDGE   WESTMORELAND GLASS COMPANY, LATE 1930S–1950S

Object	*Milk White*
Bowl, 5"	*$6.00*
Bowl, 6", Oval	*8.00*
Creamer	*12.00*
Cup	*18.00*
Plate, 6"	*6.00*
Plate, 7" or 8½"	*8.00*
Plate, 10½"	*18.00*
Plate, 15", Cake	*30.00*
Platter, 12", Oval with 2 Handle Tabs	*30.00*
Relish Dish, 3-Part	*30.00*
Salt and Pepper Shakers	*30.00*
Saucer	*3.00*
Sherbet	*8.00*
Sugar	*12.00*
Tumbler	*10.00*

The original name of this pattern is Westmoreland's "Pattern #22 Milk Glass." "Beaded Edge" is a nickname given to it by collectors. The coral-red color was named by Westmoreland and is simply milk glass with a fired-on red edge. Decorated patterns include eight different fruits as well as eight different flowers (total of 16 decorated patterns). Westmoreland also made a few pieces in a similar pattern referred to as "#108."

For coral-red or decorated patterns, double the above prices.

BLENKO GLASS COMPANY   1922–PRESENT

Object	*Price*
Ashtray, 6½" Diameter, Blue, Bubble Effect	*$10.00*
Ashtray, 7" Diameter, Green, Hinged Clam Shell Design	*10.00*

Blenko glass. Photo by Mark Pickvet.

Basket, 8³/₄" Tall, Cobalt Blue *$20.00*
Bowl, Rose, 5¹/₂" Tall, Cobalt Blue .... *.12.00*
Bowl, Rose, 7³/₄" Tall, Pale Emerald Green .... *.15.00*
Candlestick, Green with Crystal Twist Stem .... *.35.00*
Champagne Bucket, 11³/₄" Tall, Top Handle, Opaline Yellow .... *.18.00*
Compote, 7¹/₂" Tall, 9³/₄" Diameter, Opaline Yellow or Cobalt Blue .... *.18.00*
Decanter Ship's, 10" Tall, Green with Crystal Stopper .... *.22.00*
Decanter with Stopper, 13" Tall, Ruby Red .... *.50.00*
Fish, 10" Tall, Globe-Shaped, Fin Feet, Large Mouth Opening, Crystal .... *.30.00*
Fish, 16" Long, Fin Feet, Large Mouth Opening, Opaline Yellow .... *.35.00*
Fish, 22" Long, Fin Feet, Large Mouth Opening, Cobalt Blue .... *.45.00*
Goblet, Flattened Knob on Stem, Cobalt Blue .... *.25.00*
Hat Vase, 7¹/₂" Tall, 16" Diameter, Crystal with Yellow Band .... *.35.00*
Highball Glass, Crystal with Green Foot .... *.20.00*
Penguin, 9¹/₂" Tall, Sapphire Blue Cased in Crystal .... *.30.00*
Penguin, 14" Tall, Sapphire Blue Cased in Crystal .... *.40.00*
Pitcher, Milk, 5¹/₂" Tall, 32 oz. Green Crackle Design .... *.15.00*
Pitcher, Water, Deep Blue, Bubble Effect .... *.30.00*
Pitcher, Water, 14" Tall, Ruby Red .... *.65.00*
Plate, 9", Ruby Red .... *.15.00*
Plate, 12", Crimped, Blue .... *.25.00*
Platter, 13¹/₂" Circular, Circles, X's, and Squares .... *.15.00*
Punch Cup, Crystal with Ruby Red Handle .... *.10.00*
Sherbet, 6" Tall, Ruby with Crystal Twist Stem .... *.30.00*
Tumbler, Iced Tea, Footed, Dark Amethyst .... *.15.00*
Vase, 7¹/₂" Tall, Flared, Amber .... *.15.00*
Vase, 7¹/₂" Tall, 7" Diameter, Opaline Yellow .... *.30.00*
Vase, 11" Tall, Ruffled, Crystal with Circular Blue Lines .... *.35.00*
Vase, 11¹/₂" Tall, Flared, Footed, Amber with Optic Ribbing .... *.55.00*
Vase, 14¹/₂" Tall, Cylindrical, Pale Emerald Green .... *.20.00*

Vase, 22" Tall, 11½" Diameter Top, Crystal *$40.00*
Vase, 24" Tall, Tapered Neck at Top, Cobalt Blue .... *.45.00*

This company was founded by English immigrant William J. Blenko in 1922. He began as a hand producer of stained glass windows but the company later switched to more contemporary art forms. Characteristic of the company are bright vibrant colors and some art styles such as crackling, bubbling, and unique shapes.

BOYD ART GLASS   1978–PRESENT

Object	*Price*
Airplane, Black Carnival	*$18.00*
Basket, 4½" Tall, Olde Lyme (Forest Green)	*.10.00*
Bear, Fuzzy, Cambridge Blue	*.8.00*
Bear, Patrick Balloon, Carmel	*.8.00*
Bear, Patrick Balloon, Enchantment	*.25.00*
Bear, Patrick Balloon, Spinnaker Blue	*.8.00*
Bell, Owl Head Finial, Translucent, White Opal	*.12.00*
Bunny, Brian, Oxford Gray	*.10.00*
Bunny, Brian, Ruby Red	*.20.00*
Bunny, Brian, Vaseline	*.12.00*
Bunny Salt Dip, Blue	*.22.00*
Bunny Salt Dip, Sunburst	*.15.00*
Butterfly, Katie, Light Windsor Blue	*.8.00*
Candy Dish with Cover, Persimmon	*.12.00*
Car, Tucker Model, Buckeye	*.12.00*
Car Slipper, Platinum Carnival	*.16.00*
Cat, Kitten, Miss Cotton, Light Windsor Blue	*.8.00*
Chick, Bermuda, 1"	*.16.00*
Chick, Enchantment, 1"	*.8.00*
Chick, John's Surprise, 1"	*.25.00*
Chick, Royalty, 1"	*.75.00*

Boyd art glass miniatures.

Clown, Freddie Hobo, Cobalt Blue Carnival .... *.$12.00*
Dog, Bull Dog's Head, Golden Delight (Amber) .... *.8.00*
Dog, Parlour Pup #1, Mulberry Mist (Light Lilac) .... *.8.00*
Dog, Parlour Pup #2, Milk White Opal .... *.8.00*
Dog, Parlour Pup #3, Carmel .... *.8.00*
Dog, Parlour Pup #4, Bermuda Slag (Reddish-Brown) .... *.8.00*
Doll, Elizabeth, Black Satin .... *.10.00*
Doll, Elizabeth, Lime Carnival .... *.30.00*
Duck, Debbie, Shasta White (Light Tan) .... *.8.00*
Duck Salt Dip, Dove Blue .... *.12.00*
Duck Salt Dip, Light Peach .... *.8.00*
Duckling, Shasta White (Light Tan) .... *.5.00*
Elephant, Zack, Cobalt Blue .... *.40.00*
Elephant, Zack, Flame .... *.40.00*
Elephant, Zack, Furr Green .... *.25.00*
Hen, 3", Carmine .... *.65.00*
Hen, 3", Pink Champagne .... *.30.00*
Hen, 5", Ruby Gold .... *.55.00*
Hen Covered Dish, 5" Long, Shasta White (Light Tan) .... *.12.00*
Honey Jar with Cover, Lemonade (Vaseline) .... *.15.00*
Horse, Joey, Chocolate .... *.38.00*
Horse, Joey, Zack Boyd Slag .... *.12.00*
Jewel Box, Cornsilk .... *.12.00*
Jewel Box, Sam Jones Slag .... *.40.00*
Kitten with Pillow, Apricot .... *.20.00*
Kitten with Pillow, Royalty .... *.22.00*
Lamb Covered Dish, 5" Long, Golden Delight (Amber) .... *.12.00*
Lamb Salt Dip, Lime Carnival .... *.10.00*
Mouse, Willie, Lime Carnival .... *.10.00*
Owl, Mulberry Mist (Light Lilac) .... *.8.00*
Penguin, Artie, Black Carnival .... *.12.00*
Pig, Suee, Shasta White (Light Tan) .... *.8.00*
Robin Covered Dish, 5" Long, Golden Delight (Amber) .... *.12.00*
Skate Boot, Heather .... *.14.00*
Slipper, Cat, Orange Calico .... *.12.00*
Squirrel, Sammie, Shasta White (Light Tan) .... *.8.00*
Swan, 3" Long, Azure Blue .... *.8.00*
Tomahawk, Milk White .... *.12.00*
Toothpick Holder, Forget-Me-Not, Carmine .... *.36.00*
Toothpick Holder, Forget-Me-Not, Teal Swirl .... *.10.00*
Toothpick Holder, Heart, Mint Green .... *.22.00*
Train, 6-Piece, Teal .... *.60.00*
Train, 6-Piece, Yellow Engine, Baby Blue Coal Car, Dark Cobalt Blue Box Car, Candyland Coal Hopper, Bamboo Tank Car, and Ruby Red Caboose .... *.50.00*
Tucker Car, Cobalt Blue .... *.10.00*
Tugboat, Teddy, Peridot Green .... *.10.00*
Turkey Covered Dish, 5" Long, Shasta White (Light Tan) .... *.12.00*
Turtle, Alexandrite .... *.8.00*
Unicorn, Lucky, Mulberry Carnival .... *.10.00*
Vase, Candy Swirl .... *.15.00*
Vase, Dark Tangerine Slag .... *.18.00*

Boyd glass clown. Photo by Mark Pickvet.

Vase, 6" Tall, Beaded, Lilac *$15.00*
Woodchuck, Touch of Pink ....*.8.00*

Boyd is simply an amazing little company established only in 1978. All pieces are marked with a "B" in a diamond; some contain a single line under the diamond (1983–1988) as well as an additional line above the diamond (1988–present). The pieces are all miniatures, and colors come in satins, slags, iridescent, swirls, etc. The last word(s) listed above in each item describes the color.

CAMBRIDGE ANIMALS 1920S–1958

Object	Price
Blue Jay Flower Holder	*$150.00*
Buffalo Hunt Console, Mystic Blue	*.300.00*
Eagle Bookend	*.100.00*
Heron, 9", Flower Frog (Small)	*.75.00*
Heron, 12", Flower Frog (Large)	*.125.00*
Heron and Cattails' Cocktail Shaker, 10" Tall, Cobalt Blue with Sterling Silver Cover	*.75.00*
Lion Bookend	*.125.00*
Pigeon, Pouter, Bookend	*.75.00*
Scottish Terrier, Frosted	*.75.00*
Scottish Terrier Bookend	*.85.00*
Sea Gull Flower Frog	*.60.00*
Swan, 3½" Tall, Crown Tuscan	*.50.00*
Swan, 3½" Tall, Ebony	*.75.00*
Swan, 3½" Tall, Emerald Green	*.40.00*
Swan, 3½" Tall, Milk White	*.100.00*
Swan, 3½" Tall, Peach	*.45.00*
Swan, 4½" Tall, Milk White	*.125.00*
Swan, 6½" Tall, Crystal	*.50.00*
Swan, 6½" Tall, Carmen	*.275.00*
Swan, 6½" Tall, Ebony	*.100.00*
Swan, 6½" Tall, Emerald Green	*.90.00*
Swan, 6½" Tall, Milk White	*.150.00*

Swan, 8½" Tall, Carmen *$300.00*
Swan, 8½" Tall, Crown Tuscan *150.00*
Swan, 8½" Tall, Crystal *75.00*
Swan, 8½" Tall, Ebony *150.00*
Swan, 8½" Tall, Emerald Green *125.00*
Swan, 8½" Tall, Milk White *275.00*
Swan, 10½" Tall, Ebony *250.00*
Swan, 12½" Tall, Amber *75.00*
Swan, 12½" Tall, Ebony *300.00*
Swan Candlestick, 4½" Tall, Milk White *200.00*
Turkey Dish with Cover, Blue *500.00*
Turkey Dish with Cover, Green *450.00*
Turkey Dish with Cover, Pink *400.00*

Cambridge was a large producer of crystal dinnerware and especially stemware. The quality of their crystal was quite good, and they survived the Depression by making color products as well. After some good profitable years in the immediate post–World War II era, Cambridge eventually had trouble competing with cheaper products that assailed the market. The wildlife re-creations here are just some of Cambridge's collectible glassware.

CAMEO MINIATURES   MOSSER GLASS, INC.,
1980S–PRESENT

Object	*Price*
Bowl, Cereal, 2¹¹/₁₆"	*$4.00*
Bowl, Salad, 4³/₁₆", 1" Tall	*8.00*
Bowl, Soup, 4½"	*6.00*
Bowl, Fruit, 5½", 3-Footed, 1½" Tall	*12.00*
Bowl, Serving, 5" Oval (Including 2 Tab Handles) ⅞" Tall	*10.00*
Butter Dish with Cover, 2¼" Tall, 3½" Underplate Diameter, 2⅝" Dome Diameter	*12.00*
Cake Plate, 5" Diameter, 3 Feet, ⅝" Tall	*12.00*
Candlestick, 2" Tall	*7.00*
Cracker Jar with Cover, 3¾" Tall	*16.00*
Creamer, 1¹¹/₁₆" Tall	*6.00*
Creamer, 2¼" Tall	*7.00*

Miniature "Cameo" pattern. Photo by Robin Rainwater.

Miniature "Cameo" pattern. Photo by Robin Rainwater.

Cup, 1¹/₈" Tall *$3.00*
Goblet, 3" Tall *6.00*
Ice Cream Bucket, 1¹/₂" Tall, 2⁵/₈" Diameter, 2 Tab Handles *10.00*
Jam Jar with Cover, 2¹/₂" Tall, 3" Bottom Diameter *12.00*
Mayonnaise Dish, 1⁵/₈" Tall, Stemmed, 2⁵/₈" Top Diameter *8.00*
Mayonnaise Jar with Cover, 2¹/₂" Tall, 3" Bottom Diameter *12.00*
Parfait, 2³/₈" Tall, Round Foot *4.00*
Pitcher, Milk, 3" Tall, Slim *8.00*
Pitcher, Water, 3" Tall, Wide *12.00*
Plate, Dessert, 3¹/₁₆" *3.00*
Plate, Octagonal, 4³/₁₆" Across *5.00*
Plate, 4³/₄" *6.00*
Plate, Grill, 5¹/₄" *6.00*
Relish Dish, 3¹¹/₁₆" Diameter, 2 Tab Handles, ⁷/₈" Tall *8.00*
Saucer, 3" *3.00*
Sherbet, 1⁵/₈" Tall *4.00*
Sugar, 2-Handled *7.00*
Sugar Dish, 2-Handled, 1⁹/₁₆" Tall *6.00*
Tray, 5⁷/₈" Oval, (Including 2 Tab Handles) *10.00*
Tumbler, Water, 1¹³/₁₆" Tall *3.00*
Vase, 4¹/₈" Tall *14.00*

The original "Cameo" was made in full scale during the Depression (see Chapter 6, Depression Glass). Those listed here are miniature reproductions made in yellow, pink, and green (the prices are the same for all colors). The pattern is a little weaker on the small versions, but they are still very pretty, especially when an entire set is acquired. Thanks to their tiny size, there is no problem whatsoever distinguishing them from the originals. Remember that this version of "Cameo" is also referred to as "Ballerina" or "Dancing Girl" since that is what is pictured in medallion form.

CANDLEWICK **IMPERIAL GLASS COMPANY, 1936–1982**

Object   *Price*
Ashtray, 2³/₄" *$5.00*
Ashtray, 6¹/₂", Heart Design *20.00*
Ashtray, 6¹/₂", Eagle Design *50.00*
Basket, 5" Tall, Beaded Handle *175.00*

Bell, 4" Tall *$35.00*
Bowl, 5", Blue .... *.45.00*
Bowl, 5" Across, Heart-Shaped .... *.12.00*
Bowl, 5" Square .... *.55.00*
Bowl, 6", 3-Footed .... *.40.00*
Bowl, 7", 2 Handles .... *.18.00*
Bowl, 7" Square .... *.75.00*
Bowl, 8¹/₂", Divided, 2 Handles .... *.60.00*
Bowl, 9" Across, Heart-Shaped .... *.80.00*
Bowl, 10", 2 Handles .... *.40.00*
Bowl, 11" .... *.45.00*
Bowl, 14" Oval, Flared .... *.150.00*
Bowl, Rose, 7¹/₂", Footed .... *.125.00*
Brandy Glass .... *.25.00*
Bunny on Nest Dish, Blue Satin .... *.35.00*
Butter Dish with Cover, 5¹/₂" Round .... *.30.00*
Butter Dish with Cover, ¹/₄ lb. Size .... *.25.00*
Cake Stand, 10", Low Foot .... *.50.00*
Cake Stand, 11" .... *.60.00*
Calendar Desk, 1947 Edition .... *.100.00*
Candle Holder, 3¹/₂" Tall .... *.25.00*
Candle Holder, 5" Tall, Heart Design .... *.35.00*
Candle Holder, 6" Tall, Urn-Shaped .... *.60.00*
Candle Holder, 2-Light .... *.20.00*
Candy Box with Cover, 7" Tall .... *.150.00*
Celery Dish, 11" Oval .... *.50.00*
Cigarette Box with Cover .... *.30.00*
Claret Glass .... *.35.00*
Clock, 4", Circular .... *.125.00*
Coaster, 4" .... *.6.00*
Compote, 5", 2-Beaded Stem .... *.20.00*
Compote, 5¹/₂", Plain Stem .... *.12.00*
Cordial .... *.65.00*
Creamer, Footed .... *.8.00*
Creamer, Domed Feet .... *.65.00*
Cruet with Stopper, Etched "Vinegar" .... *.50.00*
Cup .... *.8.00*
Decanter with Stopper, 11¹/₂" Tall .... *.25.00*
Egg Cup .... *.35.00*
Egg Plate, 12", Center Handle .... *.100.00*
Fork, Large Serving .... *.20.00*
Goblet, Footed .... *.15.00*
Gravy Boat .... *.150.00*
Ice Tub, 5¹/₂" × 8", 2 Handles .... *.90.00*
Knife, Butter .... *.150.00*
Ladle, Mayonnaise .... *.8.00*
Mirror, Standing, 4¹/₂" Diameter .... *.85.00*
Mustard Jar with Cover .... *.35.00*
Perfume Bottle with Stopper .... *.40.00*
Pickle Dish, 7¹/₂" Oval .... *.20.00*
Pitcher, Low Foot, Small, 16 oz. .... *.225.00*

IMPERIAL GLASS CORPORATION, BELLAIRE, OHIO

IMPERIAL CANDLEWICK, CUT. No. 108

3400/C108
Goblet

3400/C108
Tall Sherbet

3400/C108
Stem Cocktail

3400/C108
Cordial

3400/C108
Finger Bowl

3400/C108
12 oz. Ftd. Tumbler

400/89/C108
4 pc. Marmalade Set

400/144/C108
5½ in. Covered Butter

400/149D/C108
9 in. Handled Mint Tray

400/163/C108
Decanter & Stopper

400/87F/C108
8 in. Fan Vase

400/75B/C108
4 pc. Salad Set

400/10D/C108
10½ in. Dinner Plate

"Candlewick" pattern. Reproduced from a 1940s advertisement.

Pitcher, 40 oz.	$225.00
Pitcher, 64 oz.	50.00
Pitcher, 80 oz.	200.00
Plate, 4½"	5.00
Plate, 8"	10.00
Plate, 8½"	10.00
Plate, 9" Oval	25.00

Plate, 10", 2 Tab Handles *$15.00*
Plate, 12¹/₂" Torte, Cupped Edge *35.00*
Plate, 14", Birthday Cake Design with Holes for 72 Candles *300.00*
Platter, 13" Oval *75.00*
Platter, 14" Round *40.00*
Punch Bowl with Matching Underplate *250.00*
Punch Cup *15.00*
Punch Ladle *25.00*
Relish Dish, 8¹/₂", 4 Divisions *20.00*
Relish Dish, 10¹/₂", 3 Divisions *35.00*
Relish Dish, 13¹/₂", 5 Divisions *70.00*
Salt Dip, 2¹/₄" *8.00*
Salt and Pepper Shakers, Chrome Tops, Beaded Foot *20.00*
Sandwich Server, 11³/₄", Center Handle *40.00*
Saucer *4.00*
Sherbet, 5 oz. *12.00*
Sherbet, 6 oz. *16.00*
Spoon, Large Serving *20.00*
Sugar Dish, Footed *20.00*
Tid-Bit, 3-Piece *100.00*
Tray, 4¹/₂" (for Salt and Pepper Shakers) *15.00*
Tray, 5¹/₂", 2 Upturned Handles *20.00*
Tray, 6¹/₂" *16.00*
Tray, 8¹/₂", 2 Handles *20.00*
Tray, 9" Oval, Beaded Foot *14.00*
Tumbler, 5 oz. *18.00*
Tumbler, 9 oz., Footed *20.00*
Tumbler, 10 oz. *15.00*
Tumbler, 12 oz. *40.00*
Tumbler, 16 oz. *50.00*
Vase, Bud, 7" Tall *150.00*
Vase, 8" Tall, Crimped *50.00*
Vase, 8¹/₂" Tall, Flared, Beaded Foot *80.00*
Vase, 10" Tall, Footed *125.00*

Another huge set that was made continuously from the 1930s until Imperial closed for good in 1982, Candlewick is unmarked except for paper labels that are naturally removed. However, it is easily identified by beaded crystal stems, handles, and rims. The name of the pattern comes from the fact that the basic design resembles tufted needlework created by pioneer women.

CANNING JARS   1850S–PRESENT

Object	*Price*
AD & H Chambers Union Fruit Jar, Blue, Wax Sealer, 1 qt.	*$150.00*
A.G. Smalley & Co., Boston and New York, ¹/₂ pt.	*15.00*
Acme LG Co., 1893, ¹/₂ gal.	*250.00*
Amazon Swift Seal, Blue, 1 qt.	*12.00*
Atlas, E-Z Seal, Amber, Glass Cover, 1 qt.	*45.00*
Atlas, E-Z Seal, Apple Green, 1 qt.	*20.00*

Atlas, E-Z Seal, Aqua, Glass Cover, 1 pt. *$30.00*
Atlas Good Luck, Clear, Clover Design, 1 qt. *3.00*
Atlas Strong Shoulder Mason, Aqua, 1 pt. *4.00*
Automatic Sealer, Aqua, 1 qt. *100.00*
Ball Eclipse, Clear, 1 pt. *5.00*
Ball Ideal, Blue, ¹/₂ pt. *30.00*
Ball Ideal, Clear with Various Bicentennial Scenes Reverse, 1 pt. *3.00*
Ball Ideal, Clear with Various Bicentennial Scenes Reverse, 1 qt. *4.00*
Ball Mason, Olive Green, 1 pt. *20.00*
Ball Perfect Mason, Amber, 2 qt. *40.00*
Ball Perfect Mason, Blue, Zinc Cover, 1 qt. *15.00*
Ball Perfect Mason, Dark Olive Green, 1 pt. *55.00*
Ball Perfect Mason, Emerald Green, 2 qt. *60.00*
Ball Sanitary Sure Seal, Blue, 1 qt. *8.00*
Brockway Sur-Grip Mason, Clear, 1 qt. *3.00*
Burlington, 1 qt. *50.00*
C.F. Spencer's Patent, Rochester, N.Y., Aqua, 1 qt. *110.00*
Canton Domestic, 1 pt. *175.00*
Canton, Cobalt Blue, 1870–90, 2 qt. *2250.00*
Carter's Butter and Fruit Preserving, Glass Lid, 1897 ....*125.00*
Clark's Peerless, Cornflower Blue, 1 pt. *30.00*
Cross Crown, 1 qt. *55.00*
Dolittle, Clear, 1 pt. *45.00*
Double Safety, Clear, 2 qt. *5.00*
Drey Square Mason, Clear, 1 qt. *7.00*
Eagle, Aqua, 1 qt. *150.00*
Electric, World Globe, Aqua, 1 qt. *90.00*
Erie Lightning, Amethyst, 1 qt. *60.00*
Excelsior, Aqua, 1 qt. *45.00*
Fearman's Mincemeat, Amber, 1 qt. *65.00*
Forest City, Amber, 1 qt. *85.00*
Forster, Clear, 1 qt. *15.00*
Franklin Dexter, Aqua, 2 qt. *45.00*
Gem, Aqua, 1 qt. *8.00*
Gem, Aqua, 2 qt. *12.00*
Globe, Wire Closure, Amber, 1 pt. *55.00*
Green Mountain CA Co., Aqua, 1 pt. *12.00*
Haines Patent March 1st 1870, Aqua, 1 qt. *100.00*
Hamilton Glass Works 1 Quart, Aqua, 1 qt. *200.00*
Hazel Atlas E-Z Seal, Aqua, 1 pt. *10.00*

American glass, canning jars. Photo by Robin Rainwater.

Hazel Preserve Jar, Clear, ½ pt. *$45.00*
Ideal Imperial, Aqua, 1 qt. .... *.25.00*
Improved Jam, 2 qt. .... *.125.00*
J.M. Clark & Co., Round Shoulder, Green, 1 qt. .... *.80.00*
Kerr Self Sealing, Mason, Clear, ½ pt. .... *.2.00*
King, Clear, Banner and Crow Design, 1 pt. .... *.16.00*
L & W, Aqua, 1 qt. .... *.50.00*
Lafayette, Aqua, ½ gal. .... *.125.00*
Lightning, Glass Cover, Amber, 2 qt. .... *.65.00*
Lightning, Aqua, 2 qt. .... *.50.00*
Lightning, Glass Cover, Aqua, 2 qt. .... *.75.00*
Magic Fruit Jar, Amber, Star Design, 1 qt. .... *.400.00*
Mason, 1858 Trademark, Aqua, 2 qt. .... *.125.00*
Mason, 3 gal. .... *.350.00*
Mason, Pat. Nov. 30th, 1858, 1 pt. .... *.10.00*
Mason, Pat. Nov. 30th, 1858, Dark Aqua .... *.30.00*
Mason, Pat. Nov. 30th, 1858, Reverse Cross, Amber, 2 qt. .... *.85.00*
Mcdonald's New Perfect Seal, Blue, 1 pt. .... *.10.00*
Millville Atmospheric, Aqua, 1 qt. .... *.40.00*
Queen Wide Mouth, Square-Shaped, Clear, 1 pt. .... *.15.00*
Quick Seal, Blue, 1 qt. .... *.3.00*
Royal, Clear, 1 qt. .... *.5.00*
Safety with Glass Cover, Aqua, 2 qt. .... *.40.00*
Schram Automatic Sealer, Flag, 1 pt. .... *.12.00*
Star Glass Co., Aqua, 1 qt. .... *.40.00*
Swayzee's Improved Mason, Dark Olive, 2 qt. .... *.50.00*
TM Lightning Reg US Patent Office, Aqua, 1 qt. .... *.3.00*
Victory, Aqua, 1 qt. .... *.50.00*
Whitney Mason, Pat'd 1858, Aqua, 1 pt. .... *.15.00*
Winslow Jar, Aqua, 1 qt. .... *.60.00*
Worcester, Aqua, 1 qt. .... *.175.00*

Although canning or fruit jars have been made in the millions for well over a century now, there exist many off-brands and rare colors from the 19th and early 20th centuries that are quite valuable today. Where a color is not designated above, the jar is clear. Nearly all jars have mold-embossed writing and/or designs.

CHARACTER GLASS VARIOUS PRODUCERS, 1930S–PRESENT

Object   *Price*
Actors Series Tumblers (Abbot and Costello, Charlie Chaplin, Laurel and Hardy, Little Rascals, Mae West, or W. C. Fields), Arby's, 1979 .... *$5.00*
Actors Series Tumblers (Jack Albertson, Monty Hall, Teddy Kollack, Jan Murray, Mary Tyler Moore, or Don Rickles), Coca Cola, 1970s .... *.12.00*
B.C. Comic Tumblers (Anteater, B.C., Broad, Grog, Thor, or Wiley), Arby's, 1981 ...*.6.00*
Bald Eagle Tumbler, Endangered Species, Burger Chef .... *.7.00*
Bullwinkle Tumblers, Ward Collector Series (over 20 Styles), Pepsi, 1960s–1970s ...*.15.00*
California Raisins Tumbler, 12 oz., 1989 .... *.3.00*
Care Bears Mug, Days of the Week, American Greetings .... *.4.00*

Care Bears Tumblers (Cheer Bear, Friends Bear, Funshine Bear, Good Luck Bear, Grumpy Bear, or Tenderheart Bear), Pizza Hut, 1983 . . . . *$4.00*

Chipmunks Tumblers (Alvin, Chipettes, Simon, or Theodore), Hardee's, 1985 . . . . . . *5.00*

Clara Peller Tumbler, Where's the Beef? Wendy's *5.00*

Flintstone Kids' Tumblers (Barney, Betty, Fred, or Wilma), Pizza Hut, 1986 . . . . *3.00*

Garfield Mugs, 4 Styles, McDonald's, 1987 . . . . *4.00*

Garfield Tumblers, 4 Styles, McDonald's, 1987 . . . . *4.00*

Great Muppet Caper Tumblers, 4 Styles, McDonald's, 1981 . . . . *3.00*

Hanna Barbera Collector Series Tumblers (Dynomutt, The Flintstones, Huckleberry Hound and Yogi Bear, Josie and The Pussycats, Mumbly, or Scooby Do), Pepsi, 1977 .*12.00*

Happy Days Tumblers (Fonzie, Richie, Joanie, Ralph, Potsie, or Cunninghams), Pizza Hut/Dr. Pepper *6.00*

Kelloggs Cartoon Tumblers, 7 Styles (Dig Um, Tony the Tiger, Tony Jr., Toucan Sam, or Snap! Crackle! Pop!), 1977 . . . . *8.00*

King Kong Tumbler, Burger Chef/Coca Cola, 1976 . . . . *5.00*

McDonaldland Action Series Tumblers, 12 Styles, 1977 . . . . *5.00*

Muppets Tumblers, The Great Muppet Caper, 4 Styles, 1981 . . . . *3.00*

Noid Tumblers, 5 Styles, Domino's Pizza, 1988 . . . . *3.00*

Pac Man Series Tumblers, 11 Styles, Bally, 1980 . . . . *5.00*

Peanuts Tumblers, 8 Styles, Dolly Madison, 1980s *4.00*

Peanuts Tumblers, 6 Styles, McDonald's, 1983 . . . . *3.00*

Popeye Kollect-a-Set Tumblers, 6 Styles, Burger King/Coca-Cola, 1975 . . . . *6.00*

Popeye Tumblers, 8 Styles, Original 1936 Series *50.00*

Shirley Temple Bowl, Cobalt Blue with White Figure *35.00*

Shirley Temple Creamer, Cobalt Blue with White Figure, 1930s *40.00*

Shirley Temple Pitcher, 9 oz. Cobalt Blue with White Figure, 1930s *40.00*

Sloth and Goonies Tumbler, Godfather's Pizza, 1985 . . . . *5.00*

Smurfs Tumblers, 14 Styles, Hardee's, 1982–1983 . . . . *4.00*

Star Trek The Motion Picture Tumblers, 3 Styles, Coca Cola, 1980 . . . . *20.00*

Star Trek Tumblers, 4 Styles, Dr. Pepper, 1978 . . . . *45.00*

Star Trek Tumblers, Cartoon Series Characters (4 Styles), Dr. Pepper, 1976 . . . . *35.00*

Star Trek III: The Search For Spock Tumblers (4 Styles), Taco Bell, 1984 . . . . . . *5.00*

Star Wars Return of the Jedi Tumblers (4 Styles), Burger King/Coca Cola, 1983 . . . . *5.00*

Star Wars The Empire Strikes Back Tumblers (4 Styles), Burger King/Coca Cola, 1980 . . . . *8.00*

Star Wars Tumblers (4 Styles), Burger King/Coca Cola, 1977 . . . . *10.00*

Superheroes Cartoon Series Tumblers (over 30 Styles), Pepsi, 1976–1979 . . . . *15.00*

Superman the Movie Tumblers (6 Styles), Pepsi, 1978 . . . . *6.00*

Tom and Jerry Jelly Tumblers, Several Styles, Welch's, 1992 . . . . *2.00*

Tom and Jerry Tumblers, Several Styles, Pepsi, 1975 . . . . *10.00*

Character glass. Photos by Robin Rainwater.

Under Dog Series Tumblers (Under Dog, Sweet Polly, or Simon Bar Sinister), Pepsi, 1970s
....*$15.00*

Universal Studios Monster Tumblers (Creature from the Black Lagoon, Dracula, Franken-stein, Mummy, Mutant, or Wolfman), 1980 ....*12.00*

Urchins Tumblers (6 Styles), Coca-Cola, 1976 ....*6.00*

Walter Lantz Cartoon Collector Series Tumblers (16 Styles—Andy Panda, Chilly Willy, Woody Woodpecker, etc.), Pepsi, 1977 ....*15.00*

Warner Brothers Collector Series Tumblers (over 30 Styles—Bugs Bunny, Porky Pig, Speedy Gonzales, Elmer Fudd, Daffy Duck, Coyote, Roadrunner, etc.), Pepsi, 1973 ...*10.00*

Warner Brothers Interaction Series Tumblers (over 25 Styles—All Major Characters), Pepsi, 1976 (Special Run Characters $20.00) *10.00*

Warner Brothers Looney Tunes Collector Series Tumblers (13 Styles), Pepsi, 1979 and 1980 ....*6.00*

Warner Brothers Tumbler (16 Styles), Welch's, 1974 and 1976 ....*5.00*

Wizard of Oz Land of Oz Tumblers (4 Styles), Kentucky Fried Chicken, 1984 ......*8.00*

Wizard of Oz Tumblers (18 Styles), Swift's Peanut Butter, 1950 ....*15.00*

Ziggy Tumblers (4 Styles), 7-Up, 1977 ....*4.00*

Ziggy Tumblers (4 Styles), Hardee's or Pizza Inn, 1979 ....*5.00*

The term "character glass" is a broad one and refers to cartoon and comic book characters, movie stars, and other figures that have been etched, enameled, trans-ferred, or reproduced in fired-on decals. In 1937, Libbey won a contract with Walt Disney to produce tumblers picturing Snow White and the Seven Dwarfs. The movie was a smash hit, and eight separate tumblers with a picture of each little character enameled on the surface were filled with cottage cheese and shipped to thousands of dairies across the country.

The immense popularity of the "character" tumbler had its beginning here. Other food items included cheese spreads (see listings under "Swanky Swigs"), jams, and jellies. Since the 1970s, fast-food restaurants, often with the backing of the soft drink industry, promote decorated tumblers far more than any other medium. See the "Disney Glass Collectibles" section for additional listings

CHINTZ   FOSTORIA GLASS COMPANY, 1940S–1950S

Object	Price
Bell	*$80.00*
Bowl, 4½"	*40.00*
Bowl, 4½" with 3 Corners	*25.00*
Bowl, 5"	*30.00*
Bowl, 5" with Handle	*25.00*
Bowl, 7½"	*35.00*
Bowl, 8½" with Handles	*50.00*
Bowl, 9½"	*70.00*
Bowl, 10" with Handles	*60.00*
Bowl, 10½" with Handles	*65.00*
Bowl, 11½" Flared	*65.00*
Bowl, #6023 Line (Large)	*70.00*
Candlestick, 3½" Tall, Double	*30.00*
Candlestick, 4" Tall	*20.00*
Candlestick, 5" Tall	*25.00*

Candlestick, 6" Tall, Triple *$40.00*
Candlestick, Double, #6023 Line (Large) *35.00*
Candy Dish with Cover, 3-Part *100.00*
Celery Dish, 11" Oval *35.00*
Champagne Glass, 5¹/₂" Tall, 6 oz. *20.00*
Claret Glass, 5¹/₂" Tall, 4¹/₂ oz. *40.00*
Cocktail Glass, 3¹/₂" Tall, 4 oz. *25.00*
Cocktail Glass, 5" Tall, 4 oz. *25.00*
Compote, 3¹/₄" *25.00*
Compote, 4³/₄" *30.00*
Compote, 5¹/₂" *35.00*
Cordial, 4" Tall, 1 oz. *45.00*
Creamer, Individual, 3¹/₈" Tall, 4 oz. (Small) *20.00*
Creamer, 3³/₄", Footed (Large) *25.00*
Cruet with Stopper, 5¹/₂" Tall, 3¹/₂ oz. *100.00*
Cup, Footed *20.00*
Goblet, 6¹/₄" Tall, 9 oz. *28.00*
Goblet, 7¹/₂" Tall, 9 oz. *30.00*
Ice Bucket with Metal Handle *125.00*
Jelly Dish with Cover, 7¹/₂" *90.00*
Mayonnaise Set, 3-Piece, 3¹/₂" Holder with Matching Underplate and Ladle *60.00*
Pickle Dish, 8" Oval *35.00*
Pitcher, 9³/₄" Tall, 1¹/₂ qt., Footed *350.00*
Plate, 6" *10.00*
Plate, 7¹/₂" *15.00*
Plate, 8¹/₂" *25.00*
Plate, 9¹/₂" *45.00*
Plate, 10¹/₂" Cake with Handles *50.00*
Plate, 11" *45.00*
Plate, 14" with Upturned Edge *50.00*
Plate, 16" Cake *100.00*
Platter, 12" Oval *90.00*
Relish, 6", Square, 2-Part *35.00*
Relish, 10", Oval, 3-Part *40.00*
Relish, 5-Part *45.00*
Salad Dressing Bottle with Stopper, 6¹/₂" Tall, 7 oz. *275.00*
Salt and Pepper Shakers, 2³/₄" Tall *90.00*
Sauce Boat, Oval *75.00*
Sauce Boat, Oval, Divided *70.00*
Sauce Boat Liner, 8", Oblong *30.00*
Saucer *6.00*
Sherbet, 4¹/₂" Tall *20.00*
Sugar, Individual, 2⁷/₈" Tall, 2 Handles (Small) *20.00*
Sugar, 3¹/₂", Footed, 2 Handles (Large) *25.00*
Syrup, Sani-cut (with Metal Tab on Pouring Spout) *300.00*
Tid-bit, 8¹/₄" with Upturned Edge, 3-Footed *30.00*
Tray, 6¹/₂" for Individual Creamer and Sugar Set, 2 Tab Handles *25.00*
Tray, 11" with Center Handle *40.00*
Tumbler, 5 oz., 4³/₄" Tall, Footed *25.00*
Tumbler, 9 oz. *25.00*
Tumbler, 13 oz., 6" Tall, Footed *30.00*

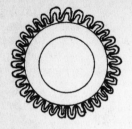

"Christmas Candy" pattern. Drawing by Mark Pickvet.

Vase, 5" (2 Styles) $80.00
Vase, 6", Footed *90.00*
Vase, 7¹/₂", Footed *110.00*

This is one of the most beautiful etched crystal patterns of the post-Depression period. Several pieces are already quite rare and desirable—therefore, very valuable. "Chintz" was also known as Fostoria's "#338 Line," and a wide variety of numbered blanks were cut for this pattern (Nos. 869, 2083, 2375 2419, 2496, 2496¹/₂, 2586, 4108, 4128, 4143, 5000, 6023, 6026, and possibly others).

CHRISTMAS CANDY   INDIANA GLASS COMPANY, 1950S

Object	Crystal	Terrace Green
Bowl, 7³/₈"	$5.00	$20.00
Creamer	8.00	16.00
Cup	5.00	15.00
Mayonnaise or Gravy Bowl with Glass Ladle	20.00	125.00
Plate, 6"	3.00	8.00
Plate, 8¹/₄"	6.00	14.00
Plate, 9¹/₂"	9.00	18.00
Plate, 11¹/₄"	12.00	30.00
Saucer	2.00	4.00
Sugar	8.00	16.00

"Christmas Candy" is sometimes referred to as the "No. 624" pattern in Indiana's advertisements. The terrace green color was also referred to as "seafoam" by Indiana. Others call it teal.

CHRISTMAS ORNAMENTS   (BLOWN AND SPUN GLASS) VARIOUS COMPANIES, 1970S–PRESENT

Object	Price
Angel with Hands Clasped, 2⁵/₈" Tall	$8.00
Angel with Hands Clasped, 3¹/₄" Tall	12.00
Angel Playing Flute, 2" Tall	8.00
Balloon, Flying with Detachable Basket, 3³/₄" Tall	25.00
Basket, 2" Tall, Red Bow at Top	8.00
Basket, 2¹/₂" Tall, Green and Red Holly and Bow, Brass Bell at Top	10.00

Bell, 1³/₄" Tall $5.00
Bell, 2" Tall, Ringer Connected to Inner Side 6.00
Bell, 2¹/₄" Tall, 10 Flutes, Pressed Diamond Pattern at Top, Crystal Ringer 15.00
Bench, Park, 2³/₈" Tall, 2¹/₄" Across 10.00
Boot, 1¹/₂" Tall 5.00
Buggy, Baby, 2¹/₄" Tall, 4 Wheels, 2³/₄" Across 12.00
Candelabra, 3¹/₄" Tall, Double—2 Sets of 4 Candles 12.00
Candle, 2¹/₄" Tall, Green and Red Holly and Bow, Brass Bell Near Bottom 8.00
Candy Cane, 2³/₄" Tall 5.00
Carousel Horse with Pole, 3³/₄" Tall 15.00
Carousel with 3 Horses, 3¹/₈" Tall, 2¹/₄" Diameter 30.00
Cello, 4" Long, 3 Strings 20.00
Fire Engine with Ladder, 2³/₄" Across, 4 Wheels 20.00
Gazebo with Dancing Couple, 4" Tall 25.00
Heart, 2" Tall, 2" Wide 5.00
Horse, Winged Rocking (Pegasus), 3¹/₄" Tall 15.00
Lamp, 3⁷/₈" Tall, Tiffany Style 15.00
Mushrooms, 2¹/₂" Tall, 1 Small and 1 Large Blown Together 8.00
Peacock, 2¹/₂" Tall, Tail Open, 2³/₄" Diameter 12.00
Peacock, 3" Tall, Tail Down 10.00
Piano, Baby Grand, 2¹/₂" Tall 10.00
Reindeer, 3¹/₈" Tall, Green and Red Holly and Bow 10.00
Rocking Chair, 3¹/₂" Tall, Songbird on Seat 10.00
Sewing Machine with Table, 2¹/₂" Tall 20.00
Ship, 3¹/₈" Tall, Nina, Pinta, or Santa Maria 15.00
Ship, Sailing, 3³/₄" Tall, Red Flag at Top 15.00
Sled, 2¹/₂" Across 6.00
Star, 2" Across (5-Pointed) 5.00
Swan, 2³/₄" Tall 10.00
Swans, 2" Tall, 3" Across, 2 Swans Blown Together 12.00
Teapot, 2¹/₈" Tall 10.00
Telephone, 1³/₄" Tall, 1³/₄" Across, Rotary Dial 10.00
Tree, Christmas, 2³/₈" Tall, Solid Glass, ¹/₂" Thick 10.00
Umbrella, 3¹/₂" Tall, Clear Bow on Top and Frosted Bow on Handle 15.00
Vase, 2⁵/₈" Tall, Pitcher-Style with Handle and Lip, Top Half Frosted with Bow 12.00
Wineglass, 2³/₄" Tall 10.00
Wishing Well with Detachable Bucket, 4" Tall 25.00

Christmas ornaments have been made by some small glass and novelty companies; others have been made in Taiwan for distribution in America.

Spun glass sailing ship, crystal Christmas ornament. Photo by Robin Rainwater.

COIN GLASS
FOSTORIA GLASS COMPANY, 1950S–EARLY 1980S

Object	Emerald Green	Olive Green	Amber	Light Blue	Ruby Red	Crystal*
Ashtray, 5"	$30.00	$18.00	$22.00	$25.00	$24.00	$15.00
Ashtray, 7½", with Center Coin	35.00	25.00	26.00	30.00	28.00	24.00
Ashtray, 7½" Round	40.00	30.00	32.00	35.00	34.00	28.00
Ashtray, 10"	55.00	40.00	35.00	50.00	45.00	35.00
Ashtray, Oblong	25.00	16.00	18.00	22.00	20.00	15.00
Ashtray with Cover	30.00	18.00	22.00	25.00	24.00	15.00
Bowl, 8"	60.00	30.00	35.00	50.00	45.00	25.00
Bowl, 8½" Footed	100.00	60.00	70.00	90.00	80.00	50.00
Bowl, 8½" Footed, with Cover	150.00	80.00	90.00	125.00	100.00	70.00
Bowl, 9" Oval	75.00	40.00	50.00	65.00	60.00	35.00
Bowl, Wedding, with Cover	125.00	70.00	80.00	100.00	90.00	60.00
Candle Holder, 4½"	30.00	18.00	22.00	25.00	24.00	15.00
Candle Holder 8"	75.00	40.00	50.00	65.00	60.00	35.00
Candy Box with Cover	75.00	40.00	50.00	65.00	60.00	35.00
Candy Jar with Cover	75.00	40.00	50.00	65.00	60.00	35.00
Cigarette Box with Cover	90.00	50.00	60.00	80.00	70.00	45.00
Cigarette Holder with Cover	90.00	50.00	60.00	80.00	70.00	45.00
Cigarette Urn, 3⅜", Footed	50.00	35.00	30.00	45.00	40.00	25.00
Condiment Set, 4-Piece (Cruet, 2 Shakers, and Tray)	350.00	200.00	225.00	300.00	250.00	175.00
Condiment Tray	90.00	50.00	60.00	80.00	70.00	45.00
Creamer	30.00	18.00	22.00	25.00	24.00	15.00
Cruet, 7 oz., with Stopper	125.00	80.00	90.00	110.00	100.00	75.00
Decanter, 16 oz., with Stopper	300.00	150.00	175.00	250.00	200.00	125.00
Goblet, 10½ oz.	80.00	40.00	50.00	70.00	60.00	35.00
Jelly Dish	35.00	25.00	26.00	30.00	28.00	24.00
Lamp, Oil 9¾", Handled	150.00	80.00	90.00	125.00	100.00	70.00
Lamp, Electric, 10⅛", Handled	150.00	80.00	90.00	125.00	100.00	70.00
Lamp, Oil, 13½"	225.00	125.00	135.00	175.00	150.00	100.00
Lamp, Electric, 13½"	225.00	125.00	135.00	175.00*	150.00	100.00
Lamp, Oil, 16⅝"	300.00	150.00	175.00	250.00	200.00	125.00
Lamp, Electric, 16⅝"	300.00	150.00	175.00	250.00	200.00	125.00
Lamp Chimney, Coach	75.00	40.00	50.00	65.00	60.00	35.00
Lamp Chimney, Handled	70.00	35.00	45.00	60.00	55.00	30.00
Nappy, 4½"	30.00	18.00	22.00	25.00	24.00	15.00
Nappy, 5⅜", with Handle	35.00	25.00	26.00	30.00	28.00	20.00
Pitcher, 32 oz., 6¼"	125.00	70.00	80.00	100.00	90.00	60.00
Plate, 8"	60.00	30.00	35.00	50.00	45.00	25.00
Punch Bowl, 14"						150.00
Punch Bowl Base						150.00

*Some crystal pieces have gold-decorated coins, and as long as the gilding is completely intact, their value is the same as that of the emerald green. The blue is more of a light coppery blue, while the ruby color is slightly dark and not as brilliant as some of the typical older ruby reds.

Object	*Emerald Green*	*Olive Green*	*Amber*	*Light Blue*	*Ruby Red*	*Crystal**
Punch Cup						*$25.00*
Salt and Pepper Shakers with Chrome Tops	*80.00*	*40.00*	*50.00*	*70.00*	*60.00*	*35.00*
Salver, Footed	*225.00*	*125.00*	*135.00*	*175.00*	*150.00*	*100.00*
Sherbet, 5¼", 9 oz.	*70.00*	*35.00*	*45.00*	*60.00*	*55.00*	*30.00*
Sugar with Cover	*60.00*	*30.00*	*35.00*	*50.00*	*45.00*	*25.00*
Tumbler, 3⅝", 9 oz.	*70.00*	*35.00*	*45.00*	*60.00*	*55.00*	*30.00*
Tumbler, 4¼",	*70.00*	*35.00*	*45.00*	*60.00*	*55.00*	*30.00*
Tumbler, 5⅛", 12 oz	*75.00*	*40.00*	*50.00*	*65.00*	*60.00*	*35.00*
Tumbler, 5⅜", 10 oz.	*35.00*	*25.00*	*26.00*	*30.00*	*28.00*	*20.00*
Tumbler, 5 3/16", 14 oz.	*70.00*	*35.00*	*45.00*	*60.00*	*55.00*	*30.00*
Urn, 12¾", Footed	*200.00*	*100.00*	*110.00*	*150.00*	*125.00*	*90.00*
Vase, 8"	*60.00*	*30.00*	*35.00*	*50.00*	*45.00*	*25.00*
Vase, 10", Footed	*90.00*	*50.00*	*60.00*	*80.00*	*70.00*	*45.00*
Wineglass, 4", 5 oz.	*75.00*	*40.00*	*50.00*	*65.00*	*60.00*	*35.00*

Fostoria's "Coin Glass" is a very popular pattern; it is still widely available, but the prices have soared the past several years. As a result some pieces are becoming quite rare and hard to come by. The original Fostoria glass has frosted coins; however, the Lancaster Colony Corporation, which purchased Fostoria, continues to reproduce many of the items *without* frosted coins. It is simply cheaper to exclude the frosting. Reproductions without frosted coins generally sell for ⅓ to ½ the original Fostoria frosted versions.

There are other "Coin" patterns available. Avon, for example, has commissioned similar Fostoria pieces.

COLUMBIA FEDERAL GLASS COMPANY, 1938–1942

Object	*Crystal*
Bowl, 5"	*$8.00*
Bowl, 8"	*10.00*
Bowl, 8½"	*10.00*
Bowl, 10½"	*12.00*
Butter Dish with Cover	*15.00*
Cup	*5.00*
Plate, 6"	*2.00*
Plate, 9½"	*4.00*
Plate, 11"	*5.00*
Saucer	*2.00*
Snack Plate	*25.00*
Tumbler, Various Styles	*12.50*

"Columbia" is borderline Depression glass since it was first made in the very late 1930s, but the majority of pieces came out in the early 1940s. A few pieces were made in pink; however, it is a bit paler and lighter than the average Depression Pink but still commands prices four or five times that of the crystal.

The butter dishes (bottoms and tops) are also available in a variety of flashed designs as well as decals. Complete flashed butter dishes are priced at about $20.00, except for the ruby red flashed version, which is worth a few dollars more at $25.00

CORREIA ART GLASS 1973–PRESENT

Object	Price
Apple, Opaque Black or Transparent Red	$100.00
Bowl, Wide Rim, Iridescent Ruby with Gold Swirls	350.00
Bowl, Rose, Iridescent Aqua with Gold Swirls	175.00
Egg, Luster White Opalescent with Gold Swirls and Red Hearts	150.00
Globe Paperweight, 2½", Luster Gold with Violet Miniature Hearts	100.00
Globe Paperweight, 2¼", Dark Opaque Green with Transparent Blue Ring, Saturn Design	110.00
Globe Paperweight, 2¼", World Globe, Iridescent Blue with Gold Continents	100.00
Globe Paperweight, 2½", Violet with Gold Waves and Crescent Moon	100.00
Globe Paperweight, 3", Black or Light Iridescent Gold with Snake in Relief	125.00
Globe Paperweight, 3", Opalescent White with Black and White Zebras	100.00
Lamp, Iridescent Blue, Gold Lustre, Etched Design	850.00
Perfume Bottle with Black Stopper, 3" Tall, Black and Aqua Striped Design	225.00
Perfume Bottle with Crystal Stopper, 3" Tall, Crystal and Aqua Swirls	125.00
Perfume Bottle with Crystal Stopper, 4½" Tall, Emerald Green and Aqua Swirls	250.00
Perfume Bottle with Crystal Stopper, 7" Tall, Cobalt Blue and Aqua	250.00
Vase, 6½" Tall, Iridescent Ruby Red with Gold Swirls	225.00
Vase, Jack-in-the-Pulpit Style, Black with Silver Swirls	300.00
Vase, Black with Silver Swirls	175.00
Vase, Cylinder Form, Black with Silver and Red Swirls	250.00

In operation since 1973, Correia has already achieved an excellent reputation for contemporary art glass. As proof of their achievements, works by Correia can be found in the permanent collections of the Corning Museum of Glass, the Chrysler Museum of Art, the Metropolitan Museum of Art, and the Smithsonian Institution, just to name a few. Everything produced by them is completely handmade without utilizing any molds; freehand blowing by superb artists is the trademark of Correia.

CREST (AQUA CREST, EMERALD CREST, AND SILVER CREST) FENTON ART GLASS COMPANY, EARLY 1940S–PRESENT

Object	Green Edge	Blue Edge	Crystal Edge
Basket, 5" (Several Styles) Varieties	$65.00	$40.00	$35.00
Basket, 6½"	70.00	50.00	40.00
Basket, 7"	75.00	55.00	45.00
Basket, 12"	85.00	65.00	55.00
Basket, 13"	90.00	70.00	60.00
Bonbon, 5½"	15.00	12.00	10.00
Bonbon, 8"	20.00	15.00	12.00
Bowl, 5"	30.00	25.00	20.00
Bowl, 5½"	40.00	35.00	30.00
Bowl, 7"	45.00	40.00	35.00
Bowl, 8½"	50.00	45.00	40.00
Bowl, 8½", Flared	50.00	45.00	40.00
Bowl, 9½"	55.00	50.00	45.00

Fenton's "Crest" pattern. Photo by Mark Pickvet.

Object	Green Edge	Blue Edge	Crystal Edge
Bowl, 10" (2 Styles)	$60.00	$55.00	$50.00
Bowl, 11"	65.00	60.00	55.00
Bowl, 13"	70.00	65.00	60.00
Bowl, 14"	70.00	65.00	60.00
Bowl, Banana, Low-Footed	55.00	50.00	45.00
Bowl, Banana, High-Footed	65.00	60.00	55.00
Bowl, Dessert, Low or Shallow	40.00	35.00	30.00
Bowl, Deep Dessert	45.00	40.00	35.00
Bowl, Finger	30.00	25.00	20.00
Bowl, Tall, Footed	70.00	65.00	60.00
Bowl, Square, Tall, Footed	75.00	70.00	65.00
Cake Plate, Low, Footed	55.00	50.00	45.00
Cake Plate, 13" Tall, Footed	65.00	60.00	55.00
Candle Holder, 6" with Crest on the Bottom	35.00	30.00	25.00
Candle Holder, Globe Holder	15.00	12.00	10.00
Candle Holder, Cornucopia-Shaped	55.00	50.00	45.00
Candle Holder with Flat Saucer-Shaped Base	30.00	25.00	20.00
Candle Holder, Low, Ruffled	15.00	12.00	10.00
Candle Holder, High, Ruffled	30.00	25.00	20.00
Candy Box	70.00	65.00	60.00
Candy Box, Tall Stem, Footed	125.00	110.00	100.00
Chip and Dip Set, 2-Piece (Low Bowl with Mayonnaise Bowl in the Center)	65.00	60.00	55.00
Comport, Footed, Low	20.00	15.00	12.00
Comport, Footed, High	15.00	12.00	10.00
Comport, 6", Flared, Footed	30.00	25.00	20.00
Comport, Footed, Crimped	30.00	25.00	20.00
Creamer, Reeded, with 1 Handle	25.00	20.00	15.00
Creamer, Reeded, with 2 Handles	30.00	25.00	20.00
Creamer, Ruffled	50.00	45.00	40.00
Creamer, Straight Sides	40.00	35.00	30.00
Creamer, Threaded Handle	25.00	20.00	15.00
Cup, Reeded Handle	30.00	25.00	20.00
Cup, Threaded Handle	30.00	25.00	20.00
Epergne Set, 2-Piece (Vase in Bowl)	60.00	55.00	50.00
Epergne Set, 3-Piece (2 Vases in Bowl)	110.00	95.00	90.00

Object	Green Edge	Blue Edge	Crystal Edge
Epergne Set, 4-Piece (3 Vases in Bowl)	$105.00	$100.00	$95.00
Epergne Set, 5-Piece (4 Vases in Bowl)	100.00	105.00	110.00
Epergne Set, 6-Piece	115.00	110.00	105.00
Flowerpot with Attached Saucer	75.00	70.00	65.00
Lamp, Hurricane	20.00	15.00	12.00
Mayonnaise Bowl	25.00	20.00	15.00
Mayonnaise Ladle (Plain Crystal $8.00)	25.00	20.00	15.00
Mayonnaise Liner	20.00	15.00	12.00
Mayonnaise Set, 3-Piece	75.00	60.00	45.00
Mustard, with Spoon and Cover	75.00	70.00	65.00
Nut, Footed	20.00	15.00	12.00
Oil Bottle with Stopper	80.00	75.00	70.00
Pitcher, Small	50.00	45.00	40.00
Pitcher, Large, 70 oz.	200.00	175.00	150.00
Plate, 5½" (2 Styles)	10.00	8.00	6.00
Plate, 6"	12.00	10.00	8.00
Plate, 6½"	15.00	12.00	10.00
Plate, 8½"	20.00	15.00	12.00
Plate, 10"	25.00	20.00	15.00
Plate, 10½"	30.00	25.00	20.00
Plate, 11½"	35.00	30.00	25.00
Plate, 12"	40.00	35.00	30.00
Plate, 12½"	45.00	40.00	35.00
Plate, 16", Cake or Torte	60.00	55.00	50.00
Punch Bowl	300.00	250.00	200.00
Punch Bowl Base	75.00	60.00	50.00
Punch Cup	15.00	12.00	10.00
Punch Ladle (Plain Crystal Only)	25.00	25.00	25.00
Relish, Divided	40.00	35.00	30.00
Relish, Heart-Shaped, with Handle	35.00	30.00	25.00
Saucer	10.00	8.00	6.00
Salt and Pepper Shakers	75.00	70.00	65.00
Sherbet, Footed	20.00	15.00	12.00
Sugar, with Reeded Handles	30.00	25.00	20.00
Sugar, with Ruffled Top	50.00	45.00	40.00
Tid-Bit, 2-Tier Plates	55.00	50.00	45.00
Tid-Bit, 2-Tier (Plate and Ruffled Bowl)	70.00	65.00	60.00

Fenton's "Crest" pattern. Photo by Mark Pickvet.

Object	Green Edge	Blue Edge	Crystal Edge
Tid-Bit, 3-Tier Plates	$75.00	$70.00	$65.00
Tid-Bit, 3-Tier (2 Plates and Ruffled Bowl)	85.00	80.00	75.00
Top Hat, 5" (Vase)	55.00	50.00	45.00
Tray, Sandwich	35.00	30.00	25.00
Tumbler, Footed	55.00	50.00	45.00
Vase, 4¹/₂" (Several Styles)	25.00	20.00	15.00
Vase, 6"	30.00	25.00	20.00
Vase, 6", Crimped	30.00	25.00	20.00
Vase, 6¹/₄", Crimped	30.00	25.00	20.00
Vase, 6¹/₄", Fan-Shaped	35.00	30.00	25.00
Vase, 7"	30.00	25.00	20.00
Vase, 8"	35.00	30.00	25.00
Vase, 8", Crimped	35.00	30.00	25.00
Vase, 8", Globe Holder	50.00	45.00	40.00
Vase, 8", Wheat	40.00	35.00	30.00
Vase, 8¹/₂"	45.00	40.00	35.00
Vase, 9"	50.00	45.00	40.00
Vase, 10"	125.00	110.00	100.00
Vase, 12"	150.00	125.00	110.00

The colors listed above are all milk glass except for the edging and in some pieces the handles or stoppers. "Aqua Crest" includes a blue trim; "Emerald Crest," obviously an emerald green trim; and "Silver Crest," interestingly enough, a clear glass trim for a unique effect.

"Aqua Crest" was the original, beginning in 1941. "Silver Crest" followed in 1943 and remains the most popular; it is still in production today. "Emerald Crest" was not made until the late 1940s and 1950s.

Rarely do glass sets contain so many pieces and varieties. In general, for the "Crest" lines the bigger the piece, the more valuable it is. This is particularly true for plates and bowls; notice how the price climbs as the pieces increase in dimension.

There were over 100 designated "lines" used for the "Crest" patterns, but some are older than others. In dating pieces, the formula for the base milk color was changed in 1958; the originals have a very light opalescence when held up to a light. The "Fenton" signature appears on all products made after 1973.

DAISY   INDIANA GLASS COMPANY, 1933–1970S

Object	Price
Bowl, 4¹/₂"	$6.00
Bowl, 6"	15.00
Bowl, 7¹/₂"	10.00
Bowl, 9³/₈"	20.00
Bowl, 10" Oval	15.00
Creamer, Footed	7.50
Cup	5.00
Plate, 6"	2.00
Plate, 7¹/₂" or 8¹/₂"	6.00
Plate, 9³/₈"	8.00

Plate, 10³/₈" with Indentation for 4¹/₂" Bowl *$20.00*
Plate, 11¹/₂" Cake *10.00*
Platter, 10³/₄" *10.00*
Relish Dish, 3 Divisions *20.00*
Saucer *2.00*
Sherbet *6.00*
Sugar, 2-Handled *7.50*
Tumbler, 9 oz., Footed *15.00*
Tumbler, 12 oz., Footed *25.00*

"Daisy" is sometimes referred to as Indiana's "No. 620" pattern run. The above-listed prices are for the original amber produced in the 1940s. Prior to that the pattern was produced in crystal (reduce the above prices by half) and a fired-on red (double the above prices). A darker forest green was added in the 1960s (reduce the above prices by half).

DEWDROP   JEANNETTE GLASS COMPANY, 1953–1956

Object	*Crystal*
Bowl, 4³/₄"	*$3.00*
Bowl, 8¹/₂"	*8.00*
Bowl, 10³/₈"	*12.00*
Butter Dish with Cover	*20.00*
Candy Dish with Cover, 7"	*20.00*
Creamer	*6.00*
Cup	*3.00*
Leaf-Shaped Dish	*8.00*
Pitcher, 1 qt.	*20.00*
Plate, 11¹/₂"	*12.00*
Punch Bowl, 1¹/₂ Gallon	*25.00*
Punch Bowl Base	*8.00*
Sugar with Cover	*12.00*
Tray, Lazy Susan, 13"	*15.00*
Tumbler, Various Styles	*7.50*

"Dewdrop" is a typical 1950s crystal pattern, nothing too fancy or difficult to obtain. The pattern contains alternating panels of clear glass and tiny horizontal rows of miniature hobs.

"Dewdrop" pattern. Drawing by Mark Pickvet.

Walt Disney's Sorcerer's Apprentice. Photo by Robin Rainwater.

DISNEY GLASS COLLECTIBLES 1930S–PRESENT

Object	*Price*
Alice in Wonderland Tumbler, 1950, 8 Styles	*$20.00*
Bell, 4¹/₂" Tall, Crystal with Gold-Plated Mickey Mouse Ringer	*20.00*
Cinderella Tumbler, 1950, 8 Styles	*10.00*
Coca-Cola Tumblers with Disney Characters, Several Styles	*10.0(*
Donald Duck Tumbler, 1942, Several Styles	*20.0(*
Dopey Crystal Figurine, 4¹/₂" Tall, Limited Edition (1,800)	*125.00*
Dumbo Crystal Figurine, 4¹/₂" Tall, Limited Edition (1,000), Val St. Lambert in Belgium	*200.00*
Dumbo Tumbler, 1941 Two-Color, 5 Styles	*40.00*
Goofy Frosted Crystal Figurine, 2⁷/₈" Tall, Goebel	*35.00*
Jiminy Cricket Crystal Figurine, 4¹/₂" Tall, Limited Edition (1,800)	*125.00*
Jungle Book Pepsi Tumblers, Several Styles	*35.00*
Lady and the Tramp Tumbler, 1955, 8 Styles	*20.00*
Little Mermaid Crystal Figurine, 4⁵/₈" Tall, Limited Edition (1,800)	*125.00*
McDonald's Disneyland Tumbler, 4 Styles	*6.00*
Mickey Mouse Club Tumbler, Several Styles	*10.00*
Mickey Mouse Crystal Figurine, 4¹/₂" Tall, Limited Edition (1,800)	*125.00*
Mickey Mouse Frosted Crystal Figurine, 2⁷/₈" Tall, Goebel	*35.00*
Mickey Mouse Sorcerer's Apprentice Crystal Figurine, 4¹/₂" Tall, Limited Edition (1,800)	*125.00*
Mickey Mouse Through the Years Mug, 1940 Fantasia, Milk White, Pepsi	*15.00*
Mickey Mouse Tumbler, Limited Edition, 1971	*12.00*
Minnie Mouse Frosted Crystal Figurine, 2⁷/₈" Tall, Goebel	*35.00*
Minnie Mouse Mug, Limited Edition, 1971	*12.00*
Pluto Frosted Crystal Figurine, 2⁷/₈" Tall, Goebel	*35.00*
The Rescuers Pepsi Tumblers, 1977, 8 Styles	*12.00*
Sleeping Beauty Crystal Castle, 4⁵/₈" Tall, Limited Edition (1,800)	*200.00*
Sleeping Beauty Tumbler, 1958, Several Styles	*15.00*
Snow White and the Seven Dwarfs Tumblers, 8 Styles, Originally Held Cottage Cheese, Libbey, Late 1930s, Complete Set	*125.00*
Sorcerer's Apprentice Sculpture, 6¹/₄" Tall, Crystal Wave with Miniature Pewter Mickey Mouse Finial, Franklin Mint	*175.00*

Tinker Bell Crystal Figurine, 4¹/₂" Tall, Limited Edition (1,800) *$125.00*
Winnie the Pooh Crystal Figurine, 4¹/₂" Tall, Limited Edition (1,800) *125.00*
Winnie the Pooh Tumbler, 1950s–1960s, Several Styles *10.00*

Disney objects range from decorated tumblers to limited-edition hand-sculpted crystal items. All have one common characteristic in that they feature Disney characters in some form. Those released in limited editions are usually sold out very quickly.

DUNCAN & MILLER ANIMALS   1920S–1955

Object	*Price*
Bird of Paradise	*$500.00*
Donkey with Cart and Peon	*500.00*
Duck, Ashtray, 4"	*15.00*
Duck, Ashtray, 8"	*20.00*
Duck, Mallard, Cigarette Box with Cover, 4¹/₂" × 3¹/₂"	*50.00*
Goose, 6" Tall	*250.00*
Grouse, Ruffled	*1750.00*
Heron, 7" Tall	*110.00*
Swan, Ashtray, 4", Blue Neck on Crystal Swan	*40.00*
Swan, 3" Tall, Crystal	*30.00*
Swan, 5" Tall, Crystal	*35.00*
Swan, 6" Tall, Ruby Red	*40.00*
Swan, 7" Tall, Chartreuse	*45.00*
Swan, 7" Tall, Crystal	*45.00*
Swan, 7" Tall, Red with Crystal Neck	*50.00*
Swan, 8" Tall, Crystal with Red Neck	*50.00*
Swan, 8" Tall, Red with Crystal Neck	*65.00*
Swan, 8" Tall, Ruby Red	*50.00*
Swan, 8" Tall, Ruby Red with Floral Design	*65.00*
Swan, 10" Tall, Crystal	*50.00*
Swan, 10" Tall, Blue Opalescent, 12¹/₂" Wingspan	*250.00*
Swan, 10" Tall, Green Opalescent, 12¹/₂" Wingspan	*225.00*
Swan, 10¹/₂" Tall, Milk White with Red Neck	*475.00*
Swan, 10¹/₂" Tall, Ruby Red with Crystal Neck, 14" Wingspan	*175.00*
Swordfish, Crystal	*175.00*
Swordfish, Blue Opalescent	*525.00*

Like so many others, Duncan and Miller created their own animal figurines from the Depression until they closed permanently in 1955. Most of their creations are water birds such as swans, ducks, etc. A few were made into practical items such as ashtrays and cigarettes boxes.

FENTON ART GLASS   1930S–PRESENT

Object	*Price*
Basket, 4¹/₂" Diameter, Crystal Handle, Opalescent Cranberry, Hobnail Pattern	*$85.00*
Basket, 4¹/₂" Diameter, Milk with Rose Trim and Handle	*75.00*

Basket, 5", Black with Crystal Handle, Enameled Floral Design *$50.00*

Basket, 5" Diameter, Opaque Cobalt Blue with Wicker Handle *150.00*

Basket, 5" Diameter, 3-Footed, Iridescent Amethyst, Pressed Daisy and Star Pattern ..*40.00*

Basket, 5" Diameter, Peking Blue (Light Blue and Milk-Colored) *85.00*

Basket, 5" Diameter, Opaque Rose Pastel with Transparent Pink Handle *80.00*

Basket, 7" Diameter, Opalescent Cranberry with Clear Handle, Coin Dot Pattern *125.00*

Basket, 7" Diameter, Milk Base, Pink Interior, Black Trim and Handle *175.00*

Basket, 7¹/₂" Diameter, Crystal Handle, Blue Opalescent, Hobnail Pattern *95.00*

Basket, 10¹/₂" Diameter, Mulberry Blue with Clear Handle *325.00*

Basket, 10¹/₂" Diameter, Wicker Handle, Ruby Red *150.00*

Bowl, 6", Cupped, Black "Fenton Ebony" *75.00*

Bowl, 13¹/₂" Diameter, 2-Handled (17" Long), Jade Green *150.00*

Candleholder, 4¹/₂" Tall, Cornucopia Style, Crystal with Silvertone *50.00*

Candlestick, 8" Tall, Milk Glass with Ebony Base *110.00*

Candy Jar with Cover, 10¹/₂" Tall, Orange "Flame" *150.00*

Compote, 7" Tall, 10" Diameter, Black, Mikado Pattern *350.00*

Cruet with Crystal Stopper and Handle, 6" Tall, Lime Opalescent, Hobnail Pattern .*95.00*

Shell Dish, 3¹/₂" Across, Embossed "Lobster Pound," Ruby Red *55.00*

Vase, 6¹/₂" Tall, Crimped, Periwinkle Blue *75.00*

Vase, 7¹/₂" Tall, Large Thumbprints, Opalescent Cranberry, Satin Finish *100.00*

Vase, 7⁵/₈" Tall, Cobalt Blue Base with Multicolored Design and Black Threading, Paper Label "Fenton Art Glass" *550.00*

Vase, 9" Tall, Blue, Dancing Ladies Pattern *250.00*

Vase, 9" Tall, Cobalt Blue Base with Multicolored Design and Black Threading *450.00*

Vase, 9" Tall, Green, Dancing Ladies Pattern *300.00*

Vase, 12" Tall, Cobalt Blue with Engraved Floral Design *125.00*

Vase, Ivory, Hanging Hearts Design *250.00*

Vase, Footed, Hearts and Vines Design, Karnak Red *550.00*

Vase with Cover, 12" Tall, Blue, Dancing Ladies Pattern *650.00*

The listings here begin in the 1930s because Fenton primarily manufactured Carnival glass prior to that time (see the "Carnival Glass" chapter for extensive listings

Fenton glass baskets. Photos by Robin Rainwater.

for Fenton). There are also a few other Fenton patterns listed in this chapter as well as in the "Depression Glass" chapter.

Fenton has had a long, distinguished career in the glassmaking industry and has survived the upheavals and downswings in the glass market for most of this century. Much of their work could easily be listed under art glass, but since it is newer, I have placed it here. The company is noted most for fancy art baskets made in a huge variety of styles—opalescent, satin, iridescent, fancy patterned, and in nearly every beautiful color that has ever been created in glass!

FIRE-KING DINNERWARE AND OVEN GLASS
ANCHOR HOCKING GLASS CORPORATION, 1940S–1960S

Anchor Hocking's "Fire-King" line was made in several patterns, as you will see on the following pages, as well as in the rare "Philbe" pattern (see Depression Glass). All "Fire-King" is heat-resistant for use in the oven, an advance over Depression glass.

Fire-King Dinnerware "Alice"   1940S

Object	Jade-ite	White with Trim
Cup	$2.00	$5.00
Plate, $9^{1}/_{2}$	10.00	8.00
Saucer	1.00	2.00

The cups and saucers were given away in boxes of oats, while the dinner plates had to be purchased separately. The trim colors of "Alice" are either light blue or red.

Fire-King Dinnerware "Charm"   1950S

Object	Jad-ite	Azur-ite
Bowl, $4^{3}/_{4}$"	$4.00	$6.00
Bowl, $7^{3}/_{8}$"	8.00	12.00
Creamer	6.00	10.00
Cup	3.00	5.00
Plate, $6^{1}/_{8}$"	4.00	6.00
Plate, $8^{3}/_{8}$"	5.00	8.00
Platter, Oval	10.00	14.00
Saucer	1.00	2.00
Sugar	6.00	10.00

Azur-ite is a very light opaque blue color. The dishes are all square, identical to An-

American glass, Fire-King, "Alice" pattern. Reproduced from a patent design.

chor Hocking's square pieces (listed under "Forest Green" and "Ruby Red" later in this chapter).

Fire-King Dinnerware "Fleurette"   1950S–1960S

Object	White with Flower Decals
Bowl, 4⅝"	$2.00
Bowl, 6⅝"	3.00
Bowl, 8¼"	4.00
Creamer	3.00
Cup	2.00
Plate, 6¼"	1.00
Plate, 7⅜"	2.00
Plate, 9⅛"	3.00
Platter, Oval	6.00
Saucer	1.00
Sugar with Cover	4.00

"Fleurette" is the sister pattern of "Honeysuckle." The pieces are identical in size and shape.

Fire-King Dinnerware "Game Bird"   1950S–1960S

Object	White with Bird Decals
Ashtray, 5¼"	$5.00
Bowl, 4⅝"	4.00
Bowl, 5"	5.00
Bowl, 8¼"	8.00
Creamer	5.00
Mug, 8 oz.	6.00
Plate, 7⅜"	3.00
Plate, 9⅛"	5.00
Sugar with Cover	6.00
Tumbler, 11 oz.	5.00

Ducks, geese, grouse, and pheasants can be found on this glassware in many combinations. Some contain pairs of one breed, while others contain all four on the same object.

Fire-King Dinnerware "Gray Laurel"   1950S

Object	Light Opaque Gray
Bowl, 4⅞"	$3.00
Bowl, 7⅝"	4.00
Bowl, 8¼"	6.00
Creamer, Footed	3.00
Cup, 8 oz.	3.00
Plate, 7⅜"	3.00

Plate, 9 1/8"	$6.00
Plate, 11"	9.00
Saucer	1.00
Sugar, Footed	3.00

"Gray Laurel" is the sister pattern of "Peach Lustre." The pieces are identical except for color, though "Gray Laurel" had a shorter production run.

Fire-King Dinnerware "Honeysuckle" 1950S–1960S

Object	*White with Flower Decals*
Bowl, 4 5/8"	$2.00
Bowl, 6 5/8"	4.00
Bowl, 8 1/4"	6.00
Creamer	3.00
Cup, 8 oz.	4.00
Plate, 6 1/4"	1.00
Plate, 7 3/8"	2.00
Plate, 9 1/8"	4.00
Platter, Oval	8.00
Saucer	1.00
Sugar with Cover	5.00
Tumbler, 5 oz.	3.00
Tumbler, 9 oz.	4.00
Tumbler, 12 oz.	5.00

"Honeysuckle" is the sister pattern of "Fleurette." Both were made in the very late 1950s and early 1960s. Nearly everything is identical except the decal work, and for some odd reason "Honeysuckle" has tumblers and "Fleurette" does not.

Fire-King Dinnerware "Jane-Ray" 1940S–1960S

Object	*Jade-ite*
Bowl, 4 7/8"	$2.00
Bowl, 5 7/8"	3.00
Bowl, 7 5/8"	4.00
Bowl, 8 1/4"	6.00
Creamer	4.00
Cup	3.00
Demitasse Cup and Saucer	15.00
Plate, 7 3/4"	3.00
Plate, 9 1/8"	4.00
Platter, 12"	10.00
Saucer	1.00
Sugar with Cover	6.00

"Jane-Ray" is a rather simple pattern with little in the way of decoration except for the light opaque jade color and the lined edges.

Fire-King Dinnerware "Peach Lustre"   1950S–1960S

Object	Opaque Peach or Iridescent
Bowl, 4⁷/₈"	$2.00
Bowl, 7⁵/₈"	3.00
Bowl, 8¹/₄"	4.00
Creamer, Footed	2.00
Cup, 8 oz.	2.00
Plate, 7³/₈"	1.00
Plate, 9¹/₈"	2.00
Plate, 11"	5.00
Saucer	1.00
Sugar, Footed	2.00

"Peach Lustre" is the sister pattern of "Gray Laurel." The pieces are identical except for the color. "Peach Lustre" was made for over a decade, while "Gray Laurel" was produced for only a few short years in the early 1950s. The color of "Peach Lustre" is much like a light marigold Carnival iridescent. It is obviously more abundant and a little cheaper than "Gray Laurel."

Fire-King Dinnerware and Oven Ware "Primrose"   EARLY 1960S

Object	White with Flower Decal
Bowl, 4⁵/₈"	$2.00
Bowl, 6⁵/₈"	3.00
Bowl, 8¹/₄"	5.00
Cake Pan, 8" Round	6.00
Cake Pan, 8" Square	6.00
Casserole, 1 pt., with Knob Cover	5.00
Casserole, ¹/₂ qt., Oval with Au Gratin Cover	10.00
Casserole, 1 qt., with Knob Cover	6.00
Casserole, 1¹/₂ qt., with Knob Cover	8.00
Casserole, 2 qt., with Knob Cover	10.00
Creamer	3.00
Cup, 5 oz. (Small)	2.00
Cup, 8 oz.	3.00
Custard, 6 oz. (Low)	2.00
Pan, 5" × 9" with Cover	10.00
Pan, 5" × 9" Loaf, Deep	7.00
Pan, 6¹/₂" × 10¹/₂"	8.00
Pan, 8" × 12¹/₂"	9.00
Plate, 6¹/₄"	1.00
Plate, 7³/₈"	2.00
Plate, 9¹/₈"	3.00
Platter, Oval	7.00
Saucer	1.00

Sugar with Cover *$4.00*
Tray, Rectangular, 11" × 6" *3.00*
Tumbler, 5 oz. *3.00*
Tumbler, 9 oz. *4.00*
Tumbler, 13 oz. *5.00*

"Primrose" is interesting in that the pieces doubled for use in the oven as well as on the table. That naturally was the object for the baking dishes all along, but the common table settings such as cups, plates, and bowls were marked as being "heat-proof." The various covers on the casserole dishes are clear crystal.

Fire-King Dinnerware "Restaurant Ware"   EARLY 1950S

Object	*Jade-ite*
Bowl, 4³/₄"	*$4.00*
Bowl, 8 oz., with Flanged Rim	*5.00*
Bowl, 10 oz.	*6.00*
Bowl, 15 oz.	*8.00*
Cup, 6 oz. (Straight)	*4.00*
Cup, 7 oz. (Heavy)	*5.00*
Cup, 7 oz., with Narrow Rim	*5.00*
Mug, 7 oz.	*5.00*
Plate, 5¹/₂"	*1.00*
Plate, 6³/₄"	*2.00*
Plate, 8"	*3.00*
Plate, 8⁷/₈", Oval with Partitions	*7.00*
Plate, 9"	*4.00*
Plate, 9⁵/₈", 3-Compartment	*6.00*
Plate, 9⁵/₈", 5-Compartment	*10.00*
Plate, 9³/₄"	*5.00*
Platter, 9¹/₂", Oval	*8.00*
Platter, 11¹/₂", Oval	*9.00*
Saucer	*1.00*

Anchor Hocking's Fire-King "Restaurant Ware" was designed for restaurants or "mass feeding establishments," as they advertised. The most interesting piece is the five-compartment serving plate, which consisted of four identical compartments and a small circle (the fifth compartment) in the very middle. The pieces were also advertised as being "inexpensive," "heat resistant," "rugged," "stain-resistant," "sanitary," and "colorful." Unfortunately for them, the pieces were not a huge seller and had a production run of only a few years.

Fire-King Oven Glass   ANCHOR HOCKING GLASS CORPORA-TION 1941–1950S

Object	*Ivory*	*Blue*
Baker, 6 oz., Individual	*$2.00*	*$3.00*
Baker, 1 pt. Round		*4.00*

Object	Ivory	Blue
Baker, 1 pt. Square	$3.00	$4.00
Baker, 1 qt.	4.00	5.00
Baker, 1½ qt.	6.00	10.00
Baker, 2 qt.	8.00	12.00
Bowl, 4⅜", Pie Plate		10.00
Bowl, 5⅜", Deep Dish Pie Plate	8.00	12.00
Bowl, 16 oz. Measuring		18.00
Cake Pan, 8¾", Deep		16.00
Cake Pan, 9"	12.00	16.00
Casserole, 10 oz. Individual		12.00
Casserole, 1 pt. with Cover (Knob Handle)	8.00	12.00
Casserole, 1 qt. with Cover (Knob Handle)	10.00	14.00
Casserole, 1 qt. with Cover (Pie Plate Cover)		15.00
Casserole, 1½ qt. with Cover (Knob Handle)	12.00	16.00
Casserole, 1½ qt. with Cover (Pie Plate Cover)		18.00
Casserole, 2 qt. with Cover (Knob Handle)	15.00	20.00
Casserole, 2 qt. with Cover (Pie Plate Cover)		22.00
Coffee Mug, 7 oz. (2 Styles) (Jade-ite $25.00)	20.00	20.00
Cup, 8 oz. Dry Measure without Spout		125.00
Cup, 8 oz. Measuring, with 1 Spout		14.00
Cup, 8 oz. Measuring, with 3 Spouts		18.00
Custard Cup, 5 oz.	2.00	3.00
Custard Cup, 6 oz. (2 Styles)	3.00	4.00
Loaf Pan, 9⅛", Deep	15.00	20.00
Nipple Cover,		100.00
Nurser, 4 oz.		12.00
Nurser, 8 oz.		18.00
Pie Plate, 8⅜"		8.00
Pie Plate, 9"	7.00	10.00
Pie Plate, 9⅝"		12.00
Pie Plate, 10⅜" Juice Saver (Jade-ite $65.00)	50.00	60.00
Refrigerator Jar with Cover, 4½" × 5" (Jade-ite $12.00)	7.00	10.00
Refrigerator Jar with Cover, 5⅛" × 9⅛" (Jade-ite $30.00)	20.00	25.00
Roaster, 8¾"		35.00
Roaster, 10⅜"		50.00
Table Server with Handles (Also Used as Hot Plate)	10.00	14.00
Utility Bowl, 6⅞"		10.00
Utility Bowl, 8⅜"		12.00
Utility Bowl, 10⅛"		14.00
Utility Pan, 8⅛" × 12½"		15.00
Utility Pan, 10½"	14.00	18.00

This pale blue ovenware by Fire-King was very popular and durable. It was a top seller by Anchor Hocking, and some of it is still being used today. It was not designed for microwave use (microwave ovens weren't around back then), and rumor has it that microwaves can cause cracks due to sudden temperature changes. Some pieces were also created in crystal, ivory, and Jade-ite. Jade-ite or Jadeite is a pale light opaque green color (the color of light jade green) and shows up on several of the Fire-King lines.

Fire-King Oven Ware "Blue Mosaic" 1960S

Object	*Cream with Blue Decoration*
Bowl, 4⅝"	$4.00
Bowl, 6⅝"	6.00
Bowl, 8¼"	10.00
Creamer	5.00
Cup	3.00
Plate, 7⅜"	3.00
Plate, 10"	4.00
Platter, Oval	12.00
Saucer	1.00
Sugar with Cover	8.00

Fire-King Oven Ware "Swirl" 1950S–1970S

Object	*Trimmed*	*Pink*	*Blue*	*White*	*Ivory*	*Jade-ite*
Bowl, 4¾"	$3.00	$4.00	$3.00	$1.00	$2.00	$2.00
Bowl, 4⅞"	4.00	5.00	4.00	2.00	3.00	3.00
Bowl, 6⅜"	4.00	5.00	4.00	2.00	3.00	3.00
Bowl, 7¼"	6.00	8.00	6.00	3.00	4.00	5.00
Bowl, 7⅝"	6.00	8.00	6.00	3.00	4.00	5.00
Bowl, 8¼"	8.00	10.00	7.00	4.00	5.00	6.00
Creamer	4.00	7.00	5.00	3.00	4.00	5.00
Creamer, Footed	3.00	6.00	4.00	2.00	3.00	4.00
Cup	3.00	4.00	3.00	2.00	2.00	3.00
Demitasse Cup and Saucer	12.00	14.00	10.00	5.00	6.00	8.00
Plate, 6⅞"	4.00	5.00	3.00	1.00	1.00	2.00
Plate, 7¼"	4.00	5.00	3.00	1.00	1.00	2.00
Plate, 7⅜"	5.00	6.00	4.00	1.00	2.00	3.00
Plate, 9⅛"	6.00	8.00	5.00	2.00	3.00	4.00
Plate, 10"	6.00	8.00	5.00	2.00	3.00	4.00
Plate, 11"	8.00	10.00	6.00	3.00	4.00	5.00
Platter, 12", Oval	9.00	11.00	7.00	4.00	6.00	8.00
Platter, 13", Oval	10.00	12.00	8.00	5.00	7.00	9.00
Saucer	2.00	2.00	1.00	1.00	1.00	1.00
Sugar, Footed, with Cover	5.00	6.00	4.00	2.00	3.00	3.00
Sugar with Cover	6.00	8.00	5.00	2.00	3.00	4.00
Tumbler, 5 oz.	4.00	5.00	3.00	1.00	2.00	3.00
Tumbler, 9 oz.	5.00	6.00	4.00	2.00	3.00	4.00
Tumbler, 12 oz.	6.00	8.00	5.00	3.00	4.00	5.00

The "Jade-ite" is very common. The white and ivory pieces are usually trimmed in gold or dark yellow. Some of the pink ones are trimmed in a darker shade of pink or red near the top. "Swirl" is rather confusing because of the numerous color variations made throughout its production.

Fire-King Oven Ware "Turquoise Blue"   LATE 1950S

Object	Blue
Ashtray, 3¹/₂"	$6.00
Ashtray, 4⁵/₈"	8.00
Ashtray, 5³/₄"	10.00
Bowl, Batter, with Spout	40.00
Bowl, 4¹/₂"	4.00
Bowl, 5"	6.00
Bowl, 6⁵/₈"	10.00
Bowl, 8"	12.00
Bowl, Tear, 1 pt.	8.00
Bowl, Round, 1 qt.	10.00
Bowl, Tear, 1 qt.	12.00
Bowl, Round, 2 qt.	12.00
Bowl, Tear, 2 qt.	14.00
Bowl, Round, 3 qt.	14.00
Bowl, Tear, 3 qt.	16.00
Bowl, Round, 4 qt.	16.00
Creamer	4.00
Cup	3.00
Egg Plate	10.00
Mug, 8 oz.	8.00
Plate, 6¹/₈	6.00
Plate, 7"	7.00
Plate, 9"	8.00
Plate, 9", with Indentation for Cup	8.00
Plate, 10"	20.00
Relish Dish, 3-Part	10.00
Saucer	1.00
Sugar	4.00

This is a fairly common opaque pattern of Fire-King glassware except for the batter bowl with the spout and the 10" plate. The relish and egg plates are usually trimmed in gold, which increases their value somewhat; but they are definitely not recommended for use in the microwave!

Fire-King Oven Ware "Wheat"   1960S

Object	White with Wheat Decal
Bowl, 4⁵/₈"	$2.00
Bowl, 6⁵/₈"	3.00
Bowl, 8¹/₄"	5.00
Cake Pan, 8" Round	7.00
Cake Pan, 8" Square	7.00
Casserole, 1 pt., with Knob Cover	4.00
Casserole, 1 qt., with Knob Cover	6.00
Casserole, 1¹/₂ qt., with Knob Cover	8.00

Casserole, 1½ qt., Oval with Au Gratin Cover *$10.00*
Casserole, 2 qt., with Knob Cover . . . .*.10.00*
Casserole, 2 qt., Round with Au Gratin Cover . . . .*.12.00*
Creamer . . . .*.3.00*
Cup, 5 oz. (Small) . . . .*.2.00*
Cup, 8 oz. . . . .*.2.00*
Custard, 6 oz. . . . .*.2.00*
Pan, Baking, 5" × 9", with Cover . . . .*.8.00*
Pan, Loaf, 5" × 9" . . . .*.7.00*
Pan, Baking, 6½" × 10½" . . . .*.7.00*
Pan, Baking 8" × 12½" . . . .*.9.00*
Plate, 7⅜" . . . .*.2.00*
Plate, 10" . . . .*.3.00*
Platter, Oval . . . .*.7.00*
Saucer . . . .*.1.00*
Sugar with Cover . . . .*.4.00*
Tray, Rectangular, 11" × 6" . . . .*.6.00*

The "Wheat" Fire-King pattern was fairly popular and lasted nearly the entire
decade of the 1960s. It is the older sister pattern of "Blue Mosaic." The two lines
are identical in dimensions and differ only in color and decal; however, the blue did
not sell as well and had a much more limited production run. As a consequence,
there are few varieties of the pieces made in blue.

FLORAGOLD LOUISA   JEANNETTE GLASS COMPANY,
1950S

Object   *Iridescent*
Bowl, 4½" Square *$5.00*
Bowl, 5½", Round . . . .*.20.00*
Bowl, 5½", Ruffled . . . .*.8.00*
Bowl, 8½", Square . . . .*.10.00*
Bowl, 9½", Deep . . . .*.25.00*
Bowl, 9½", Ruffled . . . .*.8.00*
Bowl, 12", Ruffled . . . .*.10.00*
Butter Dish with Cover, Round (6¼" Square Base) . . . .*.35.00*
Butter Dish with Cover, Oblong (for ¼ lb. Stick) . . . .*.30.00*
Candlestick . . . .*.35.00*
Candy Dish, 1 Handle . . . .*.6.00*
Candy Dish, 5¼" Long, 4-Footed . . . .*.5.00*
Candy Jar with Cover, 6¾" . . . .*.40.00*
Coaster, 4" . . . .*.5.00*
Creamer . . . .*.6.00*
Cup . . . .*.4.00*
Pitcher, 1 qt. . . . .*.25.00*
Plate, 5¼" . . . .*.8.00*
Plate, 8½" . . . .*.20.00*
Platter, 11¼" . . . .*.14.00*
Salt and Pepper Shakers with Plastic Tops . . . .*.35.00*
Saucer, 5¼" (no cup ring) . . . .*.8.00*

"Floragold Louisa" pattern. Photo by Mark Pickvet.

Sherbet, Footed *$5.00*
Sugar with Cover, 2-Handled *12.00*
Tid-bit Tray with White Wooden Post *20.00*
Tray, 13¹/₂", Oval *20.00*
Tumbler, Various Styles *20.00*
Vase *175.00*

This pattern is often confused with the true "Louisa" design of the Carnival glass era. A few crystal pieces exist that were not iridized. A few candy dishes were later reproduced in the 1960s and 1970s in light blue, reddish yellow, pink, and the light iridized marigold color.

The original salt and pepper shaker tops were plastic (brown or white plastic), but they broke easily; metal tops are a common replacement and do not lower the value of the shakers.

FOREST GREEN   ANCHOR HOCKING GLASS CORPORATION, 1950–1957

Object	Green
Ashtray, Several Styles	*$5.00*
Bowl, 4³/₄" or 5¹/₄"	*6.00*
Bowl, 6"	*10.00*
Bowl, 7¹/₂"	*10.00*
Bowl, 8¹/₂", Oval	*20.00*
Bowl with Pouring Spout	*10.00*
Creamer	*5.00*
Cup, Square	*3.00*
Goblet, Various Styles	*10.00*
Mixing Bowl Set, 3 Pieces	*20.00*
Pitcher, 1¹/₂ pt.	*15.00*
Pitcher, 1 qt.	*20.00*

Pitcher, 3 qt. *$25.00*
Plate, 6¹/₂" or 6³/₄" .... *.2.00*
Plate, 8¹/₂" .... *.4.00*
Plate, 10" .... *.15.00*
Platter, Rectangular .... *.20.00*
Punch Bowl .... *.20.00*
Punch Bowl Stand .... *.15.00*
Punch Cup, Round .... *.3.00*
Saucer .... *.1.00*
Sherbet .... *.5.00*
Sugar .... *.5.00*
Tumbler, 3"–5" Tall .... *.3.00*
Tumbler, over 5" Tall .... *.5.00*
Vase, Various Styles .... *.5.00*
Wineglass, Various Styles .... *.10.00*

The original "Forest Green" by Anchor Hocking spawned a new color era for glass. The dark green color was copied by others and sold well for the Christmas season along with the "Royal Ruby" pattern.

Depression glass collectors have an easy time distinguishing this color from the lighter Depression green colors; overall it makes dating quite easy. Anchor Hocking was the only one who actually named a pattern "Forest Green."

GIBSON GLASS   1983–PRESENT

Object   *Price*
Angel Figure, 6¹/₂" Tall, Light Blue Cased in Crystal *$45.00*
Basket, 4¹/₂" Tall, Cobalt Blue, Various Molded Pattern Designs .... *.15.00*
Basket, 4¹/₂" Tall, Carnival Cobalt Blue, Various Molded Pattern Designs .... *.20.00*
Basket, 5" Tall, Crystal with Light Iridescence, Pressed Diamond Pattern .... *.20.00*
Basket, 8¹/₂" Tall, Crimped, Cased Light Blue and Crystal .... *.55.00*
Bird, 1³/₄" Tall, 1³/₄" Long, Cobalt Blue .... *.8.00*
Bird, 1³/₄" Tall, 1³/₄" Long, Light Blue with Crystal Overlay .... *.12.00*
Candy, Glass, Multicolored with Crystal Wrapper, Various Designs .... *.5.00*
Compote, 8" Diameter, Crimped, Iridescent Pink with Crystal Base and Stem ...... *.45.00*

Left: "Forest Green" vase. Photo by Robin Rainwater. Right: Gibson miniatures. Photo by Mark Pickvet.

Cruet with Stopper, 7³/₄" Tall, Cobalt Blue with Iridescent Spatter *$30.00*
Dolphin, 5" Long, Cobalt Blue *15.00*
Duck, 3¹/₄" Tall, 4" Long, Cobalt Blue *15.00*
Duck, 3¹/₄" Tall, 4" Long, Crystal *12.00*
Egg, Cranberry or Light Blue Spatter *8.00*
Marble, 1¹/₄", Multicolored Swirls *16.00*
Marble, 1¹/₂", Multicolored Swirls *20.00*
Marble, 1³/₄", Multicolored Swirls *24.00*
Marble, 2", Sulfide, Multicolored Swirls *25.00*
Paperweight, 2" Spherical, Sulfide, Tan 7 Gray Seal Encased in Crystal *25.00*
Paperweight, Sulfide, Pastel Pink and Yellow Rabbit in Egg, Limited Edition *75.00*
Penguin, 3" Tall, Cobalt Blue *10.00*
Vase, 7" Tall, Crimped, Cranberry with Crystal Base *45.00*
Whale, 4" Long, Cobalt Blue *15.00*

Gibson opened a small shop and factory in Milton, West Virginia, in 1983. They offer a fine line of paperweights, marbles, Christmas ornaments and figurines, vases, baskets, animals, and other novelty items.

HEISEY ANIMALS   A. H. HEISEY AND COMPANY, 1920S–1957

Object   *Price*
Airedale, 5³/₄" Tall, Crystal *$350.00*
Airedale, 6" Tall, Crystal *450.00*
Bull, 4" Tall, Crystal *450.00*
Chick, 1" Tall, Head Up, Crystal *100.00*
Chick, 1" Tall, Head Down, Crystal *100.00*
Clydesdale, 7¹/₄" Tall, Crystal *500.00*
Clydesdale, 8" Tall, Crystal *600.00*
Dog, Scotty, 3¹/₂" Tall, Crystal *150.00*
Dog Head Bookends, 5" Tall, Scotty, Pair, Crystal *275.00*
Dog Head Bookends, 6¹/₄" Tall, Pair, Crystal *550.00*
Donkey, 6¹/₂" Tall, Crystal *250.00*
Duck, 2¹/₄" Tall, Floating, Crystal *125.00*
Duck, 2⁵/₈" Tall, Floating, Crystal *150.00*
Duck, Mallard, 4¹/₂" Tall, Wings Half Up, Crystal *150.00*
Duck, Mallard, 5" Tall, Wings Half Up, Crystal *200.00*
Duck, Mallard, 6³/₄" Tall, Wings Up, Crystal *225.00*
Duck, Wood, 4¹/₂" Tall, Crystal *500.00*
Duck, Wood, 5¹/₂" Tall, Crystal *700.00*
Elephant, 4" Tall, Trunk Down, Crystal *300.00*
Elephant, 4¹/₂" Tall, Trunk Up, Crystal *300.00*
Elephant, 5⁷/₈" Tall, Crystal *350.00*
Fish, Angel, Bookends, 6" Tall, Pair, Crystal *225.00*
Fish, Candlestick, 5" Tall, Crystal *225.00*
Fish, Centerpiece, 12" Tall, Tropical Fish with Coral, Crystal *1250.00*
Fish, Match Holder, 3" Tall, Crystal *175.00*
Fish Bowl, 9" Tall, Crystal *850.00*
Gazelle, 11" Tall, Crystal *1250.00*

Giraffe, 11" Tall, Head Turned to Side, Crystal $200.00
Giraffe, 11" Tall, Head Turned to Rear, Crystal ....*.200.00*
Goose, 2³/₄" Tall, Wings Down, Crystal ....*.90.00*
Goose, 4¹/₂" Tall, Wings Half Up, Crystal ....*.100.00*
Goose, 5³/₄" Tall, Wings Down, Crystal ....*.250.00*
Goose, 6¹/₂" Tall, Wings Half Up, Crystal ....*.125.00*
Goose, 6¹/₂" Tall, Wings Up, Crystal ....*.125.00*
Hen, 4¹/₄" Tall, Crystal ....*.425.00*
Hen, 5¹/₂" Tall, Crystal ....*.500.00*
Horse, Pony, 3³/₄" Tall, Rearing, Crystal ....*.125.00*
Horse, Plug, 4" Tall, Crystal ....*.100.00*
Horse, Pony, 4¹/₈" Tall, Kicking, Crystal *150.00*
Horse, Plug, 4¹/₄" Tall, Sparky, Cobalt Blue ....*.1000.00*
Horse, Pony, 5" Tall, Standing, Crystal ....*.175.00*
Horse, 7³/₈" Tall, Show, Crystal ....*.375.00*
Horse, 8¹/₄" Tall, Filly, Head Forward, Crystal ....*.450.00*
Horse, 8¹/₄" Tall, Filly, Head Backward, Crystal ....*.450.00*
Horse, 8⁷/₈" Tall, Flying Mare, Crystal ....*.1000.00*
Horse, 8⁷/₈" Tall, Flying Mare, Sahara Yellow Color ....*.2000.00*
Horse, Rearing, Bookends; 7⁷/₈" Tall, Pair, Crystal ....*.300.00*
Horse Head Bookends, 6⁷/₈" Tall, Pair, Crystal ....*.250.00*
Pheasant, Asiatic, 10¹/₂" Tall ....*.600.00*
Pheasant, Ringneck, 4³/₄" Tall, Crystal ....*.200.00*
Pig, ⁷/₈" Tall, Standing, Piglet, Crystal ....*.100.00*
Pig, 1" Tall, Sitting, Piglet, Crystal ....*.125.00*
Pig, 3¹/₈" Tall, Sow, Crystal ....*.200.00*
Pigeon, Pouter, 6¹/₂" Tall, Crystal ....*.750.00*
Rabbit, 2³/₈" Tall, Head Up, Crystal ....*.200.00*
Rabbit, 2³/₈" Tall, Head Down, Crystal ....*.225.00*
Rabbit, Paperweight, 2³/₄" Tall, Crystal ....*.225.00*
Rabbit, 4⁵/₈" Tall, Crystal ....*.250.00*
Rooster, 5⁵/₈" Tall, Crystal ....*.350.00*
Rooster, 8" Tall, Fighting, Crystal ....*.200.00*
Rooster Cocktail Glass, 4¹/₄" Tall, Crystal ....*.35.00*
Rooster Cocktail Shaker, 14" Tall ....*.150.00*
Rooster Vase, 6¹/₂" Tall, Crystal ....*.125.00*
Sparrow, 2¹/₄" Tall, Crystal ....*.125.00*
Swan, 2¹/₈" Tall, Cygnet, Crystal ....*.100.00*
Swan, 7" Tall, Crystal ....*.400.00*

The famous "Heisey Animals" were relatively inexpensive and were purchased for children and adults alike. They were rather durable and well constructed, but beware of some that might be damaged or scratched from excessive play! Of course, today they are not inexpensive at all and are quite difficult to find.

HOMESPUN OR FINE RIB   JEANNETTE GLASS COMPANY, 1939–1949

Object	Pink	Crystal
Bowl, 4¹/₂"	$5.00	$4.00

American glass, Homespun tea set.
Reproduced from a 1948 advertisement.

Object	Pink	Crystal
Bowl, 5"	$14.00	$12.00
Bowl, 8¼"	12.00	10.00
Butter Dish with Cover	45.00	40.00
Children's Tea Set:		
Cup	25.00	20.00
Plate	10.00	8.00
Saucer	5.00	4.00
Teapot with Cover	80.00	
Complete Set of 12 Pieces (Crystal Only)		130.00
Complete Set of 14 Pieces (Pink Only)	250.00	
Coaster	5.00	4.00
Creamer	8.00	6.00
Cup	5.00	4.00
Plate, 6"	3.00	2.00
Plate, 9¼"	12.00	10.00
Platter, 13", 2-Handled	10.00	8.00
Saucer	3.00	2.00
Sherbet	8.00	6.00
Sugar	8.00	6.00
Tumbler, under 5" Tall	12.00	10.00
Tumbler, over 5" Tall	20.00	17.50

This "Fine Rib" pattern is not unlike the pressed glass of old. The complete children's tea sets are particularly valuable.

IMPERIAL'S ANIMALS 1920S–1982

Object	Price
Airedale, Caramel Slag	$100.00
Airedale, Ultra Blue	75.00
Chick, Head Down or Up, Milk White	12.00
Clydesdale, Amber or Salmon	350.00
Clydesdale, Verde Green	175.00
Colt, Aqua	50.00

Cygnet, Black $60.00
Cygnet, Light Blue 30.00
Donkey, Caramel Slag 65.00
Donkey, Green Carnival 100.00
Elephant, Caramel Slag 60.00
Elephant, Green Carnival 100.00
Elephant, Pink Satin 75.00
Filly, Head Forward, Satin 80.00
Filly, Head Backward, Verde Green 150.00
Fish Candle Holder, Sunshine Yellow 50.00
Fish Match Holder, Sunshine Yellow Satin 25.00
Gazelle, Ultra Blue 125.00
Hen Covered Dish, on Nest, 4¹/₂", Beaded Brown 30.00
Horse Head Bookends, Pink 500.00
Mallard Duck, Wings Down, Caramel Slag 200.00
Mallard Duck, Wings Down, Light Blue Satin 25.00
Mallard Duck, Wings Half Up, Caramel Slag 40.00
Mallard Duck, Wings Half Up, Light Blue Satin 25.00
Mallard Duck, Wings Up, Caramel Slag 40.00
Mallard Duck, Wings Up, Light Blue Satin 25.00
Owl, Milk White 50.00
Pheasant, Asiatic, Amber 350.00
Piglet, Sitting 50.00
Piglet, Standing, Ruby Red 100.00
Piglet, Standing, Ultra Blue 50.00
Rabbit, Paperweight, Milk White 40.00
Rooster, Amber 450.00
Rooster, Fighting, Pink 200.00
Sow, Amber 350.00
Swan, Caramel Slag 40.00
Swan, Milk White 35.00
Swan Nut Dish, Footed 40.00
Terrier, 5³/₄", Caramel Slag 100.00
Tiger, Paperweight, Black 75.00
Tiger, Paperweight, Jade Green 100.00
Wood Duck, Caramel Slag, Ultra Blue Satin, or Sunshine Yellow Satin 50.00
Wood Duckling, Floating or Standing, Sunshine Yellow or Sunshine Yellow Satin .. .20.00

Imperial made their first animal figurines when the Carnival glass era ended. Imperial acquired the molds of several other companies after they had gone out of business (Central in 1940, Heisey in 1958, and Cambridge in 1960, all makers of animal figurines). Imperial was considerate enough to mark all of their new products, including reproductions, with the "IG" mark.

JAMESTOWN FOSTORIA GLASS COMPANY, 1950S–1980S

Object	Amber or Brown	Ruby Red	Other Colors	Crystal
Bowl, 4¹/₂"	.$8.00	$14.00	$10.00	$12.00
Bowl, 10"	.25.00	40.00	30.00	35.00

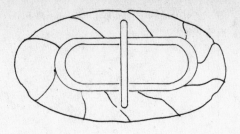

"Jamestown" pattern. Drawing by Mark Pickvet.

Object	Amber or Brown	Ruby Red	Other Colors	Crystal
Bowl, 10", with 2 Handles	$30.00	$45.00	$35.00	$40.00
Butter Dish with Cover, ¼ lb., Rectangular	35.00	50.00	40.00	45.00
Cake Plate, 9½", with 2 Handles	20.00	35.00	25.00	30.00
Celery, 9¼"	15.00	30.00	20.00	25.00
Creamer, 3½"	12.00	25.00	16.00	20.00
Goblet, Various Styles	10.00	20.00	14.00	16.00
Marmalade Dish with Cover	40.00	70.00	50.00	60.00
Pickle, 8½"	25.00	40.00	30.00	35.00
Pitcher, 1½ qt.	50.00	100.00	75.00	85.00
Plate, 8"	10.00	20.00	14.00	16.00
Plate, 14", Cake	35.00	50.00	40.00	45.00
Relish, 9", 2-Part	20.00	35.00	25.00	30.00
Salad Set, 4-Piece (10" Bowl, 14" Plate, Wooden Fork and Spoon)	65.00	100.00	75.00	85.00
Salt and Pepper Shakers with Chrome Tops	30.00	45.00	35.00	40.00
Salver, 10"	45.00	75.00	55.00	65.00
Sauce Dish with Cover	15.00	30.00	20.00	25.00
Sugar, 3½"	12.00	25.00	16.00	20.00
Tray, 9½", 2-Handled	35.00	50.00	40.00	45.00
Tumbler, under 5" Tall	12.00	25.00	16.00	20.00
Tumbler, over 5" Tall	12.00	25.00	16.00	20.00
Wineglass, Various Styles	10.00	20.00	14.00	16.00

Several lines were used for Fostoria's "Jamestown" pattern, and many pieces listed above are similar but differ slightly in dimensions. Stemware had a much longer production run and as a consequence is more easily found than some of the tableware items.

The brown and amber are not all that desirable. Fostoria usually made a fairly good grade of crystal, and the crystal "Jamestown" pieces are most in demand, followed closely by the ruby red. Other colors include amethyst, green, light blue, and pink.

MOONSTONE ANCHOR HOCKING GLASS CORPORATION, 1941–1946

Object	Light Opalescent
Bowl, 5½"	$7.50
Bowl, 6½", 2-Handled	8.00

"Moonstone" pattern. Photo by Robin Rainwater.

Bowl, 7³/₄"	*$10.00*
Bowl, 9¹/₂"	*14.00*
Candleholder	*8.00*
Candy Jar with Cover	*25.00*
Cigarette Jar with Cover	*15.00*
Cloverleaf-Shaped Dish, 3 Divisions	*12.50*
Creamer	*6.00*
Cup	*6.00*
Goblet	*15.00*
Heart-Shaped Dish, 1 Handle	*10.00*
Plate, 6¹/₄"	*3.00*
Plate, 8"	*8.00*
Plate, 10"	*16.00*
Puff Box with Cover, 4³/₄", Round	*16.00*
Relish Dish	*8.00*
Saucer	*3.00*
Sherbet	*6.00*
Sugar, 2-Handled	*6.00*
Vase	*10.00*

The large round "moonstones" on the glass articles resemble the hobs on hobnail patterns. The color is a white opalescent, which serves as edging on most pieces. The base is crystal, and the opalescent coating does not render the glass opaque. There are a few off–light green and pink opalescent pieces, but most were experimental and are housed in storage at Anchor Hocking.

The Fenton Glass Company has made a few pieces that are similar to "Moonstone," including salt and pepper shakers and cologne bottles. The hobs on Fenton's pieces are more pointed than the round ones on "Moonstone."

NAVARRE   FOSTORIA GLASS COMPANY, LATE 1930S–1982

Object	*Price*
Bell	*$35.00*
Bonbon Dish, 7³/₈" Diameter, 3-Footed	*25.00*

Bowl, 4" or 4¹/₂", 1 Handle *$12.50*
Bowl, 5", with or without Handle *15.00*
Bowl, 6" *17.50*
Bowl, 6¹/₄", 3-Footed *20.00*
Bowl, 7¹/₂" Oval, 2 Tab Handles *30.00*
Bowl, 10", Oval *40.00*
Bowl, 10¹/₂", with or without Handles or Feet *50.00*
Bowl, 12" *60.00*
Bowl, 12¹/₂", Oval *60.00*
Candlestick, 4" Tall *20.00*
Candlestick, 4¹/₂" or 5" Tall, Double *35.00*
Candlestick, 5¹/₂" Tall *25.00*
Candlestick, 6" Tall, Triple *50.00*
Candlestick, 6³/₄" Tall, Double or Triple *50.00*
Candy Dish with Cover *100.00*
Celery, 9" *25.00*
Celery, 11" *35.00*
Cheese Dish, 3¹/₄" Tall, 5¹/₄" Diameter, Stemmed *25.00*
Compote, Various Styles *30.00*
Cordial *25.00*
Cracker Dish, 11" Flat *35.00*
Creamer, Individual, 3¹/₈" Tall, 4 oz. *15.00*
Creamer, 4¹/₄" Tall, 6³/₄ oz. *20.00*
Cruet with Stopper, 6¹/₂" Tall *250.00*
Cup *15.00*
Goblet, Various Styles *35.00*
Ice Bucket, 4¹/₂" Tall *75.00*
Ice Bucket, 6" Tall *100.00*
Mayonnaise Set, 3-Piece (2 Styles) *75.00*
Pickle, 8" or 8¹/₂" *25.00*
Pitcher, Syrup *200.00*
Pitcher, 1¹/₂ qt. *300.00*
Plate, 6" *10.00*
Plate, 7¹/₂" *15.00*
Plate, 8¹/₂" *20.00*
Plate, 9¹/₂" *30.00*
Plate, 10" Cake, 2 Handles *45.00*
Plate, 10¹/₂", Oval *50.00*
Plate, 14" Cake *60.00*
Plate, 16" Cake *70.00*
Relish, 6", Square, 2 Divisions *35.00*
Relish, 10" Oval, 3 Divisions *45.00*
Relish, 10", 4 Divisions *50.00*
Relish, 13¹/₄", 5 Divisions *70.00*
Salt and Pepper Shakers *75.00*
Sauce Dish, 6¹/₂" × 5¹/₄", Oval *100.00*
Sauce Dish, 6¹/₂", Divided *40.00*
Sauce Dish Liner, 8", Oval *25.00*
Saucer *8.00*
Sugar, Individual, 2⁷/₈" Tall *15.00*
Sugar, 3⁵/₈" Tall, 2-Handled *20.00*

Syrup, 5½" Tall, Sani-cut *$200.00*
Tid-Bit, 8¼", 3-Footed .... *.25.00*
Tray, 6½" (for Individual Creamer and Sugar Set) .... *.20.00*
Tumbler, Various Styles .... *.30.00*
Vase, under 10" Tall, Various Styles .... *.75.00*
Vase, 10", Footed .... *.125.00*
Wineglass, Various Styles .... *.35.00*

"Navarre" is Fostoria's Plate Etching No. 327 and is a very beautiful and elegant etched pattern. Nearly all of the stemware and one tumbler are available in a light pink or light blue with the same etching (increase the price by 25% for pink or blue items). There are certainly quite a few pieces here, and the pitchers and cruets are already quite rare.

NEW ENGLAND CRYSTAL COMPANY 1989–
PRESENT

Object	*Price*
Bowl, 3¼" Long, Irregular Shape, Frosted Oyster Shell with Pearl Design	*$75.00*
Bowl, 8", Cut Antelope, Bird, or Fish Design	*100.00*
Cross Crystal Sculpture, 3½" Tall (Crucifix-Shaped)	*35.00*
Cross Crystal Sculpture, 3½" Tall (Crucifix-Shaped), Engraved Design	*55.00*
Cross Crystal Sculpture, 3½" Tall (Crucifix-Shaped), Diamond Cut Design	*45.00*
Fish, 2" Tall, 3¾" Long, Pink or Blue Pate de Verre Design	*100.00*
Fish, 4" Tall, 3¾" Long, Pink or Blue Pate de Verre Design on Crystal Base	*175.00*
Frog, 1⅝" Tall, 2½" Wide, Green Pate de Verre Design	*100.00*
Frog, 2⅜" Tall, 2¾" Wide, Green Pate de Verre Design on Crystal Base	*175.00*
Masquerade Crystal Prism Sculptures, 4" Tall, Copper Wheel Engraved Moon and Star, Theater Masks, or Sun and Moon Designs	*125.00*
Paperweight, 2¼", Copper Wheel Engraved Federal or Primrose Pattern	*50.00*
Paperweight, Cut Triple Diamond Pattern	*50.00*
Paperweight, 2¾", Copper Wheel Engraved "Arbor" Floral Pattern	*100.00*
Paperweight, 2¾", Copper Wheel Engraved "Jefferson" Foliage Pattern	*75.00*
Paperweight, 3", Cut Hobstar Pattern	*50.00*
Perfume Bottle with Atomizer, 4½" Tall, Copper Wheel Engraved Federal or Primrose Pattern	*125.00*
Perfume Bottle with Atomizer, 4½" Tall, Cut Triple Diamond Pattern	*125.00*
Perfume Bottle with Stopper, 5" Tall, Copper Wheel Engraved Federal or Primrose Pattern	*100.00*
Perfume Bottle with Stopper, 5" Tall, Cut Triple Diamond Pattern	*100.00*
Scrimshaw Crystal Sculpture, 4¾" Tall, Copper Wheel Engraved Ship and Ocean Scene ("The Chase")	*400.00*
Scrimshaw Crystal Sculpture, 5" Long, Copper Wheel Engraved Ship and Ocean Scene ("Going Home")	*400.00*
Scrimshaw Crystal Sculpture, 9½" Long, Copper Wheel Engraved Ship, Whale, and Boat Scene ("The Capture")	*450.00*
Shot Glass, 2¼" Tall, 1 oz., Copper Wheel Engraved Fly Caster Pattern	*80.00*
Shot Glass, 2⅝" Tall, Copper Wheel Engraved Federal or Primrose Pattern	*75.00*
Shot Glass, 2⅝" Tall, Cut Triple Diamond Pattern	*75.00*

Tumbler, 11.5 oz. Old-Fashioned Glass, Copper Wheel Engraved Fly Caster Pattern (2 Styles) *$40.00*

One of the newest of art glass companies in America, New England Crystal in a short period of time has established itself as a producer of exciting-quality new products combined with old techniques. Fine-cut lead crystal, pate de verre, and copper wheel engraving are only just the beginning for this operation. Of particular note are the pate-de-verre animals and the unique "Crystal Scrimshaw" collections.

NEW MARTINSVILLE ANIMALS 1920S–1950S

Object	*Price*
Bear, Baby, 3" Tall, 4½" Long	*$75.00*
Bear, Mama, 4" Tall, 6" Long	*300.00*
Bear, Papa, 4¾" Tall, 6½" Long	*350.00*
Bear, Black, with Wheelbarrow (2-Piece Set)	*275.00*
Chick, 1" Tall	*75.00*
Dog Bookends, German Shepherd, Pair	*150.00*
Dog Bookends, Russian Wolfhound, 7¼" Tall, Pair	*175.00*
Dove Bookends, 6" Tall, Frosted, Pair	*80.00*
Duck, Fighting, Head Up or Down (Viking)	*40.00*
Eagle	*75.00*
Elephant Bookends, Pair	*125.00*
Gazelle Bookends, 8½" Tall, Pair	*100.00*
Hen, 5" Tall	*75.00*
Horse, 12" Tall, Pony, Oval Base	*100.00*
Pelican, 8" Tall, Lavender Tint	*65.00*
Pig, 3¾" Tall, Sow	*275.00*
Piglet, 1¼" Tall	*75.00*
Police Dog on Rectangular Base, 5" Tall, 5" Long	*100.00*
Porpoise	*500.00*
Rabbit, 1" Tall, Ears Back	*75.00*
Rabbit, 1" Tall, Ears Up	*75.00*
Rabbit, 1" Tall, Ears Down	*75.00*
Rabbit, 3" Tall	*100.00*
Rooster, 8" Tall	*100.00*
Seal with Ball Bookends, Pair	*150.00*
Seal Candlestick, 4¾" Tall, Baby Seal	*75.00*
Seal Light 7¼" Tall, with Bulb	*75.00*
Squirrel Bookends, 5¼" Tall, on Base, Pair	*150.00*
Starfish Bookends, 7¾" Tall, Pair	*150.00*
Swan Bonbon Dish, 6", Cobalt Blue	*55.00*
Swan Bowl, 10½", Amber	*45.00*
Tiger Bookends, 6¾" Tall, on Base, Pair	*300.00*

New Martinsville's line of animals was continued by Viking, which purchased the company in 1944. They continued using the New Martinsville molds but marked their products as "Rainbow Art" or with the "Viking" name. In 1991, Viking was purchased by Kenneth Dalzell (former president of Fostoria), and some of the old molds are still being utilized.

PANEL GRAPE WESTMORELAND GLASS COMPANY, 1950–1970S

Object	Price
Appetizer Set, 3-Piece (Relish Dish, Round Fruit Cocktail, and Small Ladle)	$60.00
Basket, 6½", Oval	25.00
Basket, 8"	75.00
Bottle, Water, 5 oz.	60.00
Bowl, Rose	20.00
Bowl, 6½", Oval	25.00
Bowl, 8"	40.00
Bowl, 9", 9½", or 10", Various Styles	50.00
Bowl, 9" with Cover, Round or Square	60.00
Bowl, 10½", 11", or 11½", Round or Oval	60.00
Bowl, 12"	90.00
Bowl, 12½", Oval or Bell-Shaped	100.00
Bowl, 14", Shallow	125.00
Bowl, Rose	20.00
Butter Dish with Cover, Rectangular (¼ lb.)	40.00
Cake Salver, 10½"	50.00
Cake Salver, 11", Footed	80.00
Canape Set, 3-Piece (3½" Fruit Cocktail with Ladle and 12½" Tray)	125.00
Candelabra, Triple	200.00
Candle Holder, 4" Tall, Octagonal	15.00
Candle Holder, 5" Tall	20.00
Candle Holder, 8" Tall, Double	25.00
Candy Box with Cover, 6½"	40.00
Candy Jar with Cover, with or without Feet	35.00
Canister, 7"	100.00
Canister, 9½"	125.00
Canister, 11"	150.00
Celery, 6" Tall	40.00
Cheese Dish with Cover	70.00
Compote, 4½", Crimped	20.00
Compote with Cover, 7",	25.00
Compote, 9"	75.00
Condiment Set, 5-Piece (2 Oil Bottles, Salt and Pepper Shakers, and 9" Oval Tray)	100.00
Cordial	20.00
Creamer, Individual (Tiny)	12.50
Creamer	15.00
Cruet with Stopper	25.00
Cup	12.00
Decanter	125.00
Dresser Set, 4-Piece (2 Water Bottles, Puff Box, and 13½" Oval Tray)	200.00
Egg Plate, 12"	50.00
Egg Tray, 10", with Metal Center Handle	30.00
Epergne Set, 2-Piece (9" Lipped Bowl and 8½" Vase)	75.00
Epergne Set, 2-Piece (12" Lipped Bowl and 8½" Vase)	150.00
Epergne Set, 2-Piece (14" Flared Bowl and 8½" Vase)	200.00
Epergne Set, 3-Piece (12" Lipped Bowl, 5" Bowl Base, and 8½" Vase)	225.00

Epergne Set, 3-Piece (14" Flared Bowl, 5" Bowl Base, and 8½" Vase) *$275.00*
Flowerpot *50.00*
Fruit Cocktail, Round or Bell-Shaped with 6" Plate *25.00*
Goblet, Various Styles *20.00*
Jardiniere, 5" Tall *25.00*
Jardiniere, 6½" Tall *35.00*
Jelly Dish with Cover, 4½" Tall *25.00*
Ladle, Punch *50.00*
Marmalade Dish with Ladle *60.00*
Mayonnaise, 4", Footed *25.00*
Mayonnaise Set, 3-Piece (Round Fruit Cocktail, 6" Plate, and Ladle) *35.00*
Napkin Ring *15.00*
Nappy, 4½" *12.00*
Nappy, 5", Handled or Bell-Shaped *15.00*
Nappy, 7" *20.00*
Nappy, 8½" *25.00*
Nappy, 9" *30.00*
Nappy, 10", Bell-Shaped *35.00*
Parfait *25.00*
Pickle *25.00*
Pitcher, 1 pt. *40.00*
Pitcher, 1 qt. *35.00*
Planter, Free Standing, Various Styles *35.00*
Planter, Wall, Various Styles *75.00*
Plate, 6" *12.00*
Plate, 7" *15.00*
Plate, 8½" *20.00*
Plate, 10½" *40.00*
Platter, 14½" *100.00*
Platter, 18" *150.00*
Puff Box with Cover *35.00*
Punch Bowl 13" *250.00*
Punch Bowl Base *175.00*
Punch Cup *10.00*
Relish, 9", 3-Part *35.00*
Salt and Pepper Shakers, Various Styles *35.00*
Sauce Boat and Tray *60.00*
Saucer *10.00*
Sherbet, Various Styles *17.50*
Soap Dish *60.00*
Sugar, Individual (Tiny) *12.50*
Sugar *15.00*
Sugar with Cover *25.00*
Tid-Bit, 2-Tier (8½" and 10½" Plates) *65.00*
Tid-Bit Tray with Metal Handle on the 10½" Plate *50.00*
Toothpick Holder *25.00*
Tray, 9" Oval *55.00*
Tray, 13½" Oval *75.00*
Tumbler, Various Styles *25.00*
Vase, Up to 9" Tall, Various Styles *30.00*
Vase, over 9" Tall, Several Styles *40.00*

Water Bottle, 5 oz. *$60.00*
Wineglass, Various Styles *20.00*

The white is an opaque milk white, and some pieces (mostly plates) are also available with birds, flowers, and fruits as color decoration applied on the white.

"Panel Grape" is also known as Westmoreland's "Pattern #1881" and was hugely successful. In the modern or even postmodern era of glassware, there are few patterns that can boast so many pieces (excluding different color combinations). Milk glass collectors seem to always have a few pieces of "Panel Grape," and some argue that no milk glass collection is complete without one!

PILGRIM GLASS COMPANY   1972–PRESENT

Object   *Price*
Cruet with Crystal Stopper, 7" Tall, Cranberry with Applied Crystal Handle *$35.00*
Egg, 2½" Tall, Cranberry and Crystal Rose on White Cameo *225.00*
Egg, 3" Tall, White on Red Cameo, Snowman and Evergreens Design *250.00*
Lamp, 10" Tall, Brass Base, White on Blue Cameo, Evergreens and Covered Bridge Scene
. . . .*1250.00*
Paperweight 4½", Crystal with Blue Flower and Wine Swirls *50.00*
Perfume Bottle with Stopper, 6" Tall, Cranberry *80.00*
Pitcher, Water, 7½" Tall, Ruby Red Crackle Design *30.00*
Plate, 12", Crystal, Christmas Issue, Della Robia Design *25.00*
Powder Jar with White Cover, 1½" Tall, White "Summer Meadow" on Pink Cameo, Foliage and Clover Design *325.00*
Vase, 5" Tall, Fluted Top, Crystal Base, White with Cranberry Streaking *20.00*
Vase, 7" Tall, Black Bears (with White Eyes and Red Mouths) on Green Cameo, Appalachia Folk Art Design *1100.00*
Vase, 7" Tall, Light Blue and White Daisies on Green Cameo *550.00*
Vase, 8" Tall, Bud, Crystal Globe Base, Ruby Red *18.00*
Vase, 9" Tall, 4-Color Cameo, Brown and Tan Koala Bears on Dark Gray Ground . . .*925.00*
Vase, 10" Tall, Bud, Cranberry *75.00*
Vase, 11" Tall, 5-Color Cameo: Dark Brown, Tan, and Black Night Hawk Landing Design, White Stars, Shaded Light Gray Ground *1300.00*
Vase, 12" Tall, Jack-in-the-Pulpit Style, Cranberry *110.00*
Vase, 12" Tall, Jack-in-the-Pulpit Style, Iridescent *100.00*
Vase, 12" Tall, Light Blue on Aqua Cameo, Ladies in the Aviary Design *400.00*
Vase, 12" Tall, Red and White Rhododendron and Blue Leaves on White Cameo *900.00*
Vase, 13" Tall, Dark and Light Blue on Tan Cameo, Parrots Design *425.00*

Pilgrim is one of the sparks in the contemporary art glass field. Their most impressive designs are superbly crafted cameo products. Along with cameo engraving, they have revived other older styles including cranberry, crackle, iridescent, and other designs.

ROYAL RUBY   ANCHOR HOCKING GLASS COMPANY, 1938–1970S

Object   *Price*
Ashtray, 4½", Leaf *$3.00*

Beer Bottle, 7 oz. *$15.00*
Beer Bottle, 12 oz. .... *.20.00*
Beer Bottle, 16 oz. .... *.25.00*
Beer Bottle, 32 oz. .... *.35.00*
Bowl, 4¼", 4¾", or 5", Round or Square .... *.6.00*
Bowl, 5¼" .... *.10.00*
Bowl, 7½", Round of Square .... *.12.00*
Bowl, 8", Oval .... *.30.00*
Bowl, 8½" .... *.15.00*
Bowl, 10", Deep .... *.30.00*
Bowl, 11½" .... *.25.00*
Cigarette Box or Card Holder .... *.45.00*
Cordial, ... *.6.00*
Creamer .... *.6.00*
Creamer, Footed .... *.8.00*
Cup, Round .... *.4.00*
Cup, Square .... *.5.00*
Goblet, Various Styles .... *.10.00*
Lamp .... *.25.00*
Pitcher, 1 qt. .... *.25.00*
Pitcher, 3 qt. .... *.40.00*
Plate, 6½" or 7" .... *.3.00*
Plate, 7¾" .... *.4.00*
Plate, 8½", 9", or 9¼", Round or Square .... *.7.00*
Platter, 13¾" .... *.15.00*
Punch Bowl .... *.30.00*
Punch Bowl Base .... *.25.00*
Punch Cup .... *.3.00*
Saucer, Round or Square .... *.2.00*
Sherbet .... *.7.50*
Sugar .... *.6.00*
Sugar, Footed .... *.8.00*
Sugar Cover .... *.10.00*
Tumbler, 3"–5" Tall .... *.7.50*
Tumbler, over 5" Tall .... *.10.00*
Vase, 4" or 6½" Tall, Various Styles .... *.7.50*
Vase, 9" .... *.14.00*
Wineglass, Various Styles .... *.10.00*

"Royal Ruby" is the older sister pattern of "Forest Green." "Royal Ruby" was first made in the late 1930s but is usually considered as later than the Depression era. The pattern is named for the color, which is a little darker than ruby red. Anchor Hocking has a patent on the "Royal Ruby" name. Both "Royal Ruby" and "Forest Green" were made in great quantities, and pieces are usually not too difficult to find. Assembling a complete set in both colors might still be a challenge!

SANDWICH ANCHOR HOCKING GLASS COMPANY,
1939–1970S

Object   *Price*
Bowl, 4⅜" *$4.00*

Bowl, 4⁷/₈" $4.00
Bowl, 5", Ruffled 10.00
Bowl, 5¹/₄" 6.00
Bowl, 6¹/₂" 7.00
Bowl, 7", 7¹/₄", 8", or 8¹/₄" 8.00
Bowl, 9" 20.00
Butter Dish with Cover 40.00
Cookie Jar with Cover 30.00
Creamer 5.00
Cup 2.00
Custard Cup 4.00
Custard Cup, 5 oz, Ruffled 12.00
Custard Cup Liner 12.00
Pitcher, Milk, 1 pt. 50.00
Pitcher, 2 qt. 65.00
Plate, 7" 8.00
Plate, 8" 3.00
Plate, 9" 15.00
Plate, 9", with Indentation for Punch Cup 4.00
Plate, 12" 12.00
Punch Bowl 9³/₄" 20.00
Punch Bow Stand 20.00
Punch Cup 3.00
Saucer 1.00
Sherbet 7.00
Sugar with Cover 15.00
Tumbler, Various Styles 12.50

There are several odd-colored pieces: darker royal ruby, forest green, amber (which Anchor Hocking refers to as "Desert Gold"), pink, and milk white. Green is the rarest (triple the above prices). Milk white is not that desirable (reduce the prices by 25%). For all other colors, double the above prices.

The pink and royal ruby are the oldest colors and were made for only two short years (1939–1940); the rest were made in the 1950s and 1960s. A cookie jar was reproduced in the 1970s in crystal but is an inch taller and noticeably wider by a few inches than the original (priced at $15.00).

This pattern is sometimes confused with Indiana's "Sandwich" pattern, but there are more leaves surrounding each symmetrical flower pattern in Hocking's "Sandwich" (four leaves off the main stem as opposed to Indiana's two). One other prolific "Sandwich" pattern was Duncan Miller's; there are more spiral curves in Duncan Miller's pattern than in either Hocking's or Indiana's.

SANDWICH   INDIANA GLASS COMPANY, 1920S–PRESENT

Object	Light Green	Teal Blue	Smokey Blue	Orangish Red	New Crystal
Ashtrays, Set of 4 (Card Suits)					$4.00
Basket, 10"					30.00
Basket, 10¹/₂" With Handles 8.00					6.00
Bowl, 4" 4.00					3.00

Object	Light Green	Teal Blue	Smokey Blue	Orangish Red	New Crystal
Bowl, 4¼"	$4.00				$3.00
Bowl, 6"	3.00				2.00
Bowl, 6", Hexagonal	5.00	12.00	10.00		4.00
Bowl, 8"	4.00	10.00	8.00		3.00
Bowl, 8½"	10.00				8.00
Bowl, 9"	14.00				12.00
Bowl, 11½"	18.00				16.00
Butter Dish Bottom	8.00	40.00			8.00
Butter Dish with Cover (Teal Blue Reproduction $20.00)	25.00	150.00			25.00
Butter Dish Top	15.00	110.00			15.00
Candlestick, 3½"	10.00	14.00	12.00		8.00
Candlestick, 7"	14.00	18.00	16.00	20.00	12.00
Candlestick, 8½"	8.00				6.00
Celery, 10½"	14.00				12.00
Creamer	14.00	18.00	16.00		12.00
Creamer and Sugar with Diamond-Shaped Tray	22.00	30.00	25.00		20.00
Cruet, 6½", with Stopper		125.00			
Cup, 9 oz.	3.00	8.00	6.00	25.00	2.00
Cup for Indented Plate	2.00	7.00	5.00		1.00
Decanter with Stopper	25.00		30.00		20.00
Goblet, 8 oz.	12.00		14.00		10.00
Goblet, 9 oz.	14.00		16.00	40.00	12.00
Mayonnaise, Footed	14.00				12.00
Pitcher, 68 oz.				125.00	30.00
Pitcher, 8" Tall, 68 oz., with Fluted Rim	25.00				20.00
Plate, 6"	3.00	6.00			2.00
Plate, 7"	4.00				3.00
Plate, 8"	3.00				2.00
Plate, 8", Oval, with Indentation for Sherbet		6.00		12.00	
Plate, 8⅜"	4.00			20.00	3.00
Plate, 8½", Oval	4.00				3.00
Plate, 10½"	5.00				4.00
Plate, 13"	12.00	25.00	20.00	35.00	10.00
Puff Box	16.00				14.00
Salt and Pepper Shakers	18.00				16.00
Sandwich Server with Center Handle	20.00			50.00	18.00
Saucer, 6"	3.00	5.00	4.00	6.00	2.00
Sherbet	6.00	12.00	10.00		5.00
Sugar	10.00	14.00	12.00	40.00	8.00
Sugar Cover	14.00	16.00	14.00		12.00
Tray, 10" (for Wine Decanter and Goblets)	8.00		10.00		6.00
Tumbler, 3 oz., Footed	10.00		12.00		8.00
Tumbler, 8 oz., Footed	12.00		14.00		10.00
Tumbler, 12 oz., Footed	14.00		16.00		12.00
Wine, 3", 4 oz.	8.00		10.00		6.00

The above colors are all reproductions of Indiana's "Sandwich" pattern, first made in the 1920s except for the orange-red color; a few of these were originally made in 1933 but are virtually indistinguishable from the new.

The teal blue color was made from the 1950s to the 1970s, particularly for Tiara home products. Other colors were added for Tiara (amber, crystal, light green, milk white, red, and smokey blue). Teal blue is a blue aquamarine color, while smokey blue is a darker midnight blue but much duller than a cobalt blue. There are a few odd milk-white pieces that are priced like the smokey blue. The teal blue piece that causes the most trouble is the butter dish. The $150.00 price is for the original made in the 1950s; the reproduction is priced at only $20.00

It will be helpful to refer to the "Depression Glass" chapter for pricing on the original as well as newer colors. There are some additional listings above that older pieces were not manufactured in.

SHELL PINK MILK GLASS JEANNETTE GLASS COMPANY, LATE 1950S

Object	Price
Ashtray, Butterfly-Shaped	*$15.00*
Base with Ball Bearings (for Lazy Susan)	*30.00*
Bowl, 6½", with Cover	*20.00*
Bowl, 8", Footed	*30.00*
Bowl, 8", with Cover	*25.00*
Bowl, 9", Footed	*20.00*
Bowl, 10", Footed	*25.00*
Bowl, 10½", Footed	*35.00*
Bowl, 11", 4-Footed	*40.00*
Bowl, 17½"	*25.00*
Cake Stand, 10"	*30.00*
Candle Holder, Double	*15.00*
Candle Holder, 3-Footed	*25.00*
Candy Dish, 5½", 4-Footed	*25.00*
Candy Dish with Cover, 6½" Tall, Square	*30.00*
Candy Jar with Cover 5½", 4-Footed	*25.00*
Celery, 12½", 3-Part	*40.00*
Cigarette Box	*75.00*
Compote, 6"	*20.00*
Cookie Jar with Cover, 6½" Tall	*75.00*
Creamer	*15.00*
Goblet	*15.00*
Honey Jar with Notched Cover for Spoon, Bee Hive–Shaped	*35.00*
Napco, Berry Bowl, Footed	*15.00*
Napco, Bowl with Sawtooth Top	*20.00*
Napco, Compote, Square	*15.00*
Napco, Cross-Hatched Design Pot	*15.00*
National Candy Dish	*10.00*
Pitcher, 1½ pt.	*30.00*
Powder Jar with Cover, 4¾"	*30.00*
Punch Base, 3½" Tall	*25.00*
Punch Bowl, 7½ qt.	*50.00*

Punch Cup, 5 oz. *$8.00*
Punch Ladle (Plastic) *10.00*
Relish, 12", 4-Part, Octagonal *35.00*
Sugar with Cover *20.00*
Tray, 10" × 7³/₄", Oval with Indentation for Cup (Punch Cup Fits the Indentation) *10.00*
Tray, 12¹/₂" × 9³/₄", Oval with 2 Handles *45.00*
Tray, 13¹/₂", Lazy Susan, 5-Part *35.00*
Tray, 15³/₄", 5-Part with 2 Handles *40.00*
Tray, 16¹/₂", 6-Part *45.00*
Tray Set (Lazy Susan with Base) *65.00*
Tumbler, Various Styles *10.00*
Vase, 5" Tall, Cornucopia-Shaped *20.00*
Vase, 7" Tall *35.00*
Vase, 9" Tall *50.00*
Wineglass *10.00*

The color is a very light opaque pink, nearly the color of milk glass. There are several pattern variations, but all were produced under the "Shell Pink" pattern name. There are eagles, pheasants, feathers, fruits, thumbprints, and even insects. The pieces referred to as "Napco" are marked "Napco, Cleveland" on the bottom and were made specifically for Napco Ceramics of Cleveland, Ohio.

SOUVENIR GLASS VARIOUS PRODUCERS, LATE 19TH CENTURY–PRESENT

Object	*Price*
Butter Dish, Ruby Stained, Button Arches Pattern, Atlantic City 1919	*$75.00*
Creamer, Miniature, Arched Flutes, Ruby Stained, 1908	*25.00*
Liberty Bell Covered Dish, Globe Finial, Crystal with Embossed "1776" and Various Phrases	*100.00*

Left: American souvenir glass. Reproduced from an 1876 advertisement. Right: American souvenir glass. Photo by Robert Darnold.

Mug, Arched Flutes, Ruby Stained, Boston, MA $25.00
Mug, Small Corona, Ruby Stained, St. Joseph, MO 25.00
Mug, 1¾" Tall, Ruby Flashed, 1901 Pan American Exposition 22.00
Paperweight, 2½", Ruby Flashed, Etched Bird and Rose, 1904 St. Louis Fair 75.00
Paperweight, 3¼", Crystal, Seashells, 1904 St. Louis Fair 20.00
Paperweight, 4", Crystal, 1893 Columbian Exposition Agricultural Building 90.00
Paperweight, 4", Crystal, 1901 Pan American Exposition, Temple of Music 75.00
Plate, 10", Hobnail Border, Cleveland Reform 40.00
Shot Glass, 2⅜" Tall, Ruby Stained with Etched "Souvenir Bellevue, Mich." 25.00
Shot Glass, 2⅜" Tall, Ruby Stained with Etched "Souvenir Chicago, Ill." 25.00
Shot Glass, 2⅜" Tall, Ruby Stained with Etched "State Fair 1908" 25.00
Toothpick Holder, 2⅛" Tall, Ruby Stained Co-Op's Royal, Charleston, 1903 ....40.00
Tumbler, 3½" Tall, Lacy Medallion Pattern, Atlantic City 1901 ....55.00
Tumbler, 3½" Tall, Etched Crystal, 1893 Columbian Exposition, Mines and Mining
Building 35.00
Tumbler, 3½" Tall, Custard, Rangley Lakes Maine (Heisey) 50.00
Tumbler, 3¾" Tall, Admiral George Dewey Commemorative 40.00
Tumbler, 5" Tall, Crystal, 1904 St. Louis Fair, Embossed Cascade Gardens 25.00

Some of the earliest souvenirs were made in 1876 for the nation's centennial celebration; the most popular were glass Liberty Bells. From the 1880s into the Depression years, ruby-flashed or ruby-stained over crystal was quite popular and showed
up most often in small tumblers and toothpick holders. Today, souvenirs abound
with fired-on decals or machine-applied enamels; these include tumblers, mugs,
shot glasses, and a wide variety of other items.

SPORTSMAN SERIES OR SAILBOAT AND WINDMILLS OR SHIPS AND WINDMILLS
HAZEL ATLAS GLASS COMPANY, LATE 1930S

Object	Cobalt Blue with White Designs
Cocktail Mixer with Stirrer (Metal Lid)	$20.00
Cocktail Shaker (Metal Lid)	.30.00
Cup	.10.00
Ice Bowl	.30.00
Pitcher, 2½ qt.	.50.00
Pitcher, 2½ qt., with Ice Lip	.45.00
Plate, 5⅞"	.20.00
Plate, 8"	.22.00
Plate, 9"	.25.00
Saucer	.15.00
Tumbler, 3"–4½" Tall	.10.00
Tumbler, over 4½" Tall	.15.00
Whiskey Tumbler, 2¼" Tall, 2 oz.	.100.00

White designs on this glass include not only sailboats and windmills but other
sports as well. Fishing, golfing, horseback riding, and skiing are also part of the
"Sportsman Series."

Make sure that the design is fully intact. Damaged, worn, or missing designs are worth only a fraction of completely intact decorations. Some pale yellow decorations (due to factory discoloration) exist in this pattern, but as long as the complete decoration is there, the value is the same as listed above.

The 2-oz. whiskey tumbler price is not a fluke! Take it from a longtime shot glass collector, there are a lot of collectors who would gladly pay the price to obtain this glass. There are few shot glasses worth this amount except for a few rare fancy-cut crystal, art such as Tiffany, and some rare 19th-century advertising.

SQUARE   CAMBRIDGE GLASS COMPANY, 1950S

Object	*Price*
Ashtray, 3½	.$6.00
Ashtray, 6½"	.8.00
Bonbon, 7"	.15.00
Bonbon, 8"	.20.00
Bowl, 4½"	.10.00
Bowl, 6½"	.12.00
Bowl, 9"	.25.00
Bowl, 10", Round or Oval	.25.00
Bowl, 11"	.30.00
Bowl, 12", Round or Oval	.30.00
Buffet Set, 4-Piece (Plate, Divided Bowl, and 2 Ladles)	.50.00
Candle Holder, 1¾" Tall	.8.00
Candle Holder, 2¾" Tall	.10.00
Candle Holder, 3¾" Tall	.12.00
Candy Box with Cover	.30.00
Celery, 11"	.20.00
Cocktail Glass	.14.00
Compote, 6"	.20.00
Cordial Glass, 1½ oz.	.12.00
Creamer, Individual (Small)	.8.00
Creamer	.10.00
Cruet with Stopper, 4½ oz.	.20.00
Cup	.8.00
Cup, Tea (Small)	.7.00
Decanter, 1 qt.	.75.00
Goblet, Various Styles	.15.00
Iced Tea Goblet, 12 oz.	.12.00
Ice Tub 7½"	.30.00
Icer, Cocktail with Liner	.30.00
Juice Glass, 4½ oz., Footed	.8.00
Lamp, Hurricane, 2-Piece	.40.00
Mayonnaise Set, 3-Piece (Bowl, Plate, and Ladle)	.30.00
Plate, 6"	.8.00
Plate, 7"	.12.00
Plate, 9½"	.20.00
Plate, 9½", Tid-Bit	.18.00
Plate, 11½"	.22.00
Platter, 13½"	.25.00
Relish, 6½", 2-Part	.15.00

Relish, 8", 3-Part *$20.00*
Relish, 10", 3-Part . . . . *.25.00*
Salt and Pepper Shakers . . . . *.20.00*
Saucer . . . . *.6.00*
Saucer (Small, for Teacup) . . . . *.5.00*
Sherbet . . . . *.10.00*
Sugar, Individual (Small) . . . . *.8.00*
Sugar . . . . *.10.00*
Tray, 8", Oval (for Individual Creamer and Sugar) . . . . *.15.00*
Tumbler, Various Styles . . . . *.15.00*
Vase, under 7" Tall, Various Styles . . . . *.25.00*
Vase, over 7" Tall, Various Styles . . . . *.35.00*
Wineglass, Various Styles . . . . *.16.00*

This was one of Cambridge's last patterns before going out of business. When the Imperial Glass Company acquired many of Cambridge's molds, they reproduced several "Square" pieces in colors such as red and black. Colored pieces sell for about 1½ times the crystal listed above.

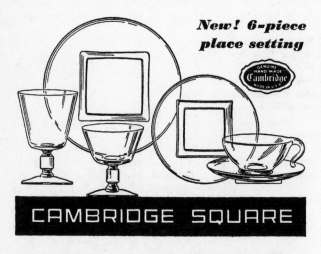

"Square" pattern. Reproduced from a 1952 trade catalog.

STEUBEN CRYSTAL   1933–PRESENT

Object	*Price*
Apple, 4" Tall, Paperweight	*$375.00*
Ashtray with Single Rest, 5" Across	*100.00*
Balloon Sculpture, 10¼" Tall, 5⅛" Width, Triangular, 6 Engraved Hot Air Balloons	*13,750.00*
Bear, 2½" Tall, Hand Cooler	*175.00*
Beaver, 4½" Long	*525.00*
Beaver, 5½" Long	*525.00*
Beaver, 6¼" Tall	*1100.00*
Beaver, 9" Long	*1100.00*
Bird, Shore, 8¼" Long, Sleek Slender Design	*500.00*
Bird, Water, 10" Tall, 9¾" Long, in Flight	*1200.00*
Bookend, 3½" Cube, Air Bubbles	*775.00*
Bowl, 6", Blocks of Cut Lines, 1936	*225.00*
Bowl, 7¾", Floret, 4 Feet	*475.00*
Bowl, 8¼", Bubbled Spherical Center/Base	*475.00*
Bowl, 8¾", Twist Base	*400.00*
Bowl, 9", Ribbed	*325.00*
Bowl, 10", Sunflower Center/Base	*475.00*
Bowl, 11½", Archaic Etruscan Design	*1725.00*
Bowl, 13½", Twist Base	*925.00*
Bowl, 15½", Sunflower Center/Base	*1025.00*
Bowl, 16", 3⅞" Tall, Sterling Frame	*17,600.00*
Bowl, 16¼", Engraved Dragonfly Design	*15,500.00*
Bull, 2½" Tall, Hand Cooler	*175.00*
Candlestick, 4" Tall, Teardrop Design	*150.00*
Candlestick, 4½" Tall, Teardrop in Stem	*550.00*
Candlestick, 6" Tall, Ruffled, Athena Design	*250.00*
Candlestick, 6" Tall, Twist Stems	*650.00*
Candlestick, 9¾" Tall, Starlight Bubble Design	*500.00*
Candlestick, 10¾" Tall, Starlight Bubble Design	*525.00*
Candy Dish with Cover, 5" Tall, 2¼" Diameter, Ram's Head Finial on Cover	*525.00*
Carousel, 7½" Tall, 4½" Diameter, Engraved Horses with Sterling Pennant	*4350.00*
Castle Sculpture, 6⅛" Tall, 10⅝" Width, Black Leather Base	*2700.00*
Cat, 2½" Width, Hand Cooler	*175.00*
Cat, Roman, 5¼" Long, Crouched Sitting Position	*475.00*
Cat, 8¾" Tall, Sitting Upright	*825.00*
Cathedral, 15¾" Tall, Prismatic Form, Engraved Cathedral with Apostles	*15,750.00*
Christmas Tree, 6¼" Tall, Cone-Shaped, Air Bubbles	*625.00*
Circle, 9¾" Diameter, Stardust Bubble Design	*2750.00*
Circle Sculpture, 6½" Tall, Cut Hemispheres, Black Leather Base	*6875.00*
Columbus Circular Sculpture on Walnut Base, Crystal Circle with 3 Ships, 4⅝" Diameter	*425.00*
Compote, 10" Diameter, "Cloud Bowl" Design	*700.00*
Crystal Ball, 4½" Diameter, Black Slate Base	*1400.00*
Decanter with Circular Stopper, 10" Tall, 32 oz., Ship's Flash Design	*1450.00*
Decanter with Eagle Finial on Ball Stopper, 10½" Tall, 32 oz.	*1150.00*
Decanter with Mushroom Stopper, 9½" Tall, 24 oz. Stardust Bubbled Base	*1375.00*
Deer, Engraved Buck Prism Sculpture, 7¼" Tall, Walnut Base	*8225.00*

Steuben crystal.
Photo by Robin Rainwater.

Dog, Puppy, 2³/₄" Width $200.00
Dog, 5" Tall, Ears Down, Head and Flowing Neck *500.00*
Domes, Flower, 5¹/₂" Diameter, Various Engraved State Flowers *750.00*
Dragon, 2" Long, Hand Cooler *175.00*
Dragon, 7¹/₂" Long *800.00*
Eagle, 2³/₄" Long, Hand Cooler *175.00*
Eagle, 3¹/₈" Tall, 4¹/₄" Width, Standing with Wings Open *375.00*
Eagle, 4³/₄" Tall, 5¹/₂" Long, Wings Closed *775.00*
Eagle, 6¹/₄" Tall, 12" Wingspan, Crystal Ball Base *725.00*
Eagle, 9¹/₂" Tall, In Flight Design *3500.00*
Eagle Bowl, 9¹/₂" Tall, 4 Copper Wheel Engraved Eagles, Feathers Form the Top Rim *27,500.00*
Eagle's Crag, 10³/₄" Tall, Crystal Ice Sculpture with Miniature Sterling Eagle at Top, Limited Edition *14,300.00*
Earth Globe on Walnut and Slate Base, Copper Wheel Engraved Continents *6050.00*
Elephant, 5¹/₂" Tall, Trunk above Head *550.00*
Elephant, 7¹/₂" Tall, Trunk above Head *900.00*
Equestrians Crystal Sculpture, 2¹/₄" Tall, 3" Width *425.00*
Excalibur, 4¹/₂" Width Crystal Rock with 8" Sterling Sword (18 kt. Gold Handle) ..*3425.00*
Fawn, Woodland, 4³/₄" Width, Semicricle *325.00*
Fig, 3¹/₄" Tall, Paperweight *225.00*
Fish, Trigger, Pair Together, 10" Tall *1500.00*
Fisherman, Arctic, 6¹/₂" Tall, Crystal Ice Sculpture with Engraved Fish and Sterling Fisherman *4250.00*
Flag, American Star Spangled Banner on Walnut Base, 6" Long, Engraved Stars and Stripes *1750.00*
Fossil Sculpture, 14¹/₄" Tall, 14" Width *6500.00*
Fox, 3¹/₄" Tall, Cub *200.00*
Fox, 4¹/₄" Tall *350.00*
Frog, 2¹/₂" Long, Hand Cooler *175.00*
Galaxy 3¹/₂" Sphere, Stardust Galaxy Bubble Design *850.00*
Gander, 5¹/₄" Tall (Matches Goose) *400.00*
Gazelle Bookends, 6³/₄" Tall, Pair *750.00*
Gazelle Bowl, 6¹/₂" Diameter, 6³/₄" Tall, Copper Wheel Engraved Gazelles *25,250.00*
Gold Prism Sculpture, 3¹/₂" Tall, 3" Width *475.00*
Goose, 4" Tall (Matches Gander) *400.00*
Heart Paperweight, 1¹/₂" Tall, 2⁵/₈" Long, Small Heart within a Large Heart *200.00*
Heart Paperweight, 2⁷/₈" Width, Heart Formed by 2 Turtle Doves *350.00*
Heart Pillar, 3¹/₂" Tall *450.00*
Heart Pillar, 4" Tall *450.00*
Heart Sculpture, 3¹/₄" Tall *400.00*

Hippopotamus, 6¼" Long *$850.00*

Horse Head, 5" Tall *350.00*

House, 3½" Trapezoidal, 3 Engraveable Lines *525.00*

Hunter, 6¼" Tall, Ice Sculpture, Frosted Arch, Sterling Hunter in Boat *4575.00*

Ice Bear (Sterling Silver) on Crystal Iceberg, 6" Width, Miniature Bear at Top *4175.00*

Jar with Cover, 15" Tall, Engraved Design from Each State in the Union (50 in All) *3250.00*

Leopard in Tree Sculpture, 7½" Tall, 8" Width, Engraved Leopard Sitting in Tree . *13,750.00*

Lion, 9½" Width, Walnut Base *2650.00*

Menorah, 9½" Width, Semicircle with 9 Silverplated Candle Cups *3925.00*

Moby Dick Sculpture, 8" Tall, 11¼"-Long Frosted Whale Curved over Boat with Harpooner and Rowers *25,750.00*

Monkey, 2¾" Tall, Hand Cooler *175.00*

Moravian Star, 2½" Tall, 2½" Width, Engraved Stars, Cube Effect *425.00*

Moth-to-Flame Bowl Sculpture, 10" Tall, 8¾" Diameter, Air Trap, Engraved Moths *21,500.00*

Mouse, Woodland, 2⅝" Width, Semicircle *150.00*

Mouse, 3½" Long *350.00*

New York Sculpture, 17" Tall, 3¾" Width, Engraved Skyscrapers (Woolworth, Chrysler, World Trade Center, and Empire State Buildings) *31,500.00*

Nut Bowl, 6" Width, Lip on Side *275.00*

Olive Dish, 5½" Diameter, Single Spiral Handle *375.00*

Owl, 2½" Tall, Hand Cooler *175.00*

Owl on Base, 5⅛" Tall *825.00*

Paperweight 2¾" Tall, Pyramidal, Old Glory Flag *375.00*

Paperweight, 3" Tall, 3" Width, Triangular Prism Effect ("Cubique") *625.00*

Paperweight 3¼" Tall, 3" Diameter, Pyramidal, with Inner Teardrop *1425.00*

Peach, 3" Tall, Paperweight *300.00*

Peacock, 10" Tall, 14½" Width, Semicircular Tail *1650.00*

Pear, 5¾" Tall, 18 kt. Gold Partridge in a Pear Tree inside Pear *4225.00*

Penguin, 3½" Tall *225.00*

Peony Jar, 6¼" Tall, 6½" Width, Copper Wheel Engraved Peony Design *3850.00*

Pig, 3⅛" Long, Hand Cooler *175.00*

Pisces Zodiac Sculpture, 2¾" Tall, 2 Fish *200.00*

Plate, 10", Various Engraved American Birds (12 Audubon Plates in All) *750.00*

Plates, 10", Various Engraved Seashell Designs (12 Plates in All). *750.00*

Plate, 10", Various Engraved Signs of the Zodiac (12 Plates in All) *750.00*

Plate, 10", Copper Wheel Engraved Aquarius Star Design, Aluminum Stand *3850.00*

Polar Bear, 5" Tall, 7½" Long *700.00*

Polo Players Sculpture, 2¼" Tall, 3" Width *425.00*

Porpoise, 6⅛" Long (Bottlenose Dolphin) *450.00*

Porpoise, 9¼" Long (Bottlenose Dolphin) *650.00*

Porpoise, 12⅛" Long (Bottlenose Dolphin) *1200.00*

Prism Sculpture, 7" Tall, 6¼" Width, Quartz Design *3575.00*

Pronghorn, 7" Tall, 14" Width, Semicircle with 5 Copper Wheel Engraved Pronghorn *24,500.00*

Quail, 5½" Tall *475.00*

Rabbit, 2¾" Long, Hand Cooler *175.00*

Sailboat, 6½" Width *575.00*

Sailboat, 12¾" Tall, Cut Sails with Engraved Lines *5200.00*

Salmon Bowl, 7½" Tall, 10¼" Width, 7 Copper Wheel Engraved Salmon, 7 Flies, Bubbles *19,500.00*

Saturn with Bubbled Ring, 5½" Diameter $525.00
Scallop Shell, 3½" Width 225.00
Seal Sculpture, 8¾" Tall, 2 Engraved Seals Pursuing 3 Tiny Fish 3500.00
Seashell, 3½" Width, Irregular Spiral Design 350.00
Skiers Prism Sculpture, 3½" Tall, 3" Width 475.00
Snail, 3¼" Tall 350.00
Snow Crystal, 2¾" Triangular, Engraved Snowflake 300.00
Snow Pine, 4¼" Width, 5 Straight Sides, Engraved Evergreen Tree 500.00
Star of David, 2½" Tall, 2½" Width, Engraved Stars of David, Cube Effect 325.00
Star Paperweight, 4¼" Width, Pentagram 875.00
Star Prism Sculpture, 5" Tall, Slate Base 1475.00
Star Stream, 5¼" Tall, Pentagram Swirl Sculpture 625.00
Starfish, 4¾" Width 225.00
Stork, 14" Tall, Slender Legs, Circular Base 625.00
Swan, 6½" Long, Straight Neck 575.00
Swan, 7½" Long, Curved Neck 575.00
Swan Bowl, 9" Diameter, 8" Tall, Bowl Formed by 3 Copper Wheel Engraved Swans
....38,500.00
Swordfish Rising from Crystal Sculpture, 7½" Tall 12,000.00
Tennis Prism Sculpture, 3½" Tall, 3" Width, 3 Engraved Tennis Players 475.00
Terebra Shell, 4⅝" Long, Spiraled 225.00
Trout, 8" Tall with 18 kt. Gold Fly 2375.00
Tumbler, Old-Fashioned, 3½" Tall, 9 oz. 225.00
Tumbler 4⅛" Tall, Stardust Bubbled Base 350.00
Tumbler, Highball, 4½" Tall 275.00
Turtle, 2½" Long, Hand Cooler 175.00
Urn, 6½" Tall, Copper Wheel Engraved Grecian People 38,500.00
Urn, 9½" Tall, 2 Scroll Handles 1025.00
Vase, 5¼" Tall, Classic "Juliet" Style 225.00
Vase, 6½" Tall, Cinched Waist 350.00
Vase, 6¾" Tall, 3½" Width, Engraved Angel with Trumpet 625.00
Vase, 7⅛" Tall, Circular Base, Engraved Gazelle 2750.00
Vase, 7¾" Tall, Ancient Lyre Design 450.00
Vase, 7¾" Tall, Concentric "Momentum" Design 1275.00
Vase, 8" Tall, Engraved by Waugh, 1935 ....1250.00
Vase, 8" Tall, Seawave Design 600.00
Vase, 8" Tall, Twist Bud Design 325.00
Vase, 8" Tall, 8½" Diameter, Sterling Frame 12,100.00
Vase, 8⅛", Twist Stem Design 650.00
Vase, 8¼" Tall, 8½" Diameter, 24 Cut Facets 11,550.00

Steuben crystal. Photo by Robin Rainwater.

Vase, 8½" Tall, Classic "Palace" Design *$400.00*
Vase, 9½" Tall, Mondo, Slender Cylindrical Design *900.00*
Vase, 10" Tall, Swirled Design *650.00*
Vase, 12¼" Tall, Seawave Design *825.00*
Vase, 16½" Tall, 6½" Diameter, Sterling Frame *14,300.00*
Vase, Handkerchief, 9½" Width *700.00*
Vase, Archaic Etruscan Design, 9¾" Width *1875.00*
Vase, Archaic Etruscan Design, 13" Width *2625.00*
Walrus with Sterling Silver Tusks, 7" Long *3250.00*
Whale, Nantucket, Limited Edition *5500.00*
Wreath, Christmas, 3½" Diameter, Engraved Snowflakes and Evergreen Bows *250.00*
Wren, 3" Width, Sitting *200.00*
Zodiac Sphere Sculpture, Engraved Constellations *13,500.00*

From 1933 on, Steuben concentrated almost exclusively on production of the highest grade of crystal. A few deviations such as silver or gold accents have been added, but no complete colored pieces have been produced since. Some pieces are one of a kind in that they were presented as awards, presentations to heads of state, gifts to museums, and so on (they are not priced here).

Steuben's grade of crystal rivals any made in the world today; copper wheel engraving, prism effects, outstanding designs, and the industry's most gifted artists are all evident in Steuben's glass products. All modern crystal items contain the "Steuben" signature in fine diamond-point script. The most inexpensive of Steuben's new pieces (i. e., small animal hand coolers a few inches long) sell for $150.00, while limited-edition major works exceed $50,000. Note that the plates, flower domes, and covered jars above are priced for each single one (the price must be multiplied for sets or for more than one).

SWANKY SWIGS DECORATED JARS FROM KRAFT CHEESE
SPREADS, 1930S–1970S

Object   *Price*
Animal Patterns, Small, under 4" *$5.00*
Animal Patterns, Large, over 4" *8.00*
Color combinations include black duck and horse, blue bear and pig, brown squirrel and deer, green cat and rabbit, orange dog and rooster, and red bird and elephant.
Antique Patterns, Small, under 4" *5.00*
Antique Patterns, Large, over 4" *8.00*
Color combinations include black coffeepot and trivet, blue kettle and lamp, brown clock and coal scuttle, green coffee grinder and plate, orange churn and cradle, and red spinning wheel and bellows.
Band Patterns, Small, under 4" (1–4 bands) *4.00*

 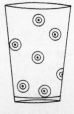

Left: American glass, Swanky Swig "Sailboat" pattern. Drawing by Mark Pickvet.
Right: American glass, Swanky Swig "Circles and Dots" pattern. Drawing by Mark Pickvet.

Band Patterns, Large, over 4" (1–4 bands) *$6.00*
Color combinations include black, blue, red, black and red, blue and red, blue and white, and
red and green.
Bicentennial Issue (1975–1976) in Green, Red, and Yellow, Small, 3¾" *4.00*
Centennial Celebration Issues (various states): Small, under 4", Enameled Colors *5.00*
Large, over 4", Enameled Colors *8.00*
Cobalt Blue Glasses, 4¾", with Enameled Colors *25.00*
Flower Patterns, Small, under 4" *5.00*
Flower Patterns, Large, over 4" *10.00*
All enameled colors for cornflowers, daisies, forget-me-nots, posies, starbursts, tulips, and
miscellaneous flower designs.
Multiple or Miscellaneous Designs, Small, under 4" *5.00*
Multiple or Miscellaneous Designs, Large, over 4" *8.00*
Enameled designs include blocks, dots, bursts, etc., in several colors.
People Patterns, Small, under 4" *5.00*
People Patterns, Large, over 4" *8.00*
All enameled colors include elderly woman, woman in plaid dress, man in pinstripe suit, and
others.
Solid Opaque Colors, Small, under 4" *6.00*
Solid Opaque Colors, Small, over 4" *10.00*
Opaque colors include blue, green, red, and yellow (may or may not have enameled designs).

Swanky Swigs were originally small jars that could be adapted to juice glasses by
soaking off the Kraft Cheese Spread label. Cheese spreads included American
Spread, Limburger Spread, Old English, Olive-Pimento, Pimento, Pimento American, Pineapple, Relish, and Zestful Roka. Even the old original lids to these jars are
selling for a dollar or two.

THIMBLES   VARIOUS COMPANIES, 1940S–PRESENT

Object   *Price*
Thimble, 1" Tall, Ruffled Edge, Shank Rim near Bottom (to Hold Rings), Crystal with Gold
Trim *$8.00*
Thimble, 1" Tall, Crystal Diamond Pattern with Ruby Red Insert in Top *20.00*
Thimble, 1" Tall, Ruffled, Crystal with Enameled Blue and White Cornflower *6.00*
Thimble, 1" Tall, Crystal with Enameled Red and Yellow Roses with Green Leaves . . .*6.00*
Thimble, 1" Tall, Scalloped, Etched White Floral Design *8.00*
Thimble, 1" Tall, Cobalt Blue with Multicolored Miniature Paperweight in Top *35.00*
Thimble, 1" Tall, Ruby Red with Multicolored Miniature Paperweight in Top *35.00*
Thimble, 1½" Tall, Teapot-Shaped with Handle, Spout, and Ball Top, Crystal with Blue Ap-
plied Porcelain Rose *12.00*
Thimble, 1½" Tall, Spun Crystal with Green and Blue Turtle Finial *12.00*
Thimble, 1¾" Tall, Crystal, Birdbath with 2 Birds Finial *14.00*
Thimble, 1¾" Tall, Spun Crystal with Multicolored Clown Finial *10.00*
Thimble, 1¾" Tall, Spun Crystal with Lavender Dragon Finial *12.00*
Thimble, 2" Tall, Bell-Shaped, Crystal, Octagonal Shape *12.00*
Thimble, 2" Tall, Spun Crystal with Amethyst Elephant Finial *10.00*
Thimble, 2⅛" Tall, Spun Crystal with Light Blue Dolphin Finial *10.00*
Thimble, 2⅛" Tall, Spun Crystal with Green Hummingbird Finial *10.00*
Thimble, 2⅛" Tall, Spun Crystal with Yellow Saxophone Finial *10.00*

Thimble, 2¼" Tall, Spun Crystal with Light Blue and Clear Sailing Ship Finial *$12.00*
Thimble, 2½" Tall, Spun Crystal, Hummingbird and Blossom Finial, Gold Trim and Accents
. . . .*30.00*

Thimbles come in a wide variety of styles and materials. Those featured here are
naturally made of glass only by American companies. All of those listed here are of
standard size except for those with a decorative finial on top. There are a few other
thimbles listed in the "Foreign Glass and Glassmaking" chapter, most notably from
Germany.

MISCELLANEOUS MODERN GLASS
COLLECTIBLES   VARIOUS COMPANIES

Object	*Price*

Apple, 4¾" Tall, Crystal, Lenox *$75.00*
Biscuit Jar with 3-Faced Frosted Finial on Cover, 9¼" Tall, Crystal, Reproduction of the
Museum of Fine Art, Boston *55.00*
Bowl, 5", Cobalt Blue, Cape Cod Pattern Reproduction, Smithsonian *65.00*
Bowl, 7", Cobalt Blue, Cape Cod Pattern Reproduction, Smithsonian *80.00*
Cake Plate, 11" Diameter, 4" Tall, Crystal with Ringed Stem, Modern Tiffany Commission
. . . .*75.00*
Candle Holder, Sparrow-Shaped, 3" Tall, 4½" Long, Crystal *8.00*
Candlestick, 4" Tall, Hexagonal Shape, Crystal, Frank Lloyd Wright Foundation *50.00*
Candlestick, 11" Tall, Square Base, Dolphin-Shape Reproductions, Crystal or Azure Blue,
Museum of Fine Art, Boston *50.00*
Candy, Glass, Old-Fashioned Clear Plastic Wrapped Design, Multicolored Glass Candy
(Several Styles) *6.00*
Chess Set, 15" Square Glass Board, 3" King, 2 Styles, 32 Pieces (16 Clear and 16 Black or
Frosted) *80.00*
Coach, Cinderella's, Crystal with Gold Frame, Wheel Borders, and Top Finial, Franklin Mint
. . . .*175.00*
Dragon, 6½" Long, 3¾" Tall, Hand-Blown Crystal with Gold and Black Accents *60.00*
Egg, 1¾" Tall, Faceted Crystal, Gold Stand, Gold and Amethyst Applied Ornamentation
. . . .*75.00*
Egg, 3½" Tall, Clear Square Base, Frosted Lavender with 3 Prancing Clear Unicorns . .*30.00*
Egg, 3½" Tall, Crystal with Iridescent Purple, White, and Blue Floral Design, from Mt. St.
Helens Volcanic Ash *30.00*
Globe, World, 4" Diameter, Frosted Crystal with Clear Continents *40.00*
Goblet, 10" Tall, 8 oz., Crystal with Frosted Stem, Applied Pink and Frosted Lalique-Style
Heart at Top of Stem *50.00*

*Mt. St. Helen's ash glass. Photo by Robin
Rainwater.*

American glass, crystal and frosted chess set, glass board.
Photo by Robin Rainwater.

Grandfather Clock 7¹/₂" Tall, Spun Crystal with Gold Ringer, String Sides, and Top Piece
....*$40.00*

Lamp, Desk, 11" Tall, Bronze Base and Stem, Tiffany Style Multicolored Grape Cluster Patterned Shade *125.00*

Lamp, Desk, 19" Tall, Bronze Base and Stem, Tiffany Style Multicolored Grape Cluster Patterned Shade *200.00*

Lamp, Desk, 23" Tall, Bronze Base and Stem, Tiffany-Style Multicolored Grape Cluster–Patterned Shade *275.00*

Lamp, Desk, 25¹/₂" Tall, Lily Pad Bronze Base and Bronze Stem, Tiffany-Style Multicolored Hummingbird Shade *300.00*

Lamp, Oil, 2¹/₂" Tall, 4³/₈" Wide, 8 oz., Iridescent Purple or Aqua from Mt. St. Helens Volcanic Ash *30.00*

Paperweight, 3" Diameter, Violet Opaline with Enameled Moon, Stars, and Waves, Lundberg Studios *100.00*

Penguin Figurine, 4¹/₄" Tall, Crystal, Dansk *50.00*

Perfume Bottle with Stopper, 6" Tall, Pastel Pink, Frosted Stopper with Applied Crystal Clear Hummingbird Finial *30.00*

Pitcher, Water, 9" Tall, 60 oz., Tinted Pale Green, Applied Emerald Green Handle and Cactus Decoration *30.00*

Pitcher, Water, 8³/₄" Tall, 64 oz., Crystal with Applied Cobalt Blue Handle *20.00*

Pitcher, Water, 68 oz., Crystal with Engraved Lily of the Valley Floral Pattern, Modern Tiffany Commission *75.00*

Plate, Christmas, 10", Bubble-Textured Crystal with Fused Green and White and Red and White Candy Canes, Limited Edition (500) *40.00*

Platter, 12" Hexagonal, Crystal with Concentric Triangle Lines, Riedel *100.00*

Platter, 13" Round, Crystal with 5 Pressed Cats *15.00*

Piggy Bank, 7" Long, 4" Tall, Ruby Red, Mouth-Blown, James Joyce *45.00*

Ram Figurine, 3¹/₂" Tall, Crystal, Dansk *50.00*

Rocking Horse, 5¹/₂" Tall, Crystal with 22 kt. Gold Saddle, Feet, and Rocker Legs *45.00*

Tumbler, 12 oz., Old-Fashioned Style, Crystal with Etched Evergreen (Canadian Hemlock, Blue Spruce, Scotch Pine, White Pine, Balsam Fir, or Eastern Red Cedar), National Wildlife Federation Commission *8.00*

Vase, 6" Tall, Iridescent Aqua Made from Mt. St. Helens Volcanic Ash *35.00*

Vase, 10" Tall, Cobalt Blue or Crystal, Classic 2-Handled Design, Smithsonian Reproduction
....*60.00*

Whale with Jonah Figure Within, 4¹/₄" Long, Hand-Blown Crystal *25.00*

To finish off the chapter, there are a wide variety of one-of-a-kind or unique items made of glass that have been produced in the United States in the past two or three decades. Some of the more interesting include chess sets, museum reproductions, items made with Mt. St. Helens volcanic ash, and pieces by new artists or companies that do not have large offerings at present.

APPENDICES

APPENDICES

APPENDIX 1

PERIODICALS AND CLUBS

Aladdin Knights
c/o J. W. Courter
Route 1
Simpson, IL 62985

American Carnival Glass Association
P. O. Box 235
Littlestown, PA 17340

American Cut Glass Association
3228 S. Boulevard Suite 221
P. O. Box 1775
Edmond, OK 73083–1775

Antique and Art Glass Salt Shaker Collectors Society
2832 Rapidan Trail
Maitland, FL 32751

The Antique Press
12403 N. Florida Ave.
Tampa, FL 33612

Antique Review
P. O. Box 538
Worthington, OH 43085–9928

Antique Week
27 N. Jefferson
P. O. Box 90
Knightstown, IN 46148

The Antiques Trader
P. O. Box 1050
Dubuque, IA 52004–1050

Arts and Crafts Quarterly
P. O. Box 3592, Station E
Trenton, NJ 08629

Avon Times
P. O. Box 9868 Dept. P
Kansas City, MO 64134

Boyd Art Glass Collectors Guild
P. O. Box 52
Hatboro, PA 19040

Cambridge Collectors, Inc.
P. O. Box 416
Cambridge, OH 43725

Candlewick Club
c/o Virginia R. Scott
275 Milledge Terrace
Athens, GA 30606

Collectible Carnival Glass Association
c/o Wilma Thurston
2360 N. Old S. R. 9
Columbus, IN 47203

Collectors of Findlay Glass
P. O. Box 256
Findlay, OH 45839–0256

Depression Glass Daze
P. O. Box 57
Otisville, MI 48463

Fenton Art Glass Collectors of America, Inc.
P. O. Box 384
Williamstown, WV 26187

The Fostoria Glass Society of America, Inc.
P. O. Box 826
Moundsville, WV 26041

Fruit Jar Newsletter
364 Gregory Ave.
West Orange, NJ 07052–3743

H. C. Fry Glass Society
P. O. Box 41
Beaver, PA 15009

The Glass Art Society
c/o Tom McGlauchlin
Toledo Museum of Art
Toledo, OH 43609

Glass Collectors Club of Toledo
2727 Middlesex Dr.
Toledo, OH 43606

Glass Collector's Digest
P. O. Box 553
Marietta, OH 45750–9979

Glass Knife Collector's Club
c/o Adrienne Escoe
P. O. Box 342
Los Alamitos, CA 90720

Glass Research Society of New Jersey
Wheaton Village
Millville, NJ 08332

Heart of America Carnival Glass
Association
c/o Lucille Britt
3048 Tamarek Dr.
Manhattan, KS 66502

Heisey Collectors of America, Inc.
P. O. Box 4367
Newark, OH 43055

Heisey Publications
P. O. Box 102
Plymouth, OH 44865

International Carnival Glass
Association
Lee Markley
R. R. #1, P. O. Box 14
Mentone, IN 46539

R. Lalique
11028 Raleigh Ct.
Rockford, IL 61111

Maine Antique Digest
P. O. Box 1429
Waldoboro, ME 04572

Marble Collector's Society
P. O. Box 222
Trumbull, CT 06611

Morgantown Collectors of America
420 1st Ave. N. W.
Plainview, MN 55964

Mount Washington Art Glass Society
60 President Ave.
Providence, RI 02906

National Association of Avon
Collectors
6100 Walnut, Dept. P
Kansas City, MO 64113

National Depression Glass Association
P. O. Box 69843
Odessa, TX 79769

The National Duncan Glass Society
P. O. Box 965
Washington, PA 15301

The National Early American Glass
Club
P. O. Box 8489
Silver Spring, MD 20907

The National Fenton Glass Society
P. O. Box 4008
Marietta, OH 45750

The National Greentown Glass
Association
1807 W. Madison St.
Kokoma, IN 46901

The National Imperial Glass Collectors
Society
P. O. Box 534
Bellaire, OH 43906

The National Insulator Association
3557 Nicklaus Dr.
Titusville, FL 32780

The National Milk Glass Collectors
Society
1113 Birchwood Dr.
Garland, TX 75043

The National Reamer Association
c/o Larry Branstad
R. R. 3, Box 67
Frederic, WI 54837

The National Westmoreland Glass Collectors Club
P. O. Box 372
Export, PA 15632

New England Antiques Journal
4 Church St.
Ware, MA 01082

New England Carnival Glass Club
12 Sherwood Dr.
West Hartford, CT 06117

Ohio Candlewick Collectors' Club
613 S. Patterson St.
Gibsonburg, OH 43431

Old Morgantown Glass Collectors'
Guild
P. O. Box 894
Morgantown, WV 26507

Pairpoint Cup Plate Collectors of
America, Inc.
P. O. Box 52 D
East Weymouth, MA 02189

Paperweight Collectors
P. O. Box 1059
Easthampton, MA 49125

Perfume and Scent Bottle Collectors
2022 E. Charleston Blvd.
Las Vegas, NV 89104

Phoenix and Consolidated Collectors
P. O. Box 81974
Chicago, IL 60681

The Shot Glass Club of America
P. O. Box 90404
Flint, MI 48509

The Stretch Glass Society
P. O. Box 770643
Lakewood, OH 44107

Thimble Collectors International
6411 Montego Rd.
Louisville, KY 40228

Three Rivers Depression Era Glass
Society
4038 Willett Rd.
Pittsburgh, PA 15227

Tiffin Glass Collectors Club
P. O. Box 554
Tiffin, OH 44883

Toothpick Holder Collectors' Club
Red Arrow Hwy.
P. O. Box 246
Sawyer, MI 49125

Whimsey Glass Club
4544 Cairo Dr.
Whitehall, PA 18052

World's Fair Collectors Society, Inc.
P. O. Box 20806
Sarasota, FL 34238

MUSEUMS

Allen Art Museum
Oberlin College
Oberlin, OH 44074

Art Institute of Chicago
Michigan Ave. and Adams St.
Chicago, IL 60603

The Bennington Museum
W. Main St.
Bennington, VT 05201

Bergstrom Art Center and Museum
165 N. Park Ave.
Neenah, WI 54956

The Cambridge Glass Museum
506 S. 9th St.
Cambridge, OH 43725

Carnegie Institute Museum of Art
4400 Forbes Ave.
Pittsburgh, PA 15213

Chrysler Museum at Norfolk
Olney Rd. and Mowbray Arch
Norfolk, VA 23510

Corning Museum of Glass and Glass
Center
1 Museum Way
Corning, NY 14830

Currier Gallery of Art
192 Orange St.
Manchester, NH 03104

Degenhart Paperweight and Glass Museum, Inc.
P. O. Box 186
Cambridge, OH 43725

Fenton Art Glass Co.
700-T Elizabeth St.
Williamstown, WV 26187

Greentown Glass Museum, Inc.
624 W. Main St.
Greentown, IN 46936

Henry Ford Museum
P. O. Box 1970
Dearborn, MI 48121

Lightner Museum
75 King St.
St. Augustine, FL 32084

Metropolitan Museum of Art
1000 5th Ave.
New York, NY 10028

Milan Historical Museum
10 Edison Dr.
Milan, OH 44846

Minneapolis Institute of Arts
2400 Third Ave. S.
Minneapolis, MN 55404

Museum of Beverage Containers and
Advertising
1055 Ridgecrest Dr.
Goodlettsville, TN 37072

Museum of Modern Art
11 West 53rd St.
New York, NY 10019

National Heisey Glass Museum
169 W. Church St.
Newark, OH 43055

Oglebay Institute-Mansion
Museum, Oglebay Park
Wheeling, WV 26003

Old Sturbridge Village
1 Old Sturbridge Village Rd.
Sturbridge, MA 01566

Philadelphia Museum of Art
P. O. Box 7646
Philadelphia, PA 19101

Portland Art Museum
7 Congress Square
Portland, ME 04101

Sandwich Glass Museum
P. O. Box 103
Sandwich, MA 02563

Seneca County Museum
28 Clay St.
Tiffin, OH 44883

Smithsonian Museum of History
Smithsonian Institution
Washington, DC 29560

Toledo Museum of Art
P. O. Box 1013
Toledo, OH 43697

Wadsworth Athenaeum
600 Main St.
Hartford, CT 06103

GLOSSARY

Acid Cut Back The process of dipping an object into acid for a controlled amount of time in order to achieve a desired cutting depth.

Acid Etching The process of covering glass with an acid-resistant protective layer, scratching on a design, and then applying hydrofluoric acid to etch the pattern into the glass.

Acid Polishing The technique of giving cut glass a polished surface by dipping it into a hydrofluoric acid bath.

Adams and Co. Founded by John Adams in Pittsburgh, Pennsylvania, in 1856, Adams was a major producer of pressed pattern glass. The firm became part of U.S. Glass in 1891.

Advertising Glass A glass vessel displaying information about a manufacturer, company, proprietor, brand, person, establishment, event, and so on.

Agata Glass Art glass characterized by mottled purple or brown finishes as a result of alcohol added on top of the color, agata glass was produced by the New England Glass Company in the late 19th century.

Air Twist An 18th-century English decorating technique where air bubbles were purposefully injected into the base of an object and then pulled down and twisted into a stem.

Akro Agate Glass Co. Akro Agate was founded in 1911 in Akron, Ohio. They were most famous for manufacturing opaque marble but added other opaque glass novelty items after they moved operations to West Virginia.

Albany Glass Co. The Albany Glass Co. was founded in the 1780s in Albany, New York, and lasted until about 1820. They made windows, bottles, and a few other items.

Albertine Glass Albertine was produced by the Mount Washington Glass Company in the late 19th century. It is characterized by opaque glass and ornate decoration that was applied primarily to show items such as vases. It is sometimes referred to as "Crown Milano."

Ale Glass An early-17th-century English glass with a capacity of 3–5 ounces; short-stemmed, it was used for drinking ale or beer.

Alexandrite Glass Art glass produced by Thomas Webb in England in the late 19th century, characterized by various shadings of blue, pink or red, and yellow, achieved through several stages of refiring.

C.G. Alford & Co. Founded in 1872 in New York City, Alford operated as a watch and jewelry store as well as a cut-glass operation. They closed in 1918.

Almy & Thomas Founded in 1903 by Charles H. Almy and G. Edwin Thomas, they purchased the Knickerbocker Cut Glass Company and continued cutting glass until 1918. The Corning Glass Works supplied them with blanks.

Amber A yellowish-brown colored glass produced by the addition of iron, carbon, and sulfur.

Amberette Pressed glassware that was frosted or stained with dark yellow or yellowish-brown colors to resemble art glass.

Amberina Art glass produced in America in the late 19th century. It is characterized by transparent glass that is lightly shaded with light amber at the base and gradually shaded darker, to ruby red, at the top. Joseph Locke received a patent for Amberina in 1883.

Amelung Glass High-quality glass made in America in the late 18th century by German immigrant John Frederick Amelung.

American Flint Glass Works Established at Wheeling, Virginia, in the 1840s (before West Virginia became a state), they produced pressed, mold-blown, and hand-blown glass in crystal (using flint and lead) and colored glass.

American Glass Co. Established in 1899 in Indiana, Pennsylvania, the firm purchased the Dugan/Northwood factory and made some pressed wares. They in turn sold out to the Diamond Glass Company in 1913.

Amethyst Purple glass produced by the addition of manganese. Some amethyst glass was made so dark that it is referred to as "Black Amethyst."

Anchor Cap and Closure Corp. An American manufacturer established in Long Island City, New York, in the early 1900s, they were a major manufacturer of containers and merged with Hocking in 1937 to form the Anchor Hocking Glass Corporation.

Anchor-Hocking Glass Corp. A huge American glass manufacturer of containers, tableware, and other items established in 1937 when the Anchor Cap and Closure Corporation merged with the Hocking Glass Company.

Animal Dishes Covered glass dishes or glass objects made in the shapes of various animals (roosters, horses, cats, dogs, elephants, etc.), animal dishes were very popular from about 1890 to 1910, a little during the Depression era, and from the 1970s on.

Annealing A process that toughens glass and eliminates stress by heating and gradually cooling in an annealing oven or lehr.

Annealing Crack A crack or fissure that develops in glass from improper cooling or annealing.

AOP Abbreviation for "allover pattern." Allover patterns generally cover the entire glass object but may be limited to the outside only.

Application Attaching molten glass rods to blanks in order to form handles, feet, pedestals, and so on.

Apricot A deep yellow or dark amber glass.

Arissing The process of removing sharp edges from glass.

Art or Art Nouveau Glass Expensive hand-blown glass with unusual effects of color, shape, and design, art glass is primarily ornamental and was most popular from the 1880s to 1920.

Ashtray A shallow bowl-like glass receptacle used for cigarette butts and tobacco ashes.

Atomizer See *Cologne Bottle* or *Perfume Bottle*.

Aurene Iridescent ornamental art glass created by Frederick Carder at the Steuben Glass Works in 1905.

Aventurine An ancient Egyptian technique of applying small flakes of metal such as gold and copper in colored glass, it was popular during the Art Nouveau period.

Averbeck Cut Glass Co. Established in New York in 1892, Averbeck ran a jewelry store and a mail-order business featuring cut-glass products. They ceased operation in 1923.

Baccarat Fine-quality glass first made in France and Belgium in the late 18th century, Baccarat glass was particularly noted for paperweights early on but also produced tableware and other decorative glass. Today, Baccarat crystal is among the finest made in the world.

Bakewell, Pears, and Co. An American company established in Pittsburgh, Pennsylvania, in 1807, they began producing glass furniture knobs and handles and then added tableware and barware. The business closed in 1882.

Ball Stopper A spherical glass object that rests at the top of a glass bottle, jug, decanter, etc., its diameter is larger than the mouth of the vessel.

Banana Boat or Dish A long flat or shallow dish, with sides that may be curved upward, with or without a separate base, and used for serving bananas or banana splits.

Bar Tumbler A glass tumbler with or without flutes produced in the United States in various shapes and sizes beginning in the mid-19th century, primarily for hotels and saloons.

Bartlett-Collins Co. An American company established in Sapulpa, Oklahoma, in 1931, they are noted for tableware, lamps, and glass decorated with Western themes.

Base Color The color of glass before any coating is applied, usually the color of Carnival glass before it is iridized.

Basket A glass receptacle with semicircular handle used for foods, decoration, or displaying flowers.

Batch The mixture of raw materials fused together before heating.

Beading The process by which chips or small relief beads are fused to a glass object in the form of a continuous row.

Bell or Dinner Bell A hollow device with ringer and single top handle used for summoning or signaling (such as to announce dinner).

Belmont Tumbler Co. An American company established in the early 1900s in Bellaire, Ohio, they produced tumblers and some Depression items. The factory burned in 1952 and was never rebuilt.

Bergen, J.D., Co. Founded in Meriden, Connecticut, by James D. Bergen and Thomas Niland, Bergen bought out Niland in 1885 and continued as a cut-glass operation until 1922.

Best Metal The highest-quality batch of glass made by a company using the purest ingredients and highest lead content.

Bevel Slanted or angle cuts, usually beginning at the bottom or sides of a glass object (sometimes referred to as flutes at the bottom).

Biscuit Jar A tall, wide-mouthed canister-shaped glass receptacle with cover used for holding biscuits, crackers, or cookies (the predecessor of the cookie jar).

Bitters Bottle A small bottle used to contain bitters or tonics that were made in the United States in the mid-19th and later 19th century.

Black Bottle A dark, opaque green English invention in the mid-17th century used for transporting and storing various beverages such as water, beer, wine, rum, etc.

Black Glass Dark, opaque ebony glass created by the combination of oxide of manganese and oxide of iron added to a batch of glass.

Blackmer Cut Glass Co. Established by Arthur L. Blackmer in New Bedford, Massachusetts, in 1894 and incorporated as A.L. Blackmer in 1902, the company produced cut-glass products until 1916.

Blank An uncut piece of glass, ordinarily a bowl or vase, that has been specifically made of heavy, high-quality lead glassware.

Blenko Glass Co. Originally founded by English immigrant William J. Blenko in

1922 in Milton, West Virginia, the company started out as a maker of stained glass windows and later switched to contemporary art forms.

Blowing The process of blowing air through a metal tube or blowpipe to shape the molten glass blob attached to its end.

Blowpipe A hollow metal tube used to gather molten glass from the pot and then to blow air through it to shape glass.

Bluerina Art glass made in America in the late 19th century that is very similar to Amberina, only the colors gradually meld from blue at the base to Amberina at the top.

Bohemian Glass German-made glass in the 17th century characterized by ornate decoration, heavy cutting, and bright colors.

Bonbon, or Bon-Bon Dish A small, usually flat or shallow circular dish, with or without handles (center handle possible), used for serving small finger foods such as nuts, bonbons, or tiny fruits.

Boot Glass A small glass vessel shaped like a boot, with a capacity of about three ounces.

Booze Bottle A flask made in America in the 1860s in the form of a two-story house by the Whitney Glass Works for Edmund G. Booze.

Boston & Sandwich Glass Co. An American company established in Boston by Deming Jarves in 1826, they produced much pressed and cut glassware before closing in 1888.

Boston Silver Glass Co. Established in 1857 by A. Young in Cambridge, Massachusetts, the company produced some pressed glassware and silverplating before closing in 1871.

Bottle A glass container with a narrow neck and mouth, may or may not have a handle. Bottles come in all shapes and sizes and can be made of other materials.

Bowl A concave hemispherical glass vessel used for holding liquids and other foods (e.g., soup, salad, cereal, berries, vegetables) in many shapes and sizes. The bowl of a wine or stemmed beverage glass is the portion that holds the liquid.

Boyd Art Glass Co. Established in Cambridge, Ohio, in 1978, Boyd is noted for highly collectible miniature art figurines created in a variety of colors and styles.

Brandy Glass A short, rounded glass with a foot and a very tiny stem; shorter but wider as compared to a rounded wine glass.

Bread and Butter Plate A round, flat object that is usually six inches in diameter.

Brides' Basket A fancy bowl held within a silver or silverplated frame, they were popular wedding gifts during the Brilliant Period after they debuted at the World's Columbian Exposition in Chicago in 1893.

Brilliant Glass Works Established by Joseph Beatty Sr. in Brilliant, Ohio, in 1880, it remained in operation only until 1893 and produced some pressed glassware.

Brilliant Period The era of American handmade glassware, 1880–1915, characterized by fine cutting, engraving, polishing, and fancy patterns.

Bristol Glass Crystal, colored, and milk glass items produced in several factories in Bristol, England, in the 17th and 18th centuries.

Bristol-Type Glass Nineteenth-century American- and English-made Victorian opaque glassware characterized by hand-enameling.

Bryce Brothers An American company formed in the mid-19th century in Mt. Pleasant, Pennsylvania, they primarily specialized in hand-blown stemware and barware and became part of the U.S. Glass Company in 1891.

Bumper Another term for a firing glass.

Burmese Glass Glass objects characterized by various light opaque shadings in pastel colors of pink, yellow, and white, produced with the addition of uranium, they were first created by the Mount Washington Glass Company in the late 19th century and then produced by others.

Butter Dish A glass dish that is ordinarily flat or footed, with or without glass dome or rectangular cover, and used for serving butter, margarine, or other spreads.

Butter Plate A miniature glass plate used for serving individual portions of butter, margarine, or other spreads.

Butter Tub A glass vessel shaped like a small bucket or pail (usually smaller than an ice bucket), with or without semicircular handle, used for serving butter balls.

Cake Plate A large, flat or footed glass plate, usually round, used for holding cakes.

Calcite Glass A brightly colored cream-white glass that resembles the mineral calcite (calcite is not used in its manufacture). Calcite glass was first produced by Frederick Carder at the Steuben Glass Works in the early 20th century.

Cambridge Glass Co. Established in Cambridge, Ohio, in the early 1900s, the Cambridge Glass Company was a major producer of cut crystal up to the 1950s, when the factory closed.

Cameo Engraving An engraving process in which the background is carved away to leave the design in relief (see *Relief Cutting*).

Campbell, Jones, and Co. Established in 1865 in Pittsburgh, Pennsylvania, by James Campbell and Jenkins Jones, they operated until 1895 and made mostly pressed-glass wares.

Camphor Glass A nearly opaque white pressed glass produced in America in the 19th century.

Canary Yellow A bright yellow glass similar to amber glass (also made with various amounts of iron, carbon, and sulfur).

Candelbra or Candelabrum A branched candlestick with several sockets for holding candles.

Candleholder A small glass tumblerlike vessel designed to hold candles of two inches in diameter or smaller.

Candlestick A raised glass object with one socket for holding a single candle.

Candlette A small bowl-like glass object with one socket for holding a single candle.

Candy Dish An open shallow bowl-like glass receptacle used for serving candy, may or may not be footed.

Candy Jar A tall, wide-mouthed glass receptacle with cover used for serving candy, may or may not be footed.

Cane A cylindrical piece or stick of glass used for stems of drinking glasses or cut up into small slices for producing millefiore paperweights.

Canton Glass Co. Established in Canton, Ohio, in 1883, the company produced pressed and novelty items before becoming part of the National Glass Company in 1900.

Cape Cod Glass Works Established in 1858 by Deming Jarves in Boston, the firm produced pressed wares and art designs such as gold-ruby, "Peachblow," and "Sandwich Alabaster," up to Jarves's death in 1869.

Carafe A large glass bottle with stopper used for serving beverages (usually water or wine).

Card Tray A flat glass object, usually rectangular, possibly with a center handle and two separate sections, used for holding standard-size playing cards.

Carder, Frederick A famous glassmaker, designer, and producer, Carder founded the Steuben Glass Company in 1903 and was responsible for most of the factory's production into the early 1930s.

Carnival Glass Pressed glassware with a fired-on iridescent finish made in the United States, 1905–1925 (reproductions were produced later, beginning in the 1960s).

Cased Glass Nineteenth-century glass that was blown in multiple layers of separate colors. The glass was then decorated by cutting away all or part of these layers.

Casserole Dish A deep round, oblong, or square dish, with or without cover, with or without handles or tabs, used to bake as well as serve food.

Cast Glass Glass made in simple molds and then surface-ground with polishing wheels fed by abrasives.

Castor Set A set of glass serving objects held on glass or metal trays. These objects might include small pitchers, cruets, small jars, salt and pepper shakers, and other small dishes.

Celery Dish A long flat or shallow narrow glass dish, usually oval in design, used for serving celery. A few odd celery dishes have been produced in tall cylindrical shapes (Celery Vases).

Centerpiece A large, circular or oval fancy glass bowl used as an adornment in the center of a table.

Central Glass Works Established in 1866 in Wheeling, West Virginia, Central was noted for pressed patterns and art "Coin Glass" and were one of the first to develop popular colors of the Depression era. Central closed permanently in 1939.

Chain Glass threads that are formed or applied to objects in interconnected links or rings.

Chalice A fancy drinking vessel with a large rounded bowl of various sizes and shapes (may or may not be stemmed).

Challinor & Taylor Ltd. Founded in 1866 by David Challinor and Taylor in 1866 in Pittsburgh, Pennsylvania, the company moved to Tarentum in 1884 and produced pressed glass, lamps, and novelties before becoming part of the U.S. Glass Co. in 1891.

Champagne Glass A tall glass with foot and stem and a large, round but shallow bowl.

Chandelier An ornate branched glass lighting fixture suspended from a ceiling.

Chartreuse Yellowish-green opaque glass.

Cheaters Small whiskey tumblers with extremely thick glass bottoms and walls that were made to look as if they had a larger capacity than in actuality.

Checkered Diamond A cut design pattern with several small diamonds inscribed within one large one.

Cheese and Cracker Dish A serving dish with two levels (two-tiered), one for holding cheese or a cheese ball (usually the upper part) and the other for crackers.

Cheese Dish A glass dish that is ordinarily flat or footed, with a separate glass cover (usually dome-shaped), that is used for serving cheese. Note that cheese dishes are a little larger than butter dishes.

Cherry Jar A small, wide-mouthed glass receptacle with cover used for holding cherries. Most are wider at the bottom and taper off somewhat near the top.

Chigger Bite A small chip or nick in a piece of glass.

Chintz A style of glass patented by A. Douglas Nash, it was characterized by colored ribbed, striped, or swirled glass marvered into opaque, opalescent, and transparent glass. The process was expensive and difficult since the separate colors often ran together.

Chocolate Glass A variegated opaque glass that shades from dark brown to light tan, it was first developed by the Indiana Tumbler and Goblet Company and is sometimes mistakenly referred to as caramel slag.

Chop Plate A large flat glass object, usually round or oval, used for serving food. A chop plate serves the same function as a platter, tray, or salver.

Chunked Glass that has been heavily damaged, usually cracked, seriously chipped, or considerably worn.

Cigar Jar A large, wide-mouthed glass canister with cover used for holding and storing cigars and tobacco.

Cigarette Box A small covered glass receptacle designed to hold a single standard pack of cigarettes.

Cigarette Holder A flat glass dish or ashtray containing notches that are used for holding cigarettes (may or may not have a cover).

Cigarette Jar or Urn A small, wide-mouthed glass canister with cover used for holding and storing cigarettes.

Clambroth or Clam Broth Grayish, semitransparent glass.

Claret Glass A tall glass with foot and stem with a large, round, deep bowl specifically designed for serving claret wine.

Clark, T.B., & Co. Established in Honesdale, Pennsylvania, in 1884 by Thomas Byron Clark, they cut blanks provided by Dorflinger and became one of the most successful cut-glass companies up until the time they closed in 1930.

Clichy A famous French glassmaking town that was noted most for paperweight production beginning in the 1840s. The factories closed in the 1880s as the popularity for paperweights declined.

Cluthra An art glass form developed by Steuben in 1920, it is characterized by a cloudy opaque design permeated by variously sized bubbles. Off-shoots of the basic design were produced by others, such as Kimble.

Coaster A very shallow or flat container used to place other glass objects on (such as tumblers) to protect the surface beneath (e.g., tabletops, counters, etc.).

Cobalt Blue Metallic coloring agent producing the most powerful deep, dark blue color in glass.

Cocktail Glass A tall glass with foot, stem, and angled or straight-edged bowl.

Cocktail Shaker A tall, tumblerlike glass vessel with cover used for mixing alcoholic drinks.

Coin Glass Originally, in the 18th and 19th centuries, a tumbler or tankard with a real coin visible in the foot or stem; 20th-century versions contain glass coin replicas inscribed within the glass.

Cologne Bottle A small glass receptacle with narrow neck and stopper used for holding colognes or perfumes.

Comport or Compote A glass serving bowl that may have a base, stem, or feet, used for serving candy, fruits, or nuts. Comports are most commonly referred to as raised candy dishes.

Condiment Set See *Castor Set*.

Console Bowl A large, concave, hemispherical glass vessel, used as a centerpiece or for serving large items. Console bowls are sometimes accompanied by a pair of matching candlesticks.

Consolidated Lamp & Glass Co. Established in 1894 in Coraopolis, Pennsylvania, the company was noted most for art glass lamps and its Martele line of art glass. The company closed in 1964.

Cookie Jar A tall, wide-mouthed, canister-shaped glass receptacle (larger than a candy jar), with cover and without feet or stem, used for holding cookies.

Copper Wheel Engraving Process of hand-engraving by holding a glass to a revolving copper wheel, which instantly cuts through the surface. Some of the best glass ever produced was done by highly skilled copper wheel engravers who kept the cutting pattern in their minds while altering the cutting with rubbing oil continuously for hours on end.

Coral Various shadings of yellow to red layers applied to glass objects with opaque bases.

Coralene Glass Art glass that was first made in 19th-century Europe and then in America, it is characterized by enamel and colored or opaque glass drops applied to raised branches that resemble coral.

Cordial Glass A miniature wineglass with foot, stem, and tiny bowl of small capacity.

Core Forming Process of glassmaking by spinning glass around a core.

Corning Glass Works An American glass factory established in Corning, New York, in 1868 as the Corning Flint Glass Works; the name was changed permanently in 1875 and the company's most notable purchase was that of Steuben in the 1930s. The company continues to operate today.

Correia Art Glass Founded in 1973 by Steven V. Correia in Santa Monica, California, the company's contemporary art products can already be found in the major art museums featuring glass in America (e.g., Smithsonian Institution, Corning Museum of Glass, Metropolitan Museum of Art).

Cosmos Pressed milk glass made in America in the early 1900s.

Cracker Jar A tall, wide-mouthed canister-shaped glass receptacle with cover, used for holding crackers.

Cracking Off The process of removing an object from the pontil. Cooled by scoring, the pipe is then gently tapped, and the object falls into a sand tray or V-shaped holder held by an assistant.

Crackling A decorating technique applied to glassware by plunging a hot object into cold water to induce cracks and then re-forming the piece within a mold.

Cranberry Glass First developed in England in the 19th century, Cranberry glass is characterized by a light red tint (the color of cranberries) produced by the addition of gold dust. Originally it was a cheaper substitute for ruby red, but now the name is applied to any glass made of the cranberry color.

Cream Soup Bowl A concave, hemispherical glass vessel, usually with two handles and used for serving soup or other foods.

Creamer A small, cuplike glass vessel, ordinarily with handle, used for serving cream (with coffee and tea), usually paired with a sugar dish.

Cremax An opaque, lightly beige glass first produced and named by the MacBeth-Evans Glass company.

Cristallo A nearly colorless, highly esteemed soda glass invented by Venetian glassmakers in the 19th century.

Crown Milano See *Albertine Glass*.

Cruet A small glass bottle or decanter with top, used to hold a condiment such as oil, vinegar, salad dressing, etc., for use at the table.

Crystal Colorless glass containing a high lead content.

Crystal Glass Works An Australian company founded in Sydney in the early 1900s, they were noted for Carnival and other glass production.

Cullets Chards or scraps of glass that are remelted and added to a new batch of glass to aid in the fusion process.

Cup An open, somewhat bowl-shaped or cylindrical vessel, usually with handle, used for drinking liquids such as coffee, tea, punch, etc.

Cuspidor A fancy glass vessel or receptacle used to contain saliva (see *Spitoon*).

Custard Cup A smaller than ordinary cup, with or without handle, used for serving desserts in small portions, such as pudding, custard, Jello, etc.

Custard Glass A yellowish or yellow-cream-colored opaque glass (the color of custard) first developed in the early 1900s.

Cut Glass Heavy flint glass with geometric patterns cut into the glass with grinding wheels and abrasives. The design is then further smoothed and polished. Cutting originated in Germany and then was introduced into the United States in the late 18th century.

Cut Velvet Colored art glass consisting of two fused, mold-blown layers that leaves the outer surface design raised in relief.

Daisy in Hexagon A cut design pattern featuring a flower inscribed within a hexagon.

Darner A glass needle with large eye for use in darning. Glass darners are sometimes whimsical creations.

Daum A French glass company established in 1875 in the town of Nancy, France. Daum or Nancy Daum or Cristalleries de Nancy are all names associated with glass produced by this company. The company began as a producer of many styles of Art Nouveau glass and continues to operate today.

De Vilbiss Co. A decorating firm established around 1900 in Toledo, Ohio, the firm primarily decorated perfume bottles and atomizers in many art glass styles until the late 1930s.

Decal A picture, design, or label from specifically prepared paper that is transferred to glass, usually by heating.

Decanter An ornamental or fancy glass bottle with cover or stopper, with or without handles, used for serving wine or other alcoholic beverages.

Delphite A lightly colored pale blue opaque glass; it is sometimes referred to as "Blue Milk Glass."

Demitasse Matching cups and saucers that are much smaller (half size or less) than their ordinary counterparts. Note that demitasse cups and saucers are still slightly larger than those found in children's miniature tea sets).

Dennis Glassworks An English glass operation founded near Stourbridge, England, by the Webb family in 1855, the company early on produced art glass and continues to operate today.

Depression Glass Mass-produced, inexpensive, and primarily machine-made glass dinner sets and giftware in clear and many colors, produced in America between 1920 and 1940.

Diamond-Daisy A cut-glass design pattern featuring daisies inscribed within diamonds or squares.

Diamond Glass Co., Ltd. A Canadian company that operated in Montreal from 1890 to 1902, they were noted for many pressed glass designs, tableware, and lamps.

Diamond Glass-Ware Co. An American company first established in Indiana, Pennsylvania, in 1891, they were noted for high-quality handmade colored glassware and closed in 1931 when their factory burned.

Diamond Point A cut-glass design pattern featuring faceted diamonds that intersect at a common point.

Diamond Point Engraving Hand cutting or machine cutting of glass with a diamond-point tool (note that hardened metal by heat treating to a sharp point has since replaced the more expensive diamonds for machine cutting).

Diatreta Glass Art glass made by applying tiny pieces of ornamental glass in patterns to other larger glass objects. This process was first developed by Frederick Carder in the early 1900s.

Dinner Plate A flat glass object, usually round and about 9–11 inches in diameter, used for serving supper or dinner.

Dip Mold A one-piece mold with an open top used for embossing or imprinting decorations and lettering.

Dispensers A large glass container or bottle with a spigot, originally used for obtaining cold water from the refrigerator.

Dithridge Flint Glass Co. Founded by Edward D. Dithridge, Jr., in 1881 in Martins Ferry, Ohio, the business moved to New Brighton, Pennsylvania, in 1887 and continued to produce cut and engraved glass as well as blanks for others. Dithridge ceased operations in 1891.

Dominion Glass Co. A Canadian company that operated from 1886 to 1898 (separate from the modern company of the same name) in Montreal, they were noted for pressed wares and lamps.

Domino Tray A serving dish with a built-in container for cream and surrounding area specifically designed for holding sugar cubes.

Dorflinger Glass Works The original factory was established in White Mills, Pennsylvania, in the 1840s by the German immigrant Christian Dorflinger. Dorflinger was noted for making high-quality cut-glass tableware and was a major supplier of lead crystal blanks. The company remained in operation as C. Dorflinger & Sons until 1921.

Double Cruet Two glass bottles (cruets) that are fused together into one larger-capacity bottle used for serving condiments.

Dram Glass Small English or Irish glasses made of metal used for drinking a single measure of strong liquor (most were made between 1750 and 1850 and imported to the United States).

Dresser Set A set of glass bath or bedroom objects held on a matching tray. These objects might include perfume or cologne bottles, jars, and tiny boxes for gloves, hair or hat pins, jewelry, and so on.

Dugan Glass Co. Established in Indiana, Pennsylvania, in 1892 by Harry White, Thomas E. Dugan, and W. G. Minnemyer, they produced a good deal of Carnival glass. The firm became the Diamond Glass Co. in 1913 and operated until a fire destroyed it in 1931.

Duncan, George & Sons See *Ripley and Co.*

Duncan Miller Glass Co. Established in 1892 by James and George Duncan, Jr., along with John Ernest Miller, in Washington, Pennsylvania, the firm produced pressed wares and novelty items through the Depression era.

Durand Art Glass Co. Established in Vineland, New Jersey, by French immigrant Victor Durand, Sr., in 1924, the company produced several art glass styles up to Durand's death in 1931.

Ebony Glass Another name for black or very dark opaque glass.

Edinburgh Crystal Glass Co. Established in the late 19th century in Edinburgh, Scotland, the company produced hand-cut crystal wares and imported some of these products to America.

Egg Cup or Holder A small cuplike vessel without handle that held a single egg. Occasionally, double egg holders have been made (room for two eggs).

Egg Plate A flat, thick plate with oval indentations for serving boiled or deviled eggs.

Eggington, O.F., Co. Established in Corning, New York, in 1899 by Oliver Eggington, the company purchased blanks from the Corning Glass Works and was a cut-glass operation until they closed in 1920.

Embossing Mold-blown or pressed glassware in which the design is applied directly upon the object from the mold. Embossed patterns are usually somewhat in relief.

Emerald Green A deep, powerful green usually made with chromium and iron (the color of the gemstone emerald).

Empire Cut Glass Co. Established in New York City in 1896 by Harry Hollis, Hollis sold the company to his employees, who operated it briefly as a cooperative. They in turn sold it to H. C. Fry in 1904, who moved operations to Flemington, New Jersey (Flemington Cut Glass Co.).

Enameling A liquid medium similar to paint applied to glassware and then permanently fused on the object by heating.

Encased Overlay A single or double overlay design further encased in clear glass.

Engraving The decoration of glass applied by holding the piece against the edge of a revolving wheel made of stone, copper, or other materials.

Enterprise Cut Glass Co. Founded by George E. Gaylord in Elmira Heights, New York, the company produced cut-glass products until it ceased operation in 1917.

Epergne A large table centerpiece that includes a large bowl surrounded by several matching smaller dishes.

Etching See *Acid Etching*.

Ewer A round glass juglike object, with or without feet, that usually contains a long handle and spout.

Favrile An American Art Nouveau style of glass created by Louis Comfort Tiffany in the late 19th century. The original pieces are often referred to as Tiffany Favrile.

Federal Glass Co. An American company established in Colombia, Ohio, in 1900, they began as a cut-glass operation, switched to automation during the Depression era, and continue to operate today as a subsidiary of the Federal Paper Board Company.

Fenton Art Glass Co. Established in Martins Ferry, Ohio, in 1907, Fenton was a major producer of Carnival, opalescent, and other pressed and molded glassware. Fenton still operates today in Williamstown, West Virginia, producing hand-decorated glassware and novelty items.

Fern Bowl or Fernery A glass container with a liner, with or without feet designed for holding ferns or other plants.

Fern Glass Glass objects decorated with etched or engraved fern or similar leaf patterns.

Figurine A small individual etched or molded statue (or figure).

Findlay Glass Art glass characterized by varying shades of brown colors.

Finger Bowl A small, concave glass vessel, usually circular and shallow, used for rinsing fingers at the table.

Finial A crowning ornament or decorative knob found most often in stemware and at the top of glass covers.

Fire Polishing Reheating a finished piece of glass at the glory hole in order to remove tool marks (more commonly replaced with acid polishing).

Fired-on Finishing colors that are baked on or fused by heating onto the outer surface of glass objects.

Fired-on Iridescence A finish applied to glass by adding metallic salts, after which the glass is refired.

Firing Glass A small glass vessel with a thick base, waisted sides, and possibly a stem or base that could withstand considerable abuse. The resulting noise of several being slammed at once was comparable to that of a musket firing. Some were made of metal, and most were produced in the 18th and early 19th centuries in both Europe and America.

Flashed-On Iridescence A finish applied to glass by dipping hot glass into a solution of metallic salts.

Flashing A very thin coating of a different color from that of the base color (thinner than a casing or an overlay).

Flask A glass container with narrow neck and mouth, with stopper or cover, used for carrying alcoholic beverages.

Flint Glass The American term for fine glassware made in the 19th century, a name for lead glass though original experimenters used powdered flints as substitutes for lead oxides.

Floret or Florette A slice from a large cane of several colored rods arranged (usually concentrically) to form a floral pattern.

Floriform A tall glass vase with narrow stem and top that is in the shape of a flower bloom.

Flower Bowl A large container, shallow, concave, and hemispherical, that is used for holding or floating flowers with relatively short stems.

Fluting Vertically cut decoration in long narrow or parallel sections such as bevels (usually wheel-cut but sometimes molded).

Flux A substance such as soda, wood ash, potash, or lead oxide added to the basic ingredients in order to stabilize and lower the melting point of a batch of glass.

Folded Foot The turned-over edge of the foot of a wine glass or similar glass object to give added strength to the vessel.

Foot The part of a glass other than the base on which it rests.

Footmaker An assistant to a glassmaker who forms the foot of the glass in the glassblowing process.

Forest Green A dark green color not as deep or rich as emerald green, first made by the Hazel Atlas Glass Company, who patented the name, in the late 1930s and early 1940s. The term has been applied to glassware made by other companies in the same color.

Fostoria Glass Co. An American glass company founded in Fostoria, Ohio, in 1887, they produced cut-crystal items early on, several Depression tableware patterns, and continued in operation until the late 1980s.

Fractional Shot A small glass tumbler with capacity of less than one ounce.

Frances Ware Mold-blown tableware, amber in color, with fluted rims and hobnail patterns; it was produced by Hobbs, Brocunier Co. in the 1880s.

Free-Blown Glass An ancient technique of hand-blowing glass by highly skilled craftsmen without the use of molds.

Frog A small but thick and heavy glass object, usually round or domed, containing perforations, holes, or spikes for holding flowers in place within a vase.

Frosted Glass A light opalescence or cloudy coloring of a batch of glass using tin, zinc, or an all-over acid etching, as in Depression glass. A frosted coating can also be applied on the surface of clear or crystal glass by spraying on white acid (a solution of ammonium bifluoride).

Fruit or Nut Dish A small flat or shallow circular container, with or without handle(s), used for serving small fruits, nuts, candies, etc.

Fry, H.C. An American glassmaker who founded the Rochester Tumbler Company in 1872 and the H.C. Fry Glass Company in 1901, both in Rochester, Pennsylvania. The glass that was produced in his later factory is sometimes referred to as Fry glass; it included some art glass as well as tableware. Fry closed for good in 1934.

Full Lead Crystal Colorless glass containing a minimum of 30% lead content.

Fusion The process of liquefying when the melting point is reached for a batch of glass. Temperature can range from 2000 to 3000 degrees Fahrenheit depending on the ingredients used.

Gadget A special rod developed to replace the pontil to avoid leaving a mark on the foot. A spring clip at the end of the gadget grips the foot of a just-finished piece of glass while the worker trims the rim and applies the finishing touches on the glass.

Gadrooning A decorative band derived from a silver form made of molded, applied, or deep-cut sections of reeding. Gadrooning is sometimes referred to as "knurling."

Gaffer A term of respect for an experienced master or head glassmaker, dating back to the 16th century.

Gall A layer of scum that forms at the surface of a batch of glass during the heating process (it is skimmed off).

Gallé, Emile A French glassmaker and pioneer in the 19th-century Art Nouveau–style glass. He is noted for art cameo and floral designs created in several color effects and styles.

Gather A blob of molten glass attached to the end of a blowpipe, pontil, or gathering iron.

Gibson Glass Established in Milton, West Virginia, by Charles Gibson in 1983, it is noted for animals, figurines, paperweights, and other novelty items produced in a variety of colors and styles.

Gilding A decorating technique with gold enamels or paints applied to finished glass objects.

Gillinder & Sons Founded by English immigrant William T. Gillinder, who once was superintendent of the New England Glass Co. Gillinder, along with his sons James and Frederick, established their own cutting and Art Glass business in 1867 in Philadelphia. The firm later became part of the U.S. Glass Co. in 1892.

Glass A hard, brittle, artificial substance made by fusing silicates (sand) with an alkali (soda or potash) and sometimes with metallic oxides (lead oxide or lime).

Glassboro Glassworks An American factory established in Glassboro, New Jersey, by Jacob Stanger in 1781, the company produced windows, bottles, and tableware into the 20th century.

Glasshouse The building that contains the glass-melting furnaces and in which the actual handling and shaping of molten glass takes place.

Glass Picture A design that is ordinarily etched on flat sheets or flat pieces of glass.

Glory Hole A small opening in the side of the furnace used for inserting cool glass objects in order to reheat them without melting or destroying the shape (sometimes named the reheating furnace).

Glove Box A rectangular glass object, with or without cover, used specifically on dressing tables or vanities for holding gloves.

Goblet A drinking vessel with a large bowl of various sizes and shapes that rests on a stemmed foot.

"Gone with the Wind" Lamp A kerosene or electric table lamp containing a glass base with a round, globe-shaped glass shade.

Grapefruit Bowl A concave, usually circular glass vessel, ordinarily with a wide foot, used for serving half of a grapefruit.

Gravy Boat An oblong bowl-like object with handle and spout used for pouring gravy (may or may not be accompanied by a matching platter or pedestal).

Green Glass The natural color of ordinary alkaline- or lime-based glassware usually produced by iron present in the sand.

Greensburg Glass Co. Established in Greensburg, Pennsylvania, in 1889, the company produced pressed glass until it became part of the National Glass Company in 1900.

Grill Plate A large individual or serving plate with divisions (similar to relish dishes only larger).

Ground The background or base glass object on which decorations are applied.

Gunderson Glass Works Robert Gunderson, along with Thomas Tripp and Isaac Babbitt, purchased the silverware and glass departments of Pairpoint in 1939 and continued production until Gunderson's death in 1952. Glass made by Gunderson is often referred to as "Gunderson's Pairpoint."

Hair Receiver A circular glass object, usually with a cover that has a large hole in the middle, used on tables, dressers, and vanities to hold hair that accumulates in a hair brush.

Hairpin Box A small square, rectangular, or circular glass container, with or without cover, used specifically on a dressing table or vanity for holding hairpins.

Half Lead Crystal Colorless glass containing a minimum of 24% lead content (lower quality than full lead crystal).

Hammonton Glassworks An American factory established at Hammonton, New Jersey, by William Coffin and Jonathan Haines in 1817, the company produced windows, bottles, and some tableware before going out of business.

Hand-Blown Glass Glass formed and shaped with a blow-pipe and other hand-manipulated tools without the use of molds.

Hand Cooler A solid ovoid or small glass object originally developed in ancient Rome for ladies to cool their hands with. Later, hand coolers were also used by ladies when being wooed or for darning.

Hand-Pressed Glass Glass that is made in hand-operated mechanical presses.

Handel, Philip J. An American glassmaker who founded the Handel Company in Meriden, Connecticut, in 1885, he was noted for producing Art Nouveau acid cut-back cameo vases and Art Nouveau lamps similar to but less expensive than Tiffany lamps.

Handkerchief Box A rectangular glass receptacle with cover used for storing handkerchiefs.

Hat Pin Holder A tall glass object in the shape of a cylinder used on tables, dressers, and vanities for holding hat pins.

Hat or Hat Vase A whimsical glass object in the shape of an upside down head covering or top hat. The space where one's head would usually rest is often used for flowers or holding tiny objects.

Hawkes, T.G., & Co. An American company established at Corning, New York, in the late 19th century by Thomas Gibbon Hawkes, the company produced high-quality cut crystal tableware and blanks for others. In 1903, T. G. Hawkes and Frederick Carder merged to form the Steuben Glass Works.

Hazel Atlas Glass Co. An American factory founded in Washington, Pennsylvania, in 1902, they produced large amounts of machine-pressed glassware, especially during the Depression period. Factories were added throughout Ohio, Pennsylvania, and West Virginia until the company sold out in 1956.

Heisey, A.H., Glass Co. An American company established at Newark, Ohio, in the 1860s, Heisey was noted early on for cut patterns and finely etched glass. They produced above-average pressed wares during the Depression era as well as collectible glass animals. The factory closed for good in 1956.

Higbee Glass Co. Established by John B. Higbee in 1900 in Bridgeville, Pennsylvania, Higbee worked with John Bryce in 1879 before opening his own business. Higbee operated for a short period, but his glass is easily identified with the famous raised bee trademark.

Highball Glass A tall narrow tumbler of at least four-ounce capacity used for mixed drinks.

Hoare, J., & Co. Established in Corning, New York, in 1868 by John Hoare. Hoare formed many partnerships, beginning in 1853 (Hoare & Burns, Gould & Hoare, Hoare and Dailey, etc.), before forming his own cut-glass department in the Corning Flint Glass Co.

Hobbs, Brocunier, & Co. Established in Wheeling, West Virginia, in 1863 by John Hobbs. Hobbs formed many partnerships, beginning as early as 1820 (Hobbs and Barnes), before teaming up with Brocunier. They were noted most for developing a cheap lime glass as a substitute for lead glass, formulated by an employee named William Leighton. They became part of the Glass Company in 1891.

Hobnail A pressed or cut pattern in glassware resembling small raised knobs referred to as "hobs" or "prunts." The name originated in England, from the large heads of hobnail fasteners.

Hocking Glass Co. An American factory established in Lancaster, Ohio, by I. J. Collins in 1905; they began as a hand operation but converted fully to automation during the Depression era. They were one of the largest manufacturers of machine-pressed tableware and merged with the Anchor Cap and Closure Corporation in 1937 to form Anchor Hocking.

Holly Amber A type of art glass made only in 1903 by the Indiana Tumbler and Goblet Company, it is a pressed design characterized by creamy opalescent to brown amber shading (golden agate) with pressed holly leaves.

Honesdale Decorating Co. An American factory founded by Christian Dorflinger and his sons at Honesdale, Pennsylvania, in 1901, they produced hand-cut quality crystal wares with some gold decoration up until the business closed in 1932.

Honey Dish A tiny flat or shallow dish used for serving honey.

Hope Glass Works Established in Providence, Rhode Island, in 1872 by Martin L. Kern, they were noted primarily for cut glass. In 1891, Kern's son resumed the business; in 1899 it was sold to the Goey family, who continued to operate under the "Hope" name until 1951.

Horseradish Jar A small to medium-sized covered glass receptacle used for serving horseradish.

Hot Plate A usually thick, sturdy flat glass object set under hot items to protect the surface below.

Humidor A glass jar or case used for holding cigars in which the air is kept properly humidified.

Hunt Glass Co. Established in Corning, New York, in 1895 by Thomas Hunt, they used blanks from the Corning Glass Works as well as pressed blanks from the Union Glass Co. They made cut glass until the early 1910s.

Hydrofluoric Acid An acid similar to but weaker than hydrochloric acid, it attacks silica and is used to finish as well as etch glass.

Ice Blue A very light shade or tint of transparent blue glass (the color of ice).

Ice Bucket or Tub A glass vessel shaped like a medium-size bucket or pail, with or without semicircular handle, used for holding ice.

Ice Cream Plate A small, flat glass plate, usually round, used for serving a single scoop of ice cream.

Ice Cream Tray A large shallow or flat glass container used for serving ice cream.

Ice Glass A type of art glass characterized by a rough surface that resembles cracked ice.

Ice Lip A rim at the top of a pitcher that prevents ice from spilling out of the spout when tilted for pouring.

Ideal Cut Glass Co. Founded by Charles E. Rose in 1904 in Corning, New York, the company moved their cut-glass business to Syracuse, New York, in 1909 and operated until 1934.

Imperial Glass Co. An American manufacturer founded in Bellaire, Ohio, by Edward Muhleman in 1901, they were a major producer of Carnival glass in the early 20th century and were responsible for many reproductions of it later.

Incising The technique of cutting or engraving designs into the surface of glass.

Indiana Glass Co. An American manufacturer founded in 1907, they were noted for many machine-pressed Depression patterns and many reproductions of them.

Indiana Tumbler & Goblet Co. An American manufacturer founded in the late 19th century, they are noted for unique though inexpensive experimental colored tableware, including caramel slag glass.

Inkwell A small but heavy glass container used for holding ink (originally for quill pens).

Intaglio An engraving or cutting made below the surface of glass so that the impression of the design leaves an image in relief.

Intarsia The name given to a type of glass produced by Steuben in the 1920s. It is characterized by a core of colored glass blown between layers of clear glass, then decorated by etching into mosaic patterns.

Iridescence A sparkling rainbow-colored finish applied to the exterior of glass objects; it is produced by adding metallic salts.

Iridized Glass that has been coated with iridescence.

Irving Cut Glass Co., Inc. Established in Honesdale, Pennsylvania, in 1900 by William Hawken and five partners, they purchased blanks from H. C. Fry and were noted for cutting flowers and figures. Many of their products were shipped to Asia, South Africa, and Spain. The company closed in 1930.

Ivory A cream-colored or off-white opaque glass (the color of ivory).

Ivrene A white opaque glass with a light pearl-like iridescent coating, originally made by Steuben.

Jack-in-the-Pulpit A style of vase made to resemble the American woodland flower, it usually consists of a circular base, thin stem, and a large open ruffled bloom at the top.

Jadeite or Jade-ite A pale lime-colored opaque green glass (the color of jade).

Jam Jar A tiny covered glass receptacle used for serving jams and jellies. The cover usually has an opening for a spoon handle.

Jardiniere An ornamental glass stand or vaselike vessel used for holding plants or flowers.

Jarves, Deming An early pioneer instrumental in getting glassmaking started in America. He founded the New England Glass Company in 1818, the Boston & Sandwich Glass Company in 1825, and several others.

Jeannette Glass Co. An American company established in Jeannette, Pennsylvania, in 1902, they were noted for several color patterns during the Depression era and continue to make glassware today.

Jelly Dish or Tray A small flat or shallow dish used for serving, jelly, jam, marmalade, and other preserves.

Jenkins, D.C., Glass Co. Once part of the Indiana Tumbler & Goblet Co. and the Kokomo Glass Co., David C. Jenkins built his own factory in Kokomo, Indiana, in 1905. His new company produced some pressed wares until the early 1910s.

Jennyware The nickname for kitchenware glass made by the Jeannette Glass Company.

Jersey Glass Co. An American company founded in Jersey City, New Jersey, by George Drummer in 1824, they produced cut- and pressed-glass tableware.

Jewel Box A glass receptacle, usually rectangular, with or without cover, used for storing jewelry.

Jewel Cut Glass Co. Established in Newark, New Jersey, in 1906 by C. H. Taylor, the company had previously begun as the C. H. Taylor Glass Co. and made cut-glass products.

Jug A large, deep glass vessel, usually with a wide mouth, pouring spout, and handle, used for storing liquids.

Juice Glass A short, narrow glass tumbler, with or without foot, with a capacity of 3–6 ounces, used for drinking fruit and vegetable juices.

Kew Blas A name given to a type of opaque art glass produced by the Union Glass Company in the 1890s. The primary color is brown with various shadings of brown and green.

Keystone Cut Glass Co. Established in Hawley, Pennsylvania, in 1902, the company produced cut glass until 1918.

Kick A small indentation in the bottom of a glass object.

Kiln An oven used for firing or refiring glass objects.

Kimble Glass Co. Colonel Evan F. Kimble purchased Durand's factory in Vineland, New Jersey, in 1931, which he operated for a short time. The company was noted for the art glass "Cluthra" style.

King, Son, and Co. An American company founded in 1859 as the Cascade Glass Works near Pittsburgh, Pennsylvania, they were another manufacturer of tableware that became part of the U.S. Glass Company in 1891.

Knife Rest A small, thick, barbell-shaped glass object used to hold knife blades off the table when eating.

Knop An ornamental ball-shaped swelling on the stem of glassware such as wineglasses.

Kosta Glassworks Established in 1742 in Sweden, it is one of the oldest glassmakers still in operation today. The factory originally produced windows, then later added chandeliers and tableware. In 1864, it merged with the Boda Glassworks to form Kosta-Boda.

LaBelle Glass Company An American Company founded in Bridgeport, Ohio, they operated in the mid-1870s to the 1880s making pressed and some limited engraved glassware.

Lace Glass A mid-16th-century Venetian-style glass characterized by transparent threaded designs layered on the sides of various glass objects.

Lacy Pressed Glass A mid-19th-century American style of pressed glass characterized by an overall angular and round braiding pattern.

Ladle A handled (long or short) spoon used for dipping jam, gravy, punch, or other foods and liquids from jars or bowls.

Lalique, René A French glassmaker and leader of the 19th-century Art Nouveau–style glass. He is noted for multiple-faced or figured crystal and colored art glass items, and his success continued well into the 20th century.

Lamp Shade Glass coverings that shelter lights in order to reduce glare. At times, large glass bowls are converted to lamp shades by drilling holes in their center to attach them above the light.

Lancaster Glass Co. Lancaster was established in the city of Lancaster, Ohio, in

1908; they sold out to the Hocking Glass Co. in 1924, which continued to use the Lancaster name through 1937.

Latticino A 16th-century Venetian-style glass characterized by white opaque glass threads applied to clear glass objects.

Laurel Cut Glass Co. Founded in 1903 as the German Cut Glass Co. in Jermyn, Pennsylvania, the name was changed to Laurel soon after. In 1906, it changed briefly to the Kohinur Cut Glass Co. but switched back to Laurel in 1907. The company produced limited cut glass and merged with the Quaker City Cut Glass Co. after World War I. The two split soon after, and Laurel disbanded in 1920.

Lava Glass A style of art glass invented by Louis Comfort Tiffany, characterized by dark blue and gray opaque hues (the color of cooled lava) and sometimes coated with gold or silver decorations.

Layered Glass Glass objects with overlapping levels or layers of glass.

Lazy Susan A large revolving tray used for serving condiments, relishes, or other foods.

Lead Crystal Crystal or colorless glass made with a high lead content (see *Half Lead Crystal* and *Full Lead Crystal*).

Lehr An annealing oven with a moving base that travels slowly through a controlled loss of heat until the objects can be taken out at the opposite end. The rate of speed is adjustable as needed.

Libbey Glass Co. An American company originally established as the New England Glass Company in 1818 and purchased by William L. Libbey in the 1870s. Libbey produced high-quality cut and pressed glass and continue to operate today as one of the nation's largest glass producers.

Liberty Works An American company established in Egg Harbor, New Jersey, in 1903, they produced some cut- and pressed-glass tableware before going out of business in 1932.

Lily Pad A name given to a decoration applied to glass objects characterized by a superimposed layer of glass. Several styles of leaves (including lily pads), flowers, and stems were then designed on this layer.

Lime Glass A glass formula developed by William Leighton as a substitute for lead glass. Calcined limestone was substituted for lead, which made glass cheaper to produce. Lime glass also cools faster than lead glassware but is lighter and less resonant.

Locke, Joseph An English pioneer in the art glass field who moved to America, he is noted for designing and creating several varieties of art glass, including Agata.

Lotz or Loetz Glass Art Nouveau glass produced by Johann Lotz of Austria in the late 19th and early 20th centuries.

Loving Cup A glass drinking vessel, with or without a foot, that usually contains three handles.

Low Relief An engraving process in which the background is cut away to a very low degree (see *Relief Cutting*).

Luncheon Plate A flat glass object, usually round and about eight inches in diameter (an inch or two smaller than a dinner plate but larger than a salad plate), used for serving lunch.

Lutz Glass A thin clear glass striped with colored twists, first created by Nicholas Lutz of the Boston & Sandwich Glass Company. It is sometimes referred to as "Candy Stripe" glass.

Luzerne Cut Glass Co. Established in the early 1900s in Pittson, Pennsylvania, the company made some cut-glass products before going out of business in the late 1920s.

MacBeth-Evans Glass Co. An American company established in Indiana in 1899, they began as a hand operation and switched to machine-pressed patterns. They continue to operate today.

Mallorytown Glass Works A Canadian Company founded in 1825 in Mallorytown, Ontario, they were Canada's first glassmaker, producing blown vessels and containers. They closed in 1840.

Maple City Glass Co. Established in 1910 in Honesdale, Pennsylvania, the company produced some limited cut glassware into the early 1920s.

Marbled Glass Glass objects with single or multiple color swirls made to resemble marble.

Marmalade Dish See *Jelly Dish.*

Marmalade Jar See *Jam Jar.*

Marver A marble plate or base on which blown glass is shaped.

Mary Gregory Clear and colored glassware (commonly pastel pink) decorated with white enamel designs of one or more boys and/or girls playing in Victorian scenes. Mary Gregory actually worked as a decorator for the Boston & Sandwich Glass Co. from 1870 to 1880, but it is not known if she ever painted the glass of her namesake.

Mayonnaise Dish A small, flat or shallow indented dish used specifically for serving mayonnaise.

McKee Brothers An American company founded in Pittsburgh, Pennsylvania, by Samuel and James McKee in 1834, they began as a hand operation and continued producing a variety of glass until 1961, when the company was purchased by the Jeannette Glass Company.

Mercury Glass Glass objects characterized by two outer layers of clear glass with an inner layer of mercury or silver nitrate between them.

Merese An ornamental notch or knob between the stem and bowl of stemware.

Meriden Cut Glass Co. Established in 1895 in Meriden, Connecticut, they operated as a subsidiary of the Meriden Silver Plate Co., which in turn became part of the International Silver Co. Cut glass was produced until 1923.

Metal A term used by chemists for a batch of glass (see *Best Metal*).

Milk Glass A semiopaque opalescent glass colored by a compound of arsenic or calcined bones or tin. The result is a white color resembling milk.

Millefiori An 18th-century European-style paperweight made with several different-colored glass rods together in a pattern and then covered with an extremely thick outer layer of glass.

Millersburg Glass Co. An American company established in Millersburg, Ohio, by John and Robert Fenton in 1920; they were a major producer of Carnival glass but closed in the early 1920s. Their glass is often referred to as "Rhodium Ware" or "Radium" because of the minor traces of radiation measurable within the glass.

Mint Dish See *Bonbon Dish* or *Fruit Dish.*

Mitre-Cut Engraving Glass cut with a sharp groove on V-edged wheel.

Moil Waste glass left on the blowpipe or pontil.

Mold A wooden or iron form used to shape glass. Pattern or half-molds are used before glass has totally expanded. Full or three-part molds are used to give identical or same-size shapes to glassware. (English spelling is "mould").

Molded Glass Blown or melted glass that is given its final shape by the use of molds.

Monart Glass An art glass of Spain characterized by opaque and clear marble swirls.

Monax A partially opaque or nearly transparent cream-colored or off-white glass first produced and named by the MacBeth Evans Glass Company.

Monroe, C.F., Co. Established in Meriden, Connecticut, in 1880, they were noted for some art glass designs, particularly "Kelva," "Nakara," and "Wave Crest" (all similar in style). They also made some cut glass and novelty items before ceasing operation in 1916.

Moser, Ludwig A famous Austrian glassmaker who opened an art glass studio in 1857 in Karlsbad, Czechoslovakia; he is noted for deeply carved and enameled wildlife scenes on glass.

Moss Agate An art glass first created by Steuben, characterized by red, brown, and other swirled or marblelike colors.

Mother-of-Pearl An art glass technique produced by trapping air between layers of glass.

Mount Vernon Glass Co. An American art glass company founded in the late 19th century, noted for fancy glass vases and glass novelty items.

Mount Washington Glass Works An American art glass manufacturer established in South Boston, Massachusetts, in 1837 by Deming Jarves; they were noted for high-quality and innovative art glass designs such as Burmese Glass, Crown Milano, and cameo-engraved designs. The company sold out to the Pairpoint Manufacturing Company in 1894.

Muffle Kiln A low-temperature oven used for refiring glass to fix or fire on enameling.

Mug A cylindrical drinking vessel with one handle; larger mugs with hinged metal lids are usually referred to as steins.

Mustard Dish or Jar A small flat or shallow dish, with or without cover, used specifically for serving mustard. If lids are present, they may or may not contain an opening for a matching spoon.

Nailsea Glass House An English glass factory established in Somerset, England, in the late 18th century, they were noted for producing many unusual glass items such as rolling pins and walking canes.

Napkin Ring A small circular glass band used for holding napkins.

Napoli Glass objects that are completely covered with gold or gold enamels, both inside and out. Additional decorations may be applied to the gold covering.

Nappy An open shallow serving bowl without a rim that may contain one or two handles.

Nash A wealthy American family of English heritage that included several glass designers and manufacturers. They are noted for expensive, high-quality art glass similar to Tiffany designs and styles.

Near Cut Pressed-glass patterns similar to designs of hand-decorated cut glass.

Neck The part of a glass vessel such as a bottle, jug, or similar article between the body and mouth.

Needle Etching A process of etching glass by machine. Fine lines are cut by a machine and then hydrofluoric acid is applied to etch the pattern into the glass.

New Bremen Glass Manufactory An American firm established at New Bremen, Maryland, by Johann F. Amelung in 1784, they were one of the first glassmakers in America of useful tableware. Many of their products were signed and dated (rare for that time).

New Carnival Reproduction iridescent glass made since 1962, sometimes with the original Carnival glass molds.

New England Crystal Company Established in 1990 by Philip E. Hopfe in Lincoln, Rhode Island, the company is noted for hand-cut and copper wheel engraved art forms, as well as pate-de-verre styles.

New England Glass Co. An American glass company established at Cambridge, Massachusetts, by Deming Jarves and associates in 1818. One of the first highly successful American glass companies, they produced pressed, cut, and a variety of art glass such as Agata, Amberina, Pomona, and Wild Rose Peachblow. They were purchased by Libbey in the 1870s.

New Geneva Glass Works An American company established in Fayette County, Pennsylvania, by Albert Gallatin in 1797, they made some tableware and windows before closing.

New Martinsville Glass Co. An American company established in 1901, they began as an art glass company and later produced pressed pattern glass, some novelty items, and Depression glass. In 1944, they sold out to the Viking Glass Company.

Nipt Diamond Waves A pattern applied to glass objects produced by compressing thick vertical threads into diamondlike shapes.

Northwood Glass Co. An American company established in Wheeling, West Virginia, in 1820, they were noted for decorated glass with gold and opalescent edges as well as for producing Carnival glass in some quantity before going out of business in 1923.

Nut Dish A small flat or shallow dish used for serving nuts.

Obsidian A mineral that resembles dark glass; black glass is sometimes referred to as obsidian glass.

Off-Hand Glass Glass objects such as whimseys, art pieces, or other novelty items created by glassmakers from leftover or scrap glass.

Ogival-Venetian Diamond A pattern applied to glass objects, produced by pressing or cutting. The shape is of large or wide diamonds and is sometimes referred to as "Reticulated Diamond" or "Expanded Diamond."

Oil Bottle A glass receptacle with top used for serving vinegar or other salad oils (see *Cruet*).

Old Gold A deep amber stain or amber applied to glass made to resemble gold.

Olive Dish A small flat or shallow glass object, oblong or rectangular; it may or may not be divided and is used specifically for serving olives.

Olive Jar A small to medium-size glass container with wide mouth and cover, used for serving olives.

Onyx Glass A dark colored glass with streaking of white or other colors, made by mixing molten glass with various color mediums.

Opal Glass An opalescent opaquelike white milk glass usually produced by tin (see *Milk Glass*).

Opalescence A milky or cloudy coloring of glass. Opalescent coating is usually made by adding tin or zinc. Opalescent glass was first made by Frederick Carder at Steuben in the early 20th century.

Opaline Glass An opaque pressed or blown art glass that was first developed by Baccarat in the early 19th century.

Opaque Glass Glass that is so dark or solid in color that it does not transmit light (milk glass, for example).

Ormolu A decorative object usually made of brass, bronze, or gold applied to glass objects (such as a knob on stemware).

Orrefors Glasbruck Established in 1898 in Sweden, the company continues to operate today. They are noted most for contemporary art glass forms, including engraving (the "Graal" line is of particular note).

Overlay Glass The technique of placing one colored glass on top or over another, with designs cut through the outermost layer only.

Overshot Glass A type of glass with a very rough or jagged finish produced by rolling molten glass objects into crushed glass.

Owens, Michael J. A glassblower who began his career at Libbey in 1888. He invented the automatic bottle-blowing machine in 1903, which produced bottles quickly and efficiently at a much lower cost. He went on to form Owens-Illinois Inc.

Owens-Illinois Inc. An American company established in Toledo, Ohio, in 1929 when the Owens Bottle Machine Company under Michael Owens merged with the Illinois Glass Company. In 1936 it acquired the Libbey Glass Company and continues to produce huge quantities of glass under the Libbey name today.

Paden City Glass Co. An American company established in Paden City, West Virginia, in 1916, they were noted for many elegant Depression glass patterns. They closed in 1951.

Pairpoint Manufacturing Co. An American company established in New Bedford, Massachusetts, in 1865, they acquired the Mount Washington Glass Company in 1894 and continued producing glass until 1958. A new Pairpoint opened in 1967 in Sagamore, Massachusetts, producing handmade glassware.

Paperweight A small, heavy glass object with an inner design, used as a weight to hold down loose papers. Paperweights are often oval or rounded and are made of extremely thick glass.

Parfait A blob of molten glass with short stem and foot used for serving ice cream.

Parison A blob of molten glass gathered at the end of the blowpipe, pontil, or gathering iron (same as *Gather*).

Pate de Verre Meaning "paste of glass," it is an ancient material made from powdered glass or glasslike substances that is formed into a pastelike material by heating and then hardened. The resulting form is carved, painted, or applied with other decorations.

Pattern Glass Glass produced by mechanically pressing it into molds. The design is cut directly in the mold.

Pattern-Molded Glass Glass that is first impressed into small molds and then removed and blown to a larger size (blown-molded).

Peachblow Glass An American art glass produced by several companies in the late 19th century. It is characterized by multicolor opaque shades such as cream, white, pink, orange, red, etc.

Pearl Ornaments A molded glass pattern consisting of diamonds, squares, and other diagonal bandings.

Pearline Glass A late-19th-century-style art glass with color variance of pale to deep opaque blues.

Pegging The technique of poking a tiny hole in a molten glass object in order to trap a small quantity of air, or a bubble. The hole is then covered with other molten glass, which expands the bubble into a tear shape, or teardrop, inside the object.

Peking Cameo Cameo-engraved glass first made in China in the late 17th century in the city of Peking, it was made to resemble more expensive Chinese porcelain.

Peloton Glass A style of art glass first made by Wilhelm Kralik in Bohemia in 1880. It is produced by rolling colored threads into colored glass directly after it was removed from the furnace.

Perfume Bottle A tiny glass receptacle with narrow neck and stopper used for holding perfume.

Perthshire Paperweights, Ltd. Established in 1970 by Stuart Drysdale in Crieff,

Scotland, Perthshire is noted for high-quality paperweights. Many are produced in limited editions.

Phoenix Glass A term usually applied to cased milk glass, also known as "Mother-of-Pearl," made by the Phoenix Glassworks Company in Pittsburgh, Pennsylvania, in the late 19th century.

Phoenix Glass Co. Established in Monaca, Pennsylvania, in 1880, they later moved to Pittsburgh and were noted for cut-glass gas and electric lighting fixtures, general glass items, and some figured art glass.

Photochromic Glass A glass developed by the Corning Glass Works in Corning, New York, in 1964. When the glass is exposed to ultraviolet radiation such as sunlight, it darkens; when the radiation is removed, the glass clears.

Pickle Castor A glass jar held within a silver or silverplated metal frame, usually with handle and matching spoon, and used for serving pickles; most popular during the Victorian period.

Pickle Dish A flat or shallow dish, usually oblong or rectangular, used specifically for serving pickles (smaller than a celery dish).

Pidgeon Blood A color of glass characterized by brown highlighting over ruby red.

Pie Plate A large shallow, round glass dish used for baking and serving pies.

Pilgrim Glass Co. A contemporary art glass company founded in 1972 in Ceredo, West Virginia, Pilgrim is noted for paperweights and modern cameo glass.

Pillar Cutting A decorative pattern of cut glass in the form of parallel vertical ribs in symmetrical pillar shapes (similar to flute cutting).

Pilsener Glass A tall, narrow glass vessel with foot, primarily used for drinking beer.

Pin Tray A tiny, flat or shallow glass dish used for holding hairpins.

Pitcher A wide-mouthed glass vessel, usually with spout and handle, with or without lip, used for pouring or serving liquids.

Pitkin & Brooks Established as a cut-glass operation and distributor of crocks and glassware in Chicago in 1872, Edward Hand Pitkin and Jonathan William Brooks operated as a partnership until 1920.

Pittsburgh Flint Glass Works The early name for Benjamin Bakewell's first glass company established in 1808 (see *Bakewll, Pears, and Co.*).

Pittsburgh Glass High-quality pressed glass made in America by several companies in and around Pittsburgh, Pennsylvania, in the late 18th and the 19th century.

Plate A flat glass object, usually round but occasionally square or oval, used for serving dinner, lunch, desserts, and other foods.

Plated Glass Glass that is covered by more than one layer, usually clear glass that is dipped or completely covered with colored glass.

Platinum Band A silver-colored metal trim applied to rims or banding around glass objects (made of genuine platinum).

Platonite A heat-resistant opaque white glass first produced and named by Hazel Atlas in the 1930s and 1940s.

Platter A large, flat glass object, usually round or oval (larger than a dinner plate), used for serving large amounts of food.

Pokal A Bohemian-style goblet with stemmed foot and cover (cover may or may not contain a finial).

Polychromic Glass Glass characterized by two or more colors.

Pomona Glass An art glass created by applying or dipping the object into acid to produce a mottled, frosted appearance. It was first developed by Joseph Locke at the New England Glass Company in the late 19th century.

Pontil A short, solid iron used to remove expanded objects from the blowing iron, which allows the top to be finished. Prior to the 19th century, it left a mark but since then has been grounded flat. Pontil is also referred to as "pontie," "ponty," and "puntee."

Pot A vessel made of fired clay in which a batch of glass ingredients is heated before being transferred to the furnace. Many varieties include open, closed, smaller (for colored glass), and so on but most last only 3–6 weeks before breaking up. Modern pots hold 1000 to 1650 pounds of glass.

Pot Arch A furnace in which a pot is fired before being transferred to the main furnace for melting.

Powder Jar A small glass receptacle, usually with cover, used for holding various body powders. Powder jars are ordinarily part of dresser sets.

Preserve Dish A small flat or shallow dish, with or without foot, and used for serving jelly, jam, and other fruit preserves.

Pressed Glass Hot molten glass mechanically forced into molds under pressure (an important American invention in the 1820s was the hand press).

Pressing The process begins with molten glass poured into a mold, which forms the outer surface of an object. A plunger lowered into the mass leaves a smooth center with a patterned exterior. Flat plates and dishes are formed in a base mold, and an upper section folds down to mold the top (like a waffle iron).

Prism Cutting Cut glass made with long horizontal grooves or lines that usually meet at a common point.

Prunts A German decoration or ornamentation characterized by small glass knobs or drops attached to drinking vessels; later became another name for hobs on hobnail-patterned glass.

Pucellas A glassmaker's tool shaped like tongs used for gripping or holding glass objects while being worked.

Puff Box A small square, rectangular, or circular glass container with cover, used on dressing tables or vanities for holding powders.

Pumice Volcanic rock that is ground into powder and used for polishing glass objects.

Punch Bowl A huge concave glass vessel, usually hemispherical, used for serving beverages.

Punch Cup An open, somewhat bowl-shaped or cylindrical vessel, usually with a single handle, used for drinking punch as dipped from a punch bowl.

Punch Stand A matching support base on which a punch bowl rests.

Purled Glass Glass characterized by a ribbing applied around the base of the object.

Pyrex A type of glass created by Corning Glass in 1912. It contains oxide of boron, which makes the glass extremely heat-resistant (sometimes referred to as "Borosilicate glass").

Quaker City Cut Glass Co. Established in Philadelphia, in 1902, they produced cut-glass products until 1927.

Quartz Glass An art glass consisting of a wide variety of colors and shades, created by Steuben (designed to imitate the appearance of quartz).

Quatrefoil A form based on four leaves or four-petaled flowers; originally applied to stained glass windows in medieval Europe, it was later applied to glass objects.

Quezal Art Glass & Decoration Co. An American company founded in Brooklyn, New York, in 1901, they were noted for producing opalescent art glass known as Quezal Glass.

Quezal Glass An iridescent semiopaque imitation of Tiffany's "Favrile" art glass made by the Quezal Art Glass & Decoration Co. in the early 20th century.

Quilling A wavy pattern applied to glass by repeated workings with pincers.

Range Sets Kitchenware glass sets developed during the Depression period. Items might include canisters, flour jars, sugar jars, shakers, etc.

Ratafia Glass A cordial glass used to serve the liquor ratafia.

Ravenscroft, George The first commercially successful glassmaker in England, he developed a high-quality, durable lead crystal formula in the 17th century (1632–1983).

Rayed A sunburst cut design usually applied to the bottoms of glass objects.

Reading Artistic Glass Works An American company established by French immigrant Lewis Kremp in Reading, Pennsylvania, in 1884 but closed soon afterward, in 1886. In their two years of operation, the factory produced several styles of high-quality art glass products.

Reamer A juice extractor with a ridge and pointed center, rising in a shallow, usually circular dish.

Reeding A decorating technique applied with very fine threads or tiny ropelike strings of glass. The strings are usually colored and applied in a variety of patterns.

Refrigerator Dish Stackable square or rectangular covered glass containers of various sizes, used for storing foods in the refrigerator.

Relief Cutting A difficult and expensive method of cutting glass by designing the outline on the surface and then cutting away the background. The design is then raised in relief similar to that of cameo engraving.

Reliquary A glass vessel used for storing sacred religious relics.

Relish Dish A small to medium-sized shallow glass serving tray with divisions, usually rectangular or oval, may contain one or two handles.

Resonance The sound that results when a glass object is struck; sometimes used as a test for crystal though other types of glass resonate with similar sounds.

Reverse Painting Designs that are painted on the back side of glass and appear in proper perspective when viewed from the front.

Rib Mold A pattern mold for bowls, bottles, tumblers, and so on that is marked with heavy vertical lines or ribbing.

Richards & Hartley An American glass company founded by Joseph Richards and William T. Hartley in Pittsburgh, Pennsylvania, in 1869. They moved to Tarentum in 1881 and manufactured press wares before becoming part of the U.S. Glass Co. in 1891.

Rigaree A narrow vertical band decoration applied to glass in various colors.

Ringtree A glass object in the shape of a miniature tree with knobs that taper upward (the knobs are used to hold finger rings).

Ripley and Co. Established in 1866 in Pittsburgh, Pennsylvania, by Daniel Ripley and George Duncan, they produced pressed-glass items until they split up in 1874. Both continued on their own (Ripley & Co. and George Duncan & Sons) until becoming part of the U.S. Glass Company in 1891.

Riverside Glass Company Established in Wellsburg, West Virginia, in 1879, the company produced pressed glass until they joined the National Glass Company in 1900.

Roaster A deep round, oblong, or angled dish, with or without cover and with or without handles, used to bake or cook foods.

Rod A thin solid cylinder or small stick of glass. Many are used together to form a cane.

Rolled Edge A curved lip or circular base on which glass objects may turn over or rotate.

Rope Edge A twirled threadlike design usually applied around the edge of glass objects.

Rose A deep-red cranberry color applied to glass by staining or flashing (not as deep or as dark as ruby red).

Rose Bowl A small, round, concave glass vessel, usually with three feet (tri-footed) and a small opening in the center for holding a single flower or a few.

Royal Flemish Glass An art glass made by the Mount Washington Glass Works, characterized by a raised gilding decoration and light staining.

Rubina Glass Glass that gradually changes in color from crystal at the bottom to a cranberry or rose color at the top.

Rubina Verde Glass that gradually changes in color from a light yellow-green at the bottom to a cranberry or rose color at the top.

Ruby Red A gold metallic coloring agent that produces the most powerful red color within glass.

Sabino, Marius-Ernest A French art glass maker noted for opalescent gold figurines produced in the 1920s–1930s and 1960s–1970s.

Sachet Jar A small glass receptacle, with or without cover, used for holding perfumed powders for scenting clothes and linens.

St. Louis A famous French glassmaking town that was producing glass as far back as the 16th century. In the 1840s, they were noted for paperweight production but most manufacturers closed when the popularity of paperweights severely declined. The art form was revived in the 1950s and continues today.

Salad Plate A flat, usually round glass object, ordinarily about 7–7½ inches in diameter (slightly smaller than a lunch plate), used for serving salads.

Salt Cellar A small open bowl, with or without a foot, used for sprinkling salt on food prior to the development of shakers (may or may not have a matching spoon).

Salts Bottle A small glass bottle with silver or silverplated top used for holding smelling salts. They were most popular during the Victorian period.

Salve Box A small jar with cover used on dressing tables and vanities for holding salves, ointments, or cold creams.

Salver A large platter or tray used for serving food or beverages.

Sand The most common form of silica used in making glass. The best sands are found along inland beds near streams of low iron content and low amounts of other impurities.

Sandblasting An American-developed process in which the design on a piece of glass is coated with a protective layer and then the exposed surfaces that remain are blasted with a pressurized gun to create the design.

Sandwich Glass An American pressed-glass produced in the eastern United States in the 19th century, it was a substitute for more expensive handcut crystal glass.

Sandwich Server A large platter or serving tray with an open or closed center handle.

Sardine Dish A small oblong or oval, flat or shallow dish, used for serving sardines.

Satin Glass An American art glass characterized by a smooth lustrous appearance obtained by giving layers of colored glass an all over acid vapor bath.

Sauce Boat A glass oblong, bowl-shaped vessel, usually with a handle on each end, used for serving sauces or gravy.

Sauce Dish A small, usually flat or shallow dish, with or without handles and possibly footed, used for serving condiments or sauces.

Saucer A small flat or shallow plate, usually with an identation for a matching cup.

Scent Bottle See *Cologne Bottle* or *Perfume Bottle*.

Sconce A glass candlestick bracket with one or more sockets for holding candles.

Seeds Tiny air bubbles in glass indicating an underheated furnace or impurities caused by flecks of dirt or dust.

Shaker A small, upright glass container, usually cylindrical or angular in shape, with metal or plastic covers containing tiny holes, used for sprinkling salt, pepper, and other spices on foods.

Sham Very thin, fragile glass tumblers.

Shaving Mug A cylindrical glass vessel, with or without handles, usually larger than a drinking mug, used for repeated dipping and rinsing of shaving cream from a razor.

Sherbet A small footed dish, with or without a small stem, used for serving desserts such as pudding, ice cream, Jello, and so on.

Sherry Glass A tall glass with foot and stem and a shallow angled or straight-edged bowl.

Shot Glass A small whiskey tumbler with a capacity of at least one ounce (but not more than two) and a height of at least $1^3/_4$ inches but strictly less than 3 inches.

Sickness Glass that is not properly tempered or annealed that ordinarily shows random cracks, flaking, and eventually breaks or disintegrates.

Signature The mark of the maker or manufacturer usually applied near the bottom or the underside of glass objects.

Silveria Glass The technique of rolling an extremely thin layer of silver over glass and then blowing it, which shatters the silver into glittery decorative flecks.

Silverina A type of art glass created by Steuben in the early 20th century using particles of silver and mica applied to the glass object.

Sinclaire, H.P., & Co. Established in Corning, New York, in 1904 by H. P. Sinclaire, the company used blanks from Dorflinger for cutting and engraving. It closed permanently in 1929.

Skittle A small fire-clay pot used for melting a specialized small batch of colored glass or enamel.

Slag Glass A type of glass made with various scrap metals, including lead, that was first produced in England in the mid-19th century.

Smith, L.E., Co. Established by Lewis E. Smith in the early 1900s in Mt. Pleasant, Pennsylvania; Smith left in 1911, but the company continued producing many unique novelty items as well as colored glass during the Depression era.

Smith Brothers Harry A. and Alfred E. Smith worked in the Art Glass decorating department of Mount Washington Glass Works in 1871. They opened their own shop in 1874 in New Bedford, Massachusetts, and produced cut, engraved, and other art glass products.

South Jersey Glass Tableware made in America in the New Jersey area in the 18th century; it was fairly crude but bold, and the style spread to Europe.

Souvenir Glass Glass objects decorated with a variety of techniques (enameled, painted, transferred, embossed, etc.) depicting cities, states, countries, advertising, tourist attractions, and so on.

Spangled Glass A late-19th-century American art glass made with flakes of mica in the clear glass inner layer and then overlaid by transparent colored glass. The majority of items produced in this style were glass baskets with fancy decorated handles and rims.

Spatter Glass An opaque white or colored glass produced in both England and

America in the late 19th century. The exterior is sometimes mottled with large spots of colored glass.

Spittoon A fancy glass vessel or receptacle used for containing saliva (or spit, hence the name "spittoon"). Spittoons are sometimes referred to as cuspidors.

Spoon Dish A flat or shallow glass object, rectangular or oval in shape, used for holding dessert spoons horizontally.

Spooner or Spoon Holder A tall cylindrical glass vessel, with or without handles, used for holding dessert spoons vertically.

Sprayed-On Iridescence Iridescence added to glass by spraying it with particles of metallic salts.

Spun Glass Glass threading that was originally spun by hand on a revolving wheel. Glass fibers are automatically spun by machine today.

Stained Glass An imitation colored glass created by painting clear glass with metallic stains or transparent paints.

Star Holly A milk glass design created by the Imperial Glass Co. in the early 1900s. It was made to duplicate pressed English Wedgewood glass and was characterized by intertwined holly leaves raised in relief with background color mattes of blue, green, or coral.

Stein A cylindrical or square drinking vessel with a single handle, ordinarily larger than a mug (originally they had a capacity of 1 pint), with or without a hinged lid (the lid as well as handles may be metal), used for serving beer.

Stem The cylindrical support connecting the foot and bowl of glass vessels (these vessels include all types of stemware—goblets, wineglasses, comports, etc.).

Sterling Cut Glass Co. Established in 1904 in Cincinnati, Ohio, by Joseph Phillips and Joseph Landenwitsch, they were noted for cut-glass production. The company closed for good in 1950.

Steuben Glass Co. An American company founded in Corning, New York, by Frederick Carder in 1903, they were a leader in art glass styles and production early on and were purchased by the Corning Glass Works in 1918. Corning continues to produce some of the finest-quality crystal in the world today.

Stevens & Williams English glassmakers who produced art glass products, including a cheaper method of making cameo glass. They operated at the Brierly Hill Glassworks in Stourbridge, England, from the 1830s to the 1920s.

Straus & Sons Established by German immigrant Lazarus Straus in 1872 in New York City, they began as a retailer of china and glass products but later began cutting glass in 1888. As the demand for cut glass declined, the company returned to the retail market.

Striped Glass An American art glass from the late 19th century, characterized by wavy bands of contrasting colors.

Sugar A small glass cuplike vessel, it may or may not have handles; used for serving sugar (often paired with a creamer for serving tea).

Sugar and Lemon Tray A two-tiered object used for serving lemons and sugar. Cut lemons are placed on the bottom level while sugar held in a bowl sits on the top level.

Sugar Shaker A small, upright glass container, usually cylindrical or angular in shape, with a metal or plastic cover containing holes; used for sprinkling sugar on various foods (larger than typical salt and pepper shakers).

Sunset-Glow Glass An early (18th century) European milk or opalescent white glass.

Superimposed Decoration A glass decoration separate from the object that it is applied to.

Sweetmeat Dish or Compote A small, flat or shallow tray or bowl-like glass object used for serving sweetmeats or hors d'oeuvres.

Syrup Pitcher A small, wide-mouthed vessel, with spout, handle, and hinged metal lid, used for pouring syrup.

Tankard A large drinking vessel, somewhat straight-edged, with a single handle; may or may not contain a hinged lid (as in steins, the lid and handle may be made of metal).

Taylor Brothers Established in 1902 in Philadelphia, by Albert Taylor and Lafayette Taylor, they operated as a cut-glass company until 1915.

Tazza An unusually wide dessert cup or serving plate, with or without handles, mounted on a stemmed foot.

Tea Caddy A large, wide-mouthed glass canister with cover, used for storing tea bags or loose tea.

Teal A bluish-green glass (a little darker than ultramarine).

Teapot A vessel with handle, spout, and lid used to serve tea. Glass teapots are typically found in children's miniature tea sets.

Tear A bubble of air trapped in glass that is sometimes purposely created for a decorative effect.

Thatcher Brothers Established by George and Richard Thatcher in 1891 in New Bedford, Massachusetts; they produced cut-glass products until going out of business in 1907.

Thread Circuit A decorative pattern applied with ropelike strings or twists of glass. The strings or threads are often colored and applied in concentric circles or other symmetrical patterns.

Thumbprint A decorative style usually made by pressing in the form of shallow oval-depressions arranged in rows. Several variations of the basic thumbprint pattern exist (i.e., almond thumbprint, diamond thumbprint, etc.).

Tid-Bit Tray A tiered dish with a pole connecting two or more levels. The pole usually runs through the center, and the size of the levels gradually decrease as they go up.

Tiffany, Louis Comfort The most celebrated and renowned leader of the Art Nouveau style of glass in America in the 19th century. he established a glass factory on Long Island, New York, in 1885 and was noted for several famous worldwide designs (including Favrile), lamps, and a host of other items (1848–1933).

Tiffin Glass Co. An American company established in Tiffin, Ohio, that became part of the United States Glass Company in 1891; glass was made at the site until 1980.

Tobacco Jar A large canisterlike glass container with cover, used for storing tobacco.

Toddy Jar A tall, wide-mouthed glass receptacle used for serving hot toddies (alcoholic beverages consisting of liquor, water, sugar, and spices).

Toilet Water Bottle A glass receptacle with narrow neck and stopper used on dressing tables and vanities for holding toilet water (larger than a cologne bottle).

Toothbrush Bottle A tall, narrow, cylindrical glass container with cap, used to store a single toothbrush.

Toothpick Holder A small glass or ceramic receptacle of small capacity designed to hold toothpicks, usually cut or patterned to taper inward at the top.

Toothpowder Jar A small glass receptacle with cover, used for holding toothpowder.

Topaz A mineral used as a coloring agent to produce a bright yellow color within glass.

Toy Mug A miniature glass vessel in the shape of a mug with a handle and a capacity of 1 to 1½ ounces.

Toy Whiskey Taster A small glass tumbler made in America around 1840 for the tasting, sampling, or consuming of whiskey in tiny amounts.

Trailing The process of pulling out a thread of glass and applying it to the surface of a glass object in spiral or other string designs.

Transfers A complete design printed on a paper backing that is removed from the backing, applied to glassware, and then fired on in a special enameling lehr.

Translucent Glass that transmits or diffuses light so that objects lying beyond cannot be seen clearly through it.

Transparents Glass that transmits light without appreciable scattering so that objects lying beyond are clearly visible.

Tray A flat glass object, usually oval or rectangular, used for holding or serving various items.

Trivet A glass plate, usually tri-footed, used under a hot dish to protect the surface (i.e., tabletop) beneath it.

Tumble-Up An inverted glass set for a dresser or night stand that usually includes a water bottle and other items, such as a tray, tumblers, etc.

Tumbler A drinking vessel ordinarily without foot, stem, or handle and with a pointed or convex base.

Tuthill Cut Glass Co. Established in 1900 in Middletown, New York, by Charles G., Tuthill, James F. Tuthill, and Susan Tuthill. They were noted for cut glass and some intaglio engraving before shutting down for good in 1923.

Ultramarine A blue-green color produced by the mineral lazulite or by a mixture of kaolin, soda ash, sulfur, and charcoal.

Unger Brothers Established in 1901 in Newark, New Jersey, they began as a silver manufacturer of household items and added cut-glass products shortly afterward. They later switched to cheaper pressed blanks before closing permanently in 1918.

Union Glass Co. Established in 1851 in Somerville, Massachusetts, by Amory Houghton as a cut-glass operation. Houghton later sold his interest to Julian de Cordova (whose initials are sometimes found on the liners of certain objects). The company closed in 1927.

U.S. Glass Co. An American glass conglomerate that was established in 1891 when 18 separate companies from the Glass Belt (Ohio, Pennsylvania, West Virginia, etc.) merged.

Urn An ornamental glass vase with or without pedestal (may or may not have handles); also a closed glass vessel with spigot used for serving liquids.

Val St. Lambert Cristalleries A Belgian factory established in the early 1900s, they are still in operation today and are noted most for engraved cameo art glass styles.

Vasa Murrhina An American 19th-century art glass characterized by an inner layer of colored glass that has powdered metals or mica added for decoration.

Vase A round or angled glass vessel, usually with a depth greater than its width, used for holding flowers.

Vaseline Glass Glass made with a small amount of uranium, which imparts a light greenish-yellow color (a greasy appearance like Vaseline).

Venetian Glass Clear and colored glassware produced in Venice, Italy, and the surrounding area (especially the Island of Murano) from the 13th century to the present.

Verre-De-Soie An art glass first produced by Steuben characterized by a smooth translucent iridescent finish.

Victorian Glass English-made glass from about the 1820s through the 1940s, characterized by colors, opalescence, and opaqueness, art glass in unusual designs and shapes (named for Queen Victoria 1837–1901).

Wafer Dish A small, flat or shallow dish, usually square or rectangular, used for serving crackers or wafers.

Watch Box A small, rectangular or circular glass vessel, with or without cover, used for storing a single wristwatch.

Water Bottle A glass container with narrow neck and mouth, usually without handle, used for drinking water or other liquids.

Waterford The first Waterford glass company was established in Waterford, Ireland, in 1783 by the Penrose family and then sold to the Gatchell family in 1799. The handmade crystal produced had a bluish-tint and heavy cuts. The factory closed in 1851. A new Waterford factory was built in 1951, and since then Waterford has become the world's largest manufacturer of handmade crystal. Today they operate as Waterford Wedgwood PLC.

Wear Marks Tiny, barely visible scratches on the base, foot, or trim, indicating normal wear and tear through years of use. Glass with wear marks is usually not considered mint glassware, but it holds much more value than damaged glass.

Webb, Thomas, & Sons Established in 1837 in Stourbridge, England, by Thomas Webb, the company has been in continuous operation since then. It is noted for several art glass styles (cameo, Peachblow, Alexandrite, Burmese, etc.).

Westmoreland Specialty Co. An American company established in Grapeville, Pennsylvania, in 1890, they were noted most for English hobnail-patterned glassware. The company closed in 1985.

Wheeling Glass Glass made in the city of Wheeling, Virginia, in the 19th century (before West Virginia became a state).

Wheels Cutting wheels developed from lapidary equipment. Large stone wheels are used for deep cuts, and smaller copper wheels of various sizes are used for finer engraving.

Whimsy A small unique decorative glass object made to display a particular glassmaker's skill (sometimes called a "frigger").

Whiskey Jug A large, deep glass vessel or decanter with a small mouth, with cover or stopper and usually with a small handle, used for serving whiskey.

Whiskey Sample Glass Small whiskey tumblers or cordials with a capacity of up to four ounces, for sampling whiskey or other distilled spirits. Sample glasses were produced in the late 19th century on up to Prohibition (1919). Most contained advertising of a distiller or brand of whiskey (also referred to as "Pre-Prohibition Advertising Glasses").

Whiskey Tumbler A small shot glass–size drinking vessel, usually without foot, stem, or handle and with a pointed or convex base; used for drinking distilled spirits in small amounts.

Whitney Glass An 18th-century American glass for bottles and flasks.

Wine Set A decanter with matching wineglasses (May or may not include a matching tray).

Wineglass A tall glass with foot and stem and a large round, deep bowl. As a unit of measure for serving size, four ounces is the most prevalent.

Witch Ball A spherical glass globe, usually 3–7 inches in diameter and dating from early-18th-century England. They were used to ward off evil and for fortune-telling and other superstitions.

Wrything Ornamentation A decoration consisting of swirled ribbing or fluting.

Zanesville Glass An American art glass produced in Ohio in the mid-19th century.

Zwischengoldglas An 18th-century Bohemian or German glass characterized by gilding and inlaid decoration within another straight-sided glass.

MANUFACTURERS' MARKS

Abraham &
Straus Inc.

Akro Agate
Company

C.G. Alford
& Company

C.G. Alford &
Company

Almay &
Thomas

American
Wholesale Corp.

Anchor-Hocking
Glass Corp.

M.J. Averback

Baccarat
Glass Co.

Bartlett-
Collins Co.

J.D. Bergen Co.

J.D. Bergen Co.

House of Birks

Blenko Glass Co.

George L.
Borden & Co.

George Borgfeldt
& Company

Boyd Crystal
Art Glass

Bradley &
Hubbard

Buffalo Cut
Glass Co.

Burley &
Tyrrell Co.

Cambridge
Glass Co.

T.B. Clark & Co.

Conlow-
Dorworth Co.

Corona Cut
Glass Co.

Crown Cut
Glass Co.

Crystal Cut
Glass Co.

Crystolyne
Cut Glass Co.

Daum Glass
Nancy, France

MADE
DeVilbiss
IN U.S.A.
De Vilbiss Co.

SILVART
Deidrick
Glass Co.

Diamond Cut
Glass Works

C. Dorflinger
& Sons

G. W. Drake & Co.

Duffner &
Kimberly

FLORAL CRYSTAL
Duncan
Dithridge

Durand Art
Glass Co.

O.F. Egginton
Company

Empire Cut
Glass Co.

VESTALIA
Eske Mfg. Co.

Federal
Glass Co.

Fenton Art Glass
Paper Label

"Iris: Fostoria"
Glass Co. Paper
Label

H.C. Fry
Glass Co.

Emile Galle

George Drake
Cut Glass Co.

GILLINDER

Gillander

Gibson Glass

Gowans, Kent,
& Co., Ltd.

Gundy-
Clapperton Co.

Handel and Co.

T.G. Hawkes
& Company

Hazel Atlas
Glass Co.

A.H. Heisey
Glass Co.

L. Hinsberger
Cut Glass

J. Hoare & Co.

Hobbs Glass Co.

Hobbs,
Brocunier & Co.

Hocking
Glass Co.

Hope GLass Works

Honedale
Decorating Co.

Hunt Glass Co.

Imperial
Glass Co.

Indiana
Glass Co.

Iorio Glass Shop

Irving Cut
Glass Co.

Jeannette Glass Co.

Jewel Cut
Glass Co.

PEERLESS
Kelly &
Steinman

Keystone Cut
Glass Co., Ltd.

**MARS
STRAND**
Kings Co. Rich
Cut Glass Works

Edward J. Kock
& Company

Krantz, Smith
& Co., Inc.

Lackawanna
Cut Glass Co.

Lansburgh & Bro.

Lansburgh &
Brother, Inc.

Laurel Cut
Glass Co.

Loetz
Glassworks

Apr. 16, 1901
(for use on pressed
[figured] blanks)

W.L Libbey & Son

Joseph Locke

Lotus Cut
Glass Co.

Lowell Cut
Glass Co.

Wm. H. Lum

Luzerne Cut
Glass Co.

Lyons Cut
Glass Co.

MacBeth-Evans
Glass Co./Corning
Glass Works

Majestic Cut
Glass Co.

Maple City
Glass Co.

McKanna Cut
Glass Co.

McKanna Cut
Glass Co.

McKee
Glass Co.

PRESCUT

McKee-Jeannette
Glass-Works

Meriden Cut
Glass Co.

"Kelva" C.F.
Monroe Co.

Moser Glass Works

NAKARA

"Nakara" C.F.
Monroe Co.

"Wavecrest"
C. F. Monroe Co.

Moses, Swan &
McLawee Co.

"Crown Milano"
Mt. Washington
Glass Works

"Royal Flemish"
Mt. Washington
Glass Works

Mt. Washington Glass
Works Paper Label

Mt. Washington Glass
Works Paper Label

Mt. Washington
Glass Works
Paper Labels

KOH-I-NOOR

Richard Murr Co.

A. Douglas Nash
Corporation

National Association of
Cut Glass Manufacturers

Newark Cut
Glass Co.

New England Glass
Works Paper Label

Northwood
Glass Co.

J.S. O'Connor Co.

The Pairpoint Corp'n

Pairpoint Mfg.
Company

Pairpoint Mfg. Co./
Mt. Washington
Glass Works

P.X. Parsche
& Son Co.

Phoenix
Glass Co.

Pilgrim Glass

Pitkin &
Brooks

DIAMONKUT
Pope Cut Glass
Co., Inc.

Quaker City
Cut Glass Co.

Quezal
Quezal Art Glass
& Decorating Co.

St. Louis, France

Roden Bros.,
Ltd.

Seattle Cut
Glass Co.

Signet
Glass Co.

H.P. Sinclaire
& Co.

Smith Brothers
Decorating Co,

Standard Cut
Glass Co.

Sterling
Glass Co.

Steuben
Glass Works

Steuben
Glass Works

"Cire Perdue"
Steuben Glass
Works

Various Frederick
Carder Signatures,
Steuben Glass Works

STEUBEN AURENE
Steuben
Glass Works

L. Straus
& Sons

Taylor
Brothers Co.

Thatcher
Bros. & Co.

"Favrile"
Tiffany

Tuthill Cut
Glass Co.

Unger
Brothers

Unger Bros.

"Kew Blas"
Union Glass Co.

United States
Glass Co.

United States
Glass Co.

Val St. Lambert

Van Heusen,
Charles Co.

E.J.S. Van
Houten Co.

Westmoreland
Glass Co.

C.E. Wheelock
& Co.

BIBLIOGRAPHY

Angus-Butterworth. *British Table and Ornamental Glass.* New York: Arco, 1956.

Archer, Margaret, and Douglas Archer. *Imperial Glass.* Paducah, KY: Collector Books, 1978.

Arwas, Victor. *Art Nouveau to Art Deco.* New York: Rizzoli International, 1977.

———. *Tiffany.* New York: Rizzoli International, 1977.

Avila, George C. *The Pairpoint Glass Story.* New Bedford, MA: Reynolds-Dewart Printing, 1968.

Baldwin, Gary, and Lee Carno. *Moser: Artistry in Glass, 1857–1938.* Marietta, OH: Antique Publications, 1988.

Barber, Edwin A. *American Glassware.* Philadelphia: Press of Patterson & White Co., 1900.

Barbour, Harriot Buxton. *Sandwich: The Town That Glass Built.* Boston: Houghton Mifflin, 1948.

Barret, Richard Carter. *A Collectors Handbook of American Art Glass.* Manchester, VT: Forward's Color Productions, 1971.

———. *A Collector's Handbook of Blown and Pressed American Glass.* Manchester, VT: Forward's Color Productions, 1971.

———. *Popular American Ruby-Stained Pattern Glass.* Manchester, VT: Richard Carter Barret and Frank L. Forward, 1968.

Battersby, Martin. *Art Nouveau: The Colour Library of Art.* Middlesex, England: Hamlyn Publishing Group, 1969.

Batty, Bob H. *A Complete Guide to Pressed Glass.* Gretna, LA: Pelican Publishing, 1978.

Belknap, E. McCamly. *Milk Glass.* New York: Crown, 1949.

Bennett, Harold, and Judy Bennett. *The Cambridge Glass Book.* Des Moines, IA: Wallace-Homestead, 1970.

Bing, S. *Artistic America, Tiffany Glass and Art Nouveau.* Cambridge, MA: Massachusetts Institute of Technology Press, 1970.

Bishop, Barbara, and Martha Hassell. *Your Obdt. Servt., Deming Jarves.* Sandwich, MA: Sandwich Historical Society, 1984.

Blount, Berniece, and Henry Blount. *French Cameo Glass.* Des Moines, IA: Authors, 1968.

Blum, John, et al. *The National Experience: A History of the United States.* New York: Harcourt Brace Jovanovich, 1981.

Boggess, Bill, and Louise Boggess. *American Brilliant Cut Glass.* New York: Crown, 1977.

Bones, Frances. *The Book of Duncan Glass.* Des Moines, IA: Wallace-Homestead, 1973.

Bossaglia, Rossana. *Art Nouveau.* New York: Crescent Books, 1971.

Boston & Sandwich Glass Co. Boston: Lee Publications, 1968.

Bredehoft, Neila, George Fogg, and Francis Maloney. *Early Duncan Glassware: Geo. Duncan & Sons, 1874–1892.* Boston: Authors, 1987.

Bridgeman, Harriet, and Elizabeth Drury. *The Encyclopedia of Victoriana.* New York: Macmillan, 1975.

Brown, Clark W. *A Supplement to Salt Dishes.* Des Moines, IA: Wallace-Homestead, 1970.

The Cambridge Glass Co. Cambridge, OH: National Cambridge Collection, 1978.

Carved and Decorated European Glass. Rutland, VT: Charles E. Tuttle Co., 1970.

Charleston, R. J. *English Glass.* London: George Allen and Unwin, 1984.

Charleston, Robert J. *Masterpieces of Glass: A World History from the Corning Museum of Glass.* New York: Harry N. Abrams, 1980.

Chase, Mark E., and Michael J. Kelly. *Contemporary Fast-Food and Drinking Glass Collectibles.* Radnor, PA: Wallace-Homestead, 1988.

Cloak, Evelyn Campbell. *Glass Paperweights of the Bergstrom Art Center.* New York: Crown, 1969.

The Complete Book of McKee. Kansas City, MO: Tuga Press, 1974.

Conder, Lyle, Editor. *Heisey's Collector's Guide to Glassware for Your Table.* Edited by Lyle Conder. Gas City, IN: L-W Book Sales, 1984.

Contemporary Art Glass. New York: Crown, 1975.

Cosentino, Geraldine, and Regina Stewart. *Carnival Glass.* New York: Western, 1976.

Cousins, Mark. *20th Century Glass.* Secaucus, NJ: Chartwell Books, 1989.

Cudd, Viola N. *Heisey Glassware.* Brenham, TX: Herrmann Print Shop, 1969.

Curtis, Jean-Louis. *Baccarat.* London: Thames and Hudson, 1992.

Daniel, Dorothy. *Cut and Engraved Glass, 1771–1905.* New York: M. Barrows, 1950.

———. *Price Guide to American Cut Glass.* New York: M. Barrows, 1967.

Davis, Derek C., and Keith Middlemas. *Colored Glass.* New York: Clarkson N. Potter, 1967.

———. *English Bottles and Decanters, 1650–1900.* New York: World Publications, 1972.

Diamond, Freda. *The Story of Glass.* New York: Harcourt, Brace, and World, 1953.

Dibartolomeo, Robert E., Editor. *American Glass: Vol. 2. Pressed and Cut.* New York: Weathervane Books, 1978.

Dorflinger, C., & Sons. *Cut Glass Catalog, 1881–1921.* Hanover, PA: Everybody's Press, 1970.

Doros, Paul E. *The Tiffany Collection of the Chrysler Museum at Norfolk.* Norfolk, VA: Chrysler Museum, 1978.

Drepperd, Carl W. *ABC's of Old Glass.* New York: Doubleday, 1968.

Duncan, Alastair. *Tiffany at Auction.* New York: Rizzoli International, 1981.

Duncan, Alastair, Martin Eidelberg, and Neil Harris. *Masterworks of Louis Comfort Tiffany.* New York: Harry N. Abrams, 1989.

Ebbott, Rex. *British Glass of the 17th and 18th Centuries.* London: Oxford University Press, 1972.

Editors of the Pyne Press. *Pennsylvania Glassware, 1870–1904.* Princeton, NJ: Pyne Press, 1972.

Edmonson, Barbara. *Old Advertising Spirits.* Oregon: Maverick Publications, 1988.

Edwards, Bill. *The Queen of Carnival Glass.* Paducah, KY: Collector Books, 1976.

———. *The Standard Encyclopedia of Carnival Glass.* Paducah, KY: Collector Books, 1982.

Ehrhardt, Alpha. *Cut Glass Price Guide.* Kansas City, MO: Heart of America Press, 1973.

Elville, E. M. *English and Irish Cut Glass, 1750–1950.* New York: Charles Scribner's Sons, 1951.

Ericson, Eric E. *A Guide to Colored Steuben.* 2 vols. Colorado: Lithographic Press, 1963–1965.

Evers, Jo. *The Standard Cut Glass Value Guide.* Paducah, KY: Collector Books, 1975.

Farrar, Estelle Sinclaire, and Jane Shadel Spillman. *The Complete Cut and Engraved Glass of Corning.* New York: Crown, 1978.

Fauster, Carl U. *Libbey Glass since 1818.* Toledo, OH: Len Beach Press, 1979.

Florence, Gene. *Collectible Glassware from the 40's, 50's, 60's.* Paducah, KY: Collector Books, 1992.

———. *The Collector's Encyclopedia of Akro Agate.* Paducah, KY: Collector Books, 1975.

———. *The Collector's Encyclopedia of Depression Glass.* Paducah, KY: Collector Books. 1990.

———. *Kitchen Glassware of the Depression Years.* Paducah, KY: Collector Books, 1981.

Frantz, Susanne K. *Contemporary Glass: A World Survey from the Corning Museum of Glass.* New York: Henry N. Abrams, 1989.

Freeman, Larry. *Iridescent Glass.* Watkins Glen, NY: Century House, 1964.

Gardner, Paul F. *Frederick Carder: Portrait of a Glassmaker.* Corning, NY: Corning Museum of Glass, 1985.

———. *The Glass of Frederick Carder.* New York: Crown, 1971.

Grimmer, Elsa H. *Wave Crest Ware.* Des Moines, IA: Wallace-Homestead, 1979.

Grover, Ray, and Lee Grover. *Art Glass Nouveau.* Rutland, VT: Charles E. Tuttle Co., 1967.

———. *Carved and Decorated European Art Glass.* Rutland, VT: Charles E. Tuttle Co. 1967.

———. *English Cameo Glass.* New York: Crown, 1980.

Hand, Sherman. *The Collector's Encyclopedia of Carnival Glass.* Paducah, KY: Collector Books, 1978.

Harrington, J. C. *Glassmaking at Jamestown: America's First Industry.* Richmond, VA: Dietz Press, 1952.

Hartung, Marion. *Carnival Glass in Color.* Emporia, KS: Author, 1967.

———. *Northwood Pattern Glass in Color.* Emporia, KS: Author, 1969.

Haslam, Malcolm. *Marks and Monograms of the Modern Movement, 1875–1930.* New York: Charles Scribner's Sons, 1977.

Hastin, Bud. *Avon Collectibles Price Guide.* Kansas City, MO: Author, 1991.

Heacock, William. *The Encyclopedia of Victorian Colored Pattern Glass.* Books 1–4, 6–9. Marietta, OH: Antique Publications, 1974–1988.

———. *Fenton Glass: The First Twenty-five Years.* Marietta, OH: O-Val Advertising Corp., 1978.

———. *Fenton Glass: The Second Twenty-five Years.* Marietta, OH: O-Val Advertising Corp., 1980.

Heacock, William, and Fred Bickenhauser. *The Encyclopedia of Victorian Colored Pattern Glass.* Book 5. Marietta, OH: Antique Publications, 1974–1988.

Hettes, Karel. "Venetian Trends in Bohemian Glassmaking in the 16th and 17th Centuries." *Journal of Glass Studies,* 5 (1963).

Hollister, Paul, and Dwight Lanmon. *Paperweights*. Corning, NY: Corning Museum of Glass, 1978.

Hollister, Paul, Jr. *The Encyclopedia of Glass Paperweights*. New York: Clarkson N. Potter, 1969.

Hotchkiss, John F. *Art Glass Handbook*. New York: Hawthorn Books, 1972.

———. *Carder's Steuben Glass Handbook and Price Guide*. New York: Hawthorn Books, 1972.

———. *Cut Glass Handbook and Price Guide*. Des Moines, IA: Wallace-Homestead, 1970.

House, Caurtman G. *Relative Values of Early American Patterned Glass*. Medina, NY: Author, 1944.

House of Collectibles. *The Official Price Guide to Carnival Glass*. New York: Random House, 1986.

House of Collectibles. *The Official Price Guide to Depression Glass*. New York: Random House, 1988.

Huether, Anne. *Glass and Man*. New York: J. B. Lippincott, 1965.

Hughes, G. Bernard. *English Glass for the Collector, 1660–1860*. New York: Macmillan, 1968.

Hunter, Frederick William. *Stiegel Glass*. New York: Dover, 1950.

Huxford, Sharon, and Bob Huxford, Editors. *Flea Market Trader*. Paducah, KY: Collector Books, 1993.

Imperial Glass Corporation. *The Story of Handmade Glass*. Imperial, 1941. (24 pages).

Innes, Lowell. *Pittsburgh Glass, 1797–1891: A History and Guide for Collectors*. Boston: Houghton Mifflin, 1976.

Jarves, Deming. *Reminiscences of Glassmaking*. Boston: Eastburn's Press, 1854.

Jefferson, Josephine. *Wheeling Glass*. Mount Vernon, OH: Guide Publishing Co., 1947.

Jenks, Bill, and Jerry Luna. *Early American Pattern Glass, 1850–1910*. Radnor, PA: Wallace-Homestead, 1990.

Jokelson, Paul. *Sulphides: The Art of Cameo Incrustation*. New York: Thomas Nelson & Sons, 1968.

Ketchum, William C., Jr. *A Treasury of American Bottles*. New York: Ridge Press, 1975.

Klamkin, Marian. *The Collector's Guide to Carnival Glass*. New York: Hawthorn Books, 1976.

———. *The Collector's Guide to Depression Glass*. New York: Hawthorne Books, 1973.

Klein, Dan, and Ward Lloyd. *The History of Glass*. New York: Crescent Books, 1989.

Koch, Robert. *Louis C. Tiffany: A Rebel in Glass*. New York: Crown, 1964.

Kovel, Ralph, and Terry Kovel. *The Complete Antiques Price List*. New York: Crown, 1973, 1976, 1980, 1981, 1982, 1985, 1986, 1990.

———. *The Kovels' Antique and Collectible Price List*. New York: Crown, 1990, 1991, 1992, 1993.

———. *Kovels' Bottles Price List*. New York: Crown, 1992.

Krantz, Susan. *Contemporary Glass*. New York: Harry N. Abrams, 1989.

Krause, Gail. *Duncan Glass*. New York: Exposition Press, 1976.

Lafferty, James R. *The Forties Revisited*. Author, 1968.

Lee, Ruth Webb. *Early American Pressed Glass*. New York: Ferris Printing Co., 1946.

———. *Nineteenth Century Art Glass*. New York: M. Barrows, 1952.

————. *Sandwich Glass*. New York: Ferris Printing Co., 1947.

Lindsey, Bessie M. *American Historical Glass*. Rutland, VT: Charles E. Tuttle, 1967.

Mackay, James. *Glass Paperweights*. New York: Facts on File, 1973.

Madigan, Mary Jean. *Steuben Glass: An American Tradition in Crystal*. New York: Harry N. Abrams, 1982.

Manley, Cyril. *Decorative Victorian Glass*. New York: Van Nostrand Reinhold, 1981.

Mannoni, Edith. *Classic French Paperweights*. Santa Cruz, CA: Paperweight Press, 1984.

Mariacher, G. *Three Centuries of Venetian Glass*. Corning, NY: Corning Museum of Glass, 1957.

Markowski, Carol, and Gene Markowski. *Tomart's Price Guide to Character and Promotional Glasses*. Radnor, PA: Wallace-Homestead, 1990.

Marshall, Jo. *Glass Source Book*. London: Quarto, 1990.

McClinton, Katharine Morrison. *Lalique for Collectors*. New York: Charles Scribner's Sons, 1975.

McKean, Hugh F. *The "Lost" Treasures of Louis Comfort Tiffany*. New York: Doubleday, 1980.

McKearin, George, and Helen McKearin. *American Glass*. New York: Crown, 1968.

————. *Nineteenth-Century Art Glass*. New York: Crown Publishers, Inc. 1966.

Mebane, John. *Collecting Brides' Baskets and Other Glass Fancies*. Des Moines, IA: Wallace-Homestead, 1976.

Melvin, Jean S. *American Glass Paperweights and Their Makers*. New York: Thomas Nelson, 1970.

Miles, Dori, and Robert W. Miller, Editors. *Wallace-Homestead Price Guide to Pattern Glass, 11th Edition*. Radnor, PA: Wallace-Homestead, 1986.

Miller, Robert. *Mary Gregory and Her Glass*. Des Moines, IA: Wallace-Homestead, 1972.

————, Editor. *Wallace-Homestead Price Guide to Antiques and Pattern Glass*. Des Moines, IA: Wallace-Homestead, 1982.

Moore, N. Hudson. *Old Glass European and American*. New York: Tudor Publishing, 1924.

Neustadt, Egon. *The Lamps of Tiffany*. New York: Fairfield Press, 1970.

Newark, Tim. *Emile Gallé*. London: Quintet Publishing, 1989.

Newman, Harold. *An Illustrated Dictionary of Glass*. London: Thames and Hudson, 1977.

Nye, Mark. *Cambridge Stemware*. Miami: Mark A. Nye, 1985.

Oliver, Elizabeth. *American Antique Glass*. New York: Golden Press, 1977.

Padgett, Leonard E. *Pairpoint Glass*. Des Moines, IA: Wallace-Homestead, 1979.

Papert, Emma. *The Illustrated Guide to American Glass*. New York: Hawthorn Books, 1972.

Paul, Tessa. *The Art of Louis Comfort Tiffany*. New York: Exeter Books, 1987.

Pears, Thomas C., III. *Bakewell, Pears & Co. Glass Catalogue*. Pittsburgh, PA: Davis & Warde, 1977.

Pearson, Michael, and Dorothy Pearson. *American Cut Glass for the Discriminating Collector*. New York: Vantage Press, 1965.

————. *A Study of American Cut Glass Collections*. Miami, FL: Authors, 1969.

Pesatova, Zuzana. *Bohemian Engraved Glass*. Prague: Knihtisk Publishing, 1968.

Peterson, Arthur G. *400 Trademarks on Glass.* Takoma Park, MD: Washington College Press, 1968.

Phillips, Phoebe, Editor. *The Encyclopedia of Glass.* New York: Crown, 1981.

Pickvet, Mark. *Shot Glasses: An American Tradition.* Marietta, OH: Antique Publications, 1989.

Polak, Ada. *Glass: Its Tradition and Its Makers.* New York: G. P. Putnam's Sons, 1975.

Rainwater, Dorothy T. *Encyclopedia of American Silver Manufacturers.* New York: Crown, 1975.

Revi, Albert Christian. *American Art Nouveau Glass.* New York: Thomas Nelson and Sons, 1968.

———. *American Cut and Engraved Glass.* New York: Thomas Nelson and Sons, 1970.

———. *American Pressed Glass and Figure Bottles.* New York: Thomas Nelson and Sons, 1968.

———. *Nineteenth Century Glass.* New York: Galahad Books, 1967.

Ring, Carolyn. *For Bitters Only.* Boston: Nimrod Press, 1980.

Rinker, Harry. *Warman's Americana and Collectibles.* Elkins Park, PA: Warman Publishing, 1986.

Rose, James H. *The Story of American Pressed Glass of the Lacy Period, 1825–1850.* Corning, NY: Corning Museum of Glass, 1954.

Rossi, Sara. *A Collector's Guide to Paperweights.* Secaucus, NJ: Wellfleet Books, 1990.

Schmutzler, Robert. *Art Nouveau.* London: Thames and Hudson, 1978.

Schroeder, Bill. *Cut Glass.* Paducah, KY: Collector Books, 1977.

Schroeder's Antiques Price Guide. Paducah, KY: Collector Books, 1993.

Schroy, Ellen. *Warman's Glass.* Radnor, PA: Wallace-Homestead, 1992.

Schwartz, Marvin D., Editor. *American Glass: Vol. 1. Blown and Molded.* New York: Weathervane Books, 1978.

Scott, Virginia R. *The Collector's Guide to Imperial Candlewick.* Athens, GA: Author, 1980.

Selman, Lawrence H. *The Art of the Paperweight.* Santa Cruz, CA: Paperweight Press, 1988.

Shuman, John, III. *American Art Glass.* Paducah, KY: Collector Books, 1988.

———. *Art Glass Sampler.* Des Moines, IA: Wallace-Homestead, 1978.

Shuman, John, III, and Susan Shuman. *Lion Pattern Glass.* Boston: Branden Press, 1977.

Sichel, Franz. *Glass Drinking Vessels.* San Francisco: Lawton & Alfred Kennedy Printing, 1969.

Spillman, Jane Schadel. *American and European Pressed Glass in the Corning Museum of Glass.* Corning, NY: Corning Museum of Glass, 1981.

———. *Glass, Tableware, Bowls, and Vases.* New York: Alfred A. Knopf, 1982.

———. *Glass from World's Fairs, 1851–1904.* Corning, NY: Corning Museum of Glass, 1986.

Spillman, Jane Schadel, and Susanne K. Frantz. *Masterpieces of American Glass.* Corning, NY: Corning Museum of Glass, 1990.

Stevens, Gerald. *Canadian Glass.* Toronto: Ryerson Press, 1967.

———. *Early Canadian Glass.* Toronto, Ryerson Press, 1967.

Stout, Sandra McPhee. *The Complete Book of McKee.* North Kansas City, Trojan Press, 1972.

Swan, Martha Louise. *American Cut and Engraved Glass of the Brilliant Period in Historical Perspective*. IL: Wallace-Homestead, Book Co. 1986.

The Toledo Museum of Art. *Libbey Glass: A Tradition of 150 Years*. Toledo, OH: Author, 1968.

Toulouse, Julian. *Fruit Jars: A Collector's Manual*. Camden, NJ: Thomas Nelson & Sons, 1969.

Traub, Jules S. *The Glass of Desire Christian*. Chicago: The Art Glass Exchange, 1978.

U.S. Patent Records

Wakefield, Hugh, *19th Century British Glass*. New York: Thomas Yoseloff Publishing, 1961.

Warman, Edwin G. *American Cut Glass*. Uniontown, PA: E.G. Warman Publishing, 1954.

Warren, Phelps. *Irish Glass*. New York: Charles Scribner's Sons, 1970.

Watkins, Lura Woodside. *Cambridge Glass*. Boston: Marshall Jones Co., 1930.

Weatherman, Hazel Marie. *Colored Glassware of the Depression Era*. MO: Weatherman Glass Books, 1974.

———. *Colored Glassware of the Depression Era II*. MO: Weatherman Glass Books, 1974.

———. *Fostoria: Its First Fifty Years*. Springfield, IL: Weatherman's Publishers, 1979.

Weatherman, Hazel Marie, and Sue Weatherman. *The Decorated Tumbler*. MO: Glassbooks, 1978.

Webber, Norman W. *Collecting Glass*. New York: Arco, 1972.

Weiner, Herbert, and Freda Lipkowitz. *Rarities in American Cut Glass*. Houston, TX: Collectors House of Books, 1975.

Whitehouse, David. *Glass of the Roman Empire*. Corning, NY: Corning Museum of Glass, 1988.

Whitmyer, Margaret, and Kenn Whitmyer. *Children's Dishes*. Paducah, KY: Collector Books, 1984.

Wilson, Jack D. *Phoenix and Consolidated Art Glass*. Marietta, OH: Antique Publications, 1989.

Wilson, Kenneth M. *New England Glass and Glassmaking*. New York: Thomas Y. Crowell, 1972.

Winter, Henry. *The Dynasty of Louis Comfort Tiffany*. Boston: Henry Winter, 1971.

Zerwick, Chloe. *A Short History of Glass*. New York: Harry N. Abrams, 1990.

ADVERTISEMENTS, TRADE CATALOGS, JOURNALS, AND OTHER PUBLICATIONS NOT LISTED ABOVE

American Glass Review

American Pottery and Glassware Reporter

M. Bazzett & Co.

A.C. Becken Co.

Butler Brothers

The Connoisseur

The Cosmopolitan

Crockery and Glass Journal

The Crockery Journal

Enos' Manual of Old Pattern Glass

Good Housekeeping

Gordon & Morrison

Harper's

Higgins & Seiter

The Jeweler's Circular-Weekly

Journal of Glass Studies

Krantz & Smith Company

Marshall Field & Co.

McClure's

Montgomery Ward
S.F. Myers Co.
N. A. & Co.
Oskamp, Nolting Co.
The Pottery, Glass & Brass
  Salesman

R. T. & Co.
Scribner's
Sears, Roebuck Co.
William Volker & Co.
Woolworth & Co.
Woman's Day

COMPANY CATALOGS, BROCHURES, TRADE JOURNALS, AND ADVERTISEMENTS NOT INCLUDED ABOVE:

Adams & Company
Akro Agate Company
Anchor Hocking Glass Company
Baccarat Glass Company
Bakewell, Pears & Company
Bergen Cut Glass Company
Blackmer Cut Glass
Blenko Glass Company
Boston & Sandwich Glass Company
Boyd Art Glass Company
Bryce Brothers
Cambridge Glass Company
Central Glass Company
T.B. Clark & Company
Consolidated Lamp & Glass
  Company
Correia Art Glass Company
De Vilbiss Company
Diamond Glass Company
Diamond Glass-Ware Company
Dominion Glass Company
C. Dorflinger & Sons
Duncan Miller Glass Company
Durand Art Glass Company
O.F. Egginton Company
Federal Glass Company
Fenton Art Glass Company
Fostoria Glass Company
H.C. Fry Glass Company
Gibson Glass Company
T.G. Hawkes & Company
Hazel Atlas Glass Company
A. H. Heisey & Company
J. Hoare & Company
Hobbs, Brocunier and Company
Hocking Glass Company
Imperial Glass Company
Indiana Glass Company
Indiana Tumbler & Goblet Company
Jeannette Glass Company

Keystone Cut Glass Company
King, Son, and Company
Lalique
Libbey Glass Company
Loetz Glass
MacBeth-Evans Glass Company
Maple City Glass Company
McKee Brothers
Meriden Cut Glass Company
C.F. Monroe Company
Moser Glass Works
Mount Washington Glass Works
New England Crystal Company
New England Glass Company
New Martinsville Glass Company
Northwood Glass Company
Orrefors Glasbruck
Paden City Glass Company
Pairpoint Manufacturing Company
Perthshire Paperweights Ltd.
Phoenix Glass Company
Pilgrim Glass Company
Pitkin & Brooks
Quaker City Cut Glass Company
Quezal Art Glass and Decorating
  Company
Sabino Art Glass Company
H. P. Sinclaire Company
L. E. Smith Company
Steuben Glass Works
L. Straus & Sons
Taylor Brothers
Tiffany
Tipperary Crystal Company
Tuthill Cut Glass Company
Unger Brothers
U.S. Glass Company
Waterford Crystal Ltd.
Thomas Webb & Sons
Westmoreland Glass Company

AUCTION HOUSES, CATALOGS, BROCHURES, AND ADVERTISEMENTS

Sanford Alderfer Auction Company, Hatfield, PA
Artfact, Inc., Computer Auction Records' Services
James Bakker, Cambridge, MA
Ron Bourgeault & Company, Portsmouth, NH
Richard A. Bourne Company, Hyannis, MA
Bullock's Auction House, Flint, MI
Christie's and Christie's East, New York, NY
William Doyle Galleries, New York, NY
Dumouchelles, Detroit, MI
Early Auction Company, Milford, OH
Robert Eldred Company, East Dennis, MA
Garth's Auction, Inc. Delaware, OH
Glass-Works Auctions, East Greenville, PA
Guerney's, New York, NY
Leslie Hindman, Inc., Chicago, IL
Milwaukee Auction Galleries, Milwaukee, WI
PK Liquidators, Flint, MI
David Rago, Trenton, NJ
Roan Brothers Auction Gallery, Cogan Station, PA
SGCA Auctions, Flint, MI
Sotheby's, New York, NY

ANTIQUE SHOWS AND DEALERS

AA Ann Arbor Antiques Mall, Ann Arbor, MI
W. D. Adams Antique Mall, Howell, MI
Antique Gallery, Detroit, MI
The Antique Gallery, Flint, MI
The Antique Warehouse, Saginaw, MI
Ark Antiques, New Haven, CT
Bankstreet Antiques Mall, Frankenmuth, MI
Bay City Antiques Center, Bay City, MI
Burton Gallery Antiques, Plymouth, MI
Cherry Street Antique Mall, Flint, MI
Flat River Antique Mall, Lowell, MI
Flushing Antique Emporium, Flushing, MI
Gallery of Antiques, Detroit, MI
Gilley's Antique Mall, Plainfield, IN
Hitching Post Antiques Mall, Tecumseh, MI
Indianapolis Antique Mall, Indianapolis, IN
Plymouth Antiques Mall, Plymouth, MI
Reminisce Antique Mall, Flint, MI
Showcase Antique Center, Sturbridge, MA
Water Tower Antiques Mall, Holly, MI

Special thanks to the numerous dealers and auction companies who allowed me to snap a few photographs and provided helpful advice on pricing and market trends.